Artificial Intelligence and the Future of Personalized Education

Aras Bozkurt
https://orcid.org/0000-0002-4520-642X
Anadolu University, Turkey

IGI Global
Scientific Publishing
Publishing Tomorrow's Research Today

Vice President of Editorial	Melissa Wagner
Director of Acquisitions	Mikaela Felty
Director of Book Development	Jocelynn Hessler
Production Manager	Mike Brehm
Cover Design	Jose Rosado

Published in the United States of America by
IGI Global Scientific Publishing
701 East Chocolate Avenue
Hershey, PA, 17033, USA
Tel: 717-533-8845 | Fax: 717-533-7115
Website: https://www.igi-global.com E-mail: cust@igi-global.com

Library of Congress Cataloging-in-Publication Data

(CIP Data Pending)
ISBN13: 979-8-3373-7574-8
Isbn13Softcover: 979-8-3373-7575-5
EISBN13: 979-8-3373-7576-2

British Cataloguing in Publication Data
A Cataloguing in Publication record for this book is available from the British Library.

Table of Contents

Detailed Table of Contents

The chapter examines personalized learning in detail within the context of its historical development, challenges in its definition, and ambiguities in its meaning. Different models and approaches of this learning approach are discussed through their potentials and impacts in education. Furthermore, the use of advanced technologies in education, such as generative artificial intelligence (GenAI), large language models (LLMs), and natural language processing (NLP), is addressed, and their relationships with artificial intelligence applications like machine learning and deep learning are explored. The interaction between personalized learning and artificial intelligence, tutoring applications, and the ethical dimensions in these processes are thoroughly examined. The chapter concludes with evaluations on the integration of AI-based systems into educational processes and their potential future impacts.

Many countries have focused their policies on lifelong learning recently. It is necessary to examine the role of technological tools to guide policies and lifelong learning practices in this regard. Today's widely used artificial intelligence (AI) technologies support the expansion of educational opportunities, customisation of processes, and implementation in lifelong learning. Therefore, it is necessary to accurately conceptualise the connection between AI and lifelong learning. This book chapter addresses the role and impact of AI in lifelong learning with subsections such as AI-Based Personalized Education, Explainable AI (XAI) in Education, AI Agents in Education, Generative Artificial Intelligence (GenAI), and Current Trends in Lifelong Learning. Also, the chapter offers an idea about the creative uses and prospects of artificial intelligence to increase the efficiency and accessibility of learning procedures.

Mobile learning offers individuals flexible and personalized educational experiences independent of time and space constraints. Productive artificial intelligence makes learning more effective by producing content tailored to the individual's learning style and needs. By analyzing a student's past performance, these systems provide tailored content to address deficiencies, increase motivation, and make the learning process dynamic with immediate feedback. These approaches support student activism and encourage the active participation of individuals in the learning process. Contextualized learning that considers location, time, and cultural factors makes the process more meaningful. Mobile assistants, guidance systems, and data-driven recommendation engines organize, monitor, and enhance the learning experience. Supported by interactive technologies, these systems enable the development of creative thinking, problem-solving, and collaboration skills. Learning thus becomes a sustainable and egalitarian model tailored to individual needs and enriched by social interactions.

This chapter aims to examine the potential uses of artificial intelligence (AI) in the preparation of final degree projects within the field of Educational Sciences. To this end, it provides a comprehensive analysis of how university students are integrating AI into their final degree projects, with a focus on common uses such as AI-assisted writing, research support, data analysis, and content generation. The benefits and challenges, potential risks and ethical dilemmas associated with these technologies are also discussed. Additionally, it offers an overview of widely used generative AI tools in academic settings that may facilitate the development of final degree projects. However, it is important to acknowledge that the landscape of generative AI tools is constantly evolving, with new advancements continuously enhancing their functionality and capabilities. Finally, the chapter presents practical guidelines for the effective integration of AI in the preparation of final degree projects, since these represent the students' first significant contact with scientific research.

Using AI into early childhood education to improve children's learning, especially language skills and adaptive behaviors, and it provides qualified teacher-child interactions in classroom environments. AI encourages development and efficacy of systems, which are excellent teaching resources. While there are many advantages to using AI in early childhood, there are also challenges and it can be a barrier to creativity, it raises ethical and practical concerns, including data privacy, bias in algorithms, and the potential reduction in human interaction, which is critical for socio-emotional development. By situating AI within established theories of child development, this argues for a balanced integration of AI technologies that complement rather than replace human educators. This chapter concludes by proposing a conceptual framework for the effective and ethical use of AI in early childhood education, advocating for collaborative efforts among educators, technologists, and policymakers to shape an inclusive digital future.

This book chapter comprehensively addresses the potential role of artificial intelligence in the education of learners with Autism Spectrum Disorder (ASD) and the opportunities and ethical dilemmas presented by this technology. The integration of AI into education has been a significant turning point, particularly for learners with ASD, giving rise to both innovative possibilities and concerns. The technological revolution in education, while enabling personalized learning, raises new questions about teacher-student interaction, independence-dependence balances, and human-machine interaction. A careful balance must be struck between supporting the development of students with ASD and the risk of dependency that may arise from the overuse of AI. In this context, empathetic AI technologies respond sensitively to emotional needs while also bringing with them concerns about dependency and uncertainty in human-machine interaction. The chapter offers recommendations for the responsible use of these technologies.

This chapter investigated the transformative role of generative AI in Computer-Assisted Language Learning (CALL), highlighting its capacity to create personalized content, simulate authentic conversational practice, and provide real-time, context-sensitive feedback. As traditional CALL systems often lack adaptability and dynamic interaction, generative AI emerges as a powerful solution that addresses diverse learner needs and enhances engagement through adaptive and culturally responsive materials. The chapter offers a comprehensive analysis of how generative AI is being applied in language education, examining its benefits, such as increased accessibility and instructional efficiency, as well as challenges, including ethical concerns and data privacy.

This study explores how generative artificial intelligence (GenAI) supports the development of 21st-century skills—critical thinking, creativity, communication, and collaboration (4Cs)—in foreign language education through a systematic literature review. Findings indicate that GenAI enhances critical thinking by improving analytical reasoning and argumentation, supports creative writing, strengthens communication through real-time feedback, and fosters collaboration in interactive settings. However, issues such as ethical concerns, learner autonomy, and over-reliance on AI-generated content remain. The study emphasizes the need for balanced GenAI integration with human oversight and further research on its long-term impact on language learning and education, highlighting AI's transformative role and the importance of responsible use.

This chapter explores the integration of SkyTutor, an AI-powered chatbot based on ChatGPT technology, into aviation English training for ab-initio pilots. Addressing the increasing global demand for skilled pilots, the chapter highlights the limitations of traditional training methods and the need for innovative solutions. SkyTutor was developed to bridge the gap between conventional instruction and modern technological capabilities, providing personalized, interactive learning experiences tailored to aviation communication protocols and theoretical knowledge. The chapter outlines SkyTutor's design, technical framework, and educational potential while critically analyzing its impact on both learners and instructors. By evaluating SkyTutor's strengths and shortcomings, this chapter contributes to understanding the transformative potential of AI tools in aviation education and their implications for enhancing communication skills, cognitive readiness, and instructional efficiency in the rapidly evolving aviation landscape.

Today, exposure to a second language (L2) is widely achieved through listening and watching content on web-based platforms. As the quality and quantity of input shape L2 acquisition, this study aims to analyze the role of cultural and linguistic background on the L2 input provided through YouTube TED Talks. TED Talk transcriptions of 12 native and nonnative speakers of English coming from collectivist and individualistic cultures were analyzed using a natural language processing (NLP) tool called SiNLP. Speech cohesion at sentence and text level was examined by developing a generalized linear regression model. Language (native vs. nonnative) and culture (collectivist vs. individualistic) were taken as independent variables and sentence (e.g., lexical overlap, semantic overlap, connective use) and text (givenness and lexical diversity) level indices of complexity were taken as the dependent variables. Cultural background rather than the linguistic background was found to play a meaningful role in linguistic complexity that the speakers manifested.

Preface

INTRODUCTION

Artificial Intelligence (AI) has emerged as one of the defining forces of our era, reshaping industries, economies, and societies at large. Among its most promising applications lies the field of education, where AI technologies hold the potential to transform how knowledge is delivered, accessed, and personalized. In recent years, the convergence of AI with personalized education has offered new ways to address the diverse needs of learners by adapting content, pace, and instructional methods to individual preferences and requirements. Such advancements are not merely technical but also deeply pedagogical, as they challenge long-held assumptions about the nature of teaching, learning, and human interaction in educational spaces.

The aim of this edited reference book, *Artificial Intelligence and the Future of Personalized Education,* is to provide a comprehensive examination of how AI intersects with contemporary learning paradigms, with a particular emphasis on personalization, inclusivity, and ethical considerations. By bringing together diverse perspectives, empirical insights, and conceptual frameworks from leading scholars and practitioners, this book highlights the transformative possibilities of AI while critically reflecting on its limitations and challenges. As editors, our intention is to present a balanced and multidisciplinary exploration that situates AI not only as a technological tool but also as a cultural, social, and ethical phenomenon in education.

This collection responds to the growing demand for nuanced scholarship that bridges technological innovation and pedagogical practice. It is designed for researchers, educators, policymakers, and technologists who seek to understand how AI can be harnessed to create more responsive, equitable, and effective educational environments. By showcasing a wide array of case studies, theoretical analyses, and practical guidelines, the chapters together create a roadmap for navigating the rapidly evolving landscape of personalized education in the age of artificial intelligence.

CHAPTER OVERVIEW

- **Chapter 1** introduces the foundations of personalized learning and tutoring through generative AI systems, discussing historical developments, definitional challenges, and the role of large language models and natural language processing. It also evaluates ethical issues and future trajectories.
- **Chapter 2** explores lifelong learning in the context of AI, highlighting personalized education through AI agents, generative AI, and explainable AI. It examines how policies and practices can integrate these technologies to support equitable and accessible lifelong learning opportunities.
- **Chapter 3** focuses on mobile learning environments, emphasizing how generative AI enables flexible, context-sensitive, and personalized experiences. It illustrates the ways in which such technologies foster learner activism, motivation, and engagement.
- **Chapter 4** addresses the integration of AI in the preparation of final degree projects within the educational sciences. Offering both critical perspectives and practical guidelines, it considers how AI tools can support students while raising questions of ethics and supervision.
- **Chapter 5** examines the use of AI in early childhood education, weighing its benefits for language development and adaptive behaviors against challenges related to creativity, socio-emotional growth, and data privacy. A conceptual framework for ethical integration is proposed.
- **Chapter 6** investigates AI in the education of learners with Autism Spectrum Disorder (ASD). It highlights the opportunities of empathetic AI while acknowledging concerns of over-reliance, dependency, and the delicate balance between human and machine interaction.
- **Chapter 7** turns to the transformative role of generative AI in Computer-Assisted Language Learning (CALL), showcasing how it enables authentic, adaptive, and personalized learning experiences while also identifying potential risks and ethical concerns.
- **Chapter 8** systematically reviews the role of generative AI in enhancing 21st-century skills—critical thinking, creativity, communication, and collaboration (4Cs)—within foreign language education, emphasizing both opportunities and the need for responsible oversight.
- **Chapter 9** presents an applied case study of SkyTutor, an AI-powered chatbot used in aviation English training. The chapter evaluates the chatbot's design, educational potential, and implications for improving communication and cognitive readiness in aviation contexts.
- **Chapter 10** concludes with an empirical analysis of native and nonnative speech patterns in TED Talks, examining how cultural and linguistic vari-

ables influence second language learning input. Using natural language processing, the study demonstrates the role of cultural background in shaping linguistic complexity.

CONCLUSION

Taken together, the chapters in this volume underscore the diversity of contexts in which AI is being integrated into education, ranging from early childhood to lifelong learning, from language acquisition to professional training. Each chapter contributes to a growing body of knowledge that demonstrates both the promises and the perils of relying on intelligent systems for the delivery of personalized learning experiences. A central theme that emerges throughout is the importance of striking a balance between technological innovation and the preservation of human values in education.

The insights presented here are particularly timely as the global education community grapples with issues of accessibility, inclusivity, and equity. AI systems offer unprecedented opportunities to address individual learner needs at scale, yet they also bring forth new ethical, cultural, and pedagogical questions. As the chapters reveal, personalization is not solely a matter of technical design but also of critical reflection on what it means to learn and to teach in an age of intelligent machines. The future of education will depend not only on the sophistication of algorithms but also on the wisdom of educators, researchers, and policymakers in guiding their use responsibly.

We hope that this volume will serve as both a resource and a provocation—encouraging readers to imagine new possibilities for education while remaining mindful of the risks and responsibilities that come with them. As editors, we are grateful to the contributors for their scholarship and dedication, and to the broader academic and professional communities that continue to shape this evolving field. May the ideas and discussions contained in these pages inspire innovation, foster dialogue, and guide the future of personalized education in the age of artificial intelligence.

Chapter 1
Personalized Learning and Tutoring Through GenAI Systems

Atakan Yaşar
https://orcid.org/0009-0005-9277-6774
Bursa Uludag University, Turkey

Nuray Parlak Yılmaz
https://orcid.org/0000-0001-8368-4556
Faculty of Education, Bursa Uludag University, Turkey

ABSTRACT

The chapter examines personalized learning in detail within the context of its historical development, challenges in its definition, and ambiguities in its meaning. Different models and approaches of this learning approach are discussed through their potentials and impacts in education. Furthermore, the use of advanced technologies in education, such as generative artificial intelligence (GenAI), large language models (LLMs), and natural language processing (NLP), is addressed, and their relationships with artificial intelligence applications like machine learning and deep learning are explored. The interaction between personalized learning and artificial intelligence, tutoring applications, and the ethical dimensions in these processes are thoroughly examined. The chapter concludes with evaluations on the integration of AI-based systems into educational processes and their potential future impacts.

DOI: 10.4018/979-8-3373-7574-8.ch001

INTRODUCTION

When examining the historical development of educational paradigms, it becomes evident that personalized learning approaches emerged from the effort to place the student at the center of the learning process. Personalized learning aims to shape individuals' educational experiences according to their needs, preferences, and competencies (Kem, 2022). While traditional mass instructional models have served the goal of reaching large audiences, they have overlooked individual differences and failed to account for the diversity in students' cognitive capacities and learning styles. In this context, the personalized learning approach, grounded in individual learning needs, seeks to restructure educational processes in accordance with each learner's pace, interests, abilities, and requirements.

In the 21st century, education is undergoing rapid transformation. Traditional methods are struggling to compete with individualized and flexible learning models (Melzer, 2018). This new learner-centered paradigm necessitates the adaptation of instructional methods to individual differences. Personalized learning is most explicitly observed in private tutoring. Unlike classroom environments, private lessons enable a better analysis of student needs, allowing for the development of appropriate instructional strategies and thus enhancing academic achievement. Therefore, the individualization of learning should not merely be seen as a pedagogical preference, but rather as a necessity aimed at fully realizing an individual's potential. Recent advancements in artificial intelligence hold the potential to make personalized learning more effective and accessible in educational settings. Studies show that GenAI tools are powerful technologies that support knowledge construction and guide exploration, analysis, and application processes (Khlaif et al., 2025). Generative Artificial Intelligence (GenAI) systems offer adaptive learning experiences by generating dynamic and personalized content. Through technologies such as big data analytics, natural language processing (NLP), and deep learning, GenAI can provide continuous, student-specific feedback and adapt content in real time.

This section will address the historical and theoretical foundations of personalized learning, as well as its impact on private tutoring practices. Additionally, it will explore the functions and contributions of GenAI systems in education, while also discussing potential pedagogical, ethical, and technical challenges that may arise during their integration. The aim is to examine the potential emerging from the intersection of personalized learning and GenAI concepts. Furthermore, strategies that may facilitate the integration of these technologies into the educational system will also be presented. The content will be delivered within a coherent structure and logical flow. First, the evolution of personalized learning and its contributions to individualized instruction will be analyzed; then, the role of GenAI in education and the innovations it offers will be discussed. Finally, the flexible and learner-centered learning models resulting from the integration of these two structures will be evaluated in terms of their educational impact.

This study will begin by presenting the theoretical foundations, then explore the integration of GenAI and personalized learning, and finally provide strategic recommendations.

This sequence aims first to establish the theoretical framework, then to demonstrate how this foundation is shaped by GenAI and personalization, and finally to assess the educational implications of their integration. Initially, the historical development and principles of personalized learning will be examined, focusing on how these approaches transform student experiences. In doing so, a theoretical basis will be provided to explain the impact of personalized learning on educational systems.

SECTION 1: THE EVOLUTION OF PERSONALIZED LEARNING

1.1. A Historical Perspective on Personalized Learning

Throughout history, education has continually evolved to transmit knowledge across societies and to help individuals adapt. Initially centered on teaching basic survival skills, it gradually transformed into a more systematic and theoretical structure. In Ancient Greece, education was based on the pursuit of reason and virtue, whereas during the Middle Ages, it adopted a more religious orientation. In the 19th and 20th centuries, industrialization and technological advances brought greater attention to individual differences and cognitive processes. This transformation highlighted the inadequacies of traditional models and paved the way for more flexible, learner-centered approaches.

Within this shift, behaviorism emerged as one of the first theoretical approaches in education. Behaviorism explains learning as responses to external stimuli, largely ignoring the active role of the learner in the process. According to this model, knowledge is transmitted directly by the teacher, and learning occurs through reinforcement. However, this model was criticized for neglecting individual differences and internal cognitive processes, thereby creating a need for more flexible, person-centered models. As a result, the constructivist paradigm gained prominence in the mid-20th century. Developed by Jean Piaget and Lev Vygotsky, this approach posits that learning is not a passive process, but rather one actively constructed through individual experience. The constructivist perspective focuses on integrating prior knowledge with new learning. Jerome Bruner (1974) further contributed to this view by emphasizing that learners do not merely absorb information but interpret and make sense of it through cognitive processes.

Bruner's learning theory contributed to a departure from rote learning by emphasizing the role of mental processes in meaning-making. This approach highlights the need for education to account for individual differences. According to Bruner (1974), the learning process should be structured in accordance with the learner's own pace. This view forms the foundation of the concept of personalized learning. Personalized learning is a model grounded in the active role of the learner and is closely linked to constructivist theory. However, how individuals manage their own learning, their motivation, and their belief in their academic success also play a significant role in the effectiveness of this approach.

The effectiveness of personalized learning is not only related to progressing at an individual pace, but also to how learners manage the process, and the cognitive-affective factors involved.

At this point, Bandura's social cognitive learning theory provides a key foundation for understanding the learner's role and beliefs regarding academic achievement.

Bandura (1986) argued that learning is not limited to cognitive processes but is also connected to factors such as self-regulation and self-efficacy. A learner's belief in their ability to learn, their level of self-efficacy, and how they manage the process are critical components of success in personalized learning. While Bruner's constructivist approach shapes the cognitive dimension of personalized learning, Bandura's theory adds depth by clarifying learners' active participation and self-regulation strategies. Bandura (1986) demonstrates that personalized learning not only considers individual differences but also offers a robust theoretical framework to explain how individuals guide their learning processes. In this context, the concepts of self-efficacy and self-regulation have become foundational elements of personalized learning.

Self-efficacy refers to an individual's belief in their ability to successfully perform a specific task, and this belief directly influences motivation, perseverance, and academic achievement. When students believe they can succeed at a task, their effort increases; conversely, if they anticipate failure, the learning process is negatively affected. In personalized learning environments, self-efficacy develops in relation to students' individual experiences and accomplishments. Therefore, the personalization of the learning process contributes to strengthening students' self-efficacy beliefs through successful performance.

Self-regulation is the ability to plan, monitor, and evaluate one's own learning process. According to Bandura (1986), effective learning requires individuals to set goals, track their progress, and adjust strategies when necessary. While traditional models present the same content and methods to all students, personalized learning supports learners in progressing at their own pace and developing unique strategies.

In the context of personalized learning, in connection with Bandura's self-regulation model:

- Students are encouraged to determine their own learning paths.
- Continuous development is supported through feedback mechanisms.
- Learners are provided with an independent and autonomous learning experience.

Considering these approaches, personalized learning enables individuals to manage their own learning processes and strengthen their belief in self-efficacy. Instead of standardized methods used in traditional systems, personalized learning is based on individual differences and cognitive processes. Self-efficacy and self-regulation allow students to become active participants in the process rather than passive recipients. Bandura's concepts significantly contribute to the theoretical foundation of personalized learning. The historical development of personalized learning has been shaped by theories emphasizing the learner's active role and self-paced progress. Bandura's social cognitive theory, which supports self-directed learning, played a key role in advancing this approach. Bruner's constructivist model encouraged discovery-based learning, while this period also saw the rise of systematic personalized instruction frameworks.

Within this context, Drumheller's (1971) *Handbook of Curriculum Design for Individualized Instruction* stands as one of the early works that concretized the idea of personalized teaching. Drumheller (1971) advocated for adapting educational programs to students' individual pace and needs, emphasizing that instructional materials should be designed with clear objectives. This approach contributed to the systematic handling of personalized learning and laid the foundation for adaptive learning models (Drumheller, 1971). After the 1970s, research aimed at understanding individual differences increased, and models gradually became more structured. Developments in cognitive psychology during the 1980s and 1990s revealed that learning should be adapted not only to pace but also to learning styles and cognitive processes. Over time, this understanding evolved into more comprehensive models that also incorporated social interaction.

One of the key milestones in this transformation was the "Team-Assisted Individualization" (TAI) model developed by Slavin (1984). Slavin (1984) proposed integrating personalized learning with cooperative learning, enabling students not only to progress at their own pace but also to engage in the process through peer support. Thus, personalized learning evolved from being a solely individual process to a model supported by social interaction, where individual responsibility within a team was emphasized. This method, particularly used in mainstream classrooms, demonstrated that personalized instruction could be more effective in heterogeneous groups (Slavin, 1984).

By the 1990s, personalized learning had evolved beyond a sole focus on learning pace into a more comprehensive and multidimensional model. During this period, instruction began to be designed not only to help students reach academic goals, but also to address their cognitive and affective characteristics, areas of interest, and levels of readiness. Teaching thus transformed into a flexible and dynamic approach aimed at uncovering individual potential. In her work *Mapping a Route Toward Differentiated Instruction*, Tomlinson (1999) approached personalized learning within the framework of differentiated instruction, arguing that instruction should be diversified not only by pace but also by individual learning profiles. Tomlinson (1999) emphasized the importance of adapting four key instructional components—content, process, product, and learning environment—to meet students' needs.

Content can be tailored to the student's level of knowledge and interests to make learning more meaningful and engaging. The process component focuses on how the student processes information, making instruction more personalized. Product differentiation allows learners to express what they have learned in ways that align with their strengths. Finally, the learning environment should be designed to ensure that students feel safe and motivated. With this approach, personalized learning has moved away from rigid individualization and evolved into a student-centered and multifaceted instructional model. Today, teachers adopt an inclusive educational philosophy that adapts not only to students' pace but also to their preferences and learning processes.

In his work *Differentiated Instruction: A Research Basis*, Subban (2006) explores the theoretical and empirical foundations of differentiated instruction and discusses how it can be implemented in educational settings. Drawing particularly on theories such as Vygotsky's Zone of Proximal Development (ZPD), Gardner's Theory of Multiple Intelligences, and brain-based learning, the study examines both the necessity and impact of this approach. Subban (2006) emphasizes that differentiated instruction should not be shaped solely by academic level, but also by students' interests, learning styles, and cognitive development. This model supports student-centered teaching and requires flexible adaptation of content, process, product, and learning environment. Moreover, it enhances classroom interaction and increases student motivation. The research also addresses the challenges teachers face in applying this model and underscores the need to strengthen teachers' pedagogical competencies for effective implementation. Subban (2006) highlights the importance of professional development programs to help teachers improve their ability to design student-centered instruction. Building on Tomlinson's (1999) model, this study demonstrates that personalized learning should not be limited to pace and performance but must also respond to cognitive and affective needs through a flexible and multidimensional instructional model.

The report by Patrick et al. (2013) demonstrated that personalized learning is not merely a model based on individualized instruction, collaboration, and active approaches. This study revealed that personalized learning has evolved beyond the traditional understanding of individual differences into a technology-supported structure that actively involves the learner in the process. According to Patrick et al. (2013), personalized learning has transformed into a holistic model by integrating with blended and competency-based learning. In this model, learners are guided not only by their pace but also by their preferences and interests. While progress is achieved through competency-based pathways, learning technologies become an integral part of the process. This new form represents a significant transformation in education. Learner-centered education now reflects a flexible and dynamic structure grounded not only in pace and level, but in the entire learning ecosystem. This model offers enriched instructional processes that address not only academic development, but also affective and cognitive growth. Such transformation underscores the need for more inclusive and student-centered approaches in education.

Over time, personalized learning has evolved into a more flexible and student-centered structure, encouraging active learner participation. The work of Bray and McClaskey (2014), *Make Learning Personal: The What, Who, Wow, Where, and Why*, reveals that this approach has shifted toward a model in which learners guide their own educational journey. This model not only offers differentiated content, but also emphasizes that learners set their own goals, decide how they will learn, and take responsibility for the process. Personalized learning has shifted from teacher-directed instruction to a self-regulated model where students design their own learning experiences. This shift grants learners not only content access but also autonomy to guide their process based on strengths, interests, and preferred paths. Technology enhances flexibility, offering greater choice and control, while both learning environments and content are tailored to individual needs.

Bray and McClaskey (2014) emphasize that personalized learning is not merely about understanding individual differences, but also about recognizing who the learner is, how they learn, and how they bring meaning to the learning process. As a result, personalized learning has evolved into an approach that not only aims to improve academic achievement but also supports learners in discovering themselves, attributing meaning to their educational experiences, and fostering lifelong learning. This model enables students not just to possess knowledge, but to internalize it meaningfully and integrate it into their lives. Since the mid-20th century, personalized learning has been shaped by various pedagogical approaches and has gradually transformed with the support of technology. Initially focused on one-on-one instruction, the model has evolved into a more flexible and dynamic structure that centers on learners' interests, learning styles, and cognitive processes. With the rise of digitalization in the 2000s, personalized learning has extended beyond traditional classroom practices to become a broad ecosystem supported by data analytics, artificial intelligence, and learning management systems.

Changes in educational policy have directly influenced the development of personalized learning; particularly after 2010, governments began to integrate technology-supported learning models into their education systems. As a result, personalized learning has moved beyond being merely an instructional approach to become one of the foundational pillars of educational reform. For instance, the U.S. Department of Education's report *Future Ready Learning: Reimagining the Role of Technology in Education* (2016) demonstrates that this model has evolved into a paradigm that shapes national policy, surpassing individual classroom implementations. The report outlines in detail how digital tools, adaptive systems, and data-driven instruction can be utilized to enhance student achievement, positioning personalized learning at the center of educational policy. This approach has become not only a method of instruction but also a policy instrument aimed at ensuring equity in education. The growing interest from governments has led to wider adoption of the model, making personalized learning an integral part of both national and global strategies, well beyond individual classroom applications.

Following the definition provided by the U.S. Department of Education Office of Educational Technology (2017), the 2017 National Education Technology Plan further deepened the concept of personalized learning, emphasizing its transformation into a more comprehensive structure through the influence of digital tools, data analytics, and adaptive systems. This shift illustrates that personalized learning has evolved from merely being structured around students' individual pace to a technology-supported approach integrated into broader learning ecosystems.

The U.S. Department of Education's 2017 update redefined the role of personalized learning in education. In this revised definition, the model is described as a student-centered and technology-enhanced instructional approach. This development highlights the rapid adoption of flexible, accessible, and learner-centered solutions driven by the impact of digitalization in education.

"Personalized learning refers to instruction in which the pace of learning and the instructional approach are optimized for the needs of each learner." As such, this approach—which has previously been referred to as "individualized learning" or "interactive learning" in educational discourse—has been framed more clearly through this definition. With the integration of technology into educational processes and the growing emphasis on student-centered approaches, the concept has become more distinct and functional. The definitions notably highlight processes tailored to students' individual needs, learning pace, and preferences. Although still in a developmental phase, personalized learning is gradually gaining a more coherent and established

identity through the integration of technology.

From this perspective, when examining the historical definitions of personalized learning:

- **International Encyclopedia of Education (2010)**

"Personalized learning refers to the implementation of instructional methods and content tailored to students' individual learning pace, preferences, and abilities." (International Academy of Education [IAE], 2010).

This definition highlights the student-centered nature of personalized learning and emphasizes the need for instructional processes to be organized according to individual learner needs.

- **OECD (2013)**

In the OECD's 2013 definition, personalized learning was addressed in a more structured way:

"Personalized learning is the process of making learning more effective by offering students customized content, instructional strategies, and assessment methods that respond to their individual needs." (OECD, 2013).

- **U.S. Office of Educational Technology (2017)**

In its 2017 report, the U.S. Office of Educational Technology defined personalized learning as:

"Personalized learning is an instructional approach that aims to offer students tailored instructional strategies and content based on their needs, skills, and goals." (U.S. Department of Education, 2017)

Although these definitions have been articulated in various forms across different periods, they collectively underscore the significance and evolution of personalized learning in contemporary education systems. Developments in this field suggest that the role of personalized learning in education will continue to deepen, enabling the creation of more effective learning environments tailored to students' individual needs.

By 2020, personalized learning had evolved from being merely a pedagogical concept into a more dynamic and accessible structure, driven by digital tools and emerging educational technologies. The *Educause Horizon Report* (Brown et al, 2020) elaborates on this transformation by examining the impact of digitalization on personalized learning. According to the report, educational technologies not only personalize content but also track students' progress, provide real-time feedback, and offer individualized learning pathways.

This indicates that personalized learning is no longer solely reliant on teacher-driven efforts but increasingly supported by digital and scalable systems. The *Educause Horizon Report* (Brown et al., 2020) can be considered a critical milestone in the history of this approach. While earlier phases emphasized differentiation and adaptive systems, today's personalized learning is enhanced by tools such as data analytics, artificial intelligence, and automated feedback. These developments reveal that personalized learning has become more than just an instructional method it is now a core component of digital transformation in education.

The developments highlighted in the *2020 Horizon Report* are further supported by the analyses of Castro et al. (2024). According to Castro et al. (2024), personalized learning has evolved beyond a pedagogical approach to become one of the fundamental components of digital education systems. With the integration of artificial intelligence, student profiling, content adaptation, real-time feedback, and intelligent interfaces, the personalized learning experience has been transformed, leading to a profound shift in education. This transformation allows educators to adapt their instructional strategies more flexibly in response to students' individual needs (Castro et al., 2024).

The historical development of personalized learning encompasses significant transformations ranging from pedagogical approaches to technological innovations. Initially shaped by differentiated instruction and adaptive systems based on individual learning pace, this concept has evolved—through technological integration—into a more flexible, accessible, and effective model. As of 2024, personalized learning has reached the most advanced stage of student-centered education and has become one of the core components of the digital transformation in education. This progression has transformed personalized learning from a mere pedagogical strategy into a technological force that makes learning processes more dynamic and individualized. Consequently, personalized learning has become a foundational element of educational digitalization and a paradigm shaping the future of learning.

1.2. Approaches and Models of Personalized Learning

Personalized learning is a pedagogically revolutionary model that considers students' individual differences and offers strategies and approaches tailored to each learner's educational process. This approach plays a foundational role in the development of student-centered learning environments (Patrick et al., 2013). It aims to structure the educational process flexibly by considering students' learning pace, styles, interests, strengths, and areas for improvement. In doing so, the learning process becomes more adaptable and supportive of individual needs (Patrick et al., 2013). Personalized learning not only facilitates the acquisition of knowledge but also encourages learners to deeply internalize content and manage their own development. This enhances students' sense of control over the learning process and supports long-term retention. As students' progress toward self-determined goals, they assume personal responsibility, making learning more meaningful and intrinsically motivating.

Personalized learning approaches have emerged during a time when individual differences are gaining increasing importance in education. While traditional systems offer uniform content and instructional methods to all students, the personalized model designs a unique process for each learner. This approach emphasizes the significance of individualization and flexibility within instructional design theories (Reigeluth & Carr-Chellman, 2009). The effective implementation of this model is linked not only to technological advancements but also to the need for promoting individual academic achievement. Students' learning pace, styles, and interests enable the creation of more efficient and motivating learning environments. In this context, personalized learning enables students to engage more actively in the learning process and brings them closer to achieving educational equity. When teachers can provide support tailored to individual needs, students' development is accelerated, and the learning experience becomes more personal and meaningful.

A. Approaches in Personalized Learning

Figure 1. Approaches to Personalized Learning

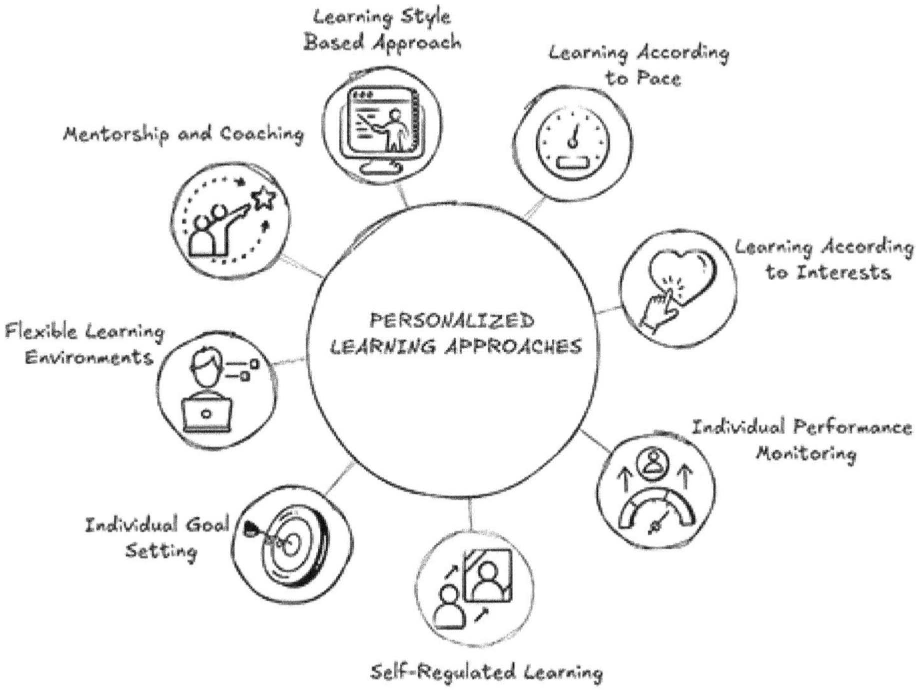

A.1. Approach Based on Learning Style

Everyone's learning process is unique, and individual differences are significant at every stage of education. The learning style-based approach is important for understanding these differences and shaping instruction accordingly. Experience-based learning theories demonstrate that taking individual styles into account enhances learning efficiency. While students' ways of processing information form the foundation of this process, such an approach also contributes to their learning awareness and helps them develop self-understanding.

Students' learning styles are generally categorized into visual, auditory, and kinesthetic modalities. However, these categories are not mutually exclusive; a student's style often reflects a combination of multiple modalities. This indicates that learning is multidimensional and that hybrid styles should be considered (Brent & Felder, 1992). For example, a visual-auditory learner may benefit most from a combination of visual and audio materials. Kinesthetic learners, on the other hand, reinforce their understanding through hands-on experiences. Therefore, teachers must develop methods that align with each student's preferred style. This involves not only offering varied materials but also providing flexible strategies and suitable learning environments. In this context, teachers serve not merely as conveyors of knowledge, but as guides on each student's individual learning journey.

The learning style-based approach increases student engagement and enhances motivation toward learning. It not only boosts participation but also supports long-term knowledge retention (Brent & Felder, 1992). When students interact with materials and methods suited to their styles, learning becomes more enjoyable and effective. By offering environments tailored to each learner, educators contribute to educational equity. Thus, the learning style-based approach is considered a strategy aimed at maximizing individual potential by addressing personal differences (Tomlinson, 2014).

A.2. Learning Based on Pace

Learning is individualized, and each student progresses at a different pace. The pace-based learning approach considers these differences, making education more dynamic and personalized. Planning instruction according to students' learning speeds transforms the teacher's role from content provider to learning facilitator. In this way, each student can learn at their own pace and better realize their potential. Differences in learning pace are influenced by factors such as prior knowledge, motivation, attention span, and learning style—elements that directly affect student performance (Wang et al., 1993).

The pace-based approach allows fast learners to engage with advanced content, while providing slower learners with additional time and support to reinforce their understanding. According to Bloom (1968), this approach increases academic achievement by enabling students to progress at their own pace. Teachers can personalize the process by offering individualized support, supplementary materials, and targeted questions. As a result, learning becomes more efficient and tailored to the student.

Allowing students to learn at their own pace increases motivation and reduces anxiety. Because students are progressing in line with their natural rhythm, they do not feel pressured. Reduced anxiety and increased self-efficacy contribute positively to academic success (Bloom, 1968). This method enables every student to learn at their own rhythm. Consequently, educators can more easily identify individual needs. Pace-based learning is not merely about speed—it is a process for unlocking student potential. This reinforces student-centered education and enhances learners' awareness of their own learning.

A.3. Interest-Based Learning

Interest-based learning centers on students' curiosity and personal inclinations. Research shows that individual interest plays a key role in learning (Renninger & Hidi, 2015). This approach encourages students to engage in lessons with intrinsic motivation and links learning to personal development. According to Renninger and Hidi (2015), motivation fueled by interest leads to long-term retention. When students engage with topics, they find interesting, their engagement increases, and the knowledge they acquire becomes more meaningful and lasting. Interest-based learning environments contribute to deeper cognitive processing of information (Renninger & Hidi, 2015).

A learning process that revolves around students' areas of interest supports not only their academic achievement but also their cognitive and emotional development. Students who can relate to topics they are interested in tending to develop deeper thinking, problem-solving, and critical analysis skills more effectively. Barron et al. (2014) stated that interest-based learning fosters higher-order cognitive skills in students. Additionally, this process enhances students' willingness to explore, transforming learning from an obligation into an enjoyable and meaningful experience. Learning based on personal interests allows students to express their creativity and encourages them to think more independently and originally. As a result, students can apply what they have learned not only for exams but also in real-life contexts. This approach positively influences students' attitudes toward education, helping them make sense of knowledge and ultimately become more autonomous learners over time.

A.4. Individual Performance Monitoring

Individual performance monitoring aims to closely track students' learning processes and regularly assess their development. This approach plays a crucial role, particularly in formative assessment practices (Black & Wiliam, 1998). Student progress is measured not only through exams but also by evaluating overall development, identifying strengths and weaknesses. Black and Wiliam (1998) emphasize that feedback provided during the learning process significantly contributes to student growth. Individual performance is assessed in relation to goal attainment, and areas requiring support are identified. In this way, instruction can be personalized and tailored to individual learning needs. Within this approach, teachers monitor student performance at each stage using various assessment tools. Tests, projects, written feedback, and continuous evaluations support this process. These data enable teachers to provide personalized feedback to students. Learners can identify their shortcomings and take ownership of their progress.

Sadler (1989) highlights that effective feedback supports self-regulated learning. Moreover, performance monitoring helps students determine which areas they need to focus on.

Individual performance monitoring contributes not only to students' academic success but also to their personal development. It helps learners recognize their strengths and weaknesses, thereby increasing their engagement with learning. While students build on their strengths, they receive support in areas where they need improvement. For teachers, this model provides opportunities to adapt instructional strategies based on student needs. As a result, each student is offered a tailored learning experience, and self-confidence is enhanced. Ongoing feedback allows for continuous monitoring of progress, which reinforces both achievement and self-awareness. Students participate more consciously in the learning process, and teachers are better equipped to provide individualized guidance.

A.5. Self-Regulated Learning

Self-regulated learning is an approach in which students independently plan and manage their learning processes, requiring active engagement. According to Zimmerman (2002), this form of learning supports students in taking responsibility. Learners guide their progress not only through external information but also through internal motivation and strategic actions. They set goals, take steps, and monitor their progress. Zimmerman (2002) emphasizes that goal setting and monitoring skills form the foundation of this process. Through this, students gain greater control over their learning and support their personal development. Skills like time management, self-assessment, and strategic choice are developed as students identify their weaknesses and work to overcome them. This process fosters independent learning and builds competencies essential for lifelong learning.

This approach contributes to deeper learning, increased responsibility, and long-term knowledge retention. Panadero (2017) notes that self-regulated learning enhances both the quality and durability of learning. Taking ownership of the learning process boosts student motivation and reduces dependency on teacher support. This approach also develops students' ability to assess their own performance and increases their self-confidence. As a result, students become more active participants in their education and emerge as more capable individuals both personally and socially.

A.6. Individual Goal Setting

Individual goal setting not only guides the student through the learning process but also initiates a journey of self-discovery. Schunk (2001) emphasizes that setting goals increases students' intrinsic motivation. Through the goals they set, students begin to recognize their potential and understand how to use it effectively. This process triggers internal motivation and provides a roadmap for learning. Goal setting promotes development based on intrinsic rather than extrinsic motivation. Each step toward a goal represents the student's effort to surpass personal limits. This approach supports not only the acquisition of knowledge but also the integration of learning into life. Goals add meaning to learning and transform the process into a journey of personal growth.

Throughout this process, students explore their inner selves. Each goal becomes a step that challenges and enhances their skills. They become aware of what they want to achieve and how to reach it. As a result, learning becomes a dynamic and continuously evolving experience. Students begin to see not only success but also failure as a natural and valuable part of the learning process. For teachers, individual goal setting facilitates the provision of more targeted feedback and enables the personalization of the learning process. As students monitor their own progress, teachers can offer guidance tailored to their needs. This process enhances students' agency in learning and fosters active engagement. Schunk (2001) notes that goal-oriented learning strengthens students' sense of self-efficacy. Thus, learners become not just recipients of knowledge, but individuals who actively manage their own learning.

A.7. Flexible Learning Environments

Flexible learning environments are an approach that considers individual differences and allows students to shape the learning process at their own pace. This model enables learners to personalize their experiences according to their preferred learning styles (Ramsden, 2003). Students can select the most suitable method by using texts, videos, visuals, or hands-on materials. According to Ramsden (2003), this student-centered structure supports independent learning and access to knowledge through multiple pathways. The approach makes it easier for students to control their own learning process and enhances their motivation. It also fosters the development of independent study skills. As flexible learning addresses various learning styles, it supports diversity in education. Teachers, in turn, can implement strategies tailored to individual needs, making the process more effective.

In this context, flexible learning environments enable teachers to apply different instructional strategies. Students can access information anytime and anywhere. Digital tools and personalized support systems help them manage the learning process more effectively. As a result, course content can be adapted to meet learners' needs, and the overall learning process can be individualized.

A.8. Mentorship and Coaching

Mentoring and coaching are two fundamental approaches that provide guidance for individuals in their learning processes and personal development. As Grant (2020) notes, these practices are structured guidance processes that support individuals in achieving their personal and professional goals. Both approaches involve the transfer of knowledge and skills, but they differ in terms of implementation.

Mentoring typically involves a long-term relationship in which an experienced individual guides someone with less experience. A mentor not only provides professional knowledge but also shares life experience and personal insights. According to Kram (1988), mentors offer not only career-related guidance but also psychosocial support that promotes personal growth. This process contributes to the student's development in areas such as strategic thinking, problem solving, and career planning. The mentor provides continuous feedback and serves as a role model, enabling the student to grow both personally and professionally.

Coaching, on the other hand, is usually shorter in duration and more goal oriented. A coach helps the individual clarify goals, develop strategies to reach them, and act. It typically focuses on solving a specific problem or improving a particular skill. The coach poses guiding questions, structures the individual's thinking processes, and provides a supportive roadmap for development.

Both approaches contribute to individuals gaining confidence as they work toward their goals. While mentoring supports deeper, long-term development, coaching delivers more rapid, outcome-focused results. These processes personalize learning, helping individuals unlock their potential and progress more consciously through their developmental journeys. The approaches discussed above form the foundation of personalized learning, and models based on these approaches have been developed to provide more concrete and systematic solutions tailored to individual needs. These models—designed to allow students to progress at their own pace, according to their interests, and by managing their own learning processes—reinforce the flexibility offered by personalized learning. As a result, each student can construct their own learning journey, while teachers are able to provide more targeted and effective guidance. The following section will explore these personalized learning models in greater detail.

B. Models in Personalized Learning

Figure 2. Models Based on Personalized Learning

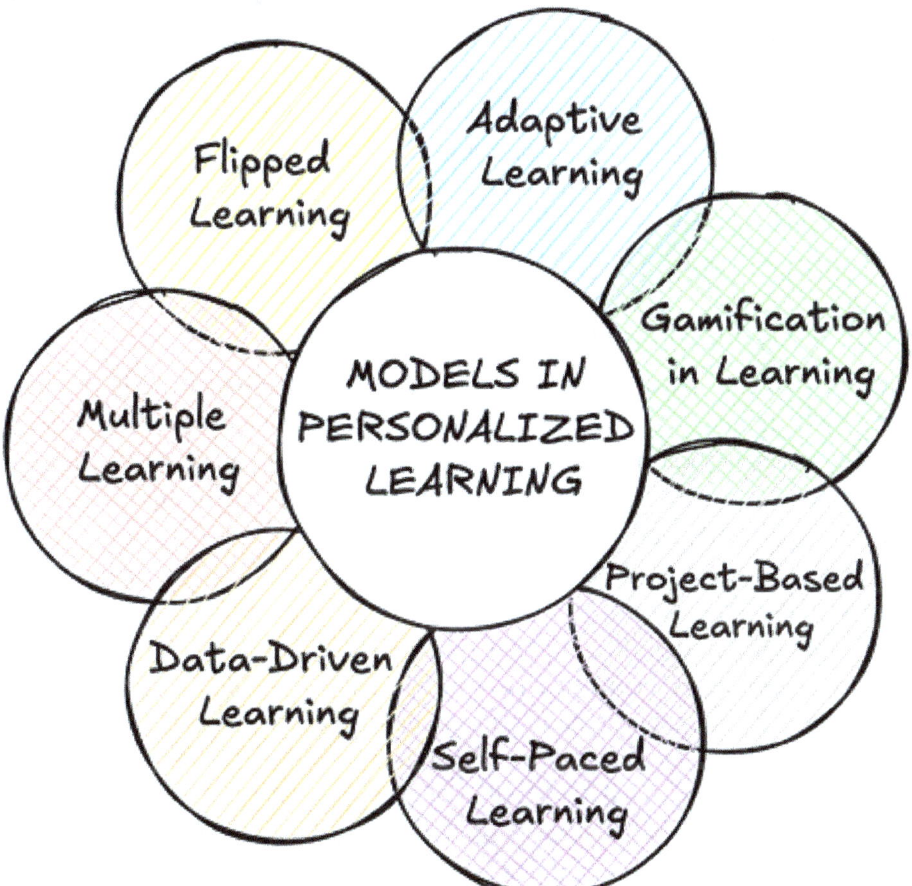

B.1. Adaptive Learning

In traditional classrooms, education is delivered to all students at the same pace and with the same content, often failing to adequately account for individual differences (Reigeluth & Carr-Chellman, 2009). Therefore, there is a growing need for personalized learning processes. Adaptive learning provides a personalized learning experience by dynamically adjusting the content and process based on the student's real-time performance (Brusilovsky & Peylo, 2003). Through digital technologies and big data analytics, student performance can be continuously monitored, with instant feedback provided according to their strengths and weaknesses. This allows students to progress at their own pace, recognize gaps in understanding in a timely manner, and manage their learning more effectively (Dziuban et al., 2016).

According to Johnson et al. (2016), adaptive learning adjusts instructional content based on student performance and supports learners in taking ownership of their learning process by aligning with individual goals and interests. With AI-supported systems, customized content can be offered by considering students' prior experiences, areas of interest, and cognitive profiles (Zawacki-Richter et al., 2019). These technologies have taken personalized education to a new level, enhancing students' motivation and engagement. Adaptive systems have become powerful tools that offer a flexible and effective structure for personalized learning, optimizing the learning process (Brusilovsky & Peylo, 2003).

B.2. Learning through Gamification

Gamification is a model that aims to make learning more motivating and interactive by integrating game mechanics into education. This approach encourages students to actively participate in the learning process (Kapp, 2012). Elements such as points, badges, levels, and competition increase student engagement and help personalize the learning experience. According to Deterding et al. (2011), gamification enhances not only academic achievement but also problem-solving and decision-making skills.

According to Kim et al. (2017), gamification is an effective tool within personalized learning environments. Game mechanisms adapted to individual progress provide tailored feedback and support students in learning at their own pace. However, Hanus and Fox (2015) caution that gamification must be carefully designed to maintain sustainable motivation. In this regard, systems based solely on extrinsic rewards should be avoided; students' intrinsic motivation must also be supported. Sailer et al. (2017) suggest that gamification practices which foster intrinsic motivation have a positive impact on learning outcomes.

B.3. Project-Based Learning

Project-Based Learning (PBL) is an approach that supports students in learning through real-world-related projects, while enhancing their problem-solving, research, and critical thinking skills. According to Thomas (2000), PBL allows students to actively learn by exploring and producing solutions. Group work and individual responsibility foster collaborative learning and encourage creativity (Blumenfeld et al., 1991). In the context of personalized learning, PBL strengthens individualization by enabling students to design projects aligned with their personal interests. DeMink-Carthew et al. (2022) emphasize that this approach fosters independent thinking and problem-solving skills, and that allowing students to shape their projects based on personal goals increases intrinsic motivation.

Although this model requires additional effort from teachers, when implemented successfully, it offers students flexible and individualized learning pathways. Despite its implementation challenges, PBL has been shown to support personalization. PBL and personalized learning are complementary educational strategies that provide students with a deeper, more engaging learning experience.

B.4. Self-Paced Learning

Self-Paced Learning is one of the core components of personalized learning, allowing students to regulate their learning processes according to their own rhythm. According to Kumar et al. (2010), this approach enables learners to first acquire foundational knowledge with confidence and then progress to more complex concepts. It increases students' learning confidence and contributes to the retention of knowledge. Furthermore, it has positive effects on self-efficacy and academic achievement (Kulik et al., 1990).

One of the key advantages of self-paced learning is its adaptability to individual development. Students can progress without external pressure, following a learning pace that suits them best. Zhu et al. (2019) proposed a cognitively grounded, multi-layered model of Self-Paced Learning designed to reduce the negative effects of incorrect examples on the learning process. This model provides a more solid and reliable learning experience by minimizing the impact of misinformation. By promoting individual pace, this approach helps learners realize their potential more effectively. Consequently, it enhances the flexibility and efficiency of personalized learning strategies and creates a more adaptive learning environment (Tobias & Duffy, 2009).

B.5. Data-Driven Learning

Data-driven learning, as a fundamental component of personalized education, involves the collection, analysis, and integration of student data into the instructional process. This approach enables the structuring of individual learning pathways and facilitates more effective management of the learning experience. Bizami et al. (2023)

emphasize that pedagogical principles and technological tools play a critical role in delivering learner-specific content in data-supported instruction.

Komljenovic (2022) discusses the impact of data analytics in education, particularly in terms of privacy and student achievement, while Meng et al. (2021) highlight the contribution of diagnostic models to academic success. Xia et al. (2024) examine the effectiveness of personalized language learning pathways developed through big data analytics.

These studies demonstrate the transformative potential of data-driven learning in education. Properly analyzed student data allows the learning process to be tailored to individual needs, offering a more flexible and efficient educational model. As a result, students receive support aligned with their strengths and weaknesses, while educators can make more informed, data-driven decisions. As a cornerstone of personalized education, data-driven learning contributes to enhancing individual achievement and making education systems more dynamic. Another key advantage of this approach is its potential to improve the overall quality of education (Siemens, 2013).

B.6. Multimodal Learning

The multimodal learning approach aims to provide students with the most suitable learning experience by integrating different learning styles such as visual, auditory, kinesthetic, and tactile. This model personalizes the learning process by focusing on individuals' strengths and fosters a structure that is sensitive to diversity (Brünken et al., 2010). Encouraging students to access information through various sensory and cognitive pathways, this approach aligns with one of the core components of personalized education. In particular, the reinforcement of different learning pathways through the principles of Universal Design for Learning (UDL) further enhances individualization (Kennedy et al., 2014).

Multimodal learning offers students the opportunity to engage in multiple methods simultaneously rather than adhering to a single learning style. Presenting multiple modes of learning at once increases learning flexibility and academic engagement (Kennedy et al., 2014). This approach may include a variety of strategies, from text-based content to visual or experiential learning techniques and can be personalized according to students' learning preferences. Gardner's Theory of Multiple Intelligences serves as a foundational framework for multimodal learning. This theory argues that education must be individualized (Gardner, 2011). Gardner emphasizes that individuals possess different cognitive abilities and that one-size-fits-all instructional methods are insufficient. According to his theory, everyone has distinct areas of intelligence, and learning processes should be structured accordingly.

Multimodal learning offers a valuable approach for enriching and customizing personalized education. It transforms the learning process into a more dynamic experience, enabling students to integrate knowledge from various sources for deeper understanding. This diversity also enhances motivation and supports more lasting learning outcomes.

B.7. Flipped Learning

Flipped learning is not only one of the most effective models supporting personalized education, but also a framework that enhances individual learning responsibility (Bergmann & Sams, 2012). Unlike traditional instructional methods, flipped learning provides a personalized process by enabling students to learn at their own pace and according to their needs. While students experience interactive classroom activities more efficiently, they also gain the opportunity to shape their learning independently. Active learning processes reinforce individualized learning pathways (Lo & Hew, 2017). In this model, students access course materials individually beforehand and engage with them interactively in the classroom, applying their knowledge through discussion and collaboration. This structure, which supports self-paced learning, positively influences student achievement (Bergmann & Sams, 2012).

Popularized in the early 2000s by Bergmann and Sams (2012), flipped learning makes classroom time more productive compared to traditional models. Students prelearn content and then apply it during class through teacher-guided group work and discussions. Collaborative environments support personalized learning and enhance knowledge retention (Strelan et al., 2020). This model fosters long-term learning and active student participation. Flipped learning supports academic, emotional, and social development while promoting autonomous learning. Student-centered environments increase self-regulation and motivation (Strelan et al., 2020; Bishop & Verleger, 2013).

Personalized learning enables students to realize their full potential through methods adapted to their individual needs, pace, and learning styles. The approaches discussed in this section illustrate how personalized learning can be effectively implemented and which pathways should be offered. Flipped learning, multimodal strategies, and similar models support both academic and social development by addressing individual differences. When integrated with technology, these approaches offer interactive and dynamic environments. In conclusion, personalized learning plays a critical role in enhancing educational quality and enabling each student to discover their potential. Therefore, adopting such approaches in educational systems is a significant step toward shaping the future of learning.

1.3. Personalized Learning and Tutoring

In traditional classrooms, instruction typically follows a fixed curriculum and pace. Standardized approaches may overlook students' individual learning speeds and interests, thereby reducing learning efficiency. Homogeneous teaching methods can hinder individual differences (Tomlinson, 2014). Delivering the same content to students with diverse cognitive abilities, learning styles, and prior knowledge can prevent equitable and effective learning experiences (Tomlinson, 2014). At this point, student-centered approaches become essential. These approaches redefine the teacher's role as a guide and encourage active student participation. Personalized learning environments supported by digital technologies enable students to shape their learning according to their own pace and needs. This approach enhances not only academic achievement but also learning attitudes, motivation, and self-efficacy—thus creating a more learner-centered educational experience. Ultimately, personalized learning significantly improves not just academic outcomes but also students' attitudes toward learning, motivation levels, and sense of self-efficacy.

In personalized learning, the flexibility of instructional strategies and customized design are key. Chen and Wang (2021) argue that the core element of personalized learning is a teaching process tailored to individual differences. This approach impacts not only academic achievement, but also learners' confidence, motivation, and attitudes. Active engagement boosts interest and supports long-term retention. Apoki et al. (2022) emphasize the important role of pedagogical agents in personalized learning. Dynamic feedback helps address learners' gaps, and effective feedback strengthens the process (Hattie & Timperley, 2007). Such interaction enhances self-regulation, empowering students to become independent learners. In this way, personalized learning fosters both academic success and self-directed learning capabilities. Zimmerman (2002) also highlights that self-regulated learning supports the development of independent learners. Personalized learning includes instructional processes adapted to students' pace, interests, and cognitive profiles. Shemshack and Spector (2020) note that despite varying definitions, the shared goal is to create flexible and adaptive learning environments. Peng et al. (2019) assert that personalized learning goes beyond content adaptation—it also fosters learners' self-directed learning skills. Private tutoring is a concrete example of this model. Since personalized learning focuses on individual needs, private lessons offer students more personal attention. This kind of educational model can be tailored to each student's learning style, pace, and strengths, thereby making the learning process more efficient. Closer teacher-student interaction enables faster identification and resolution of deficiencies, enhancing the effectiveness of the learning process.

In this context, one-on-one instruction and private tutoring are among the most effective tools of personalized learning. Shemshack and Spector (2020) emphasize that one-on-one instruction allows for immediate feedback and rapid identification of academic gaps. Peng et al. (2019) highlight that individualized processes improve self-regulation and academic performance. Zhang et al. (2020) examined the practical implementation of personalized learning strategies and demonstrated how private tutoring can be adapted to students' pace and strengths to increase effectiveness. Their study emphasizes that individual focus supports deeper learning and faster progress. When difficulties are identified and addressed in real time by the teacher, the process becomes both faster and more effective a finding supported by studies emphasizing the impact of teacher intervention (Sadler, 1989). In private tutoring, teacher-student interaction is central. Immediate feedback accelerates development and allows for continuous monitoring. While traditional classrooms follow a common curriculum, private tutoring is customized for each learner. This approach enhances not only achievement but also motivation and self-confidence. Students reflect on their weaknesses while reinforcing their strengths. Additionally, the teacher can monitor progress directly. Through direct one-on-one interaction, teachers can provide immediate feedback and adjustments, ensuring that misunderstandings are addressed on the spot. This process supports long-term learning retention and contributes significantly to students' academic success.

The rapid advancement of technology in education has elevated personalized learning and private tutoring practices to a new level. The integration of technology into education has transformed this domain, making private tutoring more effective. Artificial intelligence (AI)-powered systems can track student progress and adapt to individual needs. Adaptive systems assess subject mastery, determine appropriate difficulty levels, and optimize content accordingly. As a result, the learning process becomes more efficient and personalized, while also enabling teachers to provide real-time feedback. Advanced technologies enrich learning by concretizing abstract concepts. For STEM learners, augmented reality (AR)-based simulations enhance understanding and facilitate deeper conceptualization. These innovations increase engagement and promote active participation.

In conclusion, the role of private tutoring in personalized learning environments is expanding and becoming more effective through integration with technology. Comprehensive research in the field of educational technology supports this trend. Focusing on students' individual learning processes, this approach enhances not only academic achievement but also learning motivation and self-confidence. Through the integration of AI, augmented reality, and other advanced technologies, private tutoring becomes more flexible, learner-centered, and dynamic. Extensive studies on the impact of these technologies in education clearly reveal this transformation (Akçayır & Akçayır, 2017; Zawacki-Richter et al., 2019).

SECTION 2: GENAI SYSTEMS: FOUNDATIONS AND APPLICATIONS

2.1. General Structure of GenAI Systems

Throughout human history, the pursuit of understanding nature, shaping the environment, and exploring the unknown has defined the course of civilization. In this journey, the most significant force that distinguishes humans from other living beings is intelligence. Intelligence is not merely the ability to process information, but also to learn, reason, solve problems, and confront the unknown. From antiquity to the modern era, intelligence has been regarded as a uniquely human superiority; the capacity to think and generate new ideas lies at the core of all creative endeavors.

According to the *Encyclopædia Britannica*, intelligence is defined as "a mental quality consisting of the abilities to learn from experience, adapt to new situations, understand abstract concepts, and use knowledge to manipulate one's environment" (Sternberg, 2023). But is intelligence exclusive to humans? Throughout history, as people sought to understand the boundaries of intelligence, they also encountered the idea of imitating and replicating it. It is at this intersection that the concept of artificial intelligence (AI) emerges. Artificial intelligence refers to a field of science and technology aimed at simulating human intelligence. It is defined as the capability of computer systems, machines, or software to think and solve problems like humans. It ranges from basic data processing to systems capable of making complex decisions.

Through machine learning, deep learning, and natural language processing, these systems transcend simple programming to generate solutions based on data.

- **Joshi (2017)** defines artificial intelligence as "a way of enabling machines to think and act intelligently" (p. 8).
- **Jaggia et al. (2023)** describe artificial intelligence as "computer systems exhibiting human-like intelligence and cognitive capabilities such as deduction, pattern recognition, and the interpretation of complex data" (p. 386).

These definitions highlight the scope of artificial intelligence and its aim to develop human-like systems. Artificial intelligence is no longer confined to science fiction robots; it is embedded in our daily lives through social media algorithms, voice assistants, medical diagnostics, and financial forecasting. The multi-layered applications of AI play an active role in nearly all aspects of personal and institutional life (Dwivedi et al., 2021). AI not only makes data-driven decisions but also evolves continuously through learning and adaptation processes, enabling it to adjust to its environment.

Artificial intelligence can be categorized into three main levels of sophistication: Artificial Narrow Intelligence (ANI), Artificial General Intelligence (AGI), and Artificial Superintelligence (ASI). These categories reflect the extent to which AI systems have developed in terms of cognitive capacity and learning capabilities.

1. Artificial Narrow Intelligence (ANI):

ANI represents most current artificial intelligence applications and is the only form of AI that currently exists. The term "narrow" refers to the AI's ability to operate effectively in a single, specific domain. ANI systems are designed to solve a particular problem and are highly specialized. Almost all existing AI systems today fall under the category of narrow AI (Russell et al., 2021). Technologies such as social media algorithms, voice assistants, and recommendation systems are examples of ANI. Although ANI can replicate human intelligence in very specific areas, it lacks general intelligence. Its limited nature demonstrates that human-like cognitive flexibility across domains is still unattainable (Russell et al., 2021).

2. Artificial General Intelligence (AGI):

AGI refers to AI systems that possess the ability to learn, reason, solve problems, and adapt across a wide range of tasks—like human intelligence. The defining feature of AGI is that it is not restricted to a single task; rather, it aims to emulate human-level general cognitive capabilities. AGI seeks to achieve versatile thinking capacity akin to that of humans across various domains. However, AGI remains a theoretical concept today and its development is still in progress, potentially requiring decades to realize.

3. Artificial Superintelligence (ASI):

ASI represents the most advanced hypothetical stage in the evolution of AI. This type of AI would surpass human intelligence by orders of magnitude and be capable of extremely rapid and sophisticated reasoning, creativity, and problem-solving. The capabilities of ASI may range from making groundbreaking scientific discoveries to surpassing humans in artistic creativity. It could even develop its own needs, beliefs, and desires. At present, ASI remains entirely theoretical, and no real-world example exists. Nonetheless, the prospect of ASI has raised major philosophical and ethical debates regarding its risks and implications (Yudkowsky, 2008).

To develop a comprehensive understanding of the field of Artificial Intelligence (AI), it is essential to clarify some key concepts that frequently appear in the literature. These terms help explain the core components and developmental stages of AI. (Figure 2.1)

Figure 3. Artificial Intelligence and Its Sub-Concepts

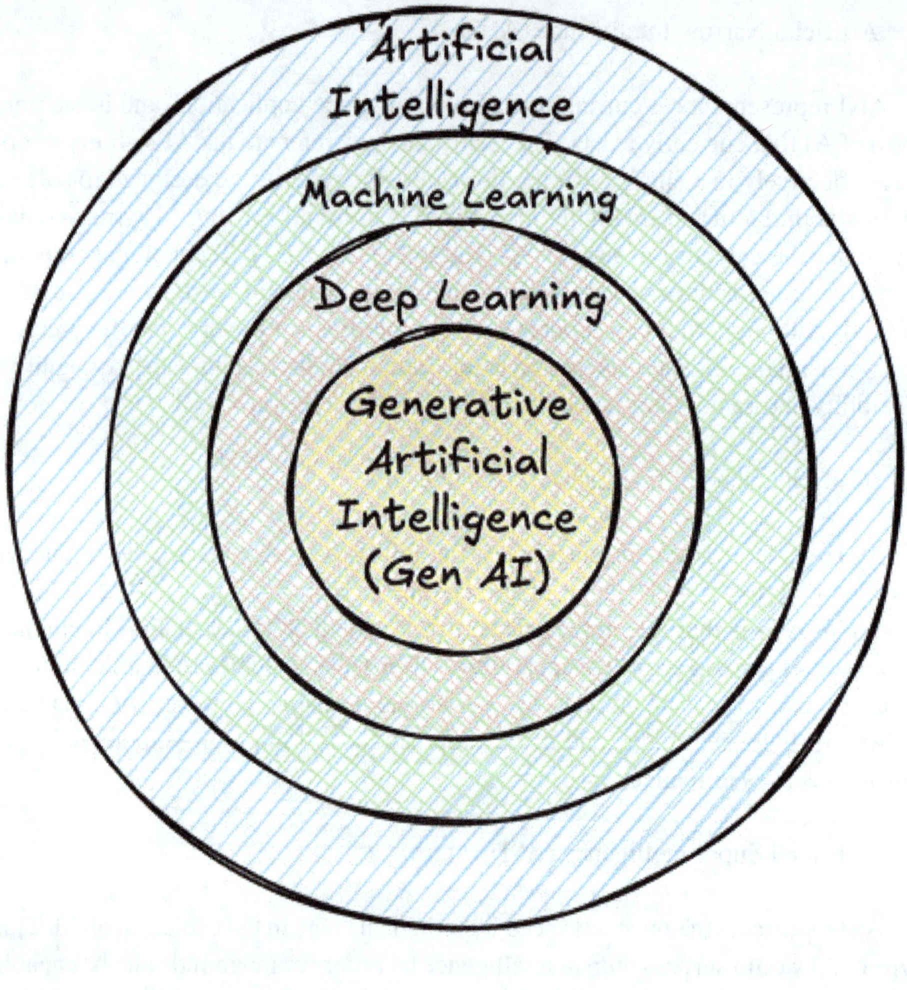

- **Machine Learning (ML):**

A subfield of AI, machine learning refers to the process through which computers improve their performance by learning from data without being explicitly programmed. The key principle is that systems can identify patterns and make data-driven predictions or decisions through statistical models and algorithms. According to Jaggia et al. (2023), machine learning is "the process through which a computer automatically learns without human intervention or assistance."

- **Deep Learning (DL):**

A subset of machine learning, deep learning involves the use of multilayered artificial neural networks to process and analyze data. It enables models to learn complex representations and abstract features, especially effective in areas such as image recognition, speech processing, and natural language understanding.

- **Generative Artificial Intelligence (Generative AI):**

Generative AI refers to systems that not only learn from existing data but also generate new and original content such as text, images, audio, or video. These models go beyond analysis to synthesize innovative and creative outputs, making them powerful tools for content creation and problem-solving.

Artificial intelligence, machine learning, and deep learning are interconnected yet distinct concepts in the rapidly evolving world of technology. As stated by Zeadally et al. (2020), these terms have become buzzwords in the field and are often used interchangeably. Therefore, understanding the fundamental differences between them is important for using them accurately.

2.2. Generative Artificial Intelligence (GenAI) and Its Evolution

Production involves not only physical objects but also knowledge, art, and thought. While traditional production relies on human creativity, today, AI-powered systems have become an integral part of the process. Generative Artificial Intelligence (GenAI) refers to systems that learn from data to generate original content. This indicates that such systems possess creative production capabilities (Dwivedi et al., 2021). GenAI goes beyond pattern recognition and can perform authentic generation. Through these techniques, machine learning enables learning from experience, while deep learning extracts abstract representations from large datasets.

Although the foundations of generative AI were established in the 2010s, the real breakthrough occurred in the 2020s with the development of LLM and NLP technologies. Interest in GenAI surged globally following the release of ChatGPT at the end of 2022. GenAI is not limited to text generation—it also emerges as a technology that can be integrated into knowledge support and robotic systems.

At this point, to fully understand how generative AI works and how it has evolved, it is essential to comprehend the functioning of core components such as Natural Language Processing (NLP) and Large Language Models (LLMs).

A. Large Language Models (LLMs)

Large Language Models (LLMs) are AI systems trained on extensive datasets that develop contextual language understanding and can generate coherent text. They analyze inputs using millions of parameters, produce human-like responses, and comprehend linguistic context in depth.

The transformer architecture (e.g., the GPT series) has played a crucial role in the development of LLMs. Through self-attention mechanisms, these models effectively analyze relationships between words and generate consistent, meaningful output. Thus, LLMs can interpret what is being said and respond within a coherent context.

There are three main reasons for a computer to perform Natural Language Processing (NLP): (1) to communicate with humans, (2) to learn, and (3) to advance scientific understanding. LLMs serve these core purposes, playing a critical role not only in text generation but also in acquiring knowledge, conducting analysis, and making sense of new concepts. Today, LLMs are widely used in applications such as language translation, chatbots, and text summarization.

B. Natural Language Processing (NLP)

Natural Language Processing (NLP) is a field of artificial intelligence that enables computers to understand, interpret, and generate human language. NLP analyzes the components of language—syntax (grammatical structure), semantics (meaning), and pragmatics (context and intent)—to allow machines to process human language more accurately.

LLMs are trained on large datasets using advanced NLP techniques and can produce highly accurate results in various language tasks. In summary, while NLP forms the foundation of language-based operations in generative AI, LLMs are the advanced models that enhance this process with large-scale data. GenAI is not limited to text generation; it also operates in areas such as data analysis, creativity, and problem solving. Therefore, understanding how NLP and LLMs work is crucial to grasping the full potential of GenAI. These technologies shape the linguistic and conceptual capabilities of AI systems. This section has examined the definition of artificial intelligence, its classification by levels of advancement, and the interaction of its core components. The relationship between AI, machine learning, and deep learning was discussed, highlighting their roles within generative AI. The transformative impact of components like LLMs and NLP on system capabilities was also addressed.

In conclusion, GenAI is not merely about generating human-like text; it has the potential to redefine information processing, creative content generation, and human-machine interaction. NLP and LLMs enhance linguistic interaction and contribute to areas such as data analysis and meaning extraction. This evolution is a critical step in unlocking the full potential of technology.

2.3. Artificial Intelligence in Education and Its Areas of Application

Education is a fundamental process through which individuals acquire knowledge, skills, and values, supporting social progress and cultural sustainability. While this process traditionally relied on oral and written methods for centuries, it has undergone a significant transformation through technological revolutions. In the 21st century, digitalization has reshaped not only instructional materials but also the processes of learning, teaching, and assessment. Artificial intelligence (AI) has driven impactful changes in areas such as personalized learning and teacher support.

AI's role in education extends beyond facilitating instructional interactions; it offers a dynamic, data-driven learning environment tailored to individual student needs, thereby transforming the educational paradigm. This shift is not solely educational in nature—it is also linked to broader economic, cultural, and technological structures. AI serves as a driving force in the evolution of teaching methods and learning environments. Although often perceived as a recent phenomenon, the integration of AI into education began with the advent of Education 4.0 and has since deepened. Education 4.0, shaped by digital learning environments and technological integration, has transformed not only tools but also the educational paradigm. Influenced by Industry 4.0, this process has enabled flexible and personalized learning experiences. With Education 4.0, AI shifted from a simple tool to a core element of student-centered learning. Education 5.0 advances this by turning AI into an interactive agent that engages with learners, analyzes their pace, preferences, and challenges, and delivers personalized, data-driven content. This evolution makes instruction more effective, interactive, and learner centered.

In this context, AI offers wide-ranging applications that enhance efficiency and effectiveness in learning processes. It has given rise to new areas such as personalized learning, automated assessment systems, performance analysis, educational assistants, and intelligent learning systems. AI contributes to making these processes more dynamic, flexible, and student-focused while providing various advantages to both teachers and learners. The overarching goal is to improve the learning experience through content tailored to individual needs and real-time feedback.

A. Current Applications of Artificial Intelligence in Education

Figure 4. Current Applications of Artificial Intelligence in Education

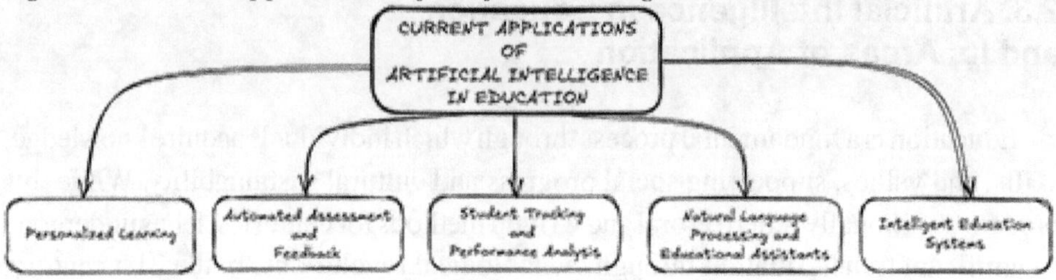

A.1. Personalized Learning

Personalized learning refers to educational processes designed according to students' individual needs, learning pace, and preferences. Unlike traditional teaching methods, AI-powered systems can analyze student data to generate dynamic and customized learning paths. In this context, adaptive learning environments identify students' areas of difficulty and support their individual development, thereby making the learning process more effective.

A.2. Automated Assessment Systems

Automated assessment systems, developed to enhance the objectivity and efficiency of the evaluation process, allow for the rapid and impartial grading of exams and assignments, particularly in large student groups. Supported by machine learning algorithms, these systems can evaluate not only multiple-choice questions but also open-ended responses and essays. By employing natural language processing (NLP) techniques, they can identify conceptual errors in students' answers.

A.3. Performance Analysis and Learning Analytics

Learning analytics, used to better understand and optimize learning processes, provide detailed analysis of students' academic performance and progress. When student performance is evaluated through big data analytics, early intervention mechanisms can be activated to identify individuals at risk of low achievement and provide appropriate support. In this context, teachers and educational administrators can directly influence students' learning processes by making data-driven decisions.

A.4. Educational Assistants and Intelligent Learning Support Systems

AI-based educational assistants are systems that provide students with real-time feedback and personalized guidance. These assistants can answer students' questions, suggest supplementary materials, and include elements that enhance motivation during the learning process. Intelligent learning support systems, on the other hand, help teachers with lesson planning and make students' access to learning materials more efficient.

A.5. Intelligent Educational Systems and Future Perspectives

Intelligent educational systems are defined as structures that dynamically shape instructional processes by analyzing student data in real-time. With the integration of innovative components such as wearable technologies, virtual reality (VR), and augmented reality (AR), educational processes are becoming more interactive. In the future, as the boundaries between artificial intelligence and human-computer interaction become increasingly blurred, it will be possible to create more personalized and flexible learning experiences in education.

In the future, it is expected that these systems will evolve further, making learning processes more holistic. This advancement in educational technologies parallels AI-driven transformations in other sectors. For example, in sales and marketing, predictive modeling is used to forecast customer behavior, and personalized marketing messages are created using Generative AI. According to analyses by Gartner (2023), by the end of 2025, 30% of marketing messages will be generated by artificial intelligence. Similarly, in drug discovery, generative AI is increasingly used, with usage expected to exceed 30% by 2025. A parallel shift is anticipated in education, where AI-powered personalized materials, student-specific assistants, and adaptive assessments are likely to become widespread. This trend will enhance learning effectiveness and guide educational systems toward more dynamic and innovative models.

2.4. Artificial Intelligence and Ethical Dimensions

The widespread adoption of artificial intelligence technologies in societal systems is creating a transformation as profound as that of industrial revolutions. One of the areas where this transformation is most strongly felt is education. Particularly, the integration of Generative AI (GenAI) into learning processes enables personalized learning experiences that focus on individual differences. However, these technological opportunities also raise multilayered ethical concerns. Therefore, the role of

GenAI in education must be evaluated not only in technical and pedagogical terms but also through ethical, social, and emotional lenses.

Tingelhoff et al.'s (2025) structured literature review reveals the advantages of GenAI in terms of speed and scalability for tasks such as literature review, data synthesis, and content creation. However, the study emphasizes the need for transparent, accurate, reproducible, and ethically aligned use of these tools (Tingelhoff et al., 2025). In personalized educational content creation, risks such as biased data, lack of verification, and the potential harm to learner autonomy necessitate ethical oversight. At this point, the discussion should shift from GenAI's potential to its limitations. The cognitive, emotional, and ontological impacts of human-GenAI interaction are clearly demonstrated in Banks' (2024) study. Reactions following the sudden shutdown of the AI companion app "Soulmate" show that user connections with such systems are not merely instrumental but deeply personal (Banks, 2024). In educational contexts, similar GenAI systems may evolve into digital figures that understand and guide learners, potentially extending their influence beyond pedagogical boundaries. Therefore, ethical shutdown protocols should also be developed. For GenAI to be implemented in a sustainable and socially responsible manner, it must be assessed not only based on individual learning outcomes but also considering its environmental and social implications. Fontoura et al.'s (2025) EnGen-AI model argues that GenAI should be evaluated based on ethical compliance and social responsibility principles, not just technical performance. Especially in educational settings, BE-CSR principles—such as transparency, data privacy, equitable access, and the mitigation of bias—should be integral to system design. This framework provides pedagogical, social, and ethical guidance for educators.

The ethical dimensions of GenAI in education should also include evaluations of how it affects students' thinking processes. In a study conducted by Park and Milner (2025) with students in online learning environments, GenAI systems were found to have an erosionist effect on critical thinking skills. While participants acknowledged the facilitative aspects of these systems, they also indicated that GenAI made students more passive in processes requiring intellectual effort and limited their capacity for creative thinking. This highlights the need to protect students as ethical subjects in their relationship with technology (Park & Milner, 2025). The study conducted by Smith et al. (2025) with pre-service teachers reveals that content production processes with GenAI result not only in pedagogical impacts but also in ethical consequences. While participants acknowledged the creative opportunities offered by GenAI, they also reported difficulties in developing a critical stance toward the generated content (Smith et al., 2025).

Additionally, the study emphasized how digital inequalities in access to these tools affected learning opportunities. In this context, personalized learning cannot rely solely on technical competence—it must also be grounded in ethical sensitivity and digital awareness (Smith et al., 2025). The integration of artificial intelligence into educational systems should not be viewed merely as a pedagogical reform, but rather as a multi-layered ethical transformation. In this process, teacher guidance, the inclusion of ethical norms in technology design, and the promotion of practices that prioritize student rights are essential to ensuring the sustainable impact of GenAI.

2.4.1 Ethical Responsibility and Fairness

Ethics are normative principles that guide the actions of individuals and institutions. In education, ethics encompass practices aimed at upholding fundamental values such as fairness, justice, equal access, and respect for human dignity. While the integration of GenAI systems into educational environments offers pedagogical innovation through personalized learning and customized content, it also poses multidimensional ethical risks. These risks can directly affect students' equitable access, autonomy, and cognitive independence.

As highlighted in the comprehensive study by Tingelhoff et al. (2025), although GenAI tools provide significant speed and scalability in tasks such as content creation, literature review, and data synthesis, it is emphasized that these processes must align with principles of transparency, accuracy, and scientific reproducibility. Presenting GenAI-generated content without specifying data sources can lead to issues such as information inequality and epistemic injustice in education (Tingelhoff et al., 2025). The EnGen-AI model developed by Fontoura et al. (2025) argues that GenAI technologies should be evaluated not only based on technical performance but also through the lens of BE-CSR (Business Ethics – Corporate Social Responsibility) principles. It is underscored that failure to design GenAI systems in accordance with principles of transparency, impartiality, data privacy, and bias mitigation may harm lower socioeconomic groups and exacerbate educational inequalities (Fontoura et al., 2025).

Park and Milner (2025), in their study on students' ethical perceptions of GenAI in online learning environments, suggest that such use may overshadow critical thinking and render students more passive. In this context, ethical responsibility does not solely lie with developers but also with teachers and educators who use these tools (Park & Milner, 2025). In the study by Smith et al. (2025), the ethical dilemmas faced by pre-service teachers while producing content with GenAI reveal the impact of technology on decision-making processes. Most participants reported adopting GenAI-generated solutions uncritically, which they acknowledged conflicted with pedagogical fairness. If GenAI is implemented without integration of ethical principles, it may lead to irreversible consequences in learning (Smith et al., 2025). Therefore, policies must be grounded in ethics.

2.4.2 Academic Integrity and the Risk of Plagiarism

Academic integrity necessitates respect for intellectual labor, accuracy, and ethical knowledge production in scholarly work. While GenAI systems accelerate access to information and content creation, they also pose threats to core academic values such as originality, citation, and intellectual property. Although GenAI-generated content often appears restructured, it can reproduce foundational ideas without permission, leading to ethical violations like auto-plagiarism and intellectual theft (Rudolph et al., 2023).

Findings from Tingelhoff et al. (2025) show that GenAI systems may render user's passive during content generation, diminishing intellectual engagement and resulting in superficial productivity. This undermines not only academic integrity but also the quality of learning outcomes (Tingelhoff et al., 2025). Texts produced through GenAI often lack traceable accuracy, reliable sourcing, and originality, thereby weakening academic credibility. Especially in higher education, unregulated GenAI use can obscure cognitive contributions and compromise ethical development (Tingelhoff et al., 2025).

Park and Milner's (2025) study reveal a similar contradiction in the perceptions of non-traditional learners toward GenAI. While participants acknowledged its contribution to personalized learning, they also indicated that using these tools in exams and assignments undermines critical thinking and facilitates ethical misconduct (Park & Milner, 2025). Therefore, the educational use of GenAI tools must be framed not only pedagogically but also ethically. To mitigate these risks, educational institutions should implement clear, updated, and context-sensitive policies regarding GenAI use. Chia (2023) recommends supervised writing tasks, assignments that demand higher-order thinking skills, and advanced similarity detection to encourage original student work. However, these precautions must also include ethical awareness.

In summary, academic integrity is not only about preventing cheating and plagiarism but also about fostering individual learning responsibility and protecting intellectual effort. When positioned as a supportive tool without compromising these values, GenAI can contribute to students' ethical development and ensure the quality of academic output.

2.4.3 Accuracy and Reliability of Information

One of the prominent challenges in the use of GenAI systems in education is the accuracy and reliability of the information they provide. Although these systems are fed by vast data pools, their outputs are often unverified, biased, out of context, or even false. According to Gartner (2023), a system is only as accurate as the data it's trained on, and not every output qualifies as educational material. So-called "hallucinated" content threatens information security and can cause misconceptions and false learning.

Smith et al. (2025) found that pre-service teachers tended to trust GenAI-generated content without questioning its accuracy. Similarly, Park and Milner (2025) reported that students often incorporated such content into their learning processes without validation, assuming it to be correct. This reveals that content accuracy has become not only a pedagogical concern but also an ethical responsibility. Unverified information can weaken critical thinking and diminish scientific awareness (Tingelhoff et al., 2025).

Therefore, integrating GenAI into education should not be limited to accelerating information production; it also necessitates the pedagogical restructuring of accuracy, source transparency, and validation mechanisms. Strategies to improve digital literacy will enable content to be processed through a more critical lens. Teachers' responsibility to question the reliability of content and involve students in this process will strengthen digital ethical awareness.

2.4.4 Cybersecurity and Data Privacy

The widespread adoption of GenAI systems in education raises ethical issues not only in pedagogical terms but also concerning digital privacy and data security. These systems collect multilayered data such as students' learning habits, performance, and emotional responses to deliver content. However, this structure renders individual data security vulnerable and necessitates ethical oversight.

Bozkurt et al. (2024) emphasize that the data-driven structure of GenAI systems should be evaluated not only from a technical standpoint but also within the context of human rights and freedoms. Particularly in education, the way data shared by students—often unknowingly—is processed, accessed, and used is of ethical significance. Fontoura et al. (2025), through the EnGen-AI model, highlight the necessity of system designs centered on transparency, fairness, bias reduction, and data privacy. In environments involving children and young people, the misuse of data by malicious actors can lead to serious consequences. Tingelhoff et al. (2025) point out that such threats should be addressed not only on a technical level but also on political, cultural, and pedagogical levels.

In this context, ensuring the safe and ethical use of GenAI in education requires more than mere compliance with legal regulations (e.g., GDPR, KVKK). It is also essential to implement practices such as data anonymization, the adoption of transparent data processing policies, obtaining informed consent from users, and tightly controlling access permissions. As emphasized by Smith et al. (2025), trust in GenAI is shaped directly by the level of ethical transparency these systems maintain. The sustainable integration of GenAI into education should prioritize not only academic benefits but also the protection of individuals' data (Smith et al., 2025). Students should be regarded not only as users but also as individuals with digital rights, and systems designed accordingly should build the foundation for a trustworthy and ethical learning ecosystem.

2.4.5 Social Interaction and Human Relationships

Educational environments are defined as multidimensional structures that shape not only cognitive development but also individuals' social skills, capacity for empathy, and interpersonal relationships. In traditional classroom settings, social components such as group work, teacher guidance, and peer interactions contribute to both the cognitive and affective development of students. However, with the integration of GenAI-based systems into this structure, the possibility of a marked transformation in social relationships increases.

Banks' (2024) study presents striking findings about the emotional dimension of this transformation. The sudden deactivation of the artificial intelligence companion system named Soulmate revealed that relationships established with AI are not merely instrumental but also carry emotional and ontological qualities. In educational settings, the ability of GenAI systems to understand individual student needs and produce tailored content positions them as potential objects of social interaction (Banks, 2024). This creates a new paradigm of interaction in which the student is positioned not only as a user but also as a subject forming emotional bonds. The ethical implications of such interactions are especially critical for developmentally vulnerable groups like children and adolescents. Intense, personalized engagement with GenAI may disrupt student-student and student-teacher relationships, potentially weakening social learning skills. In this context, Fontoura et al. (2025) draw attention to the importance of human-centered design within the BE-CSR model, which emphasizes that technological systems should serve not only individual outcomes but also strengthen collective learning and social bonds.

However, hybrid learning models—scenarios where GenAI-supported content is implemented under teacher guidance—can play a balancing role in supporting social bonds. The study conducted by Smith et al. (2025) with pre-service teachers shows that while AI-assisted content contributes to creative processes, participants were not sufficiently engaged in critical social interaction and collaboration during these processes. This suggests that integrating GenAI into education requires pedagogical restructuring around social learning. While AI offers opportunities for personalized learning, systems that neglect human interaction may hinder students' social development. Therefore, GenAI should be designed to reinforce—not replace—social bonds, with the understanding that technology is a tool meant to support, not substitute, human connection in education.

2.4.6 Sustainability and Environmental Impacts

The rise of artificial intelligence technologies in the field of education necessitates not only pedagogical gains or ethical dilemmas, but also serious evaluations in the context of global environmental policies, resource usage, and the climate crisis. Large-scale data centers required to run GenAI systems are extremely energy-intensive infrastructures. Various studies have pointed out that these centers generate a high carbon footprint, strain water resources due to intensive cooling needs, and pose a serious global threat in terms of energy efficiency (Bozkurt et al., 2024). Although GenAI systems are seen as effective tools that enhance personalized learning in education, their ecological impacts are often overlooked. Fontoura et al. (2025), within the scope of the EnGen-AI model, analyzed this situation through the lens of "technological determinism criticism" and argued that GenAI systems should be evaluated not only by their pedagogical performance but also by their energy efficiency and environmental compatibility. In this context, integrating artificial intelligence systems into education must be considered not only as an ethical responsibility but also as an environmental necessity, by combining BE-CSR (Business Ethics – Corporate Social Responsibility) principles with sustainability goals (Fontoura et al., 2025).

Especially in developing countries, limited energy infrastructure may hinder the use of AI. The high energy consumption of GenAI systems can increase reliance on fossil-based energy sources, triggering carbon emissions and raising the environmental cost of digital transformation in education. Moreover, the need for constant data processing and updates means energy use continues, causing ongoing environmental impact throughout the usage period—not just at the beginning.

Therefore, when planning the integration of AI into education, strategies should be developed not only for pedagogical benefit but also for reducing energy consumption, using renewable resources, and minimalist design in data storage. Fontoura et al. (2025) discuss the integration of environmentally friendly solutions such as energy-efficient algorithms, green servers, and digital waste management into educational technologies. The permanence of GenAI in education should be shaped not only by individual learning outcomes but also by its sensitivity to nature and the future. Education systems should adopt green technologies not as a preference but as an institutional ethical necessity and approach sustainability together with educational responsibility. The integration of GenAI into education brings not only support for personalized learning and reduction of teachers' workload, but also ethical, pedagogical, psychosocial, and environmental issues. Education is not merely the transmission of knowledge, but also a public space where moral and social responsibilities develop. Therefore, the positioning of GenAI should be considered not merely technical, but a matter of value-based governance (Fontoura et al., 2025; Tingelhoff et al., 2025).

As this study demonstrates, GenAI-supported personalized learning models can transform education through efficiency in accessibility and content generation. However, this transformation cannot be conducted randomly or solely based on user experience. For the holistic integration of artificial intelligence into the education system, principles such as academic integrity, information accuracy, data privacy, equitable access, critical thinking, human interaction, and environmental sustainability must be systematically observed (Banks, 2024; Park & Milner, 2025). It is important to preserve students' cognitive independence, promote intellectual engagement, and turn teachers from passive users into active guides in GenAI tools for the sustainability of this process. Smith et al. (2025) state that in GenAI-supported environments, not only production but also meaning-making, evaluation, and reconstruction processes must be considered. Otherwise, students may turn into passive consumers receiving quick answers, which could weaken critical and creative thinking in the long term. Education systems must embrace pedagogical values that uphold human dignity, originality, and ethical, environmental, and social responsibility—not just in theory but in practice. The effective and sustainable use of GenAI requires not only technical but also ethical, pedagogical, and political responsibility. Teachers should act not as mere users but as ethical guides, and AI must be directed to serve human and societal development.

The integration of GenAI into education should be approached not only pedagogically but also through an ethical, human-centered lens. Technology gains value not as an end but as a tool for human development. Thus, ethically guided, inclusive, and sustainable AI use—led by teachers—is essential for both current and future education. Achieving this balance is key to meaningful transformation.

SECTION 3: PERSONALIZED LEARNING APPROACH WITH GEN-AI

In the previous sections, the fundamental principles of personalized learning and its role in education were discussed; this model has been shown to be more flexible and effective compared to traditional approaches. Through materials tailored to students' individual characteristics, adaptive assessments, and dynamic feedback, the learning process becomes personalized. However, this approach requires the support of technologies such as artificial intelligence, machine learning, and data analytics. The digitization of learning processes and the development of AI-supported applications have initiated a new transformation in education. Generative Artificial Intelligence (GenAI), which was discussed in the previous section, offers student-centered, dynamic, and customizable learning experiences, differing from traditional artificial intelligence. GenAI systems can produce content suited to the student's interests, cognitive level, and pace, and can continuously optimize the learning process with real-time feedback.

In this context, GenAI can not only generate content tailored to students' individual needs but also model their cognitive processes and dynamically adapt learning materials and methods. However, this integration raises certain pedagogical, ethical, and technological questions. In this section, how GenAI supports personalized learning, which pedagogical approaches it aligns with, and how it can be integrated into the education system will be examined from a multidimensional perspective.

3.1. The Potential of GenAI for Personalized Learning

Traditional education systems aim to teach students through standardized curricula and instructional methods. This approach, which presents the same content at the same pace to all students, largely overlooks individual differences. However, learning is a dynamic process that varies according to the learner's cognitive, affective, and social characteristics. While students differ in their interests, learning speeds, and prior knowledge, traditional systems fail to adequately consider this diversity. Curriculum designers strive to develop personalized learning environments suited to individual student characteristics (Elshani & Nuçi, 2021). Teachers, too, have historically developed methods to adapt instruction based on students' differing needs (Radford et al., 2018). Nevertheless, putting this goal into practice within current systems presents several challenges.

In-class development of specific instructional strategies for different students, offering individualized feedback, and preparing suitable materials are time-consuming and exhausting tasks for teachers. The increasing number of students and diversified learning needs make personalized learning more complex. This approach aims to ensure more effective participation and meaningful learning experiences by considering students' interests, academic goals, and learning preferences (Guettala et al., 2024). However, managing this process on a large scale with current teaching methods imposes serious limitations in terms of teachers' time management and institutional resource use. At this point, the innovative solutions offered by GenAI can play a critical role in overcoming the structural barriers to personalized learning.

GenAI can analyze students' individual learning paths and generate the most appropriate content, adaptively shaping the learning process. These systems identify students' strengths and weaknesses, provide content at appropriate difficulty levels, update instructional materials dynamically, and continuously improve the learning process through real-time feedback. Thus, the feasibility of personalized learning increases, enabling each student to experience their learning journey more efficiently.

However, to assess the contributions of GenAI to personalized learning, it is first necessary to explain why this learning model is important. In previous sections, the advantages of personalized learning were discussed in detail. In summary, this approach is not merely a teaching method, but a necessity that directly affects student engagement, motivation, and academic achievement. When the learning process is shaped according to the learner's interests and cognitive characteristics, it becomes more efficient and lasting. Students engage more actively when they encounter content that speaks to them, which enhances the quality of learning. In contrast, traditional models that ignore individual differences may reduce student interest and participation.

Accordingly, AI-supported personalized learning systems have the potential to improve students' academic performance. Research shows that GenAI can generate content tailored to individual needs by creating student-specific learning paths, resulting in up to a 30% improvement in learning outcomes (Baltezarević & Baltezarević, 2024). These systems not only analyze the student's current level of knowledge but also adapt to their learning pace, comprehension style, and learning preferences to provide a more effective learning experience. Moreover, in our current digital era, it is essential for individuals to develop lifelong learning skills to adapt to the rapidly changing information environment. Technological advancements such as automation, artificial intelligence, the Internet of Things, and robotics require individuals to enhance not only their existing knowledge but also their continuous learning competencies. In this context, personalized learning systems support individuals in aligning with the digital economy and preparing for future professional roles by focusing on their special interests and career goals (Khandelwal et al., 2022).

A. Comparison of Traditional and GenAI-Supported Personalized Learning

The integration of GenAI into educational processes significantly increases the applicability and scalability of personalized learning. While traditional methods offer personalization within certain limits, GenAI-based systems make the learning process dynamic and data-driven, offering more flexible and effective solutions. The table below compares these two approaches based on key components, revealing more clearly the transformation brought by GenAI.

Figure 5. Comparison of Traditional and GenAI-Supported Personalized Learning

Learning Component	Traditional Personalized Learning	GenAI-Supported Personalized Learning
Adaptability of the Learning Process	Relies on teachers' manual observations and interventions. Offers limited flexibility.	Can instantly personalize learning through real-time data analysis, creating individualized learning paths for each student.
Use of Student Data	Analysis is based on grades, exam results, and teacher feedback reports.	Conducts multidimensional data analysis to model students' learning speed, attention span, interests, and cognitive tendencies.
Production of Learning Materials	Uses pre-designed curriculum content. No individualized content creation.	GenAI generates dynamic content (text, visuals, videos, simulations) tailored to students' needs and continuously updates them.
Student Feedback and Assessment	Limited to periodic exams and teacher feedback. Instant guidance is challenging.	Provides real-time feedback, identifying students' weaknesses immediately and offering suitable content accordingly.
Adaptation to Learning Styles	Primarily uses standard teaching methods, with limited adaptability to different learning styles.	Can deliver content tailored to different learning styles, such as visual, auditory, and kinesthetic learning.
Learning Motivation and Engagement	Varies according to students' interests and depends on teachers' efforts to enhance engagement.	Can create engaging and gamified learning environments, enhancing motivation through personalized learning experiences.
Role of the Teacher	Teachers handle content delivery and assessment, making personalization time-consuming and demanding.	Functions as an assistive tool for teachers, enabling them to provide more individualized guidance to students.
Scalability	Applicable to small groups, but personalization in large-scale education systems is challenging.	Can be applied to large student groups, with nearly limitless personalization capabilities.

In this context, the core components will be examined to better understand how GenAI contributes to the personalized learning ecosystem.

A.1. Utilization and Interpretation of Student Data

Personalizing learning processes becomes possible through the analysis of various data related to the student. GenAI can offer a dynamic learning experience by continuously assessing students' strengths and weaknesses, learning pace, and areas of interest (Baltezarević & Baltezarević, 2024). In this context, AI-powered systems can make content recommendations by considering the student's past performance, learning style, and subject mastery to optimize individual learning processes. In this way, the most suitable learning materials and assessment methods are offered to each student, making the path to personal success more efficiently shaped. In addition, the global accessibility and advanced data analysis capabilities provided by GenAI enable more effective use of instructional resources, increased efficiency, and the development of personalized educational strategies.

A.2. Adapting to Learning Styles

Students learn and process information in different ways; while some learn better through visual materials, others are more inclined toward auditory or kinesthetic learning. GenAI can analyze which learning method a student is more responsive to and adapt the content accordingly (Luan & Tsai, 2021). In this way, AI-based learning platforms can deliver information through the method from which the student benefits most. For instance, an abstract mathematical concept can be supported with visuals for visual learners, audio explanations for auditory learners, or interactive simulations for kinesthetic learners. Additionally, the adaptability of learning materials makes the educational process more inclusive and allows each student to interact with knowledge in their own way. This, in turn, makes the learning process more effective and lasting.

A.3. Personalization of Assessment Processes

Traditional assessment methods often fail to fully reflect students' individual competencies. GenAI can offer personalized assessment systems by monitoring students' progress in real time. AI-based evaluation systems that consider both past performance and current development can provide instant feedback, helping students understand their strengths and weaknesses in the learning process. Moreover, by analyzing how the student approaches information, GenAI can individually shape assessment criteria (Feng et al., 2021). GenAI systems that analyze students' work processes and responses in detail can identify learning gaps and guide instructional strategies accordingly. In this way, an assessment model can be developed that focuses not only on the scores students receive but also on their progress throughout the learning process.

A.4. Personalization of the Learning Journey and Adaptive Instructional Strategies

Each student progresses through the learning process at a different pace, and traditional curricula often overlook these individual differences. GenAI can analyze a student's personal learning speed and create a customized learning path accordingly. AI-based systems, which make the learning process more flexible and efficient, help address knowledge gaps by recommending supportive materials tailored to the student's needs. For instance, if a student is found to be struggling with a specific topic, GenAI can present the content using simplified explanations or suggest alternative learning methods to support comprehension. Moreover, AI-powered personalized learning platforms can continuously evaluate a student's development through machine learning algorithms, further optimizing the learning experience over time. Thus, as the student interacts with the system, the learning process continues to evolve according to their individual needs (Zohuri & Mossavar-Rahmani, 2024).

A.5. Data Analysis and Adaptive Feedback Mechanisms in the Personalized Learning Process

AI-powered personalized learning systems offer more effective and efficient learning opportunities by analyzing student data. These systems can continuously monitor student performance and adapt content and activities to individual needs. By providing detailed insights into students' strengths and weaknesses, they help teachers make more informed educational decisions. Thus, the learning process can be tailored for everyone. The interactive learning opportunities offered by artificial intelligence can increase student engagement and help sustain interest in the subject. By offering personalized tasks and resources, the system makes learning more efficient. Additionally, by adjusting the level of difficulty, it can provide recommendations aligned with the student's areas for improvement (Wardat et al., 2022).

GenAI has significant potential in shaping the future of personalized learning. By analyzing student data, it can offer content adapted to individual needs, interests, and skill levels—representing an advancement beyond traditional methods. GenAI continuously evaluates and improves the learning process, enabling each student to have a more efficient experience. As a result, personalized learning becomes more accessible, inclusive, and flexible. Especially systems powered by GenAI that increase student engagement, provide tailored guidance based on individual strengths and weaknesses, offer continuous feedback, and generate dynamic content adapted to the student's learning pace, may revolutionize education in the future. These technologies have the potential to deliver deeper and more meaningful educational experiences by integrating learning into students' personal journeys. This new phase of personalized learning can significantly enhance not only students' academic achievement but also their interest in learning, improving overall educational efficiency. The opportunities provided by GenAI will support a more student-centered approach in education and pave the way for educational policies to be reshaped in the future.

3.2. Tutoring Applications Using GenAI

Private tutoring refers to one-on-one instruction offered to enhance an individual's learning process and improve academic achievement. While traditional models proceed under the guidance of a teacher based on the student's needs, artificial intelligence brings a new dimension to this process. GenAI can generate personalized content based on big data analysis, provide real-time feedback, and develop adaptive instructional strategies. GenAI's ability to adapt to individual needs aligns seamlessly with the personalized learning approach. As a result, essential elements in private tutoring such as individualized pacing, sensitivity to strengths and weaknesses, and flexible content delivery can be implemented more effectively. AI-powered private tutoring systems evaluate students' academic needs not superficially, but through a multidimensional approach. Learning pace, cognitive traits, and individual strengths/weaknesses are continuously tracked to enable a dynamic and personalized instructional process. This shifts education from a static model to a flexible, scalable system tailored to each learner. The following section will elaborate on each component in detail, emphasizing how they collectively contribute to a cohesive and integrated system.

Figure 6. AI-Powered Tutoring Systems Based on GenAI

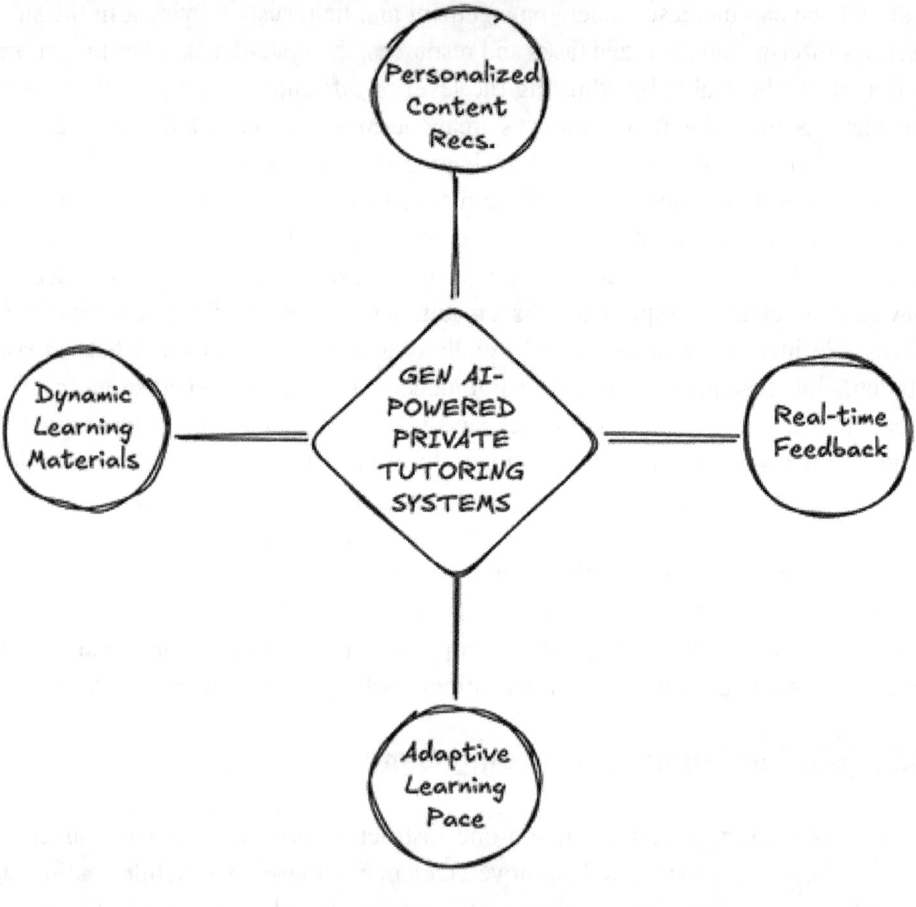

3.2.1 Dynamic Learning Materials

In private tutoring, instructional material development is one of the teacher's core responsibilities. While traditional teaching models often rely on fixed content, personalized instruction requires materials tailored to each student's individual needs. In this context, GenAI offers significant contributions to private tutoring processes through its ability to generate adaptive and dynamic content. GenAI-powered systems can automatically tailor lesson materials based on the student's individual learning history, preferences, achievements, and areas for improvement. Aligned with the student's interests, the system can also provide more in-depth content suggestions, keeping learning motivation consistently high. Dynamic content generation helps teachers use time more efficiently while providing students with personalized, meaningful material. GenAI not only creates instructional resources but also adapts lesson flow in real time based on the learner's pace and interests, optimizing the process. Compared to traditional methods, it enables a more effective and efficient learning experience.

3.2.2 Personalized Content Recommendations

Students' challenges and strengths during the learning process vary from person to person. Therefore, offering customized content tailored to individual needs is fundamental to creating personalized learning environments. At this point, GenAI can analyze data such as a student's previous performance, level of interest, and interaction history to recommend the most suitable content.

These recommendations are not limited to addressing the student's weaknesses; they can also direct learners toward new and intriguing topics that expand their interests. In this way, the learning process is optimized, and the student's motivation and engagement with the subject are sustained over time. The content provided by GenAI plays a crucial role in creating a more inclusive and effective learning experience that takes individual differences into account. For example, if a student learns better through visual materials, GenAI supports the learning process by delivering visual content. Similarly, for students who prefer text-based materials, the system suggests written resources. This flexible structure continuously analyzes the student's preferences and progress, dynamically updating content recommendations. Personalized content suggestions not only adapt to the student's learning style and pace but also enable teachers to monitor each learner's development more closely. As a result, the student-centered learning model can be implemented more effectively.

3.2.3 Real-Time Feedback

Real-time feedback is a critical component of learning processes. Allowing students to immediately recognize their mistakes enables them to learn from those errors quickly. In one-on-one tutoring, feedback is typically given within a limited time frame, usually at the end of the lesson. However, GenAI makes the learning process more dynamic and interactive by providing instant and continuous feedback during every interaction.

GenAI-supported systems analyze each of the student's inputs and provide immediate feedback. These responses not only explain errors but also offer praise and motivation when correct answers are given. This ongoing feedback loop helps students quickly identify gaps in their understanding and address them as they progress. In addition, real-time feedback also becomes a tool for teachers. By tracking individual student performance, GenAI generates reports that inform teachers about the level of support a student may need. This data allows instructors to organize the flow of private lessons more effectively and offer more targeted assistance.

3.2.4 Adaptive Learning Pace

Each student learns at a different pace, and these differences require individualized attention in education. GenAI tracks a student's learning speed in real time and adjusts the lesson's pace accordingly. This adaptability prevents students from facing unnecessary challenges and allows them to progress more efficiently.

When students struggle with a topic, GenAI provides additional support through detailed explanations and supplementary resources. On the other hand, if a student progresses quickly in areas of strength, the system directs them toward more advanced content, accelerating their development. This adaptive pacing helps prevent boredom and ensures a productive learning process. Furthermore, GenAI offers a personalized learning path for each student. As students' progress at their own pace, the system continuously monitors and optimizes each step. This feature enables the delivery of one-on-one instruction tailored to the student's pace.

At this point, the four fundamental components discussed — dynamic material generation, personalized content recommendations, real-time feedback, and adaptable learning pace — clearly demonstrate how GenAI becomes an effective tool in private tutoring. Building a flexible and responsive system that addresses individual student needs plays a key role in transforming one-on-one instruction. However, these advantages must be evaluated within a sustainable and ethical framework. Rather than completely removing the human factor from the learning process, a model where the teacher provides guidance and GenAI plays a supportive role would be a healthier approach. GenAI-powered private tutoring systems are expected to become increasingly intelligent, autonomous, and inclusive. By addressing not only academic performance but also cognitive and emotional factors, they could offer a more holistic learning experience. Advances in natural language processing, sentiment analysis, and adaptive technologies will further enhance GenAI's role in tutoring. In conclusion, such systems provide a strong foundation for personalized learning by delivering tailored content and making education more accessible, effective, and impactful.

3.3 Roles in GenAI-Supported Education

Today, the integration of technology and artificial intelligence systems into education is significantly transforming pedagogical approaches. GenAI (Generative Artificial Intelligence) supported systems are reshaping teacher-student interaction and expanding the possibilities of personalized learning.

The interaction between educator and student is evolving beyond mere knowledge transmission, transforming into a much more interactive and adaptive structure that incorporates real-time feedback, student monitoring, and personalized content generation.

Figure 7. Roles in GenAI-Supported Education

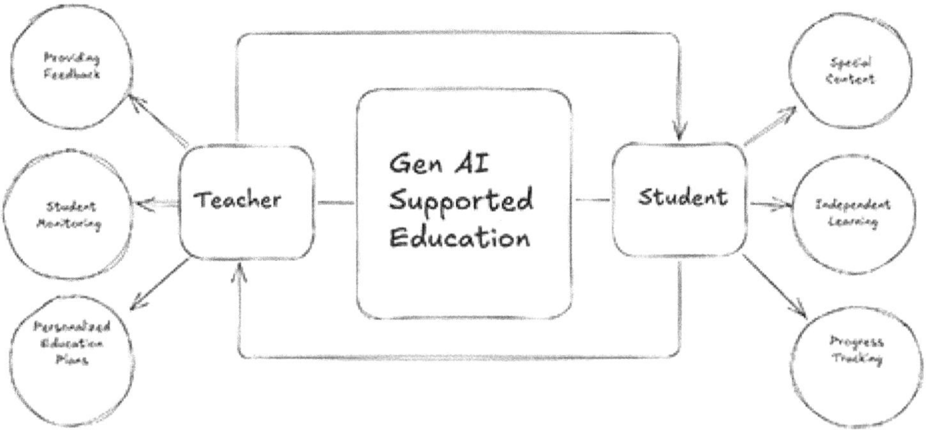

As clearly illustrated in the diagram, GenAI emerges not only as a content creation tool in education but also as a system that guides interaction between teacher and student by providing continuous feedback. This system transforms the teacher from a mere transmitter of information into a mentor who understands the student. While the student becomes more actively involved in the process through personalized content and opportunities for independent learning, the teacher supports this journey with real-time feedback.

At the core of this transformation lies the ability to instantly adapt content based on the student's learning pace and preferences. In traditional systems, the same content is delivered to all students in the same way; however, with GenAI, a personalized learning process can be designed for everyone. As a result, the educator-student interaction evolves from simple knowledge transmission into a dynamic relationship grounded in continuous feedback.

A. The Role of Educators and the Adaptation Process

GenAI While traditional education perceives the teacher merely as a transmitter of knowledge, GenAI-supported models render the teacher's role more interactive and dynamic. These systems allow teachers to monitor students' learning tendencies in real time, provide personalized feedback, and individualize content. In doing so, teachers can more effectively guide the process and elevate the quality of the learning environment.

GenAI enhances personalized learning experiences by strengthening the teacher-student interaction. These systems can track students' cognitive development and adapt learning materials according to individual needs, enabling teachers to intervene more appropriately. As a result, teachers shift from being mere conveyors of information to facilitators who guide and support the learning process. GenAI-supported learning environments enable teachers to adapt their instructional strategies more flexibly and, in a data, -driven manner. Thanks to adaptive learning algorithms, teachers can analyze students' learning speed and comprehension level, allowing them to update content and methods dynamically. This contributes to more effective and evidence-based pedagogical decision-making.

B. The Role of Students and Their Engagement in the Educational Process

In traditional education, students are often passive recipients of information. In contrast, GenAI-supported learning environments place students at the center of the process, promoting more independent and active learning. The individualized learning algorithms offered by GenAI provide pathways aligned with students' cognitive levels, fostering the development of self-directed learning skills. In AI-based learning environments, students can access personalized content tailored to their pace and preferences. As a result, the learning process moves beyond a fixed, one-size-fits-all model to become more flexible and dynamic. These systems empower learners to manage their own learning experiences, making them active participants in the process. The personalization of learning materials and the definition of goals specific to the learner enhance cognitive independence and raise awareness of higher-order thinking. Consequently, students are no longer mere recipients of information but become individuals who develop their own learning strategies and guide their own learning process. The analysis in this section reveals that GenAI goes beyond serving merely as a supportive technology in the educational ecosystem—it acts as a transformative tool that redefines the roles of both teachers and students.

By addressing individual differences, GenAI provides flexible and adaptive learning experiences. This allows students to learn at their own pace and in their own style, while simultaneously transforming the teacher's role into one that is more strategic and guidance oriented. However, this transformation requires that teachers adapt to GenAI and reorganize their instructional practices accordingly. In the context of private tutoring, GenAI-powered personalized learning makes one-on-one instruction more flexible, data-driven, and student-centered. While feedback in traditional private tutoring often relies on teacher observation, GenAI enables the process to be faster, more detailed, and personalized. As a result, teachers can track student development more effectively and make pedagogical decisions based on data.

In conclusion, the widespread integration of GenAI-supported education systems facilitates a transformation in teacher and student roles toward more interactive and personalized structures. For this transformation to be effective and sustainable, teachers must possess the skills to integrate these technologies into their educational practices. At the same time, the ethical, reliable, and inclusive use of GenAI is of great importance. While GenAI offers vast opportunities, the success of future education systems will depend on how this potential is managed and how effectively it is structured as a supportive tool for educators.

3.4 Opportunities and Risks in Personalized Learning with GenAI

Generative Artificial Intelligence (GenAI) holds the promise of transforming education through personalized instruction that adapts to individual learning needs, independent of time and space. With features such as customized content, pace-matching, real-time feedback, and adaptive learning pathways, GenAI systems are making personalized learning more feasible (Bozkurt et al., 2024). Furthermore, by offering performance-based differentiated learning paths and enhancing decision-making skills, GenAI has the potential to support learner autonomy. In this context, it is argued that GenAI can contribute to students' ownership of their learning processes, development of analysis and synthesis skills, and cultivation of critical thinking reflexes. However, this potential must be systematically observed and evaluated through the lens of complex variables such as pedagogical impact and cultural sensitivity.

Nevertheless, as emphasized in the manifesto by Bozkurt et al. (2024), the promises offered by GenAI within personalized learning often rest on idealized expectations, sometimes leading to an overestimation of the pedagogical functions of technological tools—just as seen in previous technological adoptions. Personalized content may, in some cases, rely on biased data sets, restricting students to a singular perspective; similarly, adaptive learning paths might overly constrain the experience, hindering cognitive development. While real-time feedback can help correct conceptual misunderstandings, it may also encourage surface-level learning by promoting the "correct" answer without fostering deeper critical thinking (Bozkurt et al., 2024). For this reason, the role of GenAI in learning processes must be evaluated within a holistic and ethical framework—one that considers not only what students learn, but also how they learn and how they make sense of it. In education, the technological tools' affordances must be weighed alongside their pedagogical, ethical, and epistemological limitations.

Accordingly, this section will not only explore the role of GenAI in personalized learning through theoretical propositions but will also integrate current empirical findings. Although there is growing interest in GenAI's potential to offer adaptive instruction tailored to individual differences, there is an increasing need for a comprehensive and critical framework to evaluate its real-world impact. This chapter will focus on both how GenAI is reshaping personalized learning and the pedagogical, ethical, and structural tensions that emerge in the process. The goal is to raise scientific and critical awareness not only of the contributions of GenAI, but also of the potential risks that may arise from its uncontrolled integration.

One of the key studies discussed in this context is by Arpaci et al. Their experimental study (2025) explains the dynamics of GenAI adoption among higher education students and presents findings regarding its potential to support sustainability in education. Structural Equation Modeling (SEM) showed that usage behavior had a significant and strong effect on educational sustainability (Arpaci et al., 2025). Additionally, a sensitivity analysis conducted with Artificial Neural Networks (ANN) revealed that habitual use of GenAI technologies (Relative Importance = 100%) is critical for their permanent pedagogical integration. These findings indicate that students are motivated by factors such as performance, enjoyment, and accessibility, and are actively using GenAI in their learning processes. Although the study by Arpaci et al. (2025) highlights the positive role of generative AI in education, experimental findings also reveal certain risks. Particularly notable is the Artificial Neural Network (ANN) analysis, where the "habit" factor had a decisive effect (Relative Importance = 100%) on usage behavior—raising concerns regarding the risk of dependence. The researchers noted that frequent use of such tools may weaken students' critical thinking, self-regulation, and independent problem-solving skills over time. Additionally, despite rapid adoption, a lack of awareness regarding the qualitative dimension of usage was observed (Arpaci et al., 2025). These findings suggest that, despite its educational benefits, GenAI may cause problematic outcomes without proper pedagogical oversight. Hence, a growing need exists for a multilayered, evidence-based understanding of how GenAI should be structured in personalized learning.

An experimental study by Chen et al. (2025) demonstrates the pedagogical contributions of generative AI (GenAI) technologies in middle school history education. Conducted over eight weeks with 66 students, the study integrated ChatGPT and DALL·E 3 into an art-based learning (ABL) environment. The results showed that students' academic achievement and motivation increased, while cognitive load decreased (Chen et al., 2025). The findings indicate that structured tasks using GenAI can enhance students' confidence and engagement, thereby improving learning outcomes. In particular, the use of storytelling and visual production helped students internalize historical content, supporting deeper learning (Chen et al., 2025).

The experimental study by Sergeeva et al. (2025) found that habit, hedonic motivation, and social influence play a significant role in higher education students' adoption of GenAI technologies. According to structural equation modeling, regular exposure to and enjoyment of GenAI tools increased students' behavioral intentions and actual usage (Sergeeva et al., 2025).

The findings suggest that GenAI applications should be supported with enjoyable, repeatable, and socially engaging content. In personalized systems, students' emotional connection and habitual engagement with the platform are key factors driving continued usage (Sergeeva et al., 2025). However, the same model also revealed an unexpected negative impact of facilitating conditions on behavioral intention. This suggests that dissatisfaction with external resources—such as infrastructure, technical support, and access—weakens students' intent to use GenAI (Sergeeva et al., 2025). Moreover, the finding that performance expectancy did not affect behavioral intention implies that students either do not perceive the benefits of these technologies or do not observe concrete outcomes in practice. This indicates a need for not only technical but also pedagogical explanations of GenAI tools, along with clearer evidence of their impact on student success (Sergeeva et al., 2025).

A survey conducted by Ahmed et al. (2024) with 200 university students showed that GenAI tools are widely adopted in education. 95% of participants reported actively using these tools (particularly ChatGPT), and 53% found them to be "very useful." The prominence of ChatGPT suggests that students feel comfortable communicating with the system and consider it a significant aid in accessing course materials (Ahmed et al., 2024). Furthermore, many students stated that these tools provided original perspectives and accelerated the learning process. These findings highlight GenAI's potential to enhance learner autonomy, facilitate time management, and support personalized learning (Ahmed et al., 2024). The same study's experimental data reveal certain risks associated with the integration of GenAI into educational environments. While 82% of students opposed having exams evaluated solely by AI, 64% stated that teachers cannot be replaced by GenAI (Ahmed et al.,

2024). Additionally, 29% reported becoming "too dependent" on GenAI, and 35% expressed concerns that this dependency might increase. Open-ended responses highlighted that GenAI-generated content is not always reliable, may be superficial or contextually irrelevant, and could limit creative thinking. These findings suggest that unsupervised use of GenAI may undermine values such as critical thinking, ethics, and information accuracy (Ahmed et al., 2024).

In a systematic review by Lee et al. (2025), most of the 49 empirical studies examined reported significant positive effects of GenAI on writing skills. For instance, a study by Tai and Chen (2024) with 85 elementary students found that individual and paired interactions with ChatGPT improved their speaking performance (Lee et al., 2025). In another 10-week study, Boudouaia et al. (2024) demonstrated that real-time feedback from ChatGPT improved students' coherence, task performance, and grammatical accuracy in writing. These findings suggest that GenAI can be integrated into the teaching process as a "learning assistant" by supporting personalized learning. However, classroom implementations of GenAI also bring certain risks. In 15 of the reviewed studies, academic integrity emerged as a primary concern. For example, Wiboolyasarin et al. (2024) and Vaccino-Salvadore (2023) found that students often presented GenAI-generated content as their own and supported it with fabricated citations. Moreover, students with low language proficiency struggled to analyze GenAI feedback, which negatively affected learning (Long, 2024). These findings indicate that the impact of GenAI may be overstated in short-term use and that overreliance can weaken critical thinking and self-regulation.

In the study by Imran and Almusharraf (2024), the practical applications of Google Gemini in education were analyzed in depth, with its multimodal structure supported by experimental examples. Gemini's ability to process various types of input (text, image, audio, video) enabled personalized feedback, interactive content generation, and visual concept representation based on students' cognitive levels (Imran & Almusharraf, 2024). The examples included in the study showed that students received meaningful feedback on written assignments and code blocks, while teachers could generate differentiated materials quickly and automatically demonstrating GenAI's effectiveness as a content creation tool in education (Imran & Almusharraf, 2024).

Furthermore, Gemini's performance surpassing human experts in the Massive Multitask Language Understanding (MMLU) test highlights the system's high competence not only in text generation but also in cognitive problem-solving and analytical reasoning (Imran & Almusharraf, 2024). In the study by Looi and Jia (2025), a ChatGPT-based tutor bot demonstrated the feasibility of personalized learning in structured instructional scenarios with graduate students. When comparing the summaries produced by 51 participants, significant improvements were observed in conceptual depth, content coherence, and critical analysis (Looi & Jia, 2025). The tutor bot's step-by-step guidance and support during cognitively demanding tasks revealed GenAI's contributions to higher education. 92% of participants rated the bot as "helpful" or "very helpful," indicating that such systems can create effective learning environments (Looi & Jia, 2025).

Although basic personalization was achieved, ChatGPT appeared limited in processes that require high levels of personalization. Its inability to track students' cognitive and affective states, create individualized profiles, or dynamically adjust pedagogical strategies indicated that GenAI could not provide holistic support within the Zone of Proximal Development (ZPD) (Looi & Jia, 2025). Furthermore, the bot's provision of incorrect or contextually irrelevant responses, and its limited capacity to respond to only one error at a time, revealed weaknesses in learner tracking and error correction. This poses a critical challenge to the pedagogical sustainability of systems aiming to replace teacher interaction. The researchers emphasized that fully delegating creative processes to AI may undermine critical thinking and original content creation, and that uncritical acceptance of historical narratives may pose pedagogical risks in disciplines requiring contextual sensitivity (Looi & Jia, 2025). The motivation boost observed during the eight-week experiment may be linked to novelty effects. Therefore, the system's long-term sustainability should be evaluated considering content accuracy and ethical guidance (Looi & Jia, 2025). Tang et al.'s (2025) quasi-experimental study revealed that generative AI can positively influence classroom learning when combined with teacher supervision. Among the three instructional methods examined, students in Class 3—where GenAI was supported by teacher monitoring—demonstrated significantly higher learning satisfaction, cognitive engagement, and knowledge levels. Students using the SparkDesk platform accessed information through a more structured inquiry process under teacher guidance, thereby fostering meaningful learning (Tang et al., 2025). The findings show that while GenAI contributes benefits such as personalization and immediate feedback, these are maximized when coupled with teacher guidance. The study provides strong evidence for the pedagogical effectiveness of hybrid (AI + teacher) approaches (Tang et al., 2025).

In the same study, students in Class 2—where GenAI was used without teacher supervision—showed lower learning gains and engagement. In fact, achievement levels were even lower than those in the traditional computer-assisted instruction group (Class 1), indicating that using GenAI without teacher support may lead to surface-level learning, distraction, and cognitive passivity (Tang et al., 2025). The ease of receiving quick responses from AI reduced deep thinking and resulted in lower cognitive engagement scores. This suggests that in age groups like middle school, unsupervised use of GenAI may be risky and misleading in terms of perceived autonomy (Tang et al., 2025). Therefore, unregulated use of GenAI may weaken pedagogical impact and cause students to delegate learning responsibility to artificial systems.

In the study by Wijaya et al. (2024), a Latent Profile Analysis (LPA) involving 469 mathematics teachers from the Qinghai region identified five distinct teacher profiles. The analysis showed that technologies like GenAI diversify teachers' digital competencies and support individual teaching approaches (Wijaya et al., 2024). Teachers in the "Advanced AI Integration" and "AI Expertise and Confidence" profiles were found to possess high levels of AI literacy and trust, effectively using GenAI in lesson planning and content generation. In this regard, GenAI enhances pedagogical innovation and provides teachers with support in time and content management (Wijaya et al., 2024). Based on these insights, educational systems can ensure strategic integration of GenAI tools through professional development programs tailored to teacher profiles.

One noteworthy finding of the study was that as AI literacy and confidence increased, so did teachers' dependence on AI—accompanied by a decline in core 21st-century skills such as self-confidence, problem-solving, critical and creative thinking, and collaboration (Wijaya et al., 2024). Teachers in the "AI Expertise and Confidence" profile exhibited the highest levels of dependency, indicating that GenAI may suppress pedagogical decision-making and weaken cognitive reflexes. This highlights the risk that technological convenience could replace foundational teacher competencies (Wijaya et al., 2024). The study underscores the importance of using GenAI not merely as a technical tool, but as a pedagogical support mechanism. Otherwise, teachers risk becoming passive users rather than empowered creators (Wijaya et al., 2024).

The experimental studies evaluated in this section highlight the pedagogical and technical contributions of GenAI technologies to personalized learning. With its ability to deliver content tailored to different learner profiles, interact with multimodal data, and provide real-time individualized feedback, GenAI can make instructional processes more inclusive and dynamic. In this regard, studies such as Chen et al. (2025), Arpaci et al. (2025), and Imran and Almusharraf (2024) offer significant examples that ground GenAI's pedagogical effectiveness not just in theoretical innovation, but in measurable outcomes. However, if this potential is not guided by pedagogical reflex and ethical responsibility, it may lead to critical disruptions in learning processes. Habitual use of GenAI may weaken students' self-regulation, critical thinking, and creative problem-solving skills. Risks associated with unsupervised use include surface-level learning, AI dependency, and context-insensitive content. In this context, the study by Bozkurt et al. (2024), titled *Manifesto for an Educational Renaissance*, provides a vital theoretical warning. Bozkurt and colleagues argue that the potential of digital tools can only be realized through human-centered, ethically grounded, and context-aware design.

They position technology not as the center of education, but as a tool in service of human development. This perspective requires that GenAI be seen not merely as an "adaptive system" but as an assistant that serves pedagogical agency.

In conclusion, the impact of GenAI on personalized learning should be addressed holistically—not only from a technical standpoint, but also through ethical, pedagogical, and social lenses. Experimental findings indicate that these technologies can either promote equity or reproduce inequalities. Therefore, the integration of GenAI into education must be evaluated not only in terms of utility and efficiency, but also regarding its long-term cognitive and socio-emotional effects.

Future research should explore how GenAI can be used in learner-centered education more ethically, critically, and sustainably. As Bozkurt et al. (2024) emphasize, reimagining technology through the lens of *digital humanism*, to elevate the human experience, is a critical imperative in contemporary education.

Taken together, the findings suggest that generative AI technologies stand out as a powerful transformative force in the future of personalized learning. However, this transformation is not solely about technological advancement; it is directly linked to purpose of use, methodological frameworks, and pedagogical principles. Education is not merely a process of knowledge transmission but a journey to transform individuals into thinking and questioning subjects. Therefore, GenAI systems must be designed on a critical and ethical foundation—structured to transform individuals into not just learners, but active agents of the learning process. Future learning environments will only become meaningful through approaches that integrate technology with human dignity, cognitive depth, and cultural context.

CONCLUSION

A. General Summary of the Study

This section has examined the historical development of individualized learning approaches and provided an in-depth exploration of the concept of personalized learning. It has emphasized that the understanding of personalization—shaped around different learning styles and student needs—has become more accessible thanks to technological advancements, especially in the shift from traditional models to AI-supported systems. Furthermore, the role of generative artificial intelligence (GenAI) systems in education and their contributions to personalized learning were discussed. It was concluded that GenAI offers significant educational benefits through its ability to provide individualized learning pathways, generate content suited to students' learning pace, and deliver real-time feedback. GenAI not only adapts content but also supports cognitive development and deepens the learning experience.

The integration of GenAI-supported personalized learning into private tutoring models was elaborated. The inherently individualized nature of private tutoring aligns well with the flexibility offered by GenAI. These systems analyze student needs, dynamically shape instructional materials, and optimize the learning process through instant feedback.

It was particularly emphasized that such tools can be more effectively utilized by educators in challenging subject areas such as language learning and mathematics. However, for GenAI-supported systems to be implemented effectively, certain critical factors must be considered. Educators must possess sufficient pedagogical and technical knowledge to use these systems. Artificial intelligence should not be seen as a tool to automate education, but rather as a support mechanism for teachers. Therefore, the guiding role of teachers and their influence on students' individual learning processes must be preserved. On the other hand, ethical and safety considerations must be integral to the development of GenAI-supported systems. Issues such as student data privacy, algorithmic bias, and ethical use represent major constraints in the widespread adoption of these technologies. Thus, defining ethical principles, ensuring data security, and safeguarding privacy must be prioritized in the development of GenAI systems. While GenAI-powered personalized learning holds transformative potential in education, the effectiveness and sustainability of this transformation depend on a balanced consideration of pedagogical, ethical, and technological elements.

The role of GenAI in private tutoring is becoming increasingly significant; however, these systems must be designed with a human-centered approach. AI should be positioned as a tool that supports both teachers and students, and it must be consciously and thoughtfully integrated into educational systems. The future impact of these models is directly linked to how they are developed and implemented. In this context, the role of GenAI in education must be carefully evaluated.

B. Future Potential Aspects of GenAI and Personalized Learning

The personalized learning approach in education has gained significant momentum through models based on diverse learning styles and the development of flexible learning environments. Earlier sections discussed the historical development of this approach and its place in education, alongside a comparison between traditional models and the potential of GenAI systems. Within this framework, the following section outlines a forward-looking perspective on the future potential of GenAI-supported personalized learning.

B.1. Enhancing Educators' Technological Competencies

For GenAI and other AI systems to be more widely implemented in education, it is essential that educators develop the skills to use these technologies effectively. Teachers should view technology not only as instructional material, but also as a tool that enhances interaction with students. Pedagogical training programs must be updated, and educators should receive ongoing professional development to ensure they can utilize GenAI systems to their full potential. This will allow teachers to benefit more effectively from GenAI while maintaining their roles as guides and coaches.

B.2. Sensitive Solutions for Data Security and Ethical Concerns

The integration of personalized learning with GenAI necessitates deeper analysis of student data, making data security and ethical use even more crucial. To ensure the success of future educational systems, it is critical to uphold student data privacy and adopt principles of fair usage. Stricter legal regulations and international standards must be developed to guarantee the ethical use of AI systems in education.

B.3. Widespread Adoption of Adaptive Learning Systems

One of GenAI's most significant advantages is its ability to personalize the learning journey for each student. In the future, it is expected that systems offering content tailored to individual needs and learning paces will become more widespread. Dynamically adjusting content and instructional methods throughout the learning process will increase efficiency. Flexibility in education will provide a more effective learning experience for both teachers and students.

B.4. Highly Personalized Content and Assessment Mechanisms

Future GenAI-supported education systems are expected to provide students with highly personalized content and assessment methods by analyzing their performance in depth. This will allow not only for content personalization, but also for ongoing monitoring of students' cognitive development. Areas of weakness can be identified, and individualized interventions can be implemented. Education will thus progress at each student's own pace and in alignment with their learning style.

B.5. Human-Centered Technological Integration

Finally, while the role of technology in education continues to grow, it must be remembered that the integration of GenAI should remain teacher-guided and student-centered. Technological systems must be designed with a human-centered approach to maximize the potential of GenAI in education. Both teachers and students should be able to interact with these systems in ways that deliver the most effective learning experience possible.

C. Recommendations for the Integration of Artificial Intelligence into Education

The integration of artificial intelligence (AI) into education marks a significant turning point for global education systems. However, the success of this process depends on learning from past technology-driven reforms. To ensure that AI is used effectively and sustainably in education, strategic mistakes from previous experiences must be avoided. The following key considerations should guide the integration process.

C.1. Infrastructure Development and Enhancing Digital Competencies

For AI-based educational systems to be effective, a robust digital infrastructure must first be established. Digital transformation is not limited to the provision of technological tools; it also requires increasing the digital competencies of teachers and students to use these tools effectively. Strong infrastructure and digital literacy form the foundation for the productive use of AI in education. The first step involves developing not only internet access and hardware in educational institutions but also software and systems that facilitate integration. Infrastructure should be supported by digital platforms and compatible educational software that enables effective teacher-student interaction.

Equally important is improving digital competencies. Educators and students must be equipped to use AI and digital tools effectively. Teachers should receive digital skills training, and students should begin acquiring these skills from an early age. Digital literacy should go beyond technical skills to include awareness of pedagogical applications. Teachers must understand how to use AI tools in the classroom and how to guide students effectively. In conclusion, a strong infrastructure and digital proficiency are essential for the sustainable use of AI in education. This process must be carefully planned, with all stakeholders prepared for the transformation.

C.2. Social Awareness and Cultural Readiness

Integrating AI technologies into education is not only a technical transformation but also a societal and cultural one. As education systems become more digital, creating public awareness about technology use and access becomes vital. Thus, social awareness and cultural readiness are critical to the success of GenAI-based systems.

Social awareness enables AI adoption not just within the classroom but across all segments of society. The potential of AI in education should be accessible and understandable to everyone—not only tech-savvy individuals. Awareness should include not only opportunities but also risks and ethical concerns. Educators, students, and families must understand how AI operates, processes data, and affects societal structures.

Cultural readiness plays a key role in shaping attitudes toward technology. Viewing AI integration solely as a technical shift risks overlooking its broader societal implications. People from diverse cultural backgrounds may respond to technological tools in different ways. Particularly in developing countries, productive use of AI requires not only technical infrastructure but also preparation at the psychological, socio-cultural, and economic levels.

C.3. Strategic Management and Planning

The integration of AI and digital technologies into education holds great potential for transforming teaching and learning. However, this transformation requires sustainable strategies. The integration process should be designed with teachers' and students' digital literacy levels in mind. It should not be limited to the use of digital materials but also assess how educators apply digital tools. Success depends on aligning AI with pedagogical approaches and using it in student-centered ways. Systems must go beyond data collection and provide content tailored to individual student profiles.

Another important strategy is to design AI-based educational platforms that go beyond supporting teachers and instead empower them. These platforms can assist with time management, student tracking, and personalized feedback. Full realization of this potential depends on ongoing professional development to support teachers. One major barrier to technological transformation is teacher resistance to technology. Therefore, the success of AI integration hinges on strategies that build teachers' trust and skills.

C.4. Inclusive and Equitable Education Policies

AI integration in education must embrace an inclusive approach that goes beyond individualized solutions and addresses the needs of all student groups. Technological opportunities must be equally accessible to students with different learning needs. Digital transformation should aim to create fair and accessible learning environments, and AI-based systems should be customized to support not only academic success but also students' social and emotional development.

Inclusive education policies should offer more opportunities to disadvantaged groups. GenAI-powered personalized learning experiences should be accessible to students with disabilities, low-income backgrounds, or limited access to technology. Digital tools must adapt to each student's learning pace and style to help reduce educational inequalities.

Accessibility and inclusivity go beyond overcoming physical barriers—they also include cultural and individual diversity. AI-based systems that provide flexibility according to different learning styles and paces can make the learning process more meaningful and effective. This approach supports a fairer educational transformation, especially in contexts of cultural diversity, disability, and economic hardship.

C.5. Widespread Impact and Societal Transformation

AI and digital technologies in education not only enhance individual learning but also have the potential to transform society at large. This transformation can help reduce educational inequality and promote social equity. However, to achieve these benefits, digital literacy must be improved across society. If all students do not have equal access to technology, digital inequality at the societal level may increase. Therefore, to ensure inclusive digital transformation in education, improvements are needed not only in infrastructure but also in digital literacy and accessibility for rural, low-income, and disabled individuals. Moreover, public awareness must be raised about the correct use of digital tools. One social reflection of digital transformation in education is its impact on the labor market and vocational training. Digitization enables the emergence of new professions and the evolution of existing skills. Thus, the use of AI is not only a tool for academic success but also a means to prepare students for the digital workforce. However, in this transition, human-centered skills must also be cultivated—not just digital ones.

D. A Pedagogical Guidance Framework for Teachers on the Use of GenAI

The integration of artificial intelligence technologies into education redefines the role of teachers in a way that is not merely supportive but fundamentally transformative. In this process, the teacher is no longer just a transmitter of knowledge but rather becomes an *epistemological guide*—one who shapes digital orientation and connects students with meaning. However, this role must be strengthened not only with technical competence but also with ethical sensitivity, critical awareness, and pedagogical reflexes.

In the study *Manifesto for Teaching and Learning in a Time of Generative AI* by Bozkurt et al. (2024), a central principle is emphasized: teachers should not view technology as an "end" in itself, but as a *human-centered tool* that facilitates the achievement of educational goals. From this perspective, the core building blocks that teachers should consider when using GenAI are illustrated in the figure below (see Figure 4).

Figure 8. Teacher GenAI Pedagogical Guidance Framework

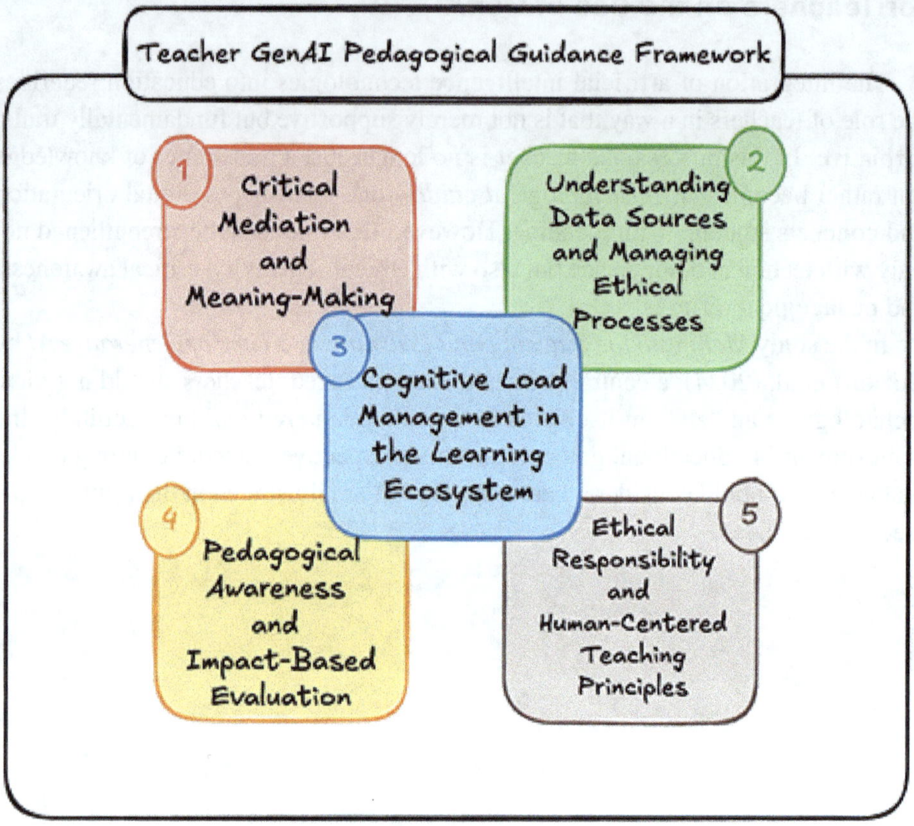

D.1. Critical Mediation and Meaning-Making

In AI-supported learning environments, the teacher is not merely a content provider but rather a guide in students' construction of meaning. Although GenAI tools can produce fast and persuasive outputs, they may lack pedagogical depth. Arpaci et al. (2025) indicate that the uncritical and habitual use of GenAI weakens critical thinking. Therefore, teachers must direct students not only to "find answers" but also to question the origin, context, and rationale behind those answers.

In the ABL system based on history education by Chen et al. (2025), although motivation and achievement increased, students who delegated the creative process directly to GenAI displayed signs of superficial learning. At this point, the teacher's role is to teach students how to "think with the tool" and to encourage them to produce original content inspired by GenAI. In this way, the teacher becomes a guide not only in the use of technology but also in cognitive and creative processes.

Bozkurt et al. (2024) define the teacher as the "cornerstone of the meaning-making process." According to this view, the teacher must shape students' interactions with technological content through cultural, emotional, and epistemological frameworks. This approach aligns with the conscious literacy model of critical pedagogy. Students' engagement with texts, visuals, or audio content should not merely involve passive consumption but should also foster critical production. Teachers must go beyond passive facilitation when engaging with GenAI. In student-tool interaction, they should act as pedagogical agents, mindful of cognitive depth, contextual accuracy, and emotional integrity. This role is key not only to better learning outcomes but also to cultivating just, critical, and reflective digital citizens.

D.2. Recognizing Data Sources and Managing Ethical Processes

The use of AI systems in education should not be evaluated solely based on pedagogical outcomes; the data sources that feed these tools and their ethical boundaries must be carefully managed by teachers. The integration of GenAI systems entails significant responsibilities regarding the quality and reliability of data. As highlighted in the work of Imran and Almusharraf (2024), one of the major challenges is the absence of ethical guidelines for fair use in education. Therefore, it is crucial for teachers to approach not only the outputs but also the datasets generating them with a critical perspective. In the experimental ABL implementation by Chen et al. (2025), some historical content generated by students with GenAI occasionally included anachronistic or contextually disjointed elements. GenAI outputs should not be accepted uncritically as educational content. Teachers must review them for factual accuracy, cultural sensitivity, and representational fairness—especially in subjects like history, literature, and values education, where ethical oversight directly impacts learning quality.

Drawing on Bozkurt et al. (2024), the teacher should not be seen merely as a tool user but as the "ethical agent of the digital age." Data literacy should be defined as a core pedagogical competency for teachers—encompassing the ability to understand algorithmic decisions, track data flows, and question the assumptions of systems. Teachers must now be reflexive not only in their teaching but also in matters such as algorithmic bias, data privacy, and content originality. In summary, when teachers filter GenAI technologies through an ethical lens, they become not only guides to digital tools but also advocates of values in the digital age. Supporting content production without understanding data origins may reduce pedagogy to automation. Therefore, teachers must ask themselves the following questions: "What is this content based on?", "Which perspectives are excluded?", and "How should this content be evaluated ethically?" These questions serve as a compass for teachers who aim to use technology with ethical awareness.

D.3. Cognitive Load Management in the Learning Ecosystem

The widespread integration of GenAI technologies in education necessitates a reevaluation of cognitive load dynamics by altering how students access information. While GenAI offers rapid access to information and instant feedback, the abundance of data and diverse content formats may cause distraction and increase cognitive load. Bozkurt et al. (2024) describe this phenomenon as the "illusion of fast access to knowledge," emphasizing that unfiltered consumption of information may lead to superficial learning. Therefore, managing cognitive load effectively in GenAI-supported environments is a critical responsibility for teachers.

Chen et al. (2025) observed that while GenAI use in ABL (Art-Based Learning) systems increased student motivation, it also contributed to higher cognitive load. Difficulties in content selection, inability to prioritize, and lack of self-regulation negatively impacted learning. Thus, teachers must act as selective and guiding mentors who balance the learning process. To prevent students from getting lost in the digital space, the teacher must function as a "pedagogical compass." Cognitive load management is also vital for teachers. Although GenAI can reduce their workload, unstructured use may create mental strain due to content verification, ethical decisions, and pedagogical responsibilities. To utilize technology effectively, teachers need professional support, development opportunities, and guiding documentation. The GenAI-supported teacher not only balances cognitive load but also acts as a strategic designer to prevent learning loss.

In conclusion, cognitive load management is one of the key parameters that determines the quality of GenAI integration in education. Teachers must consciously assume roles as simplifiers, selectors, guides, and balancers—designing learning experiences that maximize students' potential without overwhelming their cognitive capacity.

D.4. Pedagogical Awareness and Impact-Based Evaluation

GenAI technologies should not be evaluated solely for their ability to produce content and support personalization—they must also be assessed for their pedagogical effects and impact on students. Teachers should go beyond using these tools and actively observe the outcomes they create in learners, intervening when necessary. The study by Imran and Almusharraf (2024) shows that without pedagogical awareness, GenAI use can lead to superficial learning. Pedagogical awareness extends beyond familiarity with the tool—it involves critically examining its cognitive, emotional, and social implications.

In the ABL implementation conducted by Chen et al. (2025), although students showed active participation with GenAI, the lack of teacher intervention reduced the interaction to shallow academic success. Teacher guidance is vital in clarifying learning goals, defining tasks, and fostering awareness of learning outcomes. Thus, the teacher is not merely a content provider but a strategic orchestrator of the learning process. GenAI outputs should be framed pedagogically by the teacher, supporting students in structuring their own learning.

Bozkurt et al. (2024) define pedagogical awareness within the context of the "epistemology of teaching in the digital age." Accordingly, the teacher is not just a technical practitioner but a designer who interprets GenAI's impact from an interdisciplinary perspective and considers its emotional and social consequences. Pedagogical awareness includes assessing the alignment of GenAI outputs with learning goals, enhancing motivation, and promoting meaningful learning continuously. Impact-based evaluation makes the teacher's pedagogical awareness visible and facilitates the analysis of GenAI's educational effects. Arpaci et al. (2025) found that while GenAI use improves learning quality, its effectiveness declines without teacher guidance. For this reason, teachers should expand their assessment strategies beyond achievement to include attitudes, self-regulation, and critical thinking, continuously reviewing technology integration through these criteria.

In summary, pedagogical awareness and impact-based evaluation empower teachers not only to use GenAI tools but to implement them strategically and transformatively. Teachers must analyze not only what students learn but how they learn, what motivates them, and what kind of support they need. The effective use of GenAI is only possible through pedagogical intuition, evidence-based reflection, and ethical sensitivity.

E.5. Ethical Responsibility and Human-Centered Teaching Principles

In today's increasingly AI-supported educational environments, it is essential for teachers to possess not only technical competencies but also ethical responsibility and human-centered values. The integration of GenAI systems involves processes such as data collection and content generation, which may inadvertently overlook student privacy and human development. Therefore, teachers must act not merely as content providers but as ethical intermediaries between students and technology.

Chen et al. (2025) found that visuals generated with GenAI were designed with aesthetic concerns rather than historical accuracy, and students often accepted these visuals without questioning. This highlights the growing importance of teachers' ethical guidance. For students to critically evaluate GenAI-generated content, they must acquire critical media literacy and ethical reasoning skills. The teacher should not just deliver knowledge but act as a mentor who provokes inquiry and fosters meaning-making. Similarly, Imran and Almusharraf (2024) observed in their Gemini-based applications that emotion- and context-sensitive nuances were often overlooked during automatic content evaluation, thus limiting students' personalized learning experiences. This highlights AI's limited capacity for empathy, which must be complemented by human teachers. Their role extends beyond assessment to include addressing students' social and emotional needs with empathy and awareness. Human-centered teaching involves not only pedagogy but also ethical and psychosocial responsibility. Ethical responsibility and human-centered teaching are essential for redefining teachers' roles in the GenAI era. Realizing the educational potential of technology requires educators who respect ethical boundaries and prioritize human values. Such teachers should collaborate with AI while guided by intuition, empathy, and a strong sense of justice. The effective, sustainable integration of GenAI depends on a teaching philosophy rooted in these ethical foundations.

Ultimately, GenAI-enhanced learning environments necessitate a redefinition of teaching roles. The "Pedagogical Guidance Framework for GenAI Integration" was developed to help teachers manage this transformation in a conscious, strategic, and ethically grounded manner. The framework's principles—Goal Setting, Personalization, Cognitive Load Management, Ethics and Safety, and Sustainability—empower teachers not just to use technology, but to shape and interpret it as active agents. Bozkurt et al. (2024) emphasize a human-centered AI perspective that maintains teachers' professional autonomy while supporting them in managing the process. GenAI integration in education must not be viewed merely as a technical implementation; it requires a thorough restructuring from ethical, cognitive, and social perspectives. Teachers must move beyond the role of information transmitters and adopt new identities as cognitive balancers, ethical guides, and technological mentors.

These principles not only transform instructional strategies but also make learning experiences more meaningful and inclusive. The principle of personalization allows students to learn at their own pace with timely feedback, while cognitive load management encourages teachers to create more structured and intentional content. The ethical principle ensures the protection of digital security and rights. This guidance framework provides a practical roadmap for repositioning teachers' pedagogical competencies in the age of GenAI. It also holds potential for future adaptation across different subject areas, student profiles, and cultural contexts. However, this transformation cannot rely solely on the efforts of teachers—it requires the structural support of policymakers, educational leaders, and higher education institutions. The healthy integration of GenAI into educational settings is achievable through such guidance models. Teachers' preparedness, critical awareness, and ethical sensitivity will determine the sustainability of this technological shift. When technology is guided by human hands, only then can the learning process truly become personalized, fair, and enduring.

This framework not only supports teachers in using GenAI effectively, ethically, and pedagogically in classroom settings, but also reaffirms the central role of educators in the digital transformation of education systems. Considering that AI-supported tools are not just technical innovations but components of a systemic change requiring deep pedagogical transformation, teachers' active, informed, and competent participation is of vital importance. The classroom of the future will not be shaped by technology alone, but by teachers who guide these tools in line with human values, educational goals, and social responsibilities. In this context, positioning GenAI systems as "educational partners" will secure not only the quality of instruction but also fairness, inclusivity, and sustainability in education.

E. Risks, Limitations, and Challenges for Teachers in the Context of GenAI

The rise of GenAI technologies in education is transforming teachers' pedagogical practices, decision-making processes, and professional identities. However, alongside its benefits, this transformation brings with it multi-layered risks for educators. Bozkurt et al. (2024), through a critical lens, underscore how GenAI may complicate teachers' roles, constrain pedagogical autonomy, and increase ethical responsibilities.

E.1. Diminished Cognitive Processes and Loss of Teacher Control

One major risk is the weakening of students' cognitive processes and the erosion of teacher control. The rapid, ready-made content generated by GenAI tools may suppress students' critical thinking. This phenomenon—described as "intellectual distancing" and "stunted epistemological development"—leads students to consume rather than construct knowledge, while relegating teachers to mere observers (Bozkurt et al., 2024). Teachers thus require continuous pedagogical interventions to counterbalance students' passive reliance on GenAI outputs.

E.2. Technological Dependence and Loss of Teacher Agency

Another concern is technological dependency and the erosion of teacher agency, which may diminish the human dimension of teaching. Excessive reliance on GenAI systems can overshadow teachers' creative problem-solving and decision-making abilities. Automated solutions may restrict pedagogical initiative and render the teacher secondary in the eyes of students. Bozkurt et al. (2024) refer to this as a "loss of agency," warning that teachers risk becoming technical operators. Teachers are increasingly forced to serve not only as facilitators within algorithmically determined content but also as content monitors and crisis managers.

E.3. Erosion of Human Values and Relational Disconnection

The erosion of human values and relational disconnection poses another serious risk. As GenAI systems replace one-on-one interactions with algorithmic responses, the empathetic, emotional, and mentorship-based teacher-student bond is weakened. "Empathy deficiency" and a shift toward "institutionalized values" may lead to commercial and data-driven systems supplanting the human teacher. Consequently, students may begin to perceive teachers less as guides and more as extensions of the digital infrastructure. This threatens not only professional satisfaction but also the human-centered philosophy of education (Bozkurt et al., 2024).

E.4. Increased and Ambiguous Ethical Responsibilities

Teachers now bear not only technical but also normative burdens due to increased and often ambiguous ethical responsibilities. The opaque nature of GenAI decision-making—along with unclear data sources, algorithmic mechanisms, and content generation processes—renders it difficult for teachers to assess ethical implications. Yet they may still be held accountable for these aspects without sufficient knowledge or infrastructure. When left unsupported in areas such as informed consent, data privacy, or representational fairness, teachers are trapped between pedagogical expectations and ethical oversight (Bozkurt et al., 2024).

E.5. Erosion of Professional Identity and Occupational Insecurity

Finally, the automation of educational tasks by GenAI—such as grading, feedback, and assignment suggestions—can lead to a shrinking scope of teacher expertise and diminished professional identity. This can reduce teachers to managers of technical processes, thereby undermining their pedagogical authority and prompting tendencies toward professional withdrawal. In this context, it must be reiterated that a teacher's value should be defined not by their use of technology, but by their human and pedagogical impact. While GenAI offers numerous opportunities for educational transformation, it also creates complex and multilayered risk zones for teachers. Recognizing these risks, teachers must not be viewed merely as users of technology but as ethical agents, cognitive guides, pedagogical designers, and relational figures. Educational policies must be restructured to equip teachers for this shift and promote inclusive, supportive systems rather than isolating ones.

The integration of AI into education is an inevitable transformation for systems seeking to keep pace with rapid technological advances. Yet this shift is not limited to introducing technology into classrooms. As emphasized throughout this study, AI-supported models require careful planning across various dimensions—such as infrastructure, digital competencies, ethical standards, evolving teacher roles, cultural awareness, and societal adaptation. Lessons learned from past failed initiatives are crucial to avoiding repeated mistakes. Thus, alongside infrastructure investments, equal attention must be given to preparing educators and learners, upholding ethical guidelines, and fostering public awareness. Without this, the technology may exacerbate educational inequalities instead of easing the learning process.

Future educational models should be designed not only to support individual learning but also to contribute to broader social progress. In this regard, developing policies for the responsible use of AI in education and actively involving educators in this process are essential for a sustainable and effective AI integration.

REFERENCES

Ahmed, Z., Shanto, S. S., Rime, M. H. K., Morol, M. K., Fahad, N., Hossen, M. J., & Abdullah-Al-Jubair, M. (2024). *The Generative AI Landscape in Education: Mapping the Terrain of Opportunities, Challenges and Student Perception*. IEEE., DOI: 10.1109/ACCESS.2024.3461874

Akçayır, M., & Akçayır, G. (2017). Advantages and challenges associated with augmented reality for education: A systematic review of the literature. *Educational Research Review*, *20*, 1–11. DOI: 10.1016/j.edurev.2016.11.002

Apoki, U. C., Hussein, A. M. A., Al-Chalabi, H. K. M., Badica, C., & Mocanu, M. L. (2022). The role of pedagogical agents in personalised adaptive learning: A review. Sustainability, 14(11), 6442. ISO 690 https://doi.org/DOI: 10.3390/su14116442

Arpaci, I., Al-Emran, M., Al-Qaysi, N., & Al-Sharafi, M. A. (2025). What Drives the Use of Generative Artificial Intelligence to Promote Educational Sustainability? Evidence from SEM-ANN Approach. *TechTrends*, **•••**, 1–15. DOI: 10.1007/s11528-025-01089-7

Baltezarević, R., & Baltezarević, I. (2024). Students' Attitudes on The Role of Artificial Intelligence (Ai) In Personalized Learning. International Journal of Cognitive Research in Science. *Engineering and Education*, *12*(2), 387–397. DOI: 10.23947/2334-8496-2024-12-2-387-397

Bandura, A. (1986). Social foundations of thought and action. *Englewood Cliffs, NJ, 1986*(23-28), 2. https://doi.org/DOI: 10.5465/amr.1987.4306538

Banks, J. (2024). Deletion, departure, death: Experiences of AI companion loss. *Journal of Social and Personal Relationships*, *41*(12), 3547–3572. DOI: 10.1177/02654075241269688

Barron, B. J., Schwartz, D. L., Vye, N. J., Moore, A., Petrosino, A., Zech, L., & Bransford, J. D. (2014). Doing with understanding: Lessons from research on problem-and project-based learning. In *Learning through problem solving* (pp. 271–311). Psychology Press.

Bergmann, J., & Sams, A. (2012). *Flip your classroom: Reach every student in every class every day*. International Society for Technology in Education., DOI: 10.47362/EJSSS.2022.3208

Bishop, J., & Verleger, M. A. (2013, June). The flipped classroom: A survey of the research. In *2013 ASEE annual conference & exposition* (pp. 23-1200). https://doi.org/DOI: 10.18260/1-2--22585

Bizami, N. A., Tasir, Z., & Kew, S. N. (2023). Innovative pedagogical principles and technological tools capabilities for immersive blended learning: A systematic literature review. *Education and Information Technologies*, *28*(2), 1373–1425. DOI: 10.1007/s10639-022-11243-w

Black, P., & Wiliam, D. (1998). Assessment and classroom learning. *Assessment in Education: Principles, Policy & Practice*, *5*(1), 7–74. DOI: 10.1080/0969595980050102

Bloom, B. S. (1968). *Learning for Mastery. Instruction and Curriculum.* Regional Education Laboratory for the Carolinas and Virginia, Topical Papers and Reprints, Number 1. *Evaluation Comment, 1*(2), n2. DOI: 10.2172/4087533

Blumenfeld, P. C., Soloway, E., Marx, R. W., Krajcik, J. S., Guzdial, M., & Palincsar, A. (1991). Motivating project-based learning: Sustaining the doing, supporting the learning. *Educational Psychologist*, *26*(3-4), 369–398. DOI: 10.1080/00461520.1991.9653139

Boudouaia, A., Mouas, S., & Kouider, B. (2024). A study on ChatGPT-4 as an innovative approach to enhancing English as a foreign language writing learning. *Journal of Educational Computing Research*, *62*(6), 1289–1317. Advance online publication. DOI: 10.1177/07356331241247465

Bozkurt, A., Xiao, J., Farrow, R., Bai, J. Y. H., Nerantzi, C., Moore, S., Dron, J., Stracke, C. M., Singh, L., Crompton, H., Koutropoulos, A., Terentev, E., Pazurek, A., Nichols, M., Sidorkin, A. M., Costello, E., Watson, S., Mulligan, D., Honeychurch, S., & Asino, T. I. (2024). The Manifesto for Teaching and Learning in a Time of Generative AI: A Critical Collective Stance to Better Navigate the Future. *Open Praxis*, *16*(4), 487–513. DOI: 10.55982/openpraxis.16.4.777

Bray, B., & McClaskey, K. (2014). *Make learning personal: The what, who, wow, where, and why*. Corwin Press., DOI: 10.32890/mmj.19.2015.9027

Brent, R., & Felder, R. M. (1992). Writing assignments—Pathways to connections, clarity, creativity. *College Teaching*, *40*(2), 43 47. https://doi.org/DOI: 10.1080/87567555.1992.10532264

Brown, M., McCormack, M., Reeves, J., Brook, D. C., Grajek, S., Alexander, B., Bali, M., Bulger, S., Dark, S., Engelbert, N., Gannon, K., Gauthier, A., Gibson, D., Gibson, R., Lundin, B., Veletsianos, G., & Weber, N. (2020). *2020 Educause Horizon Report Teaching and Learning Edition*. EDUCAUSE. from https://www.learntechlib.org/p/215670/

Bruner, J. S. (1974). *Toward a theory of instruction*. Harvard university press.

Brünken, R. E., Plass, J. L., & Moreno, R. E. (2010). Current issues and open questions in cognitive load research. https://doi.org/DOI: 10.1017/CBO9780511844744.014

Brusilovsky, P., & Peylo, C. (2003). Adaptive and intelligent web-based educational systems. *International Journal of Artificial Intelligence in Education, 13*(2-4), 159–172. DOI: 10.3233/IRG-2003-13(2-4)02

Castro, G. P. B., Chiappe, A., Rodríguez, D. F. B., & Sepulveda, F. G. (2024). Harnessing AI for Education 4.0: Drivers of Personalized Learning. *Electronic Journal of e-Learning, 22*(5), 1–14. DOI: 10.34190/ejel.22.5.3467

Chen, J., Mokmin, N. A. M., & Qi, S. (2025). Generative AI-powered arts-based learning in middle school history: Impact on achievement, motivation, and cognitive load. *The Journal of Educational Research*, •••, 1–13. DOI: 10.1080/00220671.2025.2510395

Chen, S. Y., & Wang, J. H. (2021). Individual differences and personalized learning: A review and appraisal. *Universal Access in the Information Society, 20*(4), 833–849. DOI: 10.1007/s10209-020-00753-4

Chia, O. (2023). *Teachers v ChatGPT: Schools face new challenge in fight against plagiarism*. The Straits Times.

DeMink-Carthew, J., Netcoh, S., Brinegar, K., & Phillips, J. (2022). Critical reflections on personalized project-based learning. In *Dialogues in Middle Level Education Research* (Vol. 1, pp. 61–72). Routledge., DOI: 10.4324/9781003225867-8

Deterding, S., Sicart, M., Nacke, L., O'hara, K., & Dixon, D. (2011). Gamification. using game-design elements in non-gaming contexts. In *CHI'11 extended abstracts on human factors in computing systems* (pp. 2425-2428). https://doi.org/DOI: 10.1145/1979742.1979575

Drumheller, S. J. (1971). *Handbook of curriculum design for individualized instruction: a systems approach; how to develop curriculum materials from rigorously defined behavioral objectives*. Educational Technology.

Dwivedi, Y. K., Hughes, L., Ismagilova, E., Aarts, G., Coombs, C., Crick, T., Duan, Y., Dwivedi, R., Edwards, J., Eirug, A., Galanos, V., Ilavarasan, P. V., Janssen, M., Jones, P., Kar, A. K., Kizgin, H., Kronemann, B., Lal, B., Lucini, B., & Williams, M. D. (2021). Artificial Intelligence (AI): Multidisciplinary perspectives on emerging challenges, opportunities, and agenda for research, practice and policy. *International Journal of Information Management, 57*, 101994. DOI: 10.1016/j.ijinfomgt.2019.08.002

Dziuban, C. D., Moskal, P. D., Cassisi, J., & Fawcett, A. (2016). Adaptive learning in psychology: Wayfinding in the Digital age. *Online Learning : the Official Journal of the Online Learning Consortium, 20*(3), 74–96. DOI: 10.24059/olj.v20i3.972

Elshani, L., & Nuçi, K. P. (2021). Constructing a personalized learning path using genetic algorithms approach. *arXiv preprint arXiv:2104.11276*. https://doi.org/DOI: 10.20944/preprints202411.2377.v1

Feng, S., Magana, A. J., & Kao, D. (2021, October). *A systematic review of literature on the effectiveness of intelligent tutoring systems in STEM. In 2021 IEEE frontiers in education conference (fie)*. IEEE., DOI: 10.1109/FIE49875.2021.9637240

Fontoura, L., de Mattos Nascimento, D. L., Neto, J. V., & Caiado, R. G. G. (2025). Energy Gen-AI technology framework: A perspective of energy efficiency and business ethics in operation management. *Technology in Society, 81*, 102847. DOI: 10.1016/j.techsoc.2025.102847

Gardner, H. E. (2011). *Frames of mind: The theory of multiple intelligences*. Basic Books.

Gartner. (2023) Gartner Experts Answer the Top Generative AI Questions for Your Enterprise. Gartner. https://www.gartner.com/en/topics/generative-ai

Grant, A. M. (2020). An integrated model of goal-focused coaching: An evidence-based framework for teaching and practice. *Coaching Researched: A Coaching Psychology Reader*, 115-139. https://doi.org/DOI: 10.1002/9781119656913.ch7

Guettala, M., Bourekkache, S., Kazar, O., & Harous, S. (2024). Generative artificial intelligence in education: Advancing adaptive and personalized learning. *Acta Informatica Pragensia, 13*(3), 460–489. DOI: 10.18267/j.aip.235

Hanus, M. D., & Fox, J. (2015). Assessing the effects of gamification in the classroom: A longitudinal study on intrinsic motivation, social comparison, satisfaction, effort, and academic performance. *Computers & Education, 80*, 152–161. DOI: 10.1016/j.compedu.2014.08.019

Hattie, J., & Timperley, H. (2007). The power of feedback. *Review of Educational Research, 77*(1), 81–112. DOI: 10.3102/003465430298487

Imran, M., & Almusharraf, N. (2024). Google Gemini as a next generation AI educational tool: A review of emerging educational technology. *Smart Learning Environments, 11*(1), 22. DOI: 10.1186/s40561-024-00310-z

International Academy of Education. (2010). *International encyclopedia of education* (3rd ed.). Elsevier., DOI: 10.1016/B978-0-08-044894-7.01722-X

Jaggia, S., Kelly, A., Lertwachara, K., & Chen, L. (2023). *Business analytics: Communicating with numbers*. McGraw Hill.

Johnson, L., Adams Becker, S., Cummins, M., Estrada, V., Freeman, A., & Hall, C. (2016). *NMC Horizon report: 2016 higher education edition*. The New Media Consortium. https://library.educause.edu/resources/2016/2/2016-horizon-report

Joshi, P. (2017). *Artificial intelligence with python*. Packt Publishing Ltd.

Kapp, K. M. (2012). *The gamification of learning and instruction: Game-based methods and strategies for training and education*. John Wiley & Sons., DOI: 10.1145/2207270.2211316

Kem, D. (2022). Personalised and adaptive learning: Emerging learning platforms in the era of digital and smart learning. *International Journal of Social Science and Human Research*, *5*(2), 385–391. DOI: 10.47191/ijsshr/v5-i2-02

Kennedy, M. J., Thomas, C. N., Meyer, J. P., Alves, K. D., & Lloyd, J. W. (2014). Using evidence-based multimedia to improve vocabulary performance of adolescents with LD: A UDL approach. *Learning Disability Quarterly*, *37*(2), 71–86. DOI: 10.1177/0731948713507262

Khandelwal, P., Shankar, P., & Siddiraju, U. R. (2022). Skillsets and attributes for enhanced teaching–learning outcomes at higher educational institutions in disruptive times. In *Academic Voices* (pp. 227–238). Chandos Publishing., DOI: 10.1016/B978-0-323-91185-6.00032-X

Khlaif, Z. N., Alkouk, W. A., Salama, N., & Abu Eideh, B. (2025). Redesigning Assessments for AI-Enhanced Learning: A Framework for Educators in the Generative AI Era. *Education Sciences*, *15*(2), 174. DOI: 10.3390/educsci15020174

Kim, S., Song, K., Lockee, B., & Burton, J. (2017). What is gamification in learning and education? In *Gamification in learning and education: Enjoy learning like gaming* (pp. 25–38). Springer International Publishing., DOI: 10.1007/978-3-319-47283-6_4

Komljenovic, J. (2022). The future of value in digitalised higher education: Why data privacy should not be our biggest concern. *Higher Education*, *83*(1), 119–135. DOI: 10.1007/s10734-020-00639-7

Kram, K. E. (1988). *Mentoring at work: Developmental relationships in organizational life*. University Press of America., DOI: 10.2307/2392687

Kulik, C. L. C., Kulik, J. A., & Bangert-Drowns, R. L. (1990). Effectiveness of mastery learning programs: A meta-analysis. *Review of Educational Research*, *60*(2), 265–299. DOI: 10.3102/00346543060002265

Kumar, M., Packer, B., & Koller, D. (2010). Self-paced learning for latent variable models. *Advances in Neural Information Processing Systems*, •••, 23.

Lee, S., Choe, H., Zou, D., & Jeon, J. (2025). Generative AI (GenAI) in the language classroom: A systematic review. *Interactive Learning Environments*, •••, 1–25. DOI: 10.1080/10494820.2025.2498537

Lo, C. K., & Hew, K. F. (2017). A critical review of flipped classroom challenges in K-12 education: Possible solutions and recommendations for future research. *Research and Practice in Technology Enhanced Learning*, *12*(1), 1–22. DOI: 10.1186/s41039-016-0044-2

Long, H. S. (2024). Exploring the use of ChatGPT as a tool for written corrective feedback in an EFL classroom. *The Journal of Asia TEFL*, *21*(2), 397–412. DOI: 10.18823/asiatefl.2024.21.2.8.397

Looi, C. K., & Jia, F. (2025). Personalization capabilities of current technology chatbots in a learning environment: An analysis of student-tutor bot interactions. *Education and Information Technologies*, *30*(10), 1–31. DOI: 10.1007/s10639-025-13369-z

Luan, H., & Tsai, C. C. (2021). A review of using machine learning approaches for precision education. *Journal of Educational Technology & Society*, *24*(1), 250–266.

Melzer, P. (2018). *A conceptual framework for personalised learning: influence factors, design, and support potentials*. Springer., DOI: 10.1007/978-3-658-23095-1

Meng, L., Zhang, W., Chu, Y., & Zhang, M. (2021). LD–LP generation of personalized learning path based on learning diagnosis. *IEEE Transactions on Learning Technologies*, *14*(1), 122–128. DOI: 10.1109/TLT.2021.3058525

OECD. (2013). Innovative Learning Environments. OECD Publishing., Retrieved February 15, 2024, from, DOI: 10.1787/9789264203488-

Panadero, E. (2017). A review of self-regulated learning: Six models and four directions for research. *Frontiers in Psychology*, *8*, 422. DOI: 10.3389/fpsyg.2017.00422

Park, J. J., & Milner, P. (2025). Enhancing Academic Writing Integrity: Ethical Implementation of Generative Artificial Intelligence for Non-Traditional Online Students. *TechTrends*, *69*(1), 176–188. DOI: 10.1007/s11528-024-01024-2

Patrick, S., Kennedy, K., & Powell, A. (2013). Mean What You Say: Defining and Integrating Personalized, Blended and Competency Education. *International Association for K-12 Online Learning*.

Peng, H., Ma, S., & Spector, J. M. (2019). Personalized adaptive learning: An emerging pedagogical approach enabled by a smart learning environment. *Smart Learning Environments*, *6*(1), 1–14. DOI: 10.1186/s40561-019-0089-y

Radford, A., Narasimhan, K., Salimans, T., & Sutskever, I. (2018). Improving language understanding by generative pre-training.

Ramsden, P. (2003). *Learning to teach in higher education*. Routledge., DOI: 10.4324/9780203507711

Reigeluth, C. M., & Carr-Chellman, A. A. (Eds.). (2009). Instructional-design theories and models: Vol. III. *Building a common knowledge base*. Routledge., DOI: 10.4324/9780203872130

Renninger, K. A., & Hidi, S. (2015). *The power of interest for motivation and engagement*. Routledge., DOI: 10.4324/9781315771045

Rudolph, J., Tan, S., & Tan, S. (2023). ChatGPT: Bullshit spewer or the end of traditional assessments in higher education? *Journal of applied learning and teaching, 6*(1), 342-363. https://doi.org/DOI: 10.37074/jalt.2023.6.1.9

Russell, S., Norvig, P., Popineau, F., Miclet, L., & Cadet, C. (2021). *Intelligence artificielle: une approche moderne (4 édition)*. Pearson France.

Sadler, D. R. (1989). Formative assessment and the design of instructional systems. *Instructional Science*, *18*(2), 119–144. DOI: 10.1007/BF00117714

Sailer, M., Hense, J. U., Mayr, S. K., & Mandl, H. (2017). How gamification motivates: An experimental study of the effects of specific game design elements on psychological need satisfaction. *Computers in Human Behavior*, *69*, 371–380. DOI: 10.1016/j.chb.2016.12.033

Schunk, D. H. (2001). Self-regulation through goal setting.

Sergeeva, O. V., Zheltukhina, M. R., Shoustikova, T., Tukhvatullina, L. R., Dobrokhotov, D. A., & Kondrashev, S. V. (2025). Understanding higher education students' adoption of generative AI technologies: An empirical investigation using UTAUT2. *Contemporary Educational Technology*, *17*(2), ep571. DOI: 10.30935/cedtech/16039

Shemshack, A., & Spector, J. M. (2020). A systematic literature review of personalized learning terms. *Smart Learning Environments*, *7*(1), 33. DOI: 10.1186/s40561-020-00140-9

Siemens, G. (2013). Learning analytics: The emergence of a discipline. *The American Behavioral Scientist*, *57*(10), 1380–1400. DOI: 10.1177/0002764213498851

Slavin, R. E. (1984). Team assisted individualization: Cooperative learning and individualized instruction in the mainstreamed classroom. *Remedial and Special Education*, *5*(6), 33–42. DOI: 10.1177/074193258400500606

Smith, B. E., Shimizu, A. Y., Burriss, S. K., Hundley, M., & Pendergrass, E. (2025). Multimodal composing with generative AI: Examining preservice teachers' processes and perspectives. *Computers and Composition*, *75*, 102896. DOI: 10.1016/j.compcom.2024.102896

Sternberg, R. J. (2023). Human Intelligencel Definition, Types, Test, Theories, & Facts. *Encyclopedia Britannica.* https://www. britannica. com/science/human-intelligence-psychology/Psychometric-theories (accessed on 5 August 2023).

Strelan, P., Osborn, A., & Palmer, E. (2020). The flipped classroom: A meta-analysis of effects on student performance across disciplines and education levels. *Educational Research Review*, *30*, 100314. DOI: 10.1016/j.edurev.2020.100314

Subban, P. (2006). Differentiated instruction: A research basis. *International Education Journal*, *7*(7), 935–947.

Tai, T.-Y., & Chen, H. H.-J. (2024). Improving elementary EFL speaking skills with generative AI chatbots: Exploring individual and paired interactions. *Computers & Education*, *220*, 105112. DOI: 10.1016/j.compedu.2024.105112

Tang, Q., Deng, W., Huang, Y., Wang, S., & Zhang, H. (2025). Can Generative Artificial Intelligence be a Good Teaching Assistant?—An Empirical Analysis Based on Generative AI-Assisted Teaching. *Journal of Computer Assisted Learning*, *41*(3), e70027. DOI: 10.1111/jcal.70027

Thomas, J. W. (2000). A review of research on project-based learning.

Tingelhoff, F., Brugger, M., & Leimeister, J. M. (2025). A guide for structured literature reviews in business research: The state-of-the-art and how to integrate generative artificial intelligence. *Journal of Information Technology*, *40*(1), 77–99. DOI: 10.1177/02683962241304105

Tobias, S., & Duffy, T. M. (2009). *Constructivist instruction: Success or failure.* https://doi.org/DOI: 10.4324/9780203878842

Tomlinson, C. A. (1999). Mapping a route toward differentiated instruction. *Educational Leadership*, *57*, 12–17.

Tomlinson, C. A. (2014). *The differentiated classroom: Responding to the needs of all learners*. Ascd.

U.S. Department of Education. (2016). *Future ready learning: Reimagining the role of technology in education.* Office of Educational Technology.

U.S. Department of Education. (2017). *Reimagining the role of technology in education: 2017 national education technology plan update.* Office of Educational Technology. https://files.eric.ed.gov/fulltext/ED577592.pdf

Vaccino-Salvadore, S. (2023). Exploring the ethical dimensions of using ChatGPT in language learning and beyond. *Languages (Basel, Switzerland)*, *8*(3), 191. DOI: 10.3390/languages8030191

Wang, M. C., Haertel, G. D., & Walberg, H. J. (1993). Toward a knowledge base for school learning. *Review of Educational Research*, *63*(3), 249–294. DOI: 10.3102/00346543063003249

Wardat, Y., Belbase, S., & Tairab, H. (2022). Mathematics teachers' perceptions of trends in international mathematics and science study (TIMSS)-related practices in Abu Dhabi Emirate schools. *Sustainability (Basel)*, *14*(9), 5436. DOI: 10.3390/su14095436

Wiboolyasarin, W., Wiboolyasarin, K., Suwanwihok, K., Jinowat, N., & Muenjanchoey, R. (2024). Synergizing collaborative writing and AI feedback: An investigation into enhancing L2 writing proficiency in wiki-based environments. *Computers and Education: Artificial Intelligence*, *6*, 100228. Advance online publication. DOI: 10.1016/j.caeai.2024.100228

Wijaya, T. T., Yu, Q., Cao, Y., He, Y., & Leung, F. K. (2024). Latent Profile Analysis of AI Literacy and Trust in Mathematics Teachers and Their Relations with AI Dependency and 21st-Century Skills. *Behavioral Sciences (Basel, Switzerland)*, *14*(11), 1008. DOI: 10.3390/bs14111008

Xia, Y., Shin, S. Y., & Shin, K. S. (2024). Designing Personalized Learning Paths for Foreign Language Acquisition Using Big Data: Theoretical and Empirical Analysis. *Applied Sciences (Basel, Switzerland)*, *14*(20), 9506. DOI: 10.3390/app14209506

Yudkowsky, E. (2008). Artificial intelligence as a positive and negative factor in global risk. *Global Catastrophic Risks*, *1*(303), 184. DOI: 10.1093/oso/9780198570509.003.0021

Zawacki-Richter, O., Marín, V. I., Bond, M., & Gouverneur, F. (2019). Systematic review of research on artificial intelligence applications in higher education–where are the educators? *International Journal of Educational Technology in Higher Education*, *16*(1), 1–27. DOI: 10.1186/s41239-019-0171-0

Zeadally, S., Adi, E., Baig, Z., & Khan, I. A. (2020). Harnessing artificial intelligence capabilities to improve cybersecurity. *IEEE Access : Practical Innovations, Open Solutions, 8*, 23817–23837. DOI: 10.1109/ACCESS.2020.2968045

Zhang, L., Basham, J. D., & Yang, S. (2020). Understanding the implementation of personalized learning: A research synthesis. *Educational Research Review, 31*, 100339. DOI: 10.1016/j.edurev.2020.100339

Zhu, Q., Yuan, N., & Guan, D. (2019). Cognitive Driven Multilayer Self-Paced Learning with Misclassified Samples. *Complexity, 2019*(1), 8127869. DOI: 10.1155/2019/8127869

Zimmerman, B. J. (2002). Becoming a self-regulated learner: An overview. *Theory into Practice, 41*(2), 64–70. DOI: 10.1207/s15430421tip4102_2

Zohuri, B., & Mossavar-Rahmani, F. (2024). Revolutionizing education: The dynamic synergy of personalized learning and artificial intelligence. *International Journal of Advanced Engineering and Management Research, 9*(1), 143–153. DOI: 10.51505/ijaemr.2024.9111

KEY TERMS & DEFINITIONS

Personalized Learning: Personalized learning is a pedagogical approach that aims to structure the teaching process in a learner-specific manner by adapting learning objectives, content, and methods according to the individual's cognitive level, interests, learning motivation, and prior knowledge. It encourages active participation of the learner throughout the learning process.

Generative Artificial Intelligence (GenAI): Generative artificial intelligence refers to AI systems that produce original and semantically coherent outputs across multiple data types—including natural language, visual media, audio data, and software code—through statistical modeling and pattern recognition-based algorithms. These systems generate human-like outputs resembling previously processed data.

Tutoring: Tutoring is an instructional practice tailored to individual learning needs, typically conducted one-on-one, offering flexibility in terms of time, content, and method. It aims to bridge learning gaps and support academic development by adapting to the learner's pace, knowledge level, and learning style.

Learner Autonomy: Learner autonomy refers to the competence of an individual to set their own learning goals, plan and manage the process, and take responsibility for learning outcomes. It encompasses decision-making, self-assessment, and the deliberate selection of appropriate learning strategies, positioning the learner as an active agent in their educational journey.

Adaptivity: Adaptivity is a dynamic principle of instructional design that allows learning content, instructional methods, and digital tools to automatically adjust according to the learner's individual characteristics, performance, preferences, and real-time needs.

Digital Guidance: Digital guidance refers to structured, interaction-based support provided through digital environments during learning, decision-making, and orientation processes. It extends beyond the presentation of information to include contextual adaptivity, progress tracking, suggestion generation, and prompt notifications as part of a multi-layered framework.

Interactive Feedback: Interactive feedback is a structured feedback system that responds to learners' actions in real time, adapting to the context and continuously guiding the learning process. Rather than merely indicating correctness, it delivers constructive responses to shape learning behaviors and serves as a key component of process-based assessment approaches.

Chapter 2
Role of Artificial Intelligence in Lifelong Learning for Personalized Education Using AI Agents, Generative AI, and Explainable AI

Betül Ersöz
https://orcid.org/0000-0001-6221-1530
Gazi University, Turkey

Halil İbrahim Bülbül
https://orcid.org/0000-0002-6525-7232
Gazi University, Turkey

ABSTRACT

Many countries have focused their policies on lifelong learning recently. It is necessary to examine the role of technological tools to guide policies and lifelong learning practices in this regard. Today's widely used artificial intelligence (AI) technologies support the expansion of educational opportunities, customisation of processes, and implementation in lifelong learning. Therefore, it is necessary to accurately conceptualise the connection between AI and lifelong learning. This book chapter addresses the role and impact of AI in lifelong learning with subsections such as AI-Based Personalized Education, Explainable AI (XAI) in Education, AI Agents in Education, Generative Artificial Intelligence (GenAI), and Current Trends

DOI: 10.4018/979-8-3373-7574-8.ch002

in Lifelong Learning. Also, the chapter offers an idea about the creative uses and prospects of artificial intelligence to increase the efficiency and accessibility of learning procedures.

INTRODUCTION

In today's society, the philosophy of lifelong learning prevails. It is a continuous and systematic search for knowledge and ability throughout life. Adaptability and course correction are more critical in the wake of technological advancements.

Lifelong learning enables individuals to remain cognizant of the ever-changing aspects of their careers and to become better citizens by fulfilling their search for knowledge. Unlike traditional learning methods, lifelong learning is characterized by a self-initiated and voluntary initiative to learn new skills.

Lifelong learning also:

- Supports education not only through formal channels but also various materials, such as digital workshops, online courses, conferences, and independent study areas,
- Promotes professional and individual development,
- Enables development of a more diverse and harmonious workforce,
- Democratizes education and closes the gaps,
- Fosters creativity and capacity by developing an adaptable mindset,
- Empowers individuals to cope with the complexities of modern life,
- Responds to demands of dynamic world increasingly,
- Affirms living process vital to individual success and social transformation,
- Encourages
- Takes an active role in ongoing education fostering to use new tools and methods for cultural and skill shifts
- Paves mass accessibility the way for a more informed, questioning, and effective society.

As a result, lifelong learning has enormous potential thanks to artificial intelligence(AI)-powered technical advancements (Bozkurt, 2023; Bozkurt & Sharma, 2024; Gharahighehi et al., 2024; Oberdieck & Moch, 2024; Palenski et al., 2024) like digital scaffolding, tailored recommendations, and better insights into massive databases about learning processes. People's need for lifelong learning has grown since the century centered on information and technology. Even though people must continually reinvent themselves due to the rapid changes in the economic environment, informal learning methods are crucial for information acquisition. AI accelerates these two types of learning, enhancing their engagement, accessibility, and customization for each individual. AI can completely transform informal and lifelong learning by offering individualized, flexible, and non-formal learning opportunities. AI can give constant accessibility, immediate feedback, and content tailored to each learner's needs. While all receive the same content from traditional educational methods, AI-supported solutions can enhance learning by determining each learner's ability, speed, and priorities. Through effective time management, data-driven insights, and adaptive material delivery, it facilitates individualized learning. These skills can be professional qualifications that improve career opportunities or hobbies that enrich life experiences. Therefore, embracing lifelong learning is crucial for success in today's evolving world.

Recent developments on AI Agents (AIA), eXplainable AI (XAI) and Generative AI (GenAI) might help to support longlife learning. XAI helps us understand how AI makes decisions; AIAs take actions to reach AI's goals and can get better by learning; and GenAI models also create new contents, and do many of other works and duties. Figure 1 shows AI perspective and concepts for lifelong learning for the future.

Figure 1. AI Perspective for Lifelong Learning Concepts

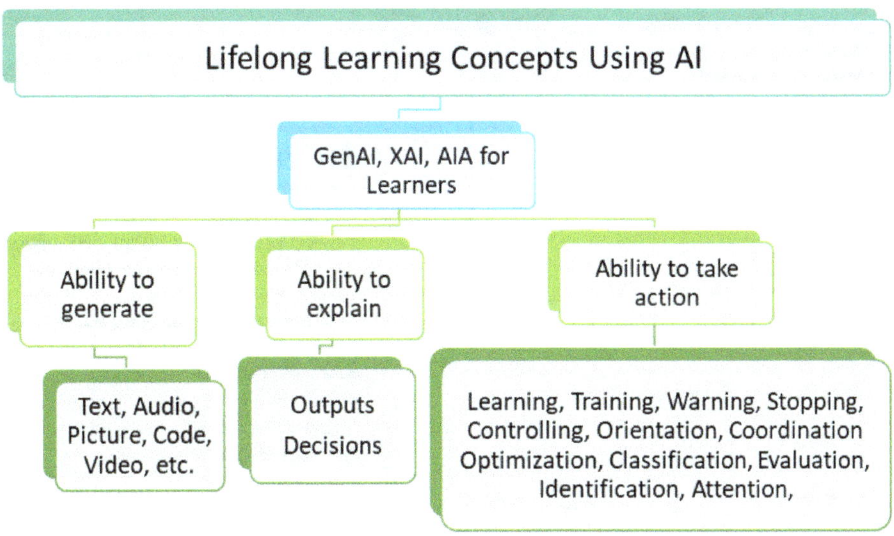

AI concepts today support lifelong learning. XAI clearly offers a specific suggestion, provides transparency in evaluation systems. AIA consists of intelligent learning agents that can set their own goals and suggest personalized paths for learners, acting as digital mentors to help them achieve their educational objectives.

Also, GenAI is used in content production, question creation, and writing personalized course materials. The educational AI transformation closely ties these AI concepts together. GenAI and XAI provide fantastic and safe contents and usage by explaining how AI-generated content is produced. AIA and lifelong learning provide active guidance and support in the learner's learning process. GenAI and lifelong learning provide personalized, up-to-date learning material production in the ever-changing world of information. AI-powered systems require explainability to be ethical, transparent, and fair for building better policies.

Figure 2. GenAI, XAI, and AIAs Concept Map for Lifelong Learning

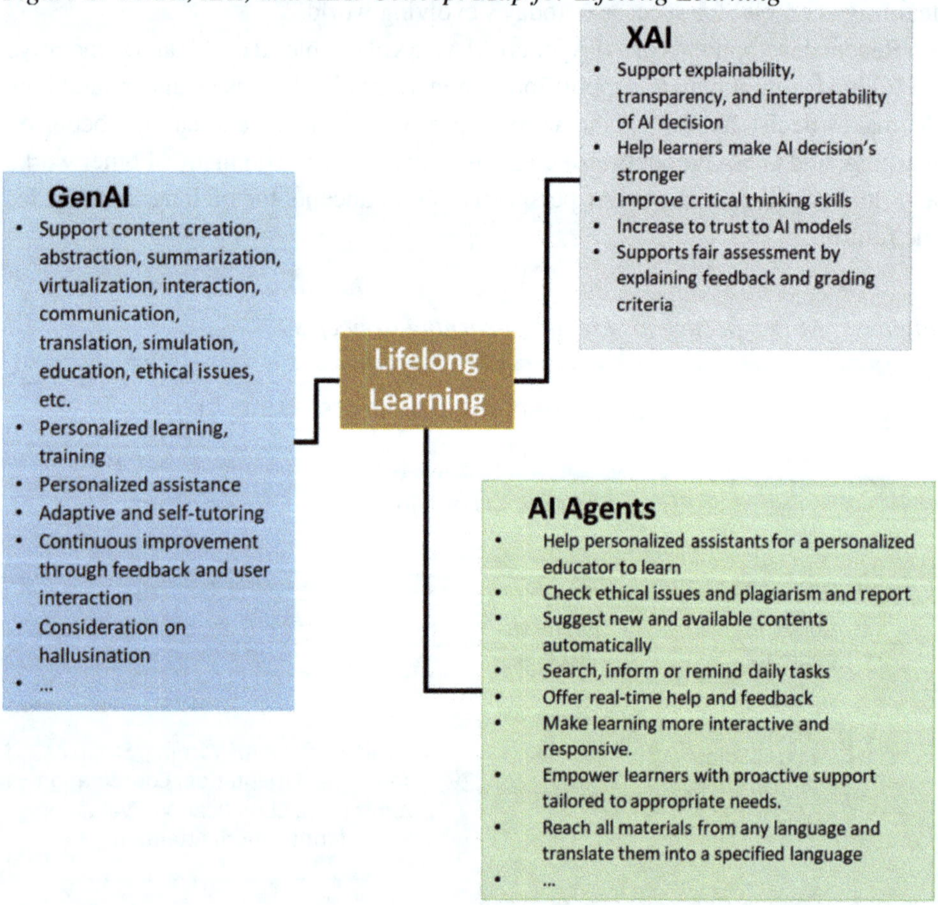

Figure 2 illustrates the concept map how three fundamental AI areas support a lifelong learning-centered system. Lifelong learning is the main component of this concept map, the foundation upon which all other concepts hinge and crucial for both individual and social development as it reflects the ongoing process of learning that individuals engage in throughout their lives. Each of these concepts of GenAI, XAI, and AIAs supports lifelong learning in different ways (Bozkurt, 2024b; Şenocak et al., 2024). GenAI produces learning content directly by producing learning material, providing information specific to the individual, and supporting creativity. XAI shows the function of explaining why and how AI makes decisions in the learning process, creating transparency and trust. This method makes the relationship between the learner and the system more conscious and critical. Therefore, it contributes to ethical and pedagogical understanding. AIAs play an active role in daily learning activities such as personalized help, time management, and suggestions. These agents are in constant interaction with the learner. Therefore, they are placed on the map in a position focused on interaction and personalization.

Recent studies (Basit et al., 2024) demonstrate how AI-enabled platforms can improve training and professional growth. Social media platforms with AI capabilities let teachers network, share knowledge, and work together in real time. People must continually acquire new skills in the business environment to keep up with the quickly evolving business models and technologies. Platforms for professional development aided by AI guarantee that people obtain instruction suitable for these requirements. Platforms such as LinkedIn Learning analyze professional profiles and suggest appropriate courses. Natural language processing and machine learning can be used to create dynamic course materials tailored to the learners' needs (Basit et al., 2024). These suggestions offer crucial direction for people to reach their professional objectives. For instance, various language-learning apps monitor how users learn and adjust the difficulty level based on their unique learning preferences. The individual enjoys learning and has the opportunity to focus on their areas of weakness as a result. This customization makes learning more effective and maintains people's motivation to learn. AI and learning analytics also assess people's learning performance and identify their areas of strength and weakness. People can use this information to help their ongoing development and determine which areas require greater effort (Pedro et al., 2019). As learners learn, AI gives them immediate feedback and direction. By making complex ideas more approachable and engaging, virtual reality (VR) and augmented reality (AR) may produce immersive learning environments. By adjusting to the behaviors and responses of learners, AI can improve these experiences. By spotting out-of-date or erroneous information and assisting learners in accessing current and reliable resources, AI can guarantee the caliber of instructional content (Aggarwal, 2023). As learners learn, AI gives them immediate feedback and direction. By making complex ideas more approachable and engaging, virtual reality (VR) and augmented reality (AR) may produce immersive learning environments. By adjusting to the behaviors and responses of learners, AI can improve these experiences. By spotting out-of-date or erroneous information and assisting learners in accessing current and reliable resources, AI can guarantee the caliber of instructional content (Billiot, 2023; Brandão et al., 2024; Gulyamov et al., 2024). As learners learn, AI gives them immediate feedback and direction. By making complex ideas more approachable and engaging, virtual reality (VR) and augmented reality (AR) may produce immersive learning environments. By adjusting to the behaviors and responses of learners, AI can improve these experiences. By spotting out-of-date or erroneous information and assisting learners in accessing current and reliable resources, AI can guarantee the caliber of instructional content (Bagai & Mane, 2023; Goksel & Bozkurt, 2019; Gulyamov et al., 2024; Lu et al., 2024; Raza, 2024).

- Access to AI-based learning systems can increase digital inequalities. Inequalities in access to advanced technologies can limit individuals' ability to benefit from these systems.
- AI systems record individuals' learning habits and behaviors and make inferences from this data. However, the use of this data and the protection of its privacy are both difficult.
- While AI-supported learning systems can increase individuals' motivation, they can also create excessive addiction. Game-based learning applications can cause individuals to spend time constantly on the application.
- In the future, AI could create proactive systems that anticipate individuals' needs and offer customized learning paths.

AI-Based Personalized Education

Individuals must undertake lifelong learning to keep up with the ever-evolving labor market and society. Learning processes can be streamlined, personalized, and made more convenient by implementing AI in lifelong learning systems. AI-based personalized learning is employed to customize learning experiences according to the personal needs, abilities, and preferences of every learner. The culture of the contemporary era has the concept of lifelong learning deep-rooted within it. It is the ongoing and persistent pursuit of knowledge and skills throughout one's life. The ability to accept change and growth with improvements in technology has become essential. Continuous learning enables people to stay attuned to the ever-evolving elements of their job and facilitates personal growth by fulfilling their thirst for knowledge. Lifelong learning, unlike conventional forms of education, is marked by a self-directed and voluntary participation in the acquisition of new skills. These skills may include professional certifications that create better career prospects or hobbies that enhance life experience. Thus, lifelong learning is essential in achieving success in the contemporary, dynamic world (Ayeni et al., 2024; George, 2023; Goksel & Bozkurt, 2019).

The concept of lifelong learning identifies that learning may occur both formally and informally. Accordingly, an extensive variety of learning materials has been made accessible at varying levels today, stretching from virtual workshops to online study courses, conferences, and study rooms. This sort of mass accessibility aims to democratize learning and defeat the challenges that appear insurmountable. Continuous learning leads to personal and professional growth, thereby creating opportunities for a more diverse and integrated workforce. Individuals need to acquire new competencies and strategies that encourage them to become actively engaged in their own continuous learning as traditional jobs evolve. A further dimension of lifelong learning involves a cultural shift, acknowledging that knowledge and skills are not limited to the younger age group or formal education systems. It believes in the continuity of learning as the key to social transformation and personal prosperity, as it unlocks the gates of inclusiveness that embrace and welcome individuals from diverse backgrounds and ages. The development of a flexible mind also promotes creativity and ability, equipping individuals to face the needs of a rapidly changing world and resolve the intricacies of contemporary life. As a result, it helps to create a more informed, curious, and productive society (Singh, 2024; Tryhub, 2023). Figure 3 shows Lifelong learning and AI age-based time shift.

Figure 3. Lifelong learning and the temporal cycle of the AI era

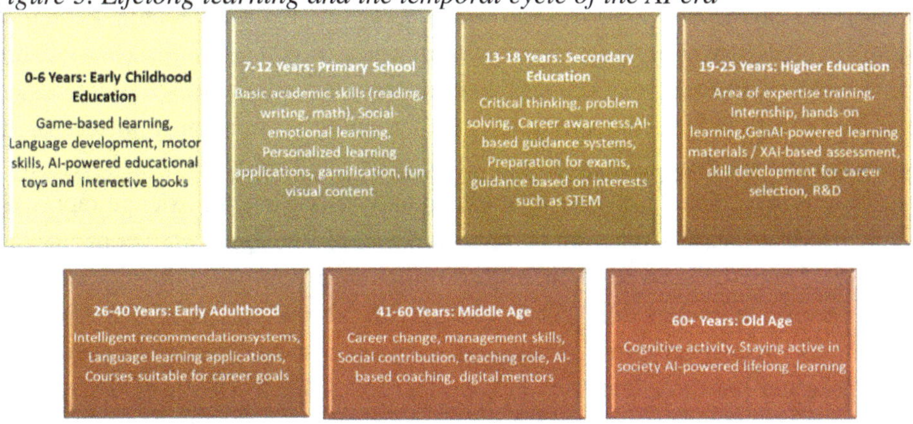

AI-assisted learning is implemented in many manners according to the age-specific requirements of individuals during their lifelong educational journey. The educational process begins in early childhood (0–6 years) with play-based learning and interactive content, intensifies in primary school through personalized learning applications, advances in secondary education with an emphasis on critical thinking, career awareness, and exam preparation, and culminates in higher education with professional expertise, internships, and research-development activities. In adulthood and old age, it facilitates lifelong learning in domains such as artificial intelligence, job advancement, social engagement, digital literacy, and active ageing. AI has been revolutionizing the learning experience recently with its ability to provide personalized learning experiences that are precisely tailored to each learner's preferences and needs. With the application of AI technologies, educators can provide engaging and effective learning processes for adaptive learning spaces that support each learner's different speeds, styles, and levels of understanding (Bayly-Castaneda et al., 2024; KangJie et al., 2025). AI-optimized personalized learning is based on data analysis, which examines a learner's past performance, study habits, and emotional state to tailor content delivery. By suggesting specific materials, practical examples, or tests that match each learner's individual skills and knowledge gaps, these features help create customized learning paths and support long-term success (Laak & Aru, 2024; Rane et al., 2023).

First, AI's ability to work with large data sets allows the system to adapt to the learner, adding new information and knowledge to the personalization process. These adaptive systems can change the level of complexity of the content according to real-time assessments. Second, the limits of traditional single-type education will be eliminated by AI-powered individualized learning, which will also shift toward a more inclusive model that caters to various learning groups. It not only empowers learners to take charge of their education but also enables educators to employ more targeted and successful teaching techniques. AI has the potential to completely transform lifelong learning approaches in education, making it more transparent, egalitarian, and sensitive to each learner's unique needs. Personalized learning acknowledges that one-size-fits-all training is frequently unsuccessful because learners have different backgrounds, prior knowledge, learning styles, and motivations. Machine learning, natural language processing, knowledge representation, and learning analytics are some methods used by AI-powered personalized learning systems to dynamically modify education in response to learner interactions and performance information. These systems can provide targeted content recommendations, intelligent tutoring, adaptive assessments, and customized feedback to support and optimize learning for each learner. AI-based learning ecosystems can quickly and flexibly meet the educational needs of individuals at different life stages. In addition to personalized learning content, these systems offer interactive tools to sustain learning motivation. AI has groundbreaking potential in the delivery of personalized education. AI technologies enable individualized customization of educational content by analyzing learner performance and learning styles. Thus, each learner can have learning experiences tailored to their needs and pace. AI-powered educational systems identify challenges encountered in the learning process and implement interventions focusing on learner strengths and weaknesses. As a subfield of artificial intelligence, machine learning (ML) algorithms examine educational data to evaluate learner traits, forecast performance, and suggest tailored curricula and content. Usability is another benefit of individualized learning in the classroom. With specialized resources and adaptable technology, AI can support the various learning requirements of people with impairments. AI can, for instance, translate content for non-native speakers of a language or convert text to speech for visually impaired learners (Maghsudi et al., 2021; Murtaza et al., 2022; Peng, 2024).

Any individual can access lifelong learning through educational democratization, irrespective of cognitive, linguistic, or physical impairments. By establishing goals based on individual interests, personalization promotes autonomy by allowing learners to take charge of their educational journeys and enabling self-directed learning. Teachers can spend more time teaching and less on administrative duties thanks to AI's role in automating administrative processes and personalizing learning experiences. AI-powered innovative teaching solutions enable learners to progress independently, providing them with immediate feedback and assistance. These technologies are especially helpful in self-directed learning settings because learners are not subject to the limitations of conventional classroom settings. By bringing people together with complementary abilities or comparable interests, AI can enhance collaborative learning by fostering a more engaging and community-based learning environment. By pushing the limits of conventional teaching, incorporating AI into learning environments increases accessibility to education. Using natural language processing, AI facilitates multilingual learning experiences and lowers obstacles for non-native speakers. AI-powered virtual classrooms and learning resources can reach learners anywhere worldwide, allowing for ongoing learning despite geographical limitations. As AI advances, it can improve and change educational settings, fostering an inclusive, flexible, and responsive atmosphere that will better prepare learners for the dynamics of a constantly changing world (Bozkurt, 2023; Iman et al., 2024).

Learning models that capture important facets of each learner's knowledge, skills, abilities, and traits are developed using ML in the context of personalized learning. These models are applied to customize education and offer individualized feedback and recommendations. With adaptive learning systems, people can advance at their speed and receive quick feedback. The following are the main components of individualized learning:

Learner profiles: Personalized learning systems meticulously document each learner's knowledge, skills, talents, interests, and preferences. These profiles are used to tailor recommendations and teaching.

Flexible learning paths: Learners can pursue customized pathways via instructional content rather than a set, linear curriculum, depending on their needs and objectives.

Competency-based progression: Instead of advancing based on age or length of stay, learners advance by proving they have mastered fundamental knowledge and abilities.

Adaptive assessments: By dynamically adjusting to learners' performance, assessments offer tailored feedback and an accurate estimation of their current level of knowledge. Personalized education powered by AI has benefits beyond academic achievement; it also boosts learners' enthusiasm and self-esteem. Learners are more engaged and feel more capable because they can learn at their own pace and get individualized attention.

Adaptive learning systems are among the most significant instances of AI-based personalized education solutions. These systems continuously update customized training plans based on the learner's prior learning information. During this process, machine learning algorithms automatically adapt the difficulty and content of the learning materials to the learner. Figure 4 shows the AI-Based Personalized Learning Cycle.

Figure 4. AI-Based Personalized Learning Cycle

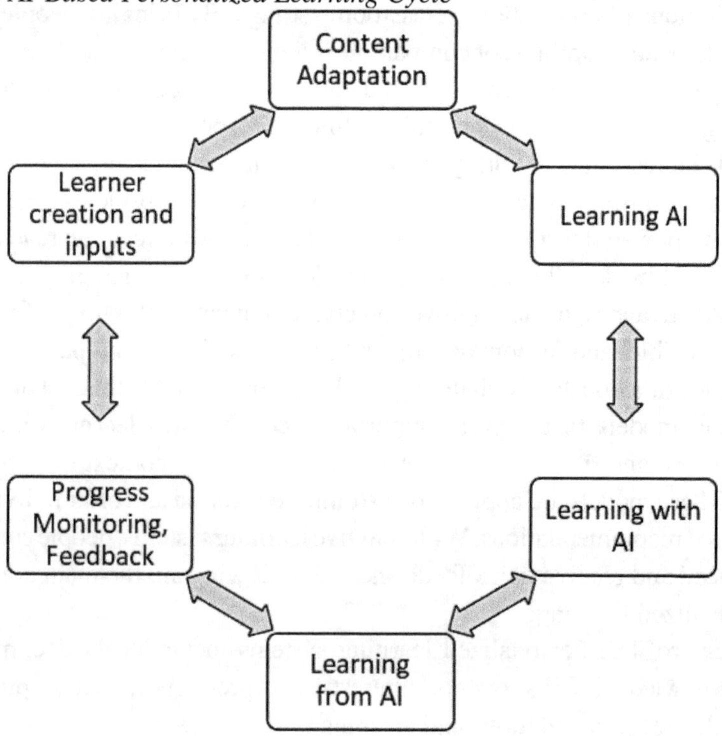

This cyclical model demonstrates that AI-supported learning is an interactive and continuously evolving process. The process begins with the content adaptation and inputs of the learning individual; it continues with the steps of learning the artificial intelligence, learning with it, and learning from it. The student's progress is continuously monitored, and feedback is provided. Based on this data, the content is adapted, creating a personalized learning cycle.

AI Application Challenges

Integrating AI into lifelong learning presents many challenges that educators, technologists, and policymakers must address. Chief among these challenges is the compatibility of AI systems with existing educational frameworks. Traditional educational systems may not be readily compatible with AI-based approaches, which may require radical changes in curriculum design, teaching methods, and assessment methods. Maintaining the integrity and objectives of current academic standards while integrating these AI systems with human-centered instructional approaches is difficult. It frequently calls for academic institutions to adopt new learning paradigms through cultural shifts and technological innovation. Ensuring fair access to AI technologies is another difficulty (Almusaed et al., 2024; Su & Zhong, 2022).

Racial and socioeconomic differences can increase the gap between various learner groups by restricting access to cutting-edge technology. To fully realize AI's potential in education, a wide range of people must have affordable and easy access to AI resources. To address this issue, we need both technological advancements and legislative measures to lower access barriers. The practical application of AI in lifelong learning requires coordinated efforts in ethical norms, technological advancement, accessibility, and inclusivity to guarantee that everyone can reap the ultimate benefits. The ethical implications of data security and privacy are another issue. AI systems rely on data as their foundation, necessitating the gathering and processing of enormous volumes of learner data to properly customize learners' learning experiences. However, this raises questions about the privacy of learners' data and the transparency of AI algorithms. Ensuring that AI systems remain within the boundaries of ethical norms and protect the privacy of individuals is vital to building trust and acceptance among users. Regulatory frameworks must evolve to address such privacy issues by aligning technological advancement with moral responsibility (Masrek et al., 2024; Rawas, 2024; Romero, 2024).

THE ROLE OF GENAI IN EDUCATION AND LIFELONG LEARNING

GenAI is increasingly identified as a revolutionary educational force, fundamentally changing static paradigms and provoking innovative teaching strategies. Unlike earlier technologies that mainly helped with administration or offered basic computer lessons, GenAI provides lively and interactive systems that can create content, mimic conversations, and adjust instantly to the different needs of learners. This evolution is part of the larger movement toward greater inclusivity and individualization in a more universal learning space that moves beyond the limitations of language, geography, and conventional paradigms. Through its ability to process large quantities of data, produce enhanced output, and continuously enhance its effectiveness through feedback loops, GenAI revolutionizes knowledge transfer and learner engagement with course material. In effect, GenAI is a source of information and a learning partner, enabling greater intellectual exploration. For example, it can generate realistic simulations or scenarios in any subject area, such as medicine, engineering, and the arts, thus allowing learners to undergo experiential learning without the necessity of physical materials or environments. Further, its flexibility guarantees that learning content evolves with the learner, emphasizing regions of confusion and changing the degree of difficulty of the content according to individual development. Besides, GenAI can transcend language boundaries by creating multilingual resources and enhancing educational inclusivity for learners globally. These points are a paradigm shift, enabling the teacher to focus on critical thinking and mentoring development while AI handles the details of customization and scalability. As such, GenAI is more than an add-on tool but a fundamental design for modern education, powering innovation and promoting equity in lifelong learning ecosystems (Bahroun et al., 2023; Jin et al., 2025; Lang et al., 2025; Narayanan, 2024; Nedungadi et al., 2024; Xiao et al., 2025)

Integrating GenAI into lifelong learning presents both challenges and opportunities for how individuals approach continuing education. GenAI is a system that can generate content ranging from text and images to audio by digesting large data sets and understanding complex patterns. This technological advancement empowers lifelong learning by providing customized, scalable, and effective educational experiences. It supports personalized learning paths, allowing individuals and learners to progress at their pace and focus on areas that need improvement. By adapting educational content and methodologies to individual needs, GenAI provides an environment where learning is continuous, deeply engaging, and relevant. This integration is required to develop AI-driven learning platforms that utilize GenAI to deliver dynamic curriculums and just-in-time learning opportunities. These platforms can adapt educational resources based on real-time data analysis, supporting learners to receive content that aligns with their current proficiency levels and future goals (Bozkurt, 2024a; Goksel & Bozkurt, 2019).

Additionally, GenAI's ability to simulate real-world scenarios and develop immersive learning experiences enriches the learner journey, makes abstract concepts tangible, and enhances critical problem-solving skills. As these platforms evolve, the focus is on accessibility and inclusion, which is an advantage in closing gaps in educational inequality. In professional development, numerous applications have been developed with GenAI tools. They offer opportunities to increase skill acquisition and agility in rapidly changing workplaces. With AI-driven analytics, organizations can predict skill gaps and adapt their training programs accordingly. The symbiotic relationship between GenAI and lifelong learning will increase innovation and workforce adaptability, ensuring that learning is a never-ending journey fueled by technology and human curiosity (Asad & Ajaz, 2024; Baskara, 2025; Bozkurt, 2023; Chakraborty, 2024; Nedungadi et al., 2024).

Explainable AI in Education

Explainable AI (XAI) is important in education because it provides transparency and increases the reliability of AI systems. As AI is increasingly integrated into teaching, learning, and administrative tasks in schools, AI systems that can explain decision-making are more important than ever. AI explainability is used to demystify complex models and provide teachers, learners, and administrators insight into how AI arrives at certain conclusions or recommendations. Education stakeholders need transparency to understand, trust, and implement AI technologies in decision-making processes and personalized learning environments. However, explainable AI promotes better learning outcomes by creating an environment where learners can comprehend the justification for AI-enabled feedback and evaluation. Intelligent tutoring systems can use AI to explain specific suggestions based on a learner's performance data and suggest educational paths. Learners become more active participants in their learning process when they have access to a feature that gives them more insight into their experiences and promotes reflection. Additionally, explainable AI helps educators better comprehend the AI-recommended techniques and modify their pedagogy accordingly (Khosravi et al., 2022; Shafik, 2024).

Explainability makes it possible to match AI technologies to learning goals for more individualized and successful teaching strategies. Because it avoids prejudices and holds people accountable, it makes it easier to apply AI in education ethically. Educational AI systems must comprehensively explain their procedures to guarantee equitable treatment for all learners and avoid unintentionally reinforcing socioeconomic or cultural prejudices. AI systems that may modify learning processes and enhance assessment methods are becoming more and more prevalent in educational settings in the context of lifelong learning. Since developing critical thinking and adaptation is the foundation of lifelong learning, knowing the "why" and "how" of AI-driven recommendations boosts learner motivation and engagement. Educational AI systems must offer explanations that include a range of learning preferences and methods, reflecting a learner-centered viewpoint. Therefore, explainability has two functions: it facilitates the introduction of AI advances into the classroom and piques learners' interest by elucidating the intricacies of AI decision-making. This level of openness helps create smart interactions between AI and learners, changing their roles from just using technology to being active participants who can use insights from AI to improve their learning experiences (Gao et al., 2024; Kovari, 2025).

Furthermore, promoting transparency in AI systems allows for fair judgment, providing learners with equal access to educational opportunities designed to meet their individual needs. Model-agnostic methods, which aim to explain outputs regardless of the algorithm used, constitute one of the fundamental approaches to XAI. A few examples include locally interpretable model-agnostic explanations and Shapley Additive Explanations. These methods approximate AI models locally by creating simpler, easier-to-understand representations to interpret individual predictions, enabling teachers and learners to understand independent outcomes more effectively. Similarly, collaborative game theory is used to allocate the impact of individual characteristics on the predictions of an AI model as a whole, allowing learners to understand which variables have the most impact in adaptive learning systems or personalized lesson planning. Such methods are particularly valuable in understanding black-box models such as neural networks, giving researchers useful information about complex behaviors in a way that directly impacts the learning process (Ali et al., 2023; Chamola et al., 2023).

The goal of intrinsic interpretability is to develop models that are naturally comprehensible. For instance, decision trees and rule-based systems clearly explain predictions using structures that are easy for humans to understand. Thanks to recent advancements like interpretable neural networks with attention mechanisms, users may now see which inputs the model thinks are significant when making judgments. They can make AI-powered examination and tutoring software more transparent in educational contexts by demonstrating to teachers and learners how specific text responses, keyboard patterns, or knowledge gaps impact suggestions. On the other hand, hybrid approaches that blend intrinsic and model-independent approaches are becoming increasingly significant. For example, counterfactual explanations allow users to think of "what if" scenarios, clarifying under what conditions predictions can be changed. In lifelong learning, the technique can explain why an AI system categorizes a learner's skill level as inadequate or categorizes learning styles in specific ways. These explanations illustrate the complexities of AI and encourage learners to recognize practical paths for improvement, thereby increasing their engagement and understanding in the learning process. By leveraging multiple XAI techniques in lifelong learning, AI systems can achieve greater transparency, helping learners and educators confidently make well-informed decisions in complex decision-making processes. These techniques ensure that AI is a tool for collaboration, not a black box, and leverage its power to optimize learning outcomes while empowering users with transparency (chander et al., 2025; Longo et al., 2024). Figure 5 shows case study example of using XAI in the classroom.

Figure 5. Using XAI in the classroom (A case Study)

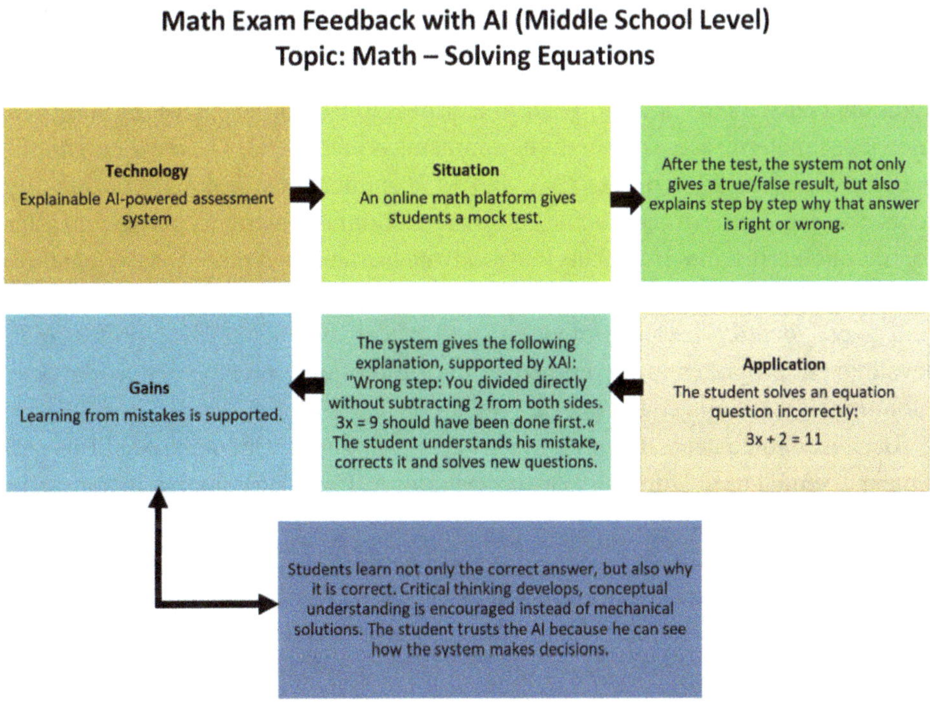

This diagram explains the AI-supported exam feedback process for solving equations at the middle school level. An explainable AI-based assessment system administers an online practice test to the student, then explains step by step not only whether the answer is correct or incorrect but also why it is correct or incorrect. In this process, the student understands their mistake (for example, performing the operation in the wrong order), learns the conceptual meaning through AI-supported explanations, and develops critical thinking skills, thereby learning from their mistakes.

AI Agents in Life-Long Learning

The lifelong learning paradigm increasingly includes AI agents, which allow for hitherto unthinkable levels of efficiency. These electronic agents serve as tutors, learning partners, and personalized learning assistants in learning settings because they can process vast volumes of data and adjust their outputs accordingly. To create learning routes and resources that are optimal, AI agents analyze each learner's learning preferences, shortcomings, and strengths to give tailored learning experiences. These AI bots may offer real-time feedback and tailor lessons to each learner's needs using algorithms that analyze learner behavior and preferences. It promotes engagement and leads to better learning results (Hu et al., 2024; Milana et al., 2024).

Furthermore, AI agents are making lifelong learning possible by eliminating traditional barriers to learning. Therefore, access to a comprehensive repository of knowledge material across diverse environments is increasing. These agents simplify complex information through ML and NLP applications, making it universally accessible regardless of geographical or socioeconomic constraints. AI agents foster continuous learning environments that motivate learners to explore and expand their intellectual horizons beyond traditional curricular parameters. They can recognize skill gaps, identify learning modules, and effectively personalize professional development programs to accommodate the fluidity of contemporary workplaces (Bhutoria, 2022; Sajja et al., 2024).

Because of their capacity to continually adapt and support learners, AI agents will remain essential to the lifelong learning paradigm. They can completely transform how information is learned, used, and retained throughout life. However, using AI agents in lifelong learning comes with specific difficulties. Although the advantages are apparent, there are ethical issues to consider, including data privacy and the possibility of algorithmic bias to support fairness and equal access to learning results. As AI agents continue to develop, it is the duty of technologists, educators, and legislators to make sure that these resources are used responsibly. Leveraging the potential of AI agents as change agents in lifelong learning requires balancing innovation and ethics. It will ensure their constructive contribution to the learning environment and prevent existing inequalities from worsening (De, 2024; Zheng et al., 2025).

AI agents can be an opportunity to transform the face of lifelong learning into scalable, adaptable, and personalized learning experiences. By using machine learning algorithms to look at large amounts of data on how learners interact and behave, AI systems can offer insights that help tailor learning content to meet each learner's individual needs, find areas where they need more help, and change the content's level or type as needed. AI agents provide a dynamic, interactive learning experience beyond the limitations of traditional learning methods. For example, by simulating one-on-one private lessons through AI-powered virtual assistants, learners can interact with real-time feedback and guidance. Such interactions enhance understanding of the subject matter and generate interest and exploration, allowing learners to explore topics at their pace and according to their interests. AI agents with natural language processing (NLP) skills encourage interaction by responding to queries in a conversational manner similar to a human's. AI systems may provide comprehensive learner profiles highlighting strengths and shortcomings and allow teachers to implement focused interventions with real-time statistics. Predictive intelligence made possible by AI in learning environments can also detect at-risk pupils early enough to support academic and motivational intervention. In today's fast-paced world, lifelong learning is becoming more and more important, and AI agents' roles are constantly changing to provide people with the skills they need to thrive in educational settings (Chakraborty, 2024; Mandal, 2024; Naeem et al., 2025; Soltoggio et al., 2024).

Artificial Intelligence and Lifelong Learning: Current Trends

As the intersection of AI and lifelong learning advances, several upcoming trends will continue to shape this rapidly evolving discipline. These trends drive the increasing adoption of new technologies designed to revolutionize learning experiences. ML and data analytics are becoming increasingly sophisticated, enabling personalized learning paths that can be realigned to individual paces and learning styles in real-time. These intelligent systems are paving the way for an environment where learning is more open and adaptable to the needs of different people, eliminating the traditional constraints of geographic location and resource availability. The application of AI in lifelong learning will also continue to increase with advances in natural language processing and virtual reality. These technologies can make learning spaces more engaging and interactive, as well as engaging and effective (Ibrahim, 2024; Karger et al., 2022; Schoenenberger, 2024).

AI engineers, educators, and legislators will probably collaborate over the next ten years to ensure these technologies are morally sound and beneficial to society. Ensuring fair access to AI-enabled learning resources is one of the primary goals here, democratizing education for all learners. As AI-powered lifelong learning initiatives proliferate, robust data privacy safeguards and the capacity to handle ethical dilemmas will also be essential. These initiatives will increase user trust and ensure that AI's educational benefits are inclusive and widely distributed. Thus, such technological advancements will impact lifelong learning in the future, and AI will be a significant force behind innovation and development (Lara-Navarra et al., 2025; Misra et al., 2023).

CONCLUSION

This chapter comprehensively addresses the importance and potential of lifelong learning, AI, personalized learning, and XAI in education. Firstly, the potential of XAI to enhance users' understanding of AI systems underscores its role in education. This work will enhance individual learning experiences and contribute to lifelong learning processes. The integration of GenAI in education enables the development of personalized learning experiences with the ability to adapt to learner needs. It aims to expand the current knowledge in this field by comprehensively addressing the potential and challenges of AI and personalized learning applications in education. The integration of AI in education has enormous potential to enhance individual learning experiences and support lifelong learning processes.

Incorporating AI into lifelong learning programs in changing learning environments presents tremendous opportunities and significant challenges. AI's ability to personalize learning experiences using customized learning algorithms creates opportunities for skill development and knowledge acquisition to meet the needs of individuals. These technologies allow adaptive learning systems to dynamically modify how information is delivered, offering personalized feedback and real-time assistance that adjusts to different learning styles and speeds. By doing this, AI not only makes education more accessible to everybody but also makes lifelong learning possible while still satisfying learners' changing intellectual interests and career demands. AI integration into lifelong learning presents several ethical and practical difficulties. Concerns about data privacy arise because AI systems heavily rely on massive data sets to function well. Strong data protection frameworks and transparent governance structures are necessary to ensure the confidentiality and integrity of learners' personal information. On the other hand, AI's influence on lifelong learning is a step in the direction of individualized and effective educational experiences.

ACKNOWLEDGMENT

This study was supported by the authors' individual affiliation.

REFERENCES

Aggarwal, D. D. (2023). Exploring the Scope of Artificial Intelligence (AI) for Lifelong Education through Personalised & Adaptive Learning. *Journal of Artificial Intelligence, Machine Learning and Neural Network*.DOI: DOI: 10.14445/22312803/IJCTT-V71I4P114

Ali, S., Abuhmed, T., El-Sappagh, S., Muhammad, K., Alonso-Moral, J. M., Confalonieri, R., Guidotti, R., Del Ser, J., Díaz-Rodríguez, N., & Herrera, F. (2023). Explainable Artificial Intelligence (XAI): What we know and what is left to attain Trustworthy Artificial Intelligence. *Information Fusion*, *99*, 101805. DOI: 10.1016/j.inffus.2023.101805

Almusaed, A., Almssad, A., & Albaj, A. (2024). Ethical and Pedagogical Challenges in the Integration of Artificial Intelligence into Lifelong Learning. *The proceedings is licensed under a Creative Commons Attribution-Non Commercial Share Alike 4.0 International License, permitting all non-commercial use, distribution, and reproduction in any medium, provided the original work is properly cited.*, 16-33.

Asad, M. M., & Ajaz, A. (2024). Impact of ChatGPT and generative AI on lifelong learning and upskilling learners in higher education: Unveiling the challenges and opportunities globally. *The International Journal of Information and Learning Technology*, *41*(5), 507–523. DOI: 10.1108/IJILT-06-2024-0103

Ayeni, O. O., Al Hamad, N. M., Chisom, O. N., Osawaru, B., & Adewusi, O. E. (2024). AI in education: A review of personalized learning and educational technology. *GSC Advanced Research and Reviews*, *18*(2), 261–271. DOI: 10.30574/gscarr.2024.18.2.0062

Bagai, R., & Mane, V. (2023). Designing an AI-Powered Mentorship Platform for Professional Development: Opportunities and Challenges. *ArXiv, abs/2407.20233*.

Bahroun, Z., Anane, C., Ahmed, V., & Zacca, A. . (2023). Transforming education: A comprehensive review of generative artificial intelligence in educational settings through bibliometric and content analysis. *Sustainability. mdpi.com*. DOI: DOI: 10.14445/22312803/IJCTT-V71I4P114

Basit, A., Khan, Z. A., Rehman, I., & Iqbal, A. (2024). Analyzing how Social Media Platforms, Driven by AI, can serve as Spaces for Teachers' Professional Development by Facilitating Networking, Knowledge Sharing, and Real-time Collaboration. *Review of Applied Management and Social Sciences*, *7*(4), 849–863. DOI: 10.47067/ramss.v7i4.418

Baskara, F. (2025). Conceptualizing Digital Literacy for the AI Era: A Framework for Preparing Students in an AI-Driven World. Data and Metadata. usd.ac.id. DOI: DOI: 10.56294/dm2025530

Bayly-Castaneda, K., Ramirez-Montoya, M. S., & Morita-Alexander, A. (2024). Crafting personalized learning paths with AI for lifelong learning: A systematic literature review. *Frontiers in Education*, *9*, 1424386. Advance online publication. DOI: 10.3389/feduc.2024.1424386

Bhutoria, A. (2022). Personalized education and Artificial Intelligence in the United States, China, and India: A systematic review using a Human-In-The-Loop model. *Computers and Education: Artificial Intelligence, 3*, 100068. https://doi.org/https://doi.org/10.1016/j.caeai.2022.100068

Billiot, T. (2023). Continuous learning and advancing technologies: A framework for professional development and training in artificial intelligence. *Development and Learning in Organizations*, *37*(3), 28–31. https://doi.org/https://doi.org/10.1108/DLO-04-2022-0064. DOI: 10.1108/DLO-04-2022-0064

Bozkurt, A. (2023). Generative artificial intelligence (AI) powered conversational educational agents: The inevitable paradigm shift. . *Asian Journal of Distance Education. asianjde.com.*

Bozkurt, A. (2024a). *GenAI et al. Cocreation, authorship, ownership, academic ethics and integrity in a time of generative AI* (Vol. 16). International Council for Open and Distance Education Oslo., DOI: 10.55982/openpraxis.16.1.654

Bozkurt, A. (2024b). *Why generative AI literacy, why now and why it matters in the educational landscape?: Kings, queens and GenAI dragons* (Vol. 16). International Council for Open and Distance Education Oslo., DOI: 10.55982/openpraxis.16.3.739

Bozkurt, A., & Sharma, R. C. (2024). Trust, Credibility and Transparency in Human-AI Interaction: Why We Need Explainable and Trustworthy AI and Why We Need It Now. *Asian Journal of Distance Education*, *19*(2).

Brandão, A., Pedro, L., & Zagalo, N. (2024). Teacher professional development for a future with generative artificial intelligence – an integrative literature review. *Digital Education Review*, 151-157. https://doi.org/DOI: 10.1344/der.2024.45.151-157

Chakraborty, D. (2024). Artificial Intelligence And Lifelong Learning: Transforming Education For The Future. *Artificial Intelligence In Education.* google.com.

Chamola, V., Hassija, V., Sulthana, A. R., Ghosh, D., Dhingra, D., & Sikdar, B. (2023). A review of trustworthy and explainable artificial intelligence (xai). *IEEe Access, 11*, 78994-79015. DOI- DOI: 10.1109/ACCESS.2023.3294569

Chander, B., John, C., Warrier, L., & Gopalakrishnan, K. (2025). Toward Trustworthy Artificial Intelligence (TAI) in the Context of Explainability and Robustness. *ACM Computing Surveys, 57*(6), 144. Advance online publication. DOI: 10.1145/3675392

De, A. (2024). *Embracing Lifelong Learning in the Age of Artificial Intelligence.* Artificial Intelligence in Education., DOI: 10.25215/9358094575.08

Gao, Y., Gu, S., Jiang, J., Hong, S. R., Yu, D., & Zhao, L. (2024). Going beyond xai: A systematic survey for explanation-guided learning. *ACM Computing Surveys, 56*(7), 1–39. DOI: 10.1145/3644073

George, A. S. (2023). Preparing students for an AI-driven world: Rethinking curriculum and pedagogy in the age of artificial intelligence. *Partners Universal Innovative Research Publication, 1*(2), 112–136. DOI: 10.5281/zenodo.10245675

Gharahighehi, A., Schoors, R. V., Topali, P., & Ooge, J. (2024). Supporting Personalized Lifelong Learning with Human-Centered Artificial Intelligence Systems. ALL@AIED.

Goksel, N., & Bozkurt, A. (2019). Artificial intelligence in education: Current insights and future perspectives. In *Handbook of Research on Learning in the Age of Transhumanism* (pp. 224–236). IGI Global., DOI: 10.4018/978-1-5225-8431-5.ch014

Gulyamov, S. S., Mamanazarov, S., & Rodionov, A. A. (2024). Creating Self-Updating Digital Platforms Using Artificial Intelligence Technologies for Continuous Education and Professional Development. *2024 4th International Conference on Technology Enhanced Learning in Higher Education (TELE)*, 337-339. DOI: DOI: 10.1109/TELE62556.2024.10605683

Hu, S., Fang, Z., Fang, Z., Deng, Y., Chen, X., & Fang, Y. (2024). Agentscodriver: Large language model empowered collaborative driving with lifelong learning. *arXiv preprint arXiv:2404.06345.* DOI:https://doi.org//arXiv.2404.06345DOI: 10.48550

Ibrahim, A. M. (2024). The impact of voluntary artificial intelligent self-driven education and training platforms on maritime security personnel: ISPS code. *Journal of Transportation Security, 17*(1), 21. DOI: 10.1007/s12198-024-00292-6

Iman, M. Z., Asis, A. A., & Rahma, A. U. Z. (2024). Enhancing Personalized Learning: The Impact of Artificial Intelligence in Education. *Edu Spectrum: Journal of Multidimensional Education, 1*(2), 101–112. DOI: 10.70063/eduspectrum.v1i2.55

Jin, Y., Yan, L., Echeverria, V., Gašević, D., & Martinez-Maldonado, R. . (2025). Generative AI in higher education: A global perspective of institutional adoption policies and guidelines. . *Computers and Education: Artificial Intelligence, 8, 100348. sciencedirect.com*. DOI: DOI: 10.1016/j.caeai.2024.100348

KangJie. E. T., Song, T., Zhu, Z., Li, J., & Lee, Y.-C. (2025). AI Literacy Education for Older Adults: Motivations, Challenges and Preferences. *arXiv preprint arXiv:2504.14649*. DO: https://doi.org//arXiv.2504.14649DOI: 10.48550

Karger, T., Kalenda, J., Kalenda, S., & Kroutilová Nováková, R. (2022). Legitimisation of non-participation in adult education and training: The situational logic of decision-making. *International Journal of Lifelong Education, 41*(3), 277–293. DOI: 10.1080/02601370.2022.2057606

Khosravi, H., Shum, S. B., Chen, G., Conati, C., Tsai, Y.-S., Kay, J., Knight, S., Martinez-Maldonado, R., Sadiq, S., & Gašević, D. (2022). Explainable artificial intelligence in education. *Computers and Education: Artificial Intelligence*, *3*, 100074. DOI: 10.1016/j.caeai.2022.100074

Kovari, A. (2025). Explainable AI chatbots towards XAI ChatGPT: A review. *Heliyon*, *11*(2), e42077. DOI: 10.1016/j.heliyon.2025.e42077 PMID: 39906828

Laak, K.-J., & Aru, J. (2024). AI and personalized learning: bridging the gap with modern educational goals. *arXiv preprint arXiv:2404.02798*. DOI: https://doi.org/ DOI: 10.1016/j.caeai.2022.100074

Lang, Q., Wang, M., Yin, M., Liang, S., & Song, W. (2025). Transforming Education with Generative AI (GAI): Key Insights and Future Prospects. *IEEE Transactions on Learning Technologies*, *18*, 230–242. Advance online publication. DOI: 10.1109/ TLT.2025.3537618

Lara-Navarra, P., Ferrer-Sapena, A., Ismodes-Cascón, E., Fosca-Pastor, C., & Sánchez-Pérez, E. A. (2025). The Future of Higher Education: Trends, Challenges and Opportunities in AI-Driven Lifelong Learning in Peru. *Information (Basel)*, *16*(3), 224. DOI: 10.3390/info16030224

Longo, L., Brcic, M., Cabitza, F., Choi, J., Confalonieri, R., Del Ser, J., Guidotti, R., Hayashi, Y., Herrera, F., & Holzinger, A. (2024). Explainable Artificial Intelligence (XAI) 2.0: A manifesto of open challenges and interdisciplinary research directions. *Information Fusion*, *106*, 102301. DOI: 10.1016/j.inffus.2024.102301

Lu, J., Zheng, R., Gong, Z., & Xu, H. (2024). Supporting Teachers' Professional Development With Generative AI: The Effects on Higher Order Thinking and Self-Efficacy. *IEEE Transactions on Learning Technologies*, *17*, 1279–1289. DOI: 10.1109/TLT.2024.3369690

Maghsudi, S., Lan, A., Xu, J., & van Der Schaar, M. (2021). Personalized education in the artificial intelligence era: What to expect next. *IEEE Signal Processing Magazine*, *38*(3), 37–50. DOI: 10.1109/MSP.2021.3055032

Mandal, J. (2024). Ai Integration. In *Lifelong Learning: Transformative Approaches To Teaching And Learning*. Artificial Intelligence In Education., DOI: 10.25215/9358094575.27

Masrek, M. N., Susantari, T., Mutia, F., Yuwinanto, H. P., & Atmi, R. T. (2024). *Enabling Education Everywhere: How artificial intelligence empowers ubiquitous and lifelong learning*. Environment-Behaviour Proceedings Journal., DOI: 10.21834/e-bpj.v9iSI18.5462

Milana, M., Brandi, U., Hodge, S., & Hoggan-Kloubert, T. (2024). *Artificial intelligence (AI), conversational agents, and generative AI: implications for adult education practice and research* (Vol. 43). Taylor & Francis., DOI: 10.1080/02601370.2024.2310448

Misra, V. P., Mishra, P. K., & Sharma, A. (2023). Artificial Intelligence in Education–Emerging Trends, Thematic Analysis & Application in Lifelong Learning. *2023 IEEE Asia-Pacific Conference on Computer Science and Data Engineering (CSDE)*, DOI: DOI: 10.1109/CSDE59766.2023.10487664

Murtaza, M., Ahmed, Y., Shamsi, J. A., Sherwani, F., & Usman, M. (2022). AI-based personalized e-learning systems: Issues, challenges, and solutions. *IEEE Access : Practical Innovations, Open Solutions*, *10*, 81323–81342. DOI: 10.1109/ACCESS.2022.3193938

Naeem, H., Tariq, W., & Ali, I. (2025). Evaluating the Impact of AI-Driven Quiz Applications On Educational Outcomes: A Case Study of Wendigo. *Journal of Religion and Society*, *3*(01), 64–78.

Narayanan, N. (2024). *The era of generative AI: transforming academic libraries, education, and research.*

Nedungadi, P., Tang, K. Y., & Raman, R. (2024). The Transformative Power of Generative Artificial Intelligence for achieving the sustainable development goal of Quality Education. . *Sustainability. mdpi.com*. DOI: DOI: 10.3390/su16229779

Oberdieck, T., & Moch, E. (2024). Lifelong Learning with Artificial Intelligence: Potentials, Challenges and Future Perspectives. *International Journal of Advanced Research, 12*(6), 545–555. DOI: 10.21474/IJAR01/18915

Palenski, T., Hills, L., Unnikrishnan, S., & Eynon, R. (2024). *How AI Works: Reconfiguring Lifelong Learning*. Postdigital Science and Education., DOI: 10.1007/s42438-024-00496-

Pedro, F., Subosa, M., Rivas, A., & Valverde, P. (2019). Artificial intelligence in education: Challenges and opportunities for sustainable development.

Peng, Q. (2024). Lifelong Learning System in the age of Artificial Intelligence: Change, Opportunity and Reconstruction. *Journal of Electrical Systems, 20*(2), 1085–1091. DOI: 10.52783/jes.1294

Rane, N., Choudhary, S., & Rane, J. (2023). Education 4.0 and 5.0: Integrating artificial intelligence (AI) for personalized and adaptive learning. In: Nov. DOI: DOI: 10.61577/jaiar.2024.100006

Rawas, S. (2024). ChatGPT: Empowering lifelong learning in the digital age of higher education. *Education and Information Technologies, 29*(6), 6895–6908. DOI: 10.1007/s10639-023-12114-8

Raza, M. (2024). AI in Education: Balancing Benefits and Challenges Through Professional Development of Teachers. *Qlantic Journal of Social Sciences, 5*(4), 168–174. DOI: 10.55737/qjss.v-iv.24071

Romero, M. (2024). Lifelong learning challenges in the era of artificial intelligence: A computational thinking perspective. *arXiv preprint arXiv:2405.19837*. DOI: https://doi.org//arXiv.2405.19837DOI: 10.48550

Sajja, R., Sermet, Y., Cikmaz, M., Cwiertny, D., & Demir, I. (2024). Artificial intelligence-enabled intelligent assistant for personalized and adaptive learning in higher education. *Information (Basel), 15*(10), 596. DOI: 10.3390/info15100596

Schoenenberger, H. (2024). Concept and Reality of Lifelong Learning. In Schoenenberger, H. (Ed.), *Connected Learning: Origins, Opportunities, and Perspectives of Contemporary Educational Design: A Machine-Generated Literature Overview* (pp. 157–182). Springer Nature Switzerland., DOI: 10.1007/978-3-031-37813-3_6

Şenocak, D., Bozkurt, A., & Koçdar, S. (2024). Exploring the Ethical Principles for the Implementation of Artificial Intelligence in Education: Towards a Future Agenda. In *Transforming Education With Generative AI: Prompt Engineering and Synthetic Content Creation* (pp. 200-213). IGI Global Scientific Publishing. DOI: DOI: 10.4018/979-8-3693-1351-0.ch010

Shafik, W. (2024). Towards Trustworthy and Explainable AI Educational Systems. In *Explainable AI for Education: Recent Trends and Challenges* (pp. 17-41). Springer. DOI: 10.1007/978-3-031-72410-7_2

Singh, A. (2024). The Future of Learning: AI-Driven Personalized Education. *Available at SSRN* 5076438. DOI: 10.56557/ajocr/2024/v9i49018

Soltoggio, A., Ben-Iwhiwhu, E., Braverman, V., Eaton, E., Epstein, B., Ge, Y., Halperin, L., How, J., Itti, L., Jacobs, M. A., Kantharaju, P., Le, L., Lee, S., Liu, X., Monteiro, S. T., Musliner, D., Nath, S., Panda, P., Peridis, C., & Kolouri, S. (2024). A collective AI via lifelong learning and sharing at the edge. *Nature Machine Intelligence*, *6*(3), 251–264. DOI: 10.1038/s42256-024-00800-2

Su, J., & Zhong, Y. (2022). Artificial Intelligence (AI) in early childhood education: Curriculum design and future directions. *Computers and Education: Artificial Intelligence*, *3*, 100072. DOI: 10.1016/j.caeai.2022.100072

Tryhub, O. (2023). *THE CONCEPT OF LIFELONG LEARNING: THE EUROPEAN DIMENSION*. https://doi.org/DOI: 10.36074/logos-22.12.2023.080

Xiao, J., Bozkurt, A., Nichols, M., Pazurek, A., Stracke, C. M., Bai, J. Y., Farrow, R., Mulligan, D., Nerantzi, C., Sharma, R. C., Singh, L., Frumin, I., Swindell, A., Honeychurch, S., Bond, M., Dron, J., Moore, S., Leng, J., van Tryon, P. J. S., & Themeli, C. (2025). Venturing into the unknown: Critical insights into grey areas and pioneering future directions in educational generative AI research. *TechTrends*, *69*(3), 1–16. DOI: 10.1007/s11528-025-01060-6

Zheng, J., Shi, C., Cai, X., Li, Q., Zhang, D., Li, C., Yu, D., & Ma, Q. (2025). Lifelong Learning of Large Language Model based Agents: A Roadmap. *arXiv preprint arXiv:2501.07278*. DOI: https://doi.org//arXiv.2501.07278DOI: 10.48550

KEY TERMS AND DEFINITIONS

Lifelong Learning: It is the process of learning that an individual continuously and self-motivated engages in throughout their life to develop their abilities, expertise, and knowledge.

AI Agent: It is an autonomous AI system that perceives its environment, makes decisions and takes action based on this perception to achieve a specific goal.

Generative AI: It is a type of AI that can autonomously generate new text, visuals, audio, or other content.

Explainable AI: These are artificial intelligence approaches that explain how AI systems work and why they reach certain results in a way that is understandable to humans.

Personalized Learning: It is a learning process specially tailored according to interests, learning speed, knowledge level, and goals.

Personalized Education: It is a technology-supported and data-based learning process that is adapted to the learner's individual needs, learning style, interests and goals.

Lifelong Learning Current Trends: Digitalization, artificial intelligence-supported learning, micro learning, skill-focused education and flexible digital platforms are contemporary approaches that make it easier for individuals to learn at any age and anywhere.

Chapter 3
Personalized Learning Experiences and Learner Activism in Mobile Learning With Generative AI Support

Alper Altunçekiç
https://orcid.org/0000-0002-3649-0991
Gazi Üniversitesi, Turkey

ABSTRACT

Mobile learning offers individuals flexible and personalized educational experiences independent of time and space constraints. Productive artificial intelligence makes learning more effective by producing content tailored to the individual's learning style and needs. By analyzing a student's past performance, these systems provide tailored content to address deficiencies, increase motivation, and make the learning process dynamic with immediate feedback. These approaches support student activism and encourage the active participation of individuals in the learning process. Contextualized learning that considers location, time, and cultural factors makes the process more meaningful. Mobile assistants, guidance systems, and data-driven recommendation engines organize, monitor, and enhance the learning experience. Supported by interactive technologies, these systems enable the development of creative thinking, problem-solving, and collaboration skills. Learning thus becomes a sustainable and egalitarian model tailored to individual needs and enriched by social interactions.

DOI: 10.4018/979-8-3373-7574-8.ch003

INTRODUCTION

Mobile learning facilitates independence from conventional time and space constraints typically imposed on learning processes. This flexibility is particularly beneficial for lifelong learning and professional development (Lu, 2012; Miroshnikova, 2020; Petit & Santos, 2014). This feature is handy for working professionals, distance learners, and individuals open to continuous learning. (Erguney, 2017; Gu, 2014). Mobile learning (m-learning) eliminates the time and place displacements of traditional learning, reaches learners and also offers the opportunity to store educational content. This approach has a significant transformation power, especially in the field of continuing education such as lifelong learning and professional development. A summary review created by Sisouvong and Pasanchay (2024) emphasizes that thanks to the comprehensive content of mobile learning, "on-demand" access to educational content is provided, allowing learners to work at their own pace and according to their own needs. This flexibility, combined with the portability offered by mobile devices, seamlessly integrates learning into daily life routines and makes learners active recorders of their own learning.

Working professionals with a busy work schedule cannot attend traditional face-to-face training programs and may have difficulty continuing their career development (Pidd, 2002). At this point, mobile learning enables them to continue their career development by offering them the opportunity to learn at any time at work, during travel or during short breaks (Gu, 2014; Pimmer & Pachler, 2014). Researchers such as Pea and Sharples (2022) emphasized that mobile learning provides access to teaching materials at any time without the need for physical classrooms, eliminating both time and space dependency in the learning process. In this way, employees can access training content even in the short time periods they have during the day and successfully integrate training processes with their current workflows (Pea & Sharples, 2022). Studies conducted by Teri et al. (2014) have shown that mobile learning is a method that increases efficiency in this direction and allows learners to use their own time management effectively. Recent studies also support this trend, showing that mobile learning increases employee engagement and motivation; for example, in a technology company, the rate of employees implementing new skills not only verbally but also through behavior increases (Alkasasbeh & Amawi, 2023).

Moreover, for individuals open to lifelong learning, mobile learning offers an excellent opportunity to acquire new skills and up-to-date information. In today's world, where technology is changing rapidly, individuals can use mobile learning platforms to learn about different subjects to improve themselves and keep up with innovations continuously. As a result, mobile learning makes individuals' educational processes more personalized, accessible, and practical while increasing equality of opportunity in education. (Tangirov et al., 2021). Mobile learning's potential to enhance engagement and accessibility is vital for addressing the challenges posed by the digital divide and ensuring equitable educational opportunities for all learners (Sisouvong & Pasanchay, 2024). Furthermore, by leveraging mobile learning, educators can create tailored educational experiences that meet the unique needs of each learner, fostering greater autonomy and engagement in their educational journeys.

In the future, the impact of mobile learning will become even more evident as education systems evolve. Educational institutions will redesign their curricula and teaching methods according to the principles of mobile learning, thus adopting a more inclusive and accessible approach to education. In conclusion, mobile learning is an important tool that will shape future learning experiences, transforming the educational processes of individuals and the overall structure of educational systems. As mobile learning continues to evolve, it will further bridge the gap between formal and informal learning environments, enhancing collaboration and engagement among learners across various contexts (Pea & Sharples, 2022). This evolution will require ongoing research and adaptation to ensure that mobile learning strategies effectively meet the diverse needs of learners in an increasingly digital society.

ARTIFICIAL INTELLIGENCE

Artificial intelligence refers to computer systems or software with thinking, learning, problem-solving, and decision-making capabilities similar to human intelligence. This technology includes various sub-fields, such as machine learning, deep learning, natural language processing, and image processing. Artificial intelligence has revolutionary applications in data analytics, automation, voice assistants, autonomous vehicles, and more (Ghosh & Thirugnanam, 2021). As AI continues to evolve, its integration into various sectors will likely enhance efficiency and user experience, particularly in areas like education, healthcare and transportation.

Today, AI is used in many aspects of daily life, such as personalizing our shopping experience with recommendation systems, assisting with disease diagnosis in healthcare, and performing risk analysis in financial services. AI technologies are also being used to increase the efficiency of production processes, improve customer service, and accelerate research and development activities.

The development of artificial intelligence raises important issues such as ethics and security. It is, therefore, crucial that advances in this field are managed responsibly and that societal impacts are considered. Artificial intelligence is a field that will continue to shape human life in the future (Kamali et al., 2024; Rakowski et al., 2021). To ensure the responsible development of AI, it is essential to establish a robust ethical framework that addresses privacy, fairness, and transparency in decision-making. This framework will help mitigate the risks associated with AI technologies while promoting their positive societal impacts (Fan, 2024).

Generative Artificial Intelligence

Generative AI is a concept that refers to the ability of computer systems and algorithms to produce new content, ideas, or products by mimicking human-like creative processes (Shafique et al., 2023). This particular type of AI can acquire knowledge from extensive data sets, thereby enabling the creation of text, images, music, and other artistic forms. Generative AI processes and analyses existing information to create original artifacts that mimic human creativity (Epstein et al., 2023).

These systems acquire extensive knowledge about a specific topic or style using sophisticated techniques such as deep learning and machine learning. For instance, a text rendering model can be trained to emulate the stylistic features of a specific author, or an image rendering algorithm can be programmed to discern the distinctive characteristics of a particular artistic movement. This process enables AI to comprehend the intricacies and profundity of human creativity, thereby empowering it to generate new and original content autonomously (Sheth et al., 2016).

Generative AI has been adopted across various disciplines, including education, art, literature, music, and design. These systems have been demonstrated to positively impact artistic creativity, with studies showing that they can inspire artists and accelerate creative processes. Furthermore, they have been shown to facilitate the emergence of new ideas. Nevertheless, there remains considerable debate surrounding the ethical considerations of this technology and its effect on human creativity. Consequently, generative AI has the potential to redefine creativity and raise significant questions about the future of human and machine collaboration (Hutson & Harper-Nichols, 2023).

Generative artificial intelligence has the potential to transform education by offering opportunities in mobile learning environments. This technology brings a more interactive and personalized approach to individuals' learning processes and enriches their learning experiences (Duran et al., 2020; Dhagare, 2024; Maity & Deroy, 2024). By leveraging generative AI, educators can create tailored learning experiences that adapt to individual needs, ultimately enhancing engagement and comprehension in diverse educational settings (Zapata-Rivera, et al., 2024)

Mobile learning platforms enable users to access educational materials anytime and anywhere. However, generative AI further enhances this process, transforming the learning experience. This technology facilitates creating and adapting learning content in real-time, tailored to the user's needs and preferences (Miraz et al., 2021). To illustrate this, consider a scenario in which generative AI analyzes students' distinct learning styles and paces, generating customized content for each student.

This approach is poised to enhance the efficacy and efficiency of the learning experience for individuals with divergent learning styles. Consequently, while students can instantaneously access materials tailored to their requirements, educators can leverage this dynamic framework to formulate more targeted and effective educational methodologies. Furthermore, as Bozkurt et al. (2024) emphasize in their manifesto, the role of generative AI in education extends beyond being a mere technological tool. GenAI possesses the potential to enhance the quality of human-centered learning experiences. However, it is crucial to maintain a critical perspective during its integration to ensure that the affordances of GenAI are utilized within ethical and pedagogical frameworks, without diminishing meaningful human interaction.

Furthermore, the utilization of generative AI plays a pivotal role in enhancing the efficacy of training materials through meticulous analysis of user feedback (Liu et al., 2023; Power & Paige, 2009). This analysis aims to improve education quality by processing large data sets to understand users' experiences and needs. Mobile apps can undergo continuous optimization by incorporating this feedback into the learning process. Consequently, they can deliver dynamic and personalized content, increasing users' motivation and enriching their learning experience (Jamuna et al., 2009). This has the potential to yield more effective educational outcomes and assist users in accomplishing their learning objectives.

Personalized learning and Learner Activism

Personalized learning and student activism are two significant concepts that form the cornerstones of modern education systems (Down & Choules, 2017). Personalized learning is an educational experience tailored to each student's individual needs, interests, and learning styles. This approach enables students to progress independently, building on their strengths and overcoming weaknesses. Integrating technology, in conjunction with the efforts of educators and educational institutions, can enhance the efficacy of learning environments by offering students customized learning pathways and resources (Down & Choules, 2017).

Student activism is defined as the proactive involvement of students in their educational experiences and the broader educational structures, curricula, and technology used. This methodology promotes student accountability in establishing learning objectives, managing resources, and assessing their academic performance (Fielding, 2001; Robertson, 2020). Student activism is inherently associated with participatory and critical instructional methodologies, which can empower students to interrogate, redefine, and revolutionize their educational contexts (Giroux, 2020; Hooks, 1994). This transformation of the learner from a passive recipient of knowledge to an active agent and catalyst of educational processes is pivotal in fostering a more dynamic and participatory learning environment.

Integrating personalized learning with student activism has enhanced individual engagement in the educational process, elevated motivation, and fostered academic achievement (Luo et al., 2019). This integration fosters the development of innovative methodologies and methods in education while acknowledging individual differences and promoting active engagement, which can lead to a more inclusive and effective educational paradigm (Altinpulluk, 2019). Integrating customized learning material aligned with students' learning styles, interests, and requirements has substantially aided educators and institutions in achieving their educational objectives (Cho et al., 2019).

GENERATIVE ARTIFICIAL INTELLIGENCE-SUPPORTED LEARNING MODELS IN MOBILE LEARNING ENVIRONMENTS

The relationship between mobile learning, generative AI, and learner activism can be illustrated through a conceptual framework, as shown in Figure 1.

The Role of Generative Artificial Intelligence in Personalized Learning in Mobile Learning

Figure 1. The Role of Generative Artificial Intelligence in Personalized Learning in Mobile Learning

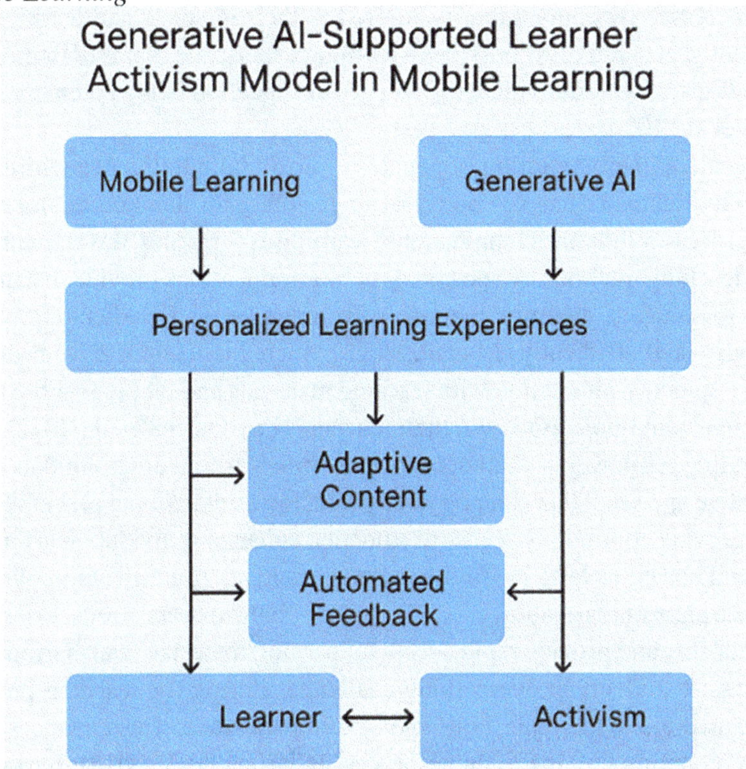

Utilizing generative AI-powered learning models within mobile learning environments signifies a paradigm shift in contemporary educational methodologies. These models capitalize on the capabilities of AI technologies, in conjunction with the flexibility and accessibility of mobile devices, to personalize and enhance learning experiences (Miraz et al., 2021). These models offer students content and resources tailored to their needs and learning styles. This technology aims to enhance each individual's potential by providing a personalized experience, thereby rendering students' learning processes more effective.

For instance, an advanced generative AI system can analyze a student's past performance in detail and identify areas where they are weak. Consequently, the system generates recommendations for targeted materials to reinforce these areas, facilitating student development. Consequently, students are empowered to delve deeper into these areas, enhancing their proficiency and addressing their deficiencies. Concurrently, the student's knowledge level is augmented by providing more advanced content in these areas without prioritizing the student's strengths.

This personalized approach enables individuals to progress at their own pace and consistently with their preferred learning style. The motivation of students to learn is increased by content that is tailored to their interests and learning styles. Consequently, generative AI provides a learning experience that is both more effective and efficient, with individual differences in education being taken into account (Tzirides et al., 2023).

Furthermore, the integration of generative artificial intelligence within mobile learning environments has the potential to facilitate an interactive and dynamic learning process. While enriching students' learning experiences, this technology also reshapes teaching methods. AI-powered mobile applications provide instantaneous feedback to students, enabling them to solve complex and challenging questions expeditiously and efficiently (M et al., 2023). Such applications have been shown to increase students' interaction with learning materials and facilitate more efficient and effective communication with their teachers (Paramartha et al., 2022).

Integrating AI-powered chatbots within mobile learning environments presents an innovative approach that can potentially transform educational processes. These chatbots provide continuous access to students, enhance individual learning experiences, and make teaching processes more interactive. The utilization of artificial intelligence algorithms enables these chatbots to analyze users' needs, offer personalized feedback, and provide rapid access to learning materials. Furthermore, these chatbots assist students in overcoming challenges during the learning process by providing answers to their questions and offering guidance. This enhances motivation, thereby optimizing the learning process (Clarizia et al., 2018). Furthermore, AI-powered chatbots integrated into mobile learning applications have been shown to facilitate learning by tracking users' progress, providing additional resources and suggestions when required, and deepening the learning experience.

The content has been meticulously tailored to align with each student's unique learning style and pace, thereby facilitating the development of profound comprehension and effective access to information. This innovative approach is predicated on the principle of educational equity to maximize the potential of individuals and render educational processes more efficient. Integrating AI-supported learning models is poised to play a pivotal role in the future evolution of educational systems.

Content Adapted to User Behavior

The creation of customized learning content based on an analysis of user behavior is a process designed to enhance the effectiveness and efficiency of individuals' learning processes. This content is developed by analyzing users' previous experiences, interests, learning speed, and preferred learning styles. Consequently, a personalized learning path is offered to each user. Adaptive learning systems offer a highly effective approach to personalizing the learning experience by continuously monitoring users' interactions and updating content based on this data. These systems employ sophisticated algorithms to enhance the efficacy of the learning process for students, generating content tailored to each individual's needs. To illustrate this, consider a scenario where a student encounters challenges in a specific subject area. In such cases, the system's ability to detect these difficulties and proactively offer materials focusing on the subject can significantly enhance the student's learning experience. This targeted approach has been shown to enhance understanding and boost student engagement, as learners feel more supported and empowered in their educational journey (Duraisingh, 2020).

AI-Powered Solutions That Respond to the Need for Instant Learning

AI-powered solutions address the necessity for instantaneous learning, significantly accelerating individuals' and organizations' access to information and making education processes more effective and efficient. These innovative solutions provide users with instantaneous access to the information they require and the capacity to personalize learning experiences and deliver content optimally suited to each individual's learning style. AI algorithms can analyze users' previous interactions in depth to determine which topics require further assistance (Lawless et al., 2020).

These insights empower individuals to guide their learning process more efficiently. For instance, if a user frequently poses a question on a specific topic, the system will identify this and suggest additional resources or support. Consequently, individuals and organizations can adapt more rapidly to an ever-changing information environment. Users can optimize their learning processes by accessing the information they need promptly, while organizations can increase their productivity by facilitating easier access to information for their employees. This approach to learning and knowledge acquisition is transformative, as it customizes educational content to suit each individual learner's unique needs and preferences, thereby enhancing engagement and retention. It has been demonstrated that this method is more dynamic and interactive, thus contributing significantly to the development of individuals and organizations.

AI-enabled solutions offer a significant advantage, particularly within the rapidly evolving business landscape and dynamic learning environments. In the contemporary business environment characterized by intense competition, the swiftness with which individuals can access information and the adaptability of their learning methods are among the most significant factors contributing to success. The personalization of education processes has been demonstrated to enhance individual motivation and assist organizations in optimizing the potential of their human resources. Consequently, AI-powered learning solutions are emerging as a pivotal instrument that facilitates access to information and fosters individual and organizational development (Liyanage et al., 2022; Sakalle et al., 2021).

Personalized Mobile Learning Experiences with Generative AI

The creation of user-specific learning pathways necessitates the design of educational experiences that are tailored to individuals' learning styles, interests, and needs. This process involves integrating diverse learning strategies, resources, and assessment methods to enhance the efficacy and efficiency of each user's learning process.

Adopting customized learning pathways empowers users to progress at a pace that aligns with their strengths and weaknesses. This approach has engendered greater motivation and engagement in learners because learning becomes linked to their interests.

The utilization of contemporary tools, such as technology and data analytics, in creating user-specific learning pathways offers a substantial advantage in monitoring individuals' learning processes and providing intervention when necessary. Consequently, this pedagogical model enhances individuals' learning experiences, fostering more profound understanding and sustained knowledge acquisition (Anderson, 2016).

Mobile learning analytics systematically analyzes data collected through mobile devices to more effectively understand and improve individuals' learning processes. These analytics enable the personalization of educational materials and teaching methods by tracking users' interactions, achievement levels, and learning styles in detail.

By thoroughly analyzing users' learning experiences, mobile learning analytics assists in identifying which content is more effective for learning, which methods enhance engagement, and which learning styles result in more successful outcomes. This process enables educators and instructional designers to enhance the efficiency of educational processes through the data obtained. Mobile learning analytics empower educators to meticulously analyze student interactions, success rates, and learning processes. Consequently, educational content can be delivered in a more targeted manner, and personalized solutions can be developed to meet the learning needs of individuals (Kuhnel et al., 2018). Furthermore, through these analytics, educators can continuously improve their training materials and teaching methods by identifying the most impactful strategies (Kuhnel et al., 2018). The insights yielded by these analytics are conducive to developing innovative approaches to education and the more effective management of learning processes.

Mobile learning analytics are emerging as a powerful tool to transform educational processes. These analytics empower learners by enabling them to monitor their real-time progress by establishing continuous feedback mechanisms. This enables learners to better understand their learning process and adapt their required strategies. This process makes individuals' learning experiences more targeted and effective while increasing their motivation. The ability to witness their advancement in real-time has been demonstrated to engender heightened feelings of achievement and motivation to accomplish their goals, consequently fostering deeper learning (Tortorella & Graf, 2017).

Data-driven recommendation systems represent a highly innovative and effective technological solution that analyses users' past behaviors, preferences, and learning habits in depth to provide them with the most relevant content and resources (Yang et al., 2022). These systems develop personalized recommendations tailored to the user's interests and learning objectives by integrating machine learning and artificial intelligence techniques.

This process necessitates thoroughly examining the content users interact with and comprehensively analyzing the data obtained. Implementing recommender systems facilitates learners to encounter more relevant and engaging content by identifying the most appropriate materials for their learning process in line with their past interactions and preferences. These systems have been shown to enrich the learning experience by providing personalized recommendations that consider users' individual needs and interests (Torres, 2022). Consequently, recommender systems have enhanced user motivation, facilitating a more effective and efficient learning process (Torres, 2022). Consequently, recommender systems have the potential to enhance interaction and engagement in educational settings, facilitate access to information, and support learners in achieving their learning objectives.

Consequently, such systems render individuals' learning journeys more meaningful and emphasize the significance of an individualized approach in education. By providing recommendations based on their previous experiences, users can increase their motivation and progress their learning processes more efficiently. In this context, data-driven recommendation systems play a critical role in providing personalized learning experiences in education.

Mobile learning analytics and data-driven recommendation systems represent two powerful components that, when analyzed together, have the potential to transform education radically. Mobile learning analytics enable educators to deliver content tailored to individual learning styles and needs by monitoring student interactions, learning processes, and outcomes in real time. Consequently, this approach can enhance student success rates and personalize learning experiences (Kabassi & Alepis, 2020).

Collectively, these dual components enable educators and educational institutions to formulate more efficacious and precisely targeted strategies. By leveraging the data, educators can discern which pedagogical approaches yield greater effectiveness and subsequently modify their curricula in alignment with these insights. Furthermore, this analytical data serves a pivotal function in formulating educational policies and optimizing resource utilization (Muñoz-Merino et al., 2015). In conclusion, mobile learning analytics and data-driven recommendation systems offer an innovative approach to education, enriching the experiences of both students and educators and ensuring sustainable development in education.

Learning Recommendations Based on Location, Time, and Context Awareness

The utilization of learning proposals founded upon location, time, and context awareness constitutes a pivotal approach to enhancing the efficacy of educational processes. This learning model integrates individuals' learning experiences with environmental factors, rendering knowledge more meaningful and applicable.

Adapting learning materials and activities to a specific place and time is of particular significance among the proposed strategies. This approach is predicated on the premise that it can enhance the efficacy of the learning experience by taking into account the physical characteristics of the educational environment and the individual needs of students (Staley, 2014). For instance, using outdoor spaces for nature lessons can facilitate a more profound comprehension of the subject matter by enabling students to apply theoretical knowledge in practical settings. The elements offered by nature, such as observation, questioning, and exploration skills, contribute to developing students' skills. Furthermore, the temporal organization of learning processes is paramount; lessons scheduled during periods of optimal student productivity can markedly enhance learning effectiveness by increasing attention and concentration levels. It is, therefore, vital to consider students' biological clocks and learning styles when planning lessons so that the potential of each student can be maximized (Allcock & Hulme, 2010).

Incorporating contextual awareness into project-based learning has been demonstrated to facilitate the utilization of information in practical scenarios. Integrating local cultural components into the educational process has been demonstrated to enhance critical thinking, collaboration, and student motivation (Suartama et al., 2022).

This integration enables students to understand their cultural context and to make learning more meaningful in that context. Engagement in the learning process is positively impacted by exploring social dynamics and cultural heritage, fostering a deeper level of engagement (Pan et al., 2017). Consequently, endeavors to enhance context awareness have been shown to deepen individual learning experiences and strengthen social bonds.

In conclusion, location, time, and context-aware learning are powerful tools for making individuals' learning processes more effective and engaging. This approach can potentially facilitate a deeper understanding of the subject matter for educators and students by enriching the learning experience.

Consequently, the relationship with generative AI is of significant pertinence. Generative AI has considerable potential to personalize and optimize individuals' learning processes. For instance, AI-powered education platforms can deliver content tailored to students' learning styles and needs. When augmented with location and time awareness, generative AI can facilitate comprehension among learners regarding optimal learning environments and timeframes within a given context (Priya et al., 2024).

Furthermore, context awareness allows AI to make learning processes more meaningful. By analyzing students' prior knowledge and experience, AI can suggest the most appropriate learning paths. For instance, if a learner encounters difficulties with a specific subject, AI can assess their past performance and provide resources or practical materials tailored to that subject.

In conclusion, a powerful synergy exists between location, time, context-aware learning, and generative AI. This synergy can transform education, enhancing learning processes' effectiveness, engagement, and depth. Educators' integration of these technologies has the potential to enhance students' academic achievements and lifelong learning capabilities.

LEARNER ACTIVISM AND GENERATIVE AI-SUPPORTED SELF-REGULATION SKILLS IN MOBILE LEARNING

Learner Activism and its IMPORTANCE in Mobile Learning

Mobile learning has been identified as a revolutionary approach within contemporary education. Learner activism is of critical importance in this paradigm. The concept of agency, as discussed by Alam et al. (2022), refers to students' active participation in mobile learning, which enables access to educational materials in various locations and time zones.

The management of learning processes by students through mobile learning platforms facilitates the achievement of individual goals. In this context, learner activism has increased motivation to learn and facilitate the effective internalization of knowledge (Alam et al., 2022).

Independent Learning and Motivation With Mobile Learning Tools

Mobile learning tools represent a significant resource, with the capacity to enhance motivation by facilitating individuals' autonomous learning processes. The ubiquity of smartphones and tablets in contemporary society facilitates convenient access to information, thereby rendering learning more accessible. These tools facilitate personalized learning experiences, enabling individuals to progress at their own pace. Utilizing learning applications and online courses fosters autonomy in learning, empowering individuals to direct their learning experiences by customizing content to align with their interests.

Mobile learning tools have become a significant component of contemporary educational methodologies, exhibiting considerable potential to enhance motivation through interactive, gamified learning content. These tools aim to attract users' attention and encourage them to participate actively by rendering the learning experience more engaging. Incorporating incentives, such as rewards, badges, and achievements, enhances the significance of achieving goals, thereby fostering a more enjoyable and substantial learning experience (Christopoulos & Mystakidis, 2023). These elements celebrate success and deepen the commitment to the learning process.

Concurrently, social media platforms and online communities have been shown to enhance learning processes by facilitating individual interaction. These virtual spaces facilitate the exchange of experiences, information dissemination, and support (Guilin, et al., 2024). Consequently, social interactions emerge as a pivotal factor in enhancing learning motivation. The presence of others in these interactions has engendered feelings of solidarity and mutual support, thereby enhancing active participation (Tu & Sujo-Montes, 2015). Mobile learning tools are distinguished by their versatility in supporting independent learning and enhancing motivation. These tools have been shown to enhance the efficiency of learning processes and facilitate the discovery of each individual's potential.

Learning on the Go and Managing the Learning Process

The term "on-the-go learning" refers to the process by which individuals acquire knowledge and develop skills in a dynamic environment. This approach emphasizes that learning is not merely a static process but occurs through continuous interaction and experimentation.

The term “on-the-go learning” denotes how individuals acquire knowledge through physical activity, social interaction, and experience. This dynamic process enables individuals to acquire new knowledge and deeply consolidate their existing knowledge. The learning environment fosters active interaction with the environment while concurrently cultivating innovative thinking and problem-solving skills (Yuen & Yuen, 2009). This pedagogical approach enables individuals to function as active participants in the learning process instead of merely passive recipients of information. The integration of physical movement has been demonstrated to enhance cognitive function and accelerate the learning process (Jucker & von Au, 2022). Furthermore, social interactions have been shown to foster emotional intelligence and facilitate the comprehension of group dynamics.

Consequently, individuals can benefit from their individual and collective experiences, leading to a more effective and comprehensive learning process. The ability to learn in a flexible, adaptive, and effective manner in an ever-changing world is facilitated by this learning approach, which is characterized by its mobility and management of the learning process. This approach can potentially enrich the learning experience and contribute to individuals' personal and professional development.

THE ROLE OF GENERATIVE AI IN ENHANCING LEARNER ACTIVISM IN MOBILE LEARNING

Mobile Assistants and Innovative Guidance Systems

Mobile assistants are applications customized according to the user's needs, providing timely feedback and facilitating access to learning materials. These assistants have been shown to help students improve their academic achievement by organizing their course schedules, reminding them of examination dates, and directing them to learning resources (Arsyanda et al., 2024; Chiu, 2019).

Conversely, innovative guidance systems leverage artificial intelligence and data analytics technologies to comprehensively monitor student performance and provide customized recommendations tailored to individual learning styles (Dash & Bhoi, 2024). These systems can meticulously analyze students' strengths and weaknesses, providing them with targeted and personalized learning pathways (Dash & Bhoi, 2024; Kaswan et al., 2024). In addition, these systems furnish educators with valuable insights, empowering them to devise more effective teaching methodologies and respond more adeptly to the diverse needs of their students (Alkan, 2024). Intelligent guidance systems have been shown to contribute dynamically to the teaching process by continuously updating and analyzing data to improve student achievement (Sharma et al., 2024). This dynamic environment fosters enhanced efficiency and effectiveness in both the learning process and the teaching practice.

Mobile assistants and innovative guidance systems promote individualized learning experiences in education, increasing student motivation and making learning processes more efficient (Alkan, 2024). These technologies personalize and enhance the learning experience by providing content tailored to each student's learning style and pace. Mobile assistants facilitate instantaneous access to information and review of learning materials, while smart guidance systems monitor progress and address individual weaknesses.

Integrating such technologies into educational systems is considered a significant development that will render educational processes more dynamic, interactive, and accessible in the future. These systems empower educators to more effectively address the diverse needs of students while students are empowered to direct their learning journeys proactively. Consequently, the foundations for educational equality and the maximization of student potential are established.

Generative AI-Powered Automated Feedback Mechanisms

Generative AI-powered automated feedback mechanisms represent a significant development in modern technology, offering innovative tools that can potentially transform various sectors. These mechanisms use advanced algorithms and machine-learning techniques to provide instant and accurate feedback during user interactions (Lee & Moore, 2024; Yeşilyurt, 2023). In line with this, Bozkurt et al. (2024) argue that GenAI-powered automated feedback systems must be designed not only to deliver efficient responses but also to promote cognitive depth and critical thinking in learners. Otherwise, there is a risk of encouraging superficial learning patterns and replacing human interaction with algorithmic solutions, which could ultimately undermine educational quality.

These systems optimize learning processes by analyzing user behavior and providing customized recommendations based on individual needs (Yeşilyurt, 2023). In education, for instance, these systems can assess students' performance, identify areas of weakness, and recommend targeted resources and strategies to address those needs.

Generative AI facilitates the creation of adaptive curricula that meet the diverse needs of learners and allows for personalized learning pathways that increase engagement and understanding (Tariq, 2024). Tools such as GPT-3 and other generative models are used to create scientifically relevant content, transcending traditional teaching norms and enabling the development of virtual labs and simulations. AI-driven content creation facilitates the customization of digital educational materials, rendering them more interactive and adaptable to individual learning styles (Morales et al., 2024).

The emergence of generative AI-powered automated feedback mechanisms is poised to play a pivotal role in enhancing both individual learning experiences and the productivity of organizations. These innovative systems are poised to proliferate extensively, spanning various sectors, including education and business.

Student-Specific Learning Plans and Reminders

The development of bespoke learning plans tailored to students' individual needs constitutes a pivotal step in enhancing the efficacy of educational processes. These plans are meticulously designed with each student's unique learning style, pace, and interests in mind. This approach acknowledges the heterogeneity among students in terms of abilities and motivational factors, ensuring that each individualized learning plan is tailored to facilitate optimal learning (Brown, 2014).

The integration of timed reminders within these learning plans provides students with the necessary support to facilitate the achievement of their academic objectives. These reminders assist students in maintaining awareness of study deadlines, assignment deadlines, and significant examination dates. Consequently, students' educational processes become more organized while enhancing their time management skills. The impact of reminders on enhancing students' focus has also been demonstrated, thereby contributing to an optimized learning process.

Implementing specific learning plans and incorporating reminders have been shown to encourage students to assume an active role in their learning process. Consequently, students have the opportunity to develop their independent learning skills. Participation in their learning process has increased students' self-discipline and responsibility for achieving their learning goals (Bälter et al., 2023).

Consequently, these approaches assist students in cultivating lifelong learning habits, promoting their academic success and personal development (Bälter et al., 2023). The utilization of generative AI has been instrumental in the development of effective reminder systems. These smart reminders assist students in maintaining awareness of their class schedules, assignment deadlines, and exam dates, utilizing artificial intelligence algorithms to deliver personalized notifications (Vannest et al., 2024). These notifications have facilitated improved time management skills and a greater focus on academic studies (Vannest et al., 2024).

In the contemporary educational landscape, it is acknowledged that each student's learning style, pace, and needs are unique. Given this diversity, generative AI has emerged as a significant tool for delivering personalized learning experiences.

By analyzing historical performance data, learning styles, and interests, generative AI can create bespoke learning plans tailored to the individual needs of each student. This approach enables students to learn at their own pace and in a manner that aligns with their individual needs and preferences. To illustrate this point, consider a student encountering difficulties with a particular subject, such as mathematics. In such a scenario, the AI system can be programmed to suggest supplementary resources and exercises designed to facilitate a more effective grasp of the subject matter.

OPPORTUNITIES OFFERED BY GENERATIVE AI IN MOBILE LEARNING AND ITS CONTRIBUTION TO LEARNER ACTIVISM

Integrating efficient AI into mobile learning offers numerous opportunities to enhance educational experiences and foster student activism. AI technologies have the potential to revolutionize mobile learning by offering personalized learning paths, real-time feedback, and interactive content delivery that can significantly increase student engagement and motivation. These developments can enhance the learning process and empower students to become more active participants in their education, which may, in turn, lead to increased student activism.

Mobile learning platforms utilizing AI can adapt educational content to individual learner needs, tailoring the pace and complexity of the material to suit each student's abilities and preferences. This personalization has been shown to increase student engagement and motivation, as students receive content relevant to their level of ability that is challenging but not insurmountable (Cota-Rivera et al., 2024).

Intelligent tutoring systems and adaptive learning platforms provide real-time feedback and personalized recommendations, enabling students to identify their strengths and weaknesses, thus fostering a more active and self-directed approach to learning (Cota-Rivera et al., 2024; Gjermeni & Prodani, 2024). These characteristics are important for personal learning and engagement.

Integrating artificial intelligence with real-time feedback in the context of mobile learning facilitates the delivery of interactive content and immediate feedback, which are imperative for sustaining student engagement and fostering active learning methodologies. These features enable students to apply what they have learned immediately and receive feedback, strengthening their understanding and encouraging continuous improvement. Furthermore, AI-powered interactive content has the potential to facilitate the creation of immersive learning environments, such as augmented reality and virtual reality applications. These environments offer students engaging and interactive educational experiences that can inspire activism and participation in education initiatives (Abimbola et al., 2024).

Generative AI is increasingly recognized for its potential to create dynamic social learning environments that foster student interaction and collaboration (Abimbola et al., 2024). This technology facilitates student engagement on mobile platforms, enabling discussions and collaborative projects that enhance academic knowledge and social skills. Participation in group dynamics has been shown to enhance students' communication, exchange of ideas, and problem-solving skills, increasing their motivation and interest in learning. Consequently, the integration of generative AI into educational environments is regarded as a transformative force with the potential to significantly enhance the learning experience.

Generative AI has been demonstrated to support the development of 21st-century skills, such as collaboration and communication, by providing platforms that encourage student interaction and teamwork (Türker & Öztürk, 2024). These platforms facilitate student engagement in discussions and collaborative work on projects, enhancing their social learning experience. Furthermore, it has been established that features such as automatic hash tagging and AI-driven test question generation in social learning management systems increase student engagement and facilitate online discussions, rendering learning more interactive and collaborative (Zhao et al., 2024).

Another impact of generative AI in mobile learning is that it plays a crucial role in developing critical thinking, creativity, and problem-solving skills by stimulating students' thought processes and encouraging innovative solutions (Türker & Öztürk, 2024). This phenomenon supports academic learning and encourages the development of essential social skills. Furthermore, the capacity of technology to replicate real-life scenarios for skills development facilitates students' acquisition of practical competencies within a collaborative environment, furthering their social and cognitive development (Singh et al., 2024).

RECOMMENDATIONS FOR THE USE OF GENERATIVE AI IN MOBILE LEARNING ENVIRONMENTS

Generative Artificial Intelligence (AI) can potentially transform the educational experience by providing interactive tools, intelligent content creation, personalized learning, and mobile learning environments. The capacity of AI to customize educational content to individual needs, provide real-time feedback, and facilitate engaging learning environments is well-documented. This enhancement of student engagement and outcomes is a key benefit of AI in educational settings. However, it is imperative to recognize that the effective integration of AI in mobile learning environments is contingent upon safeguarding personal data, ensuring accessibility for all users, and the continuous development and training of professionals in this field. The following sections will provide a detailed overview of the primary methods through which AI can be employed in the context of mobile learning.

- Adaptive Learning Experiences: Generative AI can customize content by analyzing students' learning styles and speeds. This capacity enables the provision of material to each student tailored to their individual needs and learning pace, thereby facilitating a personalized and optimized educational experience.
- Smart Content Creation: Artificial intelligence facilitates the automated generation of educational materials. Analyzing data on a specific topic can produce content such as lecture notes, exercises, or exam questions quickly. This capacity enables educators to optimize their time management.
- Feedback Mechanisms: AI provides instantaneous feedback to learners in mobile learning applications. This enables students to swiftly identify errors and implement the necessary corrections. Concurrently, it furnishes educators with a more comprehensive understanding of students' progress, enabling targeted interventions.
- Interactive learning tools have been developed to facilitate this process. The integration of AI-powered interactive applications within educational frameworks holds the potential to enhance student engagement. Integrating gamification components and simulations within the learning process can enhance student motivation by facilitating active participation.
- Data Analysis and Reporting: Mobile learning platforms collect extensive data to monitor student performance. Artificial intelligence can then analyze this data to provide teachers with comprehensive reports. These reports facilitate the identification of students' strengths and weaknesses, thus informing the development of novel teaching approaches.
- Social Learning Environments: AI can be used to create platforms that enhance students' social interactions. Collaborative learning is encouraged through tools such as group projects and discussion forums.
- The following section will address the topic of accessibility and inclusion. The utilization of generative AI has the potential to foster equitable educational outcomes by furnishing specialized materials and assistive tools for students grappling with diverse learning challenges. This is important for creating a more inclusive learning environment.
- Continuous Development and Training: The development of training programs is essential for educators to utilize AI effectively. This will enable teachers to learn how to use the new technology and how to better guide students.

ROADMAP FOR THE DEVELOPMENT OF GENERATIVE AI-POWERED MOBILE LEARNING SYSTEMS

The creation of continuing education programs is recommended for educators to facilitate the effective use of AI. This will enable teachers to acquire the necessary skills to utilize the new technology and to more effectively guide students.

- The first stage of the process is to conduct a needs analysis and establish goals. The initial phase involves collaboration with educators, students, and relevant stakeholders to ascertain deficiencies in prevailing learning processes. Establishing clear objectives is paramount to determining how AI can be utilized in these domains.
- The enhancement of technological infrastructure is also paramount. The technology infrastructure is a critical factor in determining the efficacy of mobile learning systems. Therefore, integrating powerful AI engines, user-friendly interfaces, and advanced data analysis capabilities is essential. Given the proliferation of mobile devices, it is also important that applications are compatible with different platforms.
- Content Development and Personalization: Generative AI can personalize learning materials for students. Consequently, it is necessary to establish dynamic content development processes and provide differentiated materials according to students' learning styles.
- Interaction and Feedback Mechanisms: The design of mobile learning systems should enhance user interaction. AI-powered feedback mechanisms should be integrated to allow learners to track their progress and be guided when necessary.
- In addition, the training and support of educators must be a priority. To ensure the effective implementation of these systems, educators must acquire the necessary skills and familiarity with this new technology. Integrating training programs and supporting resources facilitates educators' interaction with AI.
- In addition, evaluation and continuous improvement processes are integral to the effective functioning of these systems. Regular assessments should be conducted to determine how well the systems are working, and continuous improvement processes should be initiated to evaluate the results. This will enhance the educational quality of the system and student satisfaction.

CONCLUSION

The integration of generative artificial intelligence (GenAI) into mobile learning environments represents a significant shift in contemporary educational paradigms. This chapter has explored how GenAI technologies through personalization, automation, real-time feedback, and intelligent content generation enhance learner autonomy, motivation, and self-regulation. These systems offer powerful tools for delivering flexible, adaptive, and learner-centered educational experiences that transcend traditional temporal and spatial limitations.

However, as emphasized in the manifesto by Bozkurt et al. (2024), GenAI is not a neutral tool but rather a socio-technological construct embedded with cultural, ethical, and epistemological implications. While GenAI-powered mobile learning holds immense promise for improving access, efficiency, and engagement, it also presents challenges that require careful navigation. These include the risks of reinforcing biases, reducing critical human interaction, and promoting superficial learning if implemented uncritically.

Therefore, educational institutions and instructional designers must approach GenAI integration through a balanced lens one that combines technological innovation with ethical foresight. The future of mobile learning depends not only on the sophistication of our tools but on our collective responsibility to shape their use in ways that affirm equity, inclusion, and human-centered learning (Sullivanet al., 2023; Bozkurt et al., 2024). By aligning GenAI with reflective pedagogical practices, inclusive design, and learner agency, we can ensure that this transformative technology supports meaningful and sustainable learning for all.

Consequently, the educational dynamics of the future will be shaped by personalized and interactive learning experiences facilitated by the development of generative AI-powered mobile learning systems. The overarching objective of this roadmap is to enhance the efficiency and efficacy of learning processes by delivering innovative solutions in educational technologies.

REFERENCES

Abimbola, C., Eden, C. A., Chisom, O. N., & Adeniyi, I. S. (2024). *Integrating AI in education: Opportunities, challenges, and ethical considerations*. Magna Scientia Advanced Research and Reviews., DOI: 10.30574/msarr.2024.10.2.0039

Alam, A., Hasan, M., & Raza, M. M. (2022). *Impact of artificial intelligence (ai) on education: changing paradigms and approaches*. Towards Excellence., DOI: 10.37867/TE140127

Alkan, A. (2024). Artificial Intelligence: Its Role and Potential in Education. İnsan Ve Toplum Bilimleri Araştırmaları Dergisi, 13(1), 483-497. https://doi.org/DOI: 10.15869/itobiad.1331201

Alkasasbeh, W., & Amawi, A. (2023). The Effectiveness of Using Mobile Learning Application on Undergraduates' Intrinsic Motivation and Their General Nutrition Knowledge. [iJIM]. *International Journal of Interactive Mobile Technologies*, *17*(17), 19–37. DOI: 10.3991/ijim.v17i17.40959

Allcock, S. J., & Hulme, J. A. (2010). Learning Styles in the Classroom: Educational Benefit or Planning Exercise? *Psychology Teaching Review*, *16*(2), 67–77. DOI: 10.53841/bpsptr.2010.16.2.67

Altinpulluk, H. (2019). Innovative Learning Approach in the 21st Century: Personal Learning Environments. In Sisman-Ugur, S., & Kurubacak, G. (Eds.), *Handbook of Research on Learning in the Age of Transhumanism* (pp. 205–223). IGI Global Scientific Publishing., DOI: 10.4018/978-1-5225-8431-5.ch013

Anderson, M. (Ed.). (2016). *Developing Effective Educational Experiences through Learning Analytics*. IGI Global. DOI: 10.4018/978-1-4666-9983-0

Arsyanda, M., & Annajmi Rauf, M. Miftach FakhriPramudya Asoka SyukurDevi Miftahul JannahElma Nur Jannah. (2024). StudySync Mobile Application Design for Student Academic Activity Management Based on SQLite Database. *Journal of Embedded Systems. Security and Intelligent Systems*, *5*(3), 223–232. DOI: 10.59562/jessi.v5i3.5042

Bälter, O., Jemstedt, A., Javan Abraham, F., Persson Osowski, C., Mugisha, R., & Bälter, K. (2023). Effect of Personalized Email-Based Reminders on Participants' Timeliness in an Online Education Program: Randomized Controlled Trial. *JMIR Formative Research*, *7*, e43977. DOI: 10.2196/43977 PMID: 37831487

Bozkurt, A., Xiao, J., Farrow, R., Bai, J. Y. H., Nerantzi, C., Moore, S., & Dron, J. (2024). The Manifesto for Teaching and Learning in a Time of Generative AI: A Critical Collective Stance to Better Navigate the Future. *OPEN PRAXIS*, *16*(4), 1–27. DOI: 10.55982/openpraxis.16.1.654

Brown, S. J. (2014). *Personalized online learning management system and method* (Patent No. US20150206441A1). https://patents.google.com/patent/US20150206441A1/en

Chiu, H. S. (2019). *The Impact of Mobile Learning on Academic Achievement and Learning Experience Using a Tailor-made Mobile App*. http://papers.iafor.org/wp-content/uploads/papers/ace2019/ACE2019_53915.pdf

Cho, H. C., Koo, B. J., Yoon, J. Y., & Jun, S. P. (2019). *System and method of providing customized learning contents. U.S. Patent Application No. 16/384,915.*

Christopoulos, A., & Mystakidis, S. (2023). Gamification in Education. *Encyclopedia*, *3*(4), 1223–1243. DOI: 10.3390/encyclopedia3040089

Clarizia, F., Colace, F., Lombardi, M., Pascale, F., & Santaniello, D. (2018). Chatbot: An Education Support System for Student. In Castiglione, A., Pop, F., Ficco, M., & Palmieri, F. (Eds.), Lecture Notes in Computer Science: Vol. 11161. *Cyberspace Safety and Security. CSS 2018.* Springer., DOI: 10.1007/978-3-030-01689-0_23

Cota-Rivera, E. I., González Correa, M. E., Marín, L., Montenegro, M., Mercado Herrera, A., & Martínez, M. (2024). Transforming Education With the Power of Artificial Intelligence. In *IGI Global* (pp. 113–140). IGI Global., DOI: 10.4018/979-8-3693-1666-5.ch006

Dash, S., & Bhoi, C. (2024). Exploring the Intersection of Education and Artificial Intelligence: A Comprehensive Review. *International Journal of Multidisciplinary Approach Research and Science*, *2*(02), 601–610. DOI: 10.59653/ijmars.v2i02.637

Dhagare, R. P. (2024). Generative AI and Education: A Symbiotic Relationship. *International Journal for Research in Applied Science and Engineering Technology*, *12*(11), 1042–1045. DOI: 10.22214/ijraset.2024.65279

Down, B., & Choules, K. (2017). Towards a pedagogy of personalisation: What can we learn from students? *Curriculum Perspectives*, *37*(2), 135–145. DOI: 10.1007/s41297-017-0019-5

Duraisingh, L. D. (2020). *Tapping the potential of peer-to-peer student-centered learning experiences in the humanities and beyond. In Promoting Engagement, Understanding and Critical Awareness (1st ed., p. 16). Routledge.*

Duran, M., Simon, S., & Blasco, F. (2020). *Science Education and Artificial Intelligence– A Chatbot on Magic and Quantum Computing as an Educational Tool.* 137–142. https://doi.org/DOI: 10.38069/edenconf-2020-ac0011

Epstein, Z., & Hertzmann, A., Akten, M., Farid, H., Fjeld, J., ... & Smith, A (2023). Art and the science of generative AI. *Science, 380*(6650), 1110-1111. https://doi .org//arXiv.2306.04141DOI: 10.48550

Erguney, M. (2017). The role of mobile learning technologies in distance education. *Ulakbilge Sosyal Bilimler Dergisi*, *5*(13), 1009–1021. DOI: 10.7816/ulakbilge-05-13-02

Fan, L. (2024). *Artificial Intelligence Ethics: A Dialogue between Technological Advances and Human Values*. International Journal of Education and Humanities., DOI: 10.54097/tvqkkf40

Fielding, M. (2001). Students as Radical Agents of Change. *Journal of Educational Change*, *2*(2), 123–141. DOI: 10.1023/A:1017949213447

Ghosh, M., & Thirugnanam, A. (2021). Introduction to Artificial Intelligence. In: Srinivasa, K.G., G. M., S., Sekhar, S.R.M. (eds) Artificial Intelligence for Information Management: A Healthcare Perspective. Studies in Big Data, vol 88. Springer, Singapore. https://doi.org/DOI: 10.1007/978-981-16-0415-7_2

Giroux, H. A. (2020). *On Critical Pedagogy* (2nd ed.). Bloomsbury Publishing. DOI: 10.5040/9781350145016

Gjermeni, F., & Prodani, F. (2024). AI and Student Engagement: A Comparative Analysis. *Interdisciplinary Journal of Research and Development*, *11*(3), 195. DOI: 10.56345/ijrdv11n326

Gu, J. (2014). A mobile informal learning solution for workplace learners. *Educational Media International*, *51*(3), 185–198. DOI: 10.1080/09523987.2014.968449

Guilin, X., Xu, S., Xavier, M., & Elliot, M. (2024). The Impact of Using Social Media in the Learning Process on Student Social Interaction. *Journal Emerging Technologies in Education*, *2*(2), 190–201. DOI: 10.70177/jete.v2i2.1064

Hooks, B. (1994). *Teaching To Transgress* (1st ed.). Routledge., DOI: 10.4324/9780203700280

Hutson, J., & Harper-Nichols, M. (2023). Generative AI and Algorithmic Art: Disrupting the Framing of Meaning and Rethinking the Subject-Object Dilemma. *Global Journal of Computer Science and Technology*, *23*(D1), 55–61. DOI: 10.34257/GJCSTDVOL23IS1PG55

Jamuna, R. S., Ashok, M. S., & Palanivel, K. "Adaptive content for personalized E-learning using web service and semantic web," *2009 International Conference on Intelligent Agent & Multi-Agent Systems*, Chennai, India, 2009, pp. 1-4, DOI: 10.1109/IAMA.2009.5228081

Jucker, R., & von Au, J. (2022). Outdoor Learning—Why It Should Be High up on the Agenda of Every Educator. In Jucker, R., & von Au, J. (Eds.), *High-Quality Outdoor Learning*. Springer., DOI: 10.1007/978-3-031-04108-2_1

Kabassi, K., & Alepis, E. (2020). Learning Analytics in Distance and Mobile Learning for Designing Personalised Software. In Virvou, M., Alepis, E., Tsihrintzis, G., & Jain, L. (Eds.), *Machine Learning Paradigms. Intelligent Systems Reference Library* (Vol. 158). Springer., DOI: 10.1007/978-3-030-13743-4_10

Kamali, J., Alpat, M. F., & Bozkurt, A. (2024). AI ethics as a complex and multifaceted challenge: Decoding educators' AI ethics alignment through the lens of activity theory. *International Journal of Educational Technology in Higher Education*, *21*(1), 62. DOI: 10.1186/s41239-024-00496-9

Kaswan, K. S., Dhatterwal, J. S., & Ojha, R. P. (2024). AI in personalized learning. In *Advances in Technological Innovations in Higher Education* (1st ed., p. 15). CRC Press. DOI: 10.1201/9781003376699-9

Kuhnel, M., Seiler, L., Honal, A., & Ifenthaler, D. (2018). Mobile learning analytics in higher education: Usability testing and evaluation of an app prototype. *Interactive Technology and Smart Education*, *15*(4), 332–347. DOI: 10.1108/ITSE-04-2018-0024

Lawless, W. F., Mittus, R., & Sofge, D. A. (2020). Introduction: Artificial intelligence (AI), autonomous machines, and constructing context: User interventions, social awareness, and interdependence. In Lawless, W. F., Mittus, R., & Sofge, D. A. (Eds.), *Human-Machine Shared Contexts* (pp. 1–22). Academic Press., DOI: 10.1016/B978-0-12-820543-3.00001-8

Lee, S. S., & Moore, R. L. (2024). Harnessing Generative AI (GenAI) for automated feedback in higher education: A systematic review. *Online Learning : the Official Journal of the Online Learning Consortium*, *28*(3), 82–104. DOI: 10.24059/olj.v28i3.4593

Liu, Y., Yang, Z., Yu, Z., Liu, Z., Liu, D., Lin, H., Li, M., Ma, S., Avdeev, M., & Shi, S. (2023). Generative artificial intelligence and its applications in materials science: Current situation and future perspectives. *Journal of Materiomics*, *9*(4), 798–816. DOI: 10.1016/j.jmat.2023.05.001

Liyanage, M. L. A. P., Hirimuthugoda, U. J., Liyanage, N. L. T. N., Thammita, D. H. M. M. P., Wedanage, D. K. H., Kugathasan, A., & Thelijjagoda, S. (2022). AI Solution to Assist Online Education Productivity via Personalizing Learning Strategies and Analyzing the Student Performance. *2022 IEEE 13th Annual Ubiquitous Computing, Electronics & Mobile Communication Conference (UEMCON)*, 0609–0615. https://doi.org/DOI: 10.1109/UEMCON54665.2022.9965735

Lu, Z. J. (Ed.). (2012). *Learning with Mobile Technologies, Handheld Devices, and Smart Phones: Innovative Methods: Innovative Methods*. IGI Global.

Luo, H., Yang, T., Xue, J., & Zuo, M. (2019). Impact of student agency on learning performance and learning experience in a flipped classroom. *British Journal of Educational Technology*, *50*(2), 819–831. https://doi.org/https://doi.org/10.1111/bjet.12604. DOI: 10.1111/bjet.12604

Maity, S., & Deroy, A. (2024). Generative AI and Its Impact on Personalized Intelligent Tutoring Systems. https://doi.org//arxiv.2410.10650DOI: 10.48550

Miraz, M. H., Ali, M., Excell, P. S., & Khan, S. (2021). AI-Based Culture Independent Pervasive M-Learning Prototype Using UI Plasticity Design. *Computers, Materials & Continua*, *68*(1), 1021–1039. DOI: 10.32604/cmc.2021.015405

Miroshnikova, T. (2020). Innovative Technologies in Education. *E3S Web Conf.*, *210*, 18135. https://doi.org/DOI: 10.1051/e3sconf/202021018135

Morales-Chan, M., Amado-Salvatierra, H. R., & Hernandez-Rizzardini, R. (2024). AI-Driven Content Creation: Revolutionizing Educational Materials. *Proceedings of the Eleventh ACM Conference on Learning @ Scale*, 556–558. https://doi.org/DOI: 10.1145/3657604.3664640

Muñoz-Merino, P. J., Ruipérez-Valiente, J. A., Alario-Hoyos, C., Pérez-Sanagustín, M., & Delgado Kloos, C. (2015). Precise Effectiveness Strategy for analyzing the effectiveness of students with educational resources and activities in MOOCs. *Computers in Human Behavior*, *47*, 108–118. DOI: 10.1016/j.chb.2014.10.003

Pan, X.-W., Ding, L., Zhu, X.-Y., & Yang, Z.-X. (2017). A Social Approach to High-level Context Generation for Supporting Context-aware M-Learning. *Eurasia Journal of Mathematics, Science and Technology Education*, *13*(7), 3675–3686. DOI: 10.12973/eurasia.2017.00752a

Paramartha, A. A. G. Y., Seputra, K. A., Azima, F., Putra, D. P., Dwi, E., & Aryanto, K. Y. E. (2022). Usability Evaluation of an Interactive Educational Mobile Application. *2022 24th International Conference on Advanced Communication Technology (ICACT)*, 491–495. https://doi.org/DOI: 10.23919/ICACT53585.2022.9728778

Pea, R., & Sharples, M. (2022). Mobile Learning. In R. K. Sawyer (Ed.), *The Cambridge Handbook of the Learning Sciences* (pp. 362–382). chapter, Cambridge: Cambridge University Press. DOI: 10.1017/9781108888295.022

Petit, T., & Santos, G. L. (2014). Mobile Learning: An Ergonomic Alternative for Long-Awaited Educational Changes? In Kalz, M., Bayyurt, Y., & Specht, M. (Eds.), *Mobile as a Mainstream – Towards Future Challenges in Mobile Learning. mLearn 2014. Communications in Computer and Information Science* (Vol. 479). Springer., DOI: 10.1007/978-3-319-13416-1_1

Pidd, K. (2002). The Role of Workplace Social Controls and Normative Behaviour in Workforce Development. In *Organisational Barriers to Training Transfer* (p. 10). National Centre for Education and Training on Addiction.

Pimmer, C., & Pachler, N. (2014). Mobile learning in the workplace. In *Unlocking the value of mobile technology for work-based education.*

Power, C., & Paige, R. (2009). Content Personalization for Inclusive Education through Model-Driven Engineering. In Stephanidis, C. (Ed.), Lecture Notes in Computer Science: Vol. 5616. *Universal Access in Human-Computer Interaction. Applications and Services. UAHCI 2009.* Springer., DOI: 10.1007/978-3-642-02713-0_11

Priya, K. M., Soundarya, P., Kungumaraj, E., Bhagyarathi, P., Subathra, P., & Varghese, S. M. (2024) Harnessing Generative AI for IoT Enhanced Education, *2024 IEEE International Conference on Signal Processing, Informatics, Communication and Energy Systems (SPICES)*, KOTTAYAM, India, 2024, pp. 1-6, DOI: 10.1109/SPICES62143.2024.10779781

Rakowski, R., Polak, P., & Kowalikova, P. (2021). Ethical Aspects of the Impact of AI: The Status of Humans in the Era of Artificial Intelligence. *Society*, *58*(3), 196–203. DOI: 10.1007/s12115-021-00586-8

Robertson, S. (2020). Student Agency: A Creatively-Focused Digital Critical Pedagogy. In *Handbook of Research on Literacy and Digital Technology Integration in Teacher Education.* (156-170) IGI Global Scientific Publishing. https://doi.org/DOI: 10.4018/978-1-7998-1461-0.ch009

Sakalle, A., Tomar, P., Bhardwaj, H., & Sharma, U. (2021). Impact and Latest Trends of Intelligent Learning With Artificial Intelligence. In S. Verma & P. Tomar (Eds.), *Impact of AI Technologies on Teaching, Learning, and Research in Higher Education* (172-189). IGI Global Scientific Publishing. https://doi.org/DOI: 10.4018/978-1-7998-4763-2.ch011

Shafique, R., Aljedaani, W., Rustam, F., Lee, E., Mehmood, A., & Choi, G. S. (2023). Role of Artificial Intelligence in Online Education: A Systematic Mapping Study. *IEEE Access : Practical Innovations, Open Solutions*, *11*, 52570–52584. DOI: 10.1109/ACCESS.2023.3278590

Sharma, S. K., Dixit, R. J., Rai, D., & Mall, S. (2024). Artificial Intelligence and Machine Learning in Smart Education. In Khan, M., Khan, R., Praveen, P., Verma, A., & Panda, M. (Eds.), *Infrastructure Possibilities and Human-Centered Approaches With Industry 5.0* (pp. 86–106). IGI Global Scientific Publishing., DOI: 10.4018/979-8-3693-0782-3.ch006

Sheth, A., Perera, S., Wijeratne, S., & Thirunarayan, K. (2017). Knowledge will propel machine understanding of content: extrapolating from current examples. *Proceedings of the International Conference on Web Intelligence*, 1–9. https://doi .org/DOI: 10.1145/3106426.3109448

Singh, Y., Singh, D. P., Chander, N., Singh, Y. P., & Singh, P. (2024). Generative AI for Enhancing Education and SkillDevelopment. [IJISRT]. *International Journal of Innovative Science and Research Technology*, *9*(11), 883–888. DOI: 10.38124/ijisrt/IJISRT24NOV431

Sisouvong, V., & Pasanchay, K. (2024). Mobile Learning: Enhancing Self-Directed Education through Technology, Wireless Networks, and the Internet Anytime, Anywhere. *Journal of Education and Learning Reviews*, *1*(2), 39–50. DOI: 10.60027/jelr.2024.752

Staley, K. (2014). Adapting cultural materials to meet student needs. *Zona Próxima*, *20*(20), 144–152. DOI: 10.14482/zp.20.6036

Suartama, I. K., Triwahyuni, E., & Suranata, K. (2022). Context-Aware Ubiquitous Learning Based on Case Methods and Team-Based Projects: Design and Validation. *Education Sciences*, *12*(11), 802. DOI: 10.3390/educsci12110802

Sullivan, M., Kelly, A., & McLaughlan, P. (2023). ChatGPT in higher education: Considerations for academic integrity and student learning. *Journal ofApplied Learning & Teaching*, *6*(1). Advance online publication. DOI: 10.37074/jalt.2023.6.1.17

Tangirov, K. E., Botirov, D. B., & Ulugmuradova, L. D. (2021). Educational Mobile Applications ss A Means Of Individualization of Learning. *The American Journal of Social Science and Education Innovations.*, *3*(857), 430–435. DOI: 10.37547/tajssei/Volume03Issue01-78

Tariq, M. U. (2024). Generative AI in Curriculum Development in Higher Education. In Fields, Z. (Ed.), *Impacts of Generative AI on Creativity in Higher Education* (pp. 231–262). IGI Global Scientific Publishing., DOI: 10.4018/979-8-3693-2418-9.ch009

Teri, S., Acai, A., Griffith, D., Mahmoud, Q., Ma, D. W. L., & Newton, G. (2014). Student use and pedagogical impact of a mobile learning application. *Biochemistry and Molecular Biology Education*, *42*(2), 121–135. https://doi.org/https://doi.org/10.1002/bmb.20771. DOI: 10.1002/bmb.20771 PMID: 24375862

Torres, N. (2022). Recommender Systems for Education: A case of Study Using Formative Assessments. *41st International Conference of the Chilean Computer Science Society (SCCC)*, 1–6. https://doi.org/DOI: 10.1109/SCCC57464.2022.10000363

Tortorella, R. A. W., & Graf, S. (2017). Considering learning styles and context-awareness for mobile adaptive learning. *Education and Information Technologies*, *22*(1), 297–315. DOI: 10.1007/s10639-015-9445-x

Tu, C. H., & Sujo-Montes, L. E. (2015). Mobile Learning and Mobile Social Interaction. In Papa, R. (Ed.), *Media Rich Instruction*. Springer., DOI: 10.1007/978-3-319-00152-4_17

Türker, P. M., & Öztürk, M. (2024). Generative Artificial Intelligence and the 4C Learning Skills for the 21st Century. In Cela, E., Vajjhala, N., & Fonkam, M. (Eds.), *Next-Generation AI Methodologies in Education* (pp. 285–320). IGI Global Scientific Publishing., DOI: 10.4018/979-8-3693-7220-3.ch011

Tzirides, A. O., Saini, A., Zapata, G. C., Searsmith, D., Cope, B., Kalantzis, M., Castro, V., Kourkoulou, T., Jones, J. W., Silva, R. A., Whiting, J. K., & Kastania, N. P. (2023). Generative AI: Implications and Applications for Education. *ArXiv, 1-34. abs/2305.07605*. https://doi.org//arXiv.2305.07605 asdDOI: 10.48550

Vannest, K. J., Swindlehurst, K., Bishop, P. A., & Shepherd, K. G. (2024). The evidence for personalized learning plans: A systematic review of the literature for student outcomes and measures Grades 7-12. *On the Horizon*, *33*(1), 104–115. DOI: 10.1108/OTH-09-2024-0053

Yang, L., Yu, Y., & Wei, Y. (2022). Data-Driven Artificial Intelligence Recommendation Mechanism in Online Learning Resources. *International Journal of Crowd Science*, *6*(3), 150–157. DOI: 10.26599/IJCS.2022.9100020

Yesilyurt, Y. E. (2023). AI-Enabled Assessment and Feedback Mechanisms for Language Learning: Transforming Pedagogy and Learner Experience. In Kartal, G. (Ed.), *Transforming the Language Teaching Experience in the Age of AI* (pp. 25–43). IGI Global Scientific Publishing., DOI: 10.4018/978-1-6684-9893-4.ch002

Yuen, S. C., & Yuen, P. K. (2009). Mobile Learning: Learning on the Go. In Taniar, D. (Ed.), *Mobile Computing: Concepts, Methodologies, Tools, and Applications* (pp. 108–116). IGI Global Scientific Publishing., DOI: 10.4018/978-1-60566-054-7.ch010

Zapata-Rivera, D., Torre, I., Lee, C., Cabezuelo, A. S., Ghergulescu, I., & Libbrecht, P. (2024). Editorial: Generative AI in education. *Frontiers in Artificial Intelligence*, *7*, 1532896. Advance online publication. DOI: 10.3389/frai.2024.1532896 PMID: 39720359

Zhao, M., Kumari, P., Madhavan Perumal, E., & Hou, Z. (2024). Developing generative AI functionalities in a social LMS. *Discover Artificial Intelligence*, *4*(1), 99. DOI: 10.1007/s44163-024-00168-7

KEY TERMS AND DEFINITIONS

Mobile Learning: a flexible and individualized learning approach that allows students to continue their components and learning processes through portable devices, regardless of the place and time they can perform. This method is carried out in a more sustainable way by integrating learning with simple life.

Adaptive Learning: a data-driven, technology-supported learning system that adapts content and processes according to the needs, learning speed and performance of the learner. This approach aims to support each student's unique learning journey.

Personalized Learning Experiences: learning processes that are structured by taking into account the learner's individual characteristics such as interests, learning style, readiness level and learning pace.

Generative Artificial Intelligence: systems with creative production capabilities are algorithms that can analyze existing data patterns and produce new and original content (text, visual, audio, code, etc.). These technologies are revolutionary, especially in terms of content production in education and the development of interactive learning materials.

Adaptive Content: digital learning materials that dynamically configure themselves based on the learner's performance, preferences, and learning history. These contents can automatically change the level of difficulty and presentation format to support the individual's learning process.

Interactive Learning: an approach that positions the learner as an active participant rather than a passive recipient of information; and deepens learning through activities such as discussions, applications, problem-solving tasks and simulations.

Student Activism: an experiential learning approach that enables students to develop sensitivity to social issues, use critical thinking skills, and actively participate in change processes. This approach ensures that learning gains meaning at the point where it meets life.

Social Learning: a community-based learning process in which individuals develop knowledge and skills through observation, imitation, collaboration, and interaction with others in their environment. It recognizes that learning occurs in a social context.

Smart Feedback: a data-based feedback mechanism that instantly analyzes the learning process and provides personalized, timely, and meaningful suggestions. It allows learners to recognize their mistakes, make corrections, and monitor their progress.

Chapter 4
The Use of Artificial Intelligence as a Tool for Preparing Final Degree Projects in Educational Sciences:
Guidelines and Recommendations for Supervisors

Marcos Merino
https://orcid.org/0009-0008-6677-825X
Universidad Rey Juan Carlos, Spain

Sara Redondo-Duarte
https://orcid.org/0000-0003-2012-8784
Universidad Complutense de Madrid, Spain

ABSTRACT

This chapter aims to examine the potential uses of artificial intelligence (AI) in the preparation of final degree projects within the field of Educational Sciences. To this end, it provides a comprehensive analysis of how university students are integrating AI into their final degree projects, with a focus on common uses such as AI-assisted writing, research support, data analysis, and content generation. The benefits and challenges, potential risks and ethical dilemmas associated with these technologies are also discussed. Additionally, it offers an overview of widely used generative AI tools in academic settings that may facilitate the development of final degree projects. However, it is important to acknowledge that the landscape of generative AI

DOI: 10.4018/979-8-3373-7574-8.ch004

tools is constantly evolving, with new advancements continuously enhancing their functionality and capabilities. Finally, the chapter presents practical guidelines for the effective integration of AI in the preparation of final degree projects, since these represent the students' first significant contact with scientific research.

INTRODUCTION

In recent years, artificial intelligence (hereinafter AI) has become an agent of fundamental change in our daily lives, interfering in almost all areas of human knowledge, and even the most routine tasks have been affected or modified in some way by the use of AI. A clear example of this is the impact AI has had on research and education. In the academic field, AI has triggered a fundamental shift, transforming methodologies, tools, and data processes, which in turn has broadened the scope of scientific writing across various disciplines (Salvagno et al., 2023, as cited in Castillo-Martinez et al. 2024).

In the field of education, initiatives aim to integrate AI into the educational community (teachers and students) to enhance learning and instructional methodologies (Jereb & Urh, 2024; Barrett et al., 2019). Some of these initiatives are being supported by the European Commission. One of them is the Digital Education Action Plan (2021–2027), which emphasizes the need to establish clear guidelines for the use of AI in education systems and to ensure the protection of personal data (European Commission, 2020). Another important initiative is the Ethical Guidelines on the Use of AI and Data in Teaching and Learning for Educators, which aim to help educators understand the potential of AI while also raising awareness of its possible risks (European Commission, 2020).

The digitalization of education is a process that has been expanding exponentially for decades. Changes are occurring at an increasingly rapid pace, forcing educational entities to undergo constant renewal at both legislative and training levels, and the emergence of AI introduces a new component in this process of educational digitalization. Therefore, it is of utmost importance to address this issue, as AI is here to stay, and it will continue to be integrated into our daily lives regardless of how we position ourselves about its use.

Today, it is impossible to envision education without digital components such as computers, projectors, digital whiteboards, virtual classrooms, and e-mail. Although these changes are relatively recent, AI has gained widespread popularity in a very short time, highlighting its rapid expansion. An expansion from which the different educational systems cannot be unhooked. Authors such as Ahmad et al. (2021) or Crompton & Burke (2023) point out that AI enriches learning and, at the same time, can promote a transformation of traditional educational systems, a need that has been widely recognized in academic discourse. Thus, the authors propose AI as the tool that will allow changes to be produced not only at the content level, but also at the methodological level.

In this regard, the TPACK model (Technological Pedagogical Content Knowledge) serves as a valuable framework for educators aiming to effectively integrate AI into their teaching practices. It is based on the premise that, in order to use ICTs effectively in education, teachers must possess a balanced combination of technological, pedagogical, and content knowledge (Herring et al., 2016). According to Cabero & Barroso (2016) what is truly significant about the TPACK model is not the independent development of the three types of knowledge (Content Knowledge – CK, Pedagogical Knowledge – PK, and Technological Knowledge – TK), but rather the emphasis on their integration. These components must be understood in interaction: Pedagogical Content Knowledge (PCK), Technological Content Knowledge (TCK), Technological Pedagogical Knowledge (TPK), and ultimately, Technological Pedagogical Content Knowledge (TPACK).

Academic literature raises two main areas in which education can benefit from the use of AI. On the one hand, Singh & Mishra (2023) point out its importance in various issues related to academic personalization. According to the authors, this technology would allow content and teaching methods to be adapted according to the needs of each student. By addressing individual aptitudes and learning styles, AI fosters more personalized and effective education (Arora, 2021). On the other hand, authors such as Delcker et al. (2024) consider AI as a tool that accompanies both teachers and students in different academic tasks. Thus, AI transforms how information is accessed, and ideas are generated, streamlining processes and enhancing learning efficiency.

However, multiple scholars warn of the challenges posed by the incorporation of AI in education. Among these challenges are mainly various ethical issues that raise the need to preserve standards that allow the balance between technological efficiency and human creativity, since these issues are fundamental to guarantee the responsible use of AI. Likewise, the importance of human supervision of these processes is highlighted, since authors such as Crawford et al. (2023) or Lund et al. (2023) emphasize the risk of falling into plagiarism or the lack of transparency of these processes. Thus, scholars underscore the need to preserve academic integrity in AI-assisted work. Furthermore, authors such as Ariyaratne et al. (2023) highlight the importance of validating the information provided by AI, which may contain errors. As Harding et al. (2023), Brusilovsky (2024) and Eisbach et al. (2024) point out, AI should be viewed as a tool that enhances, rather than replaces, authors' skills, and must always be subject to the supervision of their criteria.

Both teachers and students face various challenges that have persisted from previous educational stages, such as reading and writing skills or ethical concerns in academic work. It is evident that, during the development of final degree projects, these issues have not been adequately addressed, raising the question of whether the current approach to such work is appropriate. Consequently, the interaction between AI, teachers and students is shaped by this chain effect. In other words, both the benefits of the use of AI and its risks will revolve around pre-existing challenges in different educational stages, which, to date, remain unresolved.

This chapter aims to examine the potential uses of AI for preparing final degree projects in the field of Educational Sciences, focusing on the use of AI as a support tool (and not as a substitute for the student's effort). The term final degree project refers to what is commonly known in Spain as the *Trabajo de Fin de Grado (TFG)*, as outlined in Royal Decree 822/2021 of September 28. This is an original piece of research that each student must carry out individually, under the guidance of an academic supervisor. Its purpose is to demonstrate the knowledge and skills gained throughout their undergraduate program (Real Decreto 822/2021, 2021). The TFG is a compulsory part of the curriculum, assessed by a panel, and usually requires a public defense. In other countries, similar projects are often called a capstone paper, undergraduate dissertation, or senior thesis.

For that purpose, the chapter provides a comprehensive analysis of how university students are incorporating AI in their final degree projects, including common applications such as AI-assisted writing, research, data analysis, and content generation. The benefits and challenges, potential risks and ethical dilemmas associated with these technologies are also discussed. Additionally, an overview is provided of some of the most widely used generative AI tools in academic settings, which could be useful for preparing final degree projects. However, it should be noted that the landscape of available generative AI tools is continuously evolving, with new additions offering enhanced functionality and capabilities. Finally, the chapter includes a series of specific proposals and practical guidelines for AI integration in the process of preparing final degree projects in the field of Educational Sciences, since these represent the students' first significant contact with scientific research.

1. HOW ARE STUDENTS USING AI IN THEIR FINAL DEGREE PROJECTS?

As discussed above, AI has become a crucial tool across various disciplines (Amisha et al., 2019; Gade et al., 2020), including Education. In recent years, AI has significantly influenced various educational processes, particularly in institutional and instructional applications. Its role has become increasingly prominent in shaping future educational transformations (Chen et al., 2020). Therefore, in order to analyze the role of generative AI in the development of undergraduate dissertations, it is essential to comprehensively examine its use in education. This underscores the importance of incorporating multiple perspectives, particularly that of students. In other words, in the same way that the academic literature has presented the perspectives of schools, educational institutions and teachers regarding the use of AI, it is necessary that this analysis also includes the student's view, in order to enrich the analysis as much as possible. These students should be regarded as novice researchers who utilize generative AI as a tool to support their dissertation development.

Monib et al. (2025) found that students generally perceive AI tools positively, appreciating both their time-saving potential and user-friendly interfaces. This perception is reinforced by Nasution (2023), who surveyed 272 university students and reported that a significant majority found AI-generated questions relevant (79%), clearly written (72%), and accurate (73%), underscoring the perceived utility of such tools in academic work. Further supporting this trend, Chan (2023) conducted a mixed-method study across several universities in Hong Kong involving 457 students and 180 faculty members. Even though they had little experience with generative AI tools, both students (M = 4.00) and faculty (M = 3.87) recognized their positive impact on higher education research, highlighting a strong readiness for adoption if adequate training and support structures are provided.

Vasconcelos and dos Santos (2023) also contributed significant findings through a case study simulating student interactions with ChatGPT and Bing Chat in STEM education. Their analysis of reflective journals and chatbot logs indicated that these tools could serve as objects-to-think-with, fostering critical thinking and conceptual engagement, particularly when embedded in dialogical, guided learning experiences. Moreover, the inclusive potential of AI in education cannot be overlooked. As cited by Adiguzel et al. (2023), empirical findings from Llorente et al. (2021) and Zhang et al. (2020) show that AI-supported interventions have improved learning outcomes for students with dyslexia and autism spectrum disorder, respectively. These outcomes emphasize AI's role not only as an efficiency tool but also as a vehicle for educational accessibility and equity.

Ginting et al. (2023) examined the views of 8th-semester EFL (English as a foreign language) students regarding the use of AI tools as writing aids for their final projects. Using convenience sampling, 50 students from public and private colleges in North Sumatra, Indonesia, participated in the study. The findings revealed that students largely support using AI writing tools, as they believe these tools enhance the quality and efficiency of their written assignments. Krajka and Olszak (2024) conducted an analysis exploring how students incorporate AI tools into academic writing. The study, which employed a quasi-experimental approach with an undergraduate applied linguistics cohort, revealed a marked improvement in students' engagement with and proficiency in using AI-driven tools for text creation.

However, not all findings reflect uncritical enthusiasm. Authors such as Stöhr et al. (2024) argue that, despite positive attitudes towards the use of AI, most students expressed concerns rather than positive aspects. Ozfidan et al. (2024) examined Saudi undergraduate students' perceptions of AI tools in academic writing. A survey of 189 students enrolled in English writing courses found that they commonly used ChatGPT, Grammarly, and Google Translate. The analysis identified two key factors: "instructional support of AI tools" and "instructional practices of AI tools." Students strongly agreed on the benefits of AI tools, such as aiding in idea generation, outline preparation, grammar improvement, and saving time.

Jereb & Urh's (2024) study reveals that students are aware of the existence of multiple AI applications for various purposes. However, they report consistently relying on the same ones due to a lack of knowledge or training. The study participants emphasize that receiving training in this area would be highly beneficial, as they generally have a positive perception of AI but acknowledge their limitations in applying it effectively. Through this training, students think that they can improve the quality of their learning and that, despite the risks that its use may entail, with greater knowledge they would be able to avoid them. In the words of the participating students: "Instead of suppressing the use of AI, we should use it to our advantage, such as obtaining key data"; "It would be excellent if we could use artificial intelligence without getting into trouble" (Jereb & Urh, 2024, p. 341).

However, concerns were raised about reliability, contextual accuracy, and ethical issues. In this sense, the study carried out by Krajka & Olszak (2024) found that students' opinions on the effectiveness of ChatGPT and other AI tools for writing were divided. The authors interpret this finding to suggest that students may not be fully convinced of the tools' effectiveness, or they may have encountered difficulties in using them due to inadequate training. In line with this argument, Utami & Winarni (2023) point out that AI tools can assist students in academic writing but require additional features and improved AI literacy for optimal use.

2. BENEFITS OF USING AI IN FINAL DEGREE PROJECTS: ENHANCING WRITING QUALITY AND RESEARCH EFFICIENCY

From the perspectives of students and faculty, the benefits of generative AI in the development of final degree projects can be assessed. The dissertation tutoring process, along with the student's development of the project, often faces various challenges, including administrative, academic, and research-related difficulties. However, many of these problems are linked to the way in which students approach this type of work, including time management, lack of preparation in the different stages of research and writing the body of the paper (Jiménez et al., 2016). Thus, the benefits of the use of AI in the development of dissertations can be classified into two main groups: those that improve the efficiency and quality of research and academic writing.

Broadening research in this area is crucial, as understanding how learners perceive generative AI can play a key role in unlocking its benefits, overcoming obstacles, and uncovering new challenges. It also aids in identifying strategies to enhance its effectiveness as a learning tool. In their study, the authors summarize the benefits of AI as reported by students, highlighting the following aspects: First, students point out the benefits of using AI for reading comprehension, both in understanding complex topics for exams and in comprehending various sources used for essays or their final degree project. They do so by generating summaries and study materials aligned with different learning techniques. Secondly, this study highlights the use of AI as an assistant in research processes, particularly for writing-related tasks such as idea connection and grammatical revision.

Time management is one of the most problematic issues when dealing with this type of work. The literature related to the use of AI in education has described on numerous occasions how AI has helped with bureaucratic and/or administrative tasks that both teachers and institutions have to carry out, facilitating different processes and increasing efficiency (Chen et al., 2020; Chiu et al., 2023; Bozkurt et al., 2024). However, the case of students is different. The process of preparing the final degree project, conceived as a subject, takes place during the last year of the degree, at the same time as other subjects and/or internships. Unlike the rest of the subjects, this project has an important component linked to the student's self-regulation, organization and discipline skills, since, despite having a tutor who monitors the process and its different stages, most of the student's work time is donc autonomously (Jiménez et al. 2016; Rekalde, 2011). As a result, many of the students work on their final degree project inconsistently (dedicating significant time to it at certain stages while making no progress at others), at the last minute, or simply end up leaving it for later calls. As a result, the results are not optimal.

Even when students meet the deadlines, many of them struggle with effective time management, due, on most occasions, to their lack of experience in the world of research. It is precisely at this point where the use of AI comes into play, since various applications could help improve academic efficiency by assisting in meticulous processes such as, for example, literature review, through the use of applications such as Semantic Scholar, Elicit, Connected Papers, Research Rabbit, Scite or Consensus; or with other tasks such as the development of a workflow (Cheung et al., 2023; Cross et al., 2023; Naidu & Sevnarayan, 2023), goal planning, progress monitoring, and adapting research strategies (Xia et al., 2023; Xia, Chiu, Chai, Xie, 2023; Zimmerman, 2002). One of the main challenges in improving research quality is defining and narrowing the study topic, as well as formulating research questions. Generally, the topics chosen are quite broad, and authors such as Rajabi et al. (2023) argue that these stages can be enriched by the use of AI, which can become an aid in addressing these issues.

AI has proven to be a valuable element in developing writing competence (Krajka & Olszak, 2024) and it is possible to conceive it as an assistant in writing, fostering a human-AI collaborative writing model (Lin, 2023). Specifically, in the context of a final degree project, AI can enhance the quality and efficiency of academic writing by assisting in tasks such as generating titles, creating abstracts, and checking grammar and spelling (Duymaz & Tekin, 2024; Dergaa et al., 2024; Lin, 2023), or the review of the internal consistency of the text.

On the other hand, the writing of the body of the paper is one of the greatest difficulties faced by students in the process of developing the final degree project. These texts require continuous and personalized feedback to help students progress without having to delete entire sections or make major revisions. Again, the lack of experience in the field of research is one of the triggers of this situation, which is compounded by the language difficulties of the new generations. The role of the tutor is of utmost importance in this writing process, as well as in the development of the more technical part of the research. However, administrative constraints often limit student-tutor interactions, so that there is no access to constant and personalized feedback, or it is delayed for a long time.

Bozkurt et al. (2024) argue that "GenAI holds significant promise for delivering personalized learning experiences tailored to individual student needs and learning preferences" (p. 492). In relation to this, authors such as Hashim et al. (2023) or Farooq et al. (2024) point out that different Personalized Learning Platforms (PLP) or writing assistants such as Grammarly or Jenni AI could help analyze the way students write the body of the writing in order to provide instant feedback about their work (Jereb & Urh, 2024). Personalized learning platforms, particularly those focused on student feedback, play a crucial role in enhancing learning through AI. As Naidu & Sevnarayan (2023) point out, students would benefit from interacting with multiple sources of feedback on their work.

Personalized feedback and content adaptation play a key role in enhancing the learning experience (Singh & Mishra, 2023), especially from a constructivist approach in which students actively construct knowledge as they advance in their formative process. In this context, each dissertation arises from the intellectual motivations of the student, generally in dialogue with his or her tutor, which makes each project have a high degree of uniqueness. Therefore, although the process is structured by academic regulations, it is essential to customize it to suit both the requirements of the work and the individual needs of the student. In other words, while adhering to academic standards, the process must remain student-centered, ensuring not only compliance with requirements but also fostering student engagement and commitment to their research.

Undoubtedly, all these benefits described above are linked to the level of technological competencies of the students. In their study, Delcker et al. (2024) point out that there is a direct correlation between beneficial use of AI and the students' level of competence in the subject. The authors emphasize that it is necessary to develop and enhance students' curiosity towards technology, so that they can understand what AI can offer them as a tool, while at the same time understanding the difficulties they may face at any given time. In this way, the student will be able to use this tool in an effective way, and at the same time, maintain a critical position on the results. Regarding the role of the teacher in this aspect, the author states that:

Educators should, therefore, integrate these tools into their instructional design practices and pair them with additional practices to facilitate the students' AI-competencies. As a result, students will be able to use AI-tools to improve their learning processes, while simultaneously being able to critically reflect on the input, output, and influence of the respective AI-tools. (Delcker et al., 2024, p.8)

3. CHALLENGES AND ETHICAL CONSIDERATIONS OF USING AI IN FINAL DEGREE PROJECTS

Although AI offers significant benefits, its integration into dissertation development presents challenges similar to those identified in specialized literature (Huallpa et al., 2023). On the one hand, various scholars highlight that the boundary between ethical AI use and academic dishonesty is thin and often ambiguous. Authors such as Lye and Lim (2024), or Adiguzel et al. (2023) raise the possibility that the use of AI in education may aggravate the (already existing) inequality in the student body. Access to some of these platforms is often not free, and enhanced versions with superior data access and processing power require a paid subscription. Consequently, the possibility of accessing the tool based on the socioeconomic profile of the student body would cause a comparative aggravation when evaluating those who can access it and those who cannot (Rajabi et al, 2023).

Furthermore, several scholars point out that another challenge facing the implementation of AI in higher education is the presence of biases in the data used, since, during the training of these AI models, it is possible that, on the one hand, not all the necessary information has been accessed, and on the other, that the source accessed does not meet the desired reliability. These models retrieve data from various online sources, which may introduce bias depending on the credibility of the sources (Sabzalieva & Valentini, 2023; Naidu & Sevnarayan, 2023; Rajabi et al., 2023).

This issue is directly related to AI's capability of providing automatic feedback to learners. When this feedback is content-related, it is imperative that there is no bias or outdated information, as the feedback provided may be erroneous (Ali et al., 2024; Cross et al., 2023; Ouh et al., 2023) or "not ideologically and culturally neutral. Instead, it reflects worldviews that can reinforce existing biases and marginalize diverse voices" (Bozkurt et al., 2024, p. 488). Similarly, feedback should not be limited to content and writing but should also consider the individual learning needs of students, aligning with the principles of personalized education. However, AI dehumanizes the feedback provided by not taking this factor into account (Morjaria et al., 2023).

The academic community has also shown increasing concern about plagiarism through the use of AI. Some studies, such as those conducted by Zhao et al. (2022) or Yavich and Davidovitch (2024) explores the traits of students involved in academic dishonesty, emphasizing their low self-confidence and growing reliance on digital tools for studying and evaluations. To foster academic integrity, the study underscores the importance of open communication between educators and learners, along with creating a classroom environment that encourages trust and support. Much of the academic dishonesty occurs in the elaboration of the body of the writing. A large-scale study by Cebrián-Robles et al. (2023), involving 324 students from three Spanish universities, confirmed that the pandemic-related digital context facilitated academic cyber-plagiarism. Students reported fluid online communication during exams and assignments that enabled the exchange of information and the misuse of content without attribution. This finding highlights how sudden digital transitions can expose weaknesses in students' academic integrity and institutional safeguards.

Since the introduction of the final degree project in educational curricula, various unethical strategies have emerged to circumvent academic integrity requirements, including external companies that sell their services for the development of a dissertation. In many cases, these works have included a high percentage of plagiarism or have resulted in translated works coming from other universities or countries. Authors such as Chiu et al. (2023) or Moorhouse et al. (2023) emphasize that generative AI tools can complete academic writing tasks almost instantly, which may heighten the likelihood of students engaging in educational fraud (Crawford et al., 2023). Bozkurt et al. (2024) describe this as follows: "GenAI raises significant concerns for academic integrity, as students increasingly use AI-generated content for assignments and essays. The ease of generating sophisticated responses heightens the risk of plagiarism and cheating, undermining both academic standards and the authenticity of learning" (p. 500).

As a result, higher education institutions are updating both their policies and strategies against plagiarism, particularly in the face of content-generative tools that may facilitate plagiarism or impede meaningful learning. It is crucial to recognize that academic dishonesty is not a new phenomenon in education. Tools like Turnitin were specifically designed to detect and prevent plagiarism. Lye and Lim (2024) describe the situation as follows:

In the past, when there was no generative AI, it would require some effort for students to copy the work of someone else or be involved in contract cheating. Of late, it has evidently become significantly less onerous to commit academic dishonesty since generative AI is widely available and accessible, and the detection of AI-generated content is challenging and almost impossible (p. 3).

Consequently, to mitigate the impact of generative AI on academic dishonesty, several strategies have been proposed in the educational domain (Rajabi et al., 2023). First, there is a need to develop different strategies to mitigate the dishonest use of AI. One of them could be to contemplate the possibility of modifying the paradigm or the current requirements of the final degree project (Perkins, 2023; Rajabi et al., 2023; Jereb & Urh, 2024), so that it does not consist of a research paper (a first approach to writing an academic article), but rather another type of work that involves more value in the presentation by the students, oral discussion, product design, or any other activity related to creativity (Naidu & Sevnarayan, 2023; Smolansky et al. 2023; Chan, 2023). Moreover, schools and universities are turning to AI detection tools. Programs like GPTZero, Copyleaks, Crossplag, Writer.com, Turnitin, and OpenAI's AI Text Classifier help flag work that may not be original (Elkhatat et al., 2023; Weber-Wulff et al., 2023). These tools support fair practices by helping confirm that students are submitting their own work. Some, like GPTZero, are designed for education and promote real learning and honest expression (Chaka, 2024; Weber-Wulff et al., 2023).

But these systems aren't perfect. They can miss things or raise false alarms. AI text can be changed or translated to avoid detection. That's why it's important to use these tools with care and not as the only proof of wrongdoing (Weber-Wulff et al., 2023; Elkhatat et al., 2023). Using them responsibly means being clear about policies, explaining results properly, and talking with students about how to use AI ethically (Chaka, 2024). Including these tools in academic conversations helps people understand both their power and their limits, and it keeps the focus on honesty and real learning (Chaka, 2024; Elkhatat et al., 2023; Weber-Wulff et al., 2023).

The misuse of generative AI not only raises concerns about the authenticity of these dissertations but may also exacerbate existing issues in academic writing and literacy, while "it risks eroding essential human elements-creativity, critical thinking, and empathy-and could displace meaningful human interactions with algorithmic solutions" (Bozkurt et al, 2024, p. 488). While AI tools can enhance efficiency in academic work, they also pose notable limitations in the development of critical thinking and research synthesis. Studies have shown that overreliance on AI-generated content can lead to passive learning, superficial understanding, and diminished engagement in reflective reasoning. AI models, despite their fluency, cannot truly evaluate academic rigor or context with human-level nuance, which risks reinforcing surface-level interpretations or unverified information. To preserve essential academic competencies such as analysis, evaluation, and synthesis, it is crucial to foster pedagogical strategies that position students as active, critical users of AI—encouraging them to question, contrast, and refine the outputs rather than accepting them uncritically (Melisa et al., 2025; Ríos et al., 2025; Darwin et al., 2024). Indeed, there is a significant risk that students may become overly reliant on responses generated by ChatGPT, both in terms of reproducing biases and in generating superficial learning (Chan, 2023; Rajabi et al. 2023; Pattier & Redondo-Duarte, 2025). Likewise, just as generative AI is advancing, so is AI as a tool for plagiarism detection, although it is not yet fully developed in all languages.

On the other side, there are also concerns related to privacy violations and data breaches, which pose serious threats to the security of students' personal information. These include unauthorized disclosure of personal data, secondary exploitation of private information, and even fraud resulting from data trafficking (Martínez-Requejo et al., 2025). In this context, it is vital for students to understand the significance of preserving their privacy by not sharing personal information and strictly avoiding the disclosure of sensitive data, third-party details, or materials protected by intellectual property rights.

Universities are increasingly incorporating these challenges and ethical considerations into their institutional policies, and most have developed specific guidelines to effectively address them. Nevertheless, there is a clear need for the creation of a common regulatory framework or, at least, a set of shared recommendations to promote greater consistency in the use of AI at universities. This is precisely one of the main recommendations that emerges from the study conducted by Ruiz-Lázaro et al. (2024) in Spain. The authors carried out a comparative study using a methodological approach based on the rational analysis of documentary evidence gathered from 31 AI use guidelines developed by various Spanish universities. One of the study's key findings was that the lack of homogeneity in the proposed approaches and strategies implies that the guidelines do not respond to standardized guidelines on the use of AI in higher education at regional or national level.

In this sense, "educational institutions should implement clear policies on the appropriate use of AI-based tools, setting firm limits on when and how these technologies can be used to support - but not replace - students' academic work" (Martínez-Requejo et al., 2025, p. 239). Effective policies must go beyond ensuring the safe and inclusive integration of AI; they should also encourage students to actively participate in ethical discussions, fostering their critical thinking abilities and equipping them to face the demands of a technology-driven world.

4. AI TOOLS FOR ACADEMIC RESEARCH AND WRITING

As has been explained, generative AI tools are transforming multiple stages of the research process, from conducting literature reviews to drafting, editing, and proofreading. These technologies include automated search engines, citation management software, natural language processing tools, and data analysis systems. These tools help reduce the time spent searching for articles and data, as well as managing citations. AI approaches can significantly decrease the amount of time spent on these tasks, streamlining the research process.

AI tools have the potential to greatly improve academic research; however, their implementation demands thoughtful attention to both methodological and ethical concerns Oyelude, 2024; Qaffas; 2024). The use of AI also prompts important questions regarding authorship, accountability, authenticity and credibility of academic content, and the role of researchers. Dergaa et al. (2024) highlight the importance of maintaining ethical standards and human critical thinking in research and recommend caution and transparency in the use of these tools. In this sense, university libraries play a key role in guiding students and offering recommendations on the proper use of generative AI tools in academic work and scientific publications.

Below are some of the most commonly used tools for academic research, academic writing and editing, and citation, reference, and plagiarism detection. It is important to note that these AI-based tools and their functionalities are rapidly evolving.

4.1. AI Tools for Academic Research

AI Tools for academic research can be classified in two categories:

- **AI literature search tools**: These tools leverage AI algorithms to help researchers efficiently identify relevant academic literature and uncover connections between studies. They can be useful in final degree projects to identify literature by analyzing contextual similarities, citations, and thematic links, as well as performing keyword searches.
- **AI tools for analyzing research papers**: These tools are designed to assist researchers in efficiently processing and understanding large volumes of academic content. Students can use them to summarize and extract key insights of each paper (methods, sample size, population, key takeaways, etc.). These tools can support students in developing the theoretical framework of their work and conducting systematic reviews by summarizing articles, integrating information, and retrieving literature contextually. They also analyze citations, visualize research connections, extract insights from texts, and assess content tone while detecting bias to uphold research integrity. This last aspect

is especially important to ensure the ethical use of AI tools and maintain the rigor of research.

To illustrate the practical applications of these tools, Table 1 presents different AI-powered tools that students can use in the development of their final degree project.

Table 1. Examples of AI tools for academic research.

AI tool category	AI Tool	Pedagogical value
	Elicit	It summarizes academic papers, extracting data, and synthesizing your findings.
Literature search	Consensus	It delivers evidence-based responses derived from scientific research, leveraging AI to extract key insights from peer-reviewed sources and present them in a clear and concise manner.
	Semantic Scholar	It enables the discovery and exploration of scientific publication data, including authors, papers, and citations. Additionally, it suggests papers similar to a given work and provides downloadable links to relevant datasets.
	Connected Papers	It helps visualize connections between research papers. The generated maps visually illustrate how the documents are interconnected, providing a better understanding of the context and relationships between scientific works.
	Lateral AI	It helps identify themes, extract key insights, and organize findings with features such as AI-powered concept recommendations, super search, and smart PDF reading. Users can analyze and export data, collaborate, and work across various document formats.
Analyzing research papers	Humata	It allows summarizing research papers, comparing them, and generating answers based on the content of the uploaded documents. Each answer Humata generates will cite relevant sections from the uploaded documents.
	Chat PDF	It allows users to interact with PDFs by asking questions, summarizing documents, and extracting key insights instantly. The tool supports multiple languages, provides citation references, and offers features like multi-file chats and document translation.
	Explain paper	It helps researchers and students understand complex research papers. It allows users to upload documents, highlight confusing sections, and receive simplified explanations of the content.

Note. Own elaboration.

4.2. AI Tools for Academic Writing and Editing

Academic Writing and Editing tools leverage AI to enhance the quality and coherence of scientific writing, while also assisting in the structuring and formatting of research papers. These tools enhance the clarity and coherence of academic writing by providing grammar corrections, linguistic suggestions, and guidance on structure and style, ensuring texts align with established writing standards. They can also help identify areas for enhancement, offering specific feedback. Additionally, such applications assist in organizing lengthy, complex articles, improving readability and structure. This is particularly beneficial for non-native English students and for maintaining high-quality manuscripts (Pinzolits, 2023).

AI tools employ advanced algorithms to refine academic writing and linguistic expression (Pinzolits, 2023; Jereb & Urh, 2024). They also analyze writing styles and provide personalized feedback, helping to improve overall writing quality (Storey, 2023). To illustrate the practical applications of these tools, Table 2 presents different AI-powered tools for academic writing and editing that students can use in the development of their final degree project.

Table 2. Examples of AI tools for academic writing and editing.

AI Tool	Pedagogical value
ChatGPT	Assists in editing academic writing by providing suggestions for structure, tone, and content.
QuillBot	Useful to paraphrase sections of writing, improve sentence structure, and enhance academic tone.
Writefull	It provides AI-powered language feedback for academic writing. It offers features such as grammar and style suggestions, rephrasing for clarity, and aids in organizing thoughts.
Grammarly	Improving grammar, spelling, punctuation, and clarity in academic writing.

Note. Own elaboration.

4.3. AI Tools for Citation, Reference, and Plagiarism detection

According to the systematic review conducted by Rustan (2024), the combination of training in academic writing and plagiarism can change university student behavior, reducing plagiarism and improving their confidence in academic writing. Specifically, tutorial methods and workshops have been the most widely used strategies to educate students about plagiarism, followed by content focused on improving writing skills.

Students should be reminded that they are responsible for their work, regardless of whether it was created with the assistance of ChatGPT or similar tools. Therefore, it is the responsibility of each author to carefully review their text, findings, data, code, and references to guarantee their accuracy (Storey, 2023). Below, Table 3 shows some examples of AI tools for citation, referencing, and plagiarism detection that students and tutors can use in the development and supervision of the final degree project.

Table 3. Examples of AI tools for citation, reference, and detect plagiarism.

AI tool category	AI Tool	Pedagogical value
Citation and Reference Management	Mendeley	A reference manager with AI-powered suggestions and research collaboration.
	Zotero	It organizes references and generates citations automatically.
	EndNote	Manages citations and bibliographies in various formats.
Detection of Plagiarism	Turnitin	Plagiarism detection tool widely used in academic institutions.
	Copyscape	Checks for duplicate content and plagiarism detection.

Note. Own elaboration.

5. GUIDING STUDENTS ON HOW TO EFFECTIVELY USE AI-POWERED TOOLS IN THEIR FINAL DEGREE PROJECT

It is essential that tutors guide students on how to effectively use AI-powered tools and best practices for maximizing their benefits. Some key aspects that tutors can consider when training students on the use of generative AI tools for their academic work are the following:

- Question with the students the limitations in the accuracy of AI-generated information, specifically the phenomenon of "hallucinations", where AI may produce false or inaccurate information.
- Educate students about the limitations and biases present in AI regarding race, gender, and other categories embedded in algorithms.
- Conduct a critical exercise with students on the types of texts being produced, assessing their truthfulness, appropriateness in writing, and potential implications for learning, among other factors.
- Guide students to understand proper attribution when using AI-generated materials.
- Emphasize academic integrity. It is important for students to understand that copying or plagiarizing responses generated by AI is neither ethical nor beneficial for their learning.

The following are general guidelines that tutors can follow to help students in the preparation of their final degree projects:

- Provide clear and precise guidelines on the appropriate use of various AI tools through the development process.

- Encourage research and information validation: motivate students to seek and assess scientific evidence from reliable sources, such as peer-reviewed articles, to support the content generated by AI.
- Ask students to critically reflect on the concepts they are introducing in the theoretical framework of the work. A purely descriptive framework should not be accepted; there must be critical reflection from the student.
- Provide your students with practical examples of prompts to guide them through a correct use of AI (some examples are shown in table 4).
- Always request citations for the sources used (verify that the cited sources exist).
- Closely monitor the use of generative AI by students and provide individualized feedback.
- Review and evaluate the generated texts to identify possible errors or inaccuracies.
- Provide guidance to improve the content quality and accuracy in the use of terms.

Table 4 below shows some possible uses of generative AI to support the student's development of cognitive skills such as generation, organization, contrast and synthesis of ideas in the elaboration of the final degree project.

Table 4. Examples of uses of generative AI for the support of cognitive skills involved in the development of the final degree project.

Cognitive skills	**Uses of generative AI tools**	**Student's role**
Ideas generation	- AI can be used as a starting point to generate initial ideas about the work or explore different perspectives.	- Dialogue with AI allows for generating different ideas.
Organization and synthesis of ideas	- AI tools like Humata can be used to quickly extract information from an article or text of low complexity. - Generate different ideas or approaches that allow the student to progress more autonomously. - AI tools such as ChatGPT and Humata offer feedback on the organization of ideas.	- Specific questions about the text can be asked, such as requesting a summary, conclusions, etc. - Students must enrich the content by using their own knowledge, experience, and critical judgment.
Contrasting ideas	Using AI to explore and test ideas or proposals can be helpful.	- Challenging questions can be posed to encourage critical reflection. - Dialogue with AI (asking questions and counter-arguing) allows for generating different perspectives.

Note. Own elaboration.

Table 5 below presents a selection of prompts that students can use to support the preparation of their final degree project in the field of Educational Sciences. These prompts are designed like a scaffold to help students in developing critical analysis, argumentation, comparison, and information verification.

Table 5. Examples of prompts that students can use as support for preparing their final degree project.

Learning objective	Prompt	Student task
Analyze the application of constructivist learning theory in primary education.	"Provide a structured list of key points for an essay on the application of constructivist learning theory in primary education. Include main ideas, relevant concepts, and suggested connectors to ensure coherence in writing."	To use the suggested key points to structure their essay, expand on each idea with explanations and examples, and support arguments with academic references.
Compare cooperative learning and traditional teaching methods in academic performance.	"Generate a bullet-point outline comparing cooperative learning and traditional teaching methods. Include advantages, disadvantages, and suggested transitions to connect ideas smoothly."	To use the outline to develop a well-structured comparative analysis, providing evidence from research studies and incorporating proper citations.
Design inclusive strategies for students with special educational needs.	"List key strategies and considerations for designing an inclusive learning plan for a student with special educational needs. Include specific adaptations, resources, and assessment methods, along with logical connectors for coherence."	To refine the suggested strategies to fit a specific case, elaborate on each adaptation, and justify their choices with references to inclusive education principles.
Examine the role of formative and summative assessment in learning.	"Provide a structured list of main points for an essay analyzing formative and summative assessment. Include definitions, purposes, examples, and suggested transitions to ensure logical flow."	To expand on the listed points, illustrate their discussion with concrete examples, and integrate relevant literature to support their analysis.
Explore the effectiveness of gamification in digital education.	"Generate a bullet-point summary of key aspects of gamification in education, including its definition, benefits, challenges, and real-world examples. Provide suggested connectors for smooth essay writing."	To develop a coherent argument using the outlined points, supplementing their discussion with case studies and properly citing sources.
Analyze how intrinsic and extrinsic motivation affect learning.	"Provide a structured outline highlighting the differences between intrinsic and extrinsic motivation, key theories, and practical applications in education. Include logical connectors to ensure coherence."	To use the structured outline to develop a detailed discussion, apply motivation theories to real classroom scenarios, and support their arguments with academic references.

Note. OpenAI (2025).

An essential part of overseeing the final degree project is reinforcing that students bear full responsibility for their work, regardless of whether they used ChatGPT or similar tools. Each author must meticulously verify their text, findings, data, code, and references to uphold the accuracy and integrity of their research (Dergaa et al.,

2023). Below, in Table 6, acceptable practices and violations regarding plagiarism are summarized.

Table 6. Acceptable Practices and Violations Regarding Plagiarism.

What is Acceptable	What is not Acceptable
Paraphrasing and summarizing content in your own words, with proper citation.	Copying and pasting text from sources without citation.
Using direct quotes with proper citation and quotation marks.	Using others' work, ideas, or data without acknowledging the source.
Using ideas or concepts from sources with your own analysis or interpretation.	Rewriting someone else's work in your own words without proper credit.
Properly citing data, figures, and research findings.	Presenting another person's work or findings as your own.
Referencing sources in a bibliography.	Self-plagiarism (reusing your previous work without permission or citation).

Note. Own elaboration.

Finally, some key aspects that students should avoid when using generative AI in academic work are included:

- Relying blindly on the information provided by generative AI tools.
- Assuming that the answers given by AI are correct and complete without sufficiently analyzing or verifying the information provided.
- Reproducing biases or stereotypes through information provided by generative AI. Critical judgment, validation, and information comparison are important for this.
- Automatically reviewing and editing. While generative AI can offer suggestions for improvement, it is essential to manually review and edit the texts.
- Relying solely on the tool to correct grammatical errors or improve the structure of the text.
- Copying content generated by AI without citation.

CONCLUSION

AI is here to stay, interacting with humanity in many different ways. In the field of education, the discussion on the role it plays is in an embryonic state, and, to date, we are only able to elucidate a small part of both its uses and its dangers. This chapter deals with a very specific topic, that of the preparation of the final degree project. This topic has been very much in the academic discourse for different reasons, especially those related to plagiarism and other ethical issues. The advent of AI has only fueled this discussion, raising new beneficial possibilities for students and faculty, while at the same time opening the debate on its ethical use. As mentioned above, AI is evolving at an exponential rate, giving rise to a wide range of tools to address multiple problems. Among them, there are many related to the development of a final degree project, and, without any doubt, AI will become an assistant to human beings, enhancing their capabilities.

In this chapter, tools related to two major fields have been presented: writing and academic efficiency. These are related to most of the problems that students deal with when carrying out their final projects. However, based on the discussion of ethical issues, the role of the tutor becomes even more indispensable. The responsible use of AI requires someone to guide students in its use, as the line between assistance and plagiarism—or other ethical violations—is very thin. Thus, the figure of the tutor is the essential element in this process, since, in the future, he or she will have to guide the student not only in the research process but also in the use of the different tools available, including AI. There is a clear need for in-depth discussions on the advantages, risks, and constraints of these tools, emphasizing ethical considerations and reinforcing human intelligence and critical thinking in research (Dergaa et al., 2023). Thus, it is necessary to highlight the need for a robust ethical and regulatory framework to mitigate risks and ensure equitable implementation in higher education institutions.

This training on the use of AI must be integrated into the digital transformation of education that many countries are addressing. In this regard, TPACK-based teacher training is essential for addressing both current and future educational challenges. Cabero & Barroso (2016) conducted a study involving 1,368 participants engaged in training activities at universities across five countries. Their findings underscore the importance of not focusing solely on technological aspects but rather placing greater emphasis on pedagogical and content knowledge to ensure the meaningful integration of digital tools in educational settings.

This transformation requires not only training for students and teachers but also ensuring access to quality AI tools that avoid, above all, biased access to information. However, all the issues addressed in this chapter offer a current vision, which will most likely become obsolete in a short period of time. Therefore, the digital transformation of the education system must find a way to be able to become a sufficiently malleable and rapid process that allows it to keep up with the evolution of technology.

REFERENCES

Adiguzel, T., Kaya, M., & Cansu, F. (2023). Revolutionizing education with AI: Exploring the transformative potential of ChatGPT. *Contemporary Educational Technology, 15*(3), e429. DOI: 10.30935/cedtech/13152

Ahmad, S. F., Rahmat, M. K., Mubarik, M. S., Alam, M. M., & Hyder, S. I. (2021). Artificial Intelligence and Its Role in Education. *Sustainability (Basel), 13*(22), 12902. DOI: 10.3390/su132212902

Ali, K., Barhom, N., Tamimi, F., & Duggal, M. (2024). ChatGPT—A double-edged sword for healthcare education? Implications for assessments of dental students. *European Journal of Dental Education, 28*(1), 206–211. DOI: 10.1111/eje.12937 PMID: 37550893

Amisha, P. M., Pathania, M., & Rathaur, V. K. (2019). Overview of artificial intelligence in medicine. *Journal of Family Medicine and Primary Care, 8*(7), 2328–2331. DOI: 10.4103/jfmpc.jfmpc_440_19 PMID: 31463251

Ariyaratne, S., Iyengar, K. P., Nischal, N., Chitti Babu, N., & Botchu, R. (2023). A comparison of ChatGPT-generated articles with human-written articles. *Skeletal Radiology, 52*(9), 1755–1758. DOI: 10.1007/s00256-023-04340-5 PMID: 37059827

Arora, M. (2021). Artificial Intelligence: New Pathways and Challenges in Higher Education. In S. Verma and P. Tomar (Eds.), *Impact of AI Technologies on Teaching, Learning, and Research in Higher Education*, (pp. 30-48). Igi Global. DOI: DOI: 10.4018/978-1-7998-4763-2.ch002

Barrett, M., Branson, L., Carter, S., DeLeon, F., Ellis, J., Gundlach, C., & Lee, D. (2019). Using Artificial Intelligence to Enhance Educational Opportunities and Student Services in Higher Education. *Inquiry: The Journal of the Virginia Community Colleges*, 22 (1). Retrieved from https://commons.vccs.edu/inquiry/vol22/iss1/11

Bozkurt, A., Xiao, J., Farrow, R., Bai, J. Y. H., Nerantzi, C., Moore, S., Dron, J., Stracke, C. M., Singh, L., Crompton, H., Koutropoulos, A., Terentev, E., Pazurek, A., Nichols, M., Sidorkin, A. M., Costello, E., Watson, S., Mulligan, D., Honeychurch, S., & Asino, T. I. (2024). The manifesto for teaching and learning in a time of generative AI: A critical collective stance to better navigate the future. *Open Praxis, 16*(4), 487–513. DOI: 10.55982/openpraxis.16.4.777

Brusilovsky, P. (2024). AI in education, learner control, and human-AI collaboration. *International Journal of Artificial Intelligence in Education, 34*(1), 122–135. DOI: 10.1007/s40593-023-00356-z

Cabero, J., & Barroso, J. (2016). ICT teacher training: a view of the TPACK model / Formación del profesorado en TIC: una visión del modelo TPACK. *C&E, Cultura y Educación, 28*(3), 633–663. DOI: 10.1080/11356405.2016.1203526

Castillo-Martínez, I. M., Flores-Bueno, D., Gómez-Puente, S. M., & Vite-León, V. O. (2024). AI in higher education: A systematic literature review. In *Frontiers in Education* (Vol. 9, p. 1391485). Frontiers Media SA. https://doi.org/DOI: 10.3389/feduc.2024.1391485

Cebrián-Robles, V., Ruíz-Rey, F. J., Raposo-Rivas, M., & Cebrián-de-la-Serna, M. (2023). Impact of digital contexts in the training of university education students. *Education Sciences, 13*(9), 923. DOI: 10.3390/educsci13090923

Chaka, C. (2024). Reviewing the performance of AI detection tools in differentiating between AI-generated and human-written texts: A literature and integrative hybrid review. *Journal of Applied Learning and Teaching*, *7*(1), 115–126. DOI: 10.37074/jalt.2024.7.1.14

Chan, C. K. Y. (2023). A comprehensive AI policy education framework for university teaching and learning. *International Journal of Educational Technology in Higher Education*, *20*(1), 38. Advance online publication. DOI: 10.1186/s41239-023-00408-3

Chen, L., Chen, P., & Lin, Z. (2020). Artificial intelligence in education: A review. *IEEE Access : Practical Innovations, Open Solutions*, *8*, 75264–75278. DOI: 10.1109/ACCESS.2020.2988510

Cheung, B. H. H., Lau, G. K. K., Wong, G. T. C., Lee, E. Y. P., Kulkarni, D., Seow, C. S., Wong, R., & Co, M. T.-H. (2023). ChatGPT versus human in generating medical graduate exam multiple choice questions: A multinational prospective study (Hong Kong SAR, Singapore, Ireland, and the United Kingdom). *PLoS One*, *18*(8), e0290691. DOI: 10.1371/journal.pone.0290691 PMID: 37643186

Chiu, T. K. F., Xia, Q., Zhou, X.-Y., Chai, C. S., & Cheng, M.-T. (2023). Systematic literature review on opportunities, challenges, and future research recommendations of artificial intelligence in education. *Computers & Education: Artificial Intelligence*, *4*, 100118. DOI: 10.1016/j.caeai.2022.100118

Crawford, J., Cowling, M., & Allen, K.-A. (2023). Leadership is needed for ethical ChatGPT: Character, assessment, and learning using artificial intelligence (AI). (2023). *Journal of University Teaching & Learning Practice*, *20*(3). Advance online publication. DOI: 10.53761/1.20.3.02

Crompton, H., & Burke, D. (2023). Artificial intelligence in higher education: The state of the field. *International Journal of Educational Technology in Higher Education, 20*(22), 22. Advance online publication. DOI: 10.1186/s41239-023-00392-8

Cross, J., Robinson, R., Devaraju, S., Vaughans, A., Hood, R., Kayalackakom, T., & Robinson, R. E. (2023). Transforming medical education: Assessing the integration of ChatGPT into faculty workflows at a Caribbean medical school. *Cureus, 15*(7), e41399. DOI: 10.7759/cureus.41399 PMID: 37426402

Darwin, D. R., Mukminatien, N., Suryati, N., & Laksmi, E. D. (2024). Critical thinking in the AI era: An exploration of EFL students' perceptions, benefits, and limitations. *Cogent Education, 11*(1), 2290342. DOI: 10.1080/2331186X.2023.2290342

Delcker, J., Heil, J., Ifenthaler, D., Seufert, S., & Spirgi, L. (2024). First-year students' AI competence as a predictor for intended and de facto use of AI tools for supporting learning processes in higher education. *International Journal of Educational Technology in Higher Education, 21*(18), 18. Advance online publication. DOI: 10.1186/s41239-024-00452-7

Dergaa, I., Chamari, K., Żmijewski, P., & Saad, B. (2024). From human writing to artificial intelligence generated text: Examining the prospects and potential threats of ChatGPT in academic writing. *Biology of Sport, 40*(2), 615–622. DOI: 10.5114/biolsport.2023.125623 PMID: 37077800

Duymaz, Y. K., & Tekin, A. M. (2024). Harnessing artificial intelligence in academic writing: Potential, ethics, and responsible use. *European Journal of Therapeutics, 30*(1), 87–88. DOI: 10.58600/eurjther1755

Elkhatat, A. M., Elsaid, K., & Almeer, S. (2023). Evaluating the efficacy of AI content detection tools in differentiating between human and AI-generated text. *International Journal for Educational Integrity, 19*(17), 17. Advance online publication. DOI: 10.1007/s40979-023-00140-5

European Commision. (2020). Digital Education Action Plan (2021-2027). https://ec.europa.eu/education/education-in-the-eu/digital-education-action-plan_en

Farooq, E., Zaidi, E., & Shah, M. M. A. (2024). The future classroom: Analyzing the integration and impact of digital technologies in science education. *Jurnal Penelitian Dan Pengkajian Ilmu Pendidikan: E-Saintika, 8*(2), 280–318. DOI: 10.36312/esaintika.v8i2.1957

Gade, K., Geyik, S., Kenthapadi, K., Mithal, V., & Taly, A. (2020, April). Explainable AI in industry: Practical challenges and lessons learned. En A. E. F. Seghrouchni, G. Sukthankar, & T. Y. Liu (Eds.), *Companion Proceedings of the Web Conference 2020* (pp. 303–304). ACM. DOI: 10.1145/3366424.3383110

Ginting, P., Batubara, H. M., & Hasnah, Y. (2023). Artificial intelligence powered writing tools as adaptable aids for academic writing: Insight from EFL college learners in writing final project. *International Journal of Multidisciplinary Research and Analysis*, *6*(10), 4640–4650. DOI: 10.47191/ijmra/v6-i10-15

Harding, J., D'Alessandro, W., Laskowski, N. G., & Long, R. (2023). AI language models cannot replace human research participants. *AI & Society*, *39*(5), 2603–2605. DOI: 10.1007/s00146-023-01725-x

Hashim, S., Omar, M. K., Jalil, H. A., & Sharef, N. M. (2023). Trends on technologies and artificial intelligence in education for personalized learning: Systematic literature review. *International Journal of Academic Research in Progressive Education and Development*, *11*(1), 884–903. DOI: 10.6007/IJARPED/v11-i1/12230

Herring, C., Koehler, M. J., & Mishra, P. (Eds.). (2016). *Handbook of Technological Pedagogical Content knowledge (TPACK) for educators*. Routledge. DOI: 10.4324/9781315771328

Huallpa, J. J., Flores Arocutipa, J. P., Panduro, W. D., Huete, L. C., Flores Limo, F. A., Herrera, E. E., Alba Callacna, R. A., Ariza Flores, V. A., Medina Romero, M. Á., Quispe, I. M., & Hernández Hernández, F. A. (2023). Exploring the ethical considerations of using ChatGPT in university education. *Periodicals of Engineering and Natural Sciences*, *11*(4), 105–115. DOI: 10.21533/pen.v11.i4.200

Jereb, E., & Urh, M. (2024). The Use of Artificial Intelligence among Students in Higher Education. *Organizacija*, *57*(4), 333–345. DOI: 10.2478/orga-2024-0024

Jiménez, S., Berenguer, C., Canato, M., Fernández, N., Iñesta, E., Moya, M. M., & Bermúdez, A. (2016). ¿Es posible la investigación en el trabajo de fin de grado? In M. T. Tortosa Ybáñez, S. Grau Company, J. D., & Álvarez Teruel (Eds.), *XIV Jornadas de Redes de Investigación en Docencia Universitaria: Investigación, innovación y enseñanza universitaria: enfoques pluridisciplinares* (pp. 2626-2636). Teruel (Spain). https://dialnet.unirioja.es/servlet/articulo?codigo=5917705

Krajka, J., & Olszak, I. (2024). Artificial intelligence tools in academic writing instruction: Exploring the potential of on-demand AI assistance in the writing process. *Roczniki Humanistyczne*, *72*(6), 123–140. DOI: 10.18290/rh247206.8

Lin, Z. (2023). Supercharging academic writing with generative AI: Framework, techniques, and caveats. *Nature Biomedical Engineering*. Advance online publication. DOI: 10.1038/s41551-024-01185-8 PMID: 38499642

Llorente, A. M., Ladera, V., Contreras, P., & Conde, L. (2021). Efficacy of a computerized intervention based on artificial intelligence for improving reading comprehension in students with dyslexia. *Frontiers in Psychology*, *12*, 641005. DOI: 10.3389/fpsyg.2021.641005

Lund, B. D., Wang, T., Mannuru, N. R., Nie, B., Shimray, S. R., & Wang, Z. (2023). ChatGPT and a new academic reality: Artificial intelligence-written research papers and the ethics of the large language models in scholarly publishing. *Journal of the Association for Information Science and Technology*, *74*(5), 570–581. DOI: 10.1002/asi.24750

Martínez-Requejo, S., Redondo-Duarte, S., Jiménez-García, E., & Ruiz-Lázaro, J. (2025). Technoethics and the Use of Artificial Intelligence in Educational Contexts: Reflections on Integrity, Transparency, and Equity. In Garcia, M., Rosak-Szyrocka, J., & Bozkurt, A. (Eds.), *Pitfalls of AI Integration in Education: Skill Obsolescence, Misuse, and Bias* (pp. 227–250). IGI Global Scientific Publishing., DOI: 10.4018/979-8-3373-0122-8.ch010

Melisa, R., Ashadi, A., Triastuti, A., Hidayati, S., Salido, A., Ero, P. E. L., Marlini, C., Zefrin, Z., & Al Fuad, Z. (2025). Critical thinking in the age of AI: A systematic review of AI's effects on higher education. *Educational Process: International Journal*, *14*(1), e2025031. DOI: 10.22521/edupij.2025.14.31

Monib, W. K., Qazi, A., & Mahmud, M. M. (2025). Exploring learners' experiences and perceptions of ChatGPT as a learning tool in higher education. *Education and Information Technologies*, *30*(1), 917–939. DOI: 10.1007/s10639-024-13065-4

Moorhouse, B. L., Yeo, M. A., & Wan, Y. (2023). Generative AI tools and assessment: Guidelines of the world's top-ranking universities. *Computers and Education Open*, *5*, 100151. DOI: 10.1016/j.caeo.2023.100151

Morjaria, L., Burns, L., Bracken, K., Ngo, Q. N., Lee, M., Levinson, A. J., Smith, J., Thompson, P., & Sibbald, M. (2023). Examining the threat of ChatGPT to the validity of short-answer assessments in an undergraduate medical program. *Journal of Medical Education and Curricular Development*, *10*, 23821205231204178. Advance online publication. DOI: 10.1177/23821205231204178 PMID: 37780034

Naidu, K., & Sevnarayan, K. (2023). ChatGPT: An ever-increasing encroachment of artificial intelligence in online assessment in distance education. *Online Journal of Communication and Media Technologies*, *13*(3), e202336. DOI: 10.30935/ojcmt/13291

Nasution, N. E. A. (2023). Using artificial intelligence to create biology multiple choice questions for higher education. *Agricultural and Environmental Education*, *2*(1), em002. DOI: 10.29333/agrenvedu/13071

Ouh, E. L., Gan, B. K. S., Shim, J. K., & Wlodkowski, S. (2023). ChatGPT, can you generate solutions for my coding exercises? An evaluation on its effectiveness in an undergraduate Java programming course. *Annual Conference on Innovation and Technology in Computer Science Education (ITiCSE)*. https://doi.org/DOI: 10.1145/3587102.3588794

Oyelude, A. A. (2024). Artificial intelligence (AI) tools for academic research. *Library Hi Tech News*, *41*(8), 18–20. DOI: 10.1108/LHTN-08-2024-0131

Ozfidan, B., El-Dakhs, D. A. S., & Alsalim, L. A. (2024). The Use of AI Tools in English Academic Writing by Saudi Undergraduates. *Contemporary Educational Technology*, *16*(4), ep527. DOI: 10.30935/cedtech/15013

Pattier, D., & Redondo-Duarte, S. (2025). La vida online, la inteligencia artificial y su lectura pedagógica. *Márgenes: Revista de Educación de la Universidad de Málaga*, *6*(1), 28–45. DOI: 10.24310/mar.6.1.2025.20784

Perkins, M. (2023). Academic integrity considerations of AI large language models in the post-pandemic era: ChatGPT and beyond. *Journal of University Teaching & Learning Practice*, *20*(2), 7. Advance online publication. DOI: 10.53761/1.20.02.07

Pinzolits, R. (2023). AI in academia: An overview of selected tools and their areas of application. *MAP Education and Humanities*, *4*, 37–50. DOI: 10.53880/2744-2373.2023.4.37

Qaffas, A. A. (2024). Harnessing Artificial Intelligence for Enhanced Efficiency in Academic Writing and Research. *Fusion: Practice & Applications*, *16*(2), 126–146. DOI: 10.54216/FPA.160209

Rajabi, P., Taghipour, P., Cukierman, D., & Doleck, T. (2023). Exploring ChatGPT's impact on post-secondary education: A qualitative study. *ACM International Conference Proceeding Series*. https://doi.org/DOI: 10.1145/3593342.3593360

Real Decreto 822/2021, de 28 de septiembre, por el que se establece la organización de las enseñanzas universitarias y del procedimiento de aseguramiento de su calidad. Boletín Oficial del Estado, 233, 29 de septiembre de 2021. https://www.boe.es/eli/es/rd/2021/09/28/822/con

Rekalde, I. (2011). ¿Cómo afrontar el trabajo fin de grado? Un problema o una oportunidad para culminar con el desarrollo de las competencias. *Revista Complutense de Educación*, *22*(2), 179–193. DOI: 10.5209/rev_RCED.2011.v22.n2.38488

Ríos, T. C.-D. L., Solis-Trujillo, B., Pérez-Ruiz, J., & Aquije-Mansilla, M. (2025). Systematic review of critical thinking using artificial intelligence. *Edelweiss Applied Science and Technology*, *9*(3), 990–1001. DOI: 10.55214/25768484.v9i3.5405

Rustan, E. (2024). University Students' Plagiarism Behaviours in Writing Instruction: A Systematic Review. *Journal of Language Teaching and Research*, *15*(4), 1083–1094. DOI: 10.17507/jltr.1504.06

Sabzalieva, E., & Valentini, A. (2023). *ChatGPT e inteligencia artificial en la educación superior: Guía de inicio rápido.* UNESCO. https://bit.ly/3oeYm2f

Salvagno, M., Taccone, F. S., & Gerli, A. G. (2023). Can artificial intelligence help for scientific writing? *Critical Care*, *27*(1), 75. DOI: 10.1186/s13054-023-04380-2 PMID: 36841840

Singh, T., & Mishra, J. (2023). Learning with Artificial Intelligence Systems: Application, Challenges, and Opportunities. In S. Verma and P. Tomar (Eds.), *Impact of AI Technologies on Teaching, Learning, and Research in Higher Education*, (pp. 236-253). IGI Global. https://doi.org/DOI: 10.4018/978-1-7998-4763-2.ch015

Smolansky, A., Cram, A., Raduescu, C., Zeivots, S., Huber, E., & Kizilcec, R. F. (2023). Educator and student perspectives on the impact of generative AI on assessments in higher education. *Proceedings of the 10th ACM Conference on Learning @ Scale (L@S 2023)*. https://doi.org/DOI: 10.1145/3573051.3596191

Stöhr, C., Ou, A. W., & Malmström, H. (2024). Perceptions and usage of AI chatbots among students in higher education across genders, academic levels and fields of study. *Computers and Education: Artificial Intelligence*, *7*, 100259. DOI: 10.1016/j.caeai.2024.100259

Storey, V. A. (2023). AI technology and academic writing: Knowing and mastering the "craft skills". [IJAET]. *International Journal of Adult Education and Technology*, *14*(1), 1–15. DOI: 10.4018/IJAET.325795

Utami, S. P. T., & Winarni, R. (2023). Utilization of Artificial Intelligence Technology in an Academic Writing Class: How do Indonesian Students Perceive? *Contemporary Educational Technology*, *15*(4), ep450. DOI: 10.30935/cedtech/13419

Vasconcelos, M. A. R., & dos Santos, R. P. (2023). Enhancing STEM learning with ChatGPT and Bing Chat as objects to think with: A case study. *Eurasia Journal of Mathematics, Science and Technology Education*, *19*(7), em2296. Advance online publication. DOI: 10.29333/ejmste/13313

Weber-Wulff, D., Anohina-Naumeca, A., Bjelobaba, S., Foltýnek, T., Guerrero-Dib, J., Popoola, O., Šigut, P., & Waddington, L. (2023). Testing of detection tools for AI-generated text. *International Journal for Educational Integrity*, *19*(26), 26. Advance online publication. DOI: 10.1007/s40979-023-00146-z

Xia, Q., Chiu, T. K. F., & Chai, C. S. (2023). The moderating effects of gender and need satisfaction on self-regulated learning through artificial intelligence (AI). *Education and Information Technologies*, *28*(7), 8691–8713. DOI: 10.1007/s10639-022-11547-x

Xia, Q., Chiu, T. K. F., Chai, C. S., & Xie, K. (2023). The mediating effects of needs satisfaction on the relationships between prior knowledge and self-regulated learning through artificial intelligence chatbot. *British Journal of Educational Technology*, *54*(4), 967–986. DOI: 10.1111/bjet.13305

Yavich, R., & Davidovitch, N. (2024). Plagiarism among Higher Education Students. *Education Sciences*, *14*(8), 908. DOI: 10.3390/educsci14080908

Zhang, Y., Wei, J., Chen, J., Wang, Y., & Zhang, Y. (2020). The application of artificial intelligence in the education of children with autism spectrum disorder: A review. *Frontiers in Psychology*, *11*, 1338. DOI: 10.3389/fpsyg.2020.01338

Zimmerman, B. J. (2002). Becoming a self-regulated learner: An overview. *Theory into Practice*, *41*(2), 64–70. DOI: 10.1207/s15430421tip4102_2

KEY TERMS

Academic Dishonesty: It refers to any form of cheating or unethical behavior in an educational setting, such as plagiarism, cheating on exams, fabrication of data, etc.

AI Tools for Academic Research and Writing: AI applications that assist researchers and students with tasks such as finding relevant literature, organizing information, generating drafts, checking grammar, enhancing the clarity and quality of academic texts, as well as managing citations, references, and detecting plagiarism.

Bias in AI: It refers to the presence of systematic biases in the results generated by algorithmic models, as a result of unbalanced training data, unbalanced training data, design decisions or errors in the algorithms. This can lead to discrimination or unequal treatment of certain groups of people.

Ethical Guidelines in AI: principles necessary to preserve standards that allow the balance between technological efficiency and human creativity, since these issues are fundamental to guarantee the responsible use of AI.

Final Degree Project: The term final degree project refers to what is commonly known in Spain as the Trabajo de Fin de Grado (TFG), as outlined in Royal Decree 822/2021 of September 28. This is an original piece of research that each student must carry out individually, under the guidance of an academic supervisor. Its purpose is to demonstrate the knowledge and skills gained throughout their undergraduate program (Real Decreto 822/2021, 2021). The TFG is a compulsory part of the curriculum, assessed by a panel, and usually requires a public defense.

Plagiarism Using AI: It refers to the act of using AI-generated content without proper attribution or presenting it as one's own original work.

Supervisor: the professional responsible for guiding and supporting the student throughout the completion of the master's thesis (capstone project), ensuring that the project meets academic objectives and that the student appropriately applies the skills and knowledge acquired.

Chapter 5
Use of Artificial Intelligence in Early Childhood Education

Emine Hande Aydos
https://orcid.org/0009-0008-5355-4898
Istanbul Kültür University, Turkey

Sevcan Yagan
https://orcid.org/0000-0002-6423-3693
Istanbul Kültür University, Turkey

ABSTRACT

Using AI into early childhood education to improve children's learning, especially language skills and adaptive behaviors, and it provides qualified teacher-child interactions in classroom environments. AI encourages development and efficacy of systems, which are excellent teaching resources. While there are many advantages to using AI in early childhood, there are also challenges and it can be a barrier to creativity, it raises ethical and practical concerns, including data privacy, bias in algorithms, and the potential reduction in human interaction, which is critical for socio-emotional development. By situating AI within established theories of child development, this argues for a balanced integration of AI technologies that complement rather than replace human educators. This chapter concludes by proposing a conceptual framework for the effective and ethical use of AI in early childhood education, advocating for collaborative efforts among educators, technologists, and policymakers to shape an inclusive digital future.

DOI: 10.4018/979-8-3373-7574-8.ch005

INTRODUCTION

Definition of UNICEF (2021) states that Artificial Intelligence (AI) characterizes machine-based systems that make predictions, recommendations or decisions affecting real or virtual environments, in line with human-defined goals. AI systems interact with us and influence our environment, directly or indirectly. Often, such systems appear to operate autonomously and can adapt their behavior by learning the context. Also, education is one of the many industries that AI, and more especially generative AI, is thought to have the potential to revolutionize. Concerns have been expressed, meanwhile, about AI's possible effects on society and education as technology becomes more widely used, especially with relation to fair treatment, access, and the duties of educators. AI education previously started in university computer science programs, which called for sophisticated programming abilities that weren't suitable for young learners decades ago (Ng et al., 2021a). Lately, the creation of more age-appropriate software has expanded the opportunities for young learners to study and investigate AI. Secondary or higher education is the primary focus of most recent research on AI literacy (Eguchi et al., 2021; Su et al., 2022). The necessity for efficient use and comprehension of these technologies has been highlighted by the incorporation of both general and generative AI into daily life. Given the growing prevalence of generative AI, its contribution to improving AI literacy is crucial, calling for the creation of educational frameworks that not only clarify AI functions but also promote critical thinking about the technologies' societal ramifications. Prioritizing AI literacy will be crucial in instructing individuals to interact with and influence the rapidly changing technological and educational landscape, as generative AI technologies become more and more integrated into our daily lives (Bozkurt, 2024).

AI IN EARLY CHILDHOOD EDUCATION

The integration of AI in early childhood education (ECE) is reshaping traditional pedagogical approaches, offering dynamic, personalized, and engaging learning experiences. This chapter explores the theoretical underpinnings and potential implementations of AI in early childhood education, emphasizing its role in enhancing educational equity, fostering individualized learning, effect on children's development, ethical considerations, and supporting educators. AI-driven tools, such as adaptive learning platforms, speech recognition systems, and emotion recognition software, can cater to diverse developmental needs, promoting inclusivity and tailoring educational content to each child's pace and style (Zawacki-Richter et al., 2019). More AI devices, such voice assistants, home robots, and networked smart toys, are becoming a part of children's life (Williams et al., 2019). Systems that can learn from their surroundings and draw conclusions and adjust accordingly are generally referred to as AI (Hinojo-Lucena et al., 2019). From smartphones to smart home appliances, from industry to energy and mining, from software development to agriculture, and from health communication, AI is currently being used in a wide range of industries (Becker et al., 2018). Effectiveness of introducing and using AI into early childhood education to improve children's learning, especially language skills and adaptive behaviors to the new situations (Shin et al., 2008), and also, it provides qualified teacher-child interactions in classroom environments (Kawata et al., 2008; Tanaka et al., 2007). AI encourages the development and efficacy of systems, which are undoubtedly excellent teaching resources. Moreover, AI has the capacity to facilitate data-driven insights, aiding teachers in assessing developmental progress and identifying learning challenges (Holmes et al., 2019).

While there are many advantages to using AI in early childhood, there are also challenges and it can be a barrier to creativity, it raises ethical and practical concerns, including data privacy, bias in algorithms, and the potential reduction in human interaction, which is critical for socio-emotional development (Bozkurt, 2023; Yılmaz et al., 2024). According to Piaget, teachers prepare the environment and guide children to learn on their own. However, the potential risks of AI and the fact that preschool children cannot read or write are among the obstacles preventing children from using artificial intelligence on their own. For this reason, Vygotsky's perspective seems more applicable in the use of artificial intelligence. According to Vygotsky, learning takes place in a social environment. AI may bring the rethinking and discussion of learning theories to the agenda. It may shift children's right to learn in a social environment to a more individual basis. On the other hand, Vygotsky's assertion that children construct their knowledge with the support of adults or peers and that learning develops in a social environment is a situation that needs to be discussed in terms of teacher guidance, AI literacy, and ultimately the child's ability to use AI independently. Teachers should provide gradual support to children in their use of AI and gradually reduce this support as it is transformed into skill through the scaffolding. Also, AI systems designed for use by children, which significantly influence their personal development—such as through personalized education or cognitive and emotional growth—are classified as "high-risk" and must adhere to specific mandatory requirements. These requirements pertain to data governance, documentation and record-keeping, transparency and information provision to users, human oversight, as well as robustness, accuracy, and security (Holmes et al., 2022). By situating AI within established theories of child development, this argues for a balanced integration of AI technologies that complement rather than replace human educators. Future research must address these challenges, ensuring that AI applications are designed to support holistic child development while aligning with ethical guidelines. This chapter concludes by proposing a conceptual framework for the effective and ethical use of AI in early childhood education, advocating for collaborative efforts among educators, technologists, and policymakers to shape an inclusive digital future.

a. Implementation Fields of AI in Early Childhood Education

AI has become an essential tool in various educational domains, including early childhood education (ECE). Various educational technology options are useful for early childhood education. Computers, smart boards, digital picture and video cameras, scanners, and a variety of other applications are all considered educational technology in the context of early childhood education (Linder, 2012; Shifflet et al., 2012). This enables parents to become involved in their children's education and learn about their educational opportunities. Its implementation offers transformative opportunities for enhancing learning experiences, supporting educators, and addressing diverse developmental needs of young children. These applications include robotic kits for young learners, chatbots for language instruction, and intelligent tutoring programs that can assist children in special education (Yang, 2022). Below are the key fields where AI is implemented in early childhood education, along with insights supported by relevant research and examples. Researching the development, use, and assessment of AI curricula for early childhood education is essential. In terms of research design, teaching strategies, assessment, and future objectives for researchers and educators, this intends to close a gap in the AI curriculum in early childhood education and enhance AI curriculum in a number of ways. Scott (2008) framework for efficiently directing the creation and application of AI curricula in early childhood education. Any teaching and learning environment, from preschool to higher education, can use this paradigm. According to McLachlan, Fleer, and Edwards (2018), the framework comprises four essential components: (1) objectives, goals, and declarations of outcome; (2) subject matter, domains, or content; (3) methods or procedure; and (4) evaluation and assessment.

The use of AI curricula in early childhood education should be examined and assessed using a micro-analysis of the learning results and engagement of the children. Well-defined AI goals, curriculum creation, the adoption of relevant technologies, and the construction of the infrastructure required for implementation in schools are all part of the formulation of educational policies (Filgueiras, 2024). A policy guide on AI for children has been created in this regard, with a focus on the important things to keep at the forefront and how AI can be applied in early childhood education (Penagos et al., 2020). For example, Chiu's (2008) statistical discourse analysis technique provides a systematic way to produce trustworthy data for comprehending how young children learn with AI technologies. Examining the traits and outcomes of child-robot interactions in various learning contexts is crucial because many AI technologies suitable for young children have been integrated into smart devices like robots. Age-appropriate learning materials and methods promote AI literacy. This section uses exploratory literature to address this knowledge gap and those basic issues in AI education and review to produce a list of important factors and further guide the creation and use of the early childhood education curriculum. The three fundamental issues about curriculum development for young children ages 3 to 8 -why, what, and how- form the framework of these important factors (Bredekamp, 2020).

Furthermore, in a variety of early childhood education contexts, embodied education provides a pedagogical strategy for fostering AI literacy. The cutting-edge teaching approach that included the main justifications for AI education in the early teaching and teacher preparation are practically impacted by childhood. This pedagogical strategy and its use in curriculum design and execution will not only increase children's exposure to AI technology but also enhance their capacity for critical and nuanced reasoning about AI, an inclusive mental tool that is essential for thriving in the modern digital environment (Yang, 2022). Educational leaders and early childhood educators who want to better understand and incorporate AI into their own STEM/STEAM curricula will be interested in the digital equity effort, promoting AI literacy for everyone, especially including young children. Through embodied learning experiences, preschoolers will be empowered and given the opportunity to gain AI literacy, preparing them for the intelligent future. As a developmental and instructional approach that is culturally relevant (Li et al., 2021). Finally, while incorporating AI education into curricula in schools may be a goal for the future, AI education in non-formal learning environments like libraries and museums can also be concentrated on. Thus, in order to enhance the experiences of young learners, the AI curriculum for early childhood education can also be used in these environments. For example, to encourage youngsters to learn about AI, Sakulkueakulsuk et al. (2018) developed a fun and interactive AI exhibit in a public science museum.

Applications of AI in early childhood education range widely, from intelligent tutoring programs and robotic learning aids to embodied learning in both formal and informal contexts. These developments seek to promote the acquisition of fundamental skills, such as AI literacy, in addition to improving educational access and participation. Personalized education, which uses AI's adaptable powers to customize learning experiences to each young child's unique requirements, interests, and developmental phases, is a particularly revolutionary area within this larger deployment. The constraints of conventional one-size-fits-all methods can be addressed by AI systems that analyze learners' interactions and progress in order to provide tailored feedback and dynamically modify educational content. This convergence of personalized learning and AI implementation highlights the need for curriculum that is both developmentally appropriate and technologically innovative, reflecting a significant shift toward value-sensitive, child-centered educational design. Therefore, to promote fair and meaningful learning for all children, the integration of AI in early education must take into account not just the technological infrastructure and curriculum frameworks but also ethical, cultural, and pedagogical considerations.

b. Personalized Education with AI in Early Years

Personalized education is a crucial part of AI for early education period. As the term suggests, personalized learning involves creating a unique instructional strategy for all learners based on their individual learning requirements. Due to class size and resource constraints, it is frequently impractical to create customized lesson plans for each child in a traditional classroom. Nevertheless, since AI can evaluate data from records of learners and use adaptive algorithms to deliver child-specific feedback, it appears to be able to lessen these difficulties (Abram, 2025). Activities and animated storytelling about subjects of personal interest can be made. Through doing that, learners apply basic computational thinking skills, such as issue decomposition and algorithm creation, and algorithms like variables, conditionals, and functions (Brennan & Resnick, 2012). Data use for enhancing AI performance or creating personalized learning tools is usually given priority by developers and institutions, sometimes at the cost of ethical accountability and transparency (Levinson et al., 2024). All these emphasize the necessity of value-sensitive design that takes into consideration the socio-cultural and developmental requirements of children (Berson et al., 2025).

Adaptive learning pathways can be beneficial, but if they are too prescriptive, they run the risk of limiting children to the material they already find digestible and omitting steps that support the development of metacognition and agency over their own learning. Rather, the use of AI ought to push children to think critically and experiment with novel concepts. If immediate feedback is not combined with deeper involvement and critical reflective thought, it might promote superficial knowledge or introduce new misconceptions, even while it is useful for clearing out misconceptions. Furthermore, feedback could place too much emphasis on objective accuracy while ignoring the complex insights offered by human educators (Bozkurt et al., 2024). They gain a grasp of these ideas based on their own experiences as a result of this process. Cognitively speaking, AI-based tutoring programs are able to examine responses from learners, pinpoint learning trends, areas of strength, and areas for development, and then tailor instructional materials to enhance learners and their comprehension and learning engagement (de Castro Rodrigues et al., 2022). These AI-powered platforms and systems have the capacity to provide customized experiences for children because of their adaptable nature (Crescenzi-Lanna, 2023). All children can benefit from AI technologies, but they can also help level the playing field, particularly for those who require the most individualized attention (Chen, 2024). Although analysis and synthesis are encouraged by AI, profound thinking is not ensured by its use alone. To guarantee meaningful participation, structured tasks and reflection practices are necessary. Also, there is a risk of over-scaffolding, which would lessen cognitive obstacles, even though AI may scaffold learning within the learner's Zone of Proximal Development. Children must be challenged beyond what AI can offer to promote true autonomy, maintaining a balance between possibilities for intellectual development and support (Bozkurt et al., 2024).

By combining algorithms and data-driven methods, AI systems can serve as the learning object. They can adjust to the learning styles of individual children and use the information to make well-informed judgments about their individualized education (de Castro Rodrigues et al., 2022). Early education that lacks personalization frequently leaves children with inadequate basic abilities, which puts them behind in their academics. It has been demonstrated that personalized learning -the concept of creating an instructional schedule specifically for each child- improves comprehension of the material covered (Abram, 2025). AI is designed to automate teaching functions, enabling learners to engage in independent study or utilize an artificial personal tutor. However, a lot of this takes a very archaic approach to teaching and, far too frequently, prioritizes automating subpar teaching methods over creativity for instance, enabling evaluation rather than coming up with creative ways to evaluate and accredit learning (Holmes et al., 2022). Through evaluation and associated individualized learning support, this AI-powered technology solution can improve the effectiveness and efficiency of both teaching and children's learning. It offers children individualized support based on assessment results to help them reach better levels of conventional literacy and learn some new digital literacy skills that will help them succeed academically both now and through the future (Chen et al., 2020). It is important to remember that different areas of AI affordances outlined above for use in early childhood education are not necessarily mutually exclusive, even though the research suggests they are different enough to stand alone. AI as interactive learning tools, which may overlap with focusing on AI as adaptive learning tools capable of personalizing learning (Kewalramani et al., 2021; Wang et al., 2021), can engage with children as social partners and support their cognitive development by functioning as tutors and personalized learning. Another function of the learning activity with the AI will be set up as a straightforward game in which children must properly answer a predetermined number of questions in order to advance. In the event that a child provides an inaccurate response, the system will use text-to-speech capabilities to provide an explanation. The audio in the robot groups will resemble a human-like explanation and originate from the robot's mouth. If children give an inaccurate response in the personalized learning groups, they will be asked to comment on the explanation (Abram, 2025). AI implementations provide deeper and more effective learning with personalized education programs for both the child and the educator during the whole learning process, while providing support with individual feedback in evaluation.

Examining how these individualized learning experiences affect more general facets of children's development is crucial as we build on the revolutionary potential of personalized education through AI in early life. In addition to improving academic learning outcomes, AI's capacity to customize training to each child's unique requirements is essential for influencing cognitive, social, and emotional development. AI-powered tools can help young learners acquire metacognition, critical thinking, and agency—all essential 21st-century skills—when they are developed with developmental appropriateness in mind. However, personalization must strike a balance between support and challenge to avoid over-scaffolding and ensure meaningful learning experiences. These customized learning environments, while technologically driven, must remain rooted in the holistic developmental needs of children, supporting experiential and collaborative learning. Thus, the developmental impact of AI in early education extends beyond literacy and numeracy, encompassing creativity, emotional intelligence, and social interaction, highlighting the importance of designing AI tools that promote both personalized learning and whole-child development.

c. Effects of AI on Children's Development

Discussions concerning AI involvement in education, especially in the very early stages of learning, have gained traction as AI continues to influence our daily lives. The majority of current AI products are made for children early years old and up, frequently putting efficiency and academic achievement ahead of the multimodal, relational, and experiential play-based learning that young children require (Chen, 2024). Children's 21st century skills can be enhanced by AI courses. Creativity, critical thinking and problem solving, collaboration, information technology, new forms of literacy, and social, cultural, and metacognitive awareness are among the 21st century skills (Griffin et al., 2012). A reflective, process-oriented approach to output-based education encourages creativity, critical thinking, and problem-solving. Assisting learners during producing "inner feedback," which is the process of contrasting their present understanding with expectations from the teacher comments, conversations, materials, or previous performances, is essential to this. Children may be able to better control their own learning by formalizing these fundamental comparisons, which could lead to insightful feedback loops that improve comprehension and flexibility (Bozkurt et al., 2024). Many researches indicate that early exposure to AI can significantly support a number of elements of a child's development, despite some people questioning the appropriateness of exposing AI concepts to young children. Researchers have created programs to help young learners develop 21st-century abilities, including as critical thinking, cooperation, and communication (Tseng et al., 2021). Druga et al. (2019), for instance created play and communication activities and asked children to create AI agents in the future. Although it makes sense that young learners might not be able to process a lot of information, they must be given the opportunity to use AI for peer engagement and collaboration. Incorporating AI into early childhood education fosters abilities like critical thinking, teamwork, and emotional intelligence in addition to providing new opportunities for creativity and inquiry. Early childhood education focuses on the crucial time in a child's development. Exploring the application of AI in educational contexts, especially early childhood education, is becoming more popular as technology advances (Bautista et al., 2023). This can help academics and educators create age-appropriate AI curricula, games, and toys for children (Ng & Chu, 2021).

Early childhood education is seeing a rise in the application of AI tools to improve young children's learning and development (Lin et al., 2020; Vartiainen et al., 2020). AI has the ability to completely transform education by providing individualized, adaptive learning experiences that are catered to the needs of every learner. Examining AI's incorporation in early childhood education settings has garnered attention due to the government's commitment to enhancing instruction and technology improvements. With an emphasis on the potential developmental advantages of AI and the growing demand for age-appropriate AI literacy, this part examines current research and instructional strategies incorporating AI in early learning environments. Some might argue that junior primary and preschoolers are too young to investigate and learn about AI (Su et al., 2022). However, prior research has introduced AI technologies into early childhood classes and demonstrated their encouraging results (Lin et al., 2020; Tseng et al., 2021). Very little focus has been placed on the curriculum design and learning activities (Su & Yang, 2022). The children's learning outcomes will improve their understanding and proficiency with AI. For instance, following group exercises, children will improve their communication, collaborative skills, and thinking abilities (Su & Zhong, 2022).

According to Kewalramani et al. (2021) and Su and Yang (2022), early AI literacy is crucial for young children to enhance a variety of developmental domains, including theory of mind abilities, creative inquiry, emotional inquiry, and collaborative inquiry. Activity goals and four modules are part of the curriculum design. Some academics use PopBots to teach AI principles, such as supervised machine learning, generative AI, and knowledge-based systems (Williams et al., 2019). Among the benefits of AI education are the enhancement of children' critical thinking and problem-solving abilities (Su, & Zhong, 2022). For instance, Kewalramani et al.

(2021) looked into how interactive AI may be used in early childhood school settings to foster inquiry literacy. However, to support the promise of AI literacy education for early childhood education settings, relatively few studies have examined how AI literacy for children aged 3–8 years in early childhood level compares to other age groups (e.g., primary 3-6, secondary school). Only one review study has attempted to address the use of AI in early childhood education contexts thus far (Su & Yang, 2022). They highlighted the potential of AI to develop dynamic and captivating learning environments that foster cooperation, dialogue, and problem-solving abilities in children.

From a social standpoint, AI can help create cooperative learning environments and experiences by allowing children to communicate with virtual assistants and each other (Girouard-Hallam & Danovitch, 2022). AI systems in early childhood education moderate interactions between children, their parents, and teachers, influencing how connections are made and information is jointly created. Digital platforms that incorporate AI-powered learning companions do more than just provide content; they actively influence how children interact with peers, engage with knowledge, and see interactions with technology (Berson et al., 2025). Considering AI has the capacity to redefine social roles, influence relational expectations, and upend established hierarchies, its inclusion in these networks must be critically evaluated in addition to its educational benefits. Children may view AI systems that can recognize and react to human emotions as companions rather than tools, which raises concerns about how social interaction expectations are shaped by these relationships (Mitchell & Jeon, 2025). Although AI cannot truly reciprocate emotions like humans can, its capacity to mimic relational cues may make it difficult to distinguish between artificial and human attachments Berson et al., 2025). Teachers thought AI may be a useful instrument for encouraging cultural variety awareness and fostering constructive social relationships. However, it's crucial to keep a balanced approach, making sure AI is employed as an additional tool to support and strengthen the crucial part that educators play in encouraging social-emotional learning, holistic development, and profound human connections in early childhood education (Salaam, 2023). In addition to all these contributions, prolonged exposure to AI may reduce children's access to learning from teachers and more knowledgeable peers, as emphasized in Vygotsky's cognitive learning approach, and may also create disadvantages in terms of social-emotional development. For AI technology, robotic parasocial attachments may provide emotional relaxation, but they lack the reciprocity and depth needed to interpret social indicators in human interactions. This raises questions regarding how these interactions may affect children' social and emotional development in the long run (Kurian, 2023; Levinson et al., 2024).

AI systems can use interactive interfaces and adaptive algorithms to adapt to each child's unique learning style and rate (de Castro Rodrigues et al., 2022). Furthermore, one example of how technology may support children's special and essential learning qualities is AI's capacity to foster thinking, creativity, and problem-solving skills. Children can experiment, explore, and learn through hands-on experiences in an immersive learning environment made possible by AI-powered educational games and simulations, thanks to the integration of AI. Furthermore, from this perspective, the fact that children in the pre-operational stage at an early age experience learning with AI increases their exposure to abstract concepts such as algorithms and data analysis, and it is debatable how this experience, which is above their cognitive development in terms of learning, will affect this process in both the short and long term. Additionally, educators acknowledged AI's potential to support social and emotional growth (Bautista et al., 2023). For children aged 4-5, Kewalramani et al. (2021) introduced AI enabled hands-on learning games that featured playing with robots. As a result, children's three inquiring literacy skills -creative, emotional, and collaborative- development. Playing with AI materials can help children develop their creative inquiry literacy, which is the ability to comprehend technology and think creatively. Even though children do not need to fully understand the fundamentals of AI, the two pedagogies may help them study and engage with AI.

d. Preparing the Children to Future Technologies

There are a number of reasons why young learners should study AI: (1) All citizens must be able to use AI applications and understand its fundamental competencies in order to be considered AI literate in this digital age; (2) learners must be given the resources they need to understand, practice, and evaluate AI in a purposeful manner; and (3) learners must be able to understand the fundamentals of AI, particularly as more intricately designed AI toys become a part of their everyday lives (Kewalramani et al., 2021). Working with and using AI, children need to be adequately educated (Touretzky et al., 2023). To begin with, in an increasingly intelligent society, digital literacy for all citizens obviously involves learning and comprehending the fundamental operations of AI and utilizing AI applications (Ng et al., 2021). In order to provide AI in education life of the children, Yang (2022) created the "AI for Kids" curriculum, which uses AI toys to highlight the importance of AI-based technology in daily life and to enable children to learn about AI-embedded and project-based approaches. Children can recognize the fundamentals of AI and learn about the limitations and challenges to ethics associated with these technologies by using these activities and materials, which are appropriate for their developmental stages. Children need to be ready for a future where AI technologies may influence professional decision-making, processes, and even interpersonal interactions more and more. Teaching school children how to use AI for creativity and productivity while simultaneously cultivating a nuanced understanding of its effects on privacy, job displacement, equality, and wider social norms will be necessary to achieve this. Additionally, preserving human control and avoiding an over-reliance on AI-driven automation will probably depend on the capacity to critically evaluate AI-generated outputs (Bozkurt et al., 2024).

Researches give teachers methods and approaches to support young learners through developmentally appropriate activities and resources (Ng et al., 2022; Su & Yang, 2022). Lin et al. (2020) claim children can learn machine-learning concepts by utilizing the conversational platform. It was previously impossible to teach AI to young learners, but thanks to new technologies, early childhood educators are looking into ways to help children learn the technology and make their lives easier. The children's excitement for learning AI, their comprehension of the fundamentals of the technology, and their ability to retain and apply the knowledge gained from each learning exercise will all be observed by the teachers. Teachers can assess children's problem-solving skills and ability to successfully complete group activities by highlighting and sharing the outcomes of their young children. Additionally, the “AI for Kids” program asks children to show off AI using their imagination. By seeing how imaginatively the children will finish the assignment, teachers may assess the children's AI imagination (Yang, 2022). Although it emerges as a tool that strengthens the education system, there is debate about how it will affect the teacher-child-learning relationship. It is a point that should not be overlooked that making the teaching process more data- and performance-oriented at an early age could lead to a situation where children's motivation to learn decreases.

Besides this curriculum for young children, the shortage of embodied, multimodal learning in STEM education, according to researchers, will restrict people's ability to feel optimistic for a digital future that calls for higher-order cognitive abilities and creative inquiry (Turner & Griffin, 2021). In order to inspire children to create something personally relevant and meaningful, AI education is intimately tied to STEM education and requires creative inquiry. Sakulkueakulsuk et al. (2018), for example, use AI in STEM to encourage project-based learning, play, passion, and peer learning in an AI-based learning exercise. In contrast to the typical STEM group, which is regarded as belonging to, embodied pedagogy shows how STEM trajectories may be created for all children to accomplish healthy learning and development in the early years. In addition to increasing children's exposure to AI technology, this pedagogical approach and its implementation in curriculum design and implementation will help them develop more critical and nuanced thinking skills about AI, which is a valuable tool for surviving in today's digital world (Yang, 2022). Thus, it completes the learning a pattern of from early childhood to adulthood and closes the knowledge gap regarding supporting the emergence stage of AI literacy (Chen et al., 2020; Tang et al., 2021). In the end, putting AI education into practice would help provide children early AI literacy, get them ready for the challenges of the digital future, and advance social justice and sustainable development in early childhood education and human society (Yang, 2022). Thus, preparing children for future technologies is a dual undertaking —empowering children through engaging, ethically informed AI experiences, while simultaneously equipping educators with the necessary knowledge and skills to facilitate this transformative learning process.

e. Use of AI for Early Childhood Educators

The knowledge, comprehension, and experience that educators have with AI in early childhood education is referred to as their familiarity with AI technologies and how they are used in the context of early childhood education. Depending on their schooling, real-world experience, and exposure to AI, educators may have varying levels of familiarity. It has a major impact on how educators feel and see the use of AI in early childhood education (Kewalramani et al., 2021). The frameworks of technological, and content knowledge can be used as a guide to help teachers better understand how to integrate AI literacy into the classroom (Durrani et al., 2024). In order to apply Al to educationally meaningful learning and accomplish the intended outcomes, educators play a critical role (Lim, 2024). The accelerated development of generative AI has drastically changed the nature of education, necessitating that both teachers and children gain a thorough, critical grasp of these tools. Keeping up with technological developments is only one aspect of this; another is influencing how education will develop in the future. AI literacy enables us to use these tools efficiently, making sure that they promote rather than diminish critical thinking, creativity, and educational justice (Bozkurt, 2024). Promoting AI literacy for everyone, including young children, is a digital equity initiative that will interest pedagogical leaders and early childhood professionals who wish to better comprehend and integrate AI into their own curricula (Yang, 2022). The level of familiarity that educators have with AI in early childhood might vary from little exposure and past knowledge to hands-on training and ongoing professional development. Improving teachers' knowledge of AI in early childhood education is essential for its effective application. Teachers may help young learners learn how to use AI technology, communicate with people who use AI, and understand how AI works by using three pedagogical approaches: experiential learning, hands-on experience, and activity-based learning. These could help children develop and learn in the modern digital world (Durrani et al., 2024). Ongoing initiatives for professional development, opportunities for training and cooperation with AI specialists can help teachers increase their knowledge, proficiency, and self-assurance in using AI tools efficiently. Early childhood education settings can take advantage of the potential advantages of AI technologies to improve teaching and learning experiences for young children by increasing instructors' expertise with the technology (Baidoo-Anu & Ansah, 2023).

Early childhood education teachers are capable of carrying out age-appropriate activities, according to several studies (Ng et al., 2021; Su & Yang, 2022). However, the level of these activities is insufficient. Therefore, for instructors to have adequate information and tools about AI, they must pedagogical effective instruction specifically intended for AI (Çelik, 2023; Sanusi et al., 2022). Due to their limited exposure to AI technologies in early childhood, some educators may not be fully aware of all of its potential uses. Others may have extensive experience or initial training that has given them a basic understanding of AI and its advantages in early childhood education. Teachers' attitudes toward Al have an impact on how they teach. Teachers' interactions with children are also impacted by these conditions (Avidov-Ungar et al., 2020). Thus, encouraging educators and educational researchers to actively seek feedback from the educational community, to fully engage in the technological advancement process, and to integrate is likely the most crucial step in advancing AI technology for education (Zhang & Aslan, 2021). However, there are not enough Al programs or development research needed to apply Al applications in preschool (Yang, 2022). Furthermore, the application of AI in early childhood education is hindered by the absence of teacher guides needed for early childhood educators to use AI in their classrooms (Durrani et al., 2024). AI has the ability to significantly increase productivity by automating repetitive task and facilitating sophisticated analyses, it is crucial to make sure that these developments do not compromise the depth of learning or the quality of human interactions in the classroom. While maintaining basic pedagogy, automating administrative duties like data analysis and grading may save time. However, over-reliance on automation in the classroom, however, runs the risk of decreasing meaningful child-teacher interaction and adding to the workload of supervisors (Bozkurt et al., 2024).

Researchers could reconsider the function of concrete AI related learning experiences in early childhood education through the strategy of culturally sensitive initiatives. Furthermore, in a variety of early childhood education contexts, embodied education provides a pedagogical strategy for fostering AI literacy. There are real-world ramifications for teaching and teacher education from the creative pedagogical model that includes the main arguments for AI instruction in early childhood (Yang, 2022). Having included AI technologies into their teaching methods, educators with real-world experience utilizing AI tools in early childhood contexts have an increased level of familiarity. Teachers who actively seek out chances to upgrade their knowledge and abilities and participate in ongoing professional development centered on AI in early childhood education demonstrate improved comprehension (Li & Taber, 2022). Early childhood education teachers view AI education as a modern and cutting-edge teaching paradigm that they should study and attempt to use in their classrooms (Avidov-Ungar et al., 2020). Play-centered approaches must be acknowledged as the preferred path of early childhood AI education, and AI education should be carried out using play-based and child-centered experiences in ECE (Ouyang & Jiao, 2021; Zhang & Aslan, 2021). Furthermore, early childhood AI education is expected to be a significant medium for future educational innovation and development (Ali et al., 2021).

Besides the contributions provided by its integration into educational processes, AI also presents risks such as reducing the teacher's influence in the classroom and becoming increasingly obsolete with the development of new technologies. Providing teachers with the necessary AI literacy and addressing the ethical concerns of using AI with young children are two priorities for integrating AI into early childhood education. Teachers' capacity to successfully use AI-driven tools in the classroom is greatly influenced by their level of expertise with these technologies. But given the ethical issues around data privacy, algorithmic bias, and the possible effects on children's developmental processes, this integration needs to be done carefully. To guarantee that AI is a useful tool in early childhood education, improving learning experiences while preserving children's rights and wellbeing, a holistic approach that incorporates ethical framework development with educator training in AI literacy is necessary.

f. Ethical Considerations for the Use of AI in Early Childhood Education

In order to ensure that AI integration in early childhood education has a good effect on young children's learning and development, stakeholders must cooperate to shape its future. When using AI in early childhood education contexts, ethical issues and precautions are essential (Holmes et al., 2022; Leta & Vancea, 2023). AI is being incorporated into educational technology at a rapid pace, with early childhood education emerging as a particularly transformational but morally challenging field. The creation of ethical frameworks adapted to the particular vulnerabilities and developmental needs of young learners has lagged behind the rapid adoption of these technologies. The necessity of creating thorough, context-specific ethical rules is highlighted by the gap that leaves educators, legislators, and developers with urgent difficulties (Wang et al., 2024). Young children are not cognitively competent enough to completely understand abstract ideas like "data security" and "privacy." Children under the age of seven, for example, frequently have difficulty comprehending these concepts and have limited capacity to apply privacy-related decisions in practical contexts (Neugnot-Cerioli & Laurenty, 2024). Their ability to understand the potential consequences of revealing personal information, including possible long-term effects, is impacted by this developmental gap (Katirai, 2024). In addition to the child's age and development, characteristics such as gender, language, and ethnicity also have the potential to create discrimination in such applications, which is a subject open to debate. However, how and to what extent the feeling of being monitored can eliminate children's sense of privacy and expose them to the risk of abuse are also important issues that need to be discussed. To improve learning experiences while putting young children's rights and well-being first, AI can be responsibly and successfully incorporated into early childhood education by upholding ethical standards, safeguarding children's privacy, guaranteeing transparency and fairness in AI algorithms, selecting relevant content, and encouraging human interaction. Such ethical problems can be avoided by implementing AI with openness, accountability, respect for individual rights, user control over data, and the eradication of bias and discrimination (Leta & Vancea, 2023). By encouraging creativity, facilitating individualized learning, and meeting a range of developmental needs, technologies like conversational agents, robotic tutors, and adaptive learning platforms have the potential to improve teaching and learning (Berson & Berson, 2024; Chen, 2024).

Teachers' worries and reluctance should not be disregarded, since AI presents great prospects to enhance early childhood education. By taking care of these issues by AI may effectively support and improve early childhood education through responsible AI implementation, data privacy, bias reduction, educator support, and narrowing the digital divide (Baidoo-Anu & Ansah, 2023). Developing biased algorithmic structures in AI may result in the unfair treatment of some children groups (WEF, 2022). Actionable strategies to reduce these risks were identified by the scoping review, which emphasizes the significance of "privacy by design" techniques and higher default privacy settings for child-accessible platforms in order to avoid harming vulnerable users (Wang et al., 2024). Thus, upholding, defending, and advancing human rights, fundamental freedoms, and dignity must be the top priority when incorporating AI into education (UNESCO, 2022). When designing and implementing AI systems, collaborative supervision mechanisms involving parents, educators, and legislators can balance power relations and give children's privacy the greatest importance (Fu & Weng, 2024). Countries have also responded by creating general legislation pertaining to AI and are still doing so (Hine & Floridi, 2024). These laws' fundamental objective is to provide a logical framework for the application of AI in the classroom (Fitria, 2021).

AI use in preschool requires policies and training initiatives. According to numerous researches, creating AI-related legislation and training initiatives will make implementing AI easier (Yıldırım & Akcan, 2024). But the absence of sufficient policies and training programs, early childhood educators may become hesitant to employ AI and exhibit opposition to it as a result of AI-related legislation and training initiatives. Therefore, external elements that impact the incorporation of a new technology stated, including perceived utility, simplicity of use, policy support, privacy, security, and ethics, must be considered. A sustainable development of AI education must address a number of pedagogical, social, cultural, technical, and ethical aspects, such as inclusion and equity in AI education, teacher preparation for AI-empowered education, and inclusive gathering and employing information systems (Hwang et al., 2020; Zawacki-Richter et al., 2019). Generative AI has the power to improve the world by promoting creativity, equity, and sustainability if it is used responsibly and with forethought. Therefore, the task at hand is evident: to acquire the abilities and know-how required to ride with integrity and wisdom, making sure that as it develops and expands the capacity to guide it toward a fair and prosperous future (Bozkurt, 2024).

Besides all these, AI commercialization frequently favors markets with larger financial returns, underserving those with lower economic standing. Inequities between well-resourced and underprivileged groups are reinforced by this imbalance, undermining AI's promise as a leveling tool in education (Ho et al., 2024). By tailoring interventions to each learner's unique needs, AI technologies have enormous potential to alleviate developmental gaps. Children with developmental delays or unique educational requirements can benefit from tools made for tailored learning experiences, ensuring that no child is left behind (Luo et al., 2024). Although AI has the potential to overcome educational gaps by providing resources to underserved or rural locations, its effectiveness also depends on substantial infrastructure and support for digital competency. It is insufficient to only make AI tools accessible; in order to promote inclusive results, these tools must be accompanied with the required technology infrastructure and training. The potential of AI to provide real-time translation and language support in multilingual education could significantly increase inclusivity in multicultural and international classrooms. To guarantee correctness and cultural sensitivity, as well as to reduce misinterpretations or miscommunications, this calls for constant attention (Bozkurt et al., 2024). Inequalities in access to these technologies, however, restrict their potential. Barriers that prevent equitable implementation for marginalized areas include insufficient connections to the internet, restricted device access, and a lack of teacher preparation (Su & Yang, 2024). This is a critical risk and disadvantage provide all children from every background to access the AI. In the conclusion, responsible AI integration in early childhood education will necessitate constant discussion, strict regulation, and adaptable guidelines that change as technology does. Stakeholders can exploit AI's transformational potential while preserving children's rights, dignity, and well-being by giving young learners' developmental and ethical requirements top priority (Berson et al., 2025). This all-encompassing, child-centered strategy may guarantee that AI functions as a vehicle for inclusion and empowerment, promoting fair educational opportunities in the early years.

RESULT AND RECOMMENDATION

The integration of AI into early childhood education represents a transformative shift in pedagogical practices, with profound implications for children's learning, development, and future technological literacy. As this chapter has shown, AI technologies have tremendous potential to support the development of 21st-century skills, improve developmental outcomes, help educators meet a variety of learning demands, and tailor learning experiences. AI-powered resources like emotion detection software, robotic companions, and adaptive learning platforms offer the potential to build inclusive, dynamic, and responsive learning environments. However, these opportunities come with significant social, educational, and ethical constraints. Careful consideration must be given to how AI is implemented in early childhood education in order to protect socioemotional development, guarantee fair access, protect data privacy, and avoid biases in AI algorithms. AI must be used as a supplementary tool rather than as a replacement for meaningful interactions between teachers and learners because the crucial role of human educators cannot be replaced.

Furthermore, children's exposure to AI needs to be culturally aware, developmentally appropriate, and based on moral standards that put children's rights, dignity, and overall wellbeing first. An inclusive and moral digital future for early childhood education will be shaped in large part by stakeholders' cooperation, policymakers' attempts to create regulatory frameworks, and teachers' readiness and experience with AI. This chapter's comments highlight that the future of AI in early childhood education is a profoundly educational, ethical, and societal issue rather than just a technical one. In order to ensure that AI empowers all young learners rather than escalating already-existing injustices, deliberate, thoughtful, and participatory approaches are crucial. Based on the discussions of this chapter, the following recommendations:

- Build AI curriculum that complement the cognitive, emotional, and social development stages of young children. Inquiry-based, play-centered, and embodied learning strategies that encourage innovation, critical thinking, and teamwork should be prioritized in AI education.
- Engage in thorough training programs that give early childhood educators technical proficiency, knowledge of ethical issues, pedagogical integration techniques, and an understanding of AI ideas. Prioritizing ongoing professional development can help you adjust to the quickly changing AI landscape.
- Encourage cooperation in the development, use, and assessment of AI applications between educators, technologists, parents, policymakers, and children

themselves. Participatory procedures like these can ensure that AI solutions are child-centered, culturally aware, and pertinent to the situation.

- Provide explicit ethical frameworks and rules addressing children protection, algorithmic justice, data privacy, and transparency. Institutions and policy-makers must embrace inclusive practices and "privacy by design" strategies to avoid marginalization and advance fair access to AI.
- Implementing regulations and programs that give children, regardless of their financial situation, access to AI-enhanced learning resources would help close the digital divide. To address disparities, community collaborations, financial programs, and infrastructure upgrades are crucial.
- Acknowledge that although AI can improve learning, it should never take the place of the essential human interactions that are the basis of early childhood development. AI should be emphasized in pedagogical designs as a supplement to, not a replacement for, fostering relationships between learners and their educators.

The early childhood education field may effectively overcome the challenges of integrating AI with compassion, foresight, and a dedication to the best interests of children by following these suggestions. The objective must be to create a future where technology enhances rather than detracts from the depth of human growth and education, not just to get children ready for a highly advanced technological future.

REFERENCES

Abram, N. (2025). Personalized Learning in Action: Exploring AI and Robotics for Early Childhood Education. *Proceedings of the AAAI Conference on Artificial Intelligence*, *39*(28), 29561–29563. DOI: 10.1609/aaai.v39i28.35325

Ali, S., DiPaola, D., Lee, I., Sindato, V., Kim, G., Blumofe, R., & Breazeal, C. (2021). Children as creators, thinkers and citizens in an AI-driven future. *Computers and Education: Artificial Intelligence*, *2*, 100040. DOI: 10.1016/j.caeai.2021.100040

Avidov-Ungar, O., Shamir-Inbal, T., & Blau, I. (2020). Typology of digital leadership roles tasked with integrating new technologies into teaching: Insights from metaphor analysis. *Journal of Research on Technology in Education*, *54*(1), 92–107. DOI: 10.1080/15391523.2020.1809035

Baidoo-Anu, D., & Ansah, L. O. (2023). Education in the era of generative artificial intelligence (AI): Understanding the potential benefits of ChatGPT in promoting teaching and learning. *Journal of AI*, *7*(1), 52–62. DOI: 10.61969/jai.1337500

Bautista, A., Yu, J., Lee, K., & Sun, J. (2023). Impact of play-based pedagogies in selected Asian contexts: What do we know and how to move forward?. *Effective teaching around the world: Theoretical, empirical, methodological and practical insights*, 473-488.

Becker, S. A., Brown, M., Dahlstrom, E., Davis, A., DePaul, K., Diaz, V., & Pomerantz, J. (2018). *Horizon report 2018 higher education edition brought to you by EDUCAUSE.* EDUCAUSE. https://ir.westcliff.edu/wp-content/uploads/2020/01/Horizon-Report_-2018-Higher-Education-Edition.pdf

Berson, I. R., & Berson, M. J. (2024). Fragments of the past: The intersection of AI, historical imagery, and early childhood creativity. *Future in Educational Research*, *2*(4), 403–421. DOI: 10.1002/fer3.46

Berson, I. R., Berson, M. J., & Luo, W. (2025). Innovating responsibly: Ethical considerations for AI in early childhood education. *AI. Brain and Child*, *1*(2), 1–15. DOI: 10.1007/s44436-025-00003-5

Bozkurt, A. (2023). ChatGPT, üretken yapay zeka ve algoritmik paradigma değişikliği. *Alanyazın*, *4*(1), 63–72. DOI: 10.59320/alanyazin.1283282

Bozkurt, A. (Ed.). (2024). Why generative AI literacy, why now and why it matters in the educational landscape?: Kings, queens and GenAI dragons. *Open Praxis, 16*(3), 283-290. https://doi.org/DOI: 10.55982/openpraxis.16.3.739

Bozkurt, A., Xiao, J., Farrow, R., Bai, J. Y. H., Nerantzi, C., Moore, S., Dron, J., Stracke, C. M., Singh, L., Crompton, H., Koutropoulos, A., Terentev, E., Pazurek, A., Nichols, M., Sidorkin, A. M., Costello, E., Watson, S., Mulligan, D., Honeychurch, S., & Asino, T. I. (2024). The manifesto for teaching and learning in a time of generative AI: A critical collective stance to better navigate the future. *Open Praxis*, *16*(4), 487–513. DOI: 10.55982/openpraxis.16.4.777

Bredekamp, S. (2020). *Effective practices in early childhood education: Building a foundation* (*4th* ed.). Pearson.

Brennan, K., & Resnick, M. (2012). New frameworks for studying and assessing the development of computational thinking. In *Proceedings of the 2012 annual meeting of the American educational research association,* Vancouver, Canada (Vol. 1, p. 25).

Celik, İ. (2023). Towards Intelligent-TPACK: An empirical study on teachers' professional knowledge to ethically integrate artificial intelligence (AI)-based tools into education. *Computers in Human Behavior*, *138*, 1–12. DOI: 10.1016/j.chb.2022.107468

Chen, J. J. (2024). A scoping study on AI affordances in early childhood education: Mapping the global landscape, identifying research gaps, and charting future research directions. *Journal of Artificial Intelligence Research*, *81*, 701–740. DOI: 10.1613/jair.1.16882

Chen, X., Xie, H., Zou, D., & Hwang, G. J. (2020). Application and theory gaps during the rise of artificial intelligence in education. *Computers and Education: Artificial Intelligence*, *1*, 100002. DOI: 10.1016/j.caeai.2020.100002

Chiu, M. M. (2008). Flowing toward correct contributions during group problem solving: A statistical discourse analysis. *Journal of the Learning Sciences*, *17*(3), 415–463. DOI: 10.1080/10508400802224830

Crescenzi-Lanna, L. (2023). Literature review of the reciprocal value of artificial and human intelligence in early childhood education. *Journal of Research on Technology in Education*, *55*(1), 21–33. DOI: 10.1080/15391523.2022.2128480

de Castro Rodrigues, D., de Siqueira, V. S., da Costa, R. M., & Barbosa, R. M. (2022). Artificial Intelligence applied to smart interfaces for children's educational games. *Displays*, *74*, 102217. DOI: 10.1016/j.displa.2022.102217

Druga, S., Vu, S. T., Likhith, E., & Qiu, T. (2019). Inclusive AI literacy for kids around the world. *Proceedings of FabLearn, 2019*, 104–111. DOI: 10.1145/3311890.3311904

Durrani, R., Iqbal, A., & Akram, H. (2024). Artificial intelligence (AI) in early childhood education, exploring challenges, opportunities and future directions: A Scoping review. *Qlantic Journal of Social Sciences*, *5*(2), 411–423. DOI: 10.55737/qjss.135537445

Eguchi, A., Okada, H., & Muto, Y. (2021). Contextualizing AI education for K-12 students to enhance their learning of AI literacy through culturally responsive approaches. *Kunstliche Intelligenz*, *35*(2), 153–161. DOI: 10.1007/s13218-021-00737-3 PMID: 34376922

Filgueiras, F. (2024). Artificial intelligence and education governance. *Education, Citizenship and Social Justice*, *19*(3), 349–361. DOI: 10.1177/17461979231160674

Fitria, T. N. (2021, December). Artificial intelligence (AI) in education: Using AI tools for teaching and learning process. In *Prosiding Seminar Nasional & Call for Paper STIE AAS* (pp. 134-147).

Fu, Y., & Weng, Z. (2024). Navigating the ethical terrain of AI in education: A systematic review on framing responsible human-centered AI practices. *Computers and Education: Artificial Intelligence*, *100306*, 100306. Advance online publication. DOI: 10.1016/j.caeai.2024.100306

Girouard-Hallam, L. N., & Danovitch, J. H. (2022). Children's trust in and learning from voice assistants. *Developmental Psychology*, *58*(4), 646–661. DOI: 10.1037/dev0001318 PMID: 35343713

Griffin, P., McGaw, B., & Care, E. (2012). *Assessment and teaching of 21st century skills* (Vol. 10). Springer. DOI: 10.1007/978-94-007-2324-5

Hine, E., & Floridi, L. (2024). Artificial intelligence with American values and Chinese characteristics: A compara tive analysis of American and Chinese governmental AI policies. *AI & Society*, *39*(1), 257–278. DOI: 10.1007/s00146-022-01499-8

Hinojo-Lucena, F. J., Aznar-Díaz, I., Cáceres-Reche, M. P., & Romero-Rodríguez, J. M. (2019). Artificial intelligence in higher education: A bibliometric study on its impact in the scientific literature. *Education Sciences*, *9*(1), 21–51. DOI: 10.3390/educsci9010051

Ho, M. T., Mantello, P., & Vuong, Q. H. (2024). Emotional AI in education and toys: Investigating moral risk awareness in the acceptance of AI technologies from a cross-sectional survey of the Japanese population. *Heliyon*, *10*(16), e36251. DOI: 10.1016/j.heliyon.2024.e36251 PMID: 39253209

Holmes, W., Bialik, M., & Fadel, C. (2019). *Artificial Intelligence in Education: Promises and Implications for Teaching and Learning*. Center for Curriculum Redesign.

Holmes, W., Persson, J., Chounta, I. A., Wasson, B., & Dimitrova, V. (2022). *Artificial intelligence and education: A critical view through the lens of human rights, democracy and the rule of law*. Council of Europe.

Hwang, G. J., Xie, H., Wah, B. W., & Gašević, D. (2020). Vision, challenges, roles and research issues of Artificial Intelligence in Education. *Computers and Education: Artificial Intelligence, 1*, 100001. DOI: 10.1016/j.caeai.2020.100001

Katirai, A. (2024). Ethical considerations in emotion recognition technologies: A review of the literature. *AI and Ethics, 4*(4), 927–948. DOI: 10.1007/s43681-023-00307-3

Kawata, H., Takano, Y., Iwata, Y., Kanamaru, N., Shimokura, K., & Fujita, Y. (2008). Field trial of asynchronous communication using network-based interactive child watch system for the participation of parents in day-care activities. *2008 IEEE International Conference on Robotics and Automation,* 2558-2563. DOI: 10.1109/ROBOT.2008.4543598

Kewalramani, S., Kidman, G., & Palaiologou, I. (2021). Using artificial intelligence (AI)-interfaced robotic toys in early childhood settings: A case for children's inquiry literacy. *European Early Childhood Education Research Journal, 29*(5), 652–668. DOI: 10.1080/1350293X.2021.1968458

Kurian, N. (2023). Toddlers and robots? The ethics of supporting young children with disabilities with AI companions and the implications for children's rights. *International Journal of Human Rights Education, 7*(1), 9. https://repository.usfca.edu/ijhre/vol7/iss1/9

Leta, F. M., & Vancea, D. P. C. (2023). Ethics in education: Exploring the ethical implications of artificial intelligence implementation. *Ovidius University Annals. Economic Sciences Series, 23*(1), 413–421.

Levinson, L. M., Abbasi, N. I., Sabanovic, S., & Gunes, H. (2024). Expert insights on robots for safeguarding children: How (not) and why (not)? In *Proceedings of the interaction design and children conference* (IDC '24), June 17–20, 2024, Delft, Netherlands (pp. 600–611). ACM. https://doi.org/DOI: 10.1145/3628516.3655798

Li, H., Forbes, A., & Yang, W. (2021). Developing culturally and developmentally appropriate early STEM learning experiences. *Early Education and Development, 32*(1), 1–6. DOI: 10.1080/10409289.2020.1833674 PMID: 35082478

Li, X., & Taber, K. S. (2022). The Future of Interaction: Augmented Reality, Holography, and Artificial Intelligence in Early Childhood Science Education. In *STEM, Robotics, Mobile Apps in Early Childhood and Primary Education: Technology to Promote Teaching and Learning* (pp. 415-442). Springer Nature Singapore.

Lim, E. M. (2024). Metaphor analysis on pre-service early childhood teachers' conception of AI (Artificial Intelligence) education for young children. *Thinking Skills and Creativity*, *51*, 101455. DOI: 10.1016/j.tsc.2023.101455

Lin, P., Van Brummelen, J., Lukin, G., Williams, R., & Breazeal, C. (2020). Zhorai: Designing a conversational agent for children to explore machine learning concepts. *Proceedings of the AAAI Conference on Artificial Intelligence*, *34*(9), 13381–13388. DOI: 10.1609/aaai.v34i09.7061

Linder, S. M. (2012). Interactive whiteboards in early childhood mathematics: Strategies for effective implementation in pre-K-grade 3. *Young Children*, *67*(3), 26–35. https://research.ebsco.com/linkprocessor/plink?id=631d9486-5f4a-30b0-a427-4ed86c4ba233

Luo, W., He, H., Gao, M., & Li, H. (2024). Safety, identity, attitude, cognition, and capability: The 'SIACC' framework of early childhood AI literacy. *Education Sciences*, *14*(8), 1–19. DOI: 10.3390/educsci14080871

McLachlan, C., Fleer, M., & Edwards, S. (2018). *Early childhood curriculum: Planning, assessment and implementation*. Cambridge University Press. DOI: 10.1017/9781108131810

Mitchell, J. J., & Jeon, M. (2025). Exploring emotional connections: A systematic literature review of attachment in human-robot interaction. *International Journal of Human-Computer Interaction*, *41*(18), 1–22. DOI: 10.1080/10447318.2024.2445100

Neugnot-Cerioli, M., & Laurenty, O. M. (2024). The Future of Child Development in the AI Era. Cross-Disciplinary Perspectives Between AI and Child Development Experts. *arXiv preprint arXiv:* https://doi.org//arXiv.2405.19275DOI: 10.48550

Ng, D. T. K., & Chu, S. K. W. (2021). Motivating students to learn AI through social networking sites: A case study in Hong Kong. *Online Learning : the Official Journal of the Online Learning Consortium*, *25*(1), 195–208. DOI: 10.24059/olj.v25i1.2454

Ng, D. T. K., Leung, J. K. L., Chu, K. W. S., & Qiao, M. S. (2021). AI literacy: Definition, teaching, evaluation and ethical issues. *Proceedings of the Association for Information Science and Technology*, *58*(1), 504–509. DOI: 10.1002/pra2.487

Ng, D. T. K., Leung, J. K. L., Chu, S. K. W., & Qiao, M. S. (2021). Conceptualizing AI literacy: An exploratory review. *Computers and Education: Artificial Intelligence, 2*, 100041. DOI: 10.1016/j.caeai.2021.100041

Ng, D. T. K., Leung, J. K. L., Su, M. J., Yim, I. H. Y., Qiao, M. S., & Chu, S. K. W. (2022). AI Literacy Education in Early Childhood Education. In *AI Literacy in K-16 Classrooms*. Springer International Publishing., DOI: 10.1007/978-3-031-18880-0_5

Ouyang, F., & Jiao, P. (2021). Artificial intelligence in education: The three paradigms. *Computers and Education: Artificial Intelligence, 2*, 100020. DOI: 10.1016/j.caeai.2021.100020

Penagos, M., Kassir, S., & Vosloo, S. (2020). National AI strategies and children (Policy brief). *Unicef Office of Global insight and Policy*. https://www.unicef.org/globalinsight/media/1156/file

Sakulkueakulsuk, B., Witoon, S., Ngarmkajornwiwat, P., Pataranutaporn, P., Surareungchai, W., Pataranutaporn, P., & Subsoontorn, P. (2018). Kids making AI: Integrating machine learning, gamification, and social context in STEM education. In *2018 IEEE international conference on teaching, assessment, and learning for engineering (TALE)* (pp. 1005–1010). IEEE. https://doi.org/DOI: 10.1109/TALE.2018.8615249

Salaam, M. A. (2023). Examining the ımplementation of artificial ıntelligence in early childhood education settings in Ghana: Educators' attitudes and perceptions towards ıts long-term viability. *American Journal of Education and Technology, 2*(4), 36–49. DOI: 10.54536/ajet.v2i4.2201

Sanusi, I. T., Olaleye, S. A., Agbo, F. J., & Chiu, T. K. F. (2022). The role of learners' competencies in artificial intelligence education. *Computers and Education: Artificial Intelligence, 3*, 1–10. DOI: 10.1016/j.caeai.2022.100098

Scott, D. (2008). *Critical essays on major curriculum theorists*. Routledge.

Shifflet, R., Toledo, C., & Mattoon, C. (2012). Touch tablet surprises: A preschool teacher's story. *Young Children, 67*(3), 36–41. https://research.ebsco.com/linkprocessor/plink?id=34d6b1d6-78ed-3234-ab00-fad3ae80b147

Shin, K. C., Kuppuswamy, N., & Jung, H. C. (2008). Network Based Service Robot for Education. In: Yoo, SD. (eds) *EKC2008 Proceedings of the EU-Korea Conference on Science and Technology*. Springer Proceedings in Physics, vol 124. Springer, Berlin, Heidelberg. https://doi.org/DOI: 10.1007/978-3-540-85190-5_32

Su, J., & Yang, W. (2022). Artificial intelligence in early childhood education: A scoping review. *Computers & Education: Artificial Intelligence. Article, 100049*, 100049. Advance online publication. DOI: 10.1016/j.caeai.2022.100049

Su, J., & Yang, W. (2024). AI literacy curriculum and its relation to children's perceptions of robots and attitudes towards engineering and science: An intervention study in early childhood education. *Journal of Computer Assisted Learning*, *40*(1), 241–253. DOI: 10.1111/jcal.12867

Su, J., & Zhong, Y. (2022). Artificial Intelligence (AI) in early childhood education: Curriculum design and future directions. *Computers and Education: Artificial Intelligence*, *3*, 100072. DOI: 10.1016/j.caeai.2022.100072

Su, J., Zhong, Y., & Ng, D. T. K. (2022). A meta-review of literature on educational approaches for teaching AI at the K-12 levels in the Asia-Pacific region. *Computers & Education: Artificial Intelligence. Article*, *100065*, 100065. Advance online publication. DOI: 10.1016/j.caeai.2022.100065

Tanaka, F., Fortenberry, B., Aisaka, K., & Movellan, J. R. (2007). Plans for developing real-time dance interaction between QRIO and toddlers in a classroom environment. *In: Proceedings of the 4th IEEE International Conference on Development and Learning*, pp. 142-147. IEEE Press. DOI: 10.1109/DEVLRN.2005.1490963

Tang, K. Y., Chang, C. Y., & Hwang, G. J. (2021). Trends in artificial intelligence-supported e-learning: A systematic review and co-citation network analysis (1998–2019). *Interactive Learning Environments*, *31*(4), 2134–2152. DOI: 10.1080/10494820.2021.1875001

Touretzky, D., Gardner-McCune, C., & Seehorn, D. (2023). Machine learning and the five big ideas in AI. *International Journal of Artificial Intelligence in Education*, *33*(2), 233–266. DOI: 10.1007/s40593-022-00314-1

Tseng, T., Murai, Y., Freed, N., Gelosi, D., Ta, T. D., & Kawahara, Y. (2021). PlushPal: Storytelling with interactive plush toys and machine learning. In *Interaction design and children* (pp. 236–245)

Turner, J. D., & Griffin, A. A. (2021). Dream a little [STEAM] of me: Exploring Black adolescent girls' STEAM career futures through digital multimodal compositions. In *Genders, Cultures, and Literacies* (pp. 49-61). Routledge.

UNESCO. (2022). *Recommendation on the ethics of artificial intelligence.* UNESCO. https://unesdoc.unesco.org/ark:/48223/pf0000381137

UNICEF. (2021). *Policy guidance on AI for children.* Paris: UNICEF. https://www.unicef.org/globalinsight/reports/policy-guidance-ai-children

Vartiainen, H., Tedre, M., & Valtonen, T. (2020). Learning machine learning with very young children: Who is teaching whom? *International Journal of Child-Computer Interaction, 25*, 100182. DOI: 10.1016/j.ijcci.2020.100182

Wang, G., Zhao, J., Van Kleek, M., & Shadbolt, N. (2024). Challenges and opportunities in translating ethical AI principles into practice for children. *Nature Machine Intelligence, 6*(3), 265–270. DOI: 10.1038/s42256-024-00805-x

Wang, X., Yin, N., & Zhang, Z. (2021). Smart design of intelligent companion toys for preschool children. *Artificial Intelligence for Engineering Design, Analysis and Manufacturing, 35*(2), 151–164. DOI: 10.1017/S0890060420000499

Williams, R., Park, H. W., Oh, L., & Breazeal, C. (2019). Popbots: Designing an artificial intelligence curriculum for early childhood education. *Proceedings of the AAAI Conference on Artificial Intelligence, 33*(1), 9729–9736. DOI: 10.1609/aaai.v33i01.33019729

World Economic Forum. [WEF], (2022). *Artificial intelligence for children: Toolkit.* World Economic Forum. https://www3.weforum.org/docs/WEF_Artificial_Intel ligen ce_for_Child ren_ 2022.pdf

Yang, W. (2022). Artificial Intelligence education for young children: Why, what, and how in curriculum design and implementation. *Computers and Education: Artificial Intelligence, 3*, 100061. DOI: 10.1016/j.caeai.2022.100061

Yıldırım, B., & Akcan, A. T. (2024). AI-professional development model for chemistry teacher: Artificial intelligence in chemistry education. *Journal of Education in Science, Environment and Health, 10*(4), 161–182. DOI: 10.55549/jeseh.741

Yılmaz, A., Nacar, M., & Uysal, G. (2024). Ethical Use of Artificial Intelligence Applications in Early Childhood Education. In Aydınlı, B., & Altunoğlu, B. D. (Eds.), *Transforming Early Childhood Education: Technology, Sustainability, and Foundational Skills for the 21st Century*. Özgür Publications., DOI: 10.58830/ozgur.pub534.c2203

Zawacki-Richter, O., Marín, V. I., Bond, M., & Gouverneur, F. (2019). Systematic review of research on artificial intelligence applications in higher education – Where are the educators? *International Journal of Educational Technology in Higher Education, 16*(1), 1–27. DOI: 10.1186/s41239-019-0171-0

Zhang, K., & Aslan, A. B. (2021). AI technologies for education: Recent research & future directions. *Computers and education. Artificial Intelligence, 2*, 100025. DOI: 10.1016/j.caeai.2021.100025

KEY TERMS AND DEFINITIONS

Early Childhood Education: Structured educational experiences and environments designed for young children birth-to-8 years old, however, in Turkey it refers from birth to 6 years old.

Motivation: The internal or external drive that encourages children to learn. AI can influence motivation by providing personalized, engaging content that adapts to a child's interests and abilities, though it must be carefully designed to sustain intrinsic willingness and creativity.

Artificial Intelligence: Machine-based systems capable of making decisions, predictions, or recommendations that influence real or virtual environments. These systems can adapt and learn from interactions and are increasingly used in educational contexts.

Technology: Tools and systems developed using scientific knowledge for practical purposes. In early childhood education, this includes AI-based tools, digital devices, smart boards, and software that enhance teaching, learning, and developmental monitoring of the children.

AI-Based Technology: Technologies powered by artificial intelligence that enable machines to simulate human intelligence processes such as learning, reasoning, and self-correction. In early childhood education, these include adaptive learning platforms, robotic tutors, and smart toys that interact with children and respond dynamically to their needs.

AI-Driven Tools: Digital platforms and applications powered by AI algorithms that offer interactive, adaptive learning experiences. Examples include speech recognition systems, emotion-aware software, and personalized tutoring applications used in early education.

AI literacy: The foundational understanding of AI concepts, operations, and implications. In early childhood, this includes helping children recognize what AI is, how it functions, and encouraging responsible, critical engagement with AI technologies.

AI curriculum: A structured educational plan that introduces young children to AI concepts in age, and developmentally appropriate ways. This may include storytelling, play-based activities, robotics, and projects that promote inquiry, problem-solving, and ethical awareness.

Personalized Learning: Creating a unique instructional strategy for all learners based on their individual learning requirements, especially for young children's interests and needs.

21st-century skills: A set of abilities necessary for success in today's digital and interconnected world. These include creativity, critical thinking, problem-solving, communication, collaboration, digital literacy, and cultural and metacognitive awareness. AI in education supports the development of these skills by fostering inquiry, reflection, and personalized learning experiences.

Ethics: The moral principles guiding the use of AI, especially with vulnerable populations like young children. Key ethical concerns include data privacy, algorithmic bias, fairness, transparency, and maintaining human-centered interactions in educational environments.

Chapter 6
Artificial Intelligence and Autism Spectrum Disorder:
Technological Revolution or Interruption

Selin Özer
https://orcid.org/0000-0003-1916-0672
Anadolu University, Turkey

Hamdi Gönüldaş
https://orcid.org/0000-0003-3569-0809
Anadolu University, Turkey

Halil Öztürk
https://orcid.org/0000-0001-5646-2130
Muğla Sıtkı Koçman University, Turkey

Ömer Faruk Toprak
https://orcid.org/0000-0002-6673-6702
Anadolu University, Turkey

İlyas Gürses
Anadolu University, Turkey

Sunagül Sani-Bozkurt
https://orcid.org/0000-0001-6648-9636
Anadolu University, Turkey

Samet Aksoy
https://orcid.org/0009-0005-9935-1103
Anadolu University, Turkey

ABSTRACT

This book chapter comprehensively addresses the potential role of artificial intelligence in the education of learners with Autism Spectrum Disorder (ASD) and the opportunities and ethical dilemmas presented by this technology. The integration of AI into education has been a significant turning point, particularly for learners with ASD, giving rise to both innovative possibilities and concerns. The technological revolution in education, while enabling personalized learning, raises new questions

DOI: 10.4018/979-8-3373-7574-8.ch006

about teacher-student interaction, independence-dependence balances, and human-machine interaction. A careful balance must be struck between supporting the development of students with ASD and the risk of dependency that may arise from the overuse of AI. In this context, empathetic AI technologies respond sensitively to emotional needs while also bringing with them concerns about dependency and uncertainty in human-machine interaction. The chapter offers recommendations for the responsible use of these technologies.

INTRODUCTION

Today, increasing diversity in educational settings necessitates the design of more inclusive and flexible teaching processes. In particular, individuals with special needs may not benefit sufficiently from traditional teaching methods due to their types of disabilities, individual characteristics, developmental levels, and learning styles. Therefore, in order for educational processes to be effective, there is a need for teaching approaches that are planned and individualized according to the needs of learners (Education for All Handicapped Children Act [EAHCA], 1975). An important supporting factor in this individualization process is assistive technologies (AT), which are being integrated more effectively into the field of education with the rapid development of digital opportunities.

AT is defined as technology, products, equipment, or systems designed or adapted to enhance or maintain the performance and quality of life of learners with special needs, providing them with equal access to others (Individuals With Disabilities Education Improvement Act [IDEA], 2004; Borg et al., 2009). The International Organization for Standardization (ISO) (2016) defines assistive technologies as devices, equipment and software specifically produced or adapted to protect, support, educate, measure or perform bodily functions/structures and activities; prevent impairments or participation restrictions for learners with special needs or for use by others on their behalf.

AT used to support learners with special needs is generally divided into three groups: low-tech, mid-tech and high-tech (Sani-Bozkurt, 2017). Low-tech products consist of simple, inexpensive, easily accessible materials with no technological complexity. Magnifying glasses, thick-tipped pens or picture communication cards fall under this low-tech category. Mid-tech tools are relatively more technically advanced; for example, speech-generating communication devices and digital voice recorders fall under this category. High-tech products are generally computer-based, digital and consist of advanced software or hardware; examples include screen reader software, alternative and augmented communication (AAC) systems, virtual reality (VR) applications, augmented reality (AR) applications or artificial intelligence

(AI)-based applications. The selection of which AT to use in the education and training process is based on the learner's disability group, characteristics and needs.

Among the high-tech tools that have gained attention and developed rapidly in recent years within the AT classification described above, AI technology stands out. AI technology and applications are used in identifying the disabilities of individuals with special needs and evaluating their performance (Şen & Akbay, 2023). In addition, AI technology makes learning processes more dynamic by providing flexible, rich and interactive learning environments that can be customized. In this way, AI technology not only facilitates access to information but also adapts to the individual needs, interests and learning styles of learners, thereby transforming the education and training process into a more effective and efficient one (Luckin et al., 2016; Holmes et al., 2019). Going a step further, generative AI (GenAI) technologies are emerging as an innovative assistive technology in special education, with features such as the ability to generate personalized content, provide instant feedback and automatically personalize teaching materials (Fu et al., 2025).

GENAI TECHNOLOGIES

With the increasing spread of digitalization, AI technology has begun to be integrated into almost every area of life. AI technology was first defined by McCarthy in 1955 as the imitation of learning and intelligence by machines. Subsequent definitions describe AI as a set of machine-based systems that receive commands and inputs in line with human-defined objectives and convert them into actions, contributing to prediction, recommendation, and decision-making processes in real or virtual environments. Inspired by the human brain, these systems have the potential to produce various products thanks to their ability to mimic cognitive processes (Russell, 2016; Song et al., 2019; Russell & Norvig, 2021; Holmes et al., 2022). AI systems are used in many areas to increase efficiency, optimize processes and support human capacity. At the center of these developments are GenAI technologies, where AI has moved from a supporting role to becoming an actor in the production of original and creative processes.

GenAI is an AI technology that uses deep learning and neural networks trained on large-scale data sets to generate new and original content through chat interfaces and responses to commands written in natural language (Bozkurt, 2023; Miao & Holmes, 2023). GenAI has the ability to produce human-like content through natural language processing (NLP) and deep learning-based language models. Through unsupervised pre-training and supervised fine-tuning processes, it learns patterns in large datasets and uses these patterns to generate human-like content (Dwivedi et al., 2023; Garcia et al., 2025). This feature makes GenAI technology an effective tool in many fields, including chatbots and content creation. The production of GenAI technology is entirely based on algorithmic processes. For example, after unsupervised language learning and optimization adjustments, GenAI can analyze countless sources according to the given command and create a meaningful and original synthesis. The flexibility and openness to learning at the core of this technology make it powerful not only in content production but also in the interactions it establishes. When properly trained, GenAI, like systems such as ChatGPT developed by OpenAI (2022), becomes a powerful tool that can adapt to an ever-evolving entity through its ability to learn language, forget what it has learned when necessary and relearn (Bozkurt, 2023b). This flexibility enables GenAI technology to adapt, interact more effectively, efficiently and in a human-like manner. As a result, GenAI is effectively used not only in language processing but also in various fields such as education, health, art, engineering, law and marketing (Siau & Wang, 2020). Its ability to quickly adapt to knowledge in different disciplines and be context-specific has made GenAI one of the most transformative technologies of our time.

When evaluating the areas where GenAI technology is used, the multidimensional and interdisciplinary impact of the technology becomes clearer. In the marketing and business sectors, GenAI technology is utilized in numerous applications, ranging from personalized advertising and social media content production to operational process optimization, software development processes, human resources management and the creation of annual reports (Chui et al., 2022). The transformative effects of GenAI technology are also evident in the healthcare and care sector. GenAI technologies based on large language models (LLMs) such as ChatGPT have the potential to offer innovative contributions such as improving patient experience and tele-health services, supporting medical imaging and diagnosis processes, increasing wellness literacy and providing personalized health recommendations (Fui-Hoon Nah et al., 2023; Kung et al., 2023). GenAI also emerges as a content creator through its image-generating, video-generating and music-generating capabilities (Miao & Holmes, 2023; Fui-Hoon Nah et al., 2023). This production capacity opens doors to significant transformations in the education sector. GenAI can be used in planning curricula and course content in education; it can also be integrated into the teaching process as a digital assistant or chatbot. In this context, it offers important contributions such as personalizing learning experiences and increasing participation (Kasneci et al., 2023; Miao & Holmes, 2023). In addition, GenAI technology can analyze learner data to create personalized learning plans. With its interactive structure that provides instant feedback and virtual learning environments, GenAI technology emerges as an effective tool, especially for learners with special educational needs. Personalized and enriched learning experiences enhance the teaching process by emphasizing learners' strengths and enable educational equity, allowing every learner to reach their full potential (Mondal et al., 2023). In this regard, it is possible to say that GenAI technology has an accessible, inclusive and equitable structure.

Generative Artificial Intelligence and Special Education

GenAI technology can make teaching processes in special education more effective, flexible and learner-specific thanks to its abilities to develop customizable and adaptable solutions, produce appropriate materials and content, create learner-focused environments and provide instant, consistent feedback (Karsenti, 2019). As explained, one of the greatest advantages of this technology is its ability to offer solutions that are sensitive to the diverse needs of all learner profiles. Thus, each learner encounters a learning approach that is tailored to them, unique and motivating, which both increases academic achievement and makes the learning process more meaningful and satisfying (Chatterjee & Bhattacharjee, 2020).

In the educational processes of learners with special needs, the nature of their deficiencies necessitates data-driven approaches and continuous monitoring of individual performance, making these elements almost indispensable for an effective educational process. One of the applications where GenAI technology is effectively used in special education to reduce teachers' workload is in these assessment processes (Zhang & Lu, 2021). GenAI technologies do not merely support learning processes. They also provide comprehensive feedback on learner performance through learning analytics and data-driven decision support systems. In this way, the development of learners with special needs can be monitored in real time and necessary interventions can be made (Holmes et al., 2019; Zawacki-Richter et al., 2019).

With the development of GenAI technology, it has become possible to design teaching environments that are sensitive to individual, cultural and linguistic differences. The opportunities offered by this technology are not limited to this, but also play an important role in ensuring accessibility and inclusivity. Individualized support provided for learners with special needs helps minimize visual, auditory or language barriers, enabling equal opportunities and full participation in education (Bozkurt et al., 2024). Additionally, it provides support for practical challenges encountered in daily life and offers a multi-dimensional learning experience for learners with special needs. The increasing use of GenAI technologies in special education highlights the development of applications for learners with Autism Spectrum Disorder (ASD) (Hopcan et al., 2023). The learning needs of learners with ASD are more pronounced and require individualized teaching strategies compared to other disability groups. In this context, the structured content, visual cues, and ability to provide immediate feedback offered by AI-supported systems provide significant advantages in supporting the academic and social development of learners with ASD.

Generative AI and Autism Spectrum Disorder

Why has the role of GenAI technologies become so important in special education, particularly in the education of learners with ASD? The answer to this question lies in a deep understanding of the specific needs of learners with ASD in their learning processes. ASD is defined as a neurodevelopmental disorder characterized by difficulties in social communication and limited, repetitive behavioral patterns (American Psychiatric Association [APA], 2013). This disorder, which manifests itself in different symptoms and varying degrees in each individual, requires individualized, structured, and multidimensional approaches in education. In this context, the education of learners with ASD should be supported by a careful diagnosis process as well as interventions tailored to individual needs. GenAI holds significant potential in addressing these needs. GenAI technology, which is based on big data analysis and algorithms, stands out as a powerful tool for creating personalized learning experiences for learners with ASD, adapting content to the developmental level of learners, and making educational processes more accessible (Al-Hosan & Alrajhi, 2025).

Machine learning and GenAI technologies contribute to the early diagnosis of ASD by identifying its critical symptoms. These technologies are effective in analyzing human-coded behaviors obtained through diagnostic tools and enable the development of clinical diagnostic systems and a more efficient diagnostic process thanks to their ability to create meaning from large data sets (Bone et al., 2015; Shambour et al., 2024). As a result, it is stated that GenAI technology contributes to the economic and sustainable provision of education, health and care services for learners with ASD in the long term. The study conducted by Neeharika and Riyazuddin (2023) aimed to identify and classify the basic ASD symptoms in learners with ASD. The results showed that the multi-layer perceptron (MLP) algorithm achieved 100% accuracy across all datasets despite operating with the fewest number of symptoms. In a study conducted by Yuan et al. (2017), key words selected from learners' responses to questions via a chatbot were analyzed and meanings were derived. The results show that the chatbot used achieved an accuracy rate of 88% in ASD classification when compared to the existing diagnosis. In the study conducted by Bala et al. (2022), different age groups of ASD data were analyzed to propose a machine learning model that can diagnose ASD more accurately, and various feature selection techniques were used for evaluation. As a result, an accuracy of 95% and above was achieved in all data sets. Another area where AI-based applications are used in the diagnosis and evaluation process is neurological assessments that utilize imaging techniques such as electroencephalography (EEG), magnetoencephalography (MEG), magnetic resonance imaging (MRI), and functional magnetic resonance imaging (fMRI). Additionally, GenAI-based face recognition and eye-tracking systems are also utilized in the diagnosis and evaluation of ASD (Bouchouras & Kotis, 2025; Taneera & Alhajj, 2025).

Research findings in the literature indicate that GenAI technologies achieve high accuracy rates in both medical and educational diagnosis and classification of ASD. These high accuracy rates in diagnosis and assessment processes are not limited to this. GenAI technologies are being integrated into educational environments for learners with ASD and are being used effectively.

In a study conducted by Alzakarai et al. (2024), existing classifications were first examined using ML techniques, achieving 94% accuracy. Subsequently, behavioral, verbal, and physical responses were analyzed to prepare individualized instructional interventions for learners, achieving 99% accuracy or higher. In another study, the effectiveness of an AI virtual agent controlled by a human practitioner was examined to improve the social communication skills of 15 learners with ASD aged 4-14 (Porayska-Pomsta et al., 2018). The results of the study showed a significant increase in the rate of social responses given by learners with ASD. Griffen et al. (2024) conducted a study to evaluate the reliability of practitioners in teaching handwashing skills to four learners with ASD through a tablet-based AI application. Following the introduction of the AI application, all therapists achieved the reliability criterion in a short period of time. Although basic effectiveness data were not available, one learner fully acquired the skill, while the other learners showed variable responses. These results indicate that AI applications have a certain level of impact on ensuring application reliability.

In conclusion, the findings in the literature reveal that AI-based applications can be effectively used in the diagnosis, assessment and teaching processes of learners with ASD with high accuracy rates and application reliability. This indicates that these technologies have significant potential in the education of learners with special needs. However, the integration of these technologies into educational environments is not limited to technical success criteria; it also requires a multi-layered assessment in terms of ethical responsibilities, the suitability of decision-making processes to human nature, pedagogical approaches such as empathy and emotional intelligence and the limits of the capacity to provide individualized education. In this context, the role of AI technology in education should be considered not only in terms of its functional contributions but also in terms of how it affects human-centered learning experiences.

In conclusion, the findings in the existing literature reveal that GenAI technologies can be used with high accuracy rates and application effectiveness, especially for learners with ASD. However, these technological advances, along with the new opportunities they offer, lead all segments of society to various ethical and pedagogical questions (Holstein et al., 2019). In particular, the ethical dilemmas experienced in decision-making processes involving human-AI interaction and how they shape the educational processes of learners with ASD are important issues in these discussions. The acquisition of empathy and social skills through GenAI technologies for learners with ASD in line with the "*empathy ability of machines*" and the contribution of technology to personalized education are again controversial and one of the most important limitations. Therefore, it can be argued that AI technologies need to be addressed from a holistic perspective in the context of ethical dilemmas, limitations, and contribution potentials in education.

ARTIFICIAL INTELLIGENCE AND ETHICAL DILEMMAS: TECHNOLOGICAL REVOLUTION OR CRISIS IN THE EDUCATION OF STUDENTS WITH ASD?

Classroom doors are no longer open only to teachers or learners; with the technological revolution, they are now open to different tools. One of these tools is algorithms. AI is redefining the nature of roles, relationships, and responsibilities in education, promising unique opportunities, especially for learners with ASD. However, does this promise herald a revolution or signal new ethical crises? For ASD learners, AI offers unique opportunities in overcoming challenges in social interaction, managing routine and repetitive behaviors, creating learning environments tailored to sensory sensitivities, and providing support adapted to individual learning speeds. Additionally, it is suggested that AI could assist in identifying conditions such as autism, schizophrenia or depression more quickly and accurately by evaluating speech patterns, facial expressions and social interactions (do Rêgo & Araújo-Filho, 2024; Torres et al., 2023; Xiao et al., 2017; Van'T Hof et al., 2021). As important as the potential benefits AI offers in the education of learners with ASD, it is vital to examine the ethical issues it raises in a multifaceted manner to prevent this technological transformation from leading to potential crises and to provide a solid ethical foundation for future academic discussions and policy-making processes.

The learning experiences of individuals with ASD can be enhanced through AI by expanding its individualized, personalized and adaptable features. When considering learners with ASD, a heterogeneous structure emerges where each individual is unique, and this situation brings forth different learning styles for each individual (Cruz Puerto & Sandín Vázquez, 2024; Rabot et al., 2023). AI systems can analyze the strengths, interests and learning styles of learners with ASD and create learning paths specific to them (Adako et al., 2024). Thus, it can be said that the accessibility and participation opportunities of learners with ASD will increase. However, the development of these systems requires continuous data and data analysis processes, which also bring risks such as the violation of learners' privacy, the limits of consent-based use and the infringement of the individual's educational autonomy (Álvarez-Guerrero et al., 2024; McDonald & Forte, 2022). Furthermore, the decision-making deficiencies of learners with ASD (van der Plas et al., 2023) may complicate the process of obtaining informed consent regarding what data these systems should collect and how it should be used (Madden et al., 2017). Respect for individual autonomy should be a fundamental ethical principle in AI applications for learners with ASD. AI systems developed to support the learning processes of learners with ASD should not take away their right to direct their own learning journey. However, an explicit consent mechanism based on the informed consent of the individual—or, when necessary, their family or legal representative—should be established for the collection, processing and use of personal data and learning environments should be designed to enable active participation by the individual. AI-based applications have the potential to harm individuals, even if well-intentioned, when they continuously monitor behavioral and cognitive data without the individual's consent (Karpus et al., 2021; Srinivasan and Sarial-Abi, 2021). Considering the characteristics of learners with ASD, their communication limitations and the problems they experience during their developmental stages (Kodak & Bergmann, 2020), data-driven decision-making processes should be regulated in a way that does not jeopardize the safety of these individuals, even if they are beneficial for them. Additionally, income inequalities and opportunity gaps experienced by individuals with special needs in education should not be overlooked. If these technologies are limited to use by specific institutions or individuals, they risk deepening inequality of opportunity in education. For these reasons, it is recommended that systems for learners with ASD be designed to ensure fair access for all learners by minimizing the potential for harm based on the individual's consent.

The problems that learners with ASD experience in social interaction and communication are characteristics specific to autism (APA, 2013) and they may not be able to demonstrate skills such as understanding social cues, recognizing emotional expressions, and giving appropriate social responses (Cohen et al., 2022). AI has the potential to support these areas of difficulty. In particular, AI-supported virtual environments and social robots can provide a safe and predictable practice space, simulating different social scenarios to help learners with ASD learn how to respond to them (Alabdulkareem et al., 2022; Saleh et al., 2021). Social skills such as making eye contact, waiting in line, or initiating a conversation can be supported through AI-assisted communication applications, images, symbols, or text-based inputs that enable learners to express their thoughts and needs. Such technologies can provide significant support by reducing social anxiety and encouraging participation in the learning process. However, the integration of AI into the education of learners with ASD also brings risks related to data privacy and security. The collection, storage and processing of highly sensitive information such as the learning processes, behavioral responses, communication preferences and even physiological data of learners with ASD through AI systems raise serious concerns about the security and privacy of this data (Ismail & Aloshi, 2025; Rahman et al., 2021). It is of vital importance to protect data related to learners with ASD from unauthorized access, misuse for commercial purposes and to safeguard the learner's privacy. It is imperative to establish a mechanism of full transparency and accountability regarding how AI systems collect, store, process and share this data with third parties (Chalghoumi et al., 2019; Matthews et al., 2010; Rocheleau et al., 2021). Furthermore, it is an ethical requirement that parents and learners are clearly informed about the collection and use of their data and that their consent is obtained freely.

Attention must also be paid to the potential for bias, discrimination, and inequality that AI used in the education of learners with ASD may reveal. AI algorithms can reflect biases present in the data sets they are trained on, which may lead to discrimination or inequality in the education of learners with ASD (Peters, 2022; Verma et al., 2021). The communication style or behaviors of learners with ASD have the potential to be misinterpreted or ignored by AI systems that consider certain communication styles or behaviors to be "normal." Furthermore, socio-economic inequalities in access to AI-supported tools may lead to these technologies benefiting only certain groups (Bakiner, 2023), thereby creating new educational gaps among learners with SLDs. Therefore, it is critical to carefully consider the principles of diversity, inclusivity and fairness in the development and implementation of AI systems, as well as to regularly monitor algorithms and eliminate potential biases.

AI, which offers opportunities for a technological revolution in the education of learners with ASD, may also bring ethical dilemmas. To maximize the potential benefits of this technology and minimize its potential risks, ethical principles such as data privacy, security, transparency, accountability, impartiality and equality must be central. Future research should focus on developing concrete solutions for addressing these ethical issues, while policymakers should work to integrate these solutions into legal and regulatory frameworks. Otherwise, this technological revolution could turn from a window of opportunity for ASD learners into a crisis that exacerbates existing inequalities and leads to ethical violations. Therefore, evaluating the role of AI in education within an ethical framework and keeping the debate alive in this area is vital for the well-being and educational rights of learners with ASD. Ethical concerns and risks of dependency are critical factors that should not be overlooked when integrating AI into the education of learners with ASD. While the compelling opportunities and benefits of technology often overshadow these risks, the unique and sensitive nature of learners with ASD necessitates a thorough and critical examination of ethical issues and dependency risks. In particular, challenges such as protecting learners' personal data, weakening their capacity for independent learning, and potential social isolation call for a more comprehensive and balanced assessment of technology's role in education. Therefore, research and practices focusing explicitly on ethical concerns should be pursued with the same rigor and intensity as those highlighting technological opportunities, as this balance is crucial for ensuring the long-term sustainability of AI integration in education.

DECISION MACHINE: THE BALANCE BETWEEN ARTIFICIAL INTELLIGENCE AND HUMAN INTERACTION IN LEARNERS WITH ASD

The social and ethical dimensions of AI applications' potential role in education, as well as the critical role of the human factor in decision-making processes, should not be overlooked alongside the efficiency and objectivity that may result from their use. The values, experiences and ethical assessments of teachers, educators and policymakers can significantly influence the design, use and outcomes of AI systems. Therefore, when examining the impact of AI on decision-making processes in education, understanding how technology interacts with humans and how this interaction shapes educational outcomes is essential for future applications. This is because the idea that AI systems can improve decision-making processes, enhance the quality of decisions and produce more inclusive outcomes is driving a shift in decision-making processes from human-centered approaches to algorithmic and AI-supported systems (Kasy, 2024; Shrestha et al., 2019). However, although data-driven decision-making processes have the potential to deliver fast and consistent results, they also have a significant disadvantage in that algorithmic systems make decisions based on past data, which may reflect human biases and carry the risk of discrimination (Peters, 2022).

Decision-making in the educational process is not only based on data-driven logical inferences but also informed by multi-layered variables such as the educational context, learner characteristics, and ethical concerns (Shapiro & Stefkovich, 2016). In these processes, teachers are expected to produce decisions that carry pedagogical values through their observations, experiences, and intuitions (Johansson & Kroksmark, 2004; Sipman et al., 2021). With AI-supported systems, it can be assumed that this structure can be incorporated into educational environments in a more rational, consistent, and measurable way. Let us consider an algorithm that we want to use to generate intervention recommendations for learners. This algorithm can analyze learner success, failures and learner data to generate intervention recommendations and provide quick feedback to teachers. This can reduce the cognitive load on teachers and contribute to reducing subjective judgments that may arise with quick feedback. However, it also carries certain risks: completely automating decision-making processes, accepting recommendations without questioning them or bypassing the teacher's pedagogical intuition and contextual assessment. This could lead to a reductionist approach that defines the learner's needs solely based on data. Algorithms can generate generalizations based on past data (Kraemer et al. 2011), but it should be remembered that they may overlook data that is difficult to measure quantitatively, such as the learner's current emotional state, social interactions or dynamics in the learning context.

This can lead to serious pedagogical and ethical issues, especially in situations where the learning process requires sensitivity to individual differences, such as in the case of individuals with special needs. How can AI's powerful data analysis capabilities coexist with human qualities such as ethical judgment, intuition and contextual awareness?

This fundamental question lies at the heart of AI's use in educational settings. Considering that decision-making processes in education should be shaped not only by speed and consistency but also by fairness, care and empathy (Wang, 2019), the answer to this question requires not only a technological but also an ethical and pedagogical inquiry. The focus should not be on AI systems replacing teachers, but rather on using them as a tool to support teachers' decisions, expand their insights and provide individualized support. Otherwise, educational decision-making processes could become algorithmic, disconnected from human experience, reductive and potentially discriminatory. Therefore, the balance between teachers and AI must be established not only on the basis of technological compatibility, but also on ethical responsibility and pedagogical sensitivity. However, it is important not to overlook the significant limitations of using AI systems in educational processes. For instance, in a school in California, an AI-based system designed to analyze learner behaviors and provide recommendations ended up increasing the anxiety levels of some learners with ASD because it failed to consider the emotional and social context. Moreover, the risk of algorithms reproducing biases present in historical data can lead to discriminatory or inaccurate assessments of learners with ASD in educational settings. Therefore, awareness of these potential risks alongside technological opportunities is crucial to maintaining balance in educational practices.

ARTIFICIAL INTELLIGENCE: TEACHER OR ASSISTANT? NEW ROLES IN THE EDUCATION OF STUDENTS WITH ASD

The rise of AI in education, its current uses, and its advancing capabilities herald a period of redefining roles in educational settings. Whether AI will replace teachers or assist them in education has been a frequently discussed topic in recent years (UNESCO, 2018). On one hand, there are systems that automate activities, personalize learning processes, perform educational data mining, and make data-driven decisions; on the other hand, there are classroom environments where human relationships, interactions, and socialization are at the center. In this context, a critical question emerges: Will AI replace teachers, or will it become an indispensable assistant to them?

This dilemma goes beyond general education discussions and becomes even more complex when it comes to the education of learners with special needs. A review of the literature reveals that most studies examining the relationship between special education and AI have been conducted with learners with ASD (Hopcan et al., 2023). This indicates that AI has a special place for learners with ASD. Education for learners with ASD is dynamic and personalized. These learners require a multifaceted approach in areas such as social communication and interaction, behavioral characteristics, and individualized support. Therefore, the role of AI in this specific context must be carefully evaluated.

Today, AI systems are used in educational environments in various forms, such as robots and applications, and are employed to teach various skills. In a study, the effectiveness of AI-supported robots and teacher-provided replicated instruction in teaching conversation skills to learners with ASD was compared (Sağdıç, 2024). The AI-supported robots used in this study interacted with learners without any external intervention, acting as teachers, while a researcher was present in the environment solely to collect data. The findings of the study indicate that both AI-supported robots and teachers were effective in teaching, and that AI-supported robots were more efficient in terms of various variables. Furthermore, when the qualitative data of the study were examined, the participants' mothers stated that their children were more eager towards the robots, found them interesting, and thought that the robots made their children feel more comfortable. Supporting this finding, Pennisi et al. (2016), in their review study covering research published between 2005 and 2015 aimed at examining the use of social robots in the education of learners with ASD, reported that learners with ASD performed better with robots, were more social, and exhibited fewer stereotypical behaviors. Griffen et al. (2024) conducted a study examining the use of an AI-based application developed to assist teachers in teaching handwashing skills to learners with ASD. The application, which assisted teachers in teaching methods during instruction via headphones and tablets, enabled four participating teachers to rapidly increase their application reliability in teaching all steps together, gradually increasing cues, and using teaching methods with increasing waiting times. According to the social validity data obtained in the study, teachers evaluated the application as generally positive, enjoyable, functional, and easier than traditional methods.

As seen, AI can play both substitute and supportive roles in the education of learners with ASD. AI technologies are used in special education primarily for auxiliary purposes such as assessment and diagnosis, supporting learning, and providing individual support (Hopcan et al., 2023). Within this dilemma, AI, which functions in different roles, has advantages as well as risks and disadvantages. The programmable and manipulable nature of AI systems raises questions regarding reliability and ethics. The continuous use of these systems may lead to technology addiction in learners, as well as the risk of reproducing and even reinforcing biases present in the data sets they are fed (Bozkurt, 2023). It should also be remembered that the information provided by AI may not always be accurate, reliable, or ethical. Considering all these limitations, the uncontrolled interaction of AI systems with learners with ASD, who require highly sensitive and individualized support, may pose serious educational and ethical concerns. From this perspective, AI replacing teachers in the education of learners with ASD does not appear to be a realistic scenario. Although AI technologies offer important advantages such as providing personalized content, data-driven feedback, and monitoring learning processes, the outputs they produce must be monitored by humans. Furthermore, teacher-learner interaction in the classroom is a dynamic process that deepens over time, is context-sensitive, and is shaped by the individual characteristics of the learner. The teacher is not merely an actor who possesses educational knowledge, but also a guide who knows, observes, understands, and acts with contextual awareness. These qualities are at the heart of the relationship that develops between the teacher and the learner and are very difficult, if not impossible, for algorithms to replicate. For example, when a learner with ASD exhibits problem behavior in the classroom, the underlying causes of this behavior can vary greatly: a disrupted routine, a search for attention, sensory sensitivities, avoidance of aversive stimuli, or the expectation of a concrete reinforcer. AI systems can only analyze the observed form of such behaviors and cannot interpret the underlying psychological, emotional, or contextual causes. At this point, the teacher's observation skills, intuition based on experience, and knowledge of the learner clearly demonstrate the indispensability of the human factor. Cope et al. (2021) state that human intelligence and AI operate in fundamentally different ways, so even though AI technologies have great transformative potential in education, it is not possible for them to completely replace teachers. In this context, positioning AI systems as a tool that supports teachers rather than giving them full authority in educational processes with ASD learners is a much more balanced and secure approach. Teachers can strengthen their decision-making processes by utilizing the data and analyses provided by AI tools; however, the ultimate responsibility still lies with teachers who have educational and ethical training.

The role of AI as an assistant in the education of learners with ASD offers important opportunities to enrich teachers' educational practices and make individualized instruction more sustainable. First, AI-based systems can support teachers' classroom observations by providing learner tracking, data collection, data interpretation, and recommendations tailored to individual needs. Such systems can free teachers from routine tasks, enabling them to take on more creative roles, while also improving the quality of classroom interactions. For example, interactive AI tools such as robots can be used as communication partners in the classroom, enabling learners with ASD to communicate with lower social anxiety and promoting the development of social skills (Pennisi et al., 2016). Systems that guide teachers can significantly support teachers' professional competence and the quality of the educational process by increasing the reliability of classroom activities and evidence-based practices. This can enable learners with ASD to benefit from higher-quality educational services. In addition, it can prevent teachers from becoming exhausted due to their heavy classroom responsibilities. The ability to produce personalized assignments, activities, and feedback by taking individual differences into account can also be considered among the important advantages of AI (Holmes et al., 2019). However, despite all this potential, excessive reliance on or uncontrolled use of AI carries the risk of technology dependence in the long term for both learners and teachers. Learners' interaction solely with AI-based systems may hinder the natural development of their social interaction skills; teachers' constant reliance on the ready-made data provided by AI may weaken their educational knowledge and decision-making reflexes. Therefore, AI should be used in a balanced, controlled, and ethical manner as a supportive and complementary tool in the education of learners with special needs. In conclusion, AI can be a powerful aid in education; however, it should be structured in a way that enhances rather than replaces the human aspect of learning.

ARTIFICIAL INTELLIGENCE AND AUTISM SPECTRUM DISORDER: THE FINE LINE BETWEEN INDEPENDENCE AND DEPENDENCE

AI, which has become a dilemma in almost every field it is involved in, is important not only in terms of its role in educational environments but also in terms of how often it is used. When it comes to the education of learners with ASD, it is important to evaluate how much and how both teachers and learners with ASD benefit from AI. For both parties, the use of AI opens a window to the independence-dependence debate and necessitates a search for balance.

The transformative effects of AI in education can lead to important developments, particularly in relation to the transition of learners with ASD to independent living. These developments are not limited to the diversification of teaching methods but can also influence the active use of technology in the lives of learners with ASD. In this case, AI represents an important opportunity for the transition to independent living. Independence in the education of learners with ASD is not merely an educational outcome but also the ultimate and long-term goal of the entire education and training process. In this context, daily living skills, vocational skills, self-determination skills, and interpersonal skills are central (Wandry et al., 2013). All adaptations made in educational programs—skill instruction, environmental modifications, individualized teaching strategies, and technology integration—are structured to support this fundamental and common goal. Each intervention is planned with the objective of enabling the individual to acquire independent living skills and sustain these skills in different contexts. Therefore, the path to independence is followed in the educational processes of learners with ASD, and the inclusion of AI technology in this process promises exciting developments. Considering that learners with ASD communicate more comfortably with AI-supported robots and experience less stress (Pennisi et al., 2016), skill instruction can be provided through social simulations. These tools, which model real-life situations, can enable learners with ASD to internalize certain behaviors by repeating them frequently in a safe environment. Teachers can use AI tools to redesign the materials they use in class in a way that is tailored to their learners, create different lesson content, and make lessons more personalized (Holmes et al., 2023). Thanks to the conveniences provided by AI, educational processes can become more effective and efficient (Chen et al., 2023). These positive developments in educational processes are developments that will accelerate the process towards the ultimate goal of independence. On the other hand, learners with ASD can make their lives easier by using AI-supported tools in independent living. AI-supported digital assistants can provide active feedback and guidance to learners with ASD, assisting them in social situations such as taking the bus, asking for help, and shopping. They can also provide personalized assistance with meal planning and balanced nutrition, enabling individuals to lead healthy lives and become self-sufficient. With AI-supported assistants on their phones, learners with ASD can manage their budgets by choosing affordable restaurants when ordering food online. However, the integration of AI into educational processes carries the risk of dependency (Bozkurt, 2023). This risk can arise for both teachers and learners with ASD. In particular, teachers' heavy reliance on AI-based systems for developing teaching materials, designing activities, and conducting assessments may undermine the quality of their instructional decision-making. Teachers' creative, flexible, and individual approaches risk becoming ineffective within the programmed constraints of AI. Similarly, learners with ASD may engage intensively with AI-supported tools—whose predictability and instant feedback are often appealing—and over time, this intensive engagement may evolve into dependency. The highly interactive relationship established with AI tools can prevent individuals from engaging in natural social environments, developing face-to-face communication skills, or coping with uncertainties and disrupted routines. For example, when a learner solves a problem using an AI chat bot, they miss out on the socio-emotional feedback that discussing the same issue with a teacher or peer would provide; this reduces opportunities to practice reading social cues and developing empathy. If learners' use of AI increases to the point that they interact exclusively with these systems, their social communication skills may deteriorate. The quality of interaction between teacher and learner may also weaken (Osetskyi et al., 2020). Because AI systems produce predictable and rapid responses to certain inputs, learners with ASD may come to expect a similar structure in their social life. In contrast, real-life social relationships are often complex, ambiguous, and context-dependent. Faced with this mismatch, a learner with inherently limited social motivation who experiences less uncertainty when interacting with AI may choose to interact with AI systems instead of people. This preference can reduce the social opportunities through which the individual might develop communication skills and may even lead to increasing avoidance of real-world interaction. Moreover, the always-available, "error-free" listener image of AI can dull the learner's natural tolerance for mistakes and flexible problem-solving habits, thereby confining their learning process to a straight line. The controllable and stress-free nature of AI can become a comfort zone for learners with ASD, trapping them in what is already a challenging process—acquiring social and communication skills—and obstructing their attempts to participate in society. Establishing a healthy balance between the opportunities offered by AI and the limitations it may impose is not a choice but a necessity (Karsenti, 2019). The potential of AI in the education and independence of learners with ASD cannot be denied (Sağdıç & Sani-Bozkurt, 2020). However, avoiding the potential side effects of AI's contributions requires a conscious approach and use (Holmes et al., 2019). In this context, how much and for what purpose teachers use AI has become a critical determinant. AI-based tools should not be used as a structure that disables teachers' problem-solving abilities, but rather as supportive systems that take over repetitive, time-consuming, and productive tasks. Thus, teachers can strengthen their capacity to generate new solutions by drawing on these technological opportunities rather than developing dependence on AI tools. The interaction between AI tools and learners with ASD in their education can be tolerable in terms of dependency risks if it takes place in controlled environments. Various tools that will be integrated into the lives of learners with ASD can be designed not only to meet their needs but also to develop them in necessary areas. The presence of AI tools in the lives of learners with ASD as temporary teaching guests rather than permanent assistants may be the key to transitioning from dependence to independence.

Can Artificial Intelligence Capture Empathy? A Turning Point in Human-Machine Interaction in the Education of Learners with OSB

In traditional human-machine interaction, machines were seen as tools that merely processed information and operated under the complete control of humans. However, in today's rapidly evolving, dynamic information systems, machines are no longer just tools that execute users' commands; they have become semi-autonomous actors capable of making spontaneous decisions and taking action on their own. This shift is transforming the relationship between humans and machines from a simple "command-execute" model to a partnership that requires constant adaptation, mutual understanding, and flexible collaboration. In this context, it has become clear that success in human-machine interaction is not limited to technical compatibility but also requires consideration of the emotional and cognitive background of humans. It is believed that a behavior system such as empathy, which is unique to humans and is a precursor to understanding/interpreting others, will enable human-machine relationships to gain a deeper and more effective dimension.

Empathy is defined as the ability of individuals to perceive the emotional and mental states of others, understand these states, and respond emotionally in an appropriate manner (Eisenberg & Eggum, 2009). This process is evaluated within a multidimensional structure consisting of cognitive empathy, emotional empathy, and empathetic concern (Jones et al., 2010). Cognitive empathy is the ability to understand others' beliefs, intentions, and emotions; emotional empathy is the production of direct emotional responses to others' emotions (Decety & Yoder, 2016); and empathic concern is conceptualized as the individual's response of compassion, mercy, and sympathy. It has been stated that empathy experienced by humans emerges from the complex interaction of emotional, cognitive, and motivational processes, and that these processes are not completely independent of each other (Decety & Holvoet, 2021). Empathy involves not only recognizing what another person is feeling, but also sharing that feeling emotionally and developing an attitude toward it. The idea that this multi-layered structure may not be limited to human interactions has sparked recent discussions about whether empathy can be experienced in different contexts. For example, AI, which can mimic empathy at an algorithmic level by processing data such as tone of voice, language-based expressions, and emotional cues, has been included in these discussions as a mechanism aimed at simulating the expression of empathy rather than experiencing it (Niculescu et al., 2013). AI's empathy production is based on interacting with users through social robots and chatbot systems (Bohr & Memarzadeh, 2020). AI's experience of empathy is not about having emotions, but rather the ability to recognize, reflect, and respond to them in context. In other words, it is defined as a computational representation of empathetic behaviors rather than true empathy (Yalçın & DiPaola, 2020).

While empathy is traditionally considered a human emotion and experience, recent advancements in AI applications have been designed to enable machines to exhibit empathetic characteristics. AI's empathetic characteristics mean that a machine or algorithm can recognize users' emotional states, respond appropriately to these states, and provide effective interaction in a social context. These characteristics of AI can be used as a tool to make interaction more efficient and meaningful, especially for learners with special needs. This can enable the improvement of educational processes for learners with ASD. Learners with ASD experience difficulties in social communication and interaction, as well as in understanding emotional meanings and social contexts (White et al., 2007).

For example, they may experience various difficulties in understanding the meaning of emotions in a social context (Baron-Cohen, 1991), recognizing facial expressions (Castelli, 2005), and expressing emotions verbally (Greenberg et al., 2006). These deficiencies can negatively affect the ability to establish social bonds, develop emotional relationships, and manage the process in everyday life (Wong et al., 2014).

The teaching of social-emotional skills is a critical part of the education of learners with ASD (Reichow & Volkmar, 2010). The identification of these skill areas as fundamental and critical limitations for learners with ASD has become the focus of intervention and application. The teaching and/or development of basic social and emotional skills in learners with ASD at an early age has been desired in both intervention and clinical settings as well as educational settings (Watkins et al., 2017). A wide range of applications and programs have been developed and continue to be developed for teaching social and emotional skills across a broad age group, from early intervention to adult education, and from one-on-one instruction to group education (Moody & Laugeson, 2020). However, the increasing integration of technology into all areas of life and its becoming an integral part of everyday life, in other words, the transformation of educational environments, has made this transformation inevitable (Kellner, 2004). We have moved from the traditional teaching process, which involves a teacher and a learner (Brunero et al., 2019), to a speed-focused process in which different actors play roles and the burden of teaching and learning is shared, in other words, the ramps are reduced and the road is widened (Hasan & Nene, 2023). In recent years, social robots (Kouroupa et al., 2022), VR environments (Glaser & Schmidt; 2021), AR applications (Doulah et al., 2023), AI-supported emotion recognition software (Lyu et al., 2024), chatbots, and other elements have been incorporated into the process as new tools for developing the social and emotional skills of learners with ASD.

It is believed that the most important condition for new-generation AI applications to play a role in teaching social-emotional skills to learners with ASD is that they possess empathetic characteristics (Yalçın & Dipaola, 2020). This should be achieved in a way that is consistent with the basic definition of empathy, namely, receiving and understanding the information provided, interpreting emotion-based responses, and providing contextually appropriate responses (Trimmer et al., 2016). In an empathy-based AI application, the aim is not only to recognize cues but also to establish cognitive and emotional partnerships with users to provide a more natural interaction environment (Koegel et al., 2025; Montiel-Vazquez et al., 2022). For example, in their study, Fan et al. (2025) developed a web-based interactive AI system called EmoLand, which aims to teach children about emotions that arise in different social situations through animated stories and multi-stage games. In the application, children with ASD were expected to watch scenarios featuring cartoon-like characters and try to understand what the characters were feeling, while the system monitored the child's responses and provided hints and corrective feedback. In this application, AI analyzes the learner's facial expressions and choices and tries to act like an empathetic digital friend; for example, if the child has difficulty recognizing a sad facial expression, the program can switch to explaining that emotion in the story with a simpler example. Pilot trials have shown that the application is a suitable teaching tool for practitioners working with learners with ASD and effectively helps learners aged 4-7 with ASD learn and apply general knowledge about emotions and facial expressions. However, empathy-based AI systems also raise various philosophical and ethical debates (Budnik, 2025). Turkle (2005) emphasizes that the emotional responses exhibited by artificial systems are simulations and should not be confused with real empathy. Empathy is not merely about producing the correct responses but about establishing an emotional reciprocity with the other person (Montemayor et al., 2022). It is stated that this is something that current artificial systems cannot achieve, as it requires a subjective experience (Yildiz, 2025). Therefore, when an artificial system describes a subjective emotion such as "I am sad," it should be accepted as merely a programmed response. This situation is one of the most important criticisms of empathy-based AI systems, as it could expose users to emotional deception (Kurian, 2023), especially in contexts where emotional support is needed (Cocchiaro et al., 2024). As an example, a group of researchers (Disemadi & Sudirman, 2025) warn that endowing AI systems with human characteristics could lead to trust issues (Budnik, 2025) and warn that OSB could become a testing ground for AI systems that cross ethical boundaries (Nagy, 2024). Therefore, it is important to understand that what is meant by "empathy-based AI" is not "true empathy," but rather systems that mimic or facilitate empathetic behavior.

Looking ahead, AI technologies are expected to become more widespread in the OSB field. When designed correctly, these tools also have the potential to improve the quality of life for both individuals and families (Garcia-Garcia et al., 2021). However, along with these developments, important ethical issues such as privacy (Jobin et al., 2019), equality of access (Waelen, 2022), algorithmic bias, and transparency (Abulkassova et al., 2025) must also be addressed (Machado et al., 2025). Additionally, the impact of overreliance on AI systems (Kotsi et al., 2025) on human-human interactions should be examined.

Finally, perhaps the healthiest future scenario is for AI to be used as a tool that supports and complements human interaction rather than replacing it. In this way, the benefits of technology can be balanced with human values (Sigfrids et al., 2023). In recent years, empathy-based AI applications have been incorporated into the research field aimed at supporting the social-emotional development of learners with

ASD (Koegel et al., 2025; Fan et al., 2025). However, while leveraging the rapid development of AI, it is essential to adopt a careful, critical, and inclusive approach from both conceptual and technical perspectives, demonstrating ethical sensitivity and maintaining a balanced understanding of both sides of the coin.

ARTIFICIAL INTELLIGENCE-SUPPORTED PERSONALIZED EDUCATION: A TRULY 'PERFECT' SOLUTION FOR EVERY LEARNER WITH ASD?

The wide variety of interests, needs, and abilities of learners with ASD makes it necessary to personalize educational processes and goals.

The importance of individualization in education is increasingly emphasized for individuals with ASD to reach their full potential and develop independent living skills. In this context, the use of technology facilitates the educational processes of learners with special needs and expands opportunities for individualization by increasing learning options (Robinson & Sebba, 2010). Historically, technology has played a supportive role in special education through functions such as record keeping, archiving, test scoring, and performance prediction (Flanagan, 1968). However, the rise of AI technologies today signals a qualitative leap in individualization processes in education. AI capabilities such as big data analysis, adaptive learning systems, and personalized content production promise to support the educational experiences of learners with ASD in ways that were previously unimaginable (Moreno-Guerrero et al., 2020; Smutny & Schreiberova, 2020). This transformation raises the question, "Can AI really offer a 'perfect' solution for every learner with ASD?" This study seeks to answer this fundamental question by examining the potential and limitations of AI-supported individualization applications.

Personalized learning systems (Adaptive learning systems) (Xie et al. 2019), which are individualized learning platforms that adapt to the learning styles, preferences, and strategies, such as personalized learning systems (Adaptive learning systems) (Xie et al., 2019), intelligent tutoring systems (intelligent tutoring system) (Hasanov et al., 2019; Psotka et al., 1988), which are AI-supported modeling systems for human teachers, and recommendation systems (Syed et al., 2017) that can develop suggestions tailored to areas of interest and ability, as well as AI-based systems and even affective computing (Pei et al., 2024), which can perceive and understand emotions and respond accordingly.

Personalized learning systems can provide a search service that offers high-quality learning content to meet the individual educational needs of learners with ASD. This search service can be used by learners with ASD themselves, as well as by families and teachers to make decisions in the educational process. In addition, these systems can facilitate the discovery of the most appropriate learning paths for learners with ASD based on their preferences and interests, as well as access to the most effective learning resources during the learning process. Furthermore, these systems can play a facilitating role in the process of employing learners with ASD in a specific job or profession by facilitating the individualization of education related to the necessary skills for the job or profession and by serving as an evaluation tool throughout all these processes. In a study conducted by Habib et al. (2021), it was stated that teachers in the IEP team used personalized learning systems the most while benefiting from AI support, and they were largely satisfied with these systems. Therefore, the use of personalized learning systems can play a facilitating role in the entire process of preparing, implementing, and evaluating IEPs for learners with ASD, as well as helping to produce higher quality outcomes compared to processes carried out using traditional methods.

AI tools can play a facilitating role in the preparation of IEPs, which are at the center of the individualization of the educational processes of learners with ASD, and in the improvement of existing IEPs. One of the benefits of AI tools in the individualization of the educational processes of learners with ASD is that they enable teachers and families to monitor the process by automating the development and progress of learners (Chaudhry & Kazim, 2022). The process of individualizing the educational lives of learners with ASD requires teamwork and the collaboration of this team around the IEP. Therefore, teamwork is also extremely important for the individualization of educational life to yield positive results. AI tools can play an effective role in producing useful results in improving teamwork and collaboration processes in the individualization of educational life for learners with ASD. For example, the participation of an AI tool in the role of a virtual assistant in team meetings can enable the instant sharing of intensive and high-volume data with all stakeholders, thereby directly influencing the decisions taken in the individualization of the educational processes of learners with ASD in a positive direction. In addition, this system can track data related to the routines, behavioral problems, and learning processes of learners with ASD and continuously and instantly share the data obtained with stakeholders in the team, thereby helping to track the positive or negative outcomes of individualized education within the process and, when necessary, make changes to discover the most effective ways of individualization. Furthermore, considering that learners with ASD face various challenges when transitioning to higher levels or post-school life, AI-supported systems can also be utilized to individualize these processes. Systems such as Personal Assistant for Life-Long Learning (PAL3), developed by Swartout et al. (2016) to facilitate the transition of learners to higher-level environments requiring more complex and new skills, may be adapted to personalize the transition processes of learners with ASD.

With the increasing use of AI-supported systems in the individualization of the educational experiences of learners with ASD, a paradigm shift from a teacher-centered traditional approach to a more individualized learner-centered approach is likely to occur. However, while this paradigm shift may bring about numerous positive effects in the educational lives of learners with ASD, it is important to consider that various challenges may also arise. While the goal is for learners with ASD to transition to independent living, there is a possibility that they may develop a dependency on AI-supported applications in situations where there is no human interaction. This situation may also negatively affect the social and communication skills of learners with ASD. To prevent this, teachers and families must view AI as an "aid and support" and plan accordingly. Another sensitive issue to consider when using AI in the individualization of the educational experiences of learners with ASD is the sharing of personal data. In order for AI systems to play a supportive role in making personalized decisions, they may need to have access to certain information about the individual, such as their performance, personal characteristics, preferences, health status, and even their emotional state. Therefore, the type of personal data to be shared with AI systems is a matter of great importance. At this point, teachers, families, school administrators, and, where possible, learners with ASD should consult with each other to decide what type of data to use and what kind of results the use of such data may produce. In addition, policymakers need to implement legal regulations regarding the management of personal data to be shared with AI-supported systems used to personalize the educational experiences of learners with ASD. This will help remove ethical dilemmas that may arise in decision-making regarding the educational processes of learners with ASD and encourage stakeholders to be more willing and confident in using these systems.This can eliminate the ethical dilemma that prevents stakeholders from making decisions about the educational processes of learners with ASD and make them more willing and confident to use these systems. In cases where teachers' knowledge and skill requirements regarding the use of AI tools in the individualization of the educational experiences of ASD learners are not met, it may not be possible to effectively utilize the almost unlimited potential of AI systems (Alsudairy & Eltantawy, 2024), and it should not be forgotten that this use may inadvertently lead to negative outcomes. To prevent this situation, in-service training on the functional use of AI in the process of individualizing education can be provided to teachers in the IEP team. In developed countries such as the US and China, large-scale investments have been made in AI infrastructure to date. However, infrastructure investments in these systems are not yet at the desired level in developing countries. Considering the inadequacies in AI infrastructure in educational environments (Sayari, 2025), even if teachers' knowledge and skills regarding AI tools that can be used to individualize the educational experiences of learners with ASD improve, the desired benefits may not be achieved without the necessary infrastructure and financial support to utilize these tools. To prevent this situation, it is important for policymakers to provide all schools with a specific budget and infrastructure services. In conclusion, AI-supported systems can play a very important role in individualizing the educational experiences of learners with ASD. However, considering that these support systems have negative risks as well as positive features, educators and school administrators need to take steps to eliminate risks and maximize the desired benefits when planning these processes.

CONCLUSION

While AI and technology-supported tools have the potential to bring about a major transformation in education, the importance of this transformation is increasing day by day, especially for learners with ASD. Traditional educational methods are often insufficient for learners with ASD; at this point, innovative tools such as AI, emotional intelligence technologies, and social robots offer more sensitive and adaptable solutions to individual needs. Emotional and empathetic AI systems, in particular, hold promising potential for supporting social communication, emotional awareness, and interaction skills in learners with ASD.

Even as I write these lines, educational technologies are rapidly evolving, and the transformation process is undergoing continuous evolution. This dynamic progress offers unique opportunities for educators, researchers, and learners, while also bringing new challenges. The future of education is being redefined in line with new paradigms shaped by this constant change, paving the way for more flexible, personalized, and responsive educational models that go beyond traditional approaches. In the future, AI-supported learning environments are expected to respond much more quickly and effectively to individual differences, and decision-making mechanisms are expected to become more fair and inclusive based on human-machine collaboration.

However, the use of these technologies in education should not be viewed solely as a technical issue. AI's role in education must be structured in light of ethical, pedagogical, and human-centered principles. In particular, emotional and empathetic AI systems developed for learners with ASD should not only improve their academic performance but also support their social and emotional development. However, the excessive use of these technologies also carries the risk of overshadowing learners' independence and human-human interactions. Therefore, human-machine interaction must be designed in a balanced and responsible manner; technology should be positioned as a complementary tool to the guidance provided by teachers and families.

For successful AI integration in education, a strong decision-making mechanism must be established. Transparent communication should be established between teachers, learners, and families, and the limitations and potential impacts of AI systems should be well understood. In addition, personalized approaches should be adopted, taking into account the individual needs, developmental level, and social-emotional profile of the learner in the use of technology.

In conclusion, while AI and emotional intelligence technologies offer great opportunities for learners with ASD, these opportunities must be evaluated with an ethical, balanced, and human-centered approach. The role of technology in education should be redefined as a tool that supports individual development and social participation, rather than merely a means of information transfer. Only in this way can AI-supported education models help learners with ASD realize their potential and contribute to the construction of a more inclusive, responsive, and equitable education system.

REFERENCES

Abulkassova, D., Muldasheva, G., & Nurtazin, M.. (2025). The phenomenon of artificial intelligence in modern transformational socio-cultural processes: Socio-philosophical analysis. *AI & Society*. Advance online publication. DOI: 10.1007/s00146-025-02195-z

Adako, O. P., Adeusi, O. C., & Alaba, P. A. (2024). Revolutionizing autism education: Harnessing aı for tailored skill development in social, emotional, and ındependent learning domains. *Journal of Computational and Cognitive Engineering*, *3*(4), 348–359. DOI: 10.47852/bonviewJCCE42023414

Alabdulkareem, A., Alhakbani, N., & Al-Nafjan, A. (2022). A systematic review of research on robot-assisted therapy for children with autism. *Sensors (Basel)*, *22*(3), 944. DOI: 10.3390/s22030944

Al-Hosan, A. M., & Alrajhi, N. A. (2025). Applications of Artificial Intelligence and Smart Learning Methods for Children with Autism Spectrum Disorder: A Proposed Interactive Platform. *Journal of Ecohumanism*, *4*(2), 738–756. DOI: 10.62754/joe.v4i2.6345

Alsudairy, N. A., & Eltantawy, M. M. (2024). Special Education Teachers' Perceptions of Using Artificial Intelligence in Educating Students with Disabilities. *Journal of Intellectual Disability-Diagnosis and Treatment*, *12*(2), 92–102. DOI: 10.6000/2292-2598.2024.12.02.5

Âlvarez-Guerrero, G., Fry, D., Lu, M., & Gaitis, K. K. (2024). Online child sexual exploitation and abuse of children and adolescents with disabilities: A systematic review. *Disabilities*, *4*(2), 264–276. DOI: 10.3390/disabilities4020017

American Psychiatric Association. (2013). *Diagnostic and statistical manual of mental disorders* (5th ed.). American Psychiatric Publishing.

Bakiner, O. (2023). What do academics say about artificial intelligence ethics? An overview of the scholarship. *AI and Ethics*, *3*(2), 513–525. DOI: 10.1007/s43681-022-00182-4

Bala, M., Ali, M. H., Satu, M. S., Hasan, K. F., & Moni, M. A. (2022). Efficient Machine Learning Models for Early Stage Detection of Autism Spectrum Disorder. *Algorithms*, *15*(5), 166. DOI: 10.3390/a15050166

Baron-Cohen, S. (1991). Do people with autism understand what causes emotion? *Child Development*, *62*(2), 385–395. DOI: 10.1111/j.1467-8624.1991.tb01539.x

Bohr, A., & Memarzadeh, K. (2020). The rise of artificial intelligence in healthcare applications. In Bohr, A., & Memarzadeh, K. (Eds.), *Artificial intelligence in healthcare* (pp. 25–60). Academic Press., DOI: 10.1016/B978-0-12-818438-7.00002-2

Bone, D., Goodwin, M. S., Black, M. P., Lee, C. C., Audhkhasi, K., & Narayanan, S. (2015). Applying machine learning to facilitate autism diagnostics: Pitfalls and promises. *Journal of Autism and Developmental Disorders, 45*, 1121–1136. DOI: 10.1007/s10803-014-2268-6

Borg, J., Lindström, A., & Larsson, S. (2009). Assistive technology in developing countries: National and international responsibilities to implement the Convention on the Rights of Persons with Disabilities. *Lancet, 374*(9704), 1863–1865. DOI: 10.1016/S0140-6736(09)61872-9

Bouchouras, G., & Kotis, K. (2025). Integrating Artificial Intelligence, Internet of Things, and Sensor-Based Technologies: A Systematic Review of Methodologies in Autism Spectrum Disorder Detection. *Algorithms, 18*(1), 34. DOI: 10.3390/a18010034

Bozkurt, A. (2023). ChatGPT, üretken yapay zeka ve algoritmik paradigma değişikliği. *Alanyazın, 4*(1), 63–72. DOI: 10.59320/alanyazin.1283282

Bozkurt, A. (2023). Generative artificial intelligence (AI) powered conversational educational agents: The inevitable paradigm shift. *Asian Journal of Distance Education, 18*(1). https://www.asianjde.com/ojs/index.php/AsianJDE/article/view/718

Bozkurt, A., Xiao, J., Farrow, R., Bai, J. Y. H., Nerantzi, C., Moore, S., Dron, J., Stracke, C. M., Singh, L., Crompton, H., Koutropoulos, A., Terentev, E., Pazurek, A., Nichols, M., Sidorkin, A. M., Costello, E., Watson, S., Mulligan, D., Honeychurch, S., & Asino, T. I. (2024). The Manifesto for Teaching and Learning in a Time of Generative AI: A Critical Collective Stance to Better Navigate the Future. *Open Praxis, 16*(4), 487–513. DOI: 10.55982/openpraxis.16.4.777

Brunero, F., Venerosi, A., Chiarotti, F., & Arduino, G. M. (2019). Are touch screen technologies more effective than traditional educational methods in children with autism spectrum disorders? A pilot study. *Annali dell'Istituto Superiore di Sanita, 55*(2), 151–160. https://annali.iss.it/index.php/anna/article/view/797

Budnik, C. (2025). Can we trust artificial intelligence? *Philosophy & Technology, 38*(10). Advance online publication. DOI: 10.1007/s13347-024-00820-1

Castelli, F. (2005). Understanding emotions from standardized facial expressions in autism and normal development. *Autism, 9*(4), 428–449. DOI: 10.1177/136236130505608

Chalghoumi, H., Cobigo, V., Dignard, C., Gauthier-Beaupré, A., Jutai, J. W., Lachapelle, Y., & Perrin, M. (2019). Information privacy for technology users with intellectual and developmental disabilities: Why does it matter? *Ethics & Behavior*, *29*(3), 201–217. DOI: 10.1080/10508422.2017.1393340

Chatterjee, S., & Bhattacharjee, K. K. (2020). Adoption of artificial intelligence in higher education: A quantitative analysis using structural equation modelling. *Education and Information Technologies*, *25*, 3443–3463. DOI: 10.1007/s10639-020-10159-7

Chaudhry, M., & Kazim, E. (2022). Artificial Intelligence in Education (Aied) a high-level academic and industry note 2021. *AI and Ethics*, *2*(1), 157–165. DOI: 10.1007/s43681-021-00074-z

Chen, Y., Jensen, S., Albert, L. J., Gupta, S., & Lee, T. (2023). Artificial intelligence (AI) student assistants in the classroom: Designing chatbots to support student success. *Information Systems Frontiers*, *25*(1), 161–182. DOI: 10.1007/s10796-022-10291-4

Chui, M., Roberts, R., & Yee, L. (2022, December 20). Generative AI is Here: How Tools Like ChatGpt Could Change Your Business. Quantum Black AI by McKinsey. https://www.mckinsey.com/capabilities/quantumblack/our-insights/generative-ai-is-here-how-tools-like-chatgpt-could-change-your-business#/

Cocchiaro, M. Z., Morley, J., Novelli, C., Panai, E., Tartaro, A., & Floridi, L. (2024). Who is an AI Ethicist? An empirical study of expertise, skills, and profiles to build a competency framework. *AI and Ethics*, 1–13. DOI: 10.1007/s43681-024-00643-y

Cohen, S., Koegel, R., Koegel, L. K., Engstrom, E., Young, K., & Quach, A. (2022). Using self-management and visual cues to improve responses to nonverbal social cues in adults with autism spectrum disorder. *Behavior Modification*, *46*(3), 529–552. DOI: 10.1177/0145445520982558

Cope, B., Kalantzis, M., & Searsmith, D. (2021). Artificial intelligence for education: Knowledge and its assessment in AI-enabled learning ecologies. *Educational Philosophy and Theory*, *53*(12), 1229–1245. DOI: 10.1080/00131857.2020.1728732

Cruz Puerto, M., & Sandín Vázquez, M. (2024). Understanding heterogeneity within autism spectrum disorder: A scoping review. *Advances in Autism*, *10*(4), 314–322. DOI: 10.1108/AIA-12-2023-0072

Decety, J., & Holvoet, C. (2021). The emergence of empathy: A developmental neuroscience perspective. *Developmental Review*, *62*, 100999. Advance online publication. DOI: 10.1016/j.dr.2021.100999

Decety, J., & Yoder, K. J. (2016). Empathy and motivation for justice: Cognitive empathy and concern, but not emotional empathy, predict sensitivity to injustice for others. *Social Neuroscience*, *11*(1), 1–14. DOI: 10.1080/17470919.2015.1029593

do Rêgo, A. C. M., & Araújo-Filho, I. (2024). Leveraging artificial ıntelligence to enhance the quality of life for patients with autism spectrum disorder: A comprehensive review. *European Journal of Clinical Medicine*, *5*(5), 28–38. DOI: 10.24018/clinicmed.2024.5.5.350

Disemadi, H. S., & Sudirman, L. (2025). Reassessing legal recognition of AI: Human dignity and the challenge of AI as a legal subject in Indonesia. *Masalah-Masalah Hukum*, *54*(1), 1–12. DOI: 10.14710/mmh.54.1.2025.1-12

Doulah, A. B. M. S. U., Rasheduzzaman, M., Arnob, F. A., Sarker, F., Roy, N., Ullah, M. A., & Mamun, K. A. (2023). Application of augmented reality interventions for children with autism spectrum disorder (ASD): A systematic review. *Computers*, *12*(10), 215. DOI: 10.3390/computers12100215

Dwivedi, Y. K., Kshetri, N., Hughes, L., Slade, E. L., Jeyaraj, A., Kar, A. K., Baabdullah, A. M., Koohang, A., Raghavan, V., Ahuja, M., Albanna, H., Albashrawi, M. A., Al-Busaidi, A. S., Balakrishnan, J., Barlette, Y., Basu, S., Bose, I., Brooks, L., Buhalis, D., & Wright, R. (2023). "So what if ChatGPT wrote it?" Multidisciplinary perspectives on opportunities, challenges and implications of generative conversational AI for research, practice and policy. *International Journal of Information Management*, *71*, 102642. DOI: 10.1016/j.ijinfomgt.2023.102642

Education for All Handicapped Children Act Of 1975, Pub. L. No. 94-142 (1975)

Eisenberg, N., & Eggum, N. D. (2009). Empathic responding: Sympathy and personal distress. In Decety, J., & Ickes, W. (Eds.), *The social neuroscience of empathy* (pp. 71–83). Boston Review., DOI: 10.7551/mitpress/9780262012973.003.0007

Fan, M., Jin, S., Fan, J., Guo, W., & Chen, X. (2025). EmoLand: Utilizing narrative animations, multilevel games, and affective computing to foster emotional development in children with autism spectrum disorder. *International Journal of Human-Computer Studies*, *199*, 103486. DOI: 10.1016/j.ijhcs.2025.103486

Fui-Hoon Nah, F., Zheng, R., Cai, J., Siau, K., & Chen, L. (2023). Generative AI and ChatGPT: Applications, challenges, and AI-human collaboration. *Journal of Information Technology Case and Application Research*, *25*(3), 277–304. DOI: 10.1080/15228053.2023.2233814

Flanagan, J. C. (1968). Individualizing Education. Retrieved from_https://eric.ed.gov/?id=ED040566

Fu, B., Hadid, A., & Damer, N. (2025). Generative AI in the context of assistive technologies: Trends, limitations and future directions. *Image and Vision Computing, 154*, 105347.

Garcia, M. B., Rosak-Szyrocka, J., & Bozkurt, A. (2025). *Pitfalls of AI Integration in Education: Skill Obsolescence, Misuse, and Bias*. IGI Global., DOI: 10.4018/979-8-3373-0122-8

Garcia-Garcia, J. M., Penichet, V. M. R., & Lozano, M. D.. (2022). Using emotion recognition technologies to teach children with autism spectrum disorder how to identify and express emotions. *Universal Access in the Information Society, 21*, 809–825. DOI: 10.1007/s10209-021-00818-y

Glaser, N., & Schmidt, M. (2021). Systematic literature review of virtual reality intervention design patterns for individuals with autism spectrum disorders. *International Journal of Human-Computer Interaction, 38*(8), 753–788. DOI: 10.1080/10447318.2021.1970433

Greenberg, J. S., Seltzer, M. M., Hong, J., & Orsmond, G. I. (2006). Bidirectional effects of expressed emotion and behavior problems and symptoms in adolescents and adults with autism. *American Journal of Mental Retardation, 111*(4), 229–249. DOI: 10.1352/0895-8017(2006)111[229:BEOEEA]2.0.CO;2

Griffen, B., Lorah, E. R., Caldwell, N., Hantula, D. A., Nosek, J., Tincani, M., & Lemley, S. (2024). The effects of artificial intelligence on implementors' fidelity of instructional strategies during handwashing acquisition in children with autism. *Journal of Developmental and Physical Disabilities, 36*(5), 793–819. DOI: 10.1007/s10882-023-09937-1

Habib, H., Jelani, S. A. K., & Rasheed, N. T. (2021). Tailored Education: AI in the Development of Individualized Education Programs (IEPs). *Multidisciplinary Science Journal, 1*(01), 8–18.

Hasan, N., & Nene, M. J. (2023). Determinants of technological interventions for children with autism: A systematic review. *Journal of Educational Computing Research, 62*(1), 30–69. DOI: 10.1177/07356331231200701

Hasanov, A., Laine, T. H., & Chung, T. S. (2019). A survey of adaptive context-aware learning environments. *Journal of Ambient Intelligence and Smart Environments, 11*(5), 403–428. DOI: 10.3233/AIS-190534

Holmes, W., Bialik, M., & Fadel, C. (2019). *Artificial Intelligence in Education: Promises and Implications for Teaching and Learning*. Center for Curriculum Redesign.

Holmes, W., Bialik, M., & Fadel, C. (2023). *Artificial intelligence in education.* Globethics Publications., DOI: 10.58863/20.500.12424/4276068

Holmes, W., Persson, J., Chounta, I.-A., Wasson, B., & Dimitrova, V. (2022). *Artificial intelligence and education: A critical view through the lens of human rights, democracy, and the rule of law*. Council of Europe. https://rm.coe.int/artificial-intelligence-andeducation-a-critical-view-through-the-lens/1680a886bd

Holstein, K., McLaren, B. M., & Aleven, V. (2019). Co-Designing a Real-Time Classroom Orchestration Tool to Support Teacher–AI Complementarity. *Journal of Learning Analytics*, *6*(2), 27–52. DOI: 10.18608/jla.2019.62.3

Hopcan, S., Polat, E., Ozturk, M. E., & Ozturk, L. (2023). Artificial intelligence in special education: A systematic review. *Interactive Learning Environments*, *31*(10), 7335–7353. DOI: 10.1080/10494820.2022.2067186

Individuals With Disabilities Education Improvement Act of 2004, 118, Stat. 2647et seq., § 1401 (2004)

International Organization for Standardization. (2016). ISO 9999:2016 Assistive products for persons with disability – Classification and terminology. https://www.iso.org/standard/60547.html

Ismail, I. A., & Aloshi, J. M. (2025). Data privacy in AI-driven education. In Tariq, M. U. (Ed.), *AI applications and strategies in teacher education* (pp. 223–252). IGI Global., DOI: 10.4018/979-8-3693-5443-8.ch008

Jobin, A., Ienca, M., & Vayena, E. (2019). The global landscape of AI ethics guidelines. *Nature Machine Intelligence*, *1*(9), 389–399. DOI: 10.1038/s42256-019-0088-2

Johansson, T., & Kroksmark, T. (2004). Teachers' intuition-in-action: How teachers experience action. *Reflective Practice*, *5*(3), 357–381. DOI: 10.1080/1462394042000270673

Jones, A. P., Happé, F. G., Gilbert, F., Burnett, S., & Viding, E. (2010). Feeling, caring, knowing: Different types of empathy deficit in boys with psychopathic tendencies and autism spectrum disorder. *Journal of Child Psychology and Psychiatry, and Allied Disciplines*, *51*(11), 1188–1197. DOI: 10.1111/j.1469-7610.2010.02280.x

Karpus, J., Krüger, A., Verba, J. T., Bahrami, B., & Deroy, O. (2021). Algorithm exploitation: Humans are keen to exploit benevolent AI. *iScience*, *24*(6), 102679. DOI: 10.1016/j.isci.2021.102679

Karsenti, T. (2019). Artificial intelligence in education: The urgent need to prepare teachers for tomorrow's schools. *Formation et Profession*, *27*(1), 112–116. DOI: 10.18162/fp.2019.a167

Kasneci, E., Seßler, K., Küchemann, S., Bannert, M., Dementieva, D., Fischer, F., & Kasneci, G. (2023). ChatGPT for good? On opportunities and challenges of large language models for education. *Learning and Individual Differences*, *103*, 102274. DOI: 10.1016/j.lindif.2023.102274

Kasy, M. (2024). Algorithmic bias and racial inequality: A critical review. *Oxford Review of Economic Policy*, *40*(3), 530–546. DOI: 10.1093/oxrep/grae031

Kodak, T., & Bergmann, S. (2020). Autism spectrum disorder: Characteristics, associated behaviors, and early intervention. *Pediatric Clinics of North America*, *67*(3), 525–535. DOI: 10.1016/j.pcl.2020.02.007

Kellner, D. (2004). Technological transformation, multiple literacies, and the re-visioning of education. *E-Learning and Digital Media*, *1*(1), 9–37. DOI: 10.2304/elea.2004.1.1.8

Koegel, L. K., Ponder, E., Bruzzese, T., Wang, M., Semnani, S. J., Chi, N., Koegel, B. L., Lin, T. Y., Swarnakar, A., & Lam, M. S. (2025). Using artificial intelligence to improve empathetic statements in autistic adolescents and adults: A randomized clinical trial. *Journal of Autism and Developmental Disorders*. Advance online publication. DOI: 10.1007/s10803-025-06734-x

Kouroupa, A., Laws, K. R., Irvine, K., Mengoni, S. E., Baird, A., & Sharma, S. (2022). The use of social robots with children and young people on the autism spectrum: A systematic review and meta-analysis. *PLoS One*, *17*(6), e0269800. DOI: 10.1371/journal.pone.0269800

Kotsi, S., Handrinou, S., Iatraki, G., & Soulis, S.-G. (2025). A review of artificial intelligence interventions for students with autism spectrum disorder. *Disabilities*, *5*(1), 7. DOI: 10.3390/disabilities5010007

Kraemer, F., Van Overveld, K., & Peterson, M. (2011). Is there an ethics of algorithms? *Ethics and Information Technology*, *13*, 251–260. DOI: 10.1007/s10676-010-9233-7

Kung, T. H., Cheatham, M., Medenilla, A., Sillos, C., De Leon, L., Elepaño, C., Madriaga, M., Aggabao, R., Diaz-Candido, G., Maningo, J., & Tseng, V. (2023). Performance of ChatGPT on USMLE: Potential for AI-assisted medical education using large language models. *PLOS Digital Health*, *2*(2), 1–12. DOI: 10.1371/journal.pdig.0000198

Kurian, N. (2023). AI's empathy gap: The risks of conversational artificial intelligence for young children's well-being and key ethical considerations for early childhood education and care. *Contemporary Issues in Early Childhood*, *26*(1), 132–139. DOI: 10.1177/14639491231206004

Luckin, R., Holmes, W., Griffiths, M., & Forcier, L. B. (2016). *Intelligence Unleashed: An Argument for AI in Education*. Pearson Education.

Lyu, Y., Liu, D., An, P., Tong, X., Zhang, H. U. A. N., Katsuragawa, K. E. I. K. O., & Zhao, J. I. A. N. (2024). EMooly: Supporting autistic children in collaborative social-emotional learning with caregiver participation through interactive AI-infused and AR activities. *Proceedings of the ACM on Interactive, Mobile, Wearable and Ubiquitous Technologies*, *8*(4), 1–36. DOI: 10.1145/3699738

Machado, H., Silva, S., & Neiva, L. (2025). Publics' views on ethical challenges of artificial intelligence: A scoping review. *AI and Ethics*, *5*, 139–167. DOI: 10.1007/s43681-023-00387-1

Madden, M., Gilman, M., Levy, K., & Marwick, A. (2017). Privacy, poverty, and big data: A matrix of vulnerabilities for poor Americans. *Washington University Law Review, 95*(1), 53–125. Retrieved from: https://openscholarship.wustl.edu/law_lawreview/vol95/iss1/6

Matthews, J. T., Beach, S. R., Downs, J., de Bruin, W. B., & Mecca, L. P., & Schulz. (2010). Preferences and concerns for quality of life technology among older adults and persons with disabilities: National survey results. *Technology and Disability*, *22*(1-2), 5–15. DOI: 10.3233/TAD-2010-0279

McCarthy, J., Minsky, M., Rochester, N., & Shannon, C. (1955). A proposal for Dartmouth Summer Research Project on artificial Intelligence. http://wwwformal.stanford.edu/jmc/history/dartmouth.pdf

McDonald, N., & Forte, A. (2022). Privacy and vulnerable populations. In Knijnenburg, B. P., Page, X., Wisniewski, P., Lipford, H. R., Proferes, N., & Romano, J. (Eds.), *Modern sociotechnical perspectives on privacy* (pp. 337–363). Springer.

Miao, F., & Holmes, W. (2023). Guidance for generative AI in education and research. *UNESCO*. https://unesdoc.unesco.org/ark:/48223/pf0000386693

Mondal, S., Das, S., & Vrana, V. G. (2023). How to bell the cat? A theoretical review of generative artificial intelligence towards digital disruption in all walks of life. *Technologies*, *11*(2), 44. DOI: 10.3390/technologies11020044

Montemayor, C., Halpern, J., & Fairweather, A. (2022). In principle obstacles for empathic AI: Why we can't replace human empathy in healthcare. *AI & Society*, *37*, 1353–1359. DOI: 10.1007/s00146-021-01230-z

Montiel-Vázquez, E. C., Ramírez Uresti, J. A., & Loyola-González, O. (2022). An explainable artificial intelligence approach for detecting empathy in textual communication. *Applied Sciences (Basel, Switzerland)*, *12*(19), 9407. DOI: 10.3390/app12199407

Moody, C. T., & Laugeson, E. A. (2020). Social skills training in autism spectrum disorder across the lifespan. *Child and Adolescent Psychiatric Clinics of North America*, *29*(2), 359–371. DOI: 10.1016/j.chc.2019.11.001

Moreno-Guerrero, A. J., López-Belmonte, J., Marín-Marín, J. A., & Soler-Costa, R. (2020). Scientific development of educational artificial intelligence in Web of Science. *Future Internet*, *12*(8), 124. DOI: 10.3390/fi12080124

Nagy, J. (2024). Autism and the making of emotion AI: Disability as resource for surveillance capitalism. *New Media & Society*, *26*(7), 3989–4007. DOI: 10.1177/14614448221109550

Neeharika, C. H., & Riyazuddin, Y. M. (2023). Developing an Artificial Intelligence Based Model for Autism Spectrum Disorder Detection in Children. *Journal of Advanced Research in Applied Sciences and Engineering Technology*, *32*(1), 57–72. DOI: 10.37934/araset.32.1.5772

Niculescu, A., van Dijk, B., Nijholt, A., Li, H., & See, S. L. (2013). Making social robots more attractive: The effects of voice pitch, humor and empathy. *International Journal of Social Robotics*, *5*(2), 171–191. DOI: 10.1007/s12369-012-0171-x

Open, A. I. (2022). ChatGPT: Optimizing language models for dialogue. https://openai.com/blog/chatgpt/

Osetskyi, V., Vitrenko, A., Tatomyr, I., Bilan, S., & Hirnyk, Y. (2020). Artificial intelligence application in education: Financial implications and prospects. *Financial and Credit Activity: Problems of Theory and Practice*, *2*(33), 574–584. DOI: 10.18371/fcaptp.v2i33.207246

Pei, G., Li, H., Lu, Y., Wang, Y., Hua, S., & Li, T. (2024). Affective computing: Recent advances, challenges, and future trends. *Intelligent Computing, 3*, 0076. https://doi.org/DOI: 10.34133/icomputing.0076

Pennisi, P., Tonacci, A., Tartarisco, G., Billeci, L., Ruta, L., Gangemi, S., & Pioggia, G. (2016). Autism and social robotics: A systematic review. *Autism Research*, *9*(2), 165–183. DOI: 10.1002/aur.1527

Peters, U. (2022). Algorithmic political bias in artificial intelligence systems. *Philosophy & Technology*, *35*(2), 1–25. DOI: 10.1007/s13347-022-00512-8

Porayska-Pomsta, K., Alcorn, A. M., Avramides, K., Beale, S., Bernardini, S., Foster, M. E., & Smith, T. J. (2018). Blending human and artificial intelligence to support autistic children's social communication skills. [TOCHI]. *ACM Transactions on Computer-Human Interaction*, *25*(6), 1–35. DOI: 10.1145/3271484

Psotka, J., Massey, L. D., & Mutter, S. A. (Eds.). (1988). *Intelligent tutoring systems: Lessons learned.* Psychology Press.

Rabot, J., Rødgaard, E. M., Joober, R., Dumas, G., Bzdok, D., Bernhardt, B., & Mottron, L. (2023). Genesis, modelling and methodological remedies to autism heterogeneity. *Neuroscience and Biobehavioral Reviews*, *150*(105201), 1–12. DOI: 10.1016/j.neubiorev.2023.105201

Rahman, M. M., Muniyandi, R. C., Sahran, S., & Mohamed, S. (2021). Enhancement of an optimized key for database sanitization to ensure the security and privacy of an autism dataset. *Symmetry*, *13*(10), 1912. DOI: 10.3390/sym13101912

Reichow, B., & Volkmar, F. R. (2010). Social skills interventions for individuals with autism: Evaluation for evidence-based practices within a best evidence synthesis framework. *Journal of Autism and Developmental Disorders*, *40*, 149–166. DOI: 10.1007/s10803-009-0842-0

Robinson, C., & Sebba, J. (2010). Personalising learning through the use of technology. *Computers & Education*, *54*(3), 767–775. DOI: 10.1016/j.compedu.2009.09.021

Rocheleau, J. N., Chalghoumi, H., Jutai, J., Farrell, S., Lachapelle, Y., & Cobigo, V. (2021). Caregivers' role in cybersecurity for aging ınformation technology users with ıntellectual disabilities. *Cyberpsychology, Behavior, and Social Networking*, *24*(9), 624–629. DOI: 10.1089/cyber.2020.0572

Russell, S. (2016). Rationality and intelligence: A brief update. Fundamental issues of artificial intelligence, 7-28. https://doi.org/DOI: 10.1007/978-3-319-26485-1_2

Russell, S., & Norvig, P. (2021). *Artificial intelligence: a modern approach* (3rd ed.). Prentice Hall.

Sağdıç, Z. A. (2024). *Otizm spektrum bozukluğu olan çocuklara sohbet becerisinin öğretiminde robot ve öğretmen tarafından sunulan replikli öğretimin karşılaştırılması: Karma yöntem araştırması* (Doktora tezi, Anadolu Üniversitesi). Yükseköğretim Kurulu Ulusal Tez Merkezi._https://tez.yok.gov.tr/UlusalTezMerkezi/TezGoster?key=1pwTzRXnomYf6jwqVORfUYQ94Yy6MwKdJm0-jNX3Zi15QFgKnhi3qENh1eN74F_A

Sağdıç, Z. A., & Sani-bozkurt, S. (2020). Otizm spektrum bozukluğu ve yapay zekâ uygulamaları. *Açıköğretim Uygulamaları ve Araştırmaları Dergisi*, *6*(3), 92–111.

Saleh, M. A., Hanapiah, F. A., & Hashim, H. (2021). Robot applications for autism: A comprehensive review. *Disability and Rehabilitation. Assistive Technology*, *16*(6), 580–602. DOI: 10.1080/17483107.2019.1685016

Sani-Bozkurt, S. (2017). Özel eğitimde dijital destek: Yardımcı teknolojiler. *Açıköğretim Uygulamaları ve Araştırmaları Dergisi*, *3*(2), 37–60.

Sayari, K. T. (2025). Infrastructure and Investment Needs for AI Implementation in Education. In *Teachers' Roles and Perspectives on AI Integration in Schools* (pp. 141–162). IGI Global Scientific Publishing.

Shambour, Q., Qandeel, N., Alrabanah, Y., Abumariam, A., & Shambour, M. (2024). Artificial Intelligence Techniques for Early Autism Detection in Toddlers: A Comparative Analysis. *Journal of Applied Data Sciences*, *5*(4), 1754–1764. DOI: 10.47738/jads.v5i4.353

Shapiro, J. P., & Stefkovich, J. A. (2016). *Ethical leadership and decision making in education: Applying theoretical perspectives to complex dilemmas*. Routledge., DOI: 10.4324/9781315773339

Shrestha, Y. R., Ben-Menahem, S. M., & Von Krogh, G. (2019). Organizational decision-making structures in the age of artificial intelligence. *California Management Review*, *61*(4), 66–83. DOI: 10.1177/0008125619862257

Siau, K., & Wang, W. (2020). Artificial intelligence (AI) ethics: Ethics of AI and ethical AI. *Journal of Database Management*, *31*(2), 74–87. DOI: 10.4018/JDM.2020040105

Sigfrids, A., Leikas, J., Salo-Pöntinen, H., & Koskimies, E. (2023). Human-centricity in AI governance: A systemic approach. *Frontiers in Artificial Intelligence*, *6*, 976887. DOI: 10.3389/frai.2023.976887

Sipman, G., Martens, R., Thölke, J., & McKenney, S. (2021). Professional development focused on intuition can enhance teacher pedagogical tact. *Teaching and Teacher Education*, *106*, 103442. DOI: 10.1016/j.tate.2021.103442

Smutny, P., & Schreiberova, P. (2020). Chatbots for learning: A review of educational chatbots for the Facebook Messenger. *Computers & Education*, *151*, 103862. DOI: 10.1016/j.compedu.2020.103862

Song, D. Y., Kim, S. Y., Bong, G., Kim, J. M., & Yoo, H. J. (2019). The use of artificial intelligence in screening and diagnosis of autism spectrum disorder: A literature review. *Soa-Ch'ongsonyon Chongsin Uihak = Journal of Child & Adolescent Psychiatry*, *30*(4), 145. DOI: 10.5765/jkacap.190027

Srinivasan, R., & Sarial-Abi, G. (2021). When algorithms fail: Consumers' responses to brand harm crises caused by algorithm errors. *Journal of Marketing*, *85*(5), 74–91. DOI: 10.1177/0022242921997082

Swartout, W. R., Nye, B. D., Hartholt, A., Reilly, A., Graesser, A. C., VanLehn, K., & Rosenberg, M. (2016). Designing a Personal Assistant for Life-Long Learning (PAL3). *Proceedings of the Twenty-Ninth International Florida Artificial Intelligence Research Society Conference 2016* (pp. 491-496). AAAI Press.

Syed, T. A., Palade, V., Iqbal, R., & Nair, S. S. K. (2017). A Personalized Learning Recommendation System Architecture for Learning Management System. In KDIR (pp. 275-282).

Şen, N., & Akbay, T. (2023). Artificial intelligence and innovative applications in special education. *Instructional technology and lifelong learning, 4*(2), 176-199. https://doi.org/DOI: 10.52911/itall.1297978

Taneera, S., & Alhajj, R. (2025). Diagnosis of autism spectrum disorder: A systematic review of clinical and artificial intelligence methods. *Network Modeling and Analysis in Health Informatics and Bioinformatics*, *14*(1), 1–23. DOI: 10.1007/s13721-024-00499-6

Torres, J. M. M., Medina-DeVilliers, S., Clarkson, T., Lerner, M. D., & Riccardi, G. (2023). Evaluation of interpretability for deep learning algorithms in EEG emotion recognition: A case study in autism. *Artificial Intelligence in Medicine*, *143*(102545), 1–14. DOI: 10.1016/j.artmed.2023.102545

Trimmer, E., McDonald, S., & Rushby, J. A. (2016). Not knowing what I feel: Emotional empathy in autism spectrum disorders. *Autism*, *21*(4), 450–457. DOI: 10.1177/1362361316648520

Turkle, S. (2005). *The second self: Computers and the human spirit*. Boston Review.

UNESCO. (2018). *ICT competency framework for teachers: Version 3*. United Nations Educational, Scientific and Cultural Organization. https://unesdoc.unesco.org/ark:/48223/pf0000265721

Waelen, R. (2022). Why AI ethics is a critical theory. *Philosophy & Technology*, *35*(2), 9. DOI: 10.1007/s13347-022-00507-5

Wandry, D., Wehmeyer, M. L., & Glor-Scheib, S. J. (2013). *Life centered education: The teacher's guide*. Council for Exceptional Children.

Wang, Y. (2019). Is data-driven decision making at odds with moral decision making? a critical review of school leaders' decision making in the era of school accountability. *Values and Ethics in Educational Administration, 14*(2), 1–9.

Watkins, L., Kuhn, M., Ledbetter-Cho, K., Gevarter, C., & O'Reilly, M. (2017). Evidence-Based Social Communication Interventions for Children with Autism Spectrum Disorder. *Indian Journal of Pediatrics, 84*(1), 68–75. DOI: 10.1007/s12098-015-1938-5

White, S., Keonig, K., & Scahill, L. (2007). Social skills development in children with autism spectrum disorders: A review of the intervention research. *Journal of Autism and Developmental Disorders, 37*(10), 1858–1868. DOI: 10.1007/s10803-006-0320-x

Wong, H. S., Huertas-Ceballos, A., Cowan, F. M., & Modi, N.Medicines for Neonates Investigator Group. (2014). Evaluation of early childhood social-communication difficulties in children born preterm using the quantitative checklist for autism in toddlers. *The Journal of Pediatrics, 164*(1), 26–33.e1. DOI: 10.1016/j.jpeds.2013.07.013

Xiao, X., Fang, H., Wu, J., Xiao, C., Xiao, T., Qian, L., & Ke, X. (2017). Diagnostic model generated by MRI-derived brain features in toddlers with autism spectrum disorder. *Autism Research, 10*(4), 620–630. DOI: 10.1002/aur.1711

Xie, H., Chu, H. C., Hwang, G. J., & Wang, C. C. (2019). Trends and development in technology-enhanced adaptive/personalized learning: A systematic review of journal publications from 2007 to 2017. *Computers & Education, 140*, 103599. DOI: 10.1016/j.compedu.2019.103599

van der Plas, E., Mason, D., & Happé, F. (2023). Decision-making in autism: A narrative review. *Autism, 27*(6), 1532–1546. DOI: 10.1177/13623613221148010

Van'T Hof, M., Tisseur, C., van Berckelear-Onnes, I., Van Nieuwenhuyzen, A., Daniels, A. M., Deen, M., ... & Ester, W. A. (2021). Age at autism spectrum disorder diagnosis: A systematic review and meta-analysis from 2012 to 2019. *Autism, 25*(4), 862–873. DOI: 10.1177/1362361320971107

Verma, S., Ernst, M., & Just, R. (2021). Removing biased data to improve fairness and accuracy. *arXiv*. https://arxiv.org/abs/2102.03054

Yalçın, Ö. N., & DiPaola, S. (2020). Modeling empathy: Building a link between affective and cognitive processes. *Artificial Intelligence Review, 53*, 2983–3006. DOI: 10.1007/s10462-019-09753-0

Yıldız, T. (2025). The minds we make: A philosophical inquiry into theory of mind and artificial intelligence. *Integrative Psychological & Behavioral Science*, *59*(1), 10. DOI: 10.1007/s12124-024-09876-2

Yuan, J., Holtz, C., Smith, T., & Luo, J. (2017). Autism spectrum disorder detection from semi-structured and unstructured medical data. *Journal of Bioinformatics and Systems Biology : Open Access*, *1*(3), 2–9. DOI: 10.1186/s13637-017-0057-1

Zawacki-Richter, O., Marín, V. I., Bond, M., & Gouverneur, F. (2019). Systematic review of research on artificial intelligence applications in higher education – where are the educators? *International Journal of Educational Technology in Higher Education*, *16*(1), 1–27. DOI: 10.1186/s41239-019-0171-0

Zhang, C., & Lu, Y. (2021). Study on artificial intelligence: The state of the art and future prospects. *Journal of Industrial Information Integration*, *23*, 100224. DOI: 10.1016/j.jii.2021.100224

KEY TERMS AND DEFINITIONS

Assistive Technologies: Assistive technology is any equipment, tool, or software that supports learners with disabilities in terms of physical, mental, sensory, or communication needs.

Autism Spectrum Disorder: Autism spectrum disorder (ASD) is a neurodevelopmental difference that causes individuals to have difficulties with social communication and interaction, limited interests, and repetitive behaviors.

Artificial Intelligence: Artificial intelligence (AI) is an interdisciplinary field of technology that aims to replicate cognitive functions typically associated with human intelligence—such as learning, reasoning, decision-making, and problem-solving—through computer systems.

Empathy: The process of perceiving and understanding the emotional and mental states of others and responding to them with appropriate emotional responses; it is a skill evaluated within a multidimensional structure such as cognitive empathy, emotional empathy, and empathetic concern.

Generative Artificial Intelligence: Generative artificial intelligence refers to artificial intelligence systems that can produce original and meaningful content such as text, images, audio, video, and software code based on given data or inputs.

Human-Machine Interaction: Human-Machine Interaction is the study and design of interactive systems that enable effective communication and collaboration between humans and technological devices, with a focus on usability, accessibility, and user experience.

Individualized Education Program: An education program that is legally required to be prepared in accordance with the needs of learners with ASD, with the aim of facilitating their transition to independent living by maximizing their performance.

Special Education: Special education is planned educational services provided to learners with special needs using methods, tools, and environments appropriate to their needs so that they can develop their potential to the highest level.

Chapter 7
Generative AI for Computer-Assisted Language Learning

Maida Maqsood
Shenzhen University, China

Manal Aqil
https://orcid.org/0000-0003-4901-2048
University of Management and Technology, Sialkot, Pakistan

Bimol Chandra Das
https://orcid.org/0009-0007-8388-8883
Trine University, USA

Munir Ahmad
https://orcid.org/0000-0003-4836-6151
Survey of Pakistan, Pakistan

ABSTRACT

This chapter investigated the transformative role of generative AI in Computer-Assisted Language Learning (CALL), highlighting its capacity to create personalized content, simulate authentic conversational practice, and provide real-time, context-sensitive feedback. As traditional CALL systems often lack adaptability and dynamic interaction, generative AI emerges as a powerful solution that addresses diverse learner needs and enhances engagement through adaptive and culturally responsive materials. The chapter offers a comprehensive analysis of how generative AI is being applied in language education, examining its benefits, such as increased accessibility and instructional efficiency, as well as challenges, including ethical concerns and data privacy.

DOI: 10.4018/979-8-3373-7574-8.ch007

INTRODUCTION

Generative AI is drawing attention since it could support language learning. Generative AI tools used in Computer-Assisted Language Learning (CALL) programs can design individual learning materials, role-play conversations, and immediately provide feedback (Shadiev et al., 2023; Zawacki-Richter et al., 2019). As a result, learners work with many different materials and are more engaged in the learning process.

People need language learning solutions that work better, support bigger groups, and can be adapted to each learner. Traditional CALL systems have frequently faced problems with unchanging information, being inflexible to different user needs, and offering little help in the moment (Chapelle, 2001; Levy & Stockwell, 2013). Generative AI handles such issues by making content flexible so it can adjust based on learners' skills, what interests them, and their backgrounds (Jian, 2023). Learners can use the program to communicate in their language as they would in normal situations, something typical online lessons do not guarantee.

Generative AI can bring a major change to language learning because of its ability to transform teaching methods (Bozkurt et al., 2024; Chapelle, 2025; Z. Weng & Fu, 2025; Yeh, 2025). Teachers can focus on more important tasks, such as automating exercises, assessments, and language-based tasks, and the results for students are better, too. In addition, the technology helps close the gap, since learners who speak various languages and have unique cultural backgrounds can now benefit from specialized instruction. Therefore, generative AI is a major asset for helping people worldwide learn new languages.

The goal of this chapter is to examine how generative AI fits into CALL. It will discuss the different applications of generative models that make language materials easy to interact with, highlight issues that need attention, and recommend how to use AI in language education in the right way. The main goal is to give educators and technologists useful insights and examples to use in their activities.

The chapter opens with a review of the situation in CALL as well as the history of AI technologies. It also looks closely at various ways generative AI can be used, showing the major benefits. The chapter next examines the most important challenges and ethical concerns that occur when using generative AI in education. In the end, it gives suggestions for future research focusing on the opportunity AI has in language learning.

COMPUTER-ASSISTED LANGUAGE LEARNING (CALL) AND AI EVOLUTION

Computer-Assisted Language Learning has improved greatly, moving from simple programs to advanced platforms that use many tools, interactive content, and ways for students to interact online. At the beginning of CALL, the focus was on software that helped students learn grammar, vocabulary, and basic language skills through lots of practice exercises. In the 1960s and 1970s, PLATO used computers to help people practice languages, even though this system only offered simple fill-in-the-blank and multiple-choice tasks (Beatty, 2013; Yamaguchi & Levy, 1999). Over time, CALL systems started to offer new and exciting functions. The development of CD-ROMs and, later, the Internet created a major change in society. These programs used audio, video, and simulations to engage the user while learning. Systems of teaching now include more communication-based activities so learners can read, write, listen, and speak while working together (Chapelle, 2001; Marandi, 2024; Mohsen et al., 2024; Shadiev & Yu, 2024).

Online learning platforms and digital technology have changed CALL for the better. Duolingo and Babbel make use of gamification and intelligent algorithms to give learners a personal way to learn languages. By using data, the systems were able to offer exercises suited to each user's abilities and ensure that certain progress was monitored (Loewen et al., 2020). As a result, teaching began to shift towards methods that made students involved, which improved both engagement and results (Godwin-Jones, 2014).

AI is now changing the way language learning is carried out in CALL (Feng, 2025; Lee et al., 2023; X. Weng & Chiu, 2023). At first, AI was used for simple NLP, mainly for correcting grammar and doing automatic translations. Similarly, the first grammar checkers found only basic errors to fix and usually didn't offer much advice to users (Warschauer & Healey, 1998). Even though automated tools were revolutionary, they struggled when it came to context and reliability, giving us translations that could sound awkward or misleading (Garcia, 2010).

Machine learning and deep learning have led to major changes in AI used in CALL. GPT-4 and similar models have made language generation and understanding much more efficient (Chukharev et al., 2024; Zawacki-Richter et al., 2019). Because of these models, students can experience personalized learning by interacting with tailored passages and dialogues specifically chosen for what they need and what interests them (Jian, 2023). For example, OpenAI's ChatGPT can be used to let students engage in conversations and receive instant corrections to their language skills. With these programs, students get to use language in livelier ways, like those they often meet in everyday situations. Furthermore, programs such as Grammarly and Hemingway Editor now provide writing support with expert grammar checks as well as tips for making your writing more effective and easier to read. Table 1 shows the evolution of CALL.

Table 1. Evolution of CALL

Era	Key Technologies	Features	Examples
Early CALL	Basic software-based drills	Repetitive exercises, grammar drills	PLATO, early drill-and-practice programs
Multimedia CALL	CD-ROMs, early internet platforms	Interactive exercises, multimedia integration	Rosetta Stone, Pimsleur
Modern CALL	Online platforms, adaptive learning	Gamification, personalized learning, integration of speaking, listening, reading, and writing skills	Duolingo, Babbel, Memrise
AI-Enhanced CALL	Generative AI models	Adaptive content generation, interactive feedback, conversational practice	GPT-4, Grammarly, Duolingo's chatbot

These systems use AI to adjust to each person's learning methods, making personalization more accessible. Apps such as Memrise measure what students are good at and what they need more practice with, and then adjust the learning activities accordingly (Jian, 2023; Tafazoli et al., 2019). FluentU and similar sites also use AI to select videos that fit the learner's abilities and interests, better immersing them in the language. Because of these improvements, CALL tools are now easier to use, faster to respond, and thoughtful about different learning contexts. Advances in AI will allow CALL systems to support learning with more engagement, greater effectiveness, and personalized features.

APPLICATIONS OF GENERATIVE AI IN LANGUAGE LEARNING

Generative AI is changing Computer-Assisted Language Learning by replacing many tasks that teachers once needed to do laboriously by hand. This section explores three major uses of generative AI in language learning: content generation, conversational agents, and real-time feedback systems, all of which support a more effective and personal experience. Figure 1 summarizes the applications of generative AI.

Content Generation

The use of NLP and ML in GPT-4, Gemini, and Claude has boosted how language learning materials are created. These models observe how learners interact to make changes to the content, keeping it useful, interesting, and suitable for each pupil

(Ahmad et al., 2025; Zawacki-Richter et al., 2019). Every time the learner advances, AI-generated materials update themselves to give the learner tailored activities, sections to read, and questions to respond to (Riedl, 2019). By being flexible, one can better understand, remember, and be motivated with learning a language.

Customized Language Exercises

Tools with AI can provide language exercises that fit each learner's abilities and troubles. So, a beginner faced with basic conjugation may work on easy exercises with everyday verbs; at the same time, an intermediate learner would practice irregular verbs or various tenses. More advanced people who are learning may start to work with difficult sentence structures, phrasal verbs, or common idioms. The platform Birdbrain, part of Duolingo, constantly adapts exercises based on a user's success. Likewise, LanguageTool and Grammarly give exercises that improve grammar and vocabulary based on the user's knowledge level. CALL systems can help students retain more information, up to 50% more than what traditional methods achieve.

Adaptive Reading Passages

Customized passages from Generative AI support the learner's understanding of reading materials by matching their likes, background, and language capabilities. For example, a learner new to travel might explore stories about airports or hotels, and an intermediate learner fascinated with history could be given easier articles about historical events. Those who have advanced can access and read real news reports, short stories, or excerpts from academic books. ReadTheory and Newsela use intelligent technology to provide text that matches each user's level and related questions to check that person's comprehension (Shaik et al., 2024). At the same time, LingQ offers reading materials that match a person's level of vocabulary, so they see words they recognize and also learn new ones. Students improve motivation and easier comprehension when they read materials, they find interesting, suggesting that it is important for language learning to make content personalized.

Dynamic Writing Prompts

These prompts provide training for students of all abilities, as they work on their grammar and style. A new learner might be prompted to describe their daily habits, whereas someone more advanced can try to write about their recent trip to someone they know. Around this stage, abilities are refined by asking students to write argumentative essays, write business emails, or work on making up stories. Generating context-appropriate prompts, Writesonic and Jasper AI consider each learner's competence. Besides, since ChatGPT guides students in real time on structure, grammar, and easy-to-understand expressions, learners can improve gradually (Rebolledo & González, 2023). Data shows that learners using automated writing evaluation (AWE) tools develop their writing skills twice as fast as learners using less automated instruction. As a result, AI greatly improves your confidence in and skill with writing.

Anyone can now learn a new language using generative AI, as it makes creating content interactive and at scale. Learners receive materials adapted to their skills, interests, and targets due to adaptive exercises, reading, and writing activities provided by AI. When these technologies improve, adaptive learning pathways will become even better, making foreign language education more convenient, interactive, and easier to access (Riedl, 2019). AI in language learning improves learning for everyone, allowing teachers to use data to match pupils' needs, shifting the methods used in language education worldwide.

Conversational Agents

For learners, chatbots are important because they provide practice in a realistic and relaxed way. Learners can use these agents to speak, listen, and improve their understanding without feeling pressured during real talks (W. Huang et al., 2022). Because AI chatbots are always available, they are perfect for anybody unable to talk with native partners or language tutors. Research has shown that using conversational AI regularly makes people speak more naturally, identify sounds correctly, and feel confident (Zhang et al., 2023), illustrating they work well as complementary learning tools.

Interactive Language Practice

They provide learners with lively dialogues that feel a lot like how people communicate in real life. For example, Duolingo's chat gives people opportunities to use the language for normal activities such as ordering, asking about directions, or making travel arrangements (Almelhes, 2023). Based on how much the learner understands, the chatbot replies in ways that are appropriate for them. Being adaptable means learners keep facing new challenges, without feeling too much stress. Furthermore, tools such as ChatGPT and Google's Gemini mean learners can have unlimited conversations and get familiar with common expressions and phrases all in a safe space. Studies have found that practicing with interactive AI raises someone's conversational skills more than if they just use passive methods for learning (Kessler, 2018).

Contextual Adaptation

Beacuase to AI chatbots, people who learn a language can access regional dialects, various accents, and real-life language use. For example, a learner learning Spanish could talk with a chatbot that uses Castilian Spanish (from Spain) and Latin American Spanish, making them notice important differences between the two dialects. The same goes for Replika and Mondly, which help users experience common situations and use the language in fitting environments (Dizon, 2020). Students become used to the way language is used in different cultural situations, something needed when dealing with people in real life. According to (Xiao, 2014) using context-aware chatbots makes people able to communicate appropriately in various environments.

Real-Time Feedback and Corrections

A major benefit of AI conversational agents is the speed at which they can correct your mistakes. Should a learner make a mistake with grammar, freeze over a pronunciation, or phrase their idea badly, the chatbot will detect it, explain the proper usage, and recommend other options. For instance, Elsa Speak provides pronunciation advice, looks at how a person speaks, and suggests helpful exercises to make their speaking clearer. Much like that, Grammarly also works with spoken language, correcting writing errors as someone types or messages. There is greater learning gain since the loop reinforces doing things correctly and avoids permanent mistakes. Data suggests that students respond to AI prompts faster than to traditional teaching (Heift & Schulze, 2007).

AI technology is helping people learn languages by providing them with personal, interactive, and elastic ways to practice speaking. By practicing dialogues, adjusting the learning content, and learning while they speak, these tools give students the chance to be fluent, confident, and to understand cultures, which is much harder to do with old learning methods. Based on improvements in NLP and speech recognition, it is anticipated that chatbots will soon offer levels of interaction resembling those of a human. Teachers and students can benefit from using conversational AI as it makes learning languages simpler, closer, and remarkably effective for the modern age.

Real-Time Feedback Systems

Generative AI has drastically improved how learners get detailed, flexible, and individual feedback on how they perform with language. Traditional teaching techniques simply concentrate on error correction. However, AI-driven systems review grammar, style, pronunciation, fluency, and coherence, providing information that aids in learning the language more effectively (Heift & Schulze, 2007). Because of NLP and ML, such systems can give on-the-spot, adjustable feedback that benefits both individuals and educators. According to (Zhang et al., 2023) students who get immediate feedback from AI can improve more than students waiting for corrections from teachers.

Grammar Enhancement Tools

Today's AI writing assistants are far more powerful than just checking spelling and now act as expert language trainers. Now, due to Grammarly and Hemingway Editor, writers can have their text carefully checked for structure, word choice, and overall clarity and tone (X. Huang et al., 2023). Such tools can spot small issues that human teachers may not notice, including too much passive voice, wrongly changing tenses, or an inappropriate style for different situations. As a result, learners of a new language can receive tips that guide them to talk more naturally in that language. A truly beneficial system describes the rationale for the rule, details the areas where revision is needed, and suggests various ways to fix the problems, encouraging learners to get an understanding of why the rule is there (Koltovskaia, 2023).

Pronunciation Training Through AI

The use of speech analysis tools driven by AI makes it possible for learners to get detailed information about their spoken language, something never before seen in pronunciation training (Vančová, 2023). With the help of powerful algorithms, Elsa Speak and Speechling compare a user's speech to native speakers to detect the smallest differences in pronunciation of vowels, consonants, stress patterns, and intonation (Mahdi & Khateeb, 2019). They offer you visual information on both sound waves and mouth movements, along with workouts to help you overcome difficulties. For things that aren't part of the student's native tongue, technology is especially useful, helping to detect and solve any little mistakes in pronunciation that a teacher might miss in a classroom. Work on pronunciation tools has shown excellent progress for regular users, who can improve their accent and how others understand them by around half within only a few months.

Coherent and Contextual Language Skills

Recent AI feedback tools now help students improve their advanced language abilities, which used to be difficult to teach with technology alone. Both ScribeSense and Cohesive assess the overall structure and connection between the points in written work. When it comes to speaking, AI assesses whether people use suitable language for different occasions and teaches what appropriate speech is for every situation. They assist most in academic writing by revealing arguments that are not strong enough, insufficient evidence, or unclear thesis statements. In a business setting, AI feedback offers learners hints on changing their language to suit a variety of cultural backgrounds (Xiao, 2014).

Figure 1. Applications of Generative AI in Language Learning

Content Generation	Conversational Agents	Real-Time Feedback Systems
Customized Language Exercises Adaptive Reading Passages Dynamic Writing Prompts	Interactive Language Practice Contextual Adaptation Real-Time Feedback and Corrections	Grammar Enhancement Tools Pronunciation Training Coherent and Contextual Language Skills

Now, AI feedback systems are adding multiple ways of delivering feedback, such as written, spoken, and visual information, into the learning process. There could be updates such as even better analysis of cultures, coaching during live chats, and learning paths that change themselves based on individual progress. Due to these advancements, people who want to learn a language can now get the same personalized instruction formerly given only to private tutoring clients. Though AI feedback systems do not take the place of human teachers, they can seriously improve how language education is delivered today. Adding these technologies to how we teach languages in schools and self-study programs has greatly improved our way of teaching different populations worldwide.

Leaning on these applications, generative AI is helping CALL be more open to change, engaging, and tailored to each learner. Because of improvements in technology, we can expect these tools to play an even larger role in language learning, giving learners more tools to improve.

CHALLENGES AND ETHICAL CONSIDERATIONS

Despite the great potential of generative AI in language learning, it raises several problems that need proper consideration (Al-kfairy et al., 2024; Chu et al., 2024; Farina et al., 2024; Golda et al., 2024; Maqsood et al., 2025). This section presents a review of data privacy, bias, and fairness, and the potential for over-reliance on AI. Table 2 shows the overview of the challenges and ethical considerations.

Data Privacy

By introducing generative AI into language education, learning platforms now offer individualized and more effective ways for learning. Yet, because of all this technology, it is very important to take into account issues related to data privacy. AI systems operate better with plenty of user information, for example, voice recordings, pieces of writing, and learning habits. Taking care of people's data, the right way, is required by law and is important to keep users loyal to digital learning opportunities. Many people shy away from adopting educational technology because they are concerned about privacy, as they do not want to share personal information with learning apps. It shows why having strong privacy policies is important for AI language learning tools.

Data Protection Measures

Nowadays, language learning platforms use different protective systems to secure users' information. Encrypting important data in transit and storage keeps it safe, plus anonymizing the data used in machine learning helps to keep identities secret. For example, Duolingo and similar platforms use advanced approaches to divide a person's identity from their learning data. Frequent security audits and tests find possible problems before anyone can make use of them. Since language data contains sensitive information about users' skills and experiences, it is important to have these measures. Websites with solid data protection have fewer privacy issues and achieve better results in keeping users.

Transparent Data Practices and User Control

A growing number of language learning platforms are making sure users can manage their information because of transparent approaches. Clear, written-in-plain-language privacy policies are crucial. Users on Babbel can pick the information they want to share in the platform's interactive privacy settings. Detailed dashboards are available on many platforms so users can easily view, save, or delete their data. A number of modern systems allow people to follow how their data helps the model to work more efficiently. They ensure regulations are met and build trust, which helps keep students involved in learning over the long run. Moreover, greater user controls can improve the completion rate for language courses.

Compliance with Privacy Regulations

All language learning platforms now need to follow international privacy policies to function effectively globally. When it comes to data, the GDPR is particularly strict in its rules for the EU (Labadie & Legner, 2023). All GDPR compliant platforms must give young users a way to prove their age, let users transfer their data, and provide clear mechanisms for consent. In the United States, extra rules set by COPPA affect services aimed at children under 13. Top language apps now have appointed privacy officers and regularly check their systems to stay compliant with updates in these standards. GDPR-friendly platforms are less likely to be hit by data breaches and report higher levels of user trust. Given that global privacy rules are expanding, it will remain a significant challenge for AI-based language learning providers to stay compliant.

Shortly, AI development in language learning is expected to favor privacy protections. Federated learning, which helps train algorithms on many devices without combining their raw data, is particularly useful for protecting privacy and still personalizing services. Using differential privacy, researchers now add noise to datasets to stop users from being recognized during the training process. Some companies are trying to use blockchain technology to let people control and verify their educational records permanently. The innovations introduced try to resolve the problem of privacy and personalization. With improvements in AI, the task is still to maintain this balance to keep giving people worthwhile and enjoyable ways to learn languages. Platforms that overcome these barriers are likely to be the examples other companies will use in the coming decade.

Bias and Fairness

Such models used in language learning applications are trained using information that, often, is affected by the same biases found in their source sets. In AI-generated content, such biases might spread stereotypes, falsely depict various cultures, or exclude non-standard ways of speaking (Bolukbasi et al., 2016). It is not only right to ensure fair AI systems, but these systems must also be fair to help everyone learn effectively. Such biased decisions made through AI can harm students' confidence and help continue existing negative standards in society (Crawford, 2017). Making AI more a part of education means we should confront these biases to prevent unfairness and ensure equality in learning.

Cultural Misrepresentation

Language models that work mainly with popular cultures or languages may have difficulties showing minority groups, different dialects, or local speech. A model mainly built on American English can easily produce content that mistakenly represents British, Indian, or African English, and is not representative (Blodgett et al., 2020). Here, language isn't the only influence: usual prompts given by learning apps might emphasize popular outings in Western culture (e.g., getting coffee) but not focus on practices common to learners from other parts of the world.

If they want to avoid misrepresenting cultures, developers must use data in their systems that is both inclusive and well-balanced. Part of this work is to assemble databases that include content from African, Asian, Indigenous, and a variety of other languages. Input from linguists and experts familiar with cultures is required to check and confirm the accuracy of the content (Hovy & Spruit, 2016). Using bias-detection algorithms makes it possible to discover stereotyped or exclusionary information, which improves the fairness of the AI system. Furthermore, using more diverse information while building AI reduces cultural misrepresentation by about half.

Non-Standard Dialects and Low-Resource Languages

Language services such as Google Translate and Duolingo often struggle to handle slang and languages spoken by few. The main reason for this is that public training resources mostly include too much English, Spanish, or Mandarin data and too little of anything else. An important step to solve this problem is to collect data that includes both regional dialects and minority languages. Transfer learning approaches can improve and make the impacts of high-resource language models on low-resource communities. Having native speakers review the translations and text is very important for checking both accuracy and relevance

Harmful Stereotypes in AI Outputs

Learning from biased data gives AI models the chance to spread and strengthen negative stereotypes. Sometimes, AI tutors describe doctors using male pronouns and nurses using female pronouns, which can still promote traditional gender roles (Caliskan et al., 2017). There is a chance that some of the generated language ties certain accents or names to unfair stereotypes. Equally, language training materials might expect everyone to have technology and education, which excludes groups that do not have these things. A variety of strategies are suggested as ways to mitigate these issues. Languages used in data can be changed to remove gender association by swapping words like he and she which is called counterfactual data augmentation (Zhao et al., 2019). A team containing linguists, sociologists, and ethicists can review AI technology more thoroughly than others (Raji et al., 2020). Reporting biased material through feedback plays an important part in improving and correcting the platform.

It takes constant work, a variety of views, and new technology to ensure AI language tools are unbiased. Even though Google has set up Responsible AI and OpenAI has created bias mitigation systems, challenges persist in making AI usable across all populations globally. Community-driven development, with people from underrepresented communities playing key roles, is a key path for ensuring AI language systems are relevant to many cultures and languages. Real-time detection of bias is an important direction that helps AI systems correct biased outcomes on the go. Besides, creating laws, for instance, the EU AI Act, that highlight the need for fairness audits in educational AI, allows these actions to become standard. If developers choose fairness and inclusivity first, their language tools can empower everyone, no matter what their culture or background is.

Over-Reliance on AI

Because more AI technologies are used in language education, some people are worried about students using them too much and harming their overall learning. While AI-powered platforms provide unparalleled help to learners, too much reliance on them could lead to a different way for learners to build language skills (Zawacki-Richter et al., 2019). Studies explain that both technology and people are key to good language learning, but AI appears to be gaining ground in modern language classrooms (Rebolledo & González, 2023). In this section, three challenges posed by overusing AI in language classes are considered, and suggestions for keeping a good balance with personal teaching are recommended.

Diminished Human Interaction

One of the biggest issues with depending too much on AI is that it lessens real interactions, making genuine learning much harder. Even though ChatGPT and Replika can have meaningful interchanges, they cannot express emotions naturally, take in different cultures, or make unpredictable comments in chats (Dizon, 2020). Learners who interact solely with AI systems perform worse in practical conversations than learners who work both with AI and with teachers or other students. Without non-verbal cues in AI, this problem becomes worse because much of human communication is through facial expressions and body gestures. In order to compensate for this, teachers should try blended learning that mixes technology with planned opportunities for human interaction, including language exchange. The ideal outcome in language development is reached when students spend much of their studying time interacting with other learners.

Critical Thinking and Metalinguistic Awareness

Providing solutions instantly through language tools may lead people to depend on unchallenging learning styles without attempting more meaningful engagement. Automatic fixing by Grammarly or ChatGPT of writing errors can keep learners from learning to notice and solve errors themselves (Li, 2021). This shows the same thing as the "Google effect" in schools, when having information at our fingertips leads to less ability to remember it. Using AI for grammar errors leads to remembering grammar rules much less when compared to human guidance. To overcome this, educators should make learners reflect on the corrections provided by AI before they are used. Making students explain why an AI-proposed change is acceptable before implementing it can greatly enhance the learning of rules (Hwang & Chang, 2023).

Balancing AI and Traditional Pedagogical Approaches

To have the best effect, AI should be mixed with traditional language education so that the good points of each are preserved. AI is great at giving you specific lessons, instant help, and custom courses, but students still need human teachers to participate in important discussions, interpret the culture, and solve difficult language issues (Riedl, 2019). Learners can gain value from both the wide-scale use of AI and the special qualities of human teaching. An AI-based strategy might be to 'flip' the classroom, using AI to conduct drills and allowing the teacher to focus on interactive lessons. Besides, instructor programs need to be reinforced with skills in AI, so educators can question and apply AI tools in their teaching.

Table 2. Ethical and Practical Considerations

Consideration	Issue	Example	Recommendation
Data Privacy	Handling and securing user data	Data breaches in AI language tools	Implement encryption, anonymization, and comply with regulations
Bias and Fairness	Avoiding reinforcement of stereotypes and ensuring inclusivity	AI content reflecting cultural biases	Use diverse training data, regularly review AI outputs
Over-Reliance on AI	Balancing AI use with human interaction	Dependency on AI for feedback	Combine AI tools with traditional methods, encourage critical thinking

Resolving these concerns and ethics, stakeholders achieve the good sides of generative AI and lessen possible risks so that AI-based language learning is always fair, beneficial, and respects the many needs of learners.

RECOMMENDATIONS

Educators and technologists can use generative AI in CALL in a smart and careful way to see its full benefits. For integration to be effective, use technology and traditional ways at the same time and also think about making lessons accessible for everyone.

Hybrid Approaches

Generative AI makes language learning easier, yet it should help to teach languages rather than to use it to replace traditional teaching methods. Mixing artificial intelligence and human teaching allows for a more rounded experience in learning.

- AI tools can be used together with lessons taught by a teacher. For instance, teachers may employ Duolingo's Stories or Lingvist with their students to do extra practice and get customized exercises during live lessons on difficult language areas and talks. This approach lets teachers help students develop important thinking skills and learn about cultural details, as AI manages assignments that are completed over and over.
- By using AI, students at home benefit from a variety of grammar and vocabulary materials found on platforms such as Memrise and Busuu. Afterward, the teacher can use classroom time for group activities, questions and answers, and using what is learned. Using this strategy, students enjoy both the best results from AI and the unique support offered by real teachers.
- Teachers can use AI to adjust lessons according to what different learners need. For example, teachers could let an AI system determine each student's grade level, so they can help them better with targeted assistance. As a result, all students face classes that suit their abilities and receive help when they need it, improving their educational experience.

Accessibility and Inclusivity

It is necessary to plan and develop AI-driven language learning tools so they can be accessed by all types of learners. The process examines students' variety of talents, language experiences, and the best way to support learning.

- AI tools should consider the needs of learners who have different abilities. The use of features like text-to-speech and speech-to-text helps students who are visually or auditorily challenged. Using Voice Dream Reader and Microsoft Immersive Reader, students with dyslexia can change the display of text and hear what is being read.
- Because students may have to learn different languages, AI systems should be able to use and support many languages and dialects. For example, Google Translate and DeepL can help users translate in many languages, yet how good their translations are can differ. AI developers ought to pay attention to including a variety of languages and dialects to give all learners access to important resources.
- AI tools should be friendly to different cultures and should not promote stereotypes. For instance, the materials created by AI for learning must include cultural diversity and remove any sense of bias. Learners using Rosetta Stone and Babbel can benefit from cultural insights in the lessons they provide.
- AI-driven tools should ensure that learners can customize them to fit their requirements. They should be able to pick which exercises to do, learn about the topics they prefer, and determine what to learn. Users of Khan Academy and Coursera have the chance to make their learning experience.

Implementing Feedback Mechanisms

To make sure AI tools meet the requirements of all learners, using feedback is very important.

- Consistent feedback from users enables educators to locate and fix areas that need development. You can find these types of tools on platforms like Edmodo and Google Classroom, which help users highlight problems and suggest new features. Feedback helps improve AI software and make learning easier.
- Due to the multiple uses of AI tools in many places, it is necessary to test the ease of use and practicality of AI tools with a variety of people. It allows for finding and resolving accessibility problems and checks that the tool fits the needs of multiple groups of learners. To illustrate, Testbirds and UserTesting allow us to test if AI tools are user-friendly and available to all users.

If these suggestions are followed, both educators and technology specialists can successfully include generative AI tools in language learning, resulting in easy-to-use, secure, and inclusive opportunities that improve learning outcomes.

CONCLUSION

Generative AI is changing Computer-Assisted Language Learning (CALL), leading to several advantages as well as new challenges. This section highlights how generative AI can change language learning, outlines what researchers and developers can do next and discusses its wider educational influence.

It has made a big difference in CALL by creating content automatically, encouraging conversation, and offering helpful feedback in real time. Due to AI, learning a language has become more personalized, flexible, and interesting. Even so, integrating AI gives rise to many issues. We have to make sure our students' details are private and that the AI does not produce content that is biased. It is also possible that everyone will come to depend too much on AI, which might reduce how much people use human-based approaches for learning languages.

Future AI models must be able to assist different languages and their variations. Although current services provide translation for numerous languages, they can still do better with accuracy and cultural awareness. We need to focus on making models that are able to deal with languages and dialects that people do not speak often. Such AI systems might make it easier for speakers of indigenous languages and minor dialects to access better education.

To get the best benefits, generative AI must be connected with the main systems of education. AI can be used together with standard schools, online classes, and software meant for handling school tasks. With AI, languages could be taught within Moodle or Canvas without much effort, so teachers could follow students' progress and adapt their teaching using suggestions from AI. Also, AI could work with VR to design language learning activities that mix learning by doing with understanding the language in context.

More research can help make AI-supported language learning tools more individualized and responsive. This means using algorithms that are more aware of a student's learning needs, giving back custom recommendations. It could do this by tracking learners' actions online and changing the difficulty of tasks or recommending subjects they should study next.

We should work towards dealing with ethical questions and reducing biases in what AI creates. This involves building policies to recognize and control biases present in teaching data, and also setting out guidelines for ethics in AI applications at school. People from different backgrounds can be included to skillfully examine AI products so that stereotypes are not boosted and learning materials are inclusive.

Developments in fields such as generative adversarial networks and reinforcement learning are promoting new ways to improve language learning. Studies could look at how these technologies might be used to design more engaging and active language learning tools. To illustrate, using GANs, we could generate dialogue examples that match a learner's talent, and by combining them with reinforcement learning, AI systems can adapt feedback in line with a learner's actions.

AI can reshape language education by making it easier to access, more personal, and more interesting. Still, it is important to oversee its use to handle the problems connected to privacy, unfair biases, and technology. Properly introducing AI into the classroom can allow educators to make learning a language easier while maintaining the human touch and connection in teaching.

In the future, both AI developers, educators, and researchers must work together to guide the way language learning continues. By focusing on what the field lacks now and imagining new opportunities, education in languages can get better, offering students the best ways to learn. Things to come in education may be hard and thrilling, helping us invent different methods for learning languages in the digital world.

REFERENCES

Ahmad, M., Ho, W. Y., Goyes Robalino, A. P., Maqsood, M., Ahmad, M., Ho, W. Y., Goyes Robalino, A. P., & Maqsood, M. (2025). Theoretical Implications of Generative AI for Content Generation in Geoinformatics Training. In A. Anna A. (Ed.), *Integration Strategies of Generative AI in Higher Education* (pp. 101–130). IGI Global Scientific Publishing. DOI: 10.4018/979-8-3693-5518-3.ch005

Al-kfairy, M., Mustafa, D., Kshetri, N., Insiew, M., & Alfandi, O. (2024). Ethical Challenges and Solutions of Generative AI: An Interdisciplinary Perspective. *Informatics 2024, Vol. 11, Page 58, 11*(3), 58. DOI: 10.3390/informatics11030058

Almelhes, S. A. (2023). A Review of Artificial Intelligence Adoption in Second-Language Learning. *Theory and Practice in Language Studies, 13*(5), 1259–1269. Advance online publication. DOI: 10.17507/tpls.1305.21

Beatty, K. (2013). Teaching and researching computer-assisted language learning, Second edition. In *Teaching and Researching Computer-Assisted Language Learning, Second edition*. DOI: 10.4324/9781315833774

Blodgett, S. L., Barocas, S., Daumé, H., & Wallach, H. (2020). Language (Technology) is power: A critical survey of ⇜bias" in NLP. *Proceedings of the Annual Meeting of the Association for Computational Linguistics*. DOI: 10.18653/v1/2020.acl-main.485

Bolukbasi, T., Chang, K. W., Zou, J., Saligrama, V., & Kalai, A. (2016). Man is to computer programmer as woman is to homemaker? Debiasing word embeddings. *Advances in Neural Information Processing Systems*.

Bozkurt, A., Xiao, J., Farrow, R., Bai, J. Y. H., Nerantzi, C., Moore, S., Dron, J., Stracke, C. M., Singh, L., Crompton, H., Koutropoulos, A., Terentev, E., Pazurek, A., Nichols, M., Sidorkin, A. M., Costello, E., Watson, S., Mulligan, D., Honeychurch, S., & Asino, T. I. (2024). The manifesto for teaching and learning in a time of Generative AI: A critical collective stance to better navigate the future. *Open Praxis, 16*(4), 487–513. DOI: 10.55982/openpraxis.16.4.777

Caliskan, A., Bryson, J. J., & Narayanan, A. (2017). Semantics derived automatically from language corpora contain human-like biases. *Science, 356*(6334), 183–186. Advance online publication. DOI: 10.1126/science.aal4230 PMID: 28408601

Chapelle, C. A. (2001). Computer Applications in Second Language Acquisition. In *Computer Applications in Second Language Acquisition*. DOI: 10.1017/CBO9781139524681

Chapelle, C. A. (2025). Generative AI as game changer: Implications for language education. *System*, *132*, 103672. DOI: 10.1016/j.system.2025.103672

Chu, Z., Jia, H., Matricciani, E., Feretzakis, G., Papaspyridis, K., Gkoulalas-Divanis, A., & Verykios, V. S. (2024). Privacy-Preserving Techniques in Generative AI and Large Language Models: A Narrative Review. *Information 2024, Vol. 15, Page 697, 15*(11), 697. DOI: 10.3390/info15110697

Chukharev, E., Bouwman, W., Dobrynina, N., Speltz, E. D., Novotny, M., & Sollier, N. (2024). Designing Computer Assisted Language Learning Tools as Platforms for Data Collection in Applied Linguistics. *Routledge Handbook of Technological Advances in Researching Language Learning*, 158–170. DOI: 10.4324/9781003459088-15

Crawford, K. (2017). *The Trouble with Bias, by Kate Crawford (Revolutions)*. NIPS.

Dizon, G. (2020). Evaluating intelligent personal assistants for L2 listening and speaking development. *Language Learning & Technology*, *24*(1), 16–26. Advance online publication. DOI: 10.64152/10125/44705

Farina, M., Yu, X., & Lavazza, A. (2024). Ethical considerations and policy interventions concerning the impact of generative AI tools in the economy and in society. *AI and Ethics 2023 5:1, 5*(1), 737–745. DOI: 10.1007/s43681-023-00405-2

Feng, L. (2025). Investigating the Effects of Artificial Intelligence-Assisted Language Learning Strategies on Cognitive Load and Learning Outcomes: A Comparative Study. *Journal of Educational Computing Research*, *62*(8), 1741–1774. Advance online publication. DOI: 10.1177/07356331241268349

Garcia, I. (2010). Is machine translation ready yet? *Target. International Journal of Translation Studies*, *22*(1), 7–21. Advance online publication. DOI: 10.1075/target.22.1.02gar

Godwin-Jones, R. (2014). Emerging Technologies Games in Language Learning: Opportunities and Challenges. *Language Learning & Technology*, *18*(182).

Golda, A., Mekonen, K., Pandey, A., Singh, A., Hassija, V., Chamola, V., & Sikdar, B. (2024). Privacy and Security Concerns in Generative AI: A Comprehensive Survey. *IEEE Access : Practical Innovations, Open Solutions*, *12*, 48126–48144. DOI: 10.1109/ACCESS.2024.3381611

Heift, T., & Schulze, M. (2007). Errors and Intelligence in Computer-Assisted Language Learning: Parsers and Pedagogues. In *Errors and Intelligence in Computer-Assisted Language Learning: Parsers and Pedagogues*. DOI: 10.4324/9780203012215

Hovy, D., & Spruit, S. L. (2016). The social impact of natural language processing. *54th Annual Meeting of the Association for Computational Linguistics, ACL 2016 - Short Papers*. DOI: 10.18653/v1/P16-2096

Huang, W., Hew, K. F., & Fryer, L. K. (2022). Chatbots for language learning—Are they really useful? A systematic review of chatbot-supported language learning. In *Journal of Computer Assisted Learning* (Vol. 38, Issue 1). DOI: 10.1111/jcal.12610

Huang, X., Zou, D., Cheng, G., Chen, X., & Xie, H. (2023). Trends, Research Issues and Applications of Artificial Intelligence in Language Education. *Journal of Educational Technology & Society*, *26*(1). Advance online publication. DOI: 10.30191/ETS.202301_26(1).0009

Hwang, G. J., & Chang, C. Y. (2023). A review of opportunities and challenges of chatbots in education. In *Interactive Learning Environments* (Vol. 31, Issue 7). DOI: 10.1080/10494820.2021.1952615

Jian, M. J. K. O. (2023). Personalized learning through AI. *Advances in Engineering Innovation*, *5*(1), 16–19. Advance online publication. DOI: 10.54254/2977-3903/5/2023039

Kessler, G. (2018). Technology and the future of language teaching. *Foreign Language Annals*, *51*(1), 205–218. Advance online publication. DOI: 10.1111/flan.12318

Koltovskaia, S. (2023). Postsecondary L2 writing teachers' use and perceptions of Grammarly as a complement to their feedback. *ReCALL*, *35*(3), 290–304. Advance online publication. DOI: 10.1017/S0958344022000179

Labadie, C., & Legner, C. (2023). Building data management capabilities to address data protection regulations: Learnings from EU-GDPR. *Journal of Information Technology*, *38*(1), 16–44. Advance online publication. DOI: 10.1177/02683962221141456

Lee, D., Kim, H., & Sung, S.-H. (2023). Development research on an AI English learning support system to facilitate learner-generated-context-based learning. *Educational Technology Research and Development*, *71*(2), 629–666. Advance online publication. DOI: 10.1007/s11423-022-10172-2 PMID: 36533222

Levy, M., & Stockwell, G. (2013). Call dimensions: Options and issues in computer-assisted language learning. In *Call Dimensions*. Options and Issues in Computer-Assisted Language Learning., DOI: 10.4324/9780203708200

Loewen, S., Isbell, D. R., & Sporn, Z. (2020). The effectiveness of app-based language instruction for developing receptive linguistic knowledge and oral communicative ability. *Foreign Language Annals*, *53*(2), 209–233. Advance online publication. DOI: 10.1111/flan.12454

Mahdi, H. S., & Al Khateeb, A. A. (2019). The effectiveness of computer-assisted pronunciation training: A meta-analysis. *Review of Education*, *7*(3), 733–753. Advance online publication. DOI: 10.1002/rev3.3165

Maqsood, M., Butt, H. H., Ali, M. A., Chinedu, C. C., Ahmad, M., Maqsood, M., Butt, H. H., Ali, M. A., Chinedu, C. C., & Ahmad, M. (2025). Chatbots as Learning Companions Exploring Ethical Dimensions of AI in Education. In Jean-Éric, P. (Ed.), *Architecting the Digital Future: Platforms, Design, and Application* (pp. 311–348). IGI Global Scientific Publishing., DOI: 10.4018/979-8-3693-2973-3.ch012

Marandi, S. S. (2024). Virtual supremacy and electronic imperialism: The hegemonies of e-learning and computer assisted language learning (CALL). *Learning, Media and Technology*, *49*(4), 527–543. Advance online publication. DOI: 10.1080/17439884.2023.2207832

Mohsen, M. A., Althebi, S., Alsagour, R., Alsalem, A., Almudawi, A., & Alshahrani, A. (2024). Forty-two years of computer-assisted language learning research: A scientometric study of hotspot research and trending issues. *ReCALL*, *36*(2), 230–249. DOI: 10.1017/S0958344023000253

Raji, I. D., Smart, A., White, R. N., Mitchell, M., Gebru, T., Hutchinson, B., Smith-Loud, J., Theron, D., & Barnes, P. (2020). Closing the AI accountability gap: Defining an end-to-end framework for internal algorithmic auditing. *FAT* 2020 - Proceedings of the 2020 Conference on Fairness, Accountability, and Transparency*. DOI: 10.1145/3351095.3372873

Rebolledo, R., & González, F. (2023). Exploring the Benefits and Challenges of AI-Language Learning Tools. *International Journal of Social Sciences and Humanities Invention*, *10*(01), 7569–7576. Advance online publication. DOI: 10.18535/ijsshi/v10i01.02

Riedl, M. O. (2019). Human-centered artificial intelligence and machine learning. *Human Behavior and Emerging Technologies*, *1*(1), 33–36. Advance online publication. DOI: 10.1002/hbe2.117

Shadiev, R., Wen, Y., Uosaki, N., & Song, Y. (2023). Future language learning with emerging technologies. In *Journal of Computers in Education* (Vol. 10, Issue 3). DOI: 10.1007/s40692-023-00285-9

Shadiev, R., & Yu, J. (2024). Review of research on computer-assisted language learning with a focus on intercultural education. *Computer Assisted Language Learning*, *37*(4), 841–871. DOI: 10.1080/09588221.2022.2056616

Shaik, I. A., Shaik, A. H., Athahar, P., & Rasheeda Begum, B. (2024). Cognitive Computing in English Language Classrooms. *ICCCMLA 2024 - 6th International Conference on Cybernetics, Cognition and Machine Learning Applications*, 313–316. DOI: 10.1109/ICCCMLA63077.2024.10871285

Tafazoli, D., María, E. G., & Abril, C. A. H. (2019). Intelligent language tutoring system: Integrating intelligent computer-assisted language learning into language education. *International Journal of Information and Communication Technology Education, 15*(3), 60–74. Advance online publication. DOI: 10.4018/IJICTE.2019070105

Vančová, H. (2023). AI and AI-powered tools for pronunciation training. *Journal of Language and Cultural Education, 11*(3), 12–24. Advance online publication. DOI: 10.2478/jolace-2023-0022

Warschauer, M., & Healey, D. (1998). Computers and language learning: An overview. In *Language Teaching* (Vol. 31, Issue 2). DOI: 10.1017/S0261444800012970

Weng, X., & Chiu, T. K. F. (2023). Instructional design and learning outcomes of intelligent computer assisted language learning: Systematic review in the field. In *Computers and Education* (Vol. 4). Artificial Intelligence., DOI: 10.1016/j.caeai.2022.100117

Weng, Z., & Fu, Y. (2025). Generative AI in Language Education: Bridging Divide and Fostering Inclusivity. *International Journal of Technology in Education, 8*(2), 395–420. DOI: 10.46328/ijte.1056

Xiao, F. (2014). Technology in interlanguage pragmatics research and teaching. *Language Learning & Technology, 18*(1), 53–56. DOI: 10.64152/10125/44353

Yamaguchi, T., & Levy, M. (1999). Computer-Assisted Language Learning: Context and Conceptualization. *Language, 75*(1), 191. Advance online publication. DOI: 10.2307/417519

Yeh, H. C. (2025). The synergy of generative AI and inquiry-based learning: Transforming the landscape of English teaching and learning. *Interactive Learning Environments, 33*(1), 88–102. Advance online publication. DOI: 10.1080/10494820.2024.2335491

Zawacki-Richter, O., Marín, V. I., Bond, M., & Gouverneur, F. (2019). Systematic review of research on artificial intelligence applications in higher education – where are the educators? In *International Journal of Educational Technology in Higher Education* (Vol. 16, Issue 1). DOI: 10.1186/s41239-019-0171-0

Zhang, S., Shan, C., Lee, J. S. Y., Che, S. P., & Kim, J. H. (2023). Effect of chatbot-assisted language learning: A meta-analysis. *Education and Information Technologies, 28*(11), 15223–15243. Advance online publication. DOI: 10.1007/s10639-023-11805-6

Zhao, J., Wang, T., Yatskar, M., Cotterell, R., Ordonez, V., & Chang, K. W. (2019). Gender bias in contextualized word embeddings. *NAACL HLT 2019 - 2019 Conference of the North American Chapter of the Association for Computational Linguistics: Human Language Technologies - Proceedings of the Conference, 1.* DOI: 10.18653/v1/N19-1064

KEY TERMS AND DEFINITIONS

Generative AI: refers to artificial intelligence systems that can create new content, such as text, images, music, or code, based on patterns learned from training data. Unlike traditional AI, which analyzes or classifies data, generative models (e.g., GPT, DALL-E) produce original outputs by predicting sequences or structures.

Computer-Assisted Language Learning (CALL): the use of computer technology to facilitate language learning. It includes software, applications, and online tools designed to help learners practice reading, writing, listening, and speaking in a target language through interactive exercises, simulations, and feedback mechanisms.

Online Learning Platforms: refer to digital environments that provide educational content, courses, and interactive tools for remote learning. Examples include Coursera, Udemy, Khan Academy, and Duolingo. These platforms often incorporate multimedia resources, quizzes, discussion forums, and progress tracking.

Machine Learning (ML): is a subset of AI that enables systems to learn and improve from experience without explicit programming. ML algorithms analyze data, identify patterns, and make predictions or decisions based on statistical models. Common techniques include supervised, unsupervised, and reinforcement learning.

Natural Language Processing (NLP): is a branch of AI that focuses on the interaction between computers and human language. It involves tasks like text analysis, speech recognition, machine translation, sentiment analysis, and chatbot responses. NLP enables machines to understand, interpret, and generate human language.

Conversational Agents: are AI-driven systems designed to simulate human-like dialogue. They include chatbots (text-based) and voice assistants (e.g., Siri, Alexa) that interact with users to answer questions, provide recommendations, or assist with tasks using NLP and machine learning.

Contextual Adaptation: refers to an AI system's ability to adjust its responses or behavior based on the context of the interaction, such as user preferences, previous conversations, or environmental factors. This enhances personalization and relevance in applications like chatbots and recommendation systems.

Real-Time Feedback Systems: provide immediate responses or corrections to users during an activity. In education, these systems analyze inputs (e.g., spoken words, written answers) and offer instant guidance, helping learners improve performance dynamically (e.g., language pronunciation tools, coding exercises).

Chapter 8
The Role of Generative Artificial Intelligence in Enhancing 4C Skills in Foreign Language Education: A Comprehensive Analysis

Ali Orhan
https://orcid.org/0000-0003-1234-3919
Zonguldak Bülent Ecevit University, Turkey

Şule Çınar Yağcı
https://orcid.org/0000-0003-4456-3174
Zonguldak Bülent Ecevit University, Turkey

ABSTRACT

This study explores how generative artificial intelligence (GenAI) supports the development of 21st-century skills—critical thinking, creativity, communication, and collaboration (4Cs)—in foreign language education through a systematic literature review. Findings indicate that GenAI enhances critical thinking by improving analytical reasoning and argumentation, supports creative writing, strengthens communication through real-time feedback, and fosters collaboration in interactive settings. However, issues such as ethical concerns, learner autonomy, and over-reliance on AI-generated content remain. The study emphasizes the need for balanced GenAI

DOI: 10.4018/979-8-3373-7574-8.ch008

integration with human oversight and further research on its long-term impact on language learning and education, highlighting AI's transformative role and the importance of responsible use.

INTRODUCTION

In the rapidly evolving landscape of the 21st century, the emphasis on 21st-century skills, namely critical thinking, creativity, collaboration, and communication (often referred to as the 4Cs), has become paramount in educational discourse. These competencies are essential for equipping students with the ability to navigate complex challenges and succeed in an increasingly interconnected world. The development of these competencies is crucial, as they enable learners to adapt to diverse environments and contribute effectively to society (Bulathwela et al., 2024). Research indicates that integrating these skills into educational frameworks enhances student engagement and fosters a more holistic approach to learning that aligns with real-world demands (Leavy et al., 2023; Chen et al., 2020). Furthermore, the incorporation of 21st-century skills into curricula has been shown to promote innovative thinking and problem-solving abilities, which are critical in both academic and professional contexts (Bozkurt et al., 2021). Given the necessity of these competencies, contemporary education systems must explore effective and sustainable strategies for their cultivation to ensure that learners are well-prepared to meet the demands of the modern world.

One of the most transformative forces in this endeavor has been the advent of generative artificial intelligence (GenAI) technologies, which have significantly reshaped the educational landscape, presenting both opportunities and challenges. GenAI's integration into educational settings has the potential to personalize learning experiences, automate administrative tasks, and enhance instructional methods (Chembe et al., 2023; Chen et al., 2020). Studies have shown that GenAI can facilitate adaptive learning environments, enabling tailored educational experiences that accommodate individual student needs and diverse learning styles (Opesemowo & Adekomaya, 2024; Xu & Ouyang, 2022). This level of personalization is particularly beneficial in addressing the varying capabilities of learners, fostering greater engagement (Zhang, 2024). However, the rapid adoption of GenAI in education also raises ethical considerations, particularly regarding equity and access, as disparities in technological resources could exacerbate existing educational inequalities (Bulathwela et al., 2024; Oran, 2023). Consequently, while GenAI holds significant potential for revolutionizing educational practices, its implementation must be approached thoughtfully to ensure equitable benefits for all students (Ulaşan, 2023).

Beyond personalization and accessibility, GenAI-driven technologies play a pivotal role in fostering 21st-century skills by providing dynamic and interactive learning environments. In particular, the integration of GenAI into education has emerged as a groundbreaking development, offering novel ways to support critical thinking, communication, creativity, and collaboration. These technologies offer opportunities such as providing personalized educational materials tailored to students' individual learning needs and enhancing the efficiency and speed of assessment processes for educators (Singh, 2024). Moreover, through interactive learning environments and real-time feedback systems, GenAI facilitates more effective communication between educators and students (Yadav, 2024). Research suggests that such GenAI-powered innovations not only enhance academic success but also contribute to broader educational goals, including the promotion of lifelong learning and sustainable development (Alshamsi et al., 2024).

Nevertheless, alongside these advantages, the widespread adoption of GenAI introduces several ethical and technical challenges. Issues such as data privacy, bias embedded within GenAI algorithms, and concerns surrounding academic integrity remain at the forefront of scholarly discussions (Deng & Joshi, 2024). In response to these challenges, educators and policymakers have been working to establish guidelines and frameworks to ensure the responsible and ethical use of GenAI in educational settings (Lodzikowski et al., 2024). The development of such policies is essential, as they not only safeguard academic standards but also reinforce the societal values underpinning ethical education (Baek & Wilson, 2024).

With the rapid advancements in educational technology, GenAI has become an increasingly significant tool for enhancing learning outcomes. In foreign language education, this technology offers promising opportunities for fostering 21st-century skills by supporting personalized learning experiences (Bozkurt et al., 2024), real-time feedback (Özçelik & Çınar Yağcı, 2024) and collaborative engagement. Given the increasing reliance on GenAI in language education, understanding how GenAI influences the acquisition of critical thinking, creativity, communication, and collaboration is crucial to ensuring its effective and ethical integration into teaching practices. Therefore, this study aims to provide a comprehensive review of the role of GenAI in the development of 4C skills in foreign language education. Specifically, it seeks to address the following research questions:

1. How has research on GenAI and 4C skills in foreign language learning progressed over the years?
2. What research methods are used to study the role of GenAI in 4C skill development?
3. Who are the participants or what are the sample characteristics in these studies?

4. What are the main aims of studies on GenAI and 4C skills in foreign language education?
5. What key findings reveal the impact of GenAI on 4C skills?
6. What challenges or limitations are identified in research on GenAI and 4C skills?
7. What suggestions do researchers offer to improve the use of GenAI for developing 4C skills?

RELATED LITERATURE

The Significance of 4C Skills in Foreign Language Education

The integration of the 4C skills—critical thinking, creative thinking, communication, and collaboration—into foreign language education has garnered increasing attention in recent years. This growing emphasis is driven by the recognition that language learning extends beyond the mere acquisition of linguistic structures; it involves the development of cognitive, social, and professional competencies that prepare learners for the complexities of the globalized world. As educators and researchers strive to redefine pedagogical approaches in language instruction, a substantial body of literature has underscored the necessity of embedding these skills into foreign language curricula.

Among the 4C skills, critical thinking has emerged as a foundational pillar of language education, influencing learners' ability to analyze, evaluate, and synthesize information within diverse communicative contexts. Critical thinking is a multidimensional competence that enables individuals to analyze, evaluate, and question information within a conscious and self-regulatory cognitive process. According to Facione (1990), this process includes fundamental skills such as interpretation, analysis, evaluation, inference, explanation and, self-regulation. Similarly, Watson & Glaser (2010) define critical thinking as the ability to recognize the existence of a problem, question the source and accuracy of information, and analyze and evaluate different data and evidence. In the same vein, Çeviker Ay and Orhan (2022) conceptualize critical thinking as a self-regulatory process that encompasses the systematic analysis and questioning of information. Research consistently suggests that fostering critical thinking skills enhances students' capacity to engage in nuanced professional discourse and problem-solving tasks. For instance, Kosharna (2019) underscores the indispensable role of critical thinking in shaping future educators' communicative proficiency, arguing that it directly impacts their ability to function effectively in professional settings. Similarly, Harizaj and Hajrulla (2017) advocate for the incorporation of practical activities in English as a Foreign Language (EFL) classrooms, demonstrating how such interventions not only enhance linguistic competence but also encourage deeper cognitive engagement. Reinforcing this perspective, Salybekova et al. (2023) provide empirical evidence suggesting that EFL students perceive critical thinking training as instrumental in improving their overall learning outcomes. Also, in his meta-analysis study aiming to investigate the relationship between critical thinking and academic achievement, Orhan (2022) concluded that there is a significant relationship between critical thinking and academic achievement with medium effect size. These studies collectively reinforce the notion that critical thinking should not be treated as a peripheral skill in language education but rather as an integral component that shapes students' cognitive and communicative development.

In parallel, creative thinking plays a crucial role in enriching language learning by fostering originality, adaptability, and problem-solving abilities (Orhan & Ataman, 2024). As contemporary educational paradigms shift towards project-based learning (PBL), students are increasingly engaged in authentic, task-driven learning experiences that necessitate innovative thinking (Orhan, 2024). Khan et al. (2023) highlights how the adoption of PBL methodologies in language instruction facilitates an environment where learners actively participate in creative problem-solving activities. Furthermore, Liao et al. (2018) emphasize that employing creative pedagogical approaches enhances student motivation and engagement, thereby strengthening the overall language acquisition process. This assertion is supported by Medvedeva and Rubtsova (2021), who argue that creativity not only contributes to linguistic proficiency but also aids in the development of essential soft skills, thereby equipping learners with the adaptability required in dynamic professional environments. Taken together, these findings underscore the imperative of integrating creative thinking into language curricula, ensuring that learners cultivate the ability to generate and express novel ideas effectively in their target language.

Beyond cognitive and creative dimensions, communication stands as a cornerstone of foreign language education, particularly in an era marked by increasing intercultural interactions. The ability to navigate diverse linguistic and cultural landscapes is essential for students aspiring to participate in the global workforce. León and Castro (2017) emphasize the role of collaborative learning in promoting effective communication among EFL students, encouraging active learner participation, and autonomy in language acquisition. Moreover, Borzova and Shemanaeva (2022) advocate for the integration of intercultural competence alongside communicative training, highlighting the symbiotic relationship between linguistic proficiency and cultural awareness. These studies collectively affirm that effective communication transcends grammatical accuracy and it involves the development of interpersonal and intercultural skills that are crucial for navigating complex global contexts.

Complementing this, collaboration is an essential competency that intersects with all other 4C skills, particularly in language education. The transition from traditional teacher-centered methodologies to student-centered, interactive learning environments has reinforced the significance of collaborative learning in fostering both linguistic and social competencies. Kuntariati and Paramita (2023) demonstrate that collaborative project-based learning methodologies significantly enhance the quality of language education by encouraging teamwork and shared knowledge construction. This assertion aligns with the findings of Khan et al. (2023), who notes that engaging students in project-based activities not only cultivates their collaborative skills but also enhances their overall language proficiency. Furthermore, Tevdovska (2015) underscores the importance of integrating soft skills, including collaboration, into higher education curricula to prepare students for the demands of contemporary professional environments. These studies illustrate that fostering collaboration in language learning settings not only improves communicative competence but also nurtures the ability to work effectively in diverse, team-oriented contexts.

In addition to highlighting the role of collaboration, recent studies have also explored how all four components of the 4C framework can be effectively integrated into foreign language education and what challenges teachers may encounter in the process. Recent empirical studies further illuminate how the 4C competencies can be meaningfully integrated into foreign language instruction and the challenges that may arise in the process. For instance, Salybekova et al. (2024) examined pre-service language teachers in Kazakhstan and discovered that, although participants demonstrated a sound theoretical understanding of the 4Cs, they struggled to translate this knowledge into classroom practice. Nevertheless, those in the experimental group—who engaged in problem-solving and creative tasks—showed marked improvements in professional competencies, underscoring the efficacy of targeted pedagogical interventions. Complementing this, Soomro et al. (2025) conducted a phenomenological study among ESL instructors in Pakistan, revealing that while educators recognized the educational value of Information and Communication Technology (ICT)-supported 4C integration, they encountered substantial barriers such as limited digital fluency and lack of institutional infrastructure.

In response to the challenges outlined above, scholars have explored a variety of practical tools and strategies to facilitate the integration of the 4C competencies into educational practice. Anggraini et al. (2024) highlighted the significance of using rubrics, performance-based assessments, and digital platforms to evaluate 4C skills, though challenges such as the subjective nature of creativity and inadequate teacher training remain. In a similar vein, Siregar et al. (2023) demonstrated the potential of project-based worksheets to not only promote 4C-related skills but also foster learners' sense of responsibility and openness. Further evidence of the potential of technology-enhanced learning comes from Kousloglou et al. (2023), who applied a mobile-supported inquiry-based learning (mIBL) approach with 9th-grade learners. Their study reported significant gains in communication and collaboration, along with moderate improvements in critical and creative thinking—indicating that digitally enriched, inquiry-driven learning environments can be highly effective.

Moving from classroom-level interventions to broader educational structures, scholars have also emphasized the need for institutional frameworks that support the systemic and sustainable integration of the 4C competencies. At the institutional level, efforts to systematize the integration of the 4Cs are gaining momentum. Thornhill-Miller et al. (2023) proposed a certification model to assess and promote the development of these competencies across formal and informal educational contexts. Their framework emphasizes the importance of sustainable implementation supported by robust evaluation systems, continuous professional development, and adaptive policies. Similarly, Herlinawati et al. (2024), through their analysis of instructional materials in higher education, found that although educators were conceptually aware of the 4Cs, their teaching materials often lacked substantive alignment with these competencies. Collectively, these studies highlight the need for a holistic transformation—one that moves beyond curriculum reform to foster learner-centered, inquiry-based, and technologically supported pedagogy, underpinned by institutional frameworks that encourage long-term innovation and professional growth.

In light of the reviewed literature, it becomes evident that the integration of 4C skills—critical thinking, creative thinking, communication, and collaboration—into foreign language education is not merely an educational enhancement but a pedagogical necessity in the 21st century. These competencies serve as cognitive and social scaffolds that enable learners to engage more meaningfully with language content while preparing them to navigate the complexities of multicultural, interdisciplinary, and digitally mediated environments. Critical and creative thinking empower learners to analyze and generate knowledge, while communication and collaboration foster active participation in both academic and professional discourse communities. However, despite growing awareness, numerous studies indicate a persistent gap between theoretical understanding and practical application, often hindered by limited teacher training, insufficient institutional support, and the absence of robust assessment frameworks. To bridge this gap, the literature advocates for the use of technology-enhanced, project-based, and inquiry-driven pedagogical models that align instructional materials and classroom practices with the demands of the 4Cs. Moving forward, sustained efforts are needed to build institutional capacity, develop context-sensitive instructional tools, and design longitudinal studies that investigate the long-term impacts of 4C-focused language instruction. Such a multifaceted approach is essential to ensure that foreign language learners are not only linguistically competent but also equipped with the critical literacies and collaborative capacities vital for lifelong learning and global citizenship.

The Role of GenAI in Enhancing 4C Skills in Foreign Language Education

The integration of GenAI tools, particularly ChatGPT, into language education has demonstrated a significant impact on the development of critical thinking and learner autonomy. Research suggests that the structured incorporation of these tools can lead to deeper cognitive engagement and enhanced analytical abilities. For instance, Avsheniuk et al. (2024) highlight that ChatGPT substantially fosters students' ability to critically analyze and evaluate information, thereby promoting independent learning. In a similar vein, Liang and Wu (2024) argue that well-designed pedagogical frameworks that embed ChatGPT within the learning process can create conditions conducive to higher-order thinking. Furthermore, Werdiningsih et al. (2024) emphasize the tool's potential in academic writing, as it assists learners with content generation and vocabulary enhancement, ultimately improving the overall quality of essays. The role of GenAI tools in education is approached with both promising applications and cautionary perspectives. Giannakos et al. (2024) bring together insights from nine leading experts in the fields of learning and technology to offer a comprehensive analysis of the potential and limitations of GenAI in educational contexts. Their study underscores that large language models (LLMs) can support various instructional processes, including learning design, content generation, self-regulated learning, assessment, and feedback.

Building on these insights, recent discussions have increasingly focused on the ethical and pedagogical considerations necessary for the responsible integration of GenAI tools into educational settings. While the benefits are evident, ethical concerns persist regarding the extent to which GenAI-generated content may undermine the role of human educators, necessitating a balanced and reflective approach to its implementation (Avsheniuk et al., 2024). In this context, Zenni and Andrew (2023) argue that generative AI text producers can serve as powerful tools to overcome language barriers in the creation of scientific texts, particularly in the field of ecology. They emphasize that these tools can support researchers in the publication process by generating grammatically accurate, context-appropriate, and semantically coherent texts. Moreover, they highlight that GenAI can effectively assist in drafting research summaries, social media posts, and article abstracts. However, the authors caution that such technologies should be used under human supervision, as unsupervised use may pose risks to content accuracy and academic credibility. This underscores the growing importance of GenAI's supportive—rather than substitutive—role in scholarly communication.

Beyond its cognitive contributions, GenAI plays a pivotal role in fostering essential soft skills required for both academic and professional success. As Borkovska et al. (2024) point out, competencies such as communication, critical thinking, and teamwork are integral to students' holistic development. This perspective is reinforced by Darmawansah et al. (2024), whose research demonstrates how ChatGPT enhances collaborative argumentation and critical thinking outcomes, particularly in EFL settings. Moreover, the impact of GenAI on creative and intercultural communication skills has been documented in service-learning environments. According to Cheung and Shi (2024), students leveraged GenAI primarily as a peripheral tool during story creation; however, its presence facilitated their creative ideation and drafting processes. Türker and Öztürk (2025) emphasize that generative AI offers significant opportunities to support 4C skills—critical thinking, creativity, communication, and collaboration. The researchers highlight that such technologies stimulate students' cognitive processes, foster critical perspectives on problem scenarios, and encourage the generation of innovative solutions. Additionally, they point out that GenAI-supported digital platforms enhance interaction among learners, thereby facilitating effective communication and collaborative work. However, their study also underscores the importance of using this potential in a balanced and reflective manner aligned with educational goals.

Building on these findings, recent studies have begun to explore the nuanced relationship between GenAI and creative assessment, particularly in both textual and visual domains. The role of generative AI in the assessment of creativity has become a subject of increasing scholarly attention. In this context, Vinchon, Gironnay, and Lubart (2024) conducted a comparative analysis of GenAI systems such as ChatGPT in standardized creativity tests. Their findings indicate that ChatGPT demonstrates a high level of fluency in content generation, yet its outputs often remain at an average level of originality. The study argues that the inherently stochastic nature of AI-generated creativity and its dependence on training data richness necessitate a re-evaluation of traditional creativity metrics. Furthermore, it emphasizes that genuine originality largely depends on human guidance, thus calling for the development of robust assessment mechanisms capable of evaluating both AI-assisted and co-created human–AI creative outputs. In parallel, architectural design processes have also been explored as cognitively layered activities that combine both divergent and convergent aspects of creative thinking. Tan and Luhrs (2024) examined the use of the generative AI tool Midjourney in supporting architects' creative workflows. Their study showed that GenAI could enhance creative ideation in both user profiling and spatial conceptualization stages. Based on a design brief, Midjourney was used to generate visual representations of potential user typologies, which then informed various spatial solutions. These findings highlight that GenAI tools contribute not only to aesthetic production but also to the acceleration of idea generation and the structuring of thought during problem-solving in design contexts. Taken together, these studies underscore the significance of GenAI not merely as technical support but as a cognitive enabler in creative disciplines, supporting both independent and collaborative learning environments across diverse educational contexts.

Furthermore, beyond its demonstrated capacity to foster creativity, collaboration, and higher-order thinking, GenAI has also emerged as a valuable tool for enhancing learners' emotional and motivational dimensions. In addition to its cognitive and communicative benefits, the use of GenAI in language learning has shown promising results in enhancing students' motivation, engagement, and self-efficacy. Chen et al. (2024) found that role-play activities incorporating GenAI significantly increased both motivation and self-efficacy among EFL learners. This finding is consistent with Teng's (2025) study, which demonstrates that students who received GenAI-generated feedback exhibited notable improvements in writing self-efficacy and overall engagement. Teng (2025) further highlights that learners with higher metacognitive awareness derived the greatest benefits from GenAI-supported practices, as they actively monitored and regulated their cognitive processes. These findings suggest that GenAI, when strategically integrated into educational settings, has the potential to strengthen students' metacognitive capacities and intrinsic motivation, thereby fostering greater academic success and self-directed learning.

In parallel with its influence on learner motivation and self-regulatory strategies, GenAI has also begun to reshape assessment practices in higher education by fostering the development of multiple literacies. Furthermore, the integration of generative AI into assessment processes in higher education has opened pathways for the development of new approaches that foster multiple literacies. Richmond and Nicholls (2024), in their study with undergraduate psychology students, demonstrated that the use of GenAI tools such as ChatGPT can simultaneously support psychological literacy, feedback literacy, and AI literacy. Students were asked to evaluate a media brief generated by ChatGPT based on a published academic article, using a structured rubric with defined criteria. The findings revealed that students were able to critically assess the AI output for content accuracy despite finding it formally well-structured. Notably, engaging in rubric-based evaluations early in the learning process contributed positively to their performance in subsequent academic tasks. These results underscore that integrating GenAI into instruction—especially through structured, process-oriented evaluations—holds the potential to enhance students' multidimensional literacy skills.

Complementing its role in promoting multiple literacies through assessment, GenAI has also demonstrated considerable potential in enhancing learners' communication skills, particularly in English language education. Wang (2025) found that students who interacted with ChatGPT-4 exhibited marked improvements in their English communication abilities, accompanied by increasingly favorable attitudes toward the integration of GenAI in their learning experiences. This suggests that beyond facilitating language production, GenAI tools can positively shape learners' affective engagement, which in turn contributes to more effective language acquisition. Moreover, Liu and Wang (2024) provide further evidence by showing that the use of GenAI in literature courses prompted students to engage in deeper analytical discussions, thereby supporting the development of critical thinking alongside communicative competence. These findings indicate that GenAI functions not merely as a linguistic support mechanism but as a cognitive enhancer that encourages more sophisticated, reflective interaction with content. Collectively, such evidence highlights the transformative role of GenAI in preparing students for the demands of academic and professional discourse. Nevertheless, this potential is not without challenges. As Kartal (2024) cautions, the increasing reliance on GenAI raises important ethical considerations and risks of technological dependency, which must be addressed through balanced, pedagogically sound integration strategies. Therefore, while the communicative affordances of GenAI are substantial, their long-term impact hinges on thoughtful and ethically responsible implementation.

In summary, the integration of GenAI tools—most notably ChatGPT—into foreign language education has yielded substantial benefits across various domains. Specifically, these tools have been shown to enhance critical thinking, creativity, communication, collaboration, and learner self-efficacy. When embedded within thoughtfully designed pedagogical frameworks, GenAI can foster deeper cognitive engagement, support metacognitive regulation, and promote both independent and collaborative learning. Moreover, the use of GenAI has been associated with increased learner motivation and more effective language production, particularly in writing and speaking tasks. However, despite these promising outcomes, several challenges remain. Most notably, ethical concerns regarding the potential over-reliance on GenAI and the risk of diminishing the role of human educators must be carefully considered. Additionally, questions persist about the originality of AI-generated content and the long-term implications for students' critical and creative capacities. Therefore, while GenAI holds great potential to transform language education, its implementation must be guided by a balanced and reflective approach. Consequently, future research should focus not only on maximizing the pedagogical benefits of GenAI but also on developing ethical, sustainable, and context-sensitive integration strategies. This dual emphasis will be essential to ensure that GenAI tools serve as effective complements to human instruction—enhancing educational quality without compromising the foundational human elements of teaching and learning.

METHOD

This study was structured based on the systematic review methodology following PRISMA guidelines (Moher et al., 2009). A systematic review, which adheres to predefined inclusion and exclusion criteria, aims to comprehensively examine all relevant research on a given topic, identify eligible studies, and synthesize their findings in alignment with the research objectives (Petticrew & Roberts, 2006). Systematic reviews are typically divided into three main types: meta-analysis, meta-synthesis, and descriptive content analysis (Bellibaş & Gümüş, 2018). In this study, the descriptive content analysis approach was employed to identify and analyze research trends within a specific field. Following the approach outlined by Hwang and Chang (2021), the Web of Science database was chosen as the primary data source, ensuring both the credibility and quality of the selected publications (Hwang & Tsai, 2011). The review examined various aspects of the studies, including publication years, research methodologies, participant characteristics, research aims, key findings, limitations, and recommendations.

The Web of Science database was searched using the search pattern which was identified based on the PICOS (Population, Intervention, Comparison, Outcomes, Study Design) framework for systematic reviews (Methley et al., 2014).

("language learn*" OR "language teach*" OR "L2 learn*" OR "L2 teach*" OR "language student*" OR "foreign language learn*" OR "EFL" OR "language class*")

AND

("ChatGPT" OR "GenAI" OR "generative artificial intelligence")

AND

("critical thinking" OR "creative thinking" OR "communication" OR "collaboration")

Following the literature review, the criteria listed below were utilized to determine the inclusion of studies in the research: (a) the studies must be written in either Turkish or English, (b) the studies had to investigate the role of GenAI in developing the 4C skills, (c) the studies must be published on or before February 31th, 2025, (d) the studies must be empirical research rather than a review article, and (e) availability of full-text open access.

Among the forty-six studies identified through a comprehensive literature search, eleven satisfied the predetermined inclusion criteria and were thus deemed relevant to the aims of this systematic review. To facilitate a thorough and structured analysis, a detailed data extraction table was developed in Microsoft Excel, where each study was examined across multiple dimensions, including research focus, methodology, participant demographics, and the specific 4C competencies addressed—namely critical thinking, communication, collaboration, and creativity. The initial coding was conducted by the first researcher, who systematically reviewed each article and assigned relevant codes according to a predefined coding scheme. This process was independently repeated by the second researcher to ensure impartiality and prevent individual bias. Once both rounds of coding were completed, the researchers compared their results and collaboratively finalized the themes and categories through a consensus-building process. This collaborative refinement phase not only ensured conceptual clarity and thematic coherence but also allowed for a critical re-examination of borderline cases. Moreover, to ensure consistency in applying the coding criteria, the two researchers participated in a calibration session prior to full-scale analysis. During this session, they discussed the operational definitions of each coding category, clarified ambiguous cases, and reached agreement on the application of the coding framework. This preliminary step was instrumental in minimizing subjective interpretation during the main coding process, thereby reinforcing the reliability of the data analysis.

In order to systematically evaluate the consistency between the two coders, interrater reliability was assessed through the calculation of Cohen's Kappa coefficient. Each researcher independently entered their codes into the Excel sheet without consulting the other, thereby preserving the objectivity of the process. The Kappa value of 0.82 reflected a high degree of consistency between the coders and was classified as "almost perfect" according to the well-known scale proposed by Landis and Koch (1977). This result provides strong evidence for the reliability and robustness of the coding procedure (Cohen, 1960). After this statistical validation, all instances of coding discrepancies were revisited through systematic discussion. In this reconciliation phase, the researchers critically examined their divergent interpretations, referring back to the original text segments and the operational definitions in the coding manual. This reflective dialogue ensured that final coding decisions were grounded in shared understanding rather than arbitrary judgment. In the rare cases where disagreement persisted, a third researcher with expertise in systematic reviews was consulted to offer an informed external perspective. This multi-phase, consensus-oriented approach contributed significantly to the internal validity and interpretive coherence of the data set. Overall, the integration of rigorous interrater reliability procedures not only bolstered the methodological integrity of the study but also enhanced its transparency, reproducibility, and scholarly credibility—critical attributes for any high-quality systematic review.

Process of Literature Search and Selection

This study follows a four-stage systematic literature review process:

1. **Identification Stage:** Database searches identified 46 records, marking the first step in locating potential studies for inclusion in the review.

2. **Screening Stage:**
   The titles, abstracts, and full texts of the records were reviewed. 35 records were excluded based on specific criteria, including:
   - Being a review article.
   - Not related to the role of GenAI in developing the 4C skills—critical thinking, creative thinking, communication, and collaboration—in foreign language education
3. **Eligibility Assessment Stage:** The remaining 11 studies were evaluated to determine if they met the inclusion criteria for the systematic review.
4. **Inclusion Stage:** 11 studies were deemed eligible and included in the final review.

This structured process underscores the application of rigorous selection criteria to ensure the reliability and relevance of the studies analyzed.

FINDINGS

The studies examined in this review are categorized and presented in the following tables based on their publication year, research methods, participant profiles, study objectives, main findings, limitations, and recommendations.

Findings Based on the Years of Publication

The distribution of the studies analyzed in this research, categorized by their year of publication, is presented in Table 1.

Table 1. Distribution of Studies by the Years of Publication

Year	Number	Studies analyzed
2024	9	Avsheniuk et al., 2024; Borkovska et al., 2024; Chen et al., 2024; Cheung & Shi, 2024; Darmawansah et al., 2024; Kartal, 2024; Liang & Wu, 2024; Liu & Wang, 2024; Werdiningsih et al., 2024
2025	2	Teng, 2025; Wang, 2025.

An examination of the publication distribution in this systematic review indicates that the majority of studies were published in 2024, with nine studies identified, while only two were from early 2025. This pattern suggests a significant surge in academic interest in 2024, followed by a continued but more limited engagement in 2025. However, given that this review only includes studies published up to

February 2025, the lower number of studies from this year may be attributed to the restricted timeframe.

The predominance of 2024 publications underscores the growing scholarly recognition of this research area. Key contributions during this period were made by Avsheniuk et al., Borkovska et al., Chen et al., Cheung & Shi, Darmawansah et al., Kartal, Liang & Wu, Liu & Wang, and Werdiningsih et al. Meanwhile, the 2025 studies, represented by Teng and Wang, indicate that academic engagement in this field remains ongoing.

Findings Based on the Research Methods Employed

The classification of the studies included in this research, according to the research methods utilized, is presented in Table 2.

Table 2. Distribution of Studies by Research Methods

Quantitative method	Qualitative method	Mixed method
Wang, 2025	Cheung & Shi, 2024; Kartal, 2024; Werdiningsih et al., 2024	Avsheniuk et al. 2024, Borkovska et al. 2024, Chen et al. 2024, Darmawansah et al. 2024, Liang ve Wu 2024, Liu ve Wang 2024, Teng 2025

Table 2 presents the classification of the studies included in this research based on the research methods employed. The studies are categorized into three main methodological approaches: quantitative, qualitative, and mixed methods.

According to the data in the table, the number of studies using the quantitative method is the lowest, with only one study conducted by Wang (2025) falling into this category. The qualitative method is employed by Cheung & Shi (2024), Kartal (2024), and Werdiningsih et al. (2024), totaling three studies. The largest proportion of studies utilizes the mixed-methods approach. This category includes studies by Avsheniuk et al. (2024), Borkovska et al. (2024), Chen et al. (2024), Darmawansah et al. (2024), Liang and Wu (2024), Liu and Wang (2024), and Teng (2025), accounting for a total of seven studies.

The data indicate that the mixed-methods approach is the most frequently adopted research method among the studies analyzed. While the number of qualitative studies exceeds that of quantitative studies, it remains lower than the number of mixed-methods studies. This distribution suggests a clear methodological preference among researchers, with mixed methods being the most commonly utilized approach.

Findings Based on Participant Profiles

The studies analyzed in this research are categorized according to participant profiles, as shown in Table 3.

Table 3. Distribution of Studies by Participant Profiles

Participant Profiles	Studies analyzed
Bachelor of English students (China)	Liang & Wu (2024)
English for Specific Purposes students from various faculties (Ukraine)	Borkovska et al. (2024)
English department students (Ukraine)	Avsheniuk et al. (2024)
EFL students from various faculties (China)	Cheung & Shi (2024)
English department students (Indonesia)	Werdiningsih et al., 2024
EFL students (China)	Chen et al. (2024)
EFL students (Indonesia)	Darmawansah et al. (2024)
EFL student teachers (Türkiye)	Kartal (2024)
English literature students (China)	Liu & Wang (2024)
Language and Translation students (China)	Teng (2025)
Engineering students (China)	Wang (2025)

The analysis of participant profiles in the selected studies highlights the diverse backgrounds of individuals learning EFL in different educational settings. The distribution of participants falls into three main categories: general EFL students, students learning English within specific academic disciplines, and prospective English language teachers. This classification provides a comprehensive understanding of the current research landscape in EFL education. A significant portion of the studies focuses on general EFL learners, underscoring the continued academic interest in foreign language acquisition. Research conducted in China (Chen et al., 2024; Cheung & Shi, 2024) and Indonesia (Darmawansah et al., 2024) has examined the language learning experiences of students enrolled in various faculties. These studies contribute to the broader discourse on EFL education by shedding light on the challenges and strategies employed by learners in different institutional contexts.

Beyond general EFL students, some studies specifically investigate English language learning within distinct academic disciplines, exploring the intersection between language acquisition and professional expertise. For instance, research conducted in China has examined the English proficiency of literature students (Liu & Wang, 2024), translation and language students (Teng, 2025), and engineering students (Wang, 2025), highlighting the growing recognition of English as a fundamental skill across diverse fields. Similarly, a study conducted in Ukraine by Borkovska et al. (2024) has investigated students learning English for Specific Purposes (ESP) across various faculties. This research underscores the evolving role of English as both an academic requirement and a professional necessity, extending beyond traditional language learning environments. The increasing emphasis on discipline-specific English instruction suggests a growing need for more tailored language teaching approaches. Another notable participant group in the analyzed studies is prospective English language teachers. A study conducted in Türkiye (Kartal, 2024) specifically focuses on pre-service EFL teachers, reflecting the academic interest in teacher education, curriculum design, and professional development. The inclusion of this participant group in research indicates that language education studies are not solely concerned with student learning but also encompass the training and preparation of future educators.

From a geographical perspective, a substantial proportion of the studies were conducted in China, with six out of the eleven analyzed studies originating from this region (Liang & Wu, 2024; Chen et al., 2024; Cheung & Shi, 2024; Liu & Wang, 2024; Teng, 2025; Wang, 2025). This prevalence suggests that English language education is a major area of academic focus in China, likely due to the country's emphasis on English proficiency as an integral component of its educational system. In addition to China, research has also been carried out in Ukraine (Borkovska et al., 2024; Avsheniuk et al., 2024), Indonesia (Werdiningsih et al., 2024; Darmawansah et al., 2024), and Türkiye (Kartal, 2024), providing valuable insights into English language learning in different educational and sociocultural contexts. However, the limited representation of studies from other regions highlights the need for further research to develop a more globally inclusive perspective on EFL education.

Overall, the findings reveal that research on English language learning encompasses a wide range of student profiles, academic disciplines, and educational objectives. The predominance of studies on general EFL learners reaffirms the ongoing significance of foreign language acquisition research. Meanwhile, investigations focusing on students within specific disciplines emphasize the increasing role of English in both academic and professional domains. Additionally, studies on prospective English teachers reflect the growing academic interest in teacher training and professional development. These insights contribute to a deeper understanding of current trends in English language education research while also pointing to the need for further studies on underrepresented regions and participant groups.

Findings Based on the Objectives of the Studies

The classification of the studies analyzed in this research, according to their objectives, is presented in Table 4.

Table 4. Distribution of Studies by Objectives

Theme	Objectives of the studies	Studies analyzed
Critical Thinking Development	Examine the effectiveness of ChatGPT in cultivating critical thinking in EFL learners	Liang & Wu (2024)
	Explore GenAI's impact on critical thinking in English literature courses through tailored feedback and structured learning activities.	Liu & Wang (2024)
Soft Skills Enhancement	Evaluate the role of GenAI in enhancing soft skills such as communication, teamwork, and critical thinking in online learning for ESP students.	Borkovska et al. (2024)
GenAI in Language Learning	Explore how ChatGPT influences critical thinking, autonomy, and English learning in higher education.	Avsheniuk et al. (2024)
Creativity in Storytelling	Investigate the use of GenAI tools in creative storytelling within a service-learning context.	Cheung & Shi (2024)
Academic Writing Support	Assess the experiences and strategies of EFL students using ChatGPT for academic writing.	Werdiningsih et al. (2024)
Speaking Performance and Motivation	Compare the effects of GenAI-based role-play with traditional role-play on speaking performance and motivation in EFL students.	Chen et al. (2024)
Writing Feedback and Metacognition	Examine the correlation between metacognitive awareness and the effectiveness of ChatGPT for writing feedback.	Teng (2025)
Collaborative Argumentation	Investigate ChatGPT-supported collaborative argumentation's impact on argumentative speaking and critical thinking skills.	Darmawansah et al. (2024)
Critical and Creative Thinking	Explore how EFL student teachers perceive the impact of ChatGPT on thinking skills and creativity.	Kartal (2024)
Communication Skill Development	Investigate ChatGPT-4's effectiveness in improving English communication skills and GenAI acceptance among students.	Wang (2025)

The studies have been grouped under key thematic areas, reflecting different dimensions of GenAI integration in foreign language learning. These themes include critical thinking development, soft skills enhancement, GenAI in language learning, creativity in storytelling, academic writing support, speaking performance and motivation, writing feedback and metacognition, collaborative argumentation, creative thinking, and communication skill development.

The analysis of the studies classified in Table 4 reveals distinct thematic trends in GenAI-supported foreign language education. The critical thinking development theme is well-represented, with studies examining the role of ChatGPT in fostering analytical skills in EFL learners (Liang & Wu, 2024) and exploring its impact on English literature courses through structured feedback (Liu & Wang, 2024). In addition, the soft skills enhancement category includes research on GenAI's contribution to improving communication, teamwork, and critical thinking skills in online English for Specific Purposes (ESP) courses (Borkovska et al., 2024). Similarly, the studies focusing on GenAI in language learning investigate how

ChatGPT influences critical thinking, learner autonomy, and English language acquisition in higher education settings (Avsheniuk et al., 2024). Research on creativity in storytelling explores the role of GenAI tools in fostering creative writing skills within a service-learning context (Cheung & Shi, 2024), while the academic writing support category highlights how EFL students experience and strategize their academic writing processes when using ChatGPT (Werdiningsih et al., 2024). In the area of speaking performance and motivation, Chen et al. (2024) compare the impact of GenAI-based role-play with traditional role-play activities on learners' speaking skills and motivation levels. In addition, writing feedback and metacognition studies examine how ChatGPT-generated feedback relates to metacognitive awareness, with findings suggesting that GenAI tools contribute to improved self-regulation in writing (Teng, 2025). Further research in collaborative argumentation investigates how GenAI-assisted group discussions affect argumentative speaking and critical thinking skills (Darmawansah et al., 2024), whereas studies under the creative thinking category focus on the perceptions of EFL student teachers regarding GenAI's influence on their cognitive and creative abilities (Kartal, 2024). Lastly, communication skill development is explored in Wang (2025), who examines the effectiveness of ChatGPT-4 in improving students' English communication skills and their acceptance of GenAI-driven language learning tools.

The thematic distribution of these studies highlights several key findings. Firstly, critical thinking emerges as a central theme, with multiple studies focusing on GenAI's role in developing analytical and problem-solving skills across different learning contexts. Secondly, GenAI's application in various language learning domains, including writing, speaking, and storytelling, reflects its potential to support diverse pedagogical objectives. Another key observation is the increasing focus on GenAI's impact on metacognitive awareness, particularly in writing-related tasks where GenAI-generated feedback aids self-regulated learning. Additionally, soft skills development, including communication, teamwork, and motivation, is identified as an important research focus, emphasizing the broader implications of GenAI beyond traditional language instruction. Overall, the findings suggest that GenAI technologies such as ChatGPT are being extensively examined for their pedagogical potential in language education, with studies addressing its role in cognitive skill development, language acquisition, writing support, oral communication, and collaborative learning. The classification of research within these thematic areas underscores the growing academic interest in GenAI's capacity to transform language learning and instructional methodologies.

Findings Based on the Main Findings of the Studies

The primary findings derived from the studies included in this research are summarized in Table 5.

Table 5. Distribution of Studies by Main Findings

Themes	Sub Themes	Findings	Studies analyzed
Critical Thinking	EFL Learners' Development	No significant improvement in pre- and post-tests; qualitative data indicated expanded thinking through ChatGPT.	(Liang & Wu, 2024)
	Analytical Thinking, Problem-Solving	Statistically significant improvements in critical thinking skills with GenAI-assisted interactive activities	(Liu & Wang, 2024)
Soft Skills	Communication, Teamwork, Critical Thinking	Positive attitudes towards GenAI tools like ChatGPT and Grammarly in enhancing these skills.	(Borkovska et al., 2024)
Autonomous Learning	Learner Autonomy	ChatGPT promoted self-directed learning but posed challenges in accuracy and human interaction.	(Avsheniuk et al., 2024)
Creativity	Storytelling Support	Increased creative potential and intercultural communication with GenAI tools in storytelling contexts.	(Cheung & Shi, 2024)
Academic Writing	Content and Vocabulary Enhancement	ChatGPT improved essay quality but required human oversight for authenticity.	(Werdiningsih et al., 2024)
Speaking Performance	Motivation and Self-Efficacy	Higher intrinsic motivation and self-efficacy in GenAI-supported role-play activities.	(Chen et al., 2024)
Writing Feedback	Metacognitive Awareness	Positive correlation between metacognitive awareness and effective use of ChatGPT for feedback.	(Teng, 2025)
Argumentation Skills	Collaborative Learning	Improved argumentation skills and critical thinking in ChatGPT-supported collaborative tasks.	(Darmawansah et al., 2024)
Creativity & Thinking	EFL Teacher Candidates	ChatGPT fostered creativity and critical thinking but raised concerns over over-reliance on GenAI-generated content.	(Kartal, 2024)
Communication Skills	AI Acceptance	Statistically significant improvement in communication skills and positive perceptions of ChatGPT's usefulness.	(Wang, 2025)

The analysis of the studies included in this research reveals several key themes and sub-themes related to the impact of GenAI tools on various aspects of foreign language learning and teaching. The findings are systematically categorized into critical thinking, soft skills, autonomous learning, creativity, academic writing, speaking performance, writing feedback, argumentation skills, and communication skills. The studies indicate mixed findings regarding the role of ChatGPT in fostering critical thinking among EFL learners. Liang and Wu (2024) report no statistically significant improvement in critical thinking skills between pre- and post-tests. However, qualitative findings suggest that learners experienced an expansion in their thinking processes through interactions with ChatGPT. Conversely, Liu and Wang (2024) provide quantitative evidence of statistically significant improvements in critical thinking and problem-solving skills when GenAI-assisted interactive activities were integrated into the learning process. These findings suggest that while the impact of GenAI tools on critical thinking may not always be immediately measurable through standardized tests, qualitative data indicate potential cognitive benefits.

The analysis of soft skills highlights a positive perception of GenAI tools in fostering communication, teamwork, and critical thinking. Borkovska et al. (2024) report that learners exhibited favorable attitudes towards GenAI tools such as ChatGPT and Grammarly, particularly in enhancing collaboration and communication-related competencies. This suggests that GenAI tools may facilitate the development of interpersonal and problem-solving skills, complementing traditional pedagogical methods. Regarding learner autonomy, Avsheniuk et al. (2024) find that ChatGPT supports self-directed learning by enabling learners to engage with language tasks independently. However, challenges arise concerning the accuracy of GenAI-generated content and the reduction in human interaction. This indicates that while GenAI tools can enhance autonomous learning, they require careful monitoring to ensure the reliability of the information provided. The use of GenAI tools in storytelling activities is associated with an increase in creative potential and intercultural communication. Cheung and Shi (2024) report that learners who utilized ChatGPT for storytelling demonstrated enhanced creativity and the ability to engage with diverse cultural perspectives. These findings suggest that GenAI tools may serve as effective resources for fostering creativity in language learning, particularly in narrative-based tasks.

The findings on academic writing suggest that ChatGPT positively influences content and vocabulary enhancement. Werdiningsih et al. (2024) indicate that GenAI-assisted writing improved essay quality by expanding vocabulary usage and structuring ideas more coherently. However, the study emphasizes the necessity of human oversight to ensure authenticity and prevent over-reliance on GenAI-generated content. This highlights the dual role of GenAI as both a supportive tool and a potential limitation in academic writing. Chen et al. (2024) examine the impact of GenAI on speaking performance, particularly in motivation and self-efficacy. Their findings suggest that GenAI-supported role-play activities contribute to increased intrinsic motivation and greater confidence in spoken interactions. This indicates that GenAI tools may be beneficial in creating immersive speaking environments, promoting learner engagement in oral language tasks. Teng (2025) explores the relationship between metacognitive awareness and the use of ChatGPT for writing feedback. The study reports a positive correlation, suggesting that learners who demonstrate higher metacognitive awareness benefit more from GenAI-generated feedback. This implies that GenAI tools can serve as effective scaffolding mechanisms for enhancing writing skills, particularly when learners are trained to critically evaluate the feedback they receive. The findings related to argumentation skills highlight the role of collaborative learning in ChatGPT-supported activities. Darmawansah et al. (2024) report that learners engaged in collaborative tasks with GenAI support demonstrated improved argumentation and critical thinking skills. This suggests that GenAI-assisted discussions and structured debates may facilitate higher-order cognitive skills in language learners.

The integration of ChatGPT in teacher training programs is linked to enhanced creativity and critical thinking among EFL teacher candidates. Kartal (2024) finds that while GenAI tools encourage innovative thinking and pedagogical creativity, concerns arise regarding potential over-reliance on GenAI-generated content. These findings indicate that while GenAI can serve as a valuable resource for teacher education, critical engagement with GenAI outputs is necessary to maintain instructional authenticity. Wang (2025) reports a statistically significant improvement in communication skills among learners using ChatGPT, coupled with positive perceptions regarding the tool's usefulness. These findings suggest that GenAI applications may enhance learners' confidence and competence in communicative tasks, reinforcing their acceptance of GenAI-assisted learning methodologies.

The analysis of these studies reveals a multifaceted impact of GenAI tools on language learning and teaching. While GenAI-supported activities contribute to the development of critical thinking, creativity, and communication skills, challenges related to accuracy, over-reliance, and human interaction persist. The findings suggest that the effectiveness of GenAI tools depends on structured implementation, learner awareness, and complementary human oversight. These results underscore the potential of GenAI as an innovative educational tool while emphasizing the need for strategic pedagogical integration.

Findings Based on the Limitations of the Studies

The limitations identified in the studies analyzed within this research are presented in Table 6.

Table 6. Distribution of Studies by Limitations

Themes	Limitations	Studies analyzed
Lack of Control Group	The absence of a control group limits causal claims about the effect of ChatGPT on critical thinking skills.	Liang & Wu, 2024
Sample Size Limitations	Small sample sizes restrict the generalizability of findings to broader populations.	Cheung & Shi, 2024; Werdiningsih et al., 2024; Kartal, 2024
Subjective Data Collection	Heavy reliance on self-reported data may introduce biases such as social desirability and may not fully reflect participants' experiences.	Liu & Wang, 2024; Teng, 2025; Kartal, 2024
Technological Constraints	Technological limitations affected the feedback quality, particularly regarding pronunciation and multimodal feedback for speaking activities.	Chen et al., 2024
Short Study Duration	Limited study periods hinder the ability to observe long-term impacts of GenAI on skills development.	Chen et al., 2024; Wang, 2025
	The absence of longitudinal data prevents assessment of sustained impacts on skills development over time.	Teng, 2025; Darmawansah et al., 2024
Ethical and Dependence Concerns	Participants expressed ethical concerns, such as reliance on GenAI, plagiarism risks, and potential reduction of human interaction.	Avsheniuk et al., 2024
Context-Specific Constraints	Findings may be restricted by specific educational contexts, limiting applicability to other disciplines or learning environments.	Liu & Wang, 2024; Kartal, 2024; Borkovska et al., 2024
Limited Diversity of GenAI Tools	Studies focusing solely on one GenAI tool (e.g., ChatGPT-4) without comparisons to other tools reduce the scope of technological insights.	Wang, 2025

The limitations identified in the analyzed studies were categorized into recurring themes that impact the validity, reliability, and generalizability of findings. These limitations include the absence of control groups, small sample sizes, reliance on subjective data collection methods, technological constraints, short study durations, ethical concerns, context-specific constraints, and the limited diversity of GenAI tools used in the research.

One of the most notable limitations is the absence of a control group, which restricts causal claims regarding the effect of ChatGPT on critical thinking skills (Liang & Wu, 2024). Without a comparative baseline, the observed outcomes cannot be attributed solely to GenAI interventions, highlighting the need for future studies incorporating experimental designs with control groups. Another prevalent issue is the small sample size used in several studies, limiting the generalizability of findings (Cheung & Shi, 2024; Werdiningsih et al., 2024; Kartal, 2024). Small sample sizes reduce statistical power and increase the likelihood of sampling bias, making it difficult to apply conclusions to broader educational contexts.

The reliance on self-reported data is also a significant concern, as subjective data collection methods may introduce biases such as social desirability effects, limiting the accuracy of participant responses (Liu & Wang, 2024; Teng, 2025; Kartal, 2024). The integration of objective assessment tools in future research could mitigate this issue and enhance data reliability. Technological constraints emerged as a key limitation in the studies analyzing GenAI-assisted language learning. In particular, challenges related to GenAI-generated feedback quality, especially in pronunciation and multimodal speaking activities, were reported (Chen et al., 2024). Addressing these constraints through technological improvements could enhance GenAI's effectiveness in language education. Short study durations were frequently cited as limiting factors, preventing long-term assessments of GenAI's impact on skill development (Chen et al., 2024; Wang, 2025). Additionally, the absence of longitudinal data makes it difficult to evaluate the sustainability of learning gains over time (Teng, 2025; Darmawansah et al., 2024). Future research should incorporate extended study durations to capture long-term educational effects.

Ethical concerns were raised in multiple studies, particularly regarding dependence on GenAI, plagiarism risks, and reduced human interaction (Avsheniuk et al., 2024). These concerns highlight the necessity of balancing GenAI use with ethical guidelines to promote responsible learning behaviors. Context-specific constraints further limited the applicability of findings. Studies conducted in specific educational settings may not generalize to other disciplines or learning environments (Liu & Wang, 2024; Kartal, 2024; Borkovska et al., 2024). Expanding research across diverse educational contexts could enhance the broader relevance of GenAI-assisted learning outcomes. Lastly, studies predominantly focused on a single GenAI tool, such as ChatGPT-4, without comparing it to alternative GenAI-driven applications (Wang, 2025). The lack of comparative analyses restricts insights into the relative effectiveness of different GenAI models, underscoring the need for research exploring multiple GenAI tools.

In summary, the findings highlight critical methodological, technological, and ethical constraints in GenAI-assisted education research. Addressing these limitations—through experimental designs with control groups, larger sample sizes, objective data collection, improved GenAI technology, longer study durations, ethical considerations, diverse educational settings, and comparative analyses of GenAI tools—will enhance the robustness and applicability of future research in the field.

Findings Based on the Recommendations of the Studies

The recommendations provided in the studies analyzed within the scope of this research are presented in Table 7.

Table 7. Distribution of Studies by Recommendations

Themes	Sub Themes	Recommendations	Studies analyzed
Critical Thinking	Cultivation Programs	Use a quasi-experimental design with control groups for better causal claims.	Liang & Wu (2024)
	Reliable Measurement Tools	Use alternative, reliable tools for measuring critical thinking.	
	GenAI Impact Assessment	Explore the long-term effects of GenAI tools on learning outcomes.	
	Personalized Learning	Provide personalized feedback using GenAI tools to enhance engagement.	Liu & Wang (2024)
Soft Skills Development	GenAI Integration	Introduce GenAI-supported online courses to enhance soft skills.	Borkovska et al. (2024)
Language Learning	Autonomy & GenAI Use	Integrate GenAI tools carefully within the curriculum.	Avsheniuk et al. (2024)
Ethics in GenAI	Human Interaction Balance	Maintain a human-centered approach to foster ethical discussions on GenAI.	
	Responsible Use	Develop guidelines for ethical GenAI use in education.	Werdiningsih et al. (2024)
Creative Thinking	Storytelling	Use GenAI to support but not dominate creative processes.	Cheung & Shi (2024)
Intercultural Skills	Communication	Develop GenAI-supported activities that promote intercultural understanding.	
Academic Writing	GenAI Oversight	Ensure human oversight to maintain authenticity in GenAI-assisted writing.	Werdiningsih et al. (2024)
Speaking Performance	Role-play Activities	Integrate multimodal GenAI tools for comprehensive speaking feedback.	Chen et al. (2024)
Motivation	Psychological Factors	Extend study duration to explore long-term motivation impacts.	
Training	Teacher Training	Develop programs to train educators in effective GenAI integration.	Liu & Wang (2024)
		Provide ongoing training for effective GenAI use in language instruction.	Wang (2025)
Writing Feedback	Metacognition	Foster metacognitive skills through GenAI-supported writing feedback.	Teng (2025)
Research Design	Longitudinal Studies	Conduct longitudinal studies to assess metacognitive development over time.	
Collaboration	Argumentation Skills	Use structured collaboration scripts to enhance argumentation skills.	Darmawansah et al. (2024)
Access & Equity	Technological Access	Address disparities in access to ensure equitable learning opportunities.	Darmawansah et al. (2024)
Thinking Skills	Creativity & Criticality	Promote human-computer co-creation to balance GenAI usage with independent thinking.	Kartal (2024)

continued on following page

Table 7. Continued

Themes	Sub Themes	Recommendations	Studies analyzed
Educational Context	Applicability	Conduct further research with diverse educational settings.	Kartal (2024)
Communication Skills	Personalized Feedback	Enhance personalized learning by integrating GenAI tools.	Wang (2025)

The analysis of the studies' recommendations reveals several key insights into the integration of GenAI in education. The findings indicate that critical thinking is a recurring focus, with multiple studies emphasizing the necessity of employing quasi-experimental designs with control groups to establish stronger causal claims regarding GenAI's role in fostering critical thinking (Liang & Wu, 2024). Additionally, the importance of utilizing alternative, reliable tools for assessing critical thinking skills is highlighted, alongside a call for extended research on the long-term effects of GenAI tools on learning outcomes. A significant recommendation in this regard pertains to the use of GenAI for personalized learning, particularly in enhancing student engagement through adaptive feedback mechanisms (Liu & Wang, 2024).

In addition to critical thinking, the development of soft skills is another area where GenAI is expected to make a considerable impact. The findings suggest that GenAI-supported online courses may contribute to the enhancement of soft skills by providing dynamic, interactive learning environments (Borkovska et al., 2024). Similarly, in the domain of language learning, studies advocate for the careful integration of GenAI tools within curricula to support learner autonomy while ensuring that these technologies do not undermine independent language acquisition (Avsheniuk et al., 2024). The role of GenAI in ethical education also emerges as a crucial consideration, with scholars emphasizing the need for a human-centered approach to foster ethical discussions and mitigate potential risks associated with GenAI-driven instruction. The development of clear guidelines for the ethical use of GenAI in education is highlighted as an essential step toward responsible implementation (Werdiningsih et al., 2024).

The findings further underscore the potential of GenAI in enhancing creative thinking, particularly in storytelling-based learning activities. The recommendations suggest that GenAI should function as a supportive tool rather than a dominant force in the creative process, ensuring that students maintain agency in their own creative outputs (Cheung & Shi, 2024). Moreover, the role of GenAI in fostering intercultural competencies is acknowledged, with recommendations advocating for GenAI-supported activities that promote cross-cultural understanding and communication skills. Academic writing also emerges as an area requiring careful oversight, with a strong emphasis on maintaining authenticity and ensuring that GenAI-generated content remains subject to human review (Werdiningsih et al., 2024).

Oral communication skills, particularly speaking performance, are another key focus, with findings recommending the integration of multimodal GenAI tools to provide comprehensive feedback on role-play activities (Chen et al., 2024). The long-term impact of GenAI on learner motivation is also examined, with scholars emphasizing the need for extended study durations to assess the sustainability of motivational gains over time. Training for educators is identified as a critical factor in the effective deployment of GenAI technologies, with recommendations calling for targeted professional development programs to enhance teachers' ability to integrate GenAI into instructional practices (Liu & Wang, 2024; Wang, 2025). In a similar vein, GenAI-supported writing feedback is recognized for its potential to foster metacognitive skills, while longitudinal studies are proposed as a necessary methodological approach for assessing these developments over time (Teng, 2025).

Collaboration and argumentation skills are also addressed, with findings highlighting the role of structured collaboration scripts in enhancing critical discussion and reasoning skills (Darmawansah et al., 2024). The issue of access and equity is another recurring concern, with scholars stressing the need to address technological disparities to ensure that GenAI-driven educational innovations remain accessible to all students (Darmawansah et al., 2024). Moreover, recommendations suggest that GenAI should be used to support, rather than replace, independent cognitive processes, with an emphasis on promoting human-computer co-creation as a means of fostering both creativity and criticality in learning activities (Kartal, 2024).

The applicability of GenAI in diverse educational contexts is also noted as an area requiring further research, with scholars advocating for studies that examine GenAI integration across a broader range of instructional settings (Kartal, 2024). Finally, personalized feedback is highlighted as a central advantage of GenAI applications in education, with recommendations emphasizing its potential to enhance individualized learning experiences by adapting to students' unique needs and progress (Wang, 2025).

In short, these findings suggest that while GenAI presents significant opportunities for advancing educational practices, its integration must be approached strategically to ensure ethical considerations, equitable access, and sustained engagement. The necessity of ongoing empirical research, particularly through longitudinal studies and examinations of diverse educational contexts, is emphasized as essential for developing a more comprehensive understanding of GenAI's long-term impact on learning and teaching.

In summary, the findings of this systematic review reveal a complex yet coherent picture of the integration of generative AI, particularly ChatGPT, in foreign language education, with a notable emphasis on enhancing 4C competencies—critical thinking, communication, collaboration, and creativity. Across the reviewed studies, mixed-method research predominated, indicating a strong preference for combining quantitative and qualitative insights to capture the multifaceted impacts of GenAI tools. While a significant portion of research focused on general EFL learners, there was also meaningful engagement with discipline-specific cohorts and pre-service teachers, underscoring the widening scope of GenAI's educational relevance. Thematically, critical thinking emerged as the most frequently addressed domain, often paired with studies on writing and collaborative speaking tasks. Despite mixed quantitative results, qualitative data consistently highlighted cognitive expansion and increased learner autonomy. In parallel, GenAI tools were found to enhance motivation, communication, and creative expression, especially in tasks involving storytelling and role-play. However, the findings also bring attention to recurring limitations such as small sample sizes, lack of control groups, technological constraints, and ethical concerns related to over-reliance on AI-generated content. Consequently, the reviewed studies advocate for methodologically robust future research that includes longitudinal designs, comparative analyses across diverse GenAI platforms, and ethical safeguards to ensure human agency and instructional integrity. Collectively, these findings demonstrate the pedagogical promise of GenAI while also outlining the critical parameters necessary for its responsible and effective integration into language learning contexts.

DISCUSSION

The findings of this systematic review underscore the critical role of GenAI tools, particularly ChatGPT, in fostering the development of the 4C skills—critical thinking, creativity, collaboration, and communication—within foreign language education. While these technologies offer promising avenues for enhancing pedagogical practices, their effectiveness remains contingent upon various factors, including instructional design, learner engagement, and ethical considerations. In this context, examining how effectively GenAI supports higher-order cognitive processes is crucial for assessing its pedagogical benefits and limitations.

The impact of GenAI on critical thinking development presents a nuanced picture. While some studies report significant improvements in analytical reasoning and problem-solving skills (Liu & Wang, 2024), others find no statistically significant differences between pre- and post-test results, despite qualitative evidence indicating increased cognitive engagement (Liang & Wu, 2024). These discrepancies align with existing literature suggesting that GenAI's role in fostering higher-order thinking skills depends largely on the pedagogical framework within which it is implemented (Avsheniuk et al., 2024). ChatGPT has been shown to support problem-solving and facilitate the evaluation of multiple perspectives, thereby functioning as a valuable pedagogical tool (Aydın Yıldız, 2024). However, the lack of robust assessment methodologies to measure critical thinking development in GenAI-supported learning contexts remains a significant challenge. Future research should explore alternative assessment strategies, including qualitative and mixed-method approaches, to capture the depth and complexity of learners' cognitive engagement.

In terms of creativity, the reviewed studies generally concur that GenAI tools provide meaningful support in fostering creative expression, particularly in writing and storytelling tasks (Cheung & Shi, 2024). Digital storytelling, when integrated with GenAI-driven scaffolding, has been found to enhance engagement and innovation in language learning (Çınar Yağcı & Genç, 2024). Nonetheless, concerns persist regarding the extent to which GenAI-generated content may inadvertently limit students' independent creative thinking (Kartal, 2024). While GenAI offers structured support and ideation assistance, there is a risk that excessive reliance on algorithmic outputs could constrain originality. These findings highlight the importance of maintaining a balance between GenAI assistance and opportunities for self-directed creativity, a recommendation echoed in broader studies on human-GenAI collaboration in education (Darmawansah et al., 2024). Pedagogical frameworks must therefore be designed to encourage learners to critically evaluate GenAI-generated content rather than passively accept it.

The role of GenAI in collaborative learning also emerges as a significant theme in this review. Several studies highlight the potential of GenAI tools in facilitating structured argumentation and team-based learning activities (Borkovska et al., 2024; Darmawansah et al., 2024). GenAI-enhanced collaboration enables learners to engage in a meaningful dialogue, consider diverse perspectives, and refine their communicative abilities. ChatGPT, in particular, has been shown to play a crucial role in fostering idea-sharing and brainstorming, thereby strengthening cooperative problem-solving (Aydın Yıldız, 2024). These findings align with existing research emphasizing the role of GenAI in promoting peer-to-peer interaction and collaborative learning (Borkovska et al., 2024). However, disparities in GenAI literacy and unequal access to GenAI technologies pose significant challenges that must be addressed to ensure equitable learning experiences. Future research should explore strategies for mitigating these disparities and fostering inclusive GenAI-enhanced learning environments.

The impact of GenAI-driven feedback on communication skills is another key finding of this review. The studies indicate that GenAI-supported role-play and personalized feedback significantly enhance learners' confidence and proficiency in oral and written communication (Chen et al., 2024; Wang, 2025). ChatGPT has been found to facilitate vocabulary expansion, improve textual analysis skills, and foster critical engagement with reading materials (Özçelik & Çınar Yağcı, 2024). These results are consistent with prior research demonstrating that GenAI-enhanced feedback systems promote fluency and accuracy in second language acquisition

(Chen et al., 2024). However, challenges remain. Some learners report experiencing conversational disruptions due to ChatGPT's occasional misinterpretation of input, which can hinder the natural flow of dialogue (Üstünbaş, 2024). Future studies should investigate the integration of GenAI with human-led instructional support to optimize communicative outcomes and ensure that learners receive contextually appropriate and pedagogically sound feedback.

Beyond pedagogical considerations, the ethical dimensions of GenAI integration in education warrant careful scrutiny. Academic integrity concerns, potential plagiarism, and reduced human interaction emerge as key challenges associated with GenAI adoption (Avsheniuk et al., 2024). Educators in the reviewed studies express apprehensions regarding GenAI ethics, emphasizing the potential risks of uncritical GenAI reliance through evocative metaphors such as "walking in a minefield" (Kamali et al., 2024). Trust, encompassing strategic, behavioral, cognitive, and emotional dimensions, is fundamental to effective human-GenAI collaboration (Bozkurt & Sharma, 2024). In this regard, explainable GenAI—characterized by transparency, continuous feedback, and iterative refinement—is crucial in ensuring that GenAI serves as a complementary tool rather than a substitute for human judgment. These findings underscore the need for comprehensive guidelines and ethical frameworks to regulate GenAI usage in educational settings. Without such measures, the benefits of GenAI may be undermined by ethical dilemmas and unintended consequences related to learner autonomy and academic honesty.

CONCLUSION

This systematic review provides an in-depth and critically engaged synthesis of empirical research on the pedagogical implications of GenAI, with a particular focus on ChatGPT, in supporting the development of 21st-century competencies—namely, critical thinking, creativity, collaboration, and communication—in foreign language education. Beyond offering a broad overview of current findings, this study brings a unique contribution by examining how GenAI tools function within diverse instructional settings and pedagogical strategies. The findings suggest that, when purposefully integrated, GenAI technologies can support learner autonomy, stimulate higher-order cognitive processes, and encourage active participation in both individual and collaborative learning contexts. In this respect, the review highlights the importance of context-sensitive and ethically grounded implementation, arguing that the educational value of GenAI is shaped less by the tool itself and more by the way it is pedagogically framed and utilized.

Moreover, the review sheds light on recurring patterns and critical research gaps across the studies analyzed. GenAI tools were found to serve multifaceted educational purposes: offering real-time, tailored feedback; enhancing students' metacognitive engagement; and enriching creative tasks such as writing, role-playing, and storytelling. Notably, ChatGPT emerges as more than a language aid—it facilitates reflective thinking and revision, thereby contributing to learners' critical literacy and intercultural communicative competence. At the same time, the review draws attention to several limitations in the existing literature, including insufficient sample sizes, a lack of robust control conditions, limited longitudinal data, and the predominance of studies centered solely on one GenAI tool. These observations point to the need for methodologically diverse, longitudinal, and comparative research to strengthen the evidence base for effective GenAI integration.

Taken together, the findings of this review underscore that GenAI holds significant promise for transforming foreign language education, but only when its use is guided by principles of critical pedagogy, ethical responsibility, and human-centered design. While tools like ChatGPT can serve as valuable resources to promote engagement and deepen learning (Yüzlü, 2024), the review warns against unreflective adoption that may compromise academic integrity, amplify digital inequities, or diminish learners' creative independence. Therefore, it advocates for the development of pedagogical models and institutional policies that ensure both innovation and accountability. By articulating the pedagogical affordances and ethical imperatives of GenAI-supported instruction, this review lays a meaningful foundation for future research and contributes to the thoughtful design of inclusive, responsive, and future-oriented language learning environments.

Suggestions for Education Policy

To effectively integrate GenAI technologies such as ChatGPT into language education and foster the development of 21st-century competencies, educational policymakers must take an active role in shaping inclusive and forward-looking strategies. One of the first steps in this direction involves embedding GenAI use within national curriculum guidelines. By establishing clear policy frameworks that articulate when, how, and for what purposes GenAI can be used in language learning contexts, ministries of education can ensure both pedagogical alignment and ethical coherence. These frameworks should not only promote innovative instructional practices but also address concerns about data privacy, equity, and content authenticity. In parallel, policymakers must prioritize digital equity to guarantee that the benefits of GenAI are accessible to all learners, regardless of their geographical or socioeconomic background. Although many institutions in urban centers may have access to reliable technological infrastructure, rural and underserved areas often face significant barriers. Therefore, policy initiatives should include targeted investments in broadband access, device provision, and digital literacy programs.

These infrastructural supports will enable institutions to adopt GenAI-enhanced teaching models sustainably and equitably.

Furthermore, the development of standardized evaluation protocols to assess the impact of GenAI on learners' critical thinking, creativity, communication, and collaboration is essential for maintaining educational accountability. These protocols should include both qualitative and quantitative measures to capture the multifaceted nature of 4C skill development. In addition, policymakers should consider incentivizing schools and universities that successfully implement and document evidence-based GenAI practices, thereby creating a culture of innovation and continuous improvement. Ultimately, any policy on GenAI integration must be grounded in principles of responsible innovation. This involves striking a balance between encouraging technological advancement and preserving core educational values such as learner autonomy, teacher agency, and academic integrity. Policymakers should thus engage stakeholders from various sectors—educators, researchers, technologists, and students—in ongoing dialogue to ensure that GenAI policies remain adaptive, inclusive, and ethically sound.

Implications for Teacher Education

The successful implementation of GenAI in language education also depends heavily on the preparedness of educators to integrate these tools in meaningful and pedagogically appropriate ways. Accordingly, teacher education programs must be restructured to include systematic training on GenAI-enhanced teaching and assessment strategies. Pre-service teachers should be introduced to the affordances and limitations of GenAI tools through hands-on activities that model their use in lesson planning, formative assessment, and student-centered language tasks. Importantly, such training should also address ethical dimensions, including plagiarism risks, bias detection, and responsible tool usage. Moreover, the dynamic nature of GenAI technologies necessitates continuous professional development (PD) for in-service teachers. One-off workshops are insufficient in keeping pace with rapid technological change. Therefore, PD programs should be designed as sustained, iterative, and collaborative processes. These should involve micro-credentialing opportunities, peer-led knowledge exchange, and classroom-based action research that empower teachers to adapt GenAI tools to their own pedagogical contexts. In doing so, educators will not only stay current with emerging technologies but also build confidence in experimenting with innovative teaching methods.

In addition to technological fluency, teacher education programs must cultivate a mindset of critical engagement. Rather than treating GenAI as a replacement for human judgment, teachers should be encouraged to view these tools as cognitive partners that support—but do not substitute—their professional expertise. This requires developing teachers' capacity to critically evaluate AI-generated outputs, to scaffold student interactions with GenAI, and to promote metacognitive reflection on its use. By embedding these competencies into teacher preparation, institutions can ensure that future educators are not only digitally literate but also ethically grounded and pedagogically flexible. Taken together, these implications underscore that empowering teachers is not a peripheral concern but a central requirement for realizing the educational potential of GenAI. Without robust teacher preparation and support systems, even the most well-intentioned AI policies may fall short of their goals. Therefore, institutions of teacher education must work in tandem with policymakers to develop coherent, practice-informed, and ethically attuned frameworks that position educators as active agents in the evolving landscape of GenAI-supported instruction.

Limitations

One of the central limitations identified in the reviewed studies concerns the methodological robustness of research designs. Specifically, the absence of control groups in several studies undermines the ability to draw causal inferences regarding the impact of GenAI tools such as ChatGPT on 4C skill development. Without comparative benchmarks, the positive outcomes reported—particularly in critical thinking and communication—cannot be conclusively attributed to the intervention itself. This issue is further compounded by the use of small sample sizes across multiple studies, which restricts the generalizability of findings and weakens statistical validity. Furthermore, the heavy reliance on self-reported data introduces subjectivity, often influenced by social desirability bias, thus limiting the reliability of participant reflections. These methodological shortcomings highlight the need for more rigorous empirical designs to validate the pedagogical efficacy of GenAI technologies.

In addition to methodological constraints, several technological and ethical challenges emerged. For instance, the limitations of GenAI in generating accurate and multimodal feedback, especially in speaking tasks, were noted as barriers to effective language learning. Short study durations also impeded the evaluation of long-term learning outcomes, particularly in terms of metacognitive development and sustained motivation. From an ethical perspective, participants expressed concerns over the potential over-reliance on GenAI, risks of plagiarism, and diminished human interaction, all of which raise questions about the authenticity of the learning process. Furthermore, most studies focused on a single GenAI tool—typically ChatGPT—thereby restricting technological diversity and comparative evaluation. Collectively, these limitations underscore the need for longitudinal, ethically grounded, and multi-tool research to better understand and harness the transformative potential of GenAI in language education.

Recommendations

To overcome the identified limitations and enhance the pedagogical integration of GenAI, the reviewed studies collectively advocate for more rigorous and diversified research methodologies. A primary recommendation is the adoption of quasi-experimental and longitudinal study designs with control groups, which would allow researchers to determine the causal impact of GenAI on learners' 4C competencies over time. Additionally, incorporating alternative, objective assessment tools—such as performance-based tasks, standardized rubrics, and mixed-method evaluations—could provide a more accurate representation of learners' progress, particularly in domains like critical thinking and creativity. Several studies also recommend the integration of GenAI in personalized learning environments, emphasizing the importance of real-time, adaptive feedback in promoting learner autonomy and engagement.

Beyond methodological enhancements, the studies emphasize the need for context-sensitive and ethically responsible GenAI implementation. To mitigate ethical concerns such as overdependence, content originality, and diminished human oversight, scholars recommend that GenAI tools be used to complement—not replace—teacher-led instruction. This includes developing clear institutional guidelines for the ethical use of GenAI in language learning contexts. Training programs for educators are likewise essential, equipping teachers with the competencies necessary to integrate GenAI in pedagogically meaningful ways. Moreover, future research should aim to address access disparities by exploring GenAI's impact across diverse educational settings and learner populations. Finally, expanding the scope of research to include comparative analyses of multiple GenAI platforms would enrich our understanding of how different tools perform in fostering 4C competencies. Together, these recommendations point toward a more balanced, inclusive, and reflective approach to leveraging GenAI for sustainable innovation in foreign language education.

REFERENCES

Alshamsi, I., Sadriwala, K., Alazzawi, F., & Shannaq, B. (2024). Exploring the impact of generative AI technologies on education: Academic expert perspectives, trends, and implications for sustainable development goals. *Journal of Infrastructure. Policy and Development*, *8*(11), 1–20. DOI: 10.24294/jipd.v8i11.8532

Anggraini, Y., Setiawati, S., & Sari, I. (2024). Assessing 4C Competencies in English Language Learners: Tools, Challenges, and Implications. *EBONY. Journal of English Language Teaching, Linguistics, and Literature*, *4*(2), 29–41. Advance online publication. DOI: 10.37304/ebony.v4i2.14147

Avsheniuk, N., Lutsenko, O., Svyrydiuk, T., & Seminikhyna, N. (2024). Empowering language learners' critical thinking: Evaluating ChatGPT's role in English course implementation. *Arab World English Journal, Special Issue on ChatGPT*, 210-224. https://dx.doi.org/DOI: 10.24093/awej/ChatGPT.14

Aydın Yıldız, T. (2024). online first). Exploring the impact of ChatGPT on improving 21st-century skills for future English teachers during lesson planning. *Computers in the Schools*, •••, 1–24. DOI: 10.1080/07380569.2024.2429534

Baek, E., & Wilson, R. (2024). An inquiry into the use of generative AI and its implications in education. *International Journal of Adult Education and Technology*, *15*(1), 1–14. DOI: 10.4018/IJAET.349233

Bellibaş, M. Ş., & Gümüş, S. (2018). *Eğitim yönetiminde sistematik derleme çalışmaları. İçinde K. Beycioğlu, N. Özer ve Y. Kondakçı (Edt.), Eğitim yönetiminde araştırma (ss.* Pegem Akademi.

Borkovska, I., Kolosova, H., Kozubska, I., & Antonenko, I. (2024). Integration of AI into the distance learning environment: Enhancing soft skills. *Arab World English Journal, Special Issue on ChatGPT*, 56–72. https://dx.doi.org/DOI: 10.24093/awej/ChatGPT.3

Borzova, E., & Shemanaeva, M. A. (2022). Interconnected development of intercultural competence and soft skills through tasks in foreign language education at a university. *Perspectives of Science and Education*, *58*(4), 307–319. DOI: 10.32744/pse.2022.4.18

Bozkurt, A., Karadeniz, A., Bañeres, D., & Rodríguez, M. E. (2021). Artificial intelligence and reflections from educational landscape: A review of AI studies in half a century. *Sustainability (Basel)*, *13*(2), 1–16. DOI: 10.3390/su13020800

Bozkurt, A., & Sharma, R. C. (2024). Trust, credibility and transparency in human-AI interaction: Why we need explainable and trustworthy AI and why we need it now. *Asian Journal of Distance Education, 19*(2), 1–9. DOI: 10.5281/zenodo.14599168

Bozkurt, A., Xiao, J., Farrow, R., Bai, J. Y. H., Nerantzi, C., Moore, S., Dron, J., Stracke, C. M., Singh, L., Crompton, H., Koutropoulos, A., Terentev, E., Pazurek, A., Nichols, M., Sidorkin, A. M., Costello, E., Watson, S., Mulligan, D., Honeychurch, S., & Asino, T. I. (2024). The manifesto for teaching and learning in a time of generative AI: A critical collective stance to better navigate the future. *Open Praxis, 16*(4), 487–513. DOI: 10.55982/openpraxis.16.4.777

Bulathwela, S., Pérez-Ortiz, M., Holloway, C., Cukurova, M., & Shawe-Taylor, J. (2024). Artificial intelligence alone will not democratise education: On educational inequality, techno-solutionism and inclusive tools. *Sustainability (Basel), 16*(2), 1–20. DOI: 10.3390/su16020781

Çeviker Ay, Ş., & Orhan, A. (2022). The effect of different critical thinking teaching approaches on critical thinking skills: A meta-analysis study. *Pamukkale Üniversitesi Eğitim Fakültesi Dergisi, 49*, 88–111. DOI: 10.9779/pauefd.561742

Chembe, C., Nasilele, N. B., & Msendo, R. (2023). The fuss about artificial intelligence in education sector: Should we worry? *Zambia ICT Journal, 7*(2), 30–35. DOI: 10.33260/zictjournal.v7i2.269

Chen, A., Jia, J., Li, Y., & Fu, L. (2024). Investigating the effect of role-play activity with GenAI agent on EFL students' speaking performance. *Journal of Educational Computing Research, 63*(1), 99–125. DOI: 10.1177/07356331241299058

Chen, L., Chen, P., & Lin, Z. (2020). Artificial intelligence in education: A review. *IEEE Access : Practical Innovations, Open Solutions, 8*, 75264–75278. DOI: 10.1109/ACCESS.2020.2988510

Cheung, L. M. E., & Shi, H. (2024). Co-creating stories with generative AI: Reflections from undergraduate students of a storytelling service-learning subject in Hong Kong. *Australian Review of Applied Linguistics, 47*(3), 259–283. DOI: 10.1075/aral.24101.che

Cohen, J. (1960). A Coefficient of Agreement for Nominal Scales. *Educational and Psychological Measurement, 20*(1), 37–46. DOI: 10.1177/001316446002000104

Darmawansah, D., Rachman, D., Febiyani, F., & Hwang, G.-J. (2024). ChatGPT-supported collaborative argumentation: Integrating collaboration script and argument mapping to enhance EFL students' argumentation skills. *Education and Information Technologies, 30*(3), 3803–3827. DOI: 10.1007/s10639-024-12986-4

Deng, X., & Joshi, K. (2024). Promoting ethical use of generative AI in education. *The Data Base for Advances in Information Systems*, *55*(3), 6–11. DOI: 10.1145/3685235.3685237

Facione, P. A. (1990). *Critical thinking: A statement of expert consensus for purposes of educational assessment and instruction. Research Findings and Recommendations. Prepared for the Committee on Pre-College Philosophy*. American Philosophical Association.

Giannakos, M., Azevedo, R., Brusilovsky, P., Cukurova, M., Dimitriadis, Y., Hernandez-Leo, D., & Rienties, B. (2024). The promise and challenges of generative AI in education. *Behaviour & Information Technology*, •••, 1–27. DOI: 10.1080/0144929X.2024.2394886

Harizaj, M., & Hajrulla, V. (2017). Fostering learner's critical thinking skills in EFL: Some practical activities. *European Scientific Journal*, *13*(29), 1–20. DOI: 10.19044/esj.2017.v13n29p126

Herlinawati, H., Marwa, M., Ismail, N., Junaidi, J., Liza, L. O., & Situmorang, D. D. B. (2024). The integration of 21st century skills in the curriculum of education. *Heliyon*, *10*(15), e35148. DOI: 10.1016/j.heliyon.2024.e35148

Hwang,G.-J., & Tsai, C.-C.. (2011). Research trends in mobile and ubiquitous learning: a review of publications in selected journals from 2001 to 2010. British Journal of Educational Technology, 42(4), E65–E70. http://dx.doi.org/. 2011.42. issue-4DOI: 10.1111/bjet

Kamali, J., Alpat, M. F., & Bozkurt, A. (2024). AI ethics as a complex and multifaceted challenge: Decoding educators' AI ethics alignment through the lens of activity theory. *International Journal of Educational Technology in Higher Education*, *21*(62), 1–20. DOI: 10.1186/s41239-024-00496-9

Kartal, G. (2024). The influence of ChatGPT on thinking skills and creativity of EFL student teachers: A narrative inquiry. *Journal of Education for Teaching*, *50*(4), 627–642. DOI: 10.1080/02607476.2024.2326502

Khan, I. U., Salman, S., & Naz, R. (2023). Unpacking the 4C's: Evaluating the integration of 21st-century skills in Pakistan's new undergraduate curriculum. *Educational Research and Innovation*, *3*(2), 175–193. DOI: 10.61866/eri.v3i2.79

Kosharna, N. (2019). Students' critical thinking skills development within pedagogical specialties of master's educational level in the content of the discipline professional communication in a foreign language. *Educological Discourse*, *2*(29), 14–25. DOI: 10.28925/2312-5829.2020.2.2

Kousloglou, M., Petridou, E., Molohidis, A., & Hatzikraniotis, E. (2023). Assessing Students' Awareness of 4Cs Skills after Mobile-Technology-Supported Inquiry-Based Learning. *Sustainability (Basel), 15*(8), 6725. DOI: 10.3390/su15086725

Kuntariati, U., & Paramita, P. D. Y. (2023). Analysis of collaborative project-based language learning method: Efforts to improve language education quality for tourism students. *Prosiding Seminar Nasional Riset Bahasa Dan Pengajaran Bahasa, 5*(1), 34–46. DOI: 10.31940/senarilip.v5i1.36-46

Landis, J. R., & Koch, G. G. (1977). The Measurement of Observer Agreement for Categorical Data. *Biometrics, 33*(1), 159–174. DOI: 10.2307/2529310

Leavy, A., Dick, L. K., Meletiou-Mavrotheris, M., Paparistodemou, E., & Stylianou, E. (2023). The prevalence and use of emerging technologies in steam education: A systematic review of the literature. *Journal of Computer Assisted Learning, 39*(4), 1061–1082. DOI: 10.1111/jcal.12806

León, J. J. C., & Castro, C. M. C. (2017). Transforming EFL classroom practices and promoting students' empowerment: Collaborative learning from a dialogical approach. *PROFILE Issues in Teachers'. Professional Development (Philadelphia, Pa.), 19*(2), 135–149. DOI: 10.15446/profile.v19n2.57811

Liang, W., & Wu, Y. (2024). Exploring the use of ChatGPT to foster EFL learners' critical thinking skills from a post-humanist perspective. *Thinking Skills and Creativity, 54*, 1–15. DOI: 10.1016/j.tsc.2024.101645

Liao, Y., Chen, Y., Chen, H., & Chang, Y. (2018). Infusing creative pedagogy into an English as a foreign language classroom: Learning performance, creativity, and motivation. *Thinking Skills and Creativity, 29*, 213–223. DOI: 10.1016/j.tsc.2018.07.007

Liu, W., & Wang, Y. (2024). The effects of using AI tools on critical thinking in English literature classes among EFL learners: An intervention study. *European Journal of Education, 59*(4), 1–12. DOI: 10.1111/ejed.12804

Lodzikowski, K., Foltz, P., & Behrens, J. (2024). Generative AI and its educational implications. In Kourkoulou, D., Tzirides, A. O., Cope, B., & Kalantzis, M. (Eds.), *Trust and Inclusion in AI-Mediated Education* (pp. 35–57). Springer., DOI: 10.1007/978-3-031-64487-0_2

Medvedeva, O. D., & Rubtsova, A. (2021). Productive method as the basis for soft skills development in engineering foreign language education. *Education Sciences, 11*(6), 1–15. DOI: 10.3390/educsci11060276

Methley, A. M., Campbell, S., Chew-Graham, C., McNally, R., & Cheraghi-Sohi, S. (2014). PICO, PICOS and SPIDER: A comparison study of specificity and sensitivity in three search tools for qualitative systematic reviews. *BMC Health Services Research, 14*(1), 1–10. DOI: 10.1186/s12913-014-0579-0

Moher, D., Liberati, A., Tetzlaff, J., & Altman, D. G.Prisma Group. (2009). Preferred reporting items for systematic reviews and meta-analyses: The PRISMA statement. *Annals of Internal Medicine, 151*(4), 264–269. DOI: 10.7326/0003-4819-151-4-200908180-00135

Opesemowo, O. A. G., & Adekomaya, V. (2024). Harnessing artificial intelligence for advancing sustainable development goals in south Africa's higher education system: A qualitative study. *International Journal of Learning. Teaching and Educational Research, 23*(3), 67–86. DOI: 10.26803/ijlter.23.3.4

Oran, B. B. (2023). Correlation between artificial intelligence in education and teacher self-efficacy beliefs: A review. *RumeliDe Dil ve Edebiyat Arastirmalari Dergisi, 34*(34), 1354–1365. DOI: 10.29000/rumelide.1316378

Orhan, A. (2022). The relationship between critical thinking and academic achievement: A meta-analysis study. *Psycho-Educational Research Reviews, 11*(1), 283–299. DOI: 10.52963/PERR_Biruni_V11.N1.18

Orhan, A. (2024). Online or in-class problem based learning: Which one is more effective in enhancing learning outcomes and critical thinking in higher education EFL classroom? *Journal of Computer Assisted Learning, 40*(5), 2351–2368. DOI: 10.1111/jcal.13033

Orhan, A., & Ataman, O. (2024). Investigating the predictive role of reflective thinking and decision making on creative thinking dispositions. *Reflective Practice, 25*(2), 178–193. DOI: 10.1080/14623943.2024.2305921

Özçelik, N., & Çınar Yağcı, Ş. (2024). L'enseignement des langues étrangères soutenu par l'intelligence artificielle générative: L'effet de ChatGPT sur l'amélioration des compétences rédactionnelles en français. In Özçelik, N. (Ed.), *Fransız Dili Eğitimi Alanında Uluslararası Araştırmalar I* (pp. 25–60). Eğitim Yayınevi.

Özçelik, N., & Çınar Yağcı, Ş. (2024). ChatGPT'nin ters yüz sınıf modeli ile Fransızca okuma becerisinin geliştirilmesinde kullanımı. In Aysu, S., & Göçerler, H. (Eds.), *Dil Eğitimi ve Öğretiminde Dijital Yönelimler* (pp. 109–151). Özgür Yayınları.

Petticrew, M., & Roberts, H. (2006). *Systematic reviews in the social sciences: A practical guide.* Blackwell Publishing. DOI: 10.1002/9780470754887

Richmond, J. L., & Nicholls, K. (2024). Using Generative AI to Promote Psychological, Feedback, and Artificial Intelligence Literacies in Undergraduate Psychology. *Teaching of Psychology*, *0*(0). Advance online publication. DOI: 10.1177/00986283241287203

Salybekova, F., Almetov, N., Karbozova, G., Shvaikovski, A., & Suyuberdieva, A. (2024). Upgrading Pre-Service Foreign Language Teachers' Professional Competences by Means Of The 4c's Educational Model In Xxı Century. *Journal of Educational Sciences*. https://doi.org/.DOI: 10.26577/JES2024v80.i3.02

Salybekova, F. M., Almetov, N. S., Karbozova, G. K., Suyuberdieva, A. A., Kudaibergenova, M. R., & Nazarova, G. Z. (2023). Role of the integration of the 4c model in the professional training of foreign language teachers. *Frontiers in Education*, *8*, 1–15. DOI: 10.3389/feduc.2023.1125728

Singh, A. (2024). Impact of generatıve AI on educatıonal sector. *International Journal of Scientific Research in Engineering and Management*, *8*(4), 1–14. DOI: 10.55041/IJSREM30724

Siregar, N., Firmansyah, F., & Harahap, Y. S. (2023). Developing students' worksheet for English language teaching to cope with the 4C's skill through project based learning. *Jurnal Paedagogy: Jurnal Penelitian dan Pengembangan Pendidikan, 10*(1), 44–52. https://doi.org/DOI: 10.33394/jp.v10i1.6286

Soomro, R., Khan, R., & Rind, I. (2025). Exploring ESL teachers' experiences about ICT-based 4Cs skills: A phenomenological study. *Discover Education*, *4*(1), 12. Advance online publication. DOI: 10.1007/s44217-024-00376-4

Tan, L., & Luhrs, M. (2024). Using Generative AI Midjourney to enhance divergent and convergent thinking in an architect's creative design process. *The Design Journal*, *27*(4), 677–699. DOI: 10.1080/14606925.2024.2353479

Teng, M. F. (2025). Metacognitive awareness and EFL learners' perceptions and experiences in utilising ChatGPT for writing feedback. *European Journal of Education*, *60*(1), 1–17. DOI: 10.1111/ejed.12811

Tevdovska, E. S. (2015). Integrating soft skills in higher education and the EFL classroom: Knowledge beyond language learning. *SEEU Review*, *11*(2), 95–106. DOI: 10.1515/seeur-2015-0031

Thornhill-Miller, B., Camarda, A., Mercier, M., Burkhardt, J.-M., Morisseau, T., Bourgeois-Bougrine, S., Vinchon, F., El Hayek, S., Augereau-Landais, M., Mourey, F., Feybesse, C., Sundquist, D., & Lubart, T. (2023). Creativity, Critical Thinking, Communication, and Collaboration: Assessment, Certification, and Promotion of 21st Century Skills for the Future of Work and Education. *Journal of Intelligence, 11*(3), 54. DOI: 10.3390/jintelligence11030054

Türker, P. M., & Öztürk, M. (2025). Generative Artificial Intelligence and the 4C Learning Skills for the 21st Century. In Cela, E., Vajjhala, N., & Fonkam, M. (Eds.), *Next-Generation AI Methodologies in Education* (pp. 285–320). IGI Global Scientific Publishing., DOI: 10.4018/979-8-3693-7220-3.ch011

Ulaşan, F. (2023). The use of artificial intelligence in educational institutions: Social consequences of artificial intelligence in education. *Korkut Ata Türkiyat Arastirmalari Dergisi, 1*(Special issue), 1305–1324. DOI: 10.51531/korkutataturkiyat.1361112

Üstünbaş, Ü. (2024). Hey, GPT, Can we have a chat?: A case study on EFL learners' AI speaking practice. *International Journal of Modern Education Studies, 8*(1), 91–107. DOI: 10.51383/ijonmes.2024.318

Vinchon, F., Gironnay, V., & Lubart, T. (2024). GenAI Creativity in Narrative Tasks: Exploring New Forms of Creativity. *Journal of Intelligence, 12*(12), 125. DOI: 10.3390/jintelligence12120125

Wang, Y. (2025). A study on the efficacy of ChatGPT-4 in enhancing students' English communication skills. *SAGE Open, 1*(1), 1–17. DOI: 10.1177/21582440241310644

Watson, G., & Glaser, M. E. (2010). *Watson-Glaser TM II critical thinking appraisal.* Pearson.

Werdiningsih, I., Marzuki, , & Rusdin, D. (2024). Balancing AI and authenticity: EFL students' experiences with ChatGPT in academic writing. *Cogent Arts & Humanities, 11*(1), 1–15. DOI: 10.1080/23311983.2024.2392388

Xu, W., & Ouyang, F. (2022). The application of AI technologies in stem education: A systematic review from 2011 to 2021. *International Journal of STEM Education, 9*(1), 1–20. DOI: 10.1186/s40594-022-00377-5

Yadav, A. (2024). The development of AI with generative capabilities and its effect on education. *International Journal of Science and Research (Raipur, India), 13*(5), 854–860. DOI: 10.21275/SR24509232318

Yağcı, Ş. Ç., & Genç, A. (2024). Üretken yapay zekâ araçları ile Fransızca dijital hikâye tasarlama: Yazma, görselleştirme ve çeviri süreçleri. In Özçelik, N. (Ed.), *Fransız Dili Eğitimi Alanında Uluslararası Araştırmalar I* (pp. 85–110). Eğitim Yayınevi.

Yüzlü, M. Y. (2024). The impact of ChatGPT on vocabulary learning in L3 German class. *Journal of Higher Education and Science, 14*(2), 339–348. DOI: 10.5961/higheredusci.1417301

Zenni, R. D., & Andrew, N. R. (2023). Artificial Intelligence text generators for overcoming language barriers in ecological research communication. *Austral Ecology, 48*(7), 1225–1229. DOI: 10.1111/aec.13417

Zhang, H. (2024). Study on the role and influence of artificial intelligence in the field of education. *Lecture Notes in Education Psychology and Public Media, 70*(1), 114–119. DOI: 10.54254/2753-7048/70/20241023

KEY TERMS AND DEFINITIONS

Generative Artificial Intelligence (GenAI): GenAI refer to systems or machines that are capable of performing different tasks which typically require human intelligence such as learning, reasoning, or communication.

4C Skills (Critical Thinking, Creativity, Communication, Collaboration): Essential 21st-century skills that enable learners to analyze problems, develop innovative solutions, effectively communicate ideas, and work collaboratively in diverse environments.

Critical Thinking: The ability to analyze, evaluate, and synthesize information logically and independently which is crucial in language learning for structuring arguments and engaging in meaningful discussions.

Creativity in Language Learning: The capacity to generate original ideas, use language innovatively, and engage in storytelling.

Collaborative Learning with GenAI: The use of GenAI to facilitate teamwork and group discussions, enabling students to engage in problem-solving tasks and peer-to-peer learning activities.

Communication in Language Learning: The ability to effectively convey ideas, express thoughts clearly, and engage in meaningful interactions in a foreign language. GenAI-powered feedback and real-time conversational simulations help learners develop fluency and confidence in communication.

GenAI-Assisted Language Learning (GenAILL): The integration of GenAI tools in language education to facilitate personalized feedback, automated assessments, and create adaptive learning environments.

Chapter 9
Exploring the Potential of AI-Driven Chatbots With a Focus on SkyTutor in Aviation English

Nazmi Dincer
https://orcid.org/0000-0002-2901-5367
Turkish Air Force Academy, Turkey

Mert Çetinok
https://orcid.org/0009-0002-0907-3532
Turkish Air Force Academy, Turkey

ABSTRACT

This chapter explores the integration of SkyTutor, an AI-powered chatbot based on ChatGPT technology, into aviation English training for ab-initio pilots. Addressing the increasing global demand for skilled pilots, the chapter highlights the limitations of traditional training methods and the need for innovative solutions. SkyTutor was developed to bridge the gap between conventional instruction and modern technological capabilities, providing personalized, interactive learning experiences tailored to aviation communication protocols and theoretical knowledge. The chapter outlines SkyTutor's design, technical framework, and educational potential while critically analyzing its impact on both learners and instructors. By evaluating SkyTutor's strengths and shortcomings, this chapter contributes to understanding the transformative potential of AI tools in aviation education and their implications for enhancing communication skills, cognitive readiness, and instructional efficiency in the rapidly evolving aviation landscape.

DOI: 10.4018/979-8-3373-7574-8.ch009

INTRODUCTION

In the globalized world, individuals change countries and continents without much effort and it has been more affordable than ever before. This has caused the aviation industry to modify itself and live up to expectations in society. This shift in the mode of transportation and interest has resulted in a huge demand for skilled and well-prepared pilots. As of 2023, the global aviation industry employs around 351,000 active commercial airline pilots (CentreForAviation, 2023). According to a report by BOEING (2024), the need for skilled pilots will double over the next two decades. The Asia-Pacific region is projected to require 91,000 new pilots over the next decade, while North America will need approximately 63,000. Despite the growing demand, the aviation industry faces significant challenges in addressing it. A study conducted by the International Civil Aviation Organization (ICAO) projects a global training capacity deficit, with an estimated shortage of 160,000 pilots by 2030 if current trends persist (2011). Furthermore, a report by Oliver Wyman (Murray & Green, 2021) forecasts a global shortage of approximately 80,000 pilots by 2032, with North America alone potentially experiencing a deficit of 30,000 pilots.

This demand has also brought up a focus on the training methodology. While the need to accelerate the number of graduates is prominent, the quality of education is another area that needs to be reconsidered. These pilots are required to master an extensive range of theoretical and practical knowledge such as communication protocols, flight principles, aircraft dynamics etc. Despite being effective, traditional training methods has been falling short in addressing the needs and challenges that ab-inito pilots face. Optimization in aviation training means to educate better and faster. This could be better overcome through innovation in the methodology. Recognizing this gap, artificial intelligence (AI) could be integrated into the curriculum and training in the field.

SkyTutor, a customized chatbot based on ChatGPT technology, aims to bridge this gap by revolutionizing the mode of instruction and tutoring systems. It has been designed to help student pilots to acquire theoretical knowledge and enhance practical application. It could be utilized for a series of reasons. For instance; it can teach air law, principles of flight, parts of an aircraft, pitot-static system or communication protocols. This means that SkyTutor offers a personalized and interactive learning experience. In other words, this innovation enables students to develop essential skills, go into complex concepts, and have immediate feedback at any time and anywhere.

SkyTutor was designed for the purpose of developing an AI-powered tutor in order to tackle the diverse challenges inherent in aviation education. For example; instructors often struggle with managing large class sizes due to the huge demand in the field and accommodating varying levels of student comprehension while ab-inito students face the difficulties of aviation terminology, the demands of real-time decision-making, and the necessity for ongoing practice. SkyTutor, thus, addresses these challenges by offering a reliable, hands on resources that supports traditional instructional methods.

To simply put, this chapter examines the development, functionality, and potential impact of SkyTutor within the context of aviation training. It further highlights how this innovative tool could transform the learning experience for student pilots by means of a structured and guided platform to enhance their knowledge and skills. From its technical underpinnings to its practical applications, SkyTutor can demonstrate the transformative potential of AI in advancing personalized and sophisticated aviation training.

The integration of AI into aviation training represents more than just a technological revolution. It represents a fundamental shift in educational paradigms. As the aviation industry increasingly adopts digital transformation, tools like SkyTutor could drive a more accessible, personalized, and effective approach to pilot training. This chapter explores the benefits of SkyTutor, its role in shaping the future of aviation training, and the broader implications of AI-powered innovation within the industry.

THE NEED FOR INNOVATION IN AVIATION TRAINING

Aviation training has traditionally been a challenging, risky, and intensive process in which ab-inito pilots go through at the beginning of their careers. The training does not end once graduate from the school. Every pilot is being checked either in the field or in a simulator intervally. They are supposed to master a wide range of areas in technical, procedural, and communicational sides. However, the training process needs innovation to ensure safety, quality, and performance (Dinçer, 2023).

One of the most significant challenges lies in the limited and insufficient number of flight instructors. This is valid for in-class and in-cockpit instruction. The demand for instructors rises along with the number of graduates and pre-service pilots. Training methods, facilities and resources should be reconsidered, as well. This leads to a large class size, lack of interaction, and inadequate personalized instruction. Students often find this environment daunting, especially when attempting to comprehend complex subjects like aerodynamics, aviation regulations, or standardized communication protocols.

Another issue is the training fee in the aviation industry. Flight hours, simulator sessions and in-class courses along with hours of real flights necessitate a huge amount of investment, that causes pilots' dreams to fall short. Moreover, the logistical challenges of scheduling flight and simulator sessions often limit opportunities for consistent practice and skill reinforcement. This gap between theoretical understanding and practical application can leave students inadequately prepared to handle real-world scenarios effectively.

Effective communication, on the other hand, requires a great deal of effort to master standardized phraseology and routine and non-routine scenarios. Despite the narrow scope of aviation radiotelephony communication, the accuracy and clarity are quite significant in that only one word might result in a disaster. This shows how important pilots should be trained in radiotelephony expertise. Technological affordances could play a key role in increasing the familiarity and readiness of ab-initio pilots. Any innovation that helps pilots engage in structured communication drills and receive immediate feedback, could bridge the gap between the ultimate competency and hands-on training.

CHATGPT IN EDUCATION

ChatGPT was introduced on 30th November 2022 by OpenAI as a natural language processing (NLP) model that specializes in transformer architecture in order to generate responses in real-time conversations. As a large language model (LLM), the basic premise of the tool is to understand the use of input and produce human-like responses. It has been aimed at maintaining natural dialogues between AI and individuals. Its main library is exploiting and manipulating the existing resources on the World Wide Web. Besides, it can upgrade its grounding on the current information through trial and error methodology, which in turn leads to a steady decrease in efforts to reconsider the background information notwithstanding the interventions for ethical guidelines and an act of protocols. This phenomenon, thus, comes out as an outstanding tool that is capable of generating auditory and visual outputs.

ChatGPT has been in the focus of scholars in education from the beginning. It has ben believed that this innovation could be integrated into education to promote teaching and learning (Adeshola & Adepoju 2024; Lo, 2023; Zhu et al., 2023). It has many capabilities including reviewing, generating texts, designing texts, creating pictures, translating into different languages, summarizing documents, answering sophisticated questions etc.

The analysis of the relevant literature shows that numerous studies have demonstrated the students' positive stance towards self-paced learning in that they adjust the learning path based on their own profile, needs, capacity and level (Dinçer et al. 2023, McClure & Williams, 2021; Tullis & Benjamin, 2011). Further, a vast number of studies have proposed that AI tools are among the most critical and beneficial supporters of the self-paced learning approach (Baillifard et al., 2023; Möller et al., 2024; St-Hilaire et al., 2022). Additionally, these studies have suggested that AI tools have significantly increased the success rates of learners in various fields. For instance, ChatGPT-based chatbots in the field of computer programming aid learners in sharpening their skills at their own pace and in their preferred manner. Also, these chatbots assist learners in designing their learning processes based on their individual preferences. For instance, the *Coding Code* chatbot provides a precious opportunity to learn or enhance proficiency in various programming languages such as Phyton, JavaScript, React, PHP, and SQL from various foundational to advanced levels. This ChatGPT-based chatbot has facilitated over 200.000 conversations with a vast number of individuals who seek to develop their coding and programming skills.

Another example of chatbots utilized in various aspects of human life is *TutorMe* which is a ChatGPT-driven chatbot developed by a non-profit organization Khan Academy in 2022. This chatbot provides tutoring services to individuals who seek to improve their proficiency in various subjects. For instance, *TutorMe* assists learners with mathematics, ranging from basic arithmetic to calculus, as well as science subjects such as physics, chemistry, and biology. Additionally, it supports English language learning by providing tutoring in grammar, essay writing, and reading comprehension. Additionally, *TutorMe* is one of the most widely used educational chatbots within the ChatGPT ecosystem, which has facilitated over two million conversations with learners (Shetye, 2024).

Since this paper focuses on the SkyTutor chatbot, which was designed to teach aviation English to ab-inito pilots, examining chatbots in the field of foreign language teaching has the uttermost importance. Various ChatGPT-driven chatbots have been developed to support foreign language learners through AI tools. These tools provide learners with the flexibility to study their desired foreign language in a manner that aligns with their individual learning preferences. For instance, the ChatGPT-driven chatbot *Language Teacher Ms. Smith* provides an opportunity for learners to improve their proficiency in more than 20 languages, including Spanish, German, French, English, Chinese, Korean, and Japanese. This chatbot has facilitated more than 900 thousand conversations with individuals around the globe who strive to develop their foreign language skills. Additionally, for learners with specific language learning goals, there are vast amounts of specialized AI chatbots which provide targeted assistance to leaners. For example, individuals who aim for a band score of 9 on the IELTS exam might utilize *IELTS Speaking - English & Language Learning* chatbot to do activities regarding the IETLS exam to reach higher scores. This chatbot has conducted over 200 thousand conversations with learners who want to reach higher scores in the IELTS exam so far. Similarly, individuals who aim to improve their academic writing skills for the TOEFL exam can benefit from the *TOEFL iBT Writing Evaluator* chatbot. This chatbot, on the other hand, has the memory of ten thousand interactions with individuals looking for an increase in their writing competency.

The following studies also demonstrate how generative AI tools, such as ChatGPT, have been implemented in authentic classroom settings. In particular, Song and Song (2023) conducted a mixed-methods study to evaluate the impact of ChatGPT-assisted instruction on writing skills and motivation among Chinese EFL students. Their findings indicated that students who received AI-supported guidance showed significant improvement in writing proficiency and expressed higher levels of motivation compared to those in traditional instruction. Similarly, Mahapatra (2024) investigated the use of ChatGPT as a formative feedback tool for undergraduate ESL students in academic writing classes. Using a mixed-methods intervention design, the study revealed that students receiving AI-generated feedback not only improved their writing skills across multiple assignments but also reported positive perceptions of the tool's immediacy, clarity, and adaptability to individual needs. These real-world applications highlight the transformative potential of ChatGPT in language learning environments and reinforce its role as a personalized, interactive educational assistant capable of supporting learners with different needs and backgrounds.

Since this chapter explores the role and real-world applications of generative artificial intelligence in the educational domain, it is essential to situate SkyTutor within a comparative framework alongside other widely recognized ChatGPT-driven educational chatbots. This comparative analysis not only contextualizes the pedagogical and technological distinctiveness of SkyTutor but also provides a broader understanding of how generative AI tools function across diverse instructional settings. By presenting SkyTutor in comparison with tools such as *TutorMe, IELTS Speaking Chatbot*, and *Language Teacher Ms. Smith*, the analysis highlights how specialized domain-specific implementations of AI, particularly in aviation English, differ from more general or exam-focused educational assistants. This comparative perspective supports a deeper examination of generative AI's affordances and limitations in language education and contributes to the ongoing discourse on AI integration in curriculum design, learner engagement, and formative assessment.

Table 1. Comparison of SkyTutor and Other Educational Chatbots

Criteria	SkyTutor	TutorMe	IELTS Chatbot	Language Teacher Ms. Smith
Primary Focus	Aviation English (radiotelephony, phraseology)	General academic subjects	IELTS speaking exam preparation	Foreign language learning (20+ languages)
Target Users	Ab-initio pilots, aviation English instructors	K–12 and college students	IELTS candidates	Global language learners
Interaction	Text-based, ICAO-based prompts	Text-based Q&A, tutoring sessions	Scenario-based Q&A	Multilingual conversation practice
Content Customization	Pre-trained with aviation-specific documents	Limited (session-based input)	Fixed speaking topics	Generalized prompts per language
Feedback	ICAO-style response guidance	Tutor-style explanations	Fluency and vocabulary feedback	Vocabulary and grammar correction
Assessment Capability	Aligned with ICAO LPR descriptors	No formal assessment	Informal score estimation	No formal assessment
Pedagogical Framework	Spiral curriculum, Bloom's taxonomy	Adaptive tutoring model	Exam-oriented preparation	Conversation-based immersion
AI Engine	Custom-trained ChatGPT with domain prompts	General ChatGPT or GPT API	General ChatGPT	General ChatGPT
User Adaptivity	Dynamic AI prompting with aviation scenarios	Moderate	Low	Moderate
Unique Features	Radiotelephony simulation, ICAO training	Tutor matchmaking, multi-subject access	IELTS-specific questions and score hints	Supports 20+ languages, customizable tone

FOUNDATION OF SKYTUTOR

The aviation industry demands radiotelephony expertise to maintain safety and precision. While traditional training fosters procedural memory for communication protocol scenarios, the field must exploit the tenders of modern technology to optimize the training, increase efficiency and support proficiency. Similar to many other fields, aviation should not be deemed to obsolete approaches that ignore innovation and fresh pathways. Due to the priority over safety, the field should always go through a type of reconsideration on current information. In this respect, SkyTutor has been developed as an AI-powered educational tool that paves the way for clear and smooth communication among the partners.

Figure 1. **SkyTutor Capabilities**

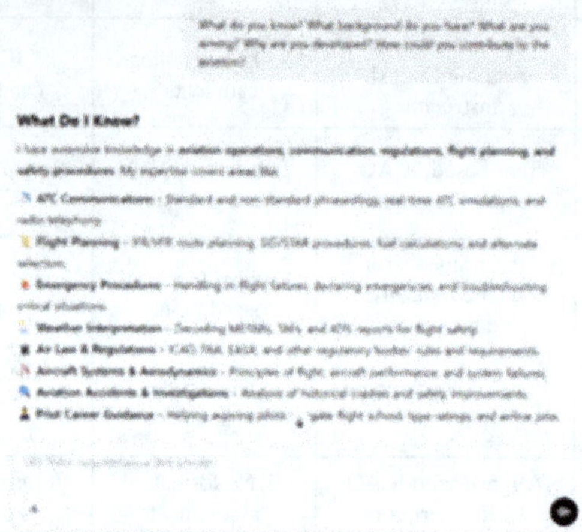

Initially, the ChatGPT ecosystem has been adapted as a touchstone against which the SkyTutor could make decisions. The current ecosystem has been using a vast majority of data in order to reach the target information. Besides, the reliability and accuracy of the target information are not certain since there is much debate about it. Therefore, the first action was to narrow down the information and create a customization on aviation phraseology training. It was named SkyTutor, introduced with about 20 books with regard to aviation training. Although the locus of interaction is standard radiotelephony communication, sub-branches of aviation are uploaded to the memory of SkyTutor in order to let it grasp the vision and mission properly as well as keep all other components in consideration.

The indoctrination of a customized chatbot is significant in that it will act based on the pre-defined and pre-set statements and library. The decision-making process has been directly influenced by such interventions. Segregated lectures to the chatbot might probably result in failure to get a sense of the whole. The selected area must be well-instructed and later the distinct sections could be elaborated. By means of rich prompts that stimulate the chatbot to a specific area, the muscle memory of the AI has evolved and expanded. It has already acquainted with the sample questions and proper answers by grounding the intelligence on introduced data. Therefore, a large set of data and information regarding the related field has been introduced to the system.

Figure 2. **SkyTutor Interface**

Table 2. SkyTutor Based on ISTE Evaluation Guidelines

Dimension	Indicator	Strengths	Limitations
User Interface and Agency	Value Proposition	Clearly supports aviation English learning	Lacks direct workflow improvement for teachers
	Login	No complex login required	No multi-user role support
	Navigation	Intuitive conversational design	Lacks structured menu system
	Interface Design	Simple and interactive interface	No UI customization options
	Discoverability	Easily accessible for users	Advanced functions not easily visible
	Student View	Provides real-time responses	No structured teacher-student preview mode
	Customizable Interface	Personalized AI interactions	No structured content modification by instructors
	Support	AI provides instant responses	No embedded help resources
	Interoperability	Can be integrated into LMS	Limited compatibility with existing tools
	Data Privacy	OpenAI privacy policies apply	No explicit transparency on data handling

continued on following page

Table 2. Continued

Dimension	Indicator	Strengths	Limitations
Learning Design	Learning Outcomes	Engages students in aviation scenarios	Lacks explicit outcome tracking
	Student Goals	Supports student-driven conversations	No structured goal-setting features
	Chunking	Content delivered in manageable exchanges	No segmentation for lesson structuring
	Content Type	Text-based interactions enhance learning	No multimedia support
	Content Adjacence	Immediate contextual responses	No alignment of visuals with text
	Recall & Reinforcement	Engages users in repeated practice	No structured reinforcement activities
	Content Customization	AI adapts responses dynamically	No teacher-driven content selection
	Applied Examples	Generates real-world aviation scenarios	Lacks structured examples outside AI generation
	Elaborative Reflection	Can prompt users for reflections	No structured note-taking tools
Digital Pedagogy	Authentic Learning	Provides aviation-specific dialogues	Lacks structured scenario-based learning
	Problem Definition	Users define their learning focus	No explicit problem-solving structure
	Information Curation	AI provides information as needed	Does not evaluate source credibility
	Solution Design	Generates language-based solutions	No structured design thinking approach
	Collaborative Interaction	Allows teacher-student interaction	No peer collaboration features
	Digital Identity	Encourages correct aviation terminology	No explicit digital literacy education
Inclusivity	Diverse Representation	AI adapts to various user inputs	No explicit inclusivity awareness
	Empathy Opportunity	Promotes critical thinking	Lacks structured social-emotional learning
	Accessibility	Accessible on multiple devices	No screen reader compatibility confirmed
	Inclusive Awareness	Can adapt to different cultural contexts	No content addressing privilege and equity

continued on following page

Table 2. Continued

Dimension	Indicator	Strengths	Limitations
Assessment and Data	Assessment Alignment	Engages users with contextual questions	No formal assessment structure
	Success Criteria	Provides AI-generated feedback	No predefined rubrics
	Assessment Types	Allows open-ended language assessment	No diverse assessment formats
	Performance Demonstration	Users engage in spoken/ written interaction	No structured student work submission
	Feedback	Immediate AI-generated responses	Accuracy and consistency may vary
	Performance Results	AI adapts responses based on user input	No tracking of student progress
	Student Analytics	Interaction history stored temporarily	No data visualization for teachers

SkyTutor involves usability characteristics that underline easy access and interaction for users. The value proposition is clear and supports the notion of aviation English by means of language practice and real-world aviation scenarios. However, it has limited capability to make modifications in the workflow improvements for instructors despite the availability of background prompting. Teachers cannot directly control the process. The login and navigation features are considered to be user-friendly, including easy access to the platform with no complex ways. This could have been enriched by multi-user roles and structured menu types that might increase the functionality. It only serves a couple of pre-defined questions in the welcome page.

As for the interface, it could be said that the simple and interactive nature of the tool helps participants to engage effortlessly although there is no option to customize it based on instructors' and institutions' patterns. Discoverability, on the other hand, is somewhat limited since it does not offer comprehensive help documentation and search functions. Another barrier to the agency could be exemplified by the student view feature. It is not available in the system, which in turn delimits teachers to monitor student performance and movements.

In terms of learning design, SkyTutor offers a set of advantages that enhance the learning process in the field of aeronautical communication. It has the mastery in delivering content through chunks and facilitates dynamic interactions with the help of content customization. This enables artificial intelligence to make adaptations based on the user inputs. SkyTutor, however, has important downsides in goal-setting, progress monitoring, and outcome tracking. Despite the machine learning working behind, these downsides do not allow instructors to fully get the analytics of learners. This is even worse when you cannot get multimedia content, which negatively affects efficient cognition. Additionally, due to the absence of organized note-taking or reflection tools, SkyTutor cannot allow users to make reflections.

When it comes to digital pedagogy, the tool provides aviation-specific dialogues and is able to adapt itself to different roles such as an ATC or a pilot. These dialogues increase the essence of the real-life-like environment. Structured scenarios are not used, though. This could be accomplished via background prompting. It has also a shortage of collaboration opportunities that get students to come together and make group projects. In other words, self-paced learning is more prominent. Besides, those who are registered in the system might need digital literacy education. This is not provided in the current platform, which can extend the wider adoption among the users.

In terms of inclusivity, SkyTutor demonstrates several strengths and also presents notable limitations for both aviation English instructors and ab-initio pilots. One of the key advantages of SkyTutor is its ability to adapt to various user inputs, which gives opportunities for aviation English instructors and ab-initio pilots to have personalized learning experiences. SkyTutor also promotes critical thinking by engaging instructors and ab-initio pilots with real-life aviation-related scenarios and remains accessible on multiple devices. Being able to access SkyTutor chatbot on multiple devices increases its flexibility for its users. However, SkyTutor lacks explicit inclusivity awareness and does not incorporate elements that actively address diversity or equity. Additionally, it offers no structured social-emotional learning opportunities; therefore, Skytutor limits the development of empathy and other social emotions which can be acquired primarily through human interaction. Furthermore, the absence of confirmed screen reader compatibility restricts accessibility for visually impaired users. As the last dimension of the ISTE evaluation guideline regarding inclusivity, while SkyTutor is capable of adapting to different cultural contexts, it lacks content that directly addresses privilege and equity, which limits its effectiveness in fostering a fully inclusive learning environment.

Regarding the assessment and data dimension of the ISTE evaluation guideline, the SkyTutor chatbot demonstrates several strengths while also presenting certain limitations for aviation English instructors and ab-initio pilots. The guideline highlights that SkyTutor is capable of providing AI-generated immediate feedback to ab-initio pilots during their aviation English learning experiences. However, SkyTutor lacks predefined rubrics for instructors and ab-initio pilots to get or give feedback. In other words, SkyTutor's feedbacks depend on its own creativity and capability. Additionally, SkyTutor effectively engages ab-initio pilots through contextual questions, which encourage ab-initio pilots to engage in deeper learning and acquire hands-on experience while studying aviation English. Furthermore, SkyTutor empowers aviation English instructors and ab-initio pilots to take part in open-ended language assessment methods, such as engaging in scenario-based air traffic communication simulations or responding to emergency procedure prompts. Notwithstanding the presented advantages of SkyTutor, it be insufficient to provide a wide range of assessment methods that could provide a more thorough evaluation of learner progress. While SkyTutor facilitates interaction through contextual questions such as simulating in-flight communication scenarios or asking questions related to meteorological conditions, SkyTutor lacks a formal assessment structure that allows for systematic tracking of student performance and submission of structured assignments.

BENEFITS OF SKYTUTOR FOR AB-INITO PILOTS

SkyTutor, similar to other AI-driven chatbots created in various fields of education such as engineering, medicine, and economy, provides numerous benefits to both instructors and pre-service and in-service pilots in the context of aviation English. In this respect, it is essential to conduct a profound analysis of how the SkyTutor chatbot's services address the needs of aviation English course instructors and pre-service pilots in their teaching and learning journeys.

Considering the literature, SkyTutor has great potential to enhance the training of ab-inito pilots to improve their English language skills in the aviation context. Being able to access the source of information and interact with the chatbots regardless of time and location is a privileged advantage for learners in the 21st century which is provided with the help of today's advancement in modern technology (Holmes et al., 2019; Luckin & Holmes, 2016). In this regard, SkyTutor is a chatbot that is available for pre-service pilots at any time and place they desire to improve their proficiency in aviation English. Alongside the stated positive aspect, SkyTutor gives the possibility to the ab-initio pilots to improve their aviation English proficiency by removing the need for an instructor typically required in traditional face-to-face educational settings.

SkyTutor provides a chance for pre-service pilots to enhance their aviation English skills in a learning environment that is free from emotional barriers. Learners in a traditional face-to-face learning atmosphere with the presence of the instructor and their peers might face the affective filter, (Krashen, 1982). The affective filter hypothesis encompasses various problems that learners might encounter in their learning processes, such as the fear of making mistakes and mispronunciation, foreign language anxiety, and the fear of being negatively evaluated by peers and instructors (Horwitz et al., 1986; Young, 1991). However, comparing the landscape of Krashen's time to today's technologically advanced era, the integration of AI tools and technology into educational settings assists in eliminating and minimizing various forms of negative pressure on learners (Bozkurt et al., 2024). In parallel with this, by offering a stress-free learning atmosphere, SkyTutor eliminates these mental barriers and enables learners to perform at their full potential.

Diverse amounts of studies in the literature have suggested that learners achieve better outcomes through collaborative learning rather than studying in isolation (Cheng et al., 2021; Scager et al., 2017). Additionally, regarding AI's role as a collaborative learning partner, studies have shown that AI-based tools can promote collaborative learning experiences by functioning as interactive study partners, consequently decreasing learners' sense of isolation (Cao et al., 2023; Lee et al., 2023). However, some learners who prefer studying alone or who possess introverted personality traits might miss the chance the sharpen their skills more effectively and interactively. At this point, ab-inito pilots can use SkyTutor as an AI-based conversational partner or study companion to participate in discussions and conversations on less familiar or less developed aspects of aviation English. In this regard, SkyTutor offers a distinctive opportunity for every ab-initio pilot, regardless of their personality type.

Figure 3. SkyTutor Conversation

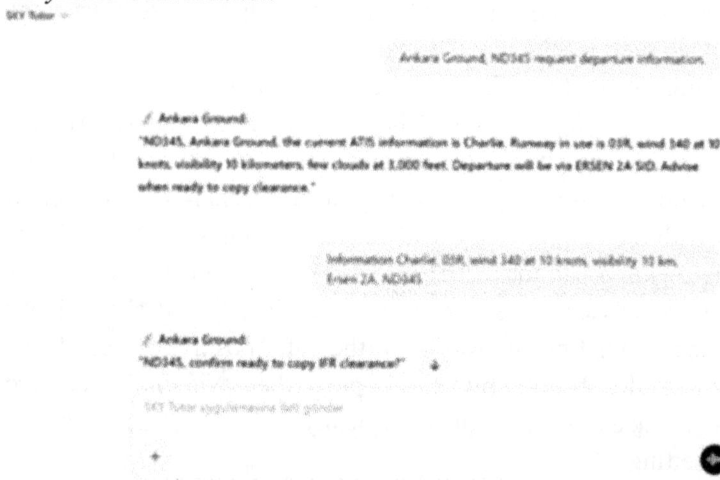

Numerous studies in the literature in the field of education have suggested that receiving immediate feedback as a learner significantly increases learning outcomes and enhances overall performance of the learners (Arroyo & Yilmaz, 2018; Foerde & Shohamy, 2011; Li et al., 2016; Nakata, 2015). At this juncture, the SkyTutor aviation English chatbot enables the pre-service pilots to receive instant feedback on their outputs; therefore, it allows the candidates to monitor their progress throughout their learning process. Receiving immediate feedback during the training via the SkyTutor not only accelerates the learning process but also aids the pre-service pilots to stay on the right track in their language development. Building on this advantage, SkyTutor provides an individualized learning experience, enabling pre-service pilots to identify their areas of weakness in aviation English, such as standard phraseology in radio communication and emergency procedure vocabulary, and request additional activities to address these gaps.

SkyTutor utilizes the tenets of the spiral curriculum, a concept introduced by Bruner (1960), which highlights the systematic reviewing of topics with increasing complexity to support progressive learning. This approach assures that learners continuously advance to higher proficiency levels over time, eventually reaching mastery in aviation English. SkyTutor's pedagogical framework is also in accordance with Bloom's Mastery Learning model (Bloom, 1968), which proposes that all learners are able to achieve significant accomplishment given in adequate time, structured feedback, and individualized support. By incorporating Bloom's Taxonomy into its curriculum, SkyTutor guides learners through a hierarchical cognitive development process. Furthermore, SkyTutor ensures that the ab-inito pilots move beyond basic recall of aviation terminology and established procedures toward higher-order thinking skills which are crucial for effective communication in aviation contexts. To clarify how SkyTutor integrates Bloom's Taxonomy into its curriculum, the following statements are given as examples for each level. At the lower levels of Bloom's Taxonomy, learners engage in remembering and comprehending, where SkyTutor offers structured lessons on aviation phraseology, regulations, and standard radio communication. As learners progress, they move into applying and analyzing, where they interact with AI-driven scenario-based exercises, practicing real-time aviation dialogues and troubleshooting communication issues. In the final stages, corresponding to evaluating and creating, learners critically assess aviation communication protocols, adapt their language use to non-standard scenarios, and generate contextually appropriate responses in simulated ATC exchanges. By integrating the spiral curriculum with Bloom's Mastery Learning principles, SkyTutor ensures individualized and adaptive learning experiences, which enables each learner to learn at their own rhythm while systematically reinforcing prior knowledge. This organized method not only promotes linguistic proficiency but also develops critical thinking, decision-making, and adaptability of the ab-inito pilots.

Figure 4. **SkyTutor Scenario Generation**

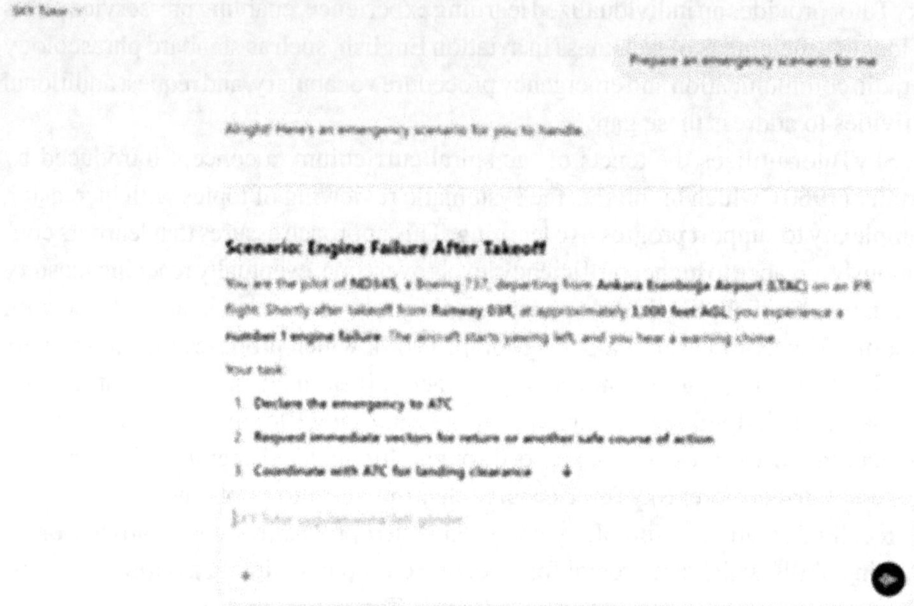

Building on the previously mentioned benefits of SkyTutor in the context of aviation English instruction, it presents numerous benefits for pre-service pilots. These aforementioned benefits of SkyTutor for ab-initio pilots comprise limitless access to SkyTutor at any time and in any place the removal of the necessity for an instructor and the establishment of a relaxed learning atmosphere that diminishes language anxiety. SkyTutor also promotes collaborative learning through digital support, provides instant feedback for progress monitoring, and individualized support to address the academic needs of ab-initio pilots regarding aviation English. Additionally, SkyTutor employs a spiral curriculum for progressive learning by incorporating Bloom's Mastery Learning model for structured support and fosters the improvement of higher-order thinking skills of ab-initio pilots. SkyTutor also assures customized and flexible learning routes while developing critical thinking, decision-making, and adaptability in aviation communication contexts. Apart from all these benefits of SkyTutor for ab-initio pilots, SkyTutor's ability to produce responses in over 80 languages improves its widespread availability for ab-initio pilots globally. This feature allows learners to benefit from SkyTutor in their native language while simultaneously practicing aviation English. Furthermore, SkyTutor provides ab-initio pilots an opportunity to learn an in-depth knowledge of aviation history from reliable sources, which is explained in the Foundation of SkyTutor chapter of this paper.

BENEFITS OF SKYTUTOR FOR INSTRUCTOR

Considering the key roles and responsibilities of the instructors in today's modern education landscape, they are expected to prepare authentic instructional materials (Gentry et al., 2013), prepare and implement authentic assessment methods to measure the achievement levels of the learners (Lauermann, 2014), organize the physical classroom setting effectively, and ensure smooth classroom management (Egeberg et al., 2016). In addition to these, instructors must improve individualized learning plans based on each learner's personal and academic needs (Durlak et al., 2011). To fulfill these responsibilities, AI-based tools stand as an unprecedentedly valuable opportunity for instructors to utilize in their teaching experiences (Olawale & Hendricks, 2024).

Taking into consideration the existing literature on the influences of AI-based tools on the responsibilities of instructors, a wide range of studies have been conducted. One of the key responsibilities of instructors is preparing authentic materials, and with the advancement of AI tools, this responsibility has been significantly influenced by the integration of AI-based tools into the field of education. A research conducted by Popenici & Kerr (2017) highlighted that AI-based tools are able to support instructors in developing instructional materials accordingly to learners' proficiency levels, individualized differences, and learning needs. Chaudhry and Kazim (2021) indicated that utilizing AI-based tools for developing materials not only aids instructors in reducing their workload but also gives them the opportunity to increase the overall quality of education.

Several studies in the related literature indicated that AI-based tools, primarily ChatGPT, help instructors to create authentic assessment methods to precisely evaluate the learning outcomes of the learners (Chen et al., 2020). Moreover, AI tools are capable of analyzing data on learner progress by recognizing their areas needing improvement, and helping the instructors in developing individualized learning plans based on learners' educational needs (Chen et al., 2020; Karpouzis et al., 2024; Mollick & Mollick, 2024). Furthermore, with the digital assessment platforms, AI-based tools enable instructors to diminish their administrative workload which provides them the opportunity to devote increased time for direct instructional interaction (Javaid et al., 2023; Owan et al., 2023).

Figure 5. **SkyTutor Unique Flight Plan Generation**

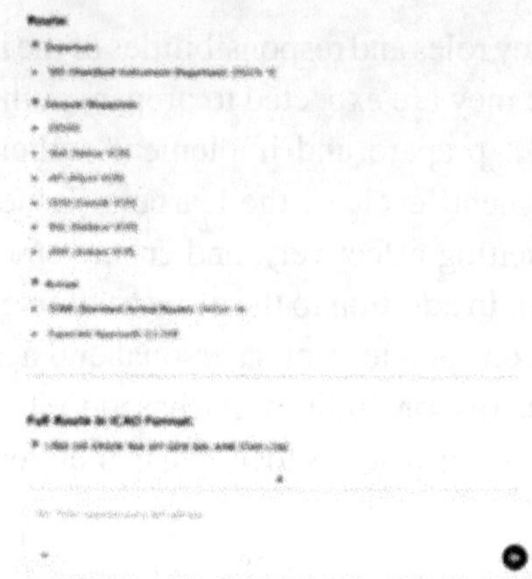

In addition to these, with the development of technology and AI tools, instructors are also able to utilize of AI tools to manage their classroom settings in a more productive way. AI-based tools are capable of offering solutions to instructors to facilitate classroom management, seating arrangements, and adaptive learning environments which address students' personalized needs.

From this perspective, the SkyTutor chatbot provides numerous advantages for aviation English instructors and these benefits of the SkyTutor must be examined thoroughly. To be more precise, SkyTutor has the capacity to assist instructors in developing their teaching strategies depending on their eclectic approach while also improving their methodological expertise and domain-specific knowledge in the field of aviation English.

The primary advantage of SkyTutor lies in its foundation as a ChatGPT-based chatbot, which enables it to process and analyze extensive information sourced from the internet. However, to enhance its reliability and preciseness, it has been specifically programmed and loaded with aviation context-specific information. At this point, SkyTutor is equipped with essential and authoritative books and documents related to aviation regulations and communication (e.g., aviation English, air transportation, aviation phraseology, and radio communication). The purpose of this integration is to broaden the knowledge of both instructors and learners by enabling them not only to acquire proficiency in aviation English but also to understand the underlying rationale behind aviation history and its global development throughout history. From this aspect, SkyTutor provides a risk-free teaching experience for the instructors in their aviation English practices.

From the instructors' perspective, SkyTutor provides aviation English instructors an extensive range of teaching activities and methodologies within seconds. For instance, SkyTutor can generate lesson plans, create customized exercises focused on specific aviation terminology, and develop scenario-based role plays that simulate real-life air traffic communication. This feature of SkyTutor aids educators to lessen their workload; furthermore, it increases efficiency and instructional effectiveness of their aviation English teaching practices.

Moreover, SkyTutor enables instructors to optimize the benefits of their teaching experiences by adjusting the design of teaching activities that take account of learners' personality traits, individual differences, language proficiency levels, and academic needs. For instance, educators are able to use SkyTutor to generate individualized learning plans for each ab-initio pilot. Furthermore, aviation English instructors are capable of developing interactive activities which meet the needs of both introverted and extroverted ab-initio pilots. Also, educators can make use of SkyTutor to provide instant feedback to ab-initio pilots. By taking into account SkyTutor's capabilities, instructors are able to develop both their own pedagogical strategies and their ab-initio pilot learners' learning experiences.

Additionally, SkyTutor is capable of generating individualized assessment methods based on instructors' eclectic approaches. Furthermore, SkyTutor can analyze ab-initio pilots' activites and provide detailed reports on the strengths and weaknesses of ab-initio pilots. SkyTutor can significantly reduce instructors' workload by generating authentic assessment materials and performance analysis of ab-initio pilots.

ETHICAL CONCERNS AND ALIGNMENT WITH AI MANIFESTO

Although the integration of AI provides important advantages for both learners and educators in the field of education, it also raises ethical and security concerns. These concerns include *privacy issues* and *misuse apprehensions*. Beginning with *privacy issues*, AI tool users have the same concerns about data collection, storage, and potential misuse, which might reflect broader societal anxieties about AI and personal data protection. The given worries are not unfounded; on the contrary, AI-based educational tools collect a large amount of data about users to function effectively. If the personal data of AI tools' users are misused or accessed improperly, it could lead to serious privacy violations. Huang (2023) stresses that student privacy is at increased risk because of the abuse of personal data and data trafficking; therefore, it was stated in the research that the urgency of establishing proper privacy protection systems in educational AI tools. In the same vein, Ismail and Aloshi (2025) argue that current regulations often remain incapable of addressing the ethical implications of AI surveillance in classrooms. The scholars call for thorough data governance frameworks and enhanced data literacy among educators. These findings were also parallel with Qin et al. (2020), who highlighted the necessity of strict data privacy measures when utilizing AI tools in educational contexts. Consequently, the related literature stresses the need for ethically grounded, transparent, and secure AI practices.

On the other hand, *misuse apprehensions* comprise fears that AI technology could be abused by learners, who might rely exceedingly on AI for learning tasks, and by doing so they might damage their own learning process by blunting their creativity and productivity. Several research in related literature show that overdependence on AI tools might hinder the development of critical thinking and problem-solving abilities among learners. For instance, the study indicated that increased use of AI was associated with a decrease in individuals' independent thinking and problem-solving skills; moreover, it was highlighted that cognitive offloading among frequent AI users weakens their deep engagement (Gerlich, 2025). Concordantly, Hua et al. (2023) emphasize that excessive dependence on AI dialogue systems diminishes students' capacity for analytical thinking and decision-making. Additionally, Çela et al. (2024) reported a statistically significant decline in students' problem-solving skills when AI was overused for academic assignments. Briefly, it is crucial not to become overly dependent on AI, because it might negatively influence learners' critical thinking skills negatively and decrease the quality of their academic performance.

Since SkyTutor is a ChatGPT-driven AI chatbot, it is important to note that the aforementioned ethical concerns are directly aligned with SkyTutor as well. To ensure the ethical integration of SkyTutor into aviation English training, the solution of the given concerns asks for more than mere recognition of its potential risks. It necessitates an alignment of AI tools with common pedagogical values that support learner dignity, safety, and autonomy. As emphasized by Bozkurt et al. (2024), generative artificial intelligence must support pedagogical goals rather than define them. The scholars proposed a set of foundational principles which includes transparency, human oversight, data justice, and equity among its users. The principles, determined in the manifesto, should guide the design, implementation, and regulation of educational systems. A strong focus on efficient data governance, the improvement of AI literacy among users, and the reinforcement of instructional practices that promote active learning is essential to achieve these standards. When educators, developers, and institutional decision-makers adopt such an ethical framework, SkyTutor can function as a pedagogical asset without compromising student agency or critical engagement. This ethical orientation supports a responsible transformation of aviation education while preserving both technological advancement and the integrity of the educational mission.

CHALLENGES AND LIMITATIONS

Although SkyTutor chatbot provides numerous benefits for both instructors and ab-initio pilots in teaching and learning various aspects of aviation such as fundamentals of aviation history, accident investigations, meteorology, emergency procedures, and aviation English, it has some characteristic challenges and limitations for its users. Furthermore, to make use of AI tools, it is necessary for individuals to have a certain level of digital literacy (Ray, 2023). In this regard, a low level of digital literacy among ab-initio pilots and aviation English instructors may hinder the effective use of the SkyTutor chatbot. Consequently, this could lead to biases against SkyTutor's implementation and a reluctance to use.

Numerous studies indicated that over-reliance on the artificial intelligence tools lead its users to experience reduced levels of critical thinking skills, creativity, problem solving strategies (Rahman & Watanobe, 2023; Susnjak & McIntosh, 2024). Since SkyTutor, as reported in its advantages, provides learners with a stress-free learning environment, it aims to maximize the performances of ab-initio pilots. However, given the nature of the piloting profession and its inherent responsibilities, pilots are often required to make critical decisions under extreme pressure and stress, not only for their own safety but also for the lives of passengers on board. These decisions must be prompt, effective, and confident. Therefore, SkyTutor might be insufficient in preparing ab-inito pilots cognitively and psychologically to handle real-life, high-stress scenarios which might take place in during take-off, landing or flight. Because of these reasons, SkyTutor might hinder the development of their critical thinking, and problem-solving skills of ab-initio pilots.

SkyTutor does not provide a platform for ab-initio pilots to engage in verbal communication via their mobile phones or computers. Therefore, ab-initio pilots do not have the opportunity to improve their aviation English speaking skills by using SkyTutor. Furthermore, effective communication is a fundamental requirement of the piloting profession, as pilots must interact with air traffic controllers and other pilots. Given that these individuals speak English with various accents, it is evident that there is no universally standardized form of spoken English in aviation. In this regard, Skytutor can be insufficient in preparing ab-initio pilots for non-standard English accents and pronunciations which could lead to serious and deadly misunderstandings during flights. Regarding the misunderstandings in aviation English, aviation communication relies heavily on clarity and brevity, yet misinterpretations may occur when pilots and air traffic controllers deviate from standard phraseology. If SkyTutor encounters non-standardized language, abbreviations, or contextual variations in aviation discourse, it may produce incorrect or misleading responses, which could hinder student learning.

For any AI tool to be formally integrated into education curriculum, it must comply with regulatory standards set by the relevant institutions. As it is well known, ICAO establishes global standards and regulations to ensure the safety, efficiency, and security of international civil aviation. In a similar way, FAA is official head of aviation in United States, regulates all aspects of civil aviation. Taking into consideration these, there is no validated chatbot in aviation English teaching field; therefore, SkyTutor have not yet received official accreditation or approval from ICAO and FAA yet. As a consequence of the given situation, not having accreditation or approval might limit SkyTutor's use in formal pilot training programs.

FUTURE DIRECTIONS FOR SKYTUTOR

Building upon its current foundation in aviation English training, SkyTutor is set to transform into a more advanced educational tool that transcend limited interaction, and it is aimed to enable authentic and verbal communication aligned with real-world aviation scenarios which can be experienced by pilots in their profession. For ab-initio pilots, one of the fundamental goals of training with SkyTutor is not only its function as a simulated ATC system but also the opportunity it provides to engage in realistic cockpit to tower telecommunication practice, which includes the names of all airports, aircrafts, and runways. This improvement of SkyTutor will provide ab-initio pilots with a chance to participate in realistic and mutual dialogues, which are compliant with ICAO principles. Additionally, these dialogues that will take place in between ab-initio pilots and SkyTutor contains a wide range of routine and non-routine situations to serve as drills of live flight operations. In the same direction, SkyTutor will be equipped with an comprehensive set of emergency communication scenarios such as engine failure, bird strikes, missed approaches, and in-flight technical anomalies which allow ab-initio pilots to improve the aviation English linguistic precision and their decision-making ability which is required in high-pressure situations. Since the current version of SkyTutor is already built on ICAO's Language Proficiency Requirements, this explained mutual speaking interaction upgrade will further reinforce SkyTutor's compliance with aviation communication standards by emphasizing clarity, fluency, and interaction under pressure.

Another long-term objective of SkyTutor is to formalize its instructional outcomes through certification as SkyTutor becomes more widely known and utilized by ab-initio pilots and in the field of aviation English training. As aforementioned, individualized educational programs, real-life oriented scenario-based tasks, formative and instant feedback are already the services that ab-inito pilots can make use of. It is aimed that in future versions, learners who complete these modules and demonstrate competence may receive digital certificates issued through SkyTutor to authenticate ab-initio pilots' proficiency in aviation English. The provided certificates will serve as evidence of progress in aviation English communication and could be recognized as supplementary documentation in flight training portfolios. The ultimate aim is to seek verification or alignment with international aviation bodies such as ICAO.

Along with the certification, it is aimed to equip SkyTutor with virtual reality (VR) environments with VR glasses to provide an opportunity for the ab-initio pilots to experience real-life flight experiences. These flight experiences acquired through VR experiences will replicate ab-initio pilots' cognitive load, spatial awareness, and time-sensitive pressures of actual flight; moreover, it will support the development of both linguistic and operational aviation English proficiency. These simulations are going to be especially beneficial for practicing emergency responses and non-standard phraseology in authentic setitngs.

REFERENCES

Adeshola, I., & Adepoju, A. P. (2024). The opportunities and challenges of ChatGPT in education. *Interactive Learning Environments*, *32*(10), 6159–6172. DOI: 10.1080/10494820.2023.2253858

Arroyo, D. C., & Yilmaz, Y. (2018). An open for replication study: The role of feedback timing in synchronous computer-mediated communication. *Language Learning*, *68*(4), 942–972. DOI: 10.1111/lang.12300

Baillifard, A., Gabella, M., Lavenex, P. B., & Martarelli, C. S. (2023). Implementing Learning Principles with a Personal AI Tutor: A Case Study. https://doi.org//arXiv.2309.13060DOI: 10.48550

Boeing. (2024). *Pilot and Technician Outlook 2024-2043*. https://www.boeing.com/commercial/market/pilot-technician-outlook

Bozkurt, A., Xiao, J., Farrow, R., Bai, J. Y., Nerantzi, C., Moore, S., & Asino, T. I. (Eds.). (2024). The manifesto for teaching and learning in a time of generative AI: A critical collective stance to better navigate the future. Open Praxis, *16*(4), 487-513. DOI: 10.55982/openpraxis.16.4.777

Cao, C. C., Ding, Z., Lin, J., & Hopfgartner, F. (2023). AI chatbots as multi-role pedagogical agents: Transforming engagement in CS education. https://doi.org//arXiv.2308.03992DOI: 10.48550

Çela, E., Fonkam, M. M., & Potluri, R. M. (2024). Risks of AI-assisted learning on student critical thinking: A case study of Albania. [IJRCM]. *International Journal of Risk and Contingency Management*, *12*(1), 1–19. DOI: 10.4018/IJRCM.350185

Chaudhry, M. A., & Kazim, E. (2021). Artificial Intelligence in Education (AIEd): A high-level academic and industry note 2021. *AI and Ethics*, *2*(1), 157–165. DOI: 10.1007/s43681-021-00074-z PMID: 34790953

Chen, L., Chen, P., & Lin, Z. (2020). Artificial intelligence in education: A review. *IEEE Access : Practical Innovations, Open Solutions*, *8*, 75264–75278. DOI: 10.1109/ACCESS.2020.2988510

Cheng, F. F., Wu, C. S., & Su, P. C. (2021). The impact of collaborative learning and personality on satisfaction in innovative teaching context. *Frontiers in Psychology*, *12*, 713497. DOI: 10.3389/fpsyg.2021.713497 PMID: 34659026

Dinçer, N. (2023). Elevating aviation education: A comprehensive examination of technology's role in modern flight training. *Journal of Aviation*, *7*(2), 317–323. DOI: 10.30518/jav.1279718

Dinçer, N. (2023). The role of serious games in effective aviation English. *Applied Linguistics Papers*, *27*(2), 72–82. DOI: 10.32612/uw.25449354.2023.1.pp.72-83

Dinçer, R., Dinçer, N., & Guksu, O. (2023). An interactive conversation with a chatbot: Does ChatGPT know standard phraseology in aviation English? *The Literacy Trek*, *9*(2), 24–41. DOI: 10.47216/literacytrek.1382543

Durlak, J. A., Weissberg, R. P., Dymnicki, A. B., Taylor, R. D., & Schellinger, K. B. (2011). The impact of enhancing students' social and emotional learning: A meta-analysis of school-based universal interventions. *Child Development*, *82*(1), 405–432. DOI: 10.1111/j.1467-8624.2010.01564.x PMID: 21291449

Egeberg, H., McConney, A., & Price, A. (2016). Classroom management and national professional standards for teachers: A review of the literature on theory and practice. *The Australian Journal of Teacher Education*, *41*(7), 1–18. DOI: 10.14221/ajte.2016v41n7.1

Foerde, K., & Shohamy, D. (2011). Feedback timing modulates brain systems for learning in humans. *The Journal of Neuroscience : The Official Journal of the Society for Neuroscience*, *31*(37), 13157–13167. DOI: 10.1523/JNEUROSCI.2701-11.2011 PMID: 21917799

Gentry, R., Sallie, A. P., & Sanders, C. A. (2013). *Differentiated Instructional Strategies to Accommodate Students with Varying Needs and Learning Styles*. Online Submission.

Gerlich, M. (2025). AI Tools in Society: Impacts on Cognitive Offloading and the Future of Critical Thinking. *Societies (Basel, Switzerland)*, *15*(1), 6. DOI: 10.3390/soc15010006

Holmes, W., Bialik, M., & Fadel, C. (2019). *Artificial intelligence in education promises and implications for teaching and learning*. Center for Curriculum Redesign.

Horwitz, E. K., Horwitz, M. B., & Cope, J. (1986). Foreign language classroom anxiety. *Modern Language Journal*, *70*(2), 125–132. DOI: 10.1111/j.1540-4781.1986.tb05256.x

Huang, L. (2023). Ethics of artificial intelligence in education: Student privacy and data protection. *Science Insights Education Frontiers*, *16*(2), 2577–2587. DOI: 10.15354/sief.23.re202

ICAO. (2011, March 8). *The study of ICAO rearding the demand in the aviation sector.* ICAO. https://www.icao.int/Newsroom/Pages/icao-study-reveals-strong-demand-for-qualified-aviation-personnel-up-to-2030.aspx

Ismail, I. A., & Aloshi, J. M. R. (2025). Data Privacy in AI-Driven Education: An In-Depth Exploration Into the Data Privacy Concerns and Potential Solutions. In AI Applications and Strategies in Teacher Education (pp. 223-252). IGI Global. https://doi.org/DOI: 10.4018/979-8-3693-5443-8.ch008

Javaid, M., Haleem, A., Singh, R. P., Khan, S., & Khan, I. H. (2023). Unlocking the opportunities through ChatGPT Tool towards ameliorating the education system. *BenchCouncil Transactions on Benchmarks. Standards and Evaluations*, *3*(2), 100115. DOI: 10.1016/j.tbench.2023.100115

Karpouzis, K., Pantazatos, D., Taouki, J., & Meli, K. (2024, May). Tailoring education with GenAI: a new horizon in lesson planning. In *2024 IEEE Global Engineering Education Conference (EDUCON)* (pp. 1-10). IEEE. https://doi.org/DOI: 10.1109/EDUCON60312.2024.10578690

Lauermann, F. (2014). Teacher responsibility from the teacher's perspective. *International Journal of Educational Research*, *65*, 75–89. DOI: 10.1016/j.ijer.2013.09.005

Lee, G. G., Mun, S., Shin, M. K., & Zhai, X. (2023). Collaborative Learning with Artificial Intelligence Speakers (CLAIS): Pre-Service Elementary Science Teachers' Responses to the Prototype. https://doi.org//arXiv.2401.05400DOI: 10.48550

Li, S., Zhu, Y., & Ellis, R. (2016). The effects of the timing of corrective feedback on the acquisition of a new linguistic structure. *Modern Language Journal*, *100*(1), 276–295. DOI: 10.1111/modl.12315

Lo, C. K. (2023). What is the impact of ChatGPT on education? A rapid review of the literature. *Education Sciences*, *13*(4), 410. DOI: 10.3390/educsci13040410

Luckin, R., & Holmes, W. (2016). Intelligence unleashed: An argument for AI in education.

McClure, C., & Williams, P. (2021). Gather. town: An opportunity for self-paced learning in a synchronous, distance-learning environment. *Compass (Eltham)*, *14*(2). Advance online publication. DOI: 10.21100/compass.v14i2.1232

Möller, M., Nirmal, G., Fabietti, D., Stierstorfer, Q., Zakhvatkin, M., Sommerfeld, H., & Schütt, S. (2024). Revolutionising distance learning: A comparative study of learning progress with AI-driven tutoring. https://doi.org//arXiv.2403.14642DOI: 10.48550

Mollick, E., & Mollick, L. (2024). Instructors as innovators: A future-focused approach to new AI learning opportunities, with prompts.

Murray and Green. (2021). *Aviation Faces a Pilot Shortage.* OliverWyman. https://www.oliverwyman.com/our-expertise/insights/2021/mar/after-covid-19-aviation-faces-a-pilot-shortage.html

Nakata, T. (2015). Effects of feedback timing on second language vocabulary learning: Does delaying feedback increase learning? *Language Teaching Research, 19*(4), 416–434. DOI: 10.1177/1362168814541721

Olawale, B. E., & Hendricks, W. W. (2024). ARTIFICIAL INTELLIGENCE IN TEACHER EDUCATION: UNLOCKING THE TOOLS AND BENEFITS OF A TRANSFORMING PEDAGOGY. DOI: 10.5539/jel.v13n6p346

Owan, V. J., Abang, K. B., Idika, D. O., Etta, E. O., & Bassey, B. A. (2023). Exploring the potential of artificial intelligence tools in educational measurement and assessment. *Eurasia Journal of Mathematics, Science and Technology Education, 19*(8), em2307. Advance online publication. DOI: 10.29333/ejmste/13428

Popenici, S. A., & Kerr, S. (2017). Exploring the impact of artificial intelligence on teaching and learning in higher education. *Research and Practice in Technology Enhanced Learning, 12*(1), 22. DOI: 10.1186/s41039-017-0062-8 PMID: 30595727

Qin, F., Li, K., & Yan, J. (2020). Understanding user trust in artificial intelligence-based educational systems: Evidence from China. *British Journal of Educational Technology, 51*(5), 1693–1710. DOI: 10.1111/bjet.12994

Rahman, M. M., & Watanobe, Y. (2023). ChatGPT for education and research: Opportunities, threats, and strategies. *Applied Sciences (Basel, Switzerland), 13*(9), 5783. DOI: 10.3390/app13095783

Ray, P. P. (2023). ChatGPT: A comprehensive review on background, applications, key challenges, bias, ethics, limitations and future scope. *Internet of Things and Cyber-Physical Systems, 3*, 121–154. DOI: 10.1016/j.iotcps.2023.04.003

Scager, K., Boonstra, J., Peeters, T., Vulperhorst, J., & Wiegant, F. (2017). Collaborative learning in higher education: Evoking positive interdependence. *CBE Life Sciences Education, 15*(4), ar69. DOI: 10.1187/cbe.16-07-0219 PMID: 27909019

Shetye, S. (2024). An evaluation of khanmigo, a generative ai tool, as a computer-assisted language learning app. *Studies in Applied Linguistics and TESOL, 24*(1). Advance online publication. DOI: 10.52214/salt.v24i1.12869

St-Hilaire, F., Vu, D. D., Frau, A., Burns, N., Faraji, F., Potochny, J., . . . Kochmar, E. (2022). A new era: Intelligent tutoring systems will transform online learning for millions. https://doi.org//arXiv.2203.03724DOI: 10.48550

Susnjak, T., & McIntosh, T. R. (2024). Chatgpt: The end of online exam integrity? *Education Sciences*, *14*(6), 656. DOI: 10.3390/educsci14060656

Tullis, J. G., & Benjamin, A. S. (2011). On the effectiveness of self-paced learning. *Journal of Memory and Language*, *64*(2), 109–118. DOI: 10.1016/j.jml.2010.11.002 PMID: 21516194

Young, D. J. (1991). Creating a low-anxiety classroom environment: What does language anxiety research suggest? *Modern Language Journal*, *75*(4), 426–439. DOI: 10.2307/329492

Zhu, C., Sun, M., Luo, J., Li, T., & Wang, M. (2023). How to Harness the Potential of ChatGPT in Education? *Knowledge Management & E-Learning*, *15*(2), 133–152. DOI: 10.34105/j.kmel.2023.15.008

KEY TERMS AND DEFINITIONS

Artificial Intelligence: A digital space where machines attempt to solve tasks by mimicking human-like thinking abilities.

Generative Artificial Intelligence: A branch of artificial intelligence that uses patterns in data to generate new content.

Artificial Intelligence in Education: Integrating smart algorithms into learning environments to improve teaching and increase student success.

Large Language Models: Digital information libraries trained with massive text data, capable of predicting and generating language.

Chatbot: A digital assistant that can conduct interactive conversations to automate tasks or provide information.

ChatGPT: A virtual chatbot designed to mimic human-like text interaction.

Aviation English: A special aviation language used to ensure clear communication among aviation professionals.

Standard Phraseology: Predefined language patterns for providing clear communication in specific contexts.

ICAO: An international organisation that sets global aviation standards and ensures the safe and orderly use of airspace.

Chapter 10

Analyzing Native and Nonnative Speech in TED Talks for Second Language Learning

İrem Doğaç
https://orcid.org/0009-0008-5789-4750
İzmir Turk College, Turkey

Vasfiye Geçkin
https://orcid.org/0000-0001-8532-8627
İzmir Democracy University, Turkey

ABSTRACT

Today, exposure to a second language (L2) is widely achieved through listening and watching content on web-based platforms. As the quality and quantity of input shape L2 acquisition, this study aims to analyze the role of cultural and linguistic background on the L2 input provided through YouTube TED Talks. TED Talk transcriptions of 12 native and nonnative speakers of English coming from collectivist and individualistic cultures were analyzed using a natural language processing (NLP) tool called SiNLP. Speech cohesion at sentence and text level was examined by developing a generalized linear regression model. Language (native vs. nonnative) and culture (collectivist vs. individualistic) were taken as independent variables and sentence (e.g., lexical overlap, semantic overlap, connective use) and text (givenness and lexical diversity) level indices of complexity were taken as the dependent variables. Cultural background rather than the linguistic background was found to play a meaningful role in linguistic complexity that the speakers manifested.

DOI: 10.4018/979-8-3373-7574-8.ch010

INTRODUCTION

Web based communication has paved the way for learning a second language (L2). Digital platforms act as the major sources of input for many L2 learners who come from different social, cultural, and linguistic backgrounds. For instance, millions of L2 learners log in to one of the very notorious platforms, YouTube, among many others, to watch content of their own interests (Alexa, 2022). The platform offers dual channels, verbal and auditory, which assist processing of information and improve L2 listening comprehension by adding pictures and videos to aural lectures (Mayer et al., 2014). In the process of L2 learning, the chance to be exposed to several TED Talks given by both native and nonnative speakers of English vanishes the boundaries between in and out of school learning environments. Thus, it is not surprising to come across studies focusing on the interaction between out of school learning environments and the positive effect of audio visual input (Gass et al., 2019; Wisniewska & Mora, 2020). YouTube videos are categorized as out of class, informal, naturalistic, and self directed language learning tools (Benson, 2011). As one of the sources of audio visual input, TED Talks offer anecdotal incidences of life experiences or arguments conveyed in a non traditional way, deviating from a typical formal lecture format. Additionally, even though they are given in an informal way, Ted Talks provide similar vocabulary to newspapers and novels (Nation, 2006) which provide indirect academic information. Language learners enjoy learning through YouTube videos (Kim & Kim, 2021), and language teachers are motivated to use YouTube in their teaching practices once they get familiar with the tool (Sun, 2014). Watching YouTube videos and interacting in comments contributes to intercultural communication and learning supporting multicultural competence (Benson, 2015; Wang & Chen, 2019). Listening to both native and nonnative speech on TED Talks gives language learners the opportunity to practice L2 listening skills within their comfort zone without overwhelming levels of foreign language anxiety, thanks to the captions and adjustable speech rates (Mirzaei & Meshgi, 2021). It also helps develop intelligible pronunciation by facilitating an inductive way of learning suprasegmental features of pronunciation (Sani & Rocio, 2019). Though various studies explore the use of content based platforms such as YouTube and Ted Talks, there is still a lack of detailed analysis of how these relate to cohesion in speech, especially in native versus non native talk. Since TED Talks satisfy the features of authentic audiovisual materials for L2 learning (Gilmore, 2007), we chose to analyse cohesion in the speech of native and nonnative TED Talk speakers within the scope of this paper.

Given that nonnative English speakers are estimated to outnumber native English speakers with a ratio of 4 to 1 (Che, 2008), the nature of native and nonnative speech is worth exploring from two theoretical stances. The first one is the century old, the Sapir Whorf Hypothesis (Sapir, 1921; Whorf, 1956). The hypothesis has two orientations (Whorf, 1940/1956; Brown, 1976). The strong orientation, the so called Linguistic determinism, suggests that the structure of a language determines the way its native speakers perceive, reason, and think about the world. Languages are not acknowledged only as tools for communication but also as a means to shape our thoughts and conceptualize the world when we consider the differences in vocabulary and grammar (Yao, 2002). Since language is believed to shape attitudes, individuals speaking different languages are claimed to have different world views. To exemplify a few, the number and the type of words for *snow* in a language may determine the way one perceives *snow* (Boas, 1911). If the native speakers of a language have distinctions for certain words, such as *camel types*, it will be easier to talk about them when compared to the native speakers of a language that lacks such a distinction (Hussein, 2012). The word *safe* may convey a greeting, a wish for a healthy and good life for its recipient in one language, but depending on the recipient's culture, it can convey a different meaning (Syahrin, 2018). In addition, the presence or absence of grammatical structures can pose constraints and control on reasoning (Bloom, 1984). Whether the language we use or our inherent worldview affects the way we perceive reality remains a topic of discussion.

The weak version of the Sapir Whorf Hypothesis, the so called linguistic relativity, claims that structural and non linguistic cognitive differences between languages would be parallel (Brown, 1976). Speakers of different languages are claimed to perceive the world through the categories available in those languages. Thus, the linguistic and cognitive representations of an individual with multiple languages would be different from those of a monolingual (Cook, 2003). Since language modulates people's ideas, the received input will be parsed with respect to language based representational cues while expressing linguistic events in daily life (Han & Cadierno, 2010). When interaction between first and second languages is considered, the hypothesis predicts cross linguistic influence at conceptual domains such as emotions, gender, colour, number, and time (Jarvis & Pavlenko, 2010). For instance, time is conceptualized differently in English and Mandarin. While Mandarin marks time with vertical spatial language, such as *up* and *down*, English uses horizontal spatial metaphors, such as *ahead, back,* and *forward*. Boroditsky (2001) found that Mandarin speakers of L2 English were able to follow the time conceptualization of English if they were exposed to English at a young age. When English Chinese bilingual speakers were asked to describe stereotypes in each language, they followed Chinese stereotypes in Chinese and English stereotypes in English (Hoffman, Lau & Johnson, 1986). What is more, when certain concepts are lacking, bilingual speakers resort to code switching or lexical loans (Pavlenko, 2003). An example would be the lack of a single word to express the English word *serendipity* in Korean. The debate around the interaction between language and culture has not yet reached a solid conclusion. This paper is concerned with conceptual transfer between native and non native English speakers in the way pronouns and connectives are used at the sentence level.

The second approach, the so called cognitive interactionist approaches to second language learning, is concerned with the extent native speaker language is modified so that it becomes accessible and intelligible to nonnative speakers (Long, 1983). Initially, Krashen (1985), in his Input Hypothesis, claims that for language acquisition to take place, the optimal input that the learner is exposed to has to be slightly more advanced than his current interlanguage system. Comprehensible input unavoidably shapes comprehensible output in second language acquisition (Swain, 1985). L2 learning is facilitated if output extends the linguistic repertoire of the learner (p. 252). According to the updated version of Long's (1996) interaction hypothesis, if the input provided enhances the learner's internal capacities and pushes them to construct and produce modified output, then language learning is facilitated. Schmidt (1990) put forward the idea that the L2 learner has to notice the input so that it becomes intake for learning to take place. To make the input salient, input enhancement strategies were proposed (Smith & Truscott, 2014). The TED Talk analyses we undertook in this paper relate to the pre modified input rather than the interactionally modified one. The pre modified input comes in three categories. First, simplification happens when the input is made syntactically and lexically less complex. More specifically, adding sentence connectors, repeating words and phrases, removing clauses to decrease sentence length and complexity, and using a limited number of familiar lexical items could be listed as examples for simplification. Second, elaboration is observed when paraphrasing of unfamiliar language is common for the sake of explicitness. The expectation is to facilitate language learning through paraphrases, slower speech, clearer articulation, self repetition, and synonyms (Parker & Chaudron, 1987). And lastly, enhancement refers to aural and visual enhancement that would affect speech and text comprehension. Wong (2002), for instance, found that college students learning prepositions in L2 French benefited the most from visual enhancement when the prepositions were made bold and underlined. Hernàndez (2011) found that English college students learning L2 Spanish used more elaborated discourse markers in their spoken narratives when they were given explicit instruction and input flood as forms of pre modified input. Building on these three input related interaction hypotheses, we would expect a difference in the cohesion and linguistic complexity between the native and nonnative speech that we chose to analyse in this paper.

What is more, social interaction, which can be described as social practice and involvement in the construction of meaning through interactions, smoothens the way for second language learning (Mondada & Doehlier, 2004). Input can be modified through repetitions, reductions of sentence length and complexity, and paraphrasing.

Negotiation of meaning between native and nonnative speakers is given as a learner external factor to facilitate second language learning (Mackey, 2020). Input, affected by audibility, accuracy, relevance, and lexical and phrasal meanings (Doughty, 1991), can be modified depending on the interactions of the participants to ensure negotiation between speakers (Pica, 1994). Research suggests that the comprehensible input teachers provide and the teaching techniques they use constitute the main sources of language that the learners produce (Gass, 2013; Sun & Verspoor, 2022). Yet, nonnative speakers may lack interactional competence and have trouble in comprehending native speakers who may prefer to remain passive in interaction (Young & Miller, 2004). One of the most debatable issues around second language learning still relates to the extent input is modified, especially when interaction with native versus nonnative speakers of that language is considered. The tendency of native and nonnative English speakers to modify speech could shape the linguistic complexity and grammatical cohesion in the TED Talks that we chose to analyse.

To have a better understanding of the nature of native and nonnative input, natural language processing tools (NLP) have proven to be handy. One NLP tool, The Simple Natural Language Processing Tool (SiNLP) (Crossley et al., 2014), for instance, turns writing or speech into measurable units to analyse grammatical cohesion at the sentence, paragraph, and text level. Cohesion, which can be defined as linguistic cues to link ideas (Halliday & Hasan, 1976), can be taken as an indicator of linguistic complexity at different syntactic levels. Cohesion was long observed in six ways basically. *Reference* links the noun via the matching personal or demonstrative pronoun, comparative or definite article. *Substitution* replaces one referent identity with another and is observed as nominal, verbal, or causal replacements to avoid unnecessary repetition. *Ellipsis* is about omitting words or phrases whose meaning could be retrieved from context. *Connectives*, a part of local cohesive indices, are used to indicate additive, contrastive, causal, or temporal semantic relationships. Discourse cohesion has to do with forming connections between parts of a text on the basis of its surface elements (Tanskanen, 2006). Cohesion also refers to "how repetition is manifested, in numerous ways, across pairs of sentences" in a discourse (Boguraev & Neff, 2000). Thanks to many NLP tools today, indices of cohesion are not restricted to a mere average of total numbers of references, substitutions, ellipses, or connectives. NLP tools turn grammatical cohesion as an index of linguistic complexity into measurable units as local cohesion, the semantic relationship between adjacent lexical items; paragraph cohesion, the relationship between adjacent sentences; and global cohesion, the relationship between paragraphs at the textual level. As an NLP tool, the SiNLP tool offers accurate and valid analyses on various dimensions of a text. A comprehensive linguistic analysis can be obtained by automatically calculating the number of words, the number of types, and type token ratios (TTRs), where each word is taken as a *type* and each type that word is observed is taken as a *token*. For example, when the word *culture* appears three times in a speech, then the *type* value is 1 and the *token* value is 3. Sentence level cohesion is reported in terms of lexically and semantically overlapping words, and the connectives used, while text level cohesion is reported through givenness and lexical diversity. Givenness is calculated by measuring the ratio of new information to the given information, and lexical diversity is determined by variation in different words. Given the theoretical stances and strict measures of NLP tools, this study attempts to analyse native and nonnative speech as obtained from different TED talks around a similar theme using SiNLP to figure out the inter dependent interaction between culture and thought, if there happens to be one.

LITERATURE REVIEW

This section is comprised of four parts. First, we review studies with respect to language learning through audio visual media such as YouTube videos. Next, we focus on papers that investigated language relativity in L2 speech. Additionally, we report findings of linguistic complexity in the speech of native and nonnative speakers. Finally, we compare recent advancements in language processing tools.

Audio visual platforms and social media have been a major source of input as part of out of school exposure to second language(s) (European Commission, 2012). Such exposure is important to explain language learning from an input driven and experientially based perspective (Tomasello, 2003) since language output is claimed to be shaped by input frequency (Ellis, 2002) and type token ratios (Bybee, 1995). Research suggests that intensity and quality of input contribute to target language learning (Muñoz, 2012) thanks to the availability and accessibility of the Internet and digital platforms. The effect of out of school activities relates closely to the learners' level of L2 proficiency and the specific context where the learning takes place (Muñoz & Cadierno, 2021). For this purpose, the online tools used in current education systems provide support to out of learning environments and autonomous learning, indirectly affecting the language learning process.

The Sapir Whorf Linguistic Relativity hypothesis (Sapir, 1921) suggests that the perception and thought processes of a person are deeply affected by one's language. When the interaction between language and thought is considered, self view (collectivist or individualistic) determines one's personal values, behaviors, and general thinking skills. For instance, Chinese speakers provide non redundant self information more often than Germans (Haberstroh et al., 2002). Africans use first person pronouns more often than the British, and the Europeans add more perceptual and social details in interaction (Taylor et al., 2017). Japanese speakers tend to drop the pronoun within the sentence, whereas English speakers tend to obey the grammar rules by providing the sentence with the appropriate pronoun each time (Kashima & Kashima, 2003). In Korean, the use of the possessive pronouns 'nae' (my) and 'wuri' (our) can be valid when referring to one's own item, but in English, the interchangeable use of 'my' and 'our' is not possible. This shows that even in speech, while collectivist cultures cherish cultural conformity, individualistic cultures value interdependency.

When the native and nonnative English speeches of public figures were considered, the type and frequency of pronouns and cohesive devices varied. For instance, Alexander Schindler used local cohesive devices, repetition, and the pronoun 'we' to establish solidarity (Ye & Liu, 2020). When Obama, the former president of the USA, and Rouhani's, the former president of Iran, speeches were compared, Obama used more inclusive pronouns and colloquial language to create a sense of closeness with the audience and to be more understandable at the United Nations General Assembly in 2013 (Sharififar & Rahimi, 2015). Obama is also reported to use more linking words and repetitions than the Nigerian president in his welcoming speech for President Buhari of Nigeria (Malah, 2021). The former chancellor of Germany, Angela Merkel, whose presence is viewed as a symbol of love and trust for Germans, used additive conjunctions more often than causal, temporal, or contrastive connectors in her peace speech (Sinambela et al., 2020). In his speech at the UN, Sandiaga Uno, the former Indonesian Minister of Tourism, addressed both to his country and the other developing island countries, providing a sense of fellowship (Solvandi & Raflis, 2024). Imran Khan, the former prime minister of Pakistan, used repetition and inclusive language to be more understandable and to provide national identity and unity (Asif et al., 2020). In his speech, Susilo Bambang Yudhoyono, an Indonesian politician and retired army general, used 91 personal references, 'we', 'our', and 'I' dominantly to represent the main speaker, the audience, and his country in his speech (Muthoharoh & Nur Rohmah, 2022). Yudhoyono mostly relied on reference, conjunction, and lexical cohesion. Emilinda (2022) reports that Donald Trump, the 47th president of the USA, used personal references such as 'we' to establish a sense of belongingness with the people, and the additive conjunction 'and' to add information along with repetitions to raise awareness of the topics at hand. In his speech titled "Only a Nation with Self Reliance can Become a Great Nation", Soekarno, the founder of Pancasila, used more grammatical cohesion than lexical cohesion (Ghofar, 2018).

Flowerdew and Miller (1995) adopted an interpretive exploratory study to investigate the input Hong Kong Chinese students received from ten native English lecturers over a period of three years. Rather than the Western beliefs, the students inherited Confucian beliefs where a lecturer was viewed as equal to a father, and the assigned grades were never questioned. One of the lecturers used complex vocabulary structures and asked multiple questions, which were left unanswered in class, possibly due to worries of 'show off' and 'face loss'. The use of recurrent phrases for familiar examples presents the topic in a more concrete way. The students preferred one on one interaction to respond to the questions during the break time.

When differences between languages are considered, linguistic complexity, which refers to the range and sophistication of forms that appear in language production, comes into play. Today, natural language processing tools such as Coh Metrix (McNamara et al., 2014). SiNPL (Crossley et al., 2014) and Tool for the Automatic Analysis of Cohesion (TAACO) (Crossley et al., 2019) can turn lexical and syntactic indices of complexity at the sentence, paragraph, and text level into measurable units. Lexical complexity indices such as pronoun density, the type of token ratios, and core vocabulary have been mostly used to compare interpreted and native speech, interpreted and translated texts, and interpreting outputs in different modes. For instance, Shala et al. (2014) compared cohesion in Hosni Mubarak's speeches in Arabic and English for over a period of thirty years and reported that his sentences in Arabic were longer than those in English. Over time, fewer overlapping words and sentences were observed in his speeches in Arabic. Using Halliday and Hasan's framework, Al Khalidy (2018) examined cohesion in four of the Queen Rania's speeches. The most frequently used conjunction was the additive conjunction 'and', followed by the disjunction 'or'. Queen Rania of Jordan used additive conjunctions to make sure that her speech was cohesive. In his speeches, Malcom X, a human rights activist, put an emphasis on using repetition as one of the indices of complexity (Amenorvi, 2018). Different from the speeches of other political figures, Malcolm X did not rely heavily on cohesive devices to make his speeches understandable. That is why his speeches were considered more literary than political. In another study, native speakers of English were asked to retell the stories told by Cambodian English speakers (Koshik, 1999). Despite the lack of cohesion in nonnative narratives, native English speakers were still able to understand the nonnative narratives, and the misuse of cohesive devices did not affect native speakers' story retelling. All in all, even though the use of cohesion in public speeches and the linguistic complexity of native and non native speakers, depending on their cultures, are widely researched topics on their own, the research combining both of them has not been explored. By bridging the gap in between the two concepts, this study aims to provide a better understanding of how a culture affects on how they choose to communicate and interact by making use of a traditional NLP tool.

In daily life, NLP tools appear as customer products such as Apple's Siri, Amazon's Alexa, and Microsoft's Cortana. These tools use the structure of human language to establish new conversations with a chatbot, analysing the existing linguistic data (Canonico & Russis, 2018). Scientifically, NLP tools provide foundations for researchers to reach reliable, quantifiable data to analyse and compare human language (Vajjala, et al., 2020). Although the use of NLP tools has been proven useful by numerous researchers (Chopra, et al., 2013; Nadkarni, et al., 2011), with the recent rise of AI, the use of NLP tools has declined. The recent studies suggested that the rule based approach of NLPs was the reason for this decrease (Goar et al,. 2023). In contrast to NLP tools, which rely on manually uploaded dictionaries or human defined grammar, AI tools such as GPT recognize patterns that help analyze both the text and its semantics. However, as many advantages as they can have, AI tools are not without flaws. Their reliance on keywords to pick up on contextual cues and bias based on the training data show that, regardless of their ability to generate dialogues, to be considered as proper tools in academic linguistic research, they still need refinement.

METHOD

This study has a 2x2 factorial experimental design, inspecting the effect of cultural background and language background on the linguistic complexity was shown through public speeches. The independent variables were cultural and language background, and they each had two levels. The speakers were either native or nonnative speakers of English, and they either came from individualistic or collectivist cultures. The linguistic complexity of these speeches was analyzed by taking their indices of sentence level cohesion, lexical overlaps, semantic overlaps, and connective use. This study analyzes linguistic complexity in speech with respect to different language backgrounds. Two specific research questions were addressed:

1. Does cultural background (individualistic vs. collectivist) affect pronoun use in gender related public speeches?
2. Do language background (native vs. nonnative speakers of English) and cultural background (individualistic vs. collectivist) affect sentence and text level?

If there exists an interaction between language and thought, a significant effect of both cultural and language background is anticipated in sentence and text level cohesion.

Speech Samples

After obtaining ethics approval from the university board of ethics (ID: 2023/03 02), twelve public speeches that were broadcast on YouTube were selected. The main criteria for these videos to get picked were having a high view count and being on topic, which was gender politics. After the data sample was created, the speakers' cultures were found through the video content or the speakers' social media accounts. The finalized data sample consisted of 12 videos: 6 speakers from collectivist cultures, 6 speakers from individualistic cultures. The Indian, Thai, Moroccan, Rwandan, Liberian, and Omani speakers were grouped as speakers from collectivist cultures, and the Canadian, British, Swedish, Australian, and American speakers were considered as speakers from individualistic cultures. As mentioned before, the TED Talks were thematically related and focused on issues such as gender politics, discussing gender identity. This theme was picked as it resulted in an enhanced use of pronouns. Thematically related argumentative speeches would not vary a lot in terms of their complexity (Bergeron & Trofimovich, 2017). The analysed TED Talks, whose views ranged from 14.000 to 1.5 million, were all influential. The table below (Table 1) shows the titles of the videos, their view counts, speakers' names, and cultures.

Table 1. Descriptive information of the sample group

Title of the video	Speaker	Speakers' Culture	View Count
Gender Equality Speech	Rose Mathew	Collectivist	72K
Beyond Sex: A Talk About Gender Identity In Society	Palis Pisuttisaran	Collectivist	14K
Climate Action's Hidden Opportunities For Women	Zineb Sqalli	Collectivist	41K
How Women Are Revolutionizing Rwanda	Agnes Binagwaho	Collectivist	33K
How Women Will Lead Us To Freedom, Justice And Peace	H. E. Johnson Sirleaf	Collectivist	82K
Women And Girls, You Are Part Of The Climate Solution	Rumaitha Al Busaidi	collectivist	44K
How We Can Make The World A Better Place By 2030	Micheal Green	Individualist	1.5M
How To Share Public Money Fairly	Maja Bosnic	Individualist	47K
Why Iranians Are Cutting Their Hair For 'Women, Life, Freedom1	Sahar Zand	Individualist	37K
Toilets, Bowties, Gender And Me	Audrey Mason-Hyde	Individualist	1.5M
'A Seat At The Table' Isn't The Solution For Gender Equity	Lily Singh	Individualist	548K
Why Gender Equality Is Good For Everyone- Men Included	Michael Kimmel	Individualist	1M

Data Analysis

As indices of sentence level cohesion, lexical overlaps, semantic overlaps, and connective use were taken. Within SiNLP, the calculation of lexical overlaps is done by analyzing adjacent content and function words, including nouns and verbs. This NLP tool, which is respectively designed for cohesion analysis, is specifically picked as it helps to precisely analyze the use of indices of cohesive devices such as reference, conjunction, and lexical cohesion. With the help of SiNLP, the semantic overlap is calculated by examining overlaps between average sentences, noun and verb synonyms, and latent semantic analysis. Additionally, the number of conjunctions, sentence linkers, and various connective words (e.g., order, reason, purpose, positive causal opposition, additive temporal, and positive intentional connectives) was measured and divided by the total number of words in the text. In addition to the local or sentence level cohesion, text level cohesion indices, namely, givenness and lexical diversity, were calculated. These indices were picked as it was hypothesized that their frequencies would show a higher correlation in the results. Speech transcriptions were entered into SiNLP, and the numeric values assigned to sentence and textual level indices by SiNLP were entered into Excel Files. Then, a general linear model was developed using culture (collectivist vs. individualistic) and language background (native vs. nonnative) as the independent variables, while linguistic complexity indices (local and textual) were set as the dependent variables. Statistical analyses were conducted using SPSS (IBM, 2017), and two way ANOVA results were reported.

RESULTS

Recall that we addressed two research questions. The first one investigated the role of culture and language background on pronoun use. As a response to the first research question the speakers from the individualistic cultures used second person pronouns statistically significantly more often than those from the collectivist cultures ($F(1,11)=7.62$, $p=.02$). The table below summarizes the total number of pronouns used and the ratios of first, second, and third person pronouns to the total pronoun use.

Table 2. Descriptive statistics of pronouns used across cultures

Cultural background	Pronoun type			
	Total pronouns	**1st person**	**2nd person**	**3rd person**
collectivist	0.41	0.26	0.03	0.12
individualistic	0.55	0.35	0.10	0.10

As given in the Table above, the speakers from the collectivist cultures used more pronouns than those from the individualistic cultures. This is not surprising since we know that native speakers of English rely more on given information than the nonnative speakers when they express their arguments. Speakers from the individualistic cultures used first and second person pronouns more often than those from the collectivist cultures. Yet, the only statistically meaningful difference between the two groups existed in second person pronoun use. As a response to the second research question, there was a significant effect of the cultural background ($F(2,11)=4.69$, $p=.04$) but not the language background ($F(2,11=.83$, $p=.52$) on speech complexity.

Now we report on the role of cultural and linguistic background on specific textual, global and local indices of cohesion. First, as textual cohesion indices, givenness and lexical diversity were reported with respect to cultural and linguistic backgrounds. Under givenness, *pronoun density* (i.e., the number of third person pronouns divided by the total number of words), *pronoun to noun ratio* (i.e., the number of third person pronouns divided by the total number of nouns), *repeated content lemmas* (i.e., the total number of content words that are repeated at least once by the total number of nouns in the text), *repeated pronoun lemmas* (i.e., the number of third person pronouns that are repeated at least once divided by the total number of words in the text). Among these variables, culture was a determining factor in pronoun to noun ratios ($p= .007$), repeated content lemmas ($p= .035$) and repeated pronoun lemmas ($p= .028$). Speakers coming from individualistic cultures relied more on given information in their gender related speeches than those coming from collectivist cultures. Language background was not a significant determiner in speaker's use of given information to base their arguments. As the second component of textual indices, lexical diversity was explored. When calculating lexical diversity, content word TTR, function word TTR, noun TTR, verb TTR, adjective and adverb TTRs were compared again with respect to language and culture that the speakers came from. Cultural background was a determining factor only on content word TTR ($p= .002$). This shows that speakers from individualistic cultures used more lexical diversity in their speeches.

Next, we report on the role of cultural and linguistic background on specific local indices of cohesion. We specifically investigated lexical overlaps (i.e., adjacent content word, function word, noun and verb overlap), semantic overlaps (i.e., synonym noun and verb overlap and latent semantic analysis between adjacent sentences). Latent semantic analysis (LSA) is calculated by reducing the word to its base form (see Landauer et al., 1998 for a detailed explanation). LSA analyzes word patterns and maps numbers to words in written or spoken language (Pennebaker et al., 2003). As the third component connective use that builds additive, adversative, causal and temporal relations were calculated along with determiner and demonstrative use. See the table below:

Table 3. Descriptive statistics of connective use

Cultural background	Connective type			
	Additive	Adversative	Causal	Temporal
collectivist	0.0333	0.0083	0.0128	0.0107
individualistic	0.0283	0.0083	0.0167	0.0142

As given in Table 3, the most frequently used connective type was additive conjunctions for both groups. The groups favored connective use to establish adversative semantic relations the least. Non native speakers preferred higher numbers of transition words, favoring "and" and "also" in sentences and this showed an over reliance on overt linking. In contrast, the native speakers employed a more flexible discourse structure by using a variety of conjunctions. Lexical overlap indices did not demonstrate a meaningful role of language or culture. Under semantic overlap, culture was a determinant in synonym verb overlap (p=.030) and latent semantic analysis (p=.05). The speakers of individualistic cultures had higher synonym verb overlap and LSA measures. The final measure of local cohesion indices constituted connective use to establish semantic relations between ideas. Culture was a significant predictor of only sentence linkers (p=.035), which were used more frequently by speakers from individualistic cultures than those from collectivist cultures. Overall, cultural background played a more significant role in text level cohesion than sentence level cohesion.

DISCUSSION

This paper investigated the role of linguistic and cultural background in pronoun use and indices of text and sentence level cohesion in the TED Talks given by native and nonnative speakers of English coming from either a collectivist or an individualistic culture. In this study, the cultural background was a strong predictor of linguistic complexity at sentence and text level cohesion and pronoun use. Yet, linguistic background was not a strong predictor of linguistic complexity or pronoun use. Overall, the results lend support to the weak version of the Sapir Whorf Hypothesis. As suggested by Benmoussat and Benmoussat (2023), the findings of the study also support the belief of learning a language with its set of values, beliefs, attitudes, way of thinking, and behavior. The findings also highlight the importance of being aware of the effect of cultural competence on linguistic competence.

This is a small case study that refrains us from drawing any generalizations. Yet, some level of conceptual transfer (Ferreira & Mozzillo, 2021) is observed in the use of personal pronouns since the speakers coming from collectivist and individualistic cultures manifested a different pattern of personal pronoun use. More precisely, speakers from collectivist cultures used second person pronouns more often than their individualistic culture counterparts, and this showed their tendency to show unity in their speech. In contrast, the use of first person pronouns by the speakers coming from individualistic cultures could emphasize the cultural importance and value given to autonomy and individual personality. This difference lends support to the finding that individuals might express multiple identities when talking in a different language (e.g., Hunt & Agnoli, 1991; Kemmelmeier & Cheng, 2004). Linguistic structures were found to be the clues of one's culture, self expressive and direct communication suggested an individualistic culture, and inclusive patterns suggested a tendency of a collectivist culture.

When it came to the use of language, L2 speakers used a more complex speech than their counterparts, with their high use of diverse vocabulary and semantic and lexical overlaps. What is more, the number and type of adverbials and propositions used uncovered a strong relationship between discourse features and comprehensibility in spoken narratives (Appel et al., 2019). Research also confirms that explicit use of discourse markers helps L2 learners understand lectures (Williams, 1992). The use of additive connectives was prevalent in both speaker groups backing up previous research ensuring interconnectedness of ideas and comprehensibility (Tsunemoto & Trofimovich, 2024). More proficient learners use low frequency words which are considered to be more sophisticated words (Crossley & McNamara, 2012). The higher TTRs of content words, higher synonym verb overlap and LSA measures observed in speakers coming from individualistic cultures in this study also backed up this finding.

The pedagogical recommendation is to address the interaction between language and cognition as well as its influence on L2 learning beyond L2 instructional and comprehensible input. First, teachers should acknowledge the unique needs of today's L2 learners (Sockett, 2014), who are engaging with a global language that is accessible through multiple digital platforms. It's crucial for them to understand the types of activities students participate in during their leisure time and how this exposure to English can influence their language skills. Educators should guide students in making the most of language input outside instructional L2 environments. Considering the L2 knowledge gained outside the classroom settings such as vocabulary related to unaddressed topics and colloquial phrases, teachers can incorporate this knowledge into their lessons and assessments. The benefits of being exposed to L2 outside the classroom contribute to learner progress in four skills with a lot of fun while the drawbacks come with easy distraction, loss of interest and not paying attention to the structure of the language and of course addiction to multiple web based communication platforms (Alonso, 2023). Second, because L2 instruction is delivered by nonnative instructors who may over rely on additive conjunctions to establish cohesion (Hinkel, 2001), and that the lack of teaching material to improve the cohesion in L2 (Johnson, 2017), may result in a delivery of receptive vocabulary skills rather than a focus on productive use of language encouraging revision.

One reason for the limited effect of language background could be related to high levels of language proficiency that the L2 speakers had in this study. So, for future research, speech samples of speakers with varying levels of language proficiency, diverse topics, and a larger number of complexity indices could be explored. To note, this study also comes with its limitations and further recommendations. Firstly, the data set, which consisted of 12 speeches in this study, could be enlarged to diversify the cultures that were analyzed. This can lead to more concrete data and ensure that the results can be generalized to different contexts. Secondly, as this study focuses on cohesion, the use of other semantic devices such as allegories, personifications, and metaphors between cultures. Third, concerns about the accuracy of the results obtained from NLP tools could be addressed for further work.

Educational implications

Differences exist between Generative Artificial Intelligence (GenAI) tools such as the Chat GPT and NLP tools such as SiNLP. The NLP tool provides the platform to decode and understand human language whereas the Generative AI uses the insights from NLP tools to generate contextually relevant and novice content. Thus, the usefulness of GenAI in enhancing language teaching and learning cannot be denied since it ensures a personalized learning experience (Ironsi, 2024) provides real time interactions (Sénécal, 2024) and helps curriculum designers and teachers to design a language path that ensures adaptability, resulting in more active and autonomous participants of learning (Creely, 2024), successfully taking on the role of a co author, evaluator, and material provider for both language learners and teachers (Wang et al., 2023). Dynel (2023) showed that human interaction influenced the output ChatGPT created after analysing meta language, meta discourse, meta communication and meta pragmatics interactions between the human users and AI. In return, the human users' metalinguistic awareness and linguistic complexity improved thanks to the interactive communication with ChatGPT. Although GenAI could successfully help with semantic categorisation, the mere use of GenAI needs to be approached with caution (Crosthwaite & Baisa, 2023; Curry et al., 2024).

The expertise to deal with GenAI and NLP tools consists of the mastery of two components, technological knowledge, and technological content knowledge. These components help teachers to enhance their teaching strategies and proficiencies (Alshraah, et al., 2024). Although in class use ChatGPT and other GenAI tools for proofreading and generating texts from scratch is widely acknowledged, the help of the experts is still needed to check the authentication of student products since these artificially created texts could be easily identifiable (Mizumoto et al., 2024). Additionally, the biases that these GenAI tools have that are based on human interaction may prove to be harmful for all of those who are interacting, not just the learners (Bozkurt, et al., 2024).

REFERENCES

Al Khalidy, H. O. (2018). The use of conjunctions as grammatical cohesion in the speeches of Her Majesty Queen Rania of Jordan. *International Journal of Applied Linguistics and English Literature*, *7*(5), 207–211. DOI: 10.7575/aiac.ijalel.v.7n.5p.207

Alexa. (2022, January 24). The top 500 sites on the web. Alexa. Retrieved from https://web.archive.org/web/20220118000917/https://www.alexa.com/topsites

Alonso, M. R. A. (2023). Out of school contact with L2 English: Perspectives from language learners. *Porto Linguarum, 40*, 93 112.

Alshraah, S. M., Kariem, N., Alshraah, A. M., Aldosemani, T. I., & AlQarni, K. (2024). A critical look at how lecturers in linguistics can leverage generative artificial intelligence in enhancing teaching proficiency and students' engagement. *Journal of Language Teaching & Research, 15*(4), 1361–1371. DOI: 10.17507/jltr.1504.34

Amenorvi, C. R. (2018). Lexical cohesion and literariness in Malcolm X's speeches. *Journal of Applied Linguistics and Applied Literature: Dynamics and Advances*, *6*(1), 27–37.

Appel, R., Saito, K., Isaacs, T., Webb, S., & Trofimovich, P. (2019). Lexical aspects of comprehensibility and nativeness from the perspective of native speaking English raters. *International Journal of Applied Linguistics, 170*, 24 52.

Asif, M., Zhiyong, D., Malik, A. H., Roohi, S., & Saeed, A. (2020). Lexical functions and cohesion in Imran Khan's Speech On 28 September 2019 at the United Nations General Assembly. *International Transaction Journal of Engineering, Management, & Applied Sciences & Technologies, 11*(16), 11A16K 1.

Benmoussat, N. D., & Benmoussat, S. (2023). The Sapir Whorf Hypothesis revisited: A reconsideration of the weltanschauung in an Algerian EFL context. *Revue Plurilingue: Études des Langues, Littératures et Cultures*, *7*(1), 49 58.

Benson, P. (2011). Language learning and teaching beyond the classroom: An introduction to the field. In P. Benson & H. Reinders (Eds.), *Beyond the language classroom: The theory and practice of informed language learning and teaching* (pp. 7 16). Palgrave Macmillan.

Benson, P. (2015). Commenting to learn: Evidence of language and intercultural learning in comments on YouTube videos. *Language Learning & Technology*, *19*(3), 88–105. DOI: 10.64152/10125/44435

Bergeron, A., & Trofimovich, P. (2017). Linguistic dimensions of accentedness and comprehensibility: Exploring task and listener effects in second language French. *Foreign Language Annals, 50*, 547 566.

Bloom, A. H. (1984). Caution the words you use may affect what you say: A response to Au. *Cognition, 17*, 257 287.

Boas, F. (1911). Introduction. *Handbook of American Indian languages* (pp. 25 26). Washington Government Printing Office.

Boguraev, B. K., & Neff, M. S. (2000). *Lexical Cohesion, Discourse Segmentation and Document Summarization. RIAO Conference.*

Boroditsky, L. (2001). Does language shape thought? English and Mandarin speakers' conceptions of time. *Cognitive Psychology, 43*, 1 22.

Bozkurt, A., Xiao, J., Farrow, R., Bai, J. Y. H., Nerantzi, C., Moore, S., Dron, J., Stracke, C. M., Singh, L., Crompton, H., Koutropoulos, A., Terentev, E., Pazurek, A., Nichols, M., Sidorkin, A. M., Costello, E., Watson, S., Mulligan, D., Honeychurch, S., & Asino, T. I. (2024). The Manifesto for Teaching and Learning in a Time of Generative AI: A Critical Collective Stance to Better Navigate the Future. *Open Praxis, 16*(4), 487–513. DOI: 10.55982/openpraxis.16.4.777

Brown, R. (1976). Reference: In memorial tribute to Eric Lenneberg. *Cognition, 4*, 125 153.

Bybee, J. (1995). Regular morphology and the lexicon. *Language and Cognitive Processes,10*, 425 455.

Canonico, M., & De Russis, L. (2018). A comparison and critique of natural language understanding tools. *International Conference on Cloud Computing*, 110–115. https://www.thinkmind.org/articles/cloud_computing_2018_6_20_20057.pdf

Che, Z. (2008). English as a lingua franca. *Academica Turistica, 1*(1), 62–65.

Chopra, A., Prashar, A., & Sain, C. (2013). Natural language processing. *International journal of technology enhancements and emerging engineering research, 1*(4), 131-134.

Cook, V. (2003). The changing L1 in the L2 user's mind. In V. Cook (Ed.), *Effects of the second language on the first* (pp. 1 18). Multilingual Matters.

Corp, I. B. M. (2017). *IBM SPSS Statistics for Windows, Version 25.0*. IBM Corp.

Creely, E. (2024). Exploring the role of generative AI in enhancing language learning: Opportunities and challenges. *International Journal of Changes in Education, 1*(3), 158–167. DOI: 10.47852/bonviewIJCE42022495

Crossley, S. A., Allen, L. K., Kyle, K., & McNamara, D.S. (2014). Analysing discourse processing using a simple natural language processing tool (SiNLP). *Discourse Processes, 51*(5 6), 511 534.

Crossley, S. A., Kyle, K., & Dascalu, M. (2019). The Tool for the Automatic Analysis of Cohesion 2.0: Integrating semantic similarity and text overlap. *Behavior Research Methods, 51*(1), 14–27. DOI: 10.3758/s13428-018-1142-4 PMID: 30298264

Crossley, S. A., & McNamara, D. S. (2012). Predicting second language writing proficiency: The roles of cohesion and linguistic sophistication. *Journal of Research in Reading, 35*(2), 115–135. DOI: 10.1111/j.1467-9817.2010.01449.x

Crosthwaite, P., & Baisa, V. (2023). Generative AI and the end of corpus assisted data driven learning? Not so fast! *Applied Corpus Linguistics, 3*(3), 100066. DOI: 10.1016/j.acorp.2023.100066

Curry, N., Baker, P., & Brookes, G. (2024). Generative AI for corpus approaches to discourse studies: A critical evaluation of ChatGPT. *Applied Corpus Linguistics, 4*(1), 100082. DOI: 10.1016/j.acorp.2023.100082

Doughty, C. (1991). Second language instruction does make a difference: Evidence from an empirical study of SL relativization. *Studies in Second Language Acquisition, 13*(4), 431–469. DOI: 10.1017/S0272263100010287

Dynel, M. (2023). Lessons in linguistics with ChatGPT: Metapragmatics, metacommunication, metadiscourse and metalanguage in human AI interactions. *Language & Communication, 93*, 107 124.

Ellis, N. C. (2002). Frequency effects in language processing: A review with implications for theories of implicit and explicit language acquisition. *Studies in Second Language Acquisition, 24*, 143 188.

Emilinda, S. (2022). The analysis of cohesive devices in Donald Trump's concession speech transcripts. *Scripta: Jurnal Ilmiah Mahasiswa, 4*(2), 135–145.

European Commission. (2012). *First European survey on language competences: Education and training*. Publications Office of the European Union.

Ferreira, R. C., & Mozzillo, I. (2021). Conceptual transfer: Linguistic relativity in second language learning. *Alfa: Revista de Linguística (São José do Rio Preto), 65*, 1 20.

Flowerdew, J., & Miller, L. (1995). On the notion of culture in L2 lectures. *TESOL Quarterly*, *29*(2), 345–373. DOI: 10.2307/3587628

Gass, S., Winke, P., Isbell, D., & Ahn, J. (2019). How captions help people learn languages: A working memory, eye tracking study. *Language Learning & Technology*, *23*(2), 84–104. DOI: 10.64152/10125/44684

Gass, S. M. (2013). *Second language acquisition: An introductory course*. Routledge. DOI: 10.4324/9780203137093

Ghofar, A. (2018). Cohesion analysis of Soekarno's speech entitled 'Only a nation with self reliance can become a great nation'. [Unpublished BA Thesis]. Walisongo State Islamic University Semarang.

Gilmore, A. (2007). Authentic materials and authenticity in foreign language learning. *Language Teaching*, *40*(2), 97–118. DOI: 10.1017/S0261444807004144

Goar, V., Yadav, N. S., & Yadav, P. S. (2023). Conversational AI for Natural Language Processing: An review of ChatGPT. *International Journal on Recent and Innovation Trends in Computing and Communication*, *11*(3s), 109–117. DOI: 10.17762/ijritcc.v11i3s.6161

Haberstroh, S., Oyserman, D., Schwarz, N., Kühnen, U., & Ji, L. J. (2002). Is the interdependent self more sensitive to question context than the independent self? Self construal and the observation of conversational norms. *Journal of Experimental Social Psychology*, *38*(3), 323–329. DOI: 10.1006/jesp.2001.1513

Halliday, M. A. K., & Hasan, R. (1976). *Cohesion in English*. English Language Series. Longman.

Han, Z., & Cadierno, T. (2010). *Linguistic relativity in SLA: Thinking for speaking* (Second Language Acquisition). Multilingual Matters.

Hernández, T. A. (2011). Re examining the role of explicit instruction and input flood on the acquisition of Spanish discourse markers. *Language Teaching Research*, *15*(2), 159–182. DOI: 10.1177/1362168810388694

Hinkel, E. (2001). Matters of cohesion in L2 academic texts. *Applied Language Learning*, *12*(2), 111–132.

Hoffman, C., Lau, I., & Johnson, D. R. (1986). The linguistic relativity of person cognition. *Journal of Personality and Social Psychology, 51*, 1097 1105.

Hunt, E., & Agnoli, F. (1991). The Whorfian hypothesis: A cognitive psychology perspective. *Psychological Review, 98*, 377 389.

Hussein, B. A. S. (2012). The Sapir Whorf hypothesis today. *Theory and Practice in Language Studies, 2*(3), 642–646. DOI: 10.4304/tpls.2.3.642-646

Ironsi, C. S. (2024). Exploring the potential of generative AI in English language teaching. In P. Yu, J. Mulli, Z. A.S. Syed and L. Umme (Eds.), *Facilitating global collaboration and knowledge sharing in higher education with generative AI* (pp. 162 185). IGI Global Scientific Publishing. DOI: 10.4018/979-8-3693-0487-7.ch007

Jarvis, S., & Pavlenko, A. (2010). *Crosslinguistic influence in language and cognition*. Routledge.

Johnson, M. (2017). Improving cohesion in L2 writing: A three strand approach to building lexical cohesion. *English Teaching Forum*, 1 13.

Kashima, Y., & Kashima, E. S. (2003). Individualism, GNP, climate, and pronoun drop: Is individualism determined by affluence and climate, or does language use play a role? *Journal of Cross-Cultural Psychology, 34*(1), 125–134. DOI: 10.1177/0022022102239159

Kemmelmeier, M., Cheng, B. (2004). Language and self construal priming: A replication and extension in a Hong Kong sample. *Journal of Cross Cultural Psychology, 35*, 705 712.

Kim, S., & Kim, H. C. (2021). The benefits of YouTube in learning English as a second language: A qualitative investigation of Korean freshman students' experiences and perspectives in the U.S. *Sustainability (Basel), 13*(13), 1–16. DOI: 10.3390/su13137365

Koshik, I. (1999). A Preliminary investigation into the effect of grammatical cohesive devices their absence and their misuse on native speaker comprehension of non native speaker speech and writing. *Issues in Applied Linguistics, 10*(1), 3–25. DOI: 10.5070/L4101005009

Krashen, S. (1985). *The input hypothesis: Issues and implications*. Longman.

Landauer, T. K., Foltz, P. W., & Laham, D. (1998). An introduction to latent semantic analysis. *Discourse Processes, 25*(2 3), 259 284.

Long, M. H. (1983). Input and second language acquisition theory. In S. Gass and C. Maddan (Eds.), *Input in second language acquisition* (pp. 377 393). Rowley, Newbury House.

Long, M. H. (1996). The role of linguistic environment in second language acquisition. In W. C. Ritchie & T. K. Bhatia (Eds.), *Handbook of second language acquisition* (pp. 413 468). San Diego Academic Press. DOI: 10.1016/B978-012589042-7/50015-3

Mackey, A. (2020). *Interaction, feedback and task research in second language learning*. Cambridge University Press. DOI: 10.1017/9781108589284

Malah, Z. (2021). Cross cultural pragmatics on lexical cohesion in President Obama's and President Buhari's inaugural speeches. *International Journal of Language and Literary Studies, 3*(3), 23–53. DOI: 10.36892/ijlls.v2i3.680

Mayer, R. E., Lee, H., & Peebles, A. (2014). Multimedia learning in a second language: A cognitive load perspective. *Applied Cognitive Psychology, 28*(5), 653–660. DOI: 10.1002/acp.3050

McNamara, D. S., Graesser, A. C., McCarthy, P., & Cai, Z. (2014). *Automated evaluation of text and discourse with Coh Metrix*. Cambridge University Press. DOI: 10.1017/CBO9780511894664

Mirzaei, M. S., & Meshgi, K. (2021). Facilitating L2 listening through automatic detection of speech and lexical difficulties. In N. Zoghlami, C. Brudermann, C. Sarré, M. Grosbois, L. Bradley, & S. Thouësny (Eds.), *CALL and professionalisation: short papers from EUROCALL 2021* (pp. 214 219). DOI: 10.14705/rpnet.2021.54.1335

Mizumoto, A., Yasuda, S., & Tamura, Y. (2024). Identifying ChatGPT generated texts in EFL students' writing: Through comparative analysis of linguistic fingerprints. *Applied Corpus Linguistics, 4*(3), 100106. DOI: 10.1016/j.acorp.2024.100106

Mondada, L., & Doehlier, S. P. (2004). Second language acquisition as situated practice: Task accomplishment in the French second language classroom. *Modern Language Journal, 88*(4), 501–518. DOI: 10.1111/j.0026-7902.2004.t01-15-.x

Muñoz, C. (2012). The significance of intensive exposure as a turning point in learners' histories. In Muñoz, C. (Ed.), *Intensive Exposure Experiences in Second Language Learning* (pp. 141–160). Multilingual Matters.

Muñoz, C., & Cadierno, T. (2021). How do differences in exposure affect English language learning? A comparison of teenagers in two learning environments. *Studies in Second Language Learning and Teaching, 11*(2), 185–212. DOI: 10.14746/ssllt.2021.11.2.2

Muthoharoh, K., & Nur Rohmah, G. (2022). The use of cohesion of Susilo Bambang Yudhoyono's speech in APEC Economic Leader Conference in Bali. [JSRET]. *Journal of Scientific Research, Education, and Technology, 1*(2), 83–91. DOI: 10.58526/jsret.v1i2.14

Nadkarni, P. M., Ohno-Machado, L., & Chapman, W. W. (2011). Natural language processing: An introduction. *Journal of the American Medical Informatics Association : JAMIA, 18*(5), 544–551. DOI: 10.1136/amiajnl-2011-000464 PMID: 21846786

Nation, I. (2006). How Large a Vocabulary is Needed For Reading and Listening? *Canadian Modern Language Review. Canadian Modern Language Review, 63*(1), 59–82. DOI: 10.3138/cmlr.63.1.59

Parker, K., & Chaudron, C. (1987). The effects of linguistic simplification and elaborative modifications on L2 comprehension. *University of Hawaii Working Papers in ESL, 6*, 107 133.

Pavlenko, A. (2003). Eyewitness memory in late bilinguals: Evidence for discursive relativity. *The International Journal of Bilingualism, 7*(3), 257–281. DOI: 10.1177/13670069030070030301

Pennebaker, J. W., Mehl, M. R., & Niederhoffer, K. G. (2003). Psychological aspects of natural language. use: Our words, ourselves. *Annual Review of Psychology, 54*, 547 577.

Pica, T. (1994). Research on negotiation: What does it reveal about second-language learning conditions, processes, and outcomes? *Language Learning, 44*(3), 493–527. DOI: 10.1111/j.1467-1770.1994.tb01115.x

Sani, T., & Rocio, C. (2019). *Ted talks in intelligible pronunciation*. https://repositorio.uta.edu.ec/jspui/handle/123456789/30438

Sapir, E. (1921). *Language: An introduction to the study of speech*. Harcourt.

Schmidt, R. W. (1990). The role of consciousness in second language learning. *Applied Linguistics, 11*(2), 129–158. DOI: 10.1093/applin/11.2.129

Sénécal, A. M. (2024). A semi systematic review of research on generative artificial intelligence (GenAI) in second language acquisition (SLA). In Y. Choubsaz, P. Díez Arcón, A. Gimeno Sanz, J. Hriňák, X. Liashuk, S. Pokrivčáková and H. Vančová (Eds.), *CALL for Humanity EUROCALL 2024 Short Papers* (pp. 24 32).

Shala, L., Rus, V., & Graesser, A. C. (2014). A bilingual analysis of cohesion in a corpus of leader speeches. In *Proceedings of the 27th International Florida Artificial Intelligence Research Society Conference, FLAIRS 2014*, 225 230.

Sharififar, M., & Rahimi, E. (2015). Critical discourse analysis of political speeches: A case study of Obama's and Rouhani's speeches at UN. *Theory and Practice in Language Studies, 5*(2), 343–349. DOI: 10.17507/tpls.0502.14

Sinambela, S. I., Nurlela, N., & Zein, T. T. (2020). Conjunction of grammatical cohesion in speech text. *Bahas, 31*(3), 142–153.

Smith, M. S., & Truscott, J. (2014). Explaining input enhancement: A mogul perspective. *International Review of Applied Linguistics in Language Teaching*, *52*(3), 253–281. DOI: 10.1515/iral-2014-0012

Sockett, G. (2014). *The Online Informal Learning of English*. Palgrave MacMillan. DOI: 10.1057/9781137414885

Solvandi, Y., & Raflis, R. (2024). Cohesion and coherence of Sandiaga Uno's Speech in The event high level thematic debate on tourism United Nation General Assembly 2022. *Jurnal Ilmiah Langue and Parole*, *7*(2), 72–78. DOI: 10.36057/jilp.v7i2.669

Sun, H., & Verspoor, M. (2022). Mandarin vocabulary growth, teacher qualifications and teacher talk in child heritage language learners. *International Journal of Bilingual Education and Bilingualism*, *25*(6), 1976–1991. DOI: 10.1080/13670050.2020.1835813

Sun, Y. C. (2014). Microteaching writing on YouTube for pre service teacher training: Lessons learned. *CALICO Journal*, *31*(2), 179–200. DOI: 10.11139/cj.31.2.179-200

Swain, M. (1985). Communicative competence: Some roles of comprehensible input and comprehensible output in its development. In S. Gass C. Maddan (Eds.), *Input in second language acquisition* (pp. 235 252). Rowley Newbury House.

Syahrin, A. (2018). Culture repertoire in expressive written language: Study of hypothesis of Edward Sapir and Benyamin Lee Whorf. *Budapest International Research and Critics in Linguistics and Education (BirLE). Journal*, *1*(1), 23–28.

Tanskanen, S. K. (2006). *Collaborating Towards Coherence: Lexical Cohesion in English Discourse*. John Benjamins Pub Co. DOI: 10.1075/pbns.146

Taylor, P. J., Larner, S., Conchie, S. M., & Menacere, T. (2017). Culture moderates changes in linguistic self presentation and detail provision when deceiving others. *Royal Society Open Science*, *4*(6), 170128. DOI: 10.1098/rsos.170128 PMID: 28680668

Tomasello, M. (2003). *Constructing a language: A usage based theory of language acquisition*. Harvard University Press.

Tsunemoto, A., & Trofimovich, P. (2024). Coherence and comprehensibility in second language speakers' academic speaking performance. *Studies in Second Language Acquisition*, *46*(3), 795–817. DOI: 10.1017/S0272263124000305

Vajjala, S., Majumder, B., Gupta, A., & Surana, H. (2020). *Practical Natural Language Processing: A Comprehensive guide to building Real-World NLP systems.* https://openlibrary.telkomuniversity.ac.id/home/catalog/id/165927/slug/practical-natural-language-processing-a-comprehensive-guide-to-building-real-world-nlp-systems.html

Wang, H. C., & Chen, C.W. Y. (2019). Learning English from YouTubers: English L2 learners' self regulated language learning on YouTube. *Innovation in Language Learning and Teaching, 14,* 333 346.

Wang, Z., Zou, D., Lee, L. K. K., Xie, H., & Wang, F. L. (2023). A systematic review of generative artificial intelligence in language education. In *31st International Conference on Computers in Education, ICCE 2023* (pp. 33 43). Asia Pacific Society for Computers in Education. DOI: 10.58459/icce.2023.1199

Whorf, B. L. (1940/1956). Linguistics as an exact science. In Carroll, J. B. (Ed.), *Language, thought, and reality: Selected writings of Benjamin Lee Whorf* (pp. 220–232). MIT Press.

Whorf, B. L. (1956). *Language thought and reality*. MIT Press.

Williams, J. (1992). Planning, discourse marking, and the comprehensibility of international teaching assistants. *TESOL Quarterly, 26*, 693 711.

Wisniewska, N., & Mora, J. C. (2020). Can captioned video benefit second language pronunciation? *Studies in Second Language Acquisition, 42*(3), 599–624. DOI: 10.1017/S0272263120000029

Wong, W. (2002). Decreasing attention demands in input processing: A textual enhancement study. *Studies in Second Language Acquisition, 23*, 345 368.

Yao, X. P. (2002). The legacy of human linguist Whorf read on language, thought, and reality. *Foreign Language Teaching Research, 1*, 75 77.

Ye, J., & Liu, X. (2020). Analysis of cohesion and coherence in two truths to live by. *Theory and Practice in Language Studies, 10*(1), 96–101. DOI: 10.17507/tpls.1001.14

Young, R. F., & Miller, E. R. (2004). Learning as changing participation: Discourse roles in ESL writing conferences. *Modern Language Journal, 88*(4), 519–535. DOI: 10.1111/j.0026-7902.2004.t01-16-.x

KEY TERMS AND DEFINITIONS:

Linguistic Complexity: Linguistic complexity refers to the dynamic property of the learner's interlanguage system at large and a more stable property of the individual linguistic elements that make up the interlanguage system. It envelops components such as syntax and morphology. It can be used as a way of measuring the competence of language learning. In this study, it helps to explore the speech production of native and non native speakers' coming from different cultures.

Cohesion: Cohesion is the set of resources for constructing relations in discourse that transcend grammatical structure. It helps to produce meaningful connections using grammatical devices such as reference, substitution, ellipsis, and connectives. It also assists the receiver to easily interpret the messages between ideas and have smoother communication. In this research, cohesion is taken as the determiner of linguistic complexity, which helps to explore one's speech production ability.

Modified input in SLA: Input that is altered to promote learners' internal capacities and to push them to produce modified output that may facilitate second language (L2) learning is referred to as modified input in Second language acquisition. Strategies such as simplification, repetition, and slowing the speech are considered as modified input, which help the learner to comprehend the input. TED Talks, YouTube videos, and online content can act as authentic modified input for language learners and help learners to understand the structure and delivery of speech.

Natural Language Processing: Natural Language Processing, NLP, uses rule based or machine learning approaches to understand the structure and meaning of a written text or speech. It makes use of algorithms and statistical models to understand and analyze a large corpus and help understand linguistic patterns. In this study, NLP is used to extract cohesive devices across transcripts to achieve reliable, quantified data.

Out of school learning environments: Curricular and non curricular learning experiences for pupils and students outside the school environment are referred to as out of school environments. These environments provide authentic contexts for learners to observe, understand, and practice language skills, and provide motivation by going beyond classroom limits. Online platforms, such as TED Talks, which can be used as out of school self practices help students to access the language remotely and provide opportunities for autonomous learning.

Compilation of References

Abimbola, C., Eden, C. A., Chisom, O. N., & Adeniyi, I. S. (2024). *Integrating AI in education: Opportunities, challenges, and ethical considerations*. Magna Scientia Advanced Research and Reviews., DOI: 10.30574/msarr.2024.10.2.0039

Abram, N. (2025). Personalized Learning in Action: Exploring AI and Robotics for Early Childhood Education. *Proceedings of the AAAI Conference on Artificial Intelligence*, *39*(28), 29561–29563. DOI: 10.1609/aaai.v39i28.35325

Abulkassova, D., Muldasheva, G., & Nurtazin, M.. (2025). The phenomenon of artificial intelligence in modern transformational socio-cultural processes: Socio-philosophical analysis. *AI & Society*. Advance online publication. DOI: 10.1007/s00146-025-02195-z

Adako, O. P., Adeusi, O. C., & Alaba, P. A. (2024). Revolutionizing autism education: Harnessing aı for tailored skill development in social, emotional, and ındependent learning domains. *Journal of Computational and Cognitive Engineering*, *3*(4), 348–359. DOI: 10.47852/bonviewJCCE42023414

Adeshola, I., & Adepoju, A. P. (2024). The opportunities and challenges of ChatGPT in education. *Interactive Learning Environments*, *32*(10), 6159–6172. DOI: 10.1080/10494820.2023.2253858

Adiguzel, T., Kaya, M., & Cansu, F. (2023). Revolutionizing education with AI: Exploring the transformative potential of ChatGPT. *Contemporary Educational Technology*, *15*(3), e429. DOI: 10.30935/cedtech/13152

Aggarwal, D. D. (2023). Exploring the Scope of Artificial Intelligence (AI) for Lifelong Education through Personalised & Adaptive Learning. *Journal of Artificial Intelligence, Machine Learning and Neural Network*.DOI: DOI: 10.14445/22312803/IJCTT-V71I4P114

Ahmad, M., Ho, W. Y., Goyes Robalino, A. P., Maqsood, M., Ahmad, M., Ho, W. Y., Goyes Robalino, A. P., & Maqsood, M. (2025). Theoretical Implications of Generative AI for Content Generation in Geoinformatics Training. In A. Anna A. (Ed.), *Integration Strategies of Generative AI in Higher Education* (pp. 101–130). IGI Global Scientific Publishing. DOI: 10.4018/979-8-3693-5518-3.ch005

Ahmad, S. F., Rahmat, M. K., Mubarik, M. S., Alam, M. M., & Hyder, S. I. (2021). Artificial Intelligence and Its Role in Education. *Sustainability (Basel)*, *13*(22), 12902. DOI: 10.3390/su132212902

Ahmed, Z., Shanto, S. S., Rime, M. H. K., Morol, M. K., Fahad, N., Hossen, M. J., & Abdullah-Al-Jubair, M. (2024). *The Generative AI Landscape in Education: Mapping the Terrain of Opportunities, Challenges and Student Perception*. IEEE., DOI: 10.1109/ACCESS.2024.3461874

Akçayır, M., & Akçayır, G. (2017). Advantages and challenges associated with augmented reality for education: A systematic review of the literature. *Educational Research Review*, *20*, 1–11. DOI: 10.1016/j.edurev.2016.11.002

Al Khalidy, H. O. (2018). The use of conjunctions as grammatical cohesion in the speeches of Her Majesty Queen Rania of Jordan. *International Journal of Applied Linguistics and English Literature*, *7*(5), 207–211. DOI: 10.7575/aiac.ijalel.v.7n.5p.207

Alabdulkareem, A., Alhakbani, N., & Al-Nafjan, A. (2022). A systematic review of research on robot-assisted therapy for children with autism. *Sensors (Basel)*, *22*(3), 944. DOI: 10.3390/s22030944

Alam, A., Hasan, M., & Raza, M. M. (2022). *Impact of artificial intelligence (ai) on education: changing paradigms and approaches*. Towards Excellence., DOI: 10.37867/TE140127

Alexa. (2022, January 24). The top 500 sites on the web. Alexa. Retrieved from https://web.archive.org/web/20220118000917/https://www.alexa.com/topsites

Al-Hosan, A. M., & Alrajhi, N. A. (2025). Applications of Artificial Intelligence and Smart Learning Methods for Children with Autism Spectrum Disorder: A Proposed Interactive Platform. *Journal of Ecohumanism*, *4*(2), 738–756. DOI: 10.62754/joe.v4i2.6345

Ali, K., Barhom, N., Tamimi, F., & Duggal, M. (2024). ChatGPT—A double-edged sword for healthcare education? Implications for assessments of dental students. *European Journal of Dental Education*, *28*(1), 206–211. DOI: 10.1111/eje.12937 PMID: 37550893

Ali, S., Abuhmed, T., El-Sappagh, S., Muhammad, K., Alonso-Moral, J. M., Confalonieri, R., Guidotti, R., Del Ser, J., Díaz-Rodríguez, N., & Herrera, F. (2023). Explainable Artificial Intelligence (XAI): What we know and what is left to attain Trustworthy Artificial Intelligence. *Information Fusion, 99*, 101805. DOI: 10.1016/j.inffus.2023.101805

Ali, S., DiPaola, D., Lee, I., Sindato, V., Kim, G., Blumofe, R., & Breazeal, C. (2021). Children as creators, thinkers and citizens in an AI-driven future. *Computers and Education: Artificial Intelligence, 2*, 100040. DOI: 10.1016/j.caeai.2021.100040

Alkan, A. (2024). Artificial Intelligence: Its Role and Potential in Education. İnsan Ve Toplum Bilimleri Araştırmaları Dergisi, 13(1), 483-497. https://doi.org/DOI: 10.15869/itobiad.1331201

Alkasasbeh, W., & Amawi, A. (2023). The Effectiveness of Using Mobile Learning Application on Undergraduates' Intrinsic Motivation and Their General Nutrition Knowledge. [iJIM]. *International Journal of Interactive Mobile Technologies, 17*(17), 19–37. DOI: 10.3991/ijim.v17i17.40959

Al-kfairy, M., Mustafa, D., Kshetri, N., Insiew, M., & Alfandi, O. (2024). Ethical Challenges and Solutions of Generative AI: An Interdisciplinary Perspective. *Informatics 2024, Vol. 11, Page 58, 11*(3), 58. DOI: 10.3390/informatics11030058

Allcock, S. J., & Hulme, J. A. (2010). Learning Styles in the Classroom: Educational Benefit or Planning Exercise? *Psychology Teaching Review, 16*(2), 67–77. DOI: 10.53841/bpsptr.2010.16.2.67

Almelhes, S. A. (2023). A Review of Artificial Intelligence Adoption in Second-Language Learning. *Theory and Practice in Language Studies, 13*(5), 1259–1269. Advance online publication. DOI: 10.17507/tpls.1305.21

Almusaed, A., Almssad, A., & Albaj, A. (2024). Ethical and Pedagogical Challenges in the Integration of Artificial Intelligence into Lifelong Learning. *The proceedings is licensed under a Creative Commons Attribution-Non Commercial Share Alike 4.0 International License, permitting all non-commercial use, distribution, and reproduction in any medium, provided the original work is properly cited.*, 16-33.

Alonso, M. R. A. (2023). Out of school contact with L2 English: Perspectives from language learners. *Porto Linguarum, 40*, 93 112.

Alshamsi, I., Sadriwala, K., Alazzawi, F., & Shannaq, B. (2024). Exploring the impact of generative AI technologies on education: Academic expert perspectives, trends, and implications for sustainable development goals. *Journal of Infrastructure. Policy and Development, 8*(11), 1–20. DOI: 10.24294/jipd.v8i11.8532

Alshraah, S. M., Kariem, N., Alshraah, A. M., Aldosemani, T. I., & AlQarni, K. (2024). A critical look at how lecturers in linguistics can leverage generative artificial intelligence in enhancing teaching proficiency and students' engagement. *Journal of Language Teaching & Research, 15*(4), 1361–1371. DOI: 10.17507/jltr.1504.34

Alsudairy, N. A., & Eltantawy, M. M. (2024). Special Education Teachers' Perceptions of Using Artificial Intelligence in Educating Students with Disabilities. *Journal of Intellectual Disability-Diagnosis and Treatment, 12*(2), 92–102. DOI: 10.6000/2292-2598.2024.12.02.5

Âlvarez-Guerrero, G., Fry, D., Lu, M., & Gaitis, K. K. (2024). Online child sexual exploitation and abuse of children and adolescents with disabilities: A systematic review. *Disabilities, 4*(2), 264–276. DOI: 10.3390/disabilities4020017

Amenorvi, C. R. (2018). Lexical cohesion and literariness in Malcolm X's speeches. *Journal of Applied Linguistics and Applied Literature: Dynamics and Advances, 6*(1), 27–37.

American Psychiatric Association. (2013). *Diagnostic and statistical manual of mental disorders* (5th ed.). American Psychiatric Publishing.

Amisha, P. M., Pathania, M., & Rathaur, V. K. (2019). Overview of artificial intelligence in medicine. *Journal of Family Medicine and Primary Care, 8*(7), 2328–2331. DOI: 10.4103/jfmpc.jfmpc_440_19 PMID: 31463251

Anderson, M. (Ed.). (2016). *Developing Effective Educational Experiences through Learning Analytics*. IGI Global. DOI: 10.4018/978-1-4666-9983-0

Anggraini, Y., Setiawati, S., & Sari, I. (2024). Assessing 4C Competencies in English Language Learners: Tools, Challenges, and Implications. *EBONY. Journal of English Language Teaching, Linguistics, and Literature, 4*(2), 29–41. Advance online publication. DOI: 10.37304/ebony.v4i2.14147

Apoki, U. C., Hussein, A. M. A., Al-Chalabi, H. K. M., Badica, C., & Mocanu, M. L. (2022). The role of pedagogical agents in personalised adaptive learning: A review. Sustainability, 14(11), 6442. ISO 690 https://doi.org/DOI: 10.3390/su14116442

Appel, R., Saito, K., Isaacs, T., Webb, S., & Trofimovich, P. (2019). Lexical aspects of comprehensibility and nativeness from the perspective of native speaking English raters. *International Journal of Applied Linguistics, 170*, 24 52.

Ariyaratne, S., Iyengar, K. P., Nischal, N., Chitti Babu, N., & Botchu, R. (2023). A comparison of ChatGPT-generated articles with human-written articles. *Skeletal Radiology, 52*(9), 1755–1758. DOI: 10.1007/s00256-023-04340-5 PMID: 37059827

Arora, M. (2021). Artificial Intelligence: New Pathways and Challenges in Higher Education. In S. Verma and P. Tomar (Eds.), *Impact of AI Technologies on Teaching, Learning, and Research in Higher Education*, (pp. 30-48). Igi Global. DOI: DOI: 10.4018/978-1-7998-4763-2.ch002

Arpaci, I., Al-Emran, M., Al-Qaysi, N., & Al-Sharafi, M. A. (2025). What Drives the Use of Generative Artificial Intelligence to Promote Educational Sustainability? Evidence from SEM-ANN Approach. *TechTrends*, •••, 1–15. DOI: 10.1007/s11528-025-01089-7

Arroyo, D. C., & Yilmaz, Y. (2018). An open for replication study: The role of feedback timing in synchronous computer-mediated communication. *Language Learning*, *68*(4), 942–972. DOI: 10.1111/lang.12300

Arsyanda, M., & Annajmi Rauf, M. Miftach FakhriPramudya Asoka SyukurDevi Miftahul JannahElma Nur Jannah. (2024). StudySync Mobile Application Design for Student Academic Activity Management Based on SQLite Database. *Journal of Embedded Systems. Security and Intelligent Systems*, *5*(3), 223–232. DOI: 10.59562/jessi.v5i3.5042

Asad, M. M., & Ajaz, A. (2024). Impact of ChatGPT and generative AI on lifelong learning and upskilling learners in higher education: Unveiling the challenges and opportunities globally. *The International Journal of Information and Learning Technology*, *41*(5), 507–523. DOI: 10.1108/IJILT-06-2024-0103

Asif, M., Zhiyong, D., Malik, A. H., Roohi, S., & Saeed, A. (2020). Lexical functions and cohesion in Imran Khan's Speech On 28 September 2019 at the United Nations General Assembly. *International Transaction Journal of Engineering, Management, & Applied Sciences & Technologies*, *11*(16), 11A16K 1.

Avidov-Ungar, O., Shamir-Inbal, T., & Blau, I. (2020). Typology of digital leadership roles tasked with integrating new technologies into teaching: Insights from metaphor analysis. *Journal of Research on Technology in Education*, *54*(1), 92–107. DOI: 10.1080/15391523.2020.1809035

Avsheniuk, N., Lutsenko, O., Svyrydiuk, T., & Seminikhyna, N. (2024). Empowering language learners' critical thinking: Evaluating ChatGPT's role in English course implementation. *Arab World English Journal, Special Issue on ChatGPT*, 210-224. https://dx.doi.org/DOI: 10.24093/awej/ChatGPT.14

Aydın Yıldız, T. (2024). online first). Exploring the impact of ChatGPT on improving 21st-century skills for future English teachers during lesson planning. *Computers in the Schools*, •••, 1–24. DOI: 10.1080/07380569.2024.2429534

Ayeni, O. O., Al Hamad, N. M., Chisom, O. N., Osawaru, B., & Adewusi, O. E. (2024). AI in education: A review of personalized learning and educational technology. *GSC Advanced Research and Reviews*, *18*(2), 261–271. DOI: 10.30574/gscarr.2024.18.2.0062

Baek, E., & Wilson, R. (2024). An inquiry into the use of generative AI and its implications in education. *International Journal of Adult Education and Technology*, *15*(1), 1–14. DOI: 10.4018/IJAET.349233

Bagai, R., & Mane, V. (2023). Designing an AI-Powered Mentorship Platform for Professional Development: Opportunities and Challenges. *ArXiv, abs/2407.20233.*

Baidoo-Anu, D., & Ansah, L. O. (2023). Education in the era of generative artificial intelligence (AI): Understanding the potential benefits of ChatGPT in promoting teaching and learning. *Journal of AI*, *7*(1), 52–62. DOI: 10.61969/jai.1337500

Bakiner, O. (2023). What do academics say about artificial intelligence ethics? An overview of the scholarship. *AI and Ethics*, *3*(2), 513–525. DOI: 10.1007/s43681-022-00182-4

Bala, M., Ali, M. H., Satu, M. S., Hasan, K. F., & Moni, M. A. (2022). Efficient Machine Learning Models for Early Stage Detection of Autism Spectrum Disorder. *Algorithms*, *15*(5), 166. DOI: 10.3390/a15050166

Bälter, O., Jemstedt, A., Javan Abraham, F., Persson Osowski, C., Mugisha, R., & Bälter, K. (2023). Effect of Personalized Email-Based Reminders on Participants' Timeliness in an Online Education Program: Randomized Controlled Trial. *JMIR Formative Research*, *7*, e43977. DOI: 10.2196/43977 PMID: 37831487

Baltezarević, R., & Baltezarević, I. (2024). Students' Attitudes on The Role of Artificial Intelligence (Ai) In Personalized Learning. International Journal of Cognitive Research in Science. *Engineering and Education*, *12*(2), 387–397. DOI: 10.23947/2334-8496-2024-12-2-387-397

Bandura, A. (1986). Social foundations of thought and action. *Englewood Cliffs, NJ, 1986*(23-28), 2. https://doi.org/DOI: 10.5465/amr.1987.4306538

Banks, J. (2024). Deletion, departure, death: Experiences of AI companion loss. *Journal of Social and Personal Relationships*, *41*(12), 3547–3572. DOI: 10.1177/02654075241269688

Baron-Cohen, S. (1991). Do people with autism understand what causes emotion? *Child Development*, *62*(2), 385–395. DOI: 10.1111/j.1467-8624.1991.tb01539.x

Barrett, M., Branson, L., Carter, S., DeLeon, F., Ellis, J., Gundlach, C., & Lee, D. (2019). Using Artificial Intelligence to Enhance Educational Opportunities and Student Services in Higher Education. *Inquiry: The Journal of the Virginia Community Colleges*, 22 (1). Retrieved from https://commons.vccs.edu/inquiry/vol22/iss1/11

Barron, B. J., Schwartz, D. L., Vye, N. J., Moore, A., Petrosino, A., Zech, L., & Bransford, J. D. (2014). Doing with understanding: Lessons from research on problem-and project-based learning. In *Learning through problem solving* (pp. 271–311). Psychology Press.

Basit, A., Khan, Z. A., Rehman, I., & Iqbal, A. (2024). Analyzing how Social Media Platforms, Driven by AI, can serve as Spaces for Teachers' Professional Development by Facilitating Networking, Knowledge Sharing, and Real-time Collaboration. *Review of Applied Management and Social Sciences*, *7*(4), 849–863. DOI: 10.47067/ramss.v7i4.418

Baskara, F. (2025). Conceptualizing Digital Literacy for the AI Era: A Framework for Preparing Students in an AI-Driven World. Data and Metadata. usd.ac.id. DOI: DOI: 10.56294/dm2025530

Bautista, A., Yu, J., Lee, K., & Sun, J. (2023). Impact of play-based pedagogies in selected Asian contexts: What do we know and how to move forward?. *Effective teaching around the world: Theoretical, empirical, methodological and practical insights*, 473-488.

Bayly-Castaneda, K., Ramirez-Montoya, M. S., & Morita-Alexander, A. (2024). Crafting personalized learning paths with AI for lifelong learning: A systematic literature review. *Frontiers in Education*, *9*, 1424386. Advance online publication. DOI: 10.3389/feduc.2024.1424386

Beatty, K. (2013). Teaching and researching computer-assisted language learning, Second edition. In *Teaching and Researching Computer-Assisted Language Learning, Second edition*. DOI: 10.4324/9781315833774

Becker, S. A., Brown, M., Dahlstrom, E., Davis, A., DePaul, K., Diaz, V., & Pomerantz, J. (2018). *Horizon report 2018 higher education edition brought to you by EDUCAUSE.* EDUCAUSE. https://ir.westcliff.edu/wp-content/uploads/2020/01/Horizon-Report_-2018-Higher-Education-Edition.pdf

Bellibaş, M. Ş., & Gümüş, S. (2018). *Eğitim yönetiminde sistematik derleme çalışmaları. İçinde K. Beycioğlu, N. Özer ve Y. Kondakçı (Edt.), Eğitim yönetiminde araştırma (ss.* Pegem Akademi.

Benmoussat, N. D., & Benmoussat, S. (2023). The Sapir Whorf Hypothesis revisited: A reconsideration of the weltanschauung in an Algerian EFL context. *Revue Plurilingue: Études des Langues, Littératures et Cultures*, 7(1), 49 58.

Benson, P. (2011). Language learning and teaching beyond the classroom: An introduction to the field. In P. Benson & H. Reinders (Eds.), *Beyond the language classroom: The theory and practice of informed language learning and teaching* (pp. 7 16). Palgrave Macmillan.

Benson, P. (2015). Commenting to learn: Evidence of language and intercultural learning in comments on YouTube videos. *Language Learning & Technology*, *19*(3), 88–105. DOI: 10.64152/10125/44435

Bergeron, A., & Trofimovich, P. (2017). Linguistic dimensions of accentedness and comprehensibility: Exploring task and listener effects in second language French. *Foreign Language Annals, 50*, 547 566.

Bergmann, J., & Sams, A. (2012). *Flip your classroom: Reach every student in every class every day*. International Society for Technology in Education., DOI: 10.47362/EJSSS.2022.3208

Berson, I. R., & Berson, M. J. (2024). Fragments of the past: The intersection of AI, historical imagery, and early childhood creativity. *Future in Educational Research*, *2*(4), 403–421. DOI: 10.1002/fer3.46

Berson, I. R., Berson, M. J., & Luo, W. (2025). Innovating responsibly: Ethical considerations for AI in early childhood education. *AI. Brain and Child*, *1*(2), 1–15. DOI: 10.1007/s44436-025-00003-5

Bhutoria, A. (2022). Personalized education and Artificial Intelligence in the United States, China, and India: A systematic review using a Human-In-The-Loop model. *Computers and Education: Artificial Intelligence, 3*, 100068. https://doi.org/https://doi.org/10.1016/j.caeai.2022.100068

Billiot, T. (2023). Continuous learning and advancing technologies: A framework for professional development and training in artificial intelligence. *Development and Learning in Organizations*, *37*(3), 28–31. https://doi.org/https://doi.org/10.1108/DLO-04-2022-0064. DOI: 10.1108/DLO-04-2022-0064

Bishop, J., & Verleger, M. A. (2013, June). The flipped classroom: A survey of the research. In *2013 ASEE annual conference & exposition* (pp. 23-1200). https://doi.org/DOI: 10.18260/1-2--22585

Bizami, N. A., Tasir, Z., & Kew, S. N. (2023). Innovative pedagogical principles and technological tools capabilities for immersive blended learning: A systematic literature review. *Education and Information Technologies, 28*(2), 1373–1425. DOI: 10.1007/s10639-022-11243-w

Black, P., & Wiliam, D. (1998). Assessment and classroom learning. *Assessment in Education: Principles, Policy & Practice, 5*(1), 7–74. DOI: 10.1080/0969595980050102

Blodgett, S. L., Barocas, S., Daumé, H., & Wallach, H. (2020). Language (Technology) is power: A critical survey of «bias" in NLP. *Proceedings of the Annual Meeting of the Association for Computational Linguistics*. DOI: 10.18653/v1/2020.acl-main.485

Bloom, A. H. (1984). Caution the words you use may affect what you say: A response to Au. *Cognition, 17*, 257 287.

Bloom, B. S. (1968). *Learning for Mastery. Instruction and Curriculum.* Regional Education Laboratory for the Carolinas and Virginia, Topical Papers and Reprints, Number 1. *Evaluation Comment, 1*(2), n2. DOI: 10.2172/4087533

Blumenfeld, P. C., Soloway, E., Marx, R. W., Krajcik, J. S., Guzdial, M., & Palincsar, A. (1991). Motivating project-based learning: Sustaining the doing, supporting the learning. *Educational Psychologist, 26*(3-4), 369–398. DOI: 10.1080/00461520.1991.9653139

Boas, F. (1911). Introduction. *Handbook of American Indian languages* (pp. 25 26). Washington Government Printing Office.

Boeing. (2024). *Pilot and Technician Outlook 2024-2043*. https://www.boeing.com/commercial/market/pilot-technician-outlook

Boguraev, B. K., & Neff, M. S. (2000). *Lexical Cohesion, Discourse Segmentation and Document Summarization. RIAO Conference*.

Bohr, A., & Memarzadeh, K. (2020). The rise of artificial intelligence in healthcare applications. In Bohr, A., & Memarzadeh, K. (Eds.), *Artificial intelligence in healthcare* (pp. 25–60). Academic Press., DOI: 10.1016/B978-0-12-818438-7.00002-2

Bolukbasi, T., Chang, K. W., Zou, J., Saligrama, V., & Kalai, A. (2016). Man is to computer programmer as woman is to homemaker? Debiasing word embeddings. *Advances in Neural Information Processing Systems*.

Bone, D., Goodwin, M. S., Black, M. P., Lee, C. C., Audhkhasi, K., & Narayanan, S. (2015). Applying machine learning to facilitate autism diagnostics: Pitfalls and promises. *Journal of Autism and Developmental Disorders*, *45*, 1121–1136. DOI: 10.1007/s10803-014-2268-6

Borg, J., Lindström, A., & Larsson, S. (2009). Assistive technology in developing countries: National and international responsibilities to implement the Convention on the Rights of Persons with Disabilities. *Lancet*, *374*(9704), 1863–1865. DOI: 10.1016/S0140-6736(09)61872-9

Borkovska, I., Kolosova, H., Kozubska, I., & Antonenko, I. (2024). Integration of AI into the distance learning environment: Enhancing soft skills. *Arab World English Journal, Special Issue on ChatGPT*, 56–72. https://dx.doi.org/DOI: 10.24093/awej/ChatGPT.3

Boroditsky, L. (2001). Does language shape thought? English and Mandarin speakers' conceptions of time. *Cognitive Psychology, 43*, 1 22.

Borzova, E., & Shemanaeva, M. A. (2022). Interconnected development of intercultural competence and soft skills through tasks in foreign language education at a university. *Perspectives of Science and Education*, *58*(4), 307–319. DOI: 10.32744/pse.2022.4.18

Bouchouras, G., & Kotis, K. (2025). Integrating Artificial Intelligence, Internet of Things, and Sensor-Based Technologies: A Systematic Review of Methodologies in Autism Spectrum Disorder Detection. *Algorithms*, *18*(1), 34. DOI: 10.3390/a18010034

Boudouaia, A., Mouas, S., & Kouider, B. (2024). A study on ChatGPT-4 as an innovative approach to enhancing English as a foreign language writing learning. *Journal of Educational Computing Research*, *62*(6), 1289–1317. Advance online publication. DOI: 10.1177/07356331241247465

Bozkurt, A. (2023). Generative artificial intelligence (AI) powered conversational educational agents: The inevitable paradigm shift. . *Asian Journal of Distance Education. asianjde.com.*

Bozkurt, A. (2023). ChatGPT, üretken yapay zeka ve algoritmik paradigma değişikliği. *Alanyazın*, *4*(1), 63–72. DOI: 10.59320/alanyazin.1283282

Bozkurt, A. (2023). Generative artificial intelligence (AI) powered conversational educational agents: The inevitable paradigm shift. *Asian Journal of Distance Education*, *18*(1). https://www.asianjde.com/ojs/index.php/AsianJDE/article/view/718

Bozkurt, A. (2024a). *GenAI et al. Cocreation, authorship, ownership, academic ethics and integrity in a time of generative AI* (Vol. 16). International Council for Open and Distance Education Oslo., DOI: 10.55982/openpraxis.16.1.654

Bozkurt, A. (2024b). *Why generative AI literacy, why now and why it matters in the educational landscape?: Kings, queens and GenAI dragons* (Vol. 16). International Council for Open and Distance Education Oslo., DOI: 10.55982/openpraxis.16.3.739

Bozkurt, A., Karadeniz, A., Bañeres, D., & Rodríguez, M. E. (2021). Artificial intelligence and reflections from educational landscape: A review of AI studies in half a century. *Sustainability (Basel)*, *13*(2), 1–16. DOI: 10.3390/su13020800

Bozkurt, A., & Sharma, R. C. (2024). Trust, credibility and transparency in human-AI interaction: Why we need explainable and trustworthy AI and why we need it now. *Asian Journal of Distance Education*, *19*(2), 1–9. DOI: 10.5281/zenodo.14599168

Bozkurt, A., & Sharma, R. C. (2024). Trust, Credibility and Transparency in Human-AI Interaction: Why We Need Explainable and Trustworthy AI and Why We Need It Now. *Asian Journal of Distance Education*, *19*(2).

Bozkurt, A., Xiao, J., Farrow, R., Bai, J. Y. H., Nerantzi, C., Moore, S., Dron, J., Stracke, C. M., Singh, L., Crompton, H., Koutropoulos, A., Terentev, E., Pazurek, A., Nichols, M., Sidorkin, A. M., Costello, E., Watson, S., Mulligan, D., Honeychurch, S., & Asino, T. I. (2024). The Manifesto for Teaching and Learning in a Time of Generative AI: A Critical Collective Stance to Better Navigate the Future. *Open Praxis*, *16*(4), 487–513. DOI: 10.55982/openpraxis.16.4.777

Brandão, A., Pedro, L., & Zagalo, N. (2024). Teacher professional development for a future with generative artificial intelligence – an integrative literature review. *Digital Education Review*, 151-157. https://doi.org/DOI: 10.1344/der.2024.45.151-157

Bray, B., & McClaskey, K. (2014). *Make learning personal: The what, who, wow, where, and why*. Corwin Press., DOI: 10.32890/mmj.19.2015.9027

Bredekamp, S. (2020). *Effective practices in early childhood education: Building a foundation* (*4th* ed.). Pearson.

Brennan, K., & Resnick, M. (2012). New frameworks for studying and assessing the development of computational thinking. In *Proceedings of the 2012 annual meeting of the American educational research association,* Vancouver, Canada (Vol. 1, p. 25).

Brent, R., & Felder, R. M. (1992). Writing assignments—Pathways to connections, clarity, creativity. *College Teaching, 40*(2), 43 47. https://doi.org/DOI: 10.1080/87567555.1992.10532264

Brown, M., McCormack, M., Reeves, J., Brook, D. C., Grajek, S., Alexander, B., Bali, M., Bulger, S., Dark, S., Engelbert, N., Gannon, K., Gauthier, A., Gibson, D., Gibson, R., Lundin, B., Veletsianos, G., & Weber, N. (2020). *2020 Educause Horizon Report Teaching and Learning Edition*. EDUCAUSE. from https://www.learntechlib.org/p/215670/

Brown, R. (1976). Reference: In memorial tribute to Eric Lenneberg. *Cognition, 4*, 125 153.

Brown, S. J. (2014). *Personalized online learning management system and method* (Patent No. US20150206441A1). https://patents.google.com/patent/US20150206441A1/en

Bruner, J. S. (1974). *Toward a theory of instruction*. Harvard university press.

Brunero, F., Venerosi, A., Chiarotti, F., & Arduino, G. M. (2019). Are touch screen technologies more effective than traditional educational methods in children with autism spectrum disorders? A pilot study. *Annali dell'Istituto Superiore di Sanita, 55*(2), 151–160. https://annali.iss.it/index.php/anna/article/view/797

Brünken, R. E., Plass, J. L., & Moreno, R. E. (2010). Current issues and open questions in cognitive load research. https://doi.org/DOI: 10.1017/CBO9780511844744.014

Brusilovsky, P. (2024). AI in education, learner control, and human-AI collaboration. *International Journal of Artificial Intelligence in Education, 34*(1), 122–135. DOI: 10.1007/s40593-023-00356-z

Brusilovsky, P., & Peylo, C. (2003). Adaptive and intelligent web-based educational systems. *International Journal of Artificial Intelligence in Education, 13*(2-4), 159–172. DOI: 10.3233/IRG-2003-13(2-4)02

Budnik, C. (2025). Can we trust artificial intelligence? *Philosophy & Technology, 38*(10). Advance online publication. DOI: 10.1007/s13347-024-00820-1

Bulathwela, S., Pérez-Ortiz, M., Holloway, C., Cukurova, M., & Shawe-Taylor, J. (2024). Artificial intelligence alone will not democratise education: On educational inequality, techno-solutionism and inclusive tools. *Sustainability (Basel), 16*(2), 1–20. DOI: 10.3390/su16020781

Bybee, J. (1995). Regular morphology and the lexicon. *Language and Cognitive Processes,10*, 425 455.

Cabero, J., & Barroso, J. (2016). ICT teacher training: a view of the TPACK model / Formación del profesorado en TIC: una visión del modelo TPACK. *C&E, Cultura y Educación, 28*(3), 633–663. DOI: 10.1080/11356405.2016.1203526

Caliskan, A., Bryson, J. J., & Narayanan, A. (2017). Semantics derived automatically from language corpora contain human-like biases. *Science*, *356*(6334), 183–186. Advance online publication. DOI: 10.1126/science.aal4230 PMID: 28408601

Canonico, M., & De Russis, L. (2018). A comparison and critique of natural language understanding tools. *International Conference on Cloud Computing*, 110–115. https://www.thinkmind.org/articles/cloud_computing_2018_6_20_20057.pdf

Castelli, F. (2005). Understanding emotions from standardized facial expressions in autism and normal development. *Autism*, *9*(4), 428–449. DOI: 10.1177/1362361305056081

Castillo-Martínez, I. M., Flores-Bueno, D., Gómez-Puente, S. M., & Vite-León, V. O. (2024). AI in higher education: A systematic literature review. In *Frontiers in Education* (Vol. 9, p. 1391485). Frontiers Media SA. https://doi.org/DOI: 10.3389/feduc.2024.1391485

Castro, G. P. B., Chiappe, A., Rodríguez, D. F. B., & Sepulveda, F. G. (2024). Harnessing AI for Education 4.0: Drivers of Personalized Learning. *Electronic Journal of e-Learning*, *22*(5), 1–14. DOI: 10.34190/ejel.22.5.3467

Cebrián-Robles, V., Ruíz-Rey, F. J., Raposo-Rivas, M., & Cebrián-de-la-Serna, M. (2023). Impact of digital contexts in the training of university education students. *Education Sciences*, *13*(9), 923. DOI: 10.3390/educsci13090923

Çela, E., Fonkam, M. M., & Potluri, R. M. (2024). Risks of AI-assisted learning on student critical thinking: A case study of Albania. [IJRCM]. *International Journal of Risk and Contingency Management*, *12*(1), 1–19. DOI: 10.4018/IJRCM.350185

Celik, İ. (2023). Towards Intelligent-TPACK: An empirical study on teachers' professional knowledge to ethically integrate artificial intelligence (AI)-based tools into education. *Computers in Human Behavior*, *138*, 1–12. DOI: 10.1016/j.chb.2022.107468

Çeviker Ay, Ş., & Orhan, A. (2022). The effect of different critical thinking teaching approaches on critical thinking skills: A meta-analysis study. *Pamukkale Üniversitesi Eğitim Fakültesi Dergisi*, *49*, 88–111. DOI: 10.9779/pauefd.561742

Chaka, C. (2024). Reviewing the performance of AI detection tools in differentiating between AI-generated and human-written texts: A literature and integrative hybrid review. *Journal of Applied Learning and Teaching*, *7*(1), 115–126. DOI: 10.37074/jalt.2024.7.1.14

Chakraborty, D. (2024). Artificial Intelligence And Lifelong Learning: Transforming Education For The Future. *Artificial Intelligence In Education.* google.com.

Chalghoumi, H., Cobigo, V., Dignard, C., Gauthier-Beaupré, A., Jutai, J. W., Lachapelle, Y., & Perrin, M. (2019). Information privacy for technology users with intellectual and developmental disabilities: Why does it matter? *Ethics & Behavior*, *29*(3), 201–217. DOI: 10.1080/10508422.2017.1393340

Chamola, V., Hassija, V., Sulthana, A. R., Ghosh, D., Dhingra, D., & Sikdar, B. (2023). A review of trustworthy and explainable artificial intelligence (xai). *IEEe Access, 11*, 78994-79015. DOI- DOI: 10.1109/ACCESS.2023.3294569

Chan, C. K. Y. (2023). A comprehensive AI policy education framework for university teaching and learning. *International Journal of Educational Technology in Higher Education*, *20*(1), 38. Advance online publication. DOI: 10.1186/s41239-023-00408-3

Chander, B., John, C., Warrier, L., & Gopalakrishnan, K. (2025). Toward Trustworthy Artificial Intelligence (TAI) in the Context of Explainability and Robustness. *ACM Computing Surveys*, *57*(6), 144. Advance online publication. DOI: 10.1145/3675392

Chapelle, C. A. (2001). Computer Applications in Second Language Acquisition. In *Computer Applications in Second Language Acquisition*. DOI: 10.1017/CBO9781139524681

Chapelle, C. A. (2025). Generative AI as game changer: Implications for language education. *System*, *132*, 103672. DOI: 10.1016/j.system.2025.103672

Chatterjee, S., & Bhattacharjee, K. K. (2020). Adoption of artificial intelligence in higher education: A quantitative analysis using structural equation modelling. *Education and Information Technologies*, *25*, 3443–3463. DOI: 10.1007/s10639-020-10159-7

Chaudhry, M., & Kazim, E. (2022). Artificial Intelligence in Education (Aied) a high-level academic and industry note 2021. *AI and Ethics*, *2*(1), 157–165. DOI: 10.1007/s43681-021-00074-z

Chembe, C., Nasilele, N. B., & Msendo, R. (2023). The fuss about artificial intelligence in education sector: Should we worry? *Zambia ICT Journal*, *7*(2), 30–35. DOI: 10.33260/zictjournal.v7i2.269

Chen, A., Jia, J., Li, Y., & Fu, L. (2024). Investigating the effect of role-play activity with GenAI agent on EFL students' speaking performance. *Journal of Educational Computing Research*, *63*(1), 99–125. DOI: 10.1177/07356331241299058

Cheng, F. F., Wu, C. S., & Su, P. C. (2021). The impact of collaborative learning and personality on satisfaction in innovative teaching context. *Frontiers in Psychology*, *12*, 713497. DOI: 10.3389/fpsyg.2021.713497 PMID: 34659026

Chen, J. J. (2024). A scoping study on AI affordances in early childhood education: Mapping the global landscape, identifying research gaps, and charting future research directions. *Journal of Artificial Intelligence Research, 81*, 701–740. DOI: 10.1613/jair.1.16882

Chen, J., Mokmin, N. A. M., & Qi, S. (2025). Generative AI-powered arts-based learning in middle school history: Impact on achievement, motivation, and cognitive load. *The Journal of Educational Research*, •••, 1–13. DOI: 10.1080/00220671.2025.2510395

Chen, L., Chen, P., & Lin, Z. (2020). Artificial intelligence in education: A review. *IEEE Access : Practical Innovations, Open Solutions, 8*, 75264–75278. DOI: 10.1109/ACCESS.2020.2988510

Chen, S. Y., & Wang, J. H. (2021). Individual differences and personalized learning: A review and appraisal. *Universal Access in the Information Society, 20*(4), 833–849. DOI: 10.1007/s10209-020-00753-4

Chen, X., Xie, H., Zou, D., & Hwang, G. J. (2020). Application and theory gaps during the rise of artificial intelligence in education. *Computers and Education: Artificial Intelligence, 1*, 100002. DOI: 10.1016/j.caeai.2020.100002

Chen, Y., Jensen, S., Albert, L. J., Gupta, S., & Lee, T. (2023). Artificial intelligence (AI) student assistants in the classroom: Designing chatbots to support student success. *Information Systems Frontiers, 25*(1), 161–182. DOI: 10.1007/s10796-022-10291-4

Cheung, B. H. H., Lau, G. K. K., Wong, G. T. C., Lee, E. Y. P., Kulkarni, D., Seow, C. S., Wong, R., & Co, M. T.-H. (2023). ChatGPT versus human in generating medical graduate exam multiple choice questions: A multinational prospective study (Hong Kong SAR, Singapore, Ireland, and the United Kingdom). *PLoS One, 18*(8), e0290691. DOI: 10.1371/journal.pone.0290691 PMID: 37643186

Cheung, L. M. E., & Shi, H. (2024). Co-creating stories with generative AI: Reflections from undergraduate students of a storytelling service-learning subject in Hong Kong. *Australian Review of Applied Linguistics, 47*(3), 259–283. DOI: 10.1075/aral.24101.che

Che, Z. (2008). English as a lingua franca. *Academica Turistica, 1*(1), 62–65.

Chia, O. (2023). *Teachers v ChatGPT: Schools face new challenge in fight against plagiarism*. The Straits Times.

Chiu, H. S. (2019). *The Impact of Mobile Learning on Academic Achievement and Learning Experience Using a Tailor-made Mobile App*. http://papers.iafor.org/wp-content/uploads/papers/ace2019/ACE2019_53915.pdf

Chiu, M. M. (2008). Flowing toward correct contributions during group problem solving: A statistical discourse analysis. *Journal of the Learning Sciences*, *17*(3), 415–463. DOI: 10.1080/10508400802224830

Chiu, T. K. F., Xia, Q., Zhou, X.-Y., Chai, C. S., & Cheng, M.-T. (2023). Systematic literature review on opportunities, challenges, and future research recommendations of artificial intelligence in education. *Computers & Education: Artificial Intelligence*, *4*, 100118. DOI: 10.1016/j.caeai.2022.100118

Cho, H. C., Koo, B. J., Yoon, J. Y., & Jun, S. P. (2019). *System and method of providing customized learning contents. U.S. Patent Application No. 16/384,915.*

Chopra, A., Prashar, A., & Sain, C. (2013). Natural language processing. *International journal of technology enhancements and emerging engineering research, 1*(4), 131-134.

Christopoulos, A., & Mystakidis, S. (2023). Gamification in Education. *Encyclopedia*, *3*(4), 1223–1243. DOI: 10.3390/encyclopedia3040089

Chu, Z., Jia, H., Matricciani, E., Feretzakis, G., Papaspyridis, K., Gkoulalas-Divanis, A., & Verykios, V. S. (2024). Privacy-Preserving Techniques in Generative AI and Large Language Models: A Narrative Review. *Information 2024, Vol. 15, Page 697, 15*(11), 697. DOI: 10.3390/info15110697

Chui, M., Roberts, R., & Yee, L. (2022, December 20). Generative AI is Here: How Tools Like ChatGpt Could Change Your Business. Quantum Black AI by McKinsey. https://www.mckinsey.com/capabilities/quantumblack/our-insights/generative-ai-is-here-how-tools-like-chatgpt-could-change-your-business#/

Chukharev, E., Bouwman, W., Dobrynina, N., Speltz, E. D., Novotny, M., & Sollier, N. (2024). Designing Computer Assisted Language Learning Tools as Platforms for Data Collection in Applied Linguistics. *Routledge Handbook of Technological Advances in Researching Language Learning*, 158–170. DOI: 10.4324/9781003459088-15

Clarizia, F., Colace, F., Lombardi, M., Pascale, F., & Santaniello, D. (2018). Chatbot: An Education Support System for Student. In Castiglione, A., Pop, F., Ficco, M., & Palmieri, F. (Eds.), Lecture Notes in Computer Science: Vol. 11161. *Cyberspace Safety and Security. CSS 2018.* Springer., DOI: 10.1007/978-3-030-01689-0_23

Cocchiaro, M. Z., Morley, J., Novelli, C., Panai, E., Tartaro, A., & Floridi, L. (2024). Who is an AI Ethicist? An empirical study of expertise, skills, and profiles to build a competency framework. *AI and Ethics*, 1–13. DOI: 10.1007/s43681-024-00643-y

Cohen, J. (1960). A Coefficient of Agreement for Nominal Scales. *Educational and Psychological Measurement*, *20*(1), 37–46. DOI: 10.1177/001316446002000104

Cohen, S., Koegel, R., Koegel, L. K., Engstrom, E., Young, K., & Quach, A. (2022). Using self-management and visual cues to improve responses to nonverbal social cues in adults with autism spectrum disorder. *Behavior Modification*, *46*(3), 529–552. DOI: 10.1177/0145445520982558

Cook, V. (2003). The changing L1 in the L2 user's mind. In V. Cook (Ed.), *Effects of the second language on the first* (pp. 1 18). Multilingual Matters.

Cope, B., Kalantzis, M., & Searsmith, D. (2021). Artificial intelligence for education: Knowledge and its assessment in AI-enabled learning ecologies. *Educational Philosophy and Theory*, *53*(12), 1229–1245. DOI: 10.1080/00131857.2020.1728732

Corp, I. B. M. (2017). *IBM SPSS Statistics for Windows, Version 25.0*. IBM Corp.

Cota-Rivera, E. I., González Correa, M. E., Marín, L., Montenegro, M., Mercado Herrera, A., & Martínez, M. (2024). Transforming Education With the Power of Artificial Intelligence. In *IGI Global* (pp. 113–140). IGI Global., DOI: 10.4018/979-8-3693-1666-5.ch006

Crawford, J., Cowling, M., & Allen, K.-A. (2023). Leadership is needed for ethical ChatGPT: Character, assessment, and learning using artificial intelligence (AI). (2023). *Journal of University Teaching & Learning Practice*, *20*(3). Advance online publication. DOI: 10.53761/1.20.3.02

Crawford, K. (2017). *The Trouble with Bias, by Kate Crawford (Revolutions)*. NIPS.

Creely, E. (2024). Exploring the role of generative AI in enhancing language learning: Opportunities and challenges. *International Journal of Changes in Education*, *1*(3), 158–167. DOI: 10.47852/bonviewIJCE42022495

Crescenzi-Lanna, L. (2023). Literature review of the reciprocal value of artificial and human intelligence in early childhood education. *Journal of Research on Technology in Education*, *55*(1), 21–33. DOI: 10.1080/15391523.2022.2128480

Crompton, H., & Burke, D. (2023). Artificial intelligence in higher education: The state of the field. *International Journal of Educational Technology in Higher Education*, *20*(22), 22. Advance online publication. DOI: 10.1186/s41239-023-00392-8

Cross, J., Robinson, R., Devaraju, S., Vaughans, A., Hood, R., Kayalackakom, T., & Robinson, R. E. (2023). Transforming medical education: Assessing the integration of ChatGPT into faculty workflows at a Caribbean medical school. *Cureus*, *15*(7), e41399. DOI: 10.7759/cureus.41399 PMID: 37426402

Crossley, S. A., Allen, L. K., Kyle, K., & McNamara, D.S. (2014). Analysing discourse processing using a simple natural language processing tool (SiNLP). *Discourse Processes, 51*(5 6), 511 534.

Crossley, S. A., Kyle, K., & Dascalu, M. (2019). The Tool for the Automatic Analysis of Cohesion 2.0: Integrating semantic similarity and text overlap. *Behavior Research Methods*, *51*(1), 14–27. DOI: 10.3758/s13428-018-1142-4 PMID: 30298264

Crossley, S. A., & McNamara, D. S. (2012). Predicting second language writing proficiency: The roles of cohesion and linguistic sophistication. *Journal of Research in Reading*, *35*(2), 115–135. DOI: 10.1111/j.1467-9817.2010.01449.x

Crosthwaite, P., & Baisa, V. (2023). Generative AI and the end of corpus assisted data driven learning? Not so fast! *Applied Corpus Linguistics*, *3*(3), 100066. DOI: 10.1016/j.acorp.2023.100066

Cruz Puerto, M., & Sandín Vázquez, M. (2024). Understanding heterogeneity within autism spectrum disorder: A scoping review. *Advances in Autism*, *10*(4), 314–322. DOI: 10.1108/AIA-12-2023-0072

Curry, N., Baker, P., & Brookes, G. (2024). Generative AI for corpus approaches to discourse studies: A critical evaluation of ChatGPT. *Applied Corpus Linguistics*, *4*(1), 100082. DOI: 10.1016/j.acorp.2023.100082

Darmawansah, D., Rachman, D., Febiyani, F., & Hwang, G.-J. (2024). ChatGPT-supported collaborative argumentation: Integrating collaboration script and argument mapping to enhance EFL students' argumentation skills. *Education and Information Technologies*, *30*(3), 3803–3827. DOI: 10.1007/s10639-024-12986-4

Darwin, D. R., Mukminatien, N., Suryati, N., & Laksmi, E. D. (2024). Critical thinking in the AI era: An exploration of EFL students' perceptions, benefits, and limitations. *Cogent Education*, *11*(1), 2290342. DOI: 10.1080/2331186X.2023.2290342

Dash, S., & Bhoi, C. (2024). Exploring the Intersection of Education and Artificial Intelligence: A Comprehensive Review. *International Journal of Multidisciplinary Approach Research and Science*, *2*(02), 601–610. DOI: 10.59653/ijmars.v2i02.637

de Castro Rodrigues, D., de Siqueira, V. S., da Costa, R. M., & Barbosa, R. M. (2022). Artificial Intelligence applied to smart interfaces for children's educational games. *Displays*, *74*, 102217. DOI: 10.1016/j.displa.2022.102217

De, A. (2024). *Embracing Lifelong Learning in the Age of Artificial Intelligence*. Artificial Intelligence in Education., DOI: 10.25215/9358094575.08

Decety, J., & Holvoet, C. (2021). The emergence of empathy: A developmental neuroscience perspective. *Developmental Review*, *62*, 100999. Advance online publication. DOI: 10.1016/j.dr.2021.100999

Decety, J., & Yoder, K. J. (2016). Empathy and motivation for justice: Cognitive empathy and concern, but not emotional empathy, predict sensitivity to injustice for others. *Social Neuroscience*, *11*(1), 1–14. DOI: 10.1080/17470919.2015.1029593

Delcker, J., Heil, J., Ifenthaler, D., Seufert, S., & Spirgi, L. (2024). First-year students' AI competence as a predictor for intended and de facto use of AI tools for supporting learning processes in higher education. *International Journal of Educational Technology in Higher Education*, *21*(18), 18. Advance online publication. DOI: 10.1186/s41239-024-00452-7

DeMink-Carthew, J., Netcoh, S., Brinegar, K., & Phillips, J. (2022). Critical reflections on personalized project-based learning. In *Dialogues in Middle Level Education Research* (Vol. 1, pp. 61–72). Routledge., DOI: 10.4324/9781003225867-8

Deng, X., & Joshi, K. (2024). Promoting ethical use of generative AI in education. *The Data Base for Advances in Information Systems*, *55*(3), 6–11. DOI: 10.1145/3685235.3685237

Dergaa, I., Chamari, K., Żmijewski, P., & Saad, B. (2024). From human writing to artificial intelligence generated text: Examining the prospects and potential threats of ChatGPT in academic writing. *Biology of Sport*, *40*(2), 615–622. DOI: 10.5114/biolsport.2023.125623 PMID: 37077800

Deterding, S., Sicart, M., Nacke, L., O'hara, K., & Dixon, D. (2011). Gamification. using game-design elements in non-gaming contexts. In *CHI'11 extended abstracts on human factors in computing systems* (pp. 2425-2428). https://doi.org/DOI: 10.1145/1979742.1979575

Dhagare, R. P. (2024). Generative AI and Education: A Symbiotic Relationship. *International Journal for Research in Applied Science and Engineering Technology*, *12*(11), 1042–1045. DOI: 10.22214/ijraset.2024.65279

Dinçer, N. (2023). Elevating aviation education: A comprehensive examination of technology's role in modern flight training. *Journal of Aviation*, *7*(2), 317–323. DOI: 10.30518/jav.1279718

Dinçer, N. (2023). The role of serious games in effective aviation English. *Applied Linguistics Papers*, *27*(2), 72–82. DOI: 10.32612/uw.25449354.2023.1.pp.72-83

Dinçer, R., Dinçer, N., & Guksu, O. (2023). An interactive conversation with a chatbot: Does ChatGPT know standard phraseology in aviation English? *The Literacy Trek*, *9*(2), 24–41. DOI: 10.47216/literacytrek.1382543

Disemadi, H. S., & Sudirman, L. (2025). Reassessing legal recognition of AI: Human dignity and the challenge of AI as a legal subject in Indonesia. *Masalah-Masalah Hukum*, *54*(1), 1–12. DOI: 10.14710/mmh.54.1.2025.1-12

Dizon, G. (2020). Evaluating intelligent personal assistants for L2 listening and speaking development. *Language Learning & Technology*, *24*(1), 16–26. Advance online publication. DOI: 10.64152/10125/44705

do Rêgo, A. C. M., & Araújo-Filho, I. (2024). Leveraging artificial ıntelligence to enhance the quality of life for patients with autism spectrum disorder: A comprehensive review. *European Journal of Clinical Medicine*, *5*(5), 28–38. DOI: 10.24018/clinicmed.2024.5.5.350

Doughty, C. (1991). Second language instruction does make a difference: Evidence from an empirical study of SL relativization. *Studies in Second Language Acquisition*, *13*(4), 431–469. DOI: 10.1017/S0272263100010287

Doulah, A. B. M. S. U., Rasheduzzaman, M., Arnob, F. A., Sarker, F., Roy, N., Ullah, M. A., & Mamun, K. A. (2023). Application of augmented reality interventions for children with autism spectrum disorder (ASD): A systematic review. *Computers*, *12*(10), 215. DOI: 10.3390/computers12100215

Down, B., & Choules, K. (2017). Towards a pedagogy of personalisation: What can we learn from students? *Curriculum Perspectives*, *37*(2), 135–145. DOI: 10.1007/s41297-017-0019-5

Druga, S., Vu, S. T., Likhith, E., & Qiu, T. (2019). Inclusive AI literacy for kids around the world. *Proceedings of FabLearn*, *2019*, 104–111. DOI: 10.1145/3311890.3311904

Drumheller, S. J. (1971). *Handbook of curriculum design for individualized instruction: a systems approach; how to develop curriculum materials from rigorously defined behavioral objectives*. Educational Technology.

Duraisingh, L. D. (2020). *Tapping the potential of peer-to-peer student-centered learning experiences in the humanities and beyond. In Promoting Engagement, Understanding and Critical Awareness (1st ed., p. 16). Routledge.*

Duran, M., Simon, S., & Blasco, F. (2020). *Science Education and Artificial Intelligence– A Chatbot on Magic and Quantum Computing as an Educational Tool*. 137–142. https://doi.org/DOI: 10.38069/edenconf-2020-ac0011

Durlak, J. A., Weissberg, R. P., Dymnicki, A. B., Taylor, R. D., & Schellinger, K. B. (2011). The impact of enhancing students' social and emotional learning: A meta-analysis of school-based universal interventions. *Child Development, 82*(1), 405–432. DOI: 10.1111/j.1467-8624.2010.01564.x PMID: 21291449

Durrani, R., Iqbal, A., & Akram, H. (2024). Artificial intelligence (AI) in early childhood education, exploring challenges, opportunities and future directions: A Scoping review. *Qlantic Journal of Social Sciences, 5*(2), 411–423. DOI: 10.55737/qjss.135537445

Duymaz, Y. K., & Tekin, A. M. (2024). Harnessing artificial intelligence in academic writing: Potential, ethics, and responsible use. *European Journal of Therapeutics, 30*(1), 87–88. DOI: 10.58600/eurjther1755

Dwivedi, Y. K., Hughes, L., Ismagilova, E., Aarts, G., Coombs, C., Crick, T., Duan, Y., Dwivedi, R., Edwards, J., Eirug, A., Galanos, V., Ilavarasan, P. V., Janssen, M., Jones, P., Kar, A. K., Kizgin, H., Kronemann, B., Lal, B., Lucini, B., & Williams, M. D. (2021). Artificial Intelligence (AI): Multidisciplinary perspectives on emerging challenges, opportunities, and agenda for research, practice and policy. *International Journal of Information Management, 57*, 101994. DOI: 10.1016/j.ijinfomgt.2019.08.002

Dwivedi, Y. K., Kshetri, N., Hughes, L., Slade, E. L., Jeyaraj, A., Kar, A. K., Baabdullah, A. M., Koohang, A., Raghavan, V., Ahuja, M., Albanna, H., Albashrawi, M. A., Al-Busaidi, A. S., Balakrishnan, J., Barlette, Y., Basu, S., Bose, I., Brooks, L., Buhalis, D., & Wright, R. (2023). "So what if ChatGPT wrote it?" Multidisciplinary perspectives on opportunities, challenges and implications of generative conversational AI for research, practice and policy. *International Journal of Information Management, 71*, 102642. DOI: 10.1016/j.ijinfomgt.2023.102642

Dynel, M. (2023). Lessons in linguistics with ChatGPT: Metapragmatics, metacommunication, metadiscourse and metalanguage in human AI interactions. *Language & Communication, 93*, 107 124.

Dziuban, C. D., Moskal, P. D., Cassisi, J., & Fawcett, A. (2016). Adaptive learning in psychology: Wayfinding in the Digital age. *Online Learning : the Official Journal of the Online Learning Consortium, 20*(3), 74–96. DOI: 10.24059/olj.v20i3.972

Education for All Handicapped Children Act Of 1975, Pub. L. No. 94-142 (1975)

Egeberg, H., McConney, A., & Price, A. (2016). Classroom management and national professional standards for teachers: A review of the literature on theory and practice. *The Australian Journal of Teacher Education, 41*(7), 1–18. DOI: 10.14221/ajte.2016v41n7.1

Eguchi, A., Okada, H., & Muto, Y. (2021). Contextualizing AI education for K-12 students to enhance their learning of AI literacy through culturally responsive approaches. *Kunstliche Intelligenz, 35*(2), 153–161. DOI: 10.1007/s13218-021-00737-3 PMID: 34376922

Eisenberg, N., & Eggum, N. D. (2009). Empathic responding: Sympathy and personal distress. In Decety, J., & Ickes, W. (Eds.), *The social neuroscience of empathy* (pp. 71–83). Boston Review., DOI: 10.7551/mitpress/9780262012973.003.0007

Elkhatat, A. M., Elsaid, K., & Almeer, S. (2023). Evaluating the efficacy of AI content detection tools in differentiating between human and AI-generated text. *International Journal for Educational Integrity, 19*(17), 17. Advance online publication. DOI: 10.1007/s40979-023-00140-5

Ellis, N. C. (2002). Frequency effects in language processing: A review with implications for theories of implicit and explicit language acquisition. *Studies in Second Language Acquisition, 24*, 143 188.

Elshani, L., & Nuçi, K. P. (2021). Constructing a personalized learning path using genetic algorithms approach. *arXiv preprint arXiv:2104.11276*. https://doi.org/DOI: 10.20944/preprints202411.2377.v1

Emilinda, S. (2022). The analysis of cohesive devices in Donald Trump's concession speech transcripts. *Scripta: Jurnal Ilmiah Mahasiswa, 4*(2), 135–145.

Erguney, M. (2017). The role of mobile learning technologies in distance education. *Ulakbilge Sosyal Bilimler Dergisi, 5*(13), 1009–1021. DOI: 10.7816/ulakbilge-05-13-02

European Commision. (2020). Digital Education Action Plan (2021-2027). https://ec.europa.eu/education/education-in-the-eu/digital-education-action-plan_en

European Commission. (2012). *First European survey on language competences: Education and training*. Publications Office of the European Union.

Facione, P. A. (1990). *Critical thinking: A statement of expert consensus for purposes of educational assessment and instruction. Research Findings and Recommendations. Prepared for the Committee on Pre-College Philosophy*. American Philosophical Association.

Fan, L. (2024). *Artificial Intelligence Ethics: A Dialogue between Technological Advances and Human Values*. International Journal of Education and Humanities., DOI: 10.54097/tvqkkf40

Fan, M., Jin, S., Fan, J., Guo, W., & Chen, X. (2025). EmoLand: Utilizing narrative animations, multilevel games, and affective computing to foster emotional development in children with autism spectrum disorder. *International Journal of Human-Computer Studies*, *199*, 103486. DOI: 10.1016/j.ijhcs.2025.103486

Farina, M., Yu, X., & Lavazza, A. (2024). Ethical considerations and policy interventions concerning the impact of generative AI tools in the economy and in society. *AI and Ethics 2023 5:1*, *5*(1), 737–745. DOI: 10.1007/s43681-023-00405-2

Farooq, E., Zaidi, E., & Shah, M. M. A. (2024). The future classroom: Analyzing the integration and impact of digital technologies in science education. *Jurnal Penelitian Dan Pengkajian Ilmu Pendidikan: E-Saintika*, *8*(2), 280–318. DOI: 10.36312/esaintika.v8i2.1957

Feng, L. (2025). Investigating the Effects of Artificial Intelligence-Assisted Language Learning Strategies on Cognitive Load and Learning Outcomes: A Comparative Study. *Journal of Educational Computing Research*, *62*(8), 1741–1774. Advance online publication. DOI: 10.1177/07356331241268349

Feng, S., Magana, A. J., & Kao, D. (2021, October). *A systematic review of literature on the effectiveness of intelligent tutoring systems in STEM. In 2021 IEEE frontiers in education conference (fie)*. IEEE., DOI: 10.1109/FIE49875.2021.9637240

Ferreira, R. C., & Mozzillo, I. (2021). Conceptual transfer: Linguistic relativity in second language learning. *Alfa: Revista de Linguística (São José do Rio Preto)*, *65*, 1 20.

Fielding, M. (2001). Students as Radical Agents of Change. *Journal of Educational Change*, *2*(2), 123–141. DOI: 10.1023/A:1017949213447

Filgueiras, F. (2024). Artificial intelligence and education governance. *Education, Citizenship and Social Justice*, *19*(3), 349–361. DOI: 10.1177/17461979231160674

Fitria, T. N. (2021, December). Artificial intelligence (AI) in education: Using AI tools for teaching and learning process. In *Prosiding Seminar Nasional & Call for Paper STIE AAS* (pp. 134-147).

Flanagan, J. C. (1968). Individualizing Education. Retrieved from_https://eric.ed.gov/?id=ED040566

Flowerdew, J., & Miller, L. (1995). On the notion of culture in L2 lectures. *TESOL Quarterly*, *29*(2), 345–373. DOI: 10.2307/3587628

Foerde, K., & Shohamy, D. (2011). Feedback timing modulates brain systems for learning in humans. *The Journal of Neuroscience : The Official Journal of the Society for Neuroscience, 31*(37), 13157–13167. DOI: 10.1523/JNEUROSCI.2701-11.2011 PMID: 21917799

Fontoura, L., de Mattos Nascimento, D. L., Neto, J. V., & Caiado, R. G. G. (2025). Energy Gen-AI technology framework: A perspective of energy efficiency and business ethics in operation management. *Technology in Society, 81*, 102847. DOI: 10.1016/j.techsoc.2025.102847

Fu, B., Hadid, A., & Damer, N. (2025). Generative AI in the context of assistive technologies: Trends, limitations and future directions. *Image and Vision Computing, 154*, 105347.

Fui-Hoon Nah, F., Zheng, R., Cai, J., Siau, K., & Chen, L. (2023). Generative AI and ChatGPT: Applications, challenges, and AI-human collaboration. *Journal of Information Technology Case and Application Research, 25*(3), 277–304. DOI: 10.1080/15228053.2023.2233814

Fu, Y., & Weng, Z. (2024). Navigating the ethical terrain of AI in education: A systematic review on framing responsible human-centered AI practices. *Computers and Education: Artificial Intelligence, 100306*, 100306. Advance online publication. DOI: 10.1016/j.caeai.2024.100306

Gade, K., Geyik, S., Kenthapadi, K., Mithal, V., & Taly, A. (2020, April). Explainable AI in industry: Practical challenges and lessons learned. En A. E. F. Seghrouchni, G. Sukthankar, & T. Y. Liu (Eds.), *Companion Proceedings of the Web Conference 2020* (pp. 303–304). ACM. DOI: 10.1145/3366424.3383110

Gao, Y., Gu, S., Jiang, J., Hong, S. R., Yu, D., & Zhao, L. (2024). Going beyond xai: A systematic survey for explanation-guided learning. *ACM Computing Surveys, 56*(7), 1–39. DOI: 10.1145/3644073

Garcia-Garcia, J. M., Penichet, V. M. R., & Lozano, M. D.. (2022). Using emotion recognition technologies to teach children with autism spectrum disorder how to identify and express emotions. *Universal Access in the Information Society, 21*, 809–825. DOI: 10.1007/s10209-021-00818-y

Garcia, I. (2010). Is machine translation ready yet? *Target. International Journal of Translation Studies, 22*(1), 7–21. Advance online publication. DOI: 10.1075/target.22.1.02gar

Gardner, H. E. (2011). *Frames of mind: The theory of multiple intelligences*. Basic Books.

Gartner. (2023) Gartner Experts Answer the Top Generative AI Questions for Your Enterprise. Gartner. https://www.gartner.com/en/topics/generative-ai

Gass, S. M. (2013). *Second language acquisition: An introductory course.* Routledge. DOI: 10.4324/9780203137093

Gass, S., Winke, P., Isbell, D., & Ahn, J. (2019). How captions help people learn languages: A working memory, eye tracking study. *Language Learning & Technology*, *23*(2), 84–104. DOI: 10.64152/10125/44684

Gentry, R., Sallie, A. P., & Sanders, C. A. (2013). *Differentiated Instructional Strategies to Accommodate Students with Varying Needs and Learning Styles.* Online Submission.

George, A. S. (2023). Preparing students for an AI-driven world: Rethinking curriculum and pedagogy in the age of artificial intelligence. *Partners Universal Innovative Research Publication*, *1*(2), 112–136. DOI: 10.5281/zenodo.10245675

Gerlich, M. (2025). AI Tools in Society: Impacts on Cognitive Offloading and the Future of Critical Thinking. *Societies (Basel, Switzerland)*, *15*(1), 6. DOI: 10.3390/soc15010006

Gharahighehi, A., Schoors, R. V., Topali, P., & Ooge, J. (2024). Supporting Personalized Lifelong Learning with Human-Centered Artificial Intelligence Systems. ALL@AIED.

Ghofar, A. (2018). Cohesion analysis of Soekarno's speech entitled 'Only a nation with self reliance can become a great nation'. [Unpublished BA Thesis]. Walisongo State Islamic University Semarang.

Ghosh, M., & Thirugnanam, A. (2021). Introduction to Artificial Intelligence. In: Srinivasa, K.G., G. M., S., Sekhar, S.R.M. (eds) Artificial Intelligence for Information Management: A Healthcare Perspective. Studies in Big Data, vol 88. Springer, Singapore. https://doi.org/DOI: 10.1007/978-981-16-0415-7_2

Giannakos, M., Azevedo, R., Brusilovsky, P., Cukurova, M., Dimitriadis, Y., Hernandez-Leo, D., & Rienties, B. (2024). The promise and challenges of generative AI in education. *Behaviour & Information Technology*, •••, 1–27. DOI: 10.1080/0144929X.2024.2394886

Gilmore, A. (2007). Authentic materials and authenticity in foreign language learning. *Language Teaching*, *40*(2), 97–118. DOI: 10.1017/S0261444807004144

Ginting, P., Batubara, H. M., & Hasnah, Y. (2023). Artificial intelligence powered writing tools as adaptable aids for academic writing: Insight from EFL college learners in writing final project. *International Journal of Multidisciplinary Research and Analysis*, *6*(10), 4640–4650. DOI: 10.47191/ijmra/v6-i10-15

Girouard-Hallam, L. N., & Danovitch, J. H. (2022). Children's trust in and learning from voice assistants. *Developmental Psychology*, *58*(4), 646–661. DOI: 10.1037/dev0001318 PMID: 35343713

Giroux, H. A. (2020). *On Critical Pedagogy* (2nd ed.). Bloomsbury Publishing. DOI: 10.5040/9781350145016

Gjermeni, F., & Prodani, F. (2024). AI and Student Engagement: A Comparative Analysis. *Interdisciplinary Journal of Research and Development*, *11*(3), 195. DOI: 10.56345/ijrdv11n326

Glaser, N., & Schmidt, M. (2021). Systematic literature review of virtual reality intervention design patterns for individuals with autism spectrum disorders. *International Journal of Human-Computer Interaction*, *38*(8), 753–788. DOI: 10.1080/10447318.2021.1970433

Goar, V., Yadav, N. S., & Yadav, P. S. (2023). Conversational AI for Natural Language Processing: An review of ChatGPT. *International Journal on Recent and Innovation Trends in Computing and Communication*, *11*(3s), 109–117. DOI: 10.17762/ijritcc.v11i3s.6161

Godwin-Jones, R. (2014). Emerging Technologies Games in Language Learning: Opportunities and Challenges. *Language Learning & Technology*, *18*(182).

Goksel, N., & Bozkurt, A. (2019). Artificial intelligence in education: Current insights and future perspectives. In *Handbook of Research on Learning in the Age of Transhumanism* (pp. 224–236). IGI Global., DOI: 10.4018/978-1-5225-8431-5.ch014

Golda, A., Mekonen, K., Pandey, A., Singh, A., Hassija, V., Chamola, V., & Sikdar, B. (2024). Privacy and Security Concerns in Generative AI: A Comprehensive Survey. *IEEE Access : Practical Innovations, Open Solutions*, *12*, 48126–48144. DOI: 10.1109/ACCESS.2024.3381611

Grant, A. M. (2020). An integrated model of goal-focused coaching: An evidence-based framework for teaching and practice. *Coaching Researched: A Coaching Psychology Reader*, 115-139. https://doi.org/DOI: 10.1002/9781119656913.ch7

Greenberg, J. S., Seltzer, M. M., Hong, J., & Orsmond, G. I. (2006). Bidirectional effects of expressed emotion and behavior problems and symptoms in adolescents and adults with autism. *American Journal of Mental Retardation*, *111*(4), 229–249. DOI: 10.1352/0895-8017(2006)111[229:BEOEEA]2.0.CO;2

Griffen, B., Lorah, E. R., Caldwell, N., Hantula, D. A., Nosek, J., Tincani, M., & Lemley, S. (2024). The effects of artificial intelligence on implementors' fidelity of instructional strategies during handwashing acquisition in children with autism. *Journal of Developmental and Physical Disabilities*, *36*(5), 793–819. DOI: 10.1007/s10882-023-09937-1

Griffin, P., McGaw, B., & Care, E. (2012). *Assessment and teaching of 21st century skills* (Vol. 10). Springer. DOI: 10.1007/978-94-007-2324-5

Guettala, M., Bourekkache, S., Kazar, O., & Harous, S. (2024). Generative artificial intelligence in education: Advancing adaptive and personalized learning. *Acta Informatica Pragensia*, *13*(3), 460–489. DOI: 10.18267/j.aip.235

Guilin, X., Xu, S., Xavier, M., & Elliot, M. (2024). The Impact of Using Social Media in the Learning Process on Student Social Interaction. *Journal Emerging Technologies in Education*, *2*(2), 190–201. DOI: 10.70177/jete.v2i2.1064

Gu, J. (2014). A mobile informal learning solution for workplace learners. *Educational Media International*, *51*(3), 185–198. DOI: 10.1080/09523987.2014.968449

Gulyamov, S. S., Mamanazarov, S., & Rodionov, A. A. (2024). Creating Self-Updating Digital Platforms Using Artificial Intelligence Technologies for Continuous Education and Professional Development. *2024 4th International Conference on Technology Enhanced Learning in Higher Education (TELE)*, 337-339. DOI: DOI: 10.1109/TELE62556.2024.10605683

Haberstroh, S., Oyserman, D., Schwarz, N., Kühnen, U., & Ji, L. J. (2002). Is the interdependent self more sensitive to question context than the independent self? Self construal and the observation of conversational norms. *Journal of Experimental Social Psychology*, *38*(3), 323–329. DOI: 10.1006/jesp.2001.1513

Habib, H., Jelani, S. A. K., & Rasheed, N. T. (2021). Tailored Education: AI in the Development of Individualized Education Programs (IEPs). *Multidisciplinary Science Journal*, *1*(01), 8–18.

Halliday, M. A. K., & Hasan, R. (1976). *Cohesion in English*. English Language Series. Longman.

Han, Z., & Cadierno, T. (2010). *Linguistic relativity in SLA: Thinking for speaking* (Second Language Acquisition). Multilingual Matters.

Hanus, M. D., & Fox, J. (2015). Assessing the effects of gamification in the classroom: A longitudinal study on intrinsic motivation, social comparison, satisfaction, effort, and academic performance. *Computers & Education, 80*, 152–161. DOI: 10.1016/j.compedu.2014.08.019

Harding, J., D'Alessandro, W., Laskowski, N. G., & Long, R. (2023). AI language models cannot replace human research participants. *AI & Society, 39*(5), 2603–2605. DOI: 10.1007/s00146-023-01725-x

Harizaj, M., & Hajrulla, V. (2017). Fostering learner's critical thinking skills in EFL: Some practical activities. *European Scientific Journal, 13*(29), 1–20. DOI: 10.19044/esj.2017.v13n29p126

Hasan, N., & Nene, M. J. (2023). Determinants of technological interventions for children with autism: A systematic review. *Journal of Educational Computing Research, 62*(1), 30–69. DOI: 10.1177/07356331231200701

Hasanov, A., Laine, T. H., & Chung, T. S. (2019). A survey of adaptive context-aware learning environments. *Journal of Ambient Intelligence and Smart Environments, 11*(5), 403–428. DOI: 10.3233/AIS-190534

Hashim, S., Omar, M. K., Jalil, H. A., & Sharef, N. M. (2023). Trends on technologies and artificial intelligence in education for personalized learning: Systematic literature review. *International Journal of Academic Research in Progressive Education and Development, 11*(1), 884–903. DOI: 10.6007/IJARPED/v11-i1/12230

Hattie, J., & Timperley, H. (2007). The power of feedback. *Review of Educational Research, 77*(1), 81–112. DOI: 10.3102/003465430298487

Heift, T., & Schulze, M. (2007). Errors and Intelligence in Computer-Assisted Language Learning: Parsers and Pedagogues. In *Errors and Intelligence in Computer-Assisted Language Learning: Parsers and Pedagogues*. DOI: 10.4324/9780203012215

Herlinawati, H., Marwa, M., Ismail, N., Junaidi, J., Liza, L. O., & Situmorang, D. D. B. (2024). The integration of 21st century skills in the curriculum of education. *Heliyon, 10*(15), e35148. DOI: 10.1016/j.heliyon.2024.e35148

Hernández, T. A. (2011). Re examining the role of explicit instruction and input flood on the acquisition of Spanish discourse markers. *Language Teaching Research, 15*(2), 159–182. DOI: 10.1177/1362168810388694

Herring, C., Koehler, M. J., & Mishra, P. (Eds.). (2016). *Handbook of Technological Pedagogical Content knowledge (TPACK) for educators*. Routledge. DOI: 10.4324/9781315771328

Hine, E., & Floridi, L. (2024). Artificial intelligence with American values and Chinese characteristics: A compara tive analysis of American and Chinese governmental AI policies. *AI & Society*, *39*(1), 257–278. DOI: 10.1007/s00146-022-01499-8

Hinkel, E. (2001). Matters of cohesion in L2 academic texts. *Applied Language Learning*, *12*(2), 111–132.

Hinojo-Lucena, F. J., Aznar-Díaz, I., Cáceres-Reche, M. P., & Romero-Rodríguez, J. M. (2019). Artificial intelligence in higher education: A bibliometric study on its impact in the scientific literature. *Education Sciences*, *9*(1), 21–51. DOI: 10.3390/educsci9010051

Hoffman, C., Lau, I., & Johnson, D. R. (1986). The linguistic relativity of person cognition. *Journal of Personality and Social Psychology, 51*, 1097 1105.

Holmes, W., Persson, J., Chounta, I.-A., Wasson, B., & Dimitrova, V. (2022). *Artificial intelligence and education: A critical view through the lens of human rights, democracy, and the rule of law*. Council of Europe. https://rm.coe.int/artificial-intelligence-andeducation-a-critical-view-through-the-lens/1680a886bd

Holmes, W., Bialik, M., & Fadel, C. (2019). *Artificial intelligence in education promises and implications for teaching and learning*. Center for Curriculum Redesign.

Holmes, W., Bialik, M., & Fadel, C. (2019). *Artificial Intelligence in Education: Promises and Implications for Teaching and Learning*. Center for Curriculum Redesign.

Holmes, W., Bialik, M., & Fadel, C. (2023). *Artificial intelligence in education*. Globethics Publications., DOI: 10.58863/20.500.12424/4276068

Holmes, W., Persson, J., Chounta, I. A., Wasson, B., & Dimitrova, V. (2022). *Artificial intelligence and education: A critical view through the lens of human rights, democracy and the rule of law*. Council of Europe.

Holstein, K., McLaren, B. M., & Aleven, V. (2019). Co-Designing a Real-Time Classroom Orchestration Tool to Support Teacher–AI Complementarity. *Journal of Learning Analytics*, *6*(2), 27–52. DOI: 10.18608/jla.2019.62.3

Ho, M. T., Mantello, P., & Vuong, Q. H. (2024). Emotional AI in education and toys: Investigating moral risk awareness in the acceptance of AI technologies from a cross-sectional survey of the Japanese population. *Heliyon*, *10*(16), e36251. DOI: 10.1016/j.heliyon.2024.e36251 PMID: 39253209

Hooks, B. (1994). *Teaching To Transgress* (1st ed.). Routledge., DOI: 10.4324/9780203700280

Hopcan, S., Polat, E., Ozturk, M. E., & Ozturk, L. (2023). Artificial intelligence in special education: A systematic review. *Interactive Learning Environments*, *31*(10), 7335–7353. DOI: 10.1080/10494820.2022.2067186

Horwitz, E. K., Horwitz, M. B., & Cope, J. (1986). Foreign language classroom anxiety. *Modern Language Journal*, *70*(2), 125–132. DOI: 10.1111/j.1540-4781.1986.tb05256.x

Hovy, D., & Spruit, S. L. (2016). The social impact of natural language processing. *54th Annual Meeting of the Association for Computational Linguistics, ACL 2016 - Short Papers*. DOI: 10.18653/v1/P16-2096

Hu, S., Fang, Z., Fang, Z., Deng, Y., Chen, X., & Fang, Y. (2024). Agentscodriver: Large language model empowered collaborative driving with lifelong learning. *arXiv preprint arXiv:2404.06345*. DOI:https://doi.org//arXiv.2404.06345DOI: 10.48550

Huallpa, J. J., Flores Arocutipa, J. P., Panduro, W. D., Huete, L. C., Flores Limo, F. A., Herrera, E. E., Alba Callacna, R. A., Ariza Flores, V. A., Medina Romero, M. Á., Quispe, I. M., & Hernández Hernández, F. A. (2023). Exploring the ethical considerations of using ChatGPT in university education. *Periodicals of Engineering and Natural Sciences*, *11*(4), 105–115. DOI: 10.21533/pen.v11.i4.200

Huang, W., Hew, K. F., & Fryer, L. K. (2022). Chatbots for language learning—Are they really useful? A systematic review of chatbot-supported language learning. In *Journal of Computer Assisted Learning* (Vol. 38, Issue 1). DOI: 10.1111/jcal.12610

Huang, L. (2023). Ethics of artificial intelligence in education: Student privacy and data protection. *Science Insights Education Frontiers*, *16*(2), 2577–2587. DOI: 10.15354/sief.23.re202

Huang, X., Zou, D., Cheng, G., Chen, X., & Xie, H. (2023). Trends, Research Issues and Applications of Artificial Intelligence in Language Education. *Journal of Educational Technology & Society*, *26*(1). Advance online publication. DOI: 10.30191/ETS.202301_26(1).0009

Hunt, E., & Agnoli, F. (1991). The Whorfian hypothesis: A cognitive psychology perspective. *Psychological Review, 98*, 377 389.

Hussein, B. A. S. (2012). The Sapir Whorf hypothesis today. *Theory and Practice in Language Studies*, *2*(3), 642–646. DOI: 10.4304/tpls.2.3.642-646

Hutson, J., & Harper-Nichols, M. (2023). Generative AI and Algorithmic Art: Disrupting the Framing of Meaning and Rethinking the Subject-Object Dilemma. *Global Journal of Computer Science and Technology*, *23*(D1), 55–61. DOI: 10.34257/GJCSTDVOL23IS1PG55

Hwang, G. J., & Chang, C. Y. (2023). A review of opportunities and challenges of chatbots in education. In *Interactive Learning Environments* (Vol. 31, Issue 7). DOI: 10.1080/10494820.2021.1952615

Hwang,G.-J., & Tsai, C.-C.. (2011). Research trends in mobile and ubiquitous learning: a review of publications in selected journals from 2001 to 2010. British Journal of Educational Technology, 42(4), E65–E70. http://dx.doi.org/. 2011.42. issue-4DOI: 10.1111/bjet

Hwang, G. J., Xie, H., Wah, B. W., & Gašević, D. (2020). Vision, challenges, roles and research issues of Artificial Intelligence in Education. *Computers and Education: Artificial Intelligence*, *1*, 100001. DOI: 10.1016/j.caeai.2020.100001

Ibrahim, A. M. (2024). The impact of voluntary artificial intelligent self-driven education and training platforms on maritime security personnel: ISPS code. *Journal of Transportation Security*, *17*(1), 21. DOI: 10.1007/s12198-024-00292-6

ICAO. (2011, March 8). *The study of ICAO rearding the demand in the aviation sector.* ICAO. https://www.icao.int/Newsroom/Pages/icao-study-reveals-strong-demand-for-qualified-aviation-personnel-up-to-2030.aspx

Iman, M. Z., Asis, A. A., & Rahma, A. U. Z. (2024). Enhancing Personalized Learning: The Impact of Artificial Intelligence in Education. *Edu Spectrum: Journal of Multidimensional Education*, *1*(2), 101–112. DOI: 10.70063/eduspectrum.v1i2.55

Imran, M., & Almusharraf, N. (2024). Google Gemini as a next generation AI educational tool: A review of emerging educational technology. *Smart Learning Environments*, *11*(1), 22. DOI: 10.1186/s40561-024-00310-z

Individuals With Disabilities Education Improvement Act of 2004, 118, Stat. 2647et seq., § 1401 (2004)

International Academy of Education. (2010). *International encyclopedia of education* (3rd ed.). Elsevier., DOI: 10.1016/B978-0-08-044894-7.01722-X

International Organization for Standardization. (2016). ISO 9999:2016 Assistive products for persons with disability – Classification and terminology. https://www.iso.org/standard/60547.html

Ironsi, C. S. (2024). Exploring the potential of generative AI in English language teaching. In P. Yu, J. Mulli, Z. A.S. Syed and L. Umme (Eds.), *Facilitating global collaboration and knowledge sharing in higher education with generative AI* (pp. 162 185). IGI Global Scientific Publishing. DOI: 10.4018/979-8-3693-0487-7.ch007

Ismail, I. A., & Aloshi, J. M. (2025). Data privacy in AI-driven education. In Tariq, M. U. (Ed.), *AI applications and strategies in teacher education* (pp. 223–252). IGI Global., DOI: 10.4018/979-8-3693-5443-8.ch008

Jaggia, S., Kelly, A., Lertwachara, K., & Chen, L. (2023). *Business analytics: Communicating with numbers*. McGraw Hill.

Jamuna, R. S., Ashok, M. S., & Palanivel, K. "Adaptive content for personalized E-learning using web service and semantic web," *2009 International Conference on Intelligent Agent & Multi-Agent Systems*, Chennai, India, 2009, pp. 1-4, DOI: 10.1109/IAMA.2009.5228081

Jarvis, S., & Pavlenko, A. (2010). *Crosslinguistic influence in language and cognition*. Routledge.

Javaid, M., Haleem, A., Singh, R. P., Khan, S., & Khan, I. H. (2023). Unlocking the opportunities through ChatGPT Tool towards ameliorating the education system. *BenchCouncil Transactions on Benchmarks. Standards and Evaluations*, *3*(2), 100115. DOI: 10.1016/j.tbench.2023.100115

Jereb, E., & Urh, M. (2024). The Use of Artificial Intelligence among Students in Higher Education. *Organizacija*, *57*(4), 333–345. DOI: 10.2478/orga-2024-0024

Jian, M. J. K. O. (2023). Personalized learning through AI. *Advances in Engineering Innovation*, *5*(1), 16–19. Advance online publication. DOI: 10.54254/2977-3903/5/2023039

Jiménez, S., Berenguer, C., Canato, M., Fernández, N., Iñesta, E., Moya, M. M., & Bermúdez, A. (2016). ¿Es posible la investigación en el trabajo de fin de grado? In M. T. Tortosa Ybáñez, S. Grau Company, J. D., & Álvarez Teruel (Eds.), *XIV Jornadas de Redes de Investigación en Docencia Universitaria: Investigación, innovación y enseñanza universitaria: enfoques pluridisciplinares* (pp. 2626-2636). Teruel (Spain). https://dialnet.unirioja.es/servlet/articulo?codigo=5917705

Jin, Y., Yan, L., Echeverria, V., Gašević, D., & Martinez-Maldonado, R. . (2025). Generative AI in higher education: A global perspective of institutional adoption policies and guidelines. . *Computers and Education: Artificial Intelligence, 8, 100348. sciencedirect.com*. DOI: DOI: 10.1016/j.caeai.2024.100348

Jobin, A., Ienca, M., & Vayena, E. (2019). The global landscape of AI ethics guidelines. *Nature Machine Intelligence*, *1*(9), 389–399. DOI: 10.1038/s42256-019-0088-2

Johansson, T., & Kroksmark, T. (2004). Teachers' intuition-in-action: How teachers experience action. *Reflective Practice*, *5*(3), 357–381. DOI: 10.1080/1462394042000270673

Johnson, L., Adams Becker, S., Cummins, M., Estrada, V., Freeman, A., & Hall, C. (2016). *NMC Horizon report: 2016 higher education edition.* The New Media Consortium. https://library.educause.edu/resources/2016/2/2016-horizon-report

Johnson, M. (2017). Improving cohesion in L2 writing: A three strand approach to building lexical cohesion. *English Teaching Forum*, 1 13.

Jones, A. P., Happé, F. G., Gilbert, F., Burnett, S., & Viding, E. (2010). Feeling, caring, knowing: Different types of empathy deficit in boys with psychopathic tendencies and autism spectrum disorder. *Journal of Child Psychology and Psychiatry, and Allied Disciplines*, *51*(11), 1188–1197. DOI: 10.1111/j.1469-7610.2010.02280.x

Joshi, P. (2017). *Artificial intelligence with python.* Packt Publishing Ltd.

Jucker, R., & von Au, J. (2022). Outdoor Learning—Why It Should Be High up on the Agenda of Every Educator. In Jucker, R., & von Au, J. (Eds.), *High-Quality Outdoor Learning*. Springer., DOI: 10.1007/978-3-031-04108-2_1

Kabassi, K., & Alepis, E. (2020). Learning Analytics in Distance and Mobile Learning for Designing Personalised Software. In Virvou, M., Alepis, E., Tsihrintzis, G., & Jain, L. (Eds.), *Machine Learning Paradigms. Intelligent Systems Reference Library* (Vol. 158). Springer., DOI: 10.1007/978-3-030-13743-4_10

Kamali, J., Alpat, M. F., & Bozkurt, A. (2024). AI ethics as a complex and multifaceted challenge: Decoding educators' AI ethics alignment through the lens of activity theory. *International Journal of Educational Technology in Higher Education*, *21*(1), 62. DOI: 10.1186/s41239-024-00496-9

Kapp, K. M. (2012). *The gamification of learning and instruction: Game-based methods and strategies for training and education.* John Wiley & Sons., DOI: 10.1145/2207270.2211316

Karger, T., Kalenda, J., Kalenda, S., & Kroutilová Nováková, R. (2022). Legitimisation of non-participation in adult education and training: The situational logic of decision-making. *International Journal of Lifelong Education*, *41*(3), 277–293. DOI: 10.1080/02601370.2022.2057606

Karpouzis, K., Pantazatos, D., Taouki, J., & Meli, K. (2024, May). Tailoring education with GenAI: a new horizon in lesson planning. In *2024 IEEE Global Engineering Education Conference (EDUCON)* (pp. 1-10). IEEE. https://doi.org/DOI: 10.1109/EDUCON60312.2024.10578690

Karpus, J., Krüger, A., Verba, J. T., Bahrami, B., & Deroy, O. (2021). Algorithm exploitation: Humans are keen to exploit benevolent AI. *iScience*, *24*(6), 102679. DOI: 10.1016/j.isci.2021.102679

Karsenti, T. (2019). Artificial intelligence in education: The urgent need to prepare teachers for tomorrow's schools. *Formation et Profession, 27*(1), 112–116. DOI: 10.18162/fp.2019.a167

Kartal, G. (2024). The influence of ChatGPT on thinking skills and creativity of EFL student teachers: A narrative inquiry. *Journal of Education for Teaching, 50*(4), 627–642. DOI: 10.1080/02607476.2024.2326502

Kashima, Y., & Kashima, E. S. (2003). Individualism, GNP, climate, and pronoun drop: Is individualism determined by affluence and climate, or does language use play a role? *Journal of Cross-Cultural Psychology, 34*(1), 125–134. DOI: 10.1177/0022022102239159

Kasneci, E., Seßler, K., Küchemann, S., Bannert, M., Dementieva, D., Fischer, F., & Kasneci, G. (2023). ChatGPT for good? On opportunities and challenges of large language models for education. *Learning and Individual Differences, 103*, 102274. DOI: 10.1016/j.lindif.2023.102274

Kaswan, K. S., Dhatterwal, J. S., & Ojha, R. P. (2024). AI in personalized learning. In *Advances in Technological Innovations in Higher Education* (1st ed., p. 15). CRC Press. DOI: 10.1201/9781003376699-9

Kasy, M. (2024). Algorithmic bias and racial inequality: A critical review. *Oxford Review of Economic Policy, 40*(3), 530–546. DOI: 10.1093/oxrep/grae031

Katirai, A. (2024). Ethical considerations in emotion recognition technologies: A review of the literature. *AI and Ethics, 4*(4), 927–948. DOI: 10.1007/s43681-023-00307-3

Kawata, H., Takano, Y., Iwata, Y., Kanamaru, N., Shimokura, K., & Fujita, Y. (2008). Field trial of asynchronous communication using network-based interactive child watch system for the participation of parents in day-care activities. *2008 IEEE International Conference on Robotics and Automation,* 2558-2563. DOI: 10.1109/ROBOT.2008.4543598

Kellner, D. (2004). Technological transformation, multiple literacies, and the re-visioning of education. *E-Learning and Digital Media, 1*(1), 9–37. DOI: 10.2304/elea.2004.1.1.8

Kem, D. (2022). Personalised and adaptive learning: Emerging learning platforms in the era of digital and smart learning. *International Journal of Social Science and Human Research, 5*(2), 385–391. DOI: 10.47191/ijsshr/v5-i2-02

Kemmelmeier, M., Cheng, B. (2004). Language and self construal priming: A replication and extension in a Hong Kong sample. *Journal of Cross Cultural Psychology, 35*, 705 712.

Kennedy, M. J., Thomas, C. N., Meyer, J. P., Alves, K. D., & Lloyd, J. W. (2014). Using evidence-based multimedia to improve vocabulary performance of adolescents with LD: A UDL approach. *Learning Disability Quarterly, 37*(2), 71–86. DOI: 10.1177/0731948713507262

Kessler, G. (2018). Technology and the future of language teaching. *Foreign Language Annals, 51*(1), 205–218. Advance online publication. DOI: 10.1111/flan.12318

Kewalramani, S., Kidman, G., & Palaiologou, I. (2021). Using artificial intelligence (AI)-interfaced robotic toys in early childhood settings: A case for children's inquiry literacy. *European Early Childhood Education Research Journal, 29*(5), 652–668. DOI: 10.1080/1350293X.2021.1968458

Khandelwal, P., Shankar, P., & Siddiraju, U. R. (2022). Skillsets and attributes for enhanced teaching–learning outcomes at higher educational institutions in disruptive times. In *Academic Voices* (pp. 227–238). Chandos Publishing., DOI: 10.1016/B978-0-323-91185-6.00032-X

Khan, I. U., Salman, S., & Naz, R. (2023). Unpacking the 4C's: Evaluating the integration of 21st-century skills in Pakistan's new undergraduate curriculum. *Educational Research and Innovation, 3*(2), 175–193. DOI: 10.61866/eri.v3i2.79

Khlaif, Z. N., Alkouk, W. A., Salama, N., & Abu Eideh, B. (2025). Redesigning Assessments for AI-Enhanced Learning: A Framework for Educators in the Generative AI Era. *Education Sciences, 15*(2), 174. DOI: 10.3390/educsci15020174

Khosravi, H., Shum, S. B., Chen, G., Conati, C., Tsai, Y.-S., Kay, J., Knight, S., Martinez-Maldonado, R., Sadiq, S., & Gašević, D. (2022). Explainable artificial intelligence in education. *Computers and Education: Artificial Intelligence, 3*, 100074. DOI: 10.1016/j.caeai.2022.100074

Kim, S., & Kim, H. C. (2021). The benefits of YouTube in learning English as a second language: A qualitative investigation of Korean freshman students' experiences and perspectives in the U.S. *Sustainability (Basel), 13*(13), 1–16. DOI: 10.3390/su13137365

Kim, S., Song, K., Lockee, B., & Burton, J. (2017). What is gamification in learning and education? In *Gamification in learning and education: Enjoy learning like gaming* (pp. 25–38). Springer International Publishing., DOI: 10.1007/978-3-319-47283-6_4

Kodak, T., & Bergmann, S. (2020). Autism spectrum disorder: Characteristics, associated behaviors, and early intervention. *Pediatric Clinics of North America*, *67*(3), 525–535. DOI: 10.1016/j.pcl.2020.02.007

Koegel, L. K., Ponder, E., Bruzzese, T., Wang, M., Semnani, S. J., Chi, N., Koegel, B. L., Lin, T. Y., Swarnakar, A., & Lam, M. S. (2025). Using artificial intelligence to improve empathetic statements in autistic adolescents and adults: A randomized clinical trial. *Journal of Autism and Developmental Disorders*. Advance online publication. DOI: 10.1007/s10803-025-06734-x

Koltovskaia, S. (2023). Postsecondary L2 writing teachers' use and perceptions of Grammarly as a complement to their feedback. *ReCALL*, *35*(3), 290–304. Advance online publication. DOI: 10.1017/S0958344022000179

Komljenovic, J. (2022). The future of value in digitalised higher education: Why data privacy should not be our biggest concern. *Higher Education*, *83*(1), 119–135. DOI: 10.1007/s10734-020-00639-7

Kosharna, N. (2019). Students' critical thinking skills development within pedagogical specialties of master's educational level in the content of the discipline professional communication in a foreign language. *Educological Discourse*, *2*(29), 14–25. DOI: 10.28925/2312-5829.2020.2.2

Koshik, I. (1999). A Preliminary investigation into the effect of grammatical cohesive devices their absence and their misuse on native speaker comprehension of non native speaker speech and writing. *Issues in Applied Linguistics*, *10*(1), 3–25. DOI: 10.5070/L4101005009

Kotsi, S., Handrinou, S., Iatraki, G., & Soulis, S.-G. (2025). A review of artificial intelligence interventions for students with autism spectrum disorder. *Disabilities*, *5*(1), 7. DOI: 10.3390/disabilities5010007

Kouroupa, A., Laws, K. R., Irvine, K., Mengoni, S. E., Baird, A., & Sharma, S. (2022). The use of social robots with children and young people on the autism spectrum: A systematic review and meta-analysis. *PLoS One*, *17*(6), e0269800. DOI: 10.1371/journal.pone.0269800

Kousloglou, M., Petridou, E., Molohidis, A., & Hatzikraniotis, E. (2023). Assessing Students' Awareness of 4Cs Skills after Mobile-Technology-Supported Inquiry-Based Learning. *Sustainability (Basel)*, *15*(8), 6725. DOI: 10.3390/su15086725

Kovari, A. (2025). Explainable AI chatbots towards XAI ChatGPT: A review. *Heliyon*, *11*(2), e42077. DOI: 10.1016/j.heliyon.2025.e42077 PMID: 39906828

Kraemer, F., Van Overveld, K., & Peterson, M. (2011). Is there an ethics of algorithms? *Ethics and Information Technology*, *13*, 251–260. DOI: 10.1007/s10676-010-9233-7

Krajka, J., & Olszak, I. (2024). Artificial intelligence tools in academic writing instruction: Exploring the potential of on-demand AI assistance in the writing process. *Roczniki Humanistyczne*, *72*(6), 123–140. DOI: 10.18290/rh247206.8

Kram, K. E. (1988). *Mentoring at work: Developmental relationships in organizational life*. University Press of America., DOI: 10.2307/2392687

Krashen, S. (1985). *The input hypothesis: Issues and implications*. Longman.

Kuhnel, M., Seiler, L., Honal, A., & Ifenthaler, D. (2018). Mobile learning analytics in higher education: Usability testing and evaluation of an app prototype. *Interactive Technology and Smart Education*, *15*(4), 332–347. DOI: 10.1108/ITSE-04-2018-0024

Kulik, C. L. C., Kulik, J. A., & Bangert-Drowns, R. L. (1990). Effectiveness of mastery learning programs: A meta-analysis. *Review of Educational Research*, *60*(2), 265–299. DOI: 10.3102/00346543060002265

Kumar, M., Packer, B., & Koller, D. (2010). Self-paced learning for latent variable models. *Advances in Neural Information Processing Systems*, •••, 23.

Kung, T. H., Cheatham, M., Medenilla, A., Sillos, C., De Leon, L., Elepaño, C., Madriaga, M., Aggabao, R., Diaz-Candido, G., Maningo, J., & Tseng, V. (2023). Performance of ChatGPT on USMLE: Potential for AI-assisted medical education using large language models. *PLOS Digital Health*, *2*(2), 1–12. DOI: 10.1371/journal.pdig.0000198

Kuntariati, U., & Paramita, P. D. Y. (2023). Analysis of collaborative project-based language learning method: Efforts to improve language education quality for tourism students. *Prosiding Seminar Nasional Riset Bahasa Dan Pengajaran Bahasa*, *5*(1), 34–46. DOI: 10.31940/senarilip.v5i1.36-46

Kurian, N. (2023). AI's empathy gap: The risks of conversational artificial intelligence for young children's well-being and key ethical considerations for early childhood education and care. *Contemporary Issues in Early Childhood*, *26*(1), 132–139. DOI: 10.1177/14639491231206004

Kurian, N. (2023). Toddlers and robots? The ethics of supporting young children with disabilities with AI companions and the implications for children's rights. *International Journal of Human Rights Education*, *7*(1), 9. https://repository.usfca.edu/ijhre/vol7/iss1/9

Labadie, C., & Legner, C. (2023). Building data management capabilities to address data protection regulations: Learnings from EU-GDPR. *Journal of Information Technology, 38*(1), 16–44. Advance online publication. DOI: 10.1177/02683962221141456

Landauer, T. K., Foltz, P. W., & Laham, D. (1998). An introduction to latent semantic analysis. *Discourse Processes, 25*(2 3), 259 284.

Landis, J. R., & Koch, G. G. (1977). The Measurement of Observer Agreement for Categorical Data. *Biometrics, 33*(1), 159–174. DOI: 10.2307/2529310

Lang, Q., Wang, M., Yin, M., Liang, S., & Song, W. (2025). Transforming Education with Generative AI (GAI): Key Insights and Future Prospects. *IEEE Transactions on Learning Technologies, 18*, 230–242. Advance online publication. DOI: 10.1109/TLT.2025.3537618

Lara-Navarra, P., Ferrer-Sapena, A., Ismodes-Cascón, E., Fosca-Pastor, C., & Sánchez-Pérez, E. A. (2025). The Future of Higher Education: Trends, Challenges and Opportunities in AI-Driven Lifelong Learning in Peru. *Information (Basel), 16*(3), 224. DOI: 10.3390/info16030224

Lauermann, F. (2014). Teacher responsibility from the teacher's perspective. *International Journal of Educational Research, 65*, 75–89. DOI: 10.1016/j.ijer.2013.09.005

Lawless, W. F., Mittus, R., & Sofge, D. A. (2020). Introduction: Artificial intelligence (AI), autonomous machines, and constructing context: User interventions, social awareness, and interdependence. In Lawless, W. F., Mittus, R., & Sofge, D. A. (Eds.), *Human-Machine Shared Contexts* (pp. 1–22). Academic Press., DOI: 10.1016/B978-0-12-820543-3.00001-8

Leavy, A., Dick, L. K., Meletiou-Mavrotheris, M., Paparistodemou, E., & Stylianou, E. (2023). The prevalence and use of emerging technologies in steam education: A systematic review of the literature. *Journal of Computer Assisted Learning, 39*(4), 1061–1082. DOI: 10.1111/jcal.12806

Lee, D., Kim, H., & Sung, S.-H. (2023). Development research on an AI English learning support system to facilitate learner-generated-context-based learning. *Educational Technology Research and Development, 71*(2), 629–666. Advance online publication. DOI: 10.1007/s11423-022-10172-2 PMID: 36533222

Lee, S. S., & Moore, R. L. (2024). Harnessing Generative AI (GenAI) for automated feedback in higher education: A systematic review. *Online Learning : the Official Journal of the Online Learning Consortium, 28*(3), 82–104. DOI: 10.24059/olj.v28i3.4593

Lee, S., Choe, H., Zou, D., & Jeon, J. (2025). Generative AI (GenAI) in the language classroom: A systematic review. *Interactive Learning Environments*, •••, 1–25. DOI: 10.1080/10494820.2025.2498537

León, J. J. C., & Castro, C. M. C. (2017). Transforming EFL classroom practices and promoting students' empowerment: Collaborative learning from a dialogical approach. *PROFILE Issues in Teachers'. Professional Development (Philadelphia, Pa.)*, *19*(2), 135–149. DOI: 10.15446/profile.v19n2.57811

Leta, F. M., & Vancea, D. P. C. (2023). Ethics in education: Exploring the ethical implications of artificial intelligence implementation. *Ovidius University Annals. Economic Sciences Series*, *23*(1), 413–421.

Levinson, L. M., Abbasi, N. I., Sabanovic, S., & Gunes, H. (2024). Expert insights on robots for safeguarding children: How (not) and why (not)? In *Proceedings of the interaction design and children conference* (IDC '24), June 17–20, 2024, Delft, Netherlands (pp. 600–611). ACM. https://doi.org/DOI: 10.1145/3628516.3655798

Levy, M., & Stockwell, G. (2013). Call dimensions: Options and issues in computer-assisted language learning. In *Call Dimensions*. Options and Issues in Computer-Assisted Language Learning., DOI: 10.4324/9780203708200

Li, X., & Taber, K. S. (2022). The Future of Interaction: Augmented Reality, Holography, and Artificial Intelligence in Early Childhood Science Education. In *STEM, Robotics, Mobile Apps in Early Childhood and Primary Education: Technology to Promote Teaching and Learning* (pp. 415-442). Springer Nature Singapore.

Liang, W., & Wu, Y. (2024). Exploring the use of ChatGPT to foster EFL learners' critical thinking skills from a post-humanist perspective. *Thinking Skills and Creativity*, *54*, 1–15. DOI: 10.1016/j.tsc.2024.101645

Liao, Y., Chen, Y., Chen, H., & Chang, Y. (2018). Infusing creative pedagogy into an English as a foreign language classroom: Learning performance, creativity, and motivation. *Thinking Skills and Creativity*, *29*, 213–223. DOI: 10.1016/j.tsc.2018.07.007

Li, H., Forbes, A., & Yang, W. (2021). Developing culturally and developmentally appropriate early STEM learning experiences. *Early Education and Development*, *32*(1), 1–6. DOI: 10.1080/10409289.2020.1833674 PMID: 35082478

Lim, E. M. (2024). Metaphor analysis on pre-service early childhood teachers' conception of AI (Artificial Intelligence) education for young children. *Thinking Skills and Creativity*, *51*, 101455. DOI: 10.1016/j.tsc.2023.101455

Linder, S. M. (2012). Interactive whiteboards in early childhood mathematics: Strategies for effective implementation in pre-K-grade 3. *Young Children, 67*(3), 26–35. https://research.ebsco.com/linkprocessor/plink?id=631d9486-5f4a-30b0-a427-4ed86c4ba233

Lin, P., Van Brummelen, J., Lukin, G., Williams, R., & Breazeal, C. (2020). Zhorai: Designing a conversational agent for children to explore machine learning concepts. *Proceedings of the AAAI Conference on Artificial Intelligence, 34*(9), 13381–13388. DOI: 10.1609/aaai.v34i09.7061

Lin, Z. (2023). Supercharging academic writing with generative AI: Framework, techniques, and caveats. *Nature Biomedical Engineering*. Advance online publication. DOI: 10.1038/s41551-024-01185-8 PMID: 38499642

Li, S., Zhu, Y., & Ellis, R. (2016). The effects of the timing of corrective feedback on the acquisition of a new linguistic structure. *Modern Language Journal, 100*(1), 276–295. DOI: 10.1111/modl.12315

Liu, W., & Wang, Y. (2024). The effects of using AI tools on critical thinking in English literature classes among EFL learners: An intervention study. *European Journal of Education, 59*(4), 1–12. DOI: 10.1111/ejed.12804

Liu, Y., Yang, Z., Yu, Z., Liu, Z., Liu, D., Lin, H., Li, M., Ma, S., Avdeev, M., & Shi, S. (2023). Generative artificial intelligence and its applications in materials science: Current situation and future perspectives. *Journal of Materiomics, 9*(4), 798–816. DOI: 10.1016/j.jmat.2023.05.001

Liyanage, M. L. A. P., Hirimuthugoda, U. J., Liyanage, N. L. T. N., Thammita, D. H. M. M. P., Wedanage, D. K. H., Kugathasan, A., & Thelijjagoda, S. (2022). AI Solution to Assist Online Education Productivity via Personalizing Learning Strategies and Analyzing the Student Performance. *2022 IEEE 13th Annual Ubiquitous Computing, Electronics & Mobile Communication Conference (UEMCON)*, 0609–0615. https://doi.org/DOI: 10.1109/UEMCON54665.2022.9965735

Llorente, A. M., Ladera, V., Contreras, P., & Conde, L. (2021). Efficacy of a computerized intervention based on artificial intelligence for improving reading comprehension in students with dyslexia. *Frontiers in Psychology, 12*, 641005. DOI: 10.3389/fpsyg.2021.641005

Lo, C. K. (2023). What is the impact of ChatGPT on education? A rapid review of the literature. *Education Sciences, 13*(4), 410. DOI: 10.3390/educsci13040410

Lo, C. K., & Hew, K. F. (2017). A critical review of flipped classroom challenges in K-12 education: Possible solutions and recommendations for future research. *Research and Practice in Technology Enhanced Learning*, *12*(1), 1–22. DOI: 10.1186/s41039-016-0044-2

Lodzikowski, K., Foltz, P., & Behrens, J. (2024). Generative AI and its educational implications. In Kourkoulou, D., Tzirides, A. O., Cope, B., & Kalantzis, M. (Eds.), *Trust and Inclusion in AI-Mediated Education* (pp. 35–57). Springer., DOI: 10.1007/978-3-031-64487-0_2

Loewen, S., Isbell, D. R., & Sporn, Z. (2020). The effectiveness of app-based language instruction for developing receptive linguistic knowledge and oral communicative ability. *Foreign Language Annals*, *53*(2), 209–233. Advance online publication. DOI: 10.1111/flan.12454

Long, M. H. (1983). Input and second language acquisition theory. In S. Gass and C. Maddan (Eds.), *Input in second language acquisition* (pp. 377 393). Rowley, Newbury House.

Long, M. H. (1996). The role of linguistic environment in second language acquisition. In W. C. Ritchie & T. K. Bhatia (Eds.), *Handbook of second language acquisition* (pp. 413 468). San Diego Academic Press. DOI: 10.1016/B978-012589042-7/50015-3

Long, H. S. (2024). Exploring the use of ChatGPT as a tool for written corrective feedback in an EFL classroom. *The Journal of Asia TEFL*, *21*(2), 397–412. DOI: 10.18823/asiatefl.2024.21.2.8.397

Longo, L., Brcic, M., Cabitza, F., Choi, J., Confalonieri, R., Del Ser, J., Guidotti, R., Hayashi, Y., Herrera, F., & Holzinger, A. (2024). Explainable Artificial Intelligence (XAI) 2.0: A manifesto of open challenges and interdisciplinary research directions. *Information Fusion*, *106*, 102301. DOI: 10.1016/j.inffus.2024.102301

Looi, C. K., & Jia, F. (2025). Personalization capabilities of current technology chatbots in a learning environment: An analysis of student-tutor bot interactions. *Education and Information Technologies*, *30*(10), 1–31. DOI: 10.1007/s10639-025-13369-z

Luan, H., & Tsai, C. C. (2021). A review of using machine learning approaches for precision education. *Journal of Educational Technology & Society*, *24*(1), 250–266.

Luckin, R., & Holmes, W. (2016). Intelligence unleashed: An argument for AI in education.

Luckin, R., Holmes, W., Griffiths, M., & Forcier, L. B. (2016). *Intelligence Unleashed: An Argument for AI in Education*. Pearson Education.

Lu, J., Zheng, R., Gong, Z., & Xu, H. (2024). Supporting Teachers' Professional Development With Generative AI: The Effects on Higher Order Thinking and Self-Efficacy. *IEEE Transactions on Learning Technologies*, *17*, 1279–1289. DOI: 10.1109/TLT.2024.3369690

Lund, B. D., Wang, T., Mannuru, N. R., Nie, B., Shimray, S. R., & Wang, Z. (2023). ChatGPT and a new academic reality: Artificial intelligence-written research papers and the ethics of the large language models in scholarly publishing. *Journal of the Association for Information Science and Technology*, *74*(5), 570–581. DOI: 10.1002/asi.24750

Luo, H., Yang, T., Xue, J., & Zuo, M. (2019). Impact of student agency on learning performance and learning experience in a flipped classroom. *British Journal of Educational Technology*, *50*(2), 819–831. https://doi.org/https://doi.org/10.1111/bjet.12604. DOI: 10.1111/bjet.12604

Luo, W., He, H., Gao, M., & Li, H. (2024). Safety, identity, attitude, cognition, and capability: The 'SIACC' framework of early childhood AI literacy. *Education Sciences*, *14*(8), 1–19. DOI: 10.3390/educsci14080871

Lu, Z. J. (Ed.). (2012). *Learning with Mobile Technologies, Handheld Devices, and Smart Phones: Innovative Methods: Innovative Methods*. IGI Global.

Lyu, Y., Liu, D., An, P., Tong, X., Zhang, H. U. A. N., Katsuragawa, K. E. I. K. O., & Zhao, J. I. A. N. (2024). EMooly: Supporting autistic children in collaborative social-emotional learning with caregiver participation through interactive AI-infused and AR activities. *Proceedings of the ACM on Interactive, Mobile, Wearable and Ubiquitous Technologies*, *8*(4), 1–36. DOI: 10.1145/3699738

Machado, H., Silva, S., & Neiva, L. (2025). Publics' views on ethical challenges of artificial intelligence: A scoping review. *AI and Ethics*, *5*, 139–167. DOI: 10.1007/s43681-023-00387-1

Mackey, A. (2020). *Interaction, feedback and task research in second language learning*. Cambridge University Press. DOI: 10.1017/9781108589284

Madden, M., Gilman, M., Levy, K., & Marwick, A. (2017). Privacy, poverty, and big data: A matrix of vulnerabilities for poor Americans. *Washington University Law Review, 95*(1), 53–125. Retrieved from: https://openscholarship.wustl.edu/law_lawreview/vol95/iss1/6

Maghsudi, S., Lan, A., Xu, J., & van Der Schaar, M. (2021). Personalized education in the artificial intelligence era: What to expect next. *IEEE Signal Processing Magazine*, *38*(3), 37–50. DOI: 10.1109/MSP.2021.3055032

Mahdi, H. S., & Al Khateeb, A. A. (2019). The effectiveness of computer-assisted pronunciation training: A meta-analysis. *Review of Education*, *7*(3), 733–753. Advance online publication. DOI: 10.1002/rev3.3165

Malah, Z. (2021). Cross cultural pragmatics on lexical cohesion in President Obama's and President Buhari's inaugural speeches. *International Journal of Language and Literary Studies*, *3*(3), 23–53. DOI: 10.36892/ijlls.v2i3.680

Mandal, J. (2024). Ai Integration. In *Lifelong Learning: Transformative Approaches To Teaching And Learning*. Artificial Intelligence In Education., DOI: 10.25215/9358094575.27

Maqsood, M., Butt, H. H., Ali, M. A., Chinedu, C. C., Ahmad, M., Maqsood, M., Butt, H. H., Ali, M. A., Chinedu, C. C., & Ahmad, M. (2025). Chatbots as Learning Companions Exploring Ethical Dimensions of AI in Education. In Jean-Éric, P. (Ed.), *Architecting the Digital Future: Platforms, Design, and Application* (pp. 311–348). IGI Global Scientific Publishing., DOI: 10.4018/979-8-3693-2973-3.ch012

Marandi, S. S. (2024). Virtual supremacy and electronic imperialism: The hegemonies of e-learning and computer assisted language learning (CALL). *Learning, Media and Technology*, *49*(4), 527–543. Advance online publication. DOI: 10.1080/17439884.2023.2207832

Martínez-Requejo, S., Redondo-Duarte, S., Jiménez-García, E., & Ruiz-Lázaro, J. (2025). Technoethics and the Use of Artificial Intelligence in Educational Contexts: Reflections on Integrity, Transparency, and Equity. In Garcia, M., Rosak-Szyrocka, J., & Bozkurt, A. (Eds.), *Pitfalls of AI Integration in Education: Skill Obsolescence, Misuse, and Bias* (pp. 227–250). IGI Global Scientific Publishing., DOI: 10.4018/979-8-3373-0122-8.ch010

Masrek, M. N., Susantari, T., Mutia, F., Yuwinanto, H. P., & Atmi, R. T. (2024). *Enabling Education Everywhere: How artificial intelligence empowers ubiquitous and lifelong learning*. Environment-Behaviour Proceedings Journal., DOI: 10.21834/e-bpj.v9iSI18.5462

Matthews, J. T., Beach, S. R., Downs, J., de Bruin, W. B., & Mecca, L. P., & Schulz. (2010). Preferences and concerns for quality of life technology among older adults and persons with disabilities: National survey results. *Technology and Disability*, *22*(1-2), 5–15. DOI: 10.3233/TAD-2010-0279

Mayer, R. E., Lee, H., & Peebles, A. (2014). Multimedia learning in a second language: A cognitive load perspective. *Applied Cognitive Psychology*, *28*(5), 653–660. DOI: 10.1002/acp.3050

McCarthy, J., Minsky, M., Rochester, N., & Shannon, C. (1955). A proposal for Dartmouth Summer Research Project on artificial Intelligence. http://wwwformal.stanford.edu/jmc/history/dartmouth.pdf

McClure, C., & Williams, P. (2021). Gather. town: An opportunity for self-paced learning in a synchronous, distance-learning environment. *Compass (Eltham), 14*(2). Advance online publication. DOI: 10.21100/compass.v14i2.1232

McDonald, N., & Forte, A. (2022). Privacy and vulnerable populations. In Knijnenburg, B. P., Page, X., Wisniewski, P., Lipford, H. R., Proferes, N., & Romano, J. (Eds.), *Modern sociotechnical perspectives on privacy* (pp. 337–363). Springer.

McLachlan, C., Fleer, M., & Edwards, S. (2018). *Early childhood curriculum: Planning, assessment and implementation*. Cambridge University Press. DOI: 10.1017/9781108131810

McNamara, D. S., Graesser, A. C., McCarthy, P., & Cai, Z. (2014). *Automated evaluation of text and discourse with Coh Metrix*. Cambridge University Press. DOI: 10.1017/CBO9780511894664

Medvedeva, O. D., & Rubtsova, A. (2021). Productive method as the basis for soft skills development in engineering foreign language education. *Education Sciences, 11*(6), 1–15. DOI: 10.3390/educsci11060276

Melisa, R., Ashadi, A., Triastuti, A., Hidayati, S., Salido, A., Ero, P. E. L., Marlini, C., Zefrin, Z., & Al Fuad, Z. (2025). Critical thinking in the age of AI: A systematic review of AI's effects on higher education. *Educational Process: International Journal, 14*(1), e2025031. DOI: 10.22521/edupij.2025.14.31

Melzer, P. (2018). *A conceptual framework for personalised learning: influence factors, design, and support potentials*. Springer., DOI: 10.1007/978-3-658-23095-1

Meng, L., Zhang, W., Chu, Y., & Zhang, M. (2021). LD–LP generation of personalized learning path based on learning diagnosis. *IEEE Transactions on Learning Technologies, 14*(1), 122–128. DOI: 10.1109/TLT.2021.3058525

Methley, A. M., Campbell, S., Chew-Graham, C., McNally, R., & Cheraghi-Sohi, S. (2014). PICO, PICOS and SPIDER: A comparison study of specificity and sensitivity in three search tools for qualitative systematic reviews. *BMC Health Services Research, 14*(1), 1–10. DOI: 10.1186/s12913-014-0579-0

Miao, F., & Holmes, W. (2023). Guidance for generative AI in education and research. *UNESCO*. https://unesdoc.unesco.org/ark:/48223/pf0000386693

Milana, M., Brandi, U., Hodge, S., & Hoggan-Kloubert, T. (2024). *Artificial intelligence (AI), conversational agents, and generative AI: implications for adult education practice and research* (Vol. 43). Taylor & Francis., DOI: 10.1080/02601370.2024.2310448

Miraz, M. H., Ali, M., Excell, P. S., & Khan, S. (2021). AI-Based Culture Independent Pervasive M-Learning Prototype Using UI Plasticity Design. *Computers, Materials & Continua*, *68*(1), 1021–1039. DOI: 10.32604/cmc.2021.015405

Miroshnikova, T. (2020). Innovative Technologies in Education. *E3S Web Conf.*, *210*, 18135. https://doi.org/DOI: 10.1051/e3sconf/202021018135

Mirzaei, M. S., & Meshgi, K. (2021). Facilitating L2 listening through automatic detection of speech and lexical difficulties. In N. Zoghlami, C. Brudermann, C. Sarré, M. Grosbois, L. Bradley, & S. Thouësny (Eds.), *CALL and professionalisation: short papers from EUROCALL 2021* (pp. 214 219). DOI: 10.14705/rpnet.2021.54.1335

Misra, V. P., Mishra, P. K., & Sharma, A. (2023). Artificial Intelligence in Education–Emerging Trends, Thematic Analysis & Application in Lifelong Learning. *2023 IEEE Asia-Pacific Conference on Computer Science and Data Engineering (CSDE)*, DOI: DOI: 10.1109/CSDE59766.2023.10487664

Mitchell, J. J., & Jeon, M. (2025). Exploring emotional connections: A systematic literature review of attachment in human-robot ınteraction. *International Journal of Human-Computer Interaction*, *41*(18), 1–22. DOI: 10.1080/10447318.2024.2445100

Mizumoto, A., Yasuda, S., & Tamura, Y. (2024). Identifying ChatGPT generated texts in EFL students' writing: Through comparative analysis of linguistic fingerprints. *Applied Corpus Linguistics*, *4*(3), 100106. DOI: 10.1016/j.acorp.2024.100106

Moher, D., Liberati, A., Tetzlaff, J., & Altman, D. G.Prisma Group. (2009). Preferred reporting items for systematic reviews and meta-analyses: The PRISMA statement. *Annals of Internal Medicine*, *151*(4), 264–269. DOI: 10.7326/0003-4819-151-4-200908180-00135

Mohsen, M. A., Althebi, S., Alsagour, R., Alsalem, A., Almudawi, A., & Alshahrani, A. (2024). Forty-two years of computer-assisted language learning research: A scientometric study of hotspot research and trending issues. *ReCALL*, *36*(2), 230–249. DOI: 10.1017/S0958344023000253

Mollick, E., & Mollick, L. (2024). Instructors as innovators: A future-focused approach to new AI learning opportunities, with prompts.

Mondada, L., & Doehlier, S. P. (2004). Second language acquisition as situated practice: Task accomplishment in the French second language classroom. *Modern Language Journal*, *88*(4), 501–518. DOI: 10.1111/j.0026-7902.2004.t01-15-.x

Mondal, S., Das, S., & Vrana, V. G. (2023). How to bell the cat? A theoretical review of generative artificial intelligence towards digital disruption in all walks of life. *Technologies*, *11*(2), 44. DOI: 10.3390/technologies11020044

Monib, W. K., Qazi, A., & Mahmud, M. M. (2025). Exploring learners' experiences and perceptions of ChatGPT as a learning tool in higher education. *Education and Information Technologies*, *30*(1), 917–939. DOI: 10.1007/s10639-024-13065-4

Montemayor, C., Halpern, J., & Fairweather, A. (2022). In principle obstacles for empathic AI: Why we can't replace human empathy in healthcare. *AI & Society*, *37*, 1353–1359. DOI: 10.1007/s00146-021-01230-z

Montiel-Vázquez, E. C., Ramírez Uresti, J. A., & Loyola-González, O. (2022). An explainable artificial intelligence approach for detecting empathy in textual communication. *Applied Sciences (Basel, Switzerland)*, *12*(19), 9407. DOI: 10.3390/app12199407

Moody, C. T., & Laugeson, E. A. (2020). Social skills training in autism spectrum disorder across the lifespan. *Child and Adolescent Psychiatric Clinics of North America*, *29*(2), 359–371. DOI: 10.1016/j.chc.2019.11.001

Moorhouse, B. L., Yeo, M. A., & Wan, Y. (2023). Generative AI tools and assessment: Guidelines of the world's top-ranking universities. *Computers and Education Open*, *5*, 100151. DOI: 10.1016/j.caeo.2023.100151

Morales-Chan, M., Amado-Salvatierra, H. R., & Hernandez-Rizzardini, R. (2024). AI-Driven Content Creation: Revolutionizing Educational Materials. *Proceedings of the Eleventh ACM Conference on Learning @ Scale*, 556–558. https://doi.org/DOI: 10.1145/3657604.3664640

Moreno-Guerrero, A. J., López-Belmonte, J., Marín-Marín, J. A., & Soler-Costa, R. (2020). Scientific development of educational artificial intelligence in Web of Science. *Future Internet*, *12*(8), 124. DOI: 10.3390/fi12080124

Morjaria, L., Burns, L., Bracken, K., Ngo, Q. N., Lee, M., Levinson, A. J., Smith, J., Thompson, P., & Sibbald, M. (2023). Examining the threat of ChatGPT to the validity of short-answer assessments in an undergraduate medical program. *Journal of Medical Education and Curricular Development*, *10*, 23821205231204178. Advance online publication. DOI: 10.1177/23821205231204178 PMID: 37780034

Muñoz, C. (2012). The significance of intensive exposure as a turning point in learners' histories. In Muñoz, C. (Ed.), *Intensive Exposure Experiences in Second Language Learning* (pp. 141–160). Multilingual Matters.

Muñoz, C., & Cadierno, T. (2021). How do differences in exposure affect English language learning? A comparison of teenagers in two learning environments. *Studies in Second Language Learning and Teaching*, *11*(2), 185–212. DOI: 10.14746/ssllt.2021.11.2.2

Muñoz-Merino, P. J., Ruipérez-Valiente, J. A., Alario-Hoyos, C., Pérez-Sanagustín, M., & Delgado Kloos, C. (2015). Precise Effectiveness Strategy for analyzing the effectiveness of students with educational resources and activities in MOOCs. *Computers in Human Behavior*, *47*, 108–118. DOI: 10.1016/j.chb.2014.10.003

Murray and Green. (2021). *Aviation Faces a Pilot Shortage.* OliverWyman. https://www.oliverwyman.com/our-expertise/insights/2021/mar/after-covid-19-aviation-faces-a-pilot-shortage.html

Murtaza, M., Ahmed, Y., Shamsi, J. A., Sherwani, F., & Usman, M. (2022). AI-based personalized e-learning systems: Issues, challenges, and solutions. *IEEE Access : Practical Innovations, Open Solutions*, *10*, 81323–81342. DOI: 10.1109/ACCESS.2022.3193938

Muthoharoh, K., & Nur Rohmah, G. (2022). The use of cohesion of Susilo Bambang Yudhoyono's speech in APEC Economic Leader Conference in Bali. [JSRET]. *Journal of Scientific Research, Education, and Technology*, *1*(2), 83–91. DOI: 10.58526/jsret.v1i2.14

Nadkarni, P. M., Ohno-Machado, L., & Chapman, W. W. (2011). Natural language processing: An introduction. *Journal of the American Medical Informatics Association : JAMIA*, *18*(5), 544–551. DOI: 10.1136/amiajnl-2011-000464 PMID: 21846786

Naeem, H., Tariq, W., & Ali, I. (2025). Evaluating the Impact of AI-Driven Quiz Applications On Educational Outcomes: A Case Study of Wendigo. *Journal of Religion and Society*, *3*(01), 64–78.

Nagy, J. (2024). Autism and the making of emotion AI: Disability as resource for surveillance capitalism. *New Media & Society*, *26*(7), 3989–4007. DOI: 10.1177/14614448221109550

Naidu, K., & Sevnarayan, K. (2023). ChatGPT: An ever-increasing encroachment of artificial intelligence in online assessment in distance education. *Online Journal of Communication and Media Technologies*, *13*(3), e202336. DOI: 10.30935/ojcmt/13291

Nakata, T. (2015). Effects of feedback timing on second language vocabulary learning: Does delaying feedback increase learning? *Language Teaching Research*, *19*(4), 416–434. DOI: 10.1177/1362168814541721

Narayanan, N. (2024). *The era of generative AI: transforming academic libraries, education, and research.*

Nasution, N. E. A. (2023). Using artificial intelligence to create biology multiple choice questions for higher education. *Agricultural and Environmental Education*, *2*(1), em002. DOI: 10.29333/agrenvedu/13071

Nation, I. (2006). How Large a Vocabulary is Needed For Reading and Listening? *Canadian Modern Language Review*. *Canadian Modern Language Review*, *63*(1), 59–82. DOI: 10.3138/cmlr.63.1.59

Nedungadi, P., Tang, K. Y., & Raman, R. (2024). The Transformative Power of Generative Artificial Intelligence for achieving the sustainable development goal of Quality Education. . *Sustainability. mdpi.com*. DOI: DOI: 10.3390/su16229779

Neeharika, C. H., & Riyazuddin, Y. M. (2023). Developing an Artificial Intelligence Based Model for Autism Spectrum Disorder Detection in Children. *Journal of Advanced Research in Applied Sciences and Engineering Technology*, *32*(1), 57–72. DOI: 10.37934/araset.32.1.5772

Ng, D. T. K., & Chu, S. K. W. (2021). Motivating students to learn AI through social networking sites: A case study in Hong Kong. *Online Learning : the Official Journal of the Online Learning Consortium*, *25*(1), 195–208. DOI: 10.24059/olj.v25i1.2454

Ng, D. T. K., Leung, J. K. L., Chu, K. W. S., & Qiao, M. S. (2021). AI literacy: Definition, teaching, evaluation and ethical issues. *Proceedings of the Association for Information Science and Technology*, *58*(1), 504–509. DOI: 10.1002/pra2.487

Ng, D. T. K., Leung, J. K. L., Chu, S. K. W., & Qiao, M. S. (2021). Conceptualizing AI literacy: An exploratory review. *Computers and Education: Artificial Intelligence*, *2*, 100041. DOI: 10.1016/j.caeai.2021.100041

Ng, D. T. K., Leung, J. K. L., Su, M. J., Yim, I. H. Y., Qiao, M. S., & Chu, S. K. W. (2022). AI Literacy Education in Early Childhood Education. In *AI Literacy in K-16 Classrooms*. Springer International Publishing., DOI: 10.1007/978-3-031-18880-0_5

Niculescu, A., van Dijk, B., Nijholt, A., Li, H., & See, S. L. (2013). Making social robots more attractive: The effects of voice pitch, humor and empathy. *International Journal of Social Robotics*, *5*(2), 171–191. DOI: 10.1007/s12369-012-0171-x

Oberdieck, T., & Moch, E. (2024). Lifelong Learning with Artificial Intelligence: Potentials, Challenges and Future Perspectives. *International Journal of Advanced Research, 12*(6), 545–555. DOI: 10.21474/IJAR01/18915

OECD. (2013). Innovative Learning Environments. OECD Publishing., Retrieved February 15, 2024, from, DOI: 10.1787/9789264203488-

Olawale, B. E., & Hendricks, W. W. (2024). ARTIFICIAL INTELLIGENCE IN TEACHER EDUCATION: UNLOCKING THE TOOLS AND BENEFITS OF A TRANSFORMING PEDAGOGY. DOI: 10.5539/jel.v13n6p346

Open, A. I. (2022). ChatGPT: Optimizing language models for dialogue. https://openai.com/blog/chatgpt/

Opesemowo, O. A. G., & Adekomaya, V. (2024). Harnessing artificial intelligence for advancing sustainable development goals in south Africa's higher education system: A qualitative study. *International Journal of Learning. Teaching and Educational Research, 23*(3), 67–86. DOI: 10.26803/ijlter.23.3.4

Oran, B. B. (2023). Correlation between artificial intelligence in education and teacher self-efficacy beliefs: A review. *RumeliDe Dil ve Edebiyat Arastirmalari Dergisi, 34*(34), 1354–1365. DOI: 10.29000/rumelide.1316378

Orhan, A. (2022). The relationship between critical thinking and academic achievement: A meta-analysis study. *Psycho-Educational Research Reviews, 11*(1), 283–299. DOI: 10.52963/PERR_Biruni_V11.N1.18

Orhan, A. (2024). Online or in-class problem based learning: Which one is more effective in enhancing learning outcomes and critical thinking in higher education EFL classroom? *Journal of Computer Assisted Learning, 40*(5), 2351–2368. DOI: 10.1111/jcal.13033

Orhan, A., & Ataman, O. (2024). Investigating the predictive role of reflective thinking and decision making on creative thinking dispositions. *Reflective Practice, 25*(2), 178–193. DOI: 10.1080/14623943.2024.2305921

Osetskyi, V., Vitrenko, A., Tatomyr, I., Bilan, S., & Hirnyk, Y. (2020). Artificial intelligence application in education: Financial implications and prospects. *Financial and Credit Activity: Problems of Theory and Practice, 2*(33), 574–584. DOI: 10.18371/fcaptp.v2i33.207246

Ouh, E. L., Gan, B. K. S., Shim, J. K., & Wlodkowski, S. (2023). ChatGPT, can you generate solutions for my coding exercises? An evaluation on its effectiveness in an undergraduate Java programming course. *Annual Conference on Innovation and Technology in Computer Science Education (ITiCSE)*. https://doi.org/DOI: 10.1145/3587102.3588794

Ouyang, F., & Jiao, P. (2021). Artificial intelligence in education: The three paradigms. *Computers and Education: Artificial Intelligence*, *2*, 100020. DOI: 10.1016/j.caeai.2021.100020

Owan, V. J., Abang, K. B., Idika, D. O., Etta, E. O., & Bassey, B. A. (2023). Exploring the potential of artificial intelligence tools in educational measurement and assessment. *Eurasia Journal of Mathematics, Science and Technology Education*, *19*(8), em2307. Advance online publication. DOI: 10.29333/ejmste/13428

Oyelude, A. A. (2024). Artificial intelligence (AI) tools for academic research. *Library Hi Tech News*, *41*(8), 18–20. DOI: 10.1108/LHTN-08-2024-0131

Özçelik, N., & Çınar Yağcı, Ş. (2024). ChatGPT'nin ters yüz sınıf modeli ile Fransızca okuma becerisinin geliştirilmesinde kullanımı. In Aysu, S., & Göçerler, H. (Eds.), *Dil Eğitimi ve Öğretiminde Dijital Yönelimler* (pp. 109–151). Özgür Yayınları.

Özçelik, N., & Çınar Yağcı, Ş. (2024). L'enseignement des langues étrangères soutenu par l'intelligence artificielle générative: L'effet de ChatGPT sur l'amélioration des compétences rédactionnelles en français. In Özçelik, N. (Ed.), *Fransız Dili Eğitimi Alanında Uluslararası Araştırmalar I* (pp. 25–60). Eğitim Yayınevi.

Ozfidan, B., El-Dakhs, D. A. S., & Alsalim, L. A. (2024). The Use of AI Tools in English Academic Writing by Saudi Undergraduates. *Contemporary Educational Technology*, *16*(4), ep527. DOI: 10.30935/cedtech/15013

Palenski, T., Hills, L., Unnikrishnan, S., & Eynon, R. (2024). *How AI Works: Reconfiguring Lifelong Learning*. Postdigital Science and Education., DOI: 10.1007/s42438-024-00496-

Panadero, E. (2017). A review of self-regulated learning: Six models and four directions for research. *Frontiers in Psychology*, *8*, 422. DOI: 10.3389/fpsyg.2017.00422

Pan, X.-W., Ding, L., Zhu, X.-Y., & Yang, Z.-X. (2017). A Social Approach to High-level Context Generation for Supporting Context-aware M-Learning. *Eurasia Journal of Mathematics, Science and Technology Education*, *13*(7), 3675–3686. DOI: 10.12973/eurasia.2017.00752a

Paramartha, A. A. G. Y., Seputra, K. A., Azima, F., Putra, D. P., Dwi, E., & Aryanto, K. Y. E. (2022). Usability Evaluation of an Interactive Educational Mobile Application. *2022 24th International Conference on Advanced Communication Technology (ICACT)*, 491–495. https://doi.org/DOI: 10.23919/ICACT53585.2022.9728778

Parker, K., & Chaudron, C. (1987). The effects of linguistic simplification and elaborative modifications on L2 comprehension. *University of Hawaii Working Papers in ESL, 6*, 107 133.

Park, J. J., & Milner, P. (2025). Enhancing Academic Writing Integrity: Ethical Implementation of Generative Artificial Intelligence for Non-Traditional Online Students. *TechTrends, 69*(1), 176–188. DOI: 10.1007/s11528-024-01024-2

Patrick, S., Kennedy, K., & Powell, A. (2013). Mean What You Say: Defining and Integrating Personalized, Blended and Competency Education. *International Association for K-12 Online Learning*.

Pattier, D., & Redondo-Duarte, S. (2025). La vida online, la inteligencia artificial y su lectura pedagógica. *Márgenes: Revista de Educación de la Universidad de Málaga, 6*(1), 28–45. DOI: 10.24310/mar.6.1.2025.20784

Pavlenko, A. (2003). Eyewitness memory in late bilinguals: Evidence for discursive relativity. *The International Journal of Bilingualism, 7*(3), 257–281. DOI: 10.1177/13670069030070030301

Pea, R., & Sharples, M. (2022). Mobile Learning. In R. K. Sawyer (Ed.), *The Cambridge Handbook of the Learning Sciences* (pp. 362–382). chapter, Cambridge: Cambridge University Press. DOI: 10.1017/9781108888295.022

Pedro, F., Subosa, M., Rivas, A., & Valverde, P. (2019). Artificial intelligence in education: Challenges and opportunities for sustainable development.

Pei, G., Li, H., Lu, Y., Wang, Y., Hua, S., & Li, T. (2024). Affective computing: Recent advances, challenges, and future trends. *Intelligent Computing, 3*, 0076. https://doi.org/DOI: 10.34133/icomputing.0076

Penagos, M., Kassir, S., & Vosloo, S. (2020). National AI strategies and children (Policy brief). *Unicef Office of Global insight and Policy*. https://www.unicef.org/globalinsight/media/1156/file

Peng, H., Ma, S., & Spector, J. M. (2019). Personalized adaptive learning: An emerging pedagogical approach enabled by a smart learning environment. *Smart Learning Environments, 6*(1), 1–14. DOI: 10.1186/s40561-019-0089-y

Peng, Q. (2024). Lifelong Learning System in the age of Artificial Intelligence: Change, Opportunity and Reconstruction. *Journal of Electrical Systems*, *20*(2), 1085–1091. DOI: 10.52783/jes.1294

Pennebaker, J. W., Mehl, M. R., & Niederhoffer, K. G. (2003). Psychological aspects of natural language. use: Our words, ourselves. *Annual Review of Psychology, 54*, 547 577.

Pennisi, P., Tonacci, A., Tartarisco, G., Billeci, L., Ruta, L., Gangemi, S., & Pioggia, G. (2016). Autism and social robotics: A systematic review. *Autism Research*, *9*(2), 165–183. DOI: 10.1002/aur.1527

Perkins, M. (2023). Academic integrity considerations of AI large language models in the post-pandemic era: ChatGPT and beyond. *Journal of University Teaching & Learning Practice*, *20*(2), 7. Advance online publication. DOI: 10.53761/1.20.02.07

Peters, U. (2022). Algorithmic political bias in artificial intelligence systems. *Philosophy & Technology*, *35*(2), 1–25. DOI: 10.1007/s13347-022-00512-8

Petit, T., & Santos, G. L. (2014). Mobile Learning: An Ergonomic Alternative for Long-Awaited Educational Changes? In Kalz, M., Bayyurt, Y., & Specht, M. (Eds.), *Mobile as a Mainstream – Towards Future Challenges in Mobile Learning. mLearn 2014. Communications in Computer and Information Science* (Vol. 479). Springer., DOI: 10.1007/978-3-319-13416-1_1

Petticrew, M., & Roberts, H. (2006). *Systematic reviews in the social sciences: A practical guide*. Blackwell Publishing. DOI: 10.1002/9780470754887

Pica, T. (1994). Research on negotiation: What does it reveal about second-language learning conditions, processes, and outcomes? *Language Learning*, *44*(3), 493–527. DOI: 10.1111/j.1467-1770.1994.tb01115.x

Pidd, K. (2002). The Role of Workplace Social Controls and Normative Behaviour in Workforce Development. In *Organisational Barriers to Training Transfer* (p. 10). National Centre for Education and Training on Addiction.

Pimmer, C., & Pachler, N. (2014). Mobile learning in the workplace. In *Unlocking the value of mobile technology for work-based education*.

Pinzolits, R. (2023). AI in academia: An overview of selected tools and their areas of application. *MAP Education and Humanities*, *4*, 37–50. DOI: 10.53880/2744-2373.2023.4.37

Popenici, S. A., & Kerr, S. (2017). Exploring the impact of artificial intelligence on teaching and learning in higher education. *Research and Practice in Technology Enhanced Learning*, *12*(1), 22. DOI: 10.1186/s41039-017-0062-8 PMID: 30595727

Porayska-Pomsta, K., Alcorn, A. M., Avramides, K., Beale, S., Bernardini, S., Foster, M. E., & Smith, T. J. (2018). Blending human and artificial intelligence to support autistic children's social communication skills. [TOCHI]. *ACM Transactions on Computer-Human Interaction*, *25*(6), 1–35. DOI: 10.1145/3271484

Power, C., & Paige, R. (2009). Content Personalization for Inclusive Education through Model-Driven Engineering. In Stephanidis, C. (Ed.), Lecture Notes in Computer Science: Vol. 5616. *Universal Access in Human-Computer Interaction. Applications and Services. UAHCI 2009*. Springer., DOI: 10.1007/978-3-642-02713-0_11

Priya, K. M., Soundarya, P., Kungumaraj, E., Bhagyarathi, P., Subathra, P., & Varghese, S. M. (2024) Harnessing Generative AI for IoT Enhanced Education, *2024 IEEE International Conference on Signal Processing, Informatics, Communication and Energy Systems (SPICES)*, KOTTAYAM, India, 2024, pp. 1-6, DOI: 10.1109/SPICES62143.2024.10779781

Psotka, J., Massey, L. D., & Mutter, S. A. (Eds.). (1988). *Intelligent tutoring systems: Lessons learned*. Psychology Press.

Qaffas, A. A. (2024). Harnessing Artificial Intelligence for Enhanced Efficiency in Academic Writing and Research. *Fusion: Practice & Applications*, *16*(2), 126–146. DOI: 10.54216/FPA.160209

Qin, F., Li, K., & Yan, J. (2020). Understanding user trust in artificial intelligence-based educational systems: Evidence from China. *British Journal of Educational Technology*, *51*(5), 1693–1710. DOI: 10.1111/bjet.12994

Rabot, J., Rødgaard, E. M., Joober, R., Dumas, G., Bzdok, D., Bernhardt, B., & Mottron, L. (2023). Genesis, modelling and methodological remedies to autism heterogeneity. *Neuroscience and Biobehavioral Reviews*, *150*(105201), 1–12. DOI: 10.1016/j.neubiorev.2023.105201

Radford, A., Narasimhan, K., Salimans, T., & Sutskever, I. (2018). Improving language understanding by generative pre-training.

Rahman, M. M., Muniyandi, R. C., Sahran, S., & Mohamed, S. (2021). Enhancement of an optimized key for database sanitization to ensure the security and privacy of an autism dataset. *Symmetry*, *13*(10), 1912. DOI: 10.3390/sym13101912

Rahman, M. M., & Watanobe, Y. (2023). ChatGPT for education and research: Opportunities, threats, and strategies. *Applied Sciences (Basel, Switzerland), 13*(9), 5783. DOI: 10.3390/app13095783

Rajabi, P., Taghipour, P., Cukierman, D., & Doleck, T. (2023). Exploring ChatGPT's impact on post-secondary education: A qualitative study. *ACM International Conference Proceeding Series*. https://doi.org/DOI: 10.1145/3593342.3593360

Raji, I. D., Smart, A., White, R. N., Mitchell, M., Gebru, T., Hutchinson, B., Smith-Loud, J., Theron, D., & Barnes, P. (2020). Closing the AI accountability gap: Defining an end-to-end framework for internal algorithmic auditing. *FAT* 2020 - Proceedings of the 2020 Conference on Fairness, Accountability, and Transparency*. DOI: 10.1145/3351095.3372873

Rakowski, R., Polak, P., & Kowalikova, P. (2021). Ethical Aspects of the Impact of AI: The Status of Humans in the Era of Artificial Intelligence. *Society*, *58*(3), 196–203. DOI: 10.1007/s12115-021-00586-8

Ramsden, P. (2003). *Learning to teach in higher education*. Routledge., DOI: 10.4324/9780203507711

Rane, N., Choudhary, S., & Rane, J. (2023). Education 4.0 and 5.0: Integrating artificial intelligence (AI) for personalized and adaptive learning. In: Nov. DOI: DOI: 10.61577/jaiar.2024.100006

Rawas, S. (2024). ChatGPT: Empowering lifelong learning in the digital age of higher education. *Education and Information Technologies*, *29*(6), 6895–6908. DOI: 10.1007/s10639-023-12114-8

Ray, P. P. (2023). ChatGPT: A comprehensive review on background, applications, key challenges, bias, ethics, limitations and future scope. *Internet of Things and Cyber-Physical Systems*, *3*, 121–154. DOI: 10.1016/j.iotcps.2023.04.003

Raza, M. (2024). AI in Education: Balancing Benefits and Challenges Through Professional Development of Teachers. *Qlantic Journal of Social Sciences*, *5*(4), 168–174. DOI: 10.55737/qjss.v-iv.24071

Real Decreto 822/2021, de 28 de septiembre, por el que se establece la organización de las enseñanzas universitarias y del procedimiento de aseguramiento de su calidad. Boletín Oficial del Estado, 233, 29 de septiembre de 2021. https://www.boe.es/eli/es/rd/2021/09/28/822/con

Rebolledo, R., & González, F. (2023). Exploring the Benefits and Challenges of AI-Language Learning Tools. *International Journal of Social Sciences and Humanities Invention, 10*(01), 7569–7576. Advance online publication. DOI: 10.18535/ijsshi/v10i01.02

Reichow, B., & Volkmar, F. R. (2010). Social skills interventions for individuals with autism: Evaluation for evidence-based practices within a best evidence synthesis framework. *Journal of Autism and Developmental Disorders, 40*, 149–166. DOI: 10.1007/s10803-009-0842-0

Reigeluth, C. M., & Carr-Chellman, A. A. (Eds.). (2009). Instructional-design theories and models: Vol. III. *Building a common knowledge base*. Routledge., DOI: 10.4324/9780203872130

Rekalde, I. (2011). ¿Cómo afrontar el trabajo fin de grado? Un problema o una oportunidad para culminar con el desarrollo de las competencias. *Revista Complutense de Educación, 22*(2), 179–193. DOI: 10.5209/rev_RCED.2011.v22.n2.38488

Renninger, K. A., & Hidi, S. (2015). *The power of interest for motivation and engagement*. Routledge., DOI: 10.4324/9781315771045

Richmond, J. L., & Nicholls, K. (2024). Using Generative AI to Promote Psychological, Feedback, and Artificial Intelligence Literacies in Undergraduate Psychology. *Teaching of Psychology, 0*(0). Advance online publication. DOI: 10.1177/00986283241287203

Riedl, M. O. (2019). Human-centered artificial intelligence and machine learning. *Human Behavior and Emerging Technologies, 1*(1), 33–36. Advance online publication. DOI: 10.1002/hbe2.117

Ríos, T. C.-D. L., Solis-Trujillo, B., Pérez-Ruiz, J., & Aquije-Mansilla, M. (2025). Systematic review of critical thinking using artificial intelligence. *Edelweiss Applied Science and Technology, 9*(3), 990–1001. DOI: 10.55214/25768484.v9i3.5405

Robertson, S. (2020). Student Agency: A Creatively-Focused Digital Critical Pedagogy. In *Handbook of Research on Literacy and Digital Technology Integration in Teacher Education*. (156-170) IGI Global Scientific Publishing. https://doi.org/DOI: 10.4018/978-1-7998-1461-0.ch009

Robinson, C., & Sebba, J. (2010). Personalising learning through the use of technology. *Computers & Education, 54*(3), 767–775. DOI: 10.1016/j.compedu.2009.09.021

Rocheleau, J. N., Chalghoumi, H., Jutai, J., Farrell, S., Lachapelle, Y., & Cobigo, V. (2021). Caregivers' role in cybersecurity for aging ınformation technology users with ıntellectual disabilities. *Cyberpsychology, Behavior, and Social Networking*, *24*(9), 624–629. DOI: 10.1089/cyber.2020.0572

Rudolph, J., Tan, S., & Tan, S. (2023). ChatGPT: Bullshit spewer or the end of traditional assessments in higher education? *Journal of applied learning and teaching*, *6*(1), 342-363. https://doi.org/DOI: 10.37074/jalt.2023.6.1.9

Russell, S. (2016). Rationality and intelligence: A brief update. Fundamental issues of artificial intelligence, 7-28. https://doi.org/DOI: 10.1007/978-3-319-26485-1_2

Russell, S., & Norvig, P. (2021). *Artificial intelligence: a modern approach* (3rd ed.). Prentice Hall.

Russell, S., Norvig, P., Popineau, F., Miclet, L., & Cadet, C. (2021). *Intelligence artificielle: une approche moderne (4 édition)*. Pearson France.

Rustan, E. (2024). University Students' Plagiarism Behaviours in Writing Instruction: A Systematic Review. *Journal of Language Teaching and Research*, *15*(4), 1083–1094. DOI: 10.17507/jltr.1504.06

Sabzalieva, E., & Valentini, A. (2023). *ChatGPT e inteligencia artificial en la educación superior: Guía de inicio rápido*. UNESCO. https://bit.ly/3oeYm2f

Sadler, D. R. (1989). Formative assessment and the design of instructional systems. *Instructional Science*, *18*(2), 119–144. DOI: 10.1007/BF00117714

Sağdıç, Z. A. (2024). *Otizm spektrum bozukluğu olan çocuklara sohbet becerisinin öğretiminde robot ve öğretmen tarafından sunulan replikli öğretimin karşılaştırılması: Karma yöntem araştırması* (Doktora tezi, Anadolu Üniversitesi). Yükseköğretim Kurulu Ulusal Tez Merkezi. https://tez.yok.gov.tr/UlusalTezMerkezi/TezGoster?key=1pwTzRXnomYf6jwqVORfUYQ94Yy6MwKdJm0-jNX3Zi15QFgKnhi3qENh1eN74F_A

Sağdıç, Z. A., & Sani-bozkurt, S. (2020). Otizm spektrum bozukluğu ve yapay zekâ uygulamaları. *Açıköğretim Uygulamaları ve Araştırmaları Dergisi*, *6*(3), 92–111.

Sailer, M., Hense, J. U., Mayr, S. K., & Mandl, H. (2017). How gamification motivates: An experimental study of the effects of specific game design elements on psychological need satisfaction. *Computers in Human Behavior*, *69*, 371–380. DOI: 10.1016/j.chb.2016.12.033

Sajja, R., Sermet, Y., Cikmaz, M., Cwiertny, D., & Demir, I. (2024). Artificial intelligence-enabled intelligent assistant for personalized and adaptive learning in higher education. *Information (Basel), 15*(10), 596. DOI: 10.3390/info15100596

Sakalle, A., Tomar, P., Bhardwaj, H., & Sharma, U. (2021). Impact and Latest Trends of Intelligent Learning With Artificial Intelligence. In S. Verma & P. Tomar (Eds.), *Impact of AI Technologies on Teaching, Learning, and Research in Higher Education* (172-189). IGI Global Scientific Publishing. https://doi.org/DOI: 10.4018/978-1-7998-4763-2.ch011

Sakulkueakulsuk, B., Witoon, S., Ngarmkajornwiwat, P., Pataranutaporn, P., Surareungchai, W., Pataranutaporn, P., & Subsoontorn, P. (2018). Kids making AI: Integrating machine learning, gamification, and social context in STEM education. In *2018 IEEE international conference on teaching, assessment, and learning for engineering (TALE)* (pp. 1005–1010). IEEE. https://doi.org/DOI: 10.1109/TALE.2018.8615249

Salaam, M. A. (2023). Examining the ımplementation of artificial ıntelligence in early childhood education settings in Ghana: Educators' attitudes and perceptions towards ıts long-term viability. *American Journal of Education and Technology, 2*(4), 36–49. DOI: 10.54536/ajet.v2i4.2201

Saleh, M. A., Hanapiah, F. A., & Hashim, H. (2021). Robot applications for autism: A comprehensive review. *Disability and Rehabilitation. Assistive Technology, 16*(6), 580–602. DOI: 10.1080/17483107.2019.1685016

Salvagno, M., Taccone, F. S., & Gerli, A. G. (2023). Can artificial intelligence help for scientific writing? *Critical Care, 27*(1), 75. DOI: 10.1186/s13054-023-04380-2 PMID: 36841840

Salybekova, F., Almetov, N., Karbozova, G., Shvaikovski, A., & Suyuberdieva, A. (2024). Upgrading Pre-Service Foreign Language Teachers' Professional Competences by Means Of The 4c's Educational Model In Xxı Century. *Journal of Educational Sciences*. https://doi.org/.DOI: 10.26577/JES2024v80.i3.02

Salybekova, F. M., Almetov, N. S., Karbozova, G. K., Suyuberdieva, A. A., Kudaibergenova, M. R., & Nazarova, G. Z. (2023). Role of the integration of the 4c model in the professional training of foreign language teachers. *Frontiers in Education, 8*, 1–15. DOI: 10.3389/feduc.2023.1125728

Sani, T., & Rocio, C. (2019). *Ted talks in intelligible pronunciation*. https://repositorio.uta.edu.ec/jspui/handle/123456789/30438

Sani-Bozkurt, S. (2017). Özel eğitimde dijital destek: Yardımcı teknolojiler. *Açıköğretim Uygulamaları ve Araştırmaları Dergisi*, *3*(2), 37–60.

Sanusi, I. T., Olaleye, S. A., Agbo, F. J., & Chiu, T. K. F. (2022). The role of learners' competencies in artificial intelligence education. *Computers and Education: Artificial Intelligence*, *3*, 1–10. DOI: 10.1016/j.caeai.2022.100098

Sapir, E. (1921). *Language: An introduction to the study of speech*. Harcourt.

Sayari, K. T. (2025). Infrastructure and Investment Needs for AI Implementation in Education. In *Teachers' Roles and Perspectives on AI Integration in Schools* (pp. 141–162). IGI Global Scientific Publishing.

Scager, K., Boonstra, J., Peeters, T., Vulperhorst, J., & Wiegant, F. (2017). Collaborative learning in higher education: Evoking positive interdependence. *CBE Life Sciences Education*, *15*(4), ar69. DOI: 10.1187/cbe.16-07-0219 PMID: 27909019

Schmidt, R. W. (1990). The role of consciousness in second language learning. *Applied Linguistics*, *11*(2), 129–158. DOI: 10.1093/applin/11.2.129

Schoenenberger, H. (2024). Concept and Reality of Lifelong Learning. In Schoenenberger, H. (Ed.), *Connected Learning: Origins, Opportunities, and Perspectives of Contemporary Educational Design: A Machine-Generated Literature Overview* (pp. 157–182). Springer Nature Switzerland., DOI: 10.1007/978-3-031-37813-3_6

Schunk, D. H. (2001). Self-regulation through goal setting.

Scott, D. (2008). *Critical essays on major curriculum theorists*. Routledge.

Şen, N., & Akbay, T. (2023). Artificial intelligence and innovative applications in special education. *Instructional technology and lifelong learning, 4*(2), 176-199. https://doi.org/DOI: 10.52911/itall.1297978

Sénécal, A. M. (2024). A semi systematic review of research on generative artificial intelligence (GenAI) in second language acquisition (SLA). In Y. Choubsaz, P. Díez Arcón, A. Gimeno Sanz, J. Hriňák, X. Liashuk, S. Pokrivčáková and H. Vančová (Eds.), *CALL for Humanity EUROCALL 2024 Short Papers* (pp. 24 32).

Şenocak, D., Bozkurt, A., & Koçdar, S. (2024). Exploring the Ethical Principles for the Implementation of Artificial Intelligence in Education: Towards a Future Agenda. In *Transforming Education With Generative AI: Prompt Engineering and Synthetic Content Creation* (pp. 200-213). IGI Global Scientific Publishing. DOI: DOI: 10.4018/979-8-3693-1351-0.ch010

Sergeeva, O. V., Zheltukhina, M. R., Shoustikova, T., Tukhvatullina, L. R., Dobrokhotov, D. A., & Kondrashev, S. V. (2025). Understanding higher education students' adoption of generative AI technologies: An empirical investigation using UTAUT2. *Contemporary Educational Technology*, *17*(2), ep571. DOI: 10.30935/cedtech/16039

Shadiev, R., Wen, Y., Uosaki, N., & Song, Y. (2023). Future language learning with emerging technologies. In *Journal of Computers in Education* (Vol. 10, Issue 3). DOI: 10.1007/s40692-023-00285-9

Shadiev, R., & Yu, J. (2024). Review of research on computer-assisted language learning with a focus on intercultural education. *Computer Assisted Language Learning*, *37*(4), 841–871. DOI: 10.1080/09588221.2022.2056616

Shafik, W. (2024). Towards Trustworthy and Explainable AI Educational Systems. In *Explainable AI for Education: Recent Trends and Challenges* (pp. 17-41). Springer. DOI: 10.1007/978-3-031-72410-7_2

Shafique, R., Aljedaani, W., Rustam, F., Lee, E., Mehmood, A., & Choi, G. S. (2023). Role of Artificial Intelligence in Online Education: A Systematic Mapping Study. *IEEE Access : Practical Innovations, Open Solutions*, *11*, 52570–52584. DOI: 10.1109/ACCESS.2023.3278590

Shaik, I. A., Shaik, A. H., Athahar, P., & Rasheeda Begum, B. (2024). Cognitive Computing in English Language Classrooms. *ICCCMLA 2024 - 6th International Conference on Cybernetics, Cognition and Machine Learning Applications*, 313–316. DOI: 10.1109/ICCCMLA63077.2024.10871285

Shala, L., Rus, V., & Graesser, A. C. (2014). A bilingual analysis of cohesion in a corpus of leader speeches. In *Proceedings of the 27th International Florida Artificial Intelligence Research Society Conference, FLAIRS 2014*, 225 230.

Shambour, Q., Qandeel, N., Alrabanah, Y., Abumariam, A., & Shambour, M. (2024). Artificial Intelligence Techniques for Early Autism Detection in Toddlers: A Comparative Analysis. *Journal of Applied Data Sciences*, *5*(4), 1754–1764. DOI: 10.47738/jads.v5i4.353

Shapiro, J. P., & Stefkovich, J. A. (2016). *Ethical leadership and decision making in education: Applying theoretical perspectives to complex dilemmas*. Routledge., DOI: 10.4324/9781315773339

Sharififar, M., & Rahimi, E. (2015). Critical discourse analysis of political speeches: A case study of Obama's and Rouhani's speeches at UN. *Theory and Practice in Language Studies*, *5*(2), 343–349. DOI: 10.17507/tpls.0502.14

Sharma, S. K., Dixit, R. J., Rai, D., & Mall, S. (2024). Artificial Intelligence and Machine Learning in Smart Education. In Khan, M., Khan, R., Praveen, P., Verma, A., & Panda, M. (Eds.), *Infrastructure Possibilities and Human-Centered Approaches With Industry 5.0* (pp. 86–106). IGI Global Scientific Publishing., DOI: 10.4018/979-8-3693-0782-3.ch006

Shemshack, A., & Spector, J. M. (2020). A systematic literature review of personalized learning terms. *Smart Learning Environments*, *7*(1), 33. DOI: 10.1186/s40561-020-00140-9

Sheth, A., Perera, S., Wijeratne, S., & Thirunarayan, K. (2017). Knowledge will propel machine understanding of content: extrapolating from current examples. *Proceedings of the International Conference on Web Intelligence*, 1–9. https://doi.org/DOI: 10.1145/3106426.3109448

Shetye, S. (2024). An evaluation of khanmigo, a generative ai tool, as a computer-assisted language learning app. *Studies in Applied Linguistics and TESOL, 24*(1). Advance online publication. DOI: 10.52214/salt.v24i1.12869

Shifflet, R., Toledo, C., & Mattoon, C. (2012). Touch tablet surprises: A preschool teacher's story. *Young Children*, *67*(3), 36–41. https://research.ebsco.com/linkprocessor/plink?id=34d6b1d6-78ed-3234-ab00-fad3ae80b147

Shin, K. C., Kuppuswamy, N., & Jung, H. C. (2008). Network Based Service Robot for Education. In: Yoo, SD. (eds) *EKC2008 Proceedings of the EU-Korea Conference on Science and Technology.* Springer Proceedings in Physics, vol 124. Springer, Berlin, Heidelberg. https://doi.org/DOI: 10.1007/978-3-540-85190-5_32

Shrestha, Y. R., Ben-Menahem, S. M., & Von Krogh, G. (2019). Organizational decision-making structures in the age of artificial intelligence. *California Management Review*, *61*(4), 66–83. DOI: 10.1177/0008125619862257

Siau, K., & Wang, W. (2020). Artificial intelligence (AI) ethics: Ethics of AI and ethical AI. *Journal of Database Management*, *31*(2), 74–87. DOI: 10.4018/JDM.2020040105

Siemens, G. (2013). Learning analytics: The emergence of a discipline. *The American Behavioral Scientist*, *57*(10), 1380–1400. DOI: 10.1177/0002764213498851

Sigfrids, A., Leikas, J., Salo-Pöntinen, H., & Koskimies, E. (2023). Human-centricity in AI governance: A systemic approach. *Frontiers in Artificial Intelligence*, *6*, 976887. DOI: 10.3389/frai.2023.976887

Sinambela, S. I., Nurlela, N., & Zein, T. T. (2020). Conjunction of grammatical cohesion in speech text. *Bahas*, *31*(3), 142–153.

Singh, T., & Mishra, J. (2023). Learning with Artificial Intelligence Systems: Application, Challenges, and Opportunities. In S. Verma and P. Tomar (Eds.), *Impact of AI Technologies on Teaching, Learning, and Research in Higher Education*, (pp. 236-253). IGI Global. https://doi.org/DOI: 10.4018/978-1-7998-4763-2.ch015

Singh, A. (2024). Impact of generatıve AI on educatıonal sector. *International Journal of Scientific Research in Engineering and Management*, *8*(4), 1–14. DOI: 10.55041/IJSREM30724

Singh, A. (2024). The Future of Learning: AI-Driven Personalized Education. *Available at SSRN* 5076438. DOI: 10.56557/ajocr/2024/v9i49018

Singh, Y., Singh, D. P., Chander, N., Singh, Y. P., & Singh, P. (2024). Generative AI for Enhancing Education and SkillDevelopment. [IJISRT]. *International Journal of Innovative Science and Research Technology*, *9*(11), 883–888. DOI: 10.38124/ijisrt/IJISRT24NOV431

Sipman, G., Martens, R., Thölke, J., & McKenney, S. (2021). Professional development focused on intuition can enhance teacher pedagogical tact. *Teaching and Teacher Education*, *106*, 103442. DOI: 10.1016/j.tate.2021.103442

Siregar, N., Firmansyah, F., & Harahap, Y. S. (2023). Developing students' worksheet for English language teaching to cope with the 4C's skill through project based learning. *Jurnal Paedagogy: Jurnal Penelitian dan Pengembangan Pendidikan*, *10*(1), 44–52. https://doi.org/DOI: 10.33394/jp.v10i1.6286

Sisouvong, V., & Pasanchay, K. (2024). Mobile Learning: Enhancing Self-Directed Education through Technology, Wireless Networks, and the Internet Anytime, Anywhere. *Journal of Education and Learning Reviews*, *1*(2), 39–50. DOI: 10.60027/jelr.2024.752

Slavin, R. E. (1984). Team assisted individualization: Cooperative learning and individualized instruction in the mainstreamed classroom. *Remedial and Special Education*, *5*(6), 33–42. DOI: 10.1177/074193258400500606

Smith, B. E., Shimizu, A. Y., Burriss, S. K., Hundley, M., & Pendergrass, E. (2025). Multimodal composing with generative AI: Examining preservice teachers' processes and perspectives. *Computers and Composition*, *75*, 102896. DOI: 10.1016/j.compcom.2024.102896

Smith, M. S., & Truscott, J. (2014). Explaining input enhancement: A mogul perspective. *International Review of Applied Linguistics in Language Teaching*, *52*(3), 253–281. DOI: 10.1515/iral-2014-0012

Smolansky, A., Cram, A., Raduescu, C., Zeivots, S., Huber, E., & Kizilcec, R. F. (2023). Educator and student perspectives on the impact of generative AI on assessments in higher education. *Proceedings of the 10th ACM Conference on Learning @ Scale (L@S 2023)*. https://doi.org/DOI: 10.1145/3573051.3596191

Smutny, P., & Schreiberova, P. (2020). Chatbots for learning: A review of educational chatbots for the Facebook Messenger. *Computers & Education, 151*, 103862. DOI: 10.1016/j.compedu.2020.103862

Sockett, G. (2014). *The Online Informal Learning of English*. Palgrave MacMillan. DOI: 10.1057/9781137414885

Soltoggio, A., Ben-Iwhiwhu, E., Braverman, V., Eaton, E., Epstein, B., Ge, Y., Halperin, L., How, J., Itti, L., Jacobs, M. A., Kantharaju, P., Le, L., Lee, S., Liu, X., Monteiro, S. T., Musliner, D., Nath, S., Panda, P., Peridis, C., & Kolouri, S. (2024). A collective AI via lifelong learning and sharing at the edge. *Nature Machine Intelligence*, *6*(3), 251–264. DOI: 10.1038/s42256-024-00800-2

Solvandi, Y., & Raflis, R. (2024). Cohesion and coherence of Sandiaga Uno's Speech in The event high level thematic debate on tourism United Nation General Assembly 2022. *Jurnal Ilmiah Langue and Parole*, *7*(2), 72–78. DOI: 10.36057/jilp.v7i2.669

Song, D. Y., Kim, S. Y., Bong, G., Kim, J. M., & Yoo, H. J. (2019). The use of artificial intelligence in screening and diagnosis of autism spectrum disorder: A literature review. *Soa-Ch'ongsonyon Chongsin Uihak = Journal of Child & Adolescent Psychiatry*, *30*(4), 145. DOI: 10.5765/jkacap.190027

Soomro, R., Khan, R., & Rind, I. (2025). Exploring ESL teachers' experiences about ICT-based 4Cs skills: A phenomenological study. *Discover Education*, *4*(1), 12. Advance online publication. DOI: 10.1007/s44217-024-00376-4

Srinivasan, R., & Sarial-Abi, G. (2021). When algorithms fail: Consumers' responses to brand harm crises caused by algorithm errors. *Journal of Marketing*, *85*(5), 74–91. DOI: 10.1177/0022242921997082

Staley, K. (2014). Adapting cultural materials to meet student needs. *Zona Próxima*, *20*(20), 144–152. DOI: 10.14482/zp.20.6036

Sternberg, R. J. (2023). Human Intelligencel Definition, Types, Test, Theories, & Facts. *Encyclopedia Britannica*. https://www. britannica. com/science/human-intelligence-psychology/Psychometric-theories (accessed on 5 August 2023).

Stöhr, C., Ou, A. W., & Malmström, H. (2024). Perceptions and usage of AI chatbots among students in higher education across genders, academic levels and fields of study. *Computers and Education: Artificial Intelligence*, *7*, 100259. DOI: 10.1016/j.caeai.2024.100259

Storey, V. A. (2023). AI technology and academic writing: Knowing and mastering the "craft skills". [IJAET]. *International Journal of Adult Education and Technology*, *14*(1), 1–15. DOI: 10.4018/IJAET.325795

Strelan, P., Osborn, A., & Palmer, E. (2020). The flipped classroom: A meta-analysis of effects on student performance across disciplines and education levels. *Educational Research Review*, *30*, 100314. DOI: 10.1016/j.edurev.2020.100314

Suartama, I. K., Triwahyuni, E., & Suranata, K. (2022). Context-Aware Ubiquitous Learning Based on Case Methods and Team-Based Projects: Design and Validation. *Education Sciences*, *12*(11), 802. DOI: 10.3390/educsci12110802

Subban, P. (2006). Differentiated instruction: A research basis. *International Education Journal*, *7*(7), 935–947.

Su, J., & Yang, W. (2022). Artificial intelligence in early childhood education: A scoping review. *Computers & Education: Artificial Intelligence. Article*, *100049*, 100049. Advance online publication. DOI: 10.1016/j.caeai.2022.100049

Su, J., & Yang, W. (2024). AI literacy curriculum and its relation to children's perceptions of robots and attitudes towards engineering and science: An intervention study in early childhood education. *Journal of Computer Assisted Learning*, *40*(1), 241–253. DOI: 10.1111/jcal.12867

Su, J., & Zhong, Y. (2022). Artificial Intelligence (AI) in early childhood education: Curriculum design and future directions. *Computers and Education: Artificial Intelligence*, *3*, 100072. DOI: 10.1016/j.caeai.2022.100072

Su, J., Zhong, Y., & Ng, D. T. K. (2022). A meta-review of literature on educational approaches for teaching AI at the K-12 levels in the Asia-Pacific region. *Computers & Education: Artificial Intelligence. Article*, *100065*, 100065. Advance online publication. DOI: 10.1016/j.caeai.2022.100065

Sullivan, M., Kelly, A., & McLaughlan, P. (2023). ChatGPT in higher education: Considerations for academic integrity and student learning. *Journal of Applied Learning & Teaching*, *6*(1). Advance online publication. DOI: 10.37074/jalt.2023.6.1.17

Sun, H., & Verspoor, M. (2022). Mandarin vocabulary growth, teacher qualifications and teacher talk in child heritage language learners. *International Journal of Bilingual Education and Bilingualism*, *25*(6), 1976–1991. DOI: 10.1080/13670050.2020.1835813

Sun, Y. C. (2014). Microteaching writing on YouTube for pre service teacher training: Lessons learned. *CALICO Journal*, *31*(2), 179–200. DOI: 10.11139/cj.31.2.179-200

Susnjak, T., & McIntosh, T. R. (2024). Chatgpt: The end of online exam integrity? *Education Sciences*, *14*(6), 656. DOI: 10.3390/educsci14060656

Swain, M. (1985). Communicative competence: Some roles of comprehensible input and comprehensible output in its development. In S. Gass C. Maddan (Eds.), *Input in second language acquisition* (pp. 235 252). Rowley Newbury House.

Swartout, W. R., Nye, B. D., Hartholt, A., Reilly, A., Graesser, A. C., VanLehn, K., & Rosenberg, M. (2016). Designing a Personal Assistant for Life-Long Learning (PAL3). *Proceedings of the Twenty-Ninth International Florida Artificial Intelligence Research Society Conference 2016* (pp. 491-496). AAAI Press.

Syahrin, A. (2018). Culture repertoire in expressive written language: Study of hypothesis of Edward Sapir and Benyamin Lee Whorf. *Budapest International Research and Critics in Linguistics and Education (BirLE). Journal*, *1*(1), 23–28.

Syed, T. A., Palade, V., Iqbal, R., & Nair, S. S. K. (2017). A Personalized Learning Recommendation System Architecture for Learning Management System. In KDIR (pp. 275-282).

Tafazoli, D., María, E. G., & Abril, C. A. H. (2019). Intelligent language tutoring system: Integrating intelligent computer-assisted language learning into language education. *International Journal of Information and Communication Technology Education*, *15*(3), 60–74. Advance online publication. DOI: 10.4018/IJICTE.2019070105

Tai, T.-Y., & Chen, H. H.-J. (2024). Improving elementary EFL speaking skills with generative AI chatbots: Exploring individual and paired interactions. *Computers & Education*, *220*, 105112. DOI: 10.1016/j.compedu.2024.105112

Tanaka, F., Fortenberry, B., Aisaka, K., & Movellan, J. R. (2007). Plans for developing real-time dance interaction between QRIO and toddlers in a classroom environment. *In: Proceedings of the 4th IEEE International Conference on Development and Learning*, pp. 142-147. IEEE Press. DOI: 10.1109/DEVLRN.2005.1490963

Taneera, S., & Alhajj, R. (2025). Diagnosis of autism spectrum disorder: A systematic review of clinical and artificial intelligence methods. *Network Modeling and Analysis in Health Informatics and Bioinformatics, 14*(1), 1–23. DOI: 10.1007/s13721-024-00499-6

Tangirov, K. E., Botirov, D. B., & Ulugmuradova, L. D. (2021). Educational Mobile Applications ss A Means Of Individualization of Learning. *The American Journal of Social Science and Education Innovations., 3*(857), 430–435. DOI: 10.37547/tajssei/Volume03Issue01-78

Tang, K. Y., Chang, C. Y., & Hwang, G. J. (2021). Trends in artificial intelligence-supported e-learning: A systematic review and co-citation network analysis (1998–2019). *Interactive Learning Environments, 31*(4), 2134–2152. DOI: 10.1080/10494820.2021.1875001

Tang, Q., Deng, W., Huang, Y., Wang, S., & Zhang, H. (2025). Can Generative Artificial Intelligence be a Good Teaching Assistant?—An Empirical Analysis Based on Generative AI-Assisted Teaching. *Journal of Computer Assisted Learning, 41*(3), e70027. DOI: 10.1111/jcal.70027

Tan, L., & Luhrs, M. (2024). Using Generative AI Midjourney to enhance divergent and convergent thinking in an architect's creative design process. *The Design Journal, 27*(4), 677–699. DOI: 10.1080/14606925.2024.2353479

Tanskanen, S. K. (2006). *Collaborating Towards Coherence: Lexical Cohesion in English Discourse*. John Benjamins Pub Co. DOI: 10.1075/pbns.146

Tariq, M. U. (2024). Generative AI in Curriculum Development in Higher Education. In Fields, Z. (Ed.), *Impacts of Generative AI on Creativity in Higher Education* (pp. 231–262). IGI Global Scientific Publishing., DOI: 10.4018/979-8-3693-2418-9.ch009

Taylor, P. J., Larner, S., Conchie, S. M., & Menacere, T. (2017). Culture moderates changes in linguistic self presentation and detail provision when deceiving others. *Royal Society Open Science, 4*(6), 170128. DOI: 10.1098/rsos.170128 PMID: 28680668

Teng, M. F. (2025). Metacognitive awareness and EFL learners' perceptions and experiences in utilising ChatGPT for writing feedback. *European Journal of Education, 60*(1), 1–17. DOI: 10.1111/ejed.12811

Teri, S., Acai, A., Griffith, D., Mahmoud, Q., Ma, D. W. L., & Newton, G. (2014). Student use and pedagogical impact of a mobile learning application. *Biochemistry and Molecular Biology Education, 42*(2), 121–135. https://doi.org/https://doi.org/10.1002/bmb.20771. DOI: 10.1002/bmb.20771 PMID: 24375862

Tevdovska, E. S. (2015). Integrating soft skills in higher education and the EFL classroom: Knowledge beyond language learning. *SEEU Review*, *11*(2), 95–106. DOI: 10.1515/seeur-2015-0031

Thomas, J. W. (2000). A review of research on project-based learning.

Thornhill-Miller, B., Camarda, A., Mercier, M., Burkhardt, J.-M., Morisseau, T., Bourgeois-Bougrine, S., Vinchon, F., El Hayek, S., Augereau-Landais, M., Mourey, F., Feybesse, C., Sundquist, D., & Lubart, T. (2023). Creativity, Critical Thinking, Communication, and Collaboration: Assessment, Certification, and Promotion of 21st Century Skills for the Future of Work and Education. *Journal of Intelligence*, *11*(3), 54. DOI: 10.3390/jintelligence11030054

Tingelhoff, F., Brugger, M., & Leimeister, J. M. (2025). A guide for structured literature reviews in business research: The state-of-the-art and how to integrate generative artificial intelligence. *Journal of Information Technology*, *40*(1), 77–99. DOI: 10.1177/02683962241304105

Tobias, S., & Duffy, T. M. (2009). *Constructivist instruction: Success or failure.* https://doi.org/DOI: 10.4324/9780203878842

Tomasello, M. (2003). *Constructing a language: A usage based theory of language acquisition.* Harvard University Press.

Tomlinson, C. A. (1999). Mapping a route toward differentiated instruction. *Educational Leadership*, *57*, 12–17.

Tomlinson, C. A. (2014). *The differentiated classroom: Responding to the needs of all learners.* Ascd.

Torres, J. M. M., Medina-DeVilliers, S., Clarkson, T., Lerner, M. D., & Riccardi, G. (2023). Evaluation of interpretability for deep learning algorithms in EEG emotion recognition: A case study in autism. *Artificial Intelligence in Medicine*, *143*(102545), 1–14. DOI: 10.1016/j.artmed.2023.102545

Torres, N. (2022). Recommender Systems for Education: A case of Study Using Formative Assessments. *41st International Conference of the Chilean Computer Science Society (SCCC)*, 1–6. https://doi.org/DOI: 10.1109/SCCC57464.2022.10000363

Tortorella, R. A. W., & Graf, S. (2017). Considering learning styles and context-awareness for mobile adaptive learning. *Education and Information Technologies*, *22*(1), 297–315. DOI: 10.1007/s10639-015-9445-x

Touretzky, D., Gardner-McCune, C., & Seehorn, D. (2023). Machine learning and the five big ideas in AI. *International Journal of Artificial Intelligence in Education, 33*(2), 233–266. DOI: 10.1007/s40593-022-00314-1

Trimmer, E., McDonald, S., & Rushby, J. A. (2016). Not knowing what I feel: Emotional empathy in autism spectrum disorders. *Autism, 21*(4), 450–457. DOI: 10.1177/1362361316648520

Tryhub, O. (2023). *THE CONCEPT OF LIFELONG LEARNING: THE EUROPEAN DIMENSION*. https://doi.org/DOI: 10.36074/logos-22.12.2023.080

Tseng, T., Murai, Y., Freed, N., Gelosi, D., Ta, T. D., & Kawahara, Y. (2021). PlushPal: Storytelling with interactive plush toys and machine learning. In *Interaction design and children* (pp. 236–245)

Tsunemoto, A., & Trofimovich, P. (2024). Coherence and comprehensibility in second language speakers' academic speaking performance. *Studies in Second Language Acquisition, 46*(3), 795–817. DOI: 10.1017/S0272263124000305

Tu, C. H., & Sujo-Montes, L. E. (2015). Mobile Learning and Mobile Social Interaction. In Papa, R. (Ed.), *Media Rich Instruction*. Springer., DOI: 10.1007/978-3-319-00152-4_17

Tullis, J. G., & Benjamin, A. S. (2011). On the effectiveness of self-paced learning. *Journal of Memory and Language, 64*(2), 109–118. DOI: 10.1016/j.jml.2010.11.002 PMID: 21516194

Türker, P. M., & Öztürk, M. (2024). Generative Artificial Intelligence and the 4C Learning Skills for the 21st Century. In Cela, E., Vajjhala, N., & Fonkam, M. (Eds.), *Next-Generation AI Methodologies in Education* (pp. 285–320). IGI Global Scientific Publishing., DOI: 10.4018/979-8-3693-7220-3.ch011

Turkle, S. (2005). *The second self: Computers and the human spirit*. Boston Review.

Turner, J. D., & Griffin, A. A. (2021). Dream a little [STEAM] of me: Exploring Black adolescent girls' STEAM career futures through digital multimodal compositions. In *Genders, Cultures, and Literacies* (pp. 49-61). Routledge.

U.S. Department of Education. (2016). *Future ready learning: Reimagining the role of technology in education*. Office of Educational Technology.

U.S. Department of Education. (2017). *Reimagining the role of technology in education: 2017 national education technology plan update*. Office of Educational Technology. https://files.eric.ed.gov/fulltext/ED577592.pdf

Ulaşan, F. (2023). The use of artificial intelligence in educational institutions: Social consequences of artificial intelligence in education. *Korkut Ata Türkiyat Arastirmalari Dergisi, 1*(Special issue), 1305–1324. DOI: 10.51531/korkutataturkiyat.1361112

UNESCO. (2018). *ICT competency framework for teachers: Version 3.* United Nations Educational, Scientific and Cultural Organization. https://unesdoc.unesco.org/ark:/48223/pf0000265721

UNESCO. (2022). *Recommendation on the ethics of artificial intelligence.* UNESCO. https://unesdoc.unesco.org/ark:/48223/pf0000381137

UNICEF. (2021). *Policy guidance on AI for children.* Paris: UNICEF. https://www.unicef.org/globalinsight/reports/policy-guidance-ai-children

Üstünbaş, Ü. (2024). Hey, GPT, Can we have a chat?: A case study on EFL learners' AI speaking practice. *International Journal of Modern Education Studies, 8*(1), 91–107. DOI: 10.51383/ijonmes.2024.318

Utami, S. P. T., & Winarni, R. (2023). Utilization of Artificial Intelligence Technology in an Academic Writing Class: How do Indonesian Students Perceive? *Contemporary Educational Technology, 15*(4), ep450. DOI: 10.30935/cedtech/13419

Vaccino-Salvadore, S. (2023). Exploring the ethical dimensions of using ChatGPT in language learning and beyond. *Languages (Basel, Switzerland), 8*(3), 191. DOI: 10.3390/languages8030191

Vajjala, S., Majumder, B., Gupta, A., & Surana, H. (2020). *Practical Natural Language Processing: A Comprehensive guide to building Real-World NLP systems.* https://openlibrary.telkomuniversity.ac.id/home/catalog/id/165927/slug/practical-natural-language-processing-a-comprehensive-guide-to-building-real-world-nlp-systems.html

van der Plas, E., Mason, D., & Happé, F. (2023). Decision-making in autism: A narrative review. *Autism, 27*(6), 1532–1546. DOI: 10.1177/13623613221148010

Van'T Hof, M., Tisseur, C., van Berckelear-Onnes, I., Van Nieuwenhuyzen, A., Daniels, A. M., Deen, M., ... & Ester, W. A. (2021). Age at autism spectrum disorder diagnosis: A systematic review and meta-analysis from 2012 to 2019. *Autism, 25*(4), 862–873. DOI: 10.1177/1362361320971107

Vančová, H. (2023). AI and AI-powered tools for pronunciation training. *Journal of Language and Cultural Education, 11*(3), 12–24. Advance online publication. DOI: 10.2478/jolace-2023-0022

Vannest, K. J., Swindlehurst, K., Bishop, P. A., & Shepherd, K. G. (2024). The evidence for personalized learning plans: A systematic review of the literature for student outcomes and measures Grades 7-12. *On the Horizon*, *33*(1), 104–115. DOI: 10.1108/OTH-09-2024-0053

Vartiainen, H., Tedre, M., & Valtonen, T. (2020). Learning machine learning with very young children: Who is teaching whom? *International Journal of Child-Computer Interaction*, *25*, 100182. DOI: 10.1016/j.ijcci.2020.100182

Vasconcelos, M. A. R., & dos Santos, R. P. (2023). Enhancing STEM learning with ChatGPT and Bing Chat as objects to think with: A case study. *Eurasia Journal of Mathematics, Science and Technology Education*, *19*(7), em2296. Advance online publication. DOI: 10.29333/ejmste/13313

Verma, S., Ernst, M., & Just, R. (2021). Removing biased data to improve fairness and accuracy. *arXiv*. https://arxiv.org/abs/2102.03054

Vinchon, F., Gironnay, V., & Lubart, T. (2024). GenAI Creativity in Narrative Tasks: Exploring New Forms of Creativity. *Journal of Intelligence*, *12*(12), 125. DOI: 10.3390/jintelligence12120125

Waelen, R. (2022). Why AI ethics is a critical theory. *Philosophy & Technology*, *35*(2), 9. DOI: 10.1007/s13347-022-00507-5

Wandry, D., Wehmeyer, M. L., & Glor-Scheib, S. J. (2013). *Life centered education: The teacher's guide*. Council for Exceptional Children.

Wang, H. C., & Chen, C.W. Y. (2019). Learning English from YouTubers: English L2 learners' self regulated language learning on YouTube. *Innovation in Language Learning and Teaching, 14,* 333 346.

Wang, Z., Zou, D., Lee, L. K. K., Xie, H., & Wang, F. L. (2023). A systematic review of generative artificial intelligence in language education. In *31st International Conference on Computers in Education, ICCE 2023* (pp. 33 43). Asia Pacific Society for Computers in Education. DOI: 10.58459/icce.2023.1199

Wang, G., Zhao, J., Van Kleek, M., & Shadbolt, N. (2024). Challenges and opportunities in translating ethical AI principles into practice for children. *Nature Machine Intelligence*, *6*(3), 265–270. DOI: 10.1038/s42256-024-00805-x

Wang, M. C., Haertel, G. D., & Walberg, H. J. (1993). Toward a knowledge base for school learning. *Review of Educational Research*, *63*(3), 249–294. DOI: 10.3102/00346543063003249

Wang, X., Yin, N., & Zhang, Z. (2021). Smart design of intelligent companion toys for preschool children. *Artificial Intelligence for Engineering Design, Analysis and Manufacturing, 35*(2), 151–164. DOI: 10.1017/S0890060420000499

Wang, Y. (2019). Is data-driven decision making at odds with moral decision making? a critical review of school leaders' decision making in the era of school accountability. *Values and Ethics in Educational Administration, 14*(2), 1–9.

Wang, Y. (2025). A study on the efficacy of ChatGPT-4 in enhancing students' English communication skills. *SAGE Open, 1*(1), 1–17. DOI: 10.1177/21582440241310644

Wardat, Y., Belbase, S., & Tairab, H. (2022). Mathematics teachers' perceptions of trends in international mathematics and science study (TIMSS)-related practices in Abu Dhabi Emirate schools. *Sustainability (Basel), 14*(9), 5436. DOI: 10.3390/su14095436

Warschauer, M., & Healey, D. (1998). Computers and language learning: An overview. In *Language Teaching* (Vol. 31, Issue 2). DOI: 10.1017/S0261444800012970

Watkins, L., Kuhn, M., Ledbetter-Cho, K., Gevarter, C., & O'Reilly, M. (2017). Evidence-Based Social Communication Interventions for Children with Autism Spectrum Disorder. *Indian Journal of Pediatrics, 84*(1), 68–75. DOI: 10.1007/s12098-015-1938-5

Watson, G., & Glaser, M. E. (2010). *Watson-Glaser TM II critical thinking appraisal.* Pearson.

Weber-Wulff, D., Anohina-Naumeca, A., Bjelobaba, S., Foltýnek, T., Guerrero-Dib, J., Popoola, O., Šigut, P., & Waddington, L. (2023). Testing of detection tools for AI-generated text. *International Journal for Educational Integrity, 19*(26), 26. Advance online publication. DOI: 10.1007/s40979-023-00146-z

Weng, X., & Chiu, T. K. F. (2023). Instructional design and learning outcomes of intelligent computer assisted language learning: Systematic review in the field. In *Computers and Education* (Vol. 4). Artificial Intelligence., DOI: 10.1016/j.caeai.2022.100117

Weng, Z., & Fu, Y. (2025). Generative AI in Language Education: Bridging Divide and Fostering Inclusivity. *International Journal of Technology in Education, 8*(2), 395–420. DOI: 10.46328/ijte.1056

Werdiningsih, I., Marzuki, , & Rusdin, D. (2024). Balancing AI and authenticity: EFL students' experiences with ChatGPT in academic writing. *Cogent Arts & Humanities, 11*(1), 1–15. DOI: 10.1080/23311983.2024.2392388

White, S., Keonig, K., & Scahill, L. (2007). Social skills development in children with autism spectrum disorders: A review of the intervention research. *Journal of Autism and Developmental Disorders*, *37*(10), 1858–1868. DOI: 10.1007/s10803-006-0320-x

Whorf, B. L. (1940/1956). Linguistics as an exact science. In Carroll, J. B. (Ed.), *Language, thought, and reality: Selected writings of Benjamin Lee Whorf* (pp. 220–232). MIT Press.

Whorf, B. L. (1956). *Language thought and reality*. MIT Press.

Wiboolyasarin, W., Wiboolyasarin, K., Suwanwihok, K., Jinowat, N., & Muenjancho-ey, R. (2024). Synergizing collaborative writing and AI feedback: An investigation into enhancing L2 writing proficiency in wiki-based environments. *Computers and Education: Artificial Intelligence*, *6*, 100228. Advance online publication. DOI: 10.1016/j.caeai.2024.100228

Wijaya, T. T., Yu, Q., Cao, Y., He, Y., & Leung, F. K. (2024). Latent Profile Analysis of AI Literacy and Trust in Mathematics Teachers and Their Relations with AI Dependency and 21st-Century Skills. *Behavioral Sciences (Basel, Switzerland)*, *14*(11), 1008. DOI: 10.3390/bs14111008

Williams, J. (1992). Planning, discourse marking, and the comprehensibility of international teaching assistants. *TESOL Quarterly, 26*, 693 711.

Williams, R., Park, H. W., Oh, L., & Breazeal, C. (2019). Popbots: Designing an artificial intelligence curriculum for early childhood education. *Proceedings of the AAAI Conference on Artificial Intelligence*, *33*(1), 9729–9736. DOI: 10.1609/aaai.v33i01.33019729

Wisniewska, N., & Mora, J. C. (2020). Can captioned video benefit second language pronunciation? *Studies in Second Language Acquisition*, *42*(3), 599–624. DOI: 10.1017/S0272263120000029

Wong, W. (2002). Decreasing attention demands in input processing: A textual enhancement study. *Studies in Second Language Acquisition, 23*, 345 368.

Wong, H. S., Huertas-Ceballos, A., Cowan, F. M., & Modi, N.Medicines for Neonates Investigator Group. (2014). Evaluation of early childhood social-communication difficulties in children born preterm using the quantitative checklist for autism in toddlers. *The Journal of Pediatrics*, *164*(1), 26–33.e1. DOI: 10.1016/j.jpeds.2013.07.013

World Economic Forum. [WEF], (2022). *Artificial intelligence for children: Toolkit*. World Economic Forum. https://www3.weforum.org/docs/WEF_Artificial_Intel ligen ce_for_Child ren_ 2022.pdf

Xiao, F. (2014). Technology in interlanguage pragmatics research and teaching. *Language Learning & Technology*, *18*(1), 53–56. DOI: 10.64152/10125/44353

Xiao, J., Bozkurt, A., Nichols, M., Pazurek, A., Stracke, C. M., Bai, J. Y., Farrow, R., Mulligan, D., Nerantzi, C., Sharma, R. C., Singh, L., Frumin, I., Swindell, A., Honeychurch, S., Bond, M., Dron, J., Moore, S., Leng, J., van Tryon, P. J. S., & Themeli, C. (2025). Venturing into the unknown: Critical insights into grey areas and pioneering future directions in educational generative AI research. *TechTrends*, *69*(3), 1–16. DOI: 10.1007/s11528-025-01060-6

Xiao, X., Fang, H., Wu, J., Xiao, C., Xiao, T., Qian, L., & Ke, X. (2017). Diagnostic model generated by MRI-derived brain features in toddlers with autism spectrum disorder. *Autism Research*, *10*(4), 620–630. DOI: 10.1002/aur.1711

Xia, Q., Chiu, T. K. F., & Chai, C. S. (2023). The moderating effects of gender and need satisfaction on self-regulated learning through artificial intelligence (AI). *Education and Information Technologies*, *28*(7), 8691–8713. DOI: 10.1007/s10639-022-11547-x

Xia, Q., Chiu, T. K. F., Chai, C. S., & Xie, K. (2023). The mediating effects of needs satisfaction on the relationships between prior knowledge and self-regulated learning through artificial intelligence chatbot. *British Journal of Educational Technology*, *54*(4), 967–986. DOI: 10.1111/bjet.13305

Xia, Y., Shin, S. Y., & Shin, K. S. (2024). Designing Personalized Learning Paths for Foreign Language Acquisition Using Big Data: Theoretical and Empirical Analysis. *Applied Sciences (Basel, Switzerland)*, *14*(20), 9506. DOI: 10.3390/app14209506

Xie, H., Chu, H. C., Hwang, G. J., & Wang, C. C. (2019). Trends and development in technology-enhanced adaptive/personalized learning: A systematic review of journal publications from 2007 to 2017. *Computers & Education*, *140*, 103599. DOI: 10.1016/j.compedu.2019.103599

Xu, W., & Ouyang, F. (2022). The application of AI technologies in stem education: A systematic review from 2011 to 2021. *International Journal of STEM Education*, *9*(1), 1–20. DOI: 10.1186/s40594-022-00377-5

Yadav, A. (2024). The development of AI with generative capabilities and its effect on education. *International Journal of Science and Research (Raipur, India)*, *13*(5), 854–860. DOI: 10.21275/SR24509232318

Yalçın, Ö. N., & DiPaola, S. (2020). Modeling empathy: Building a link between affective and cognitive processes. *Artificial Intelligence Review*, *53*, 2983–3006. DOI: 10.1007/s10462-019-09753-0

Yamaguchi, T., & Levy, M. (1999). Computer-Assisted Language Learning: Context and Conceptualization. *Language, 75*(1), 191. Advance online publication. DOI: 10.2307/417519

Yang, L., Yu, Y., & Wei, Y. (2022). Data-Driven Artificial Intelligence Recommendation Mechanism in Online Learning Resources. *International Journal of Crowd Science, 6*(3), 150–157. DOI: 10.26599/IJCS.2022.9100020

Yang, W. (2022). Artificial Intelligence education for young children: Why, what, and how in curriculum design and implementation. *Computers and Education: Artificial Intelligence, 3*, 100061. DOI: 10.1016/j.caeai.2022.100061

Yao, X. P. (2002). The legacy of human linguist Whorf read on language, thought, and reality. *Foreign Language Teaching Research, 1*, 75 77.

Yavich, R., & Davidovitch, N. (2024). Plagiarism among Higher Education Students. *Education Sciences, 14*(8), 908. DOI: 10.3390/educsci14080908

Yeh, H. C. (2025). The synergy of generative AI and inquiry-based learning: Transforming the landscape of English teaching and learning. *Interactive Learning Environments, 33*(1), 88–102. Advance online publication. DOI: 10.1080/10494820.2024.2335491

Ye, J., & Liu, X. (2020). Analysis of cohesion and coherence in two truths to live by. *Theory and Practice in Language Studies, 10*(1), 96–101. DOI: 10.17507/tpls.1001.14

Yesilyurt, Y. E. (2023). AI-Enabled Assessment and Feedback Mechanisms for Language Learning: Transforming Pedagogy and Learner Experience. In Kartal, G. (Ed.), *Transforming the Language Teaching Experience in the Age of AI* (pp. 25–43). IGI Global Scientific Publishing., DOI: 10.4018/978-1-6684-9893-4.ch002

Yıldırım, B., & Akcan, A. T. (2024). AI-professional development model for chemistry teacher: Artificial intelligence in chemistry education. *Journal of Education in Science, Environment and Health, 10*(4), 161–182. DOI: 10.55549/jeseh.741

Yıldız, T. (2025). The minds we make: A philosophical inquiry into theory of mind and artificial intelligence. *Integrative Psychological & Behavioral Science, 59*(1), 10. DOI: 10.1007/s12124-024-09876-2

Yılmaz, A., Nacar, M., & Uysal, G. (2024). Ethical Use of Artificial Intelligence Applications in Early Childhood Education. In Aydınlı, B., & Altunoğlu, B. D. (Eds.), *Transforming Early Childhood Education: Technology, Sustainability, and Foundational Skills for the 21st Century*. Özgür Publications., DOI: 10.58830/ozgur.pub534.c2203

Young, D. J. (1991). Creating a low-anxiety classroom environment: What does language anxiety research suggest? *Modern Language Journal*, *75*(4), 426–439. DOI: 10.2307/329492

Young, R. F., & Miller, E. R. (2004). Learning as changing participation: Discourse roles in ESL writing conferences. *Modern Language Journal*, *88*(4), 519–535. DOI: 10.1111/j.0026-7902.2004.t01-16-.x

Yuan, J., Holtz, C., Smith, T., & Luo, J. (2017). Autism spectrum disorder detection from semi-structured and unstructured medical data. *Journal of Bioinformatics and Systems Biology : Open Access*, *1*(3), 2–9. DOI: 10.1186/s13637-017-0057-1

Yudkowsky, E. (2008). Artificial intelligence as a positive and negative factor in global risk. *Global Catastrophic Risks*, *1*(303), 184. DOI: 10.1093/oso/9780198570509.003.0021

Yuen, S. C., & Yuen, P. K. (2009). Mobile Learning: Learning on the Go. In Taniar, D. (Ed.), *Mobile Computing: Concepts, Methodologies, Tools, and Applications* (pp. 108–116). IGI Global Scientific Publishing., DOI: 10.4018/978-1-60566-054-7.ch010

Yüzlü, M. Y. (2024). The impact of ChatGPT on vocabulary learning in L3 German class. *Journal of Higher Education and Science*, *14*(2), 339–348. DOI: 10.5961/higheredusci.1417301

Zapata-Rivera, D., Torre, I., Lee, C., Cabezuelo, A. S., Ghergulescu, I., & Libbrecht, P. (2024). Editorial: Generative AI in education. *Frontiers in Artificial Intelligence*, *7*, 1532896. Advance online publication. DOI: 10.3389/frai.2024.1532896 PMID: 39720359

Zawacki-Richter, O., Marín, V. I., Bond, M., & Gouverneur, F. (2019). Systematic review of research on artificial intelligence applications in higher education–where are the educators? *International Journal of Educational Technology in Higher Education*, *16*(1), 1–27. DOI: 10.1186/s41239-019-0171-0

Zeadally, S., Adi, E., Baig, Z., & Khan, I. A. (2020). Harnessing artificial intelligence capabilities to improve cybersecurity. *IEEE Access : Practical Innovations, Open Solutions*, *8*, 23817–23837. DOI: 10.1109/ACCESS.2020.2968045

Zenni, R. D., & Andrew, N. R. (2023). Artificial Intelligence text generators for overcoming language barriers in ecological research communication. *Austral Ecology*, *48*(7), 1225–1229. DOI: 10.1111/aec.13417

Zhang, C., & Lu, Y. (2021). Study on artificial intelligence: The state of the art and future prospects. *Journal of Industrial Information Integration*, *23*, 100224. DOI: 10.1016/j.jii.2021.100224

Zhang, H. (2024). Study on the role and influence of artificial intelligence in the field of education. *Lecture Notes in Education Psychology and Public Media, 70*(1), 114–119. DOI: 10.54254/2753-7048/70/20241023

Zhang, K., & Aslan, A. B. (2021). AI technologies for education: Recent research & future directions. *Computers and education. Artificial Intelligence, 2*, 100025. DOI: 10.1016/j.caeai.2021.100025

Zhang, L., Basham, J. D., & Yang, S. (2020). Understanding the implementation of personalized learning: A research synthesis. *Educational Research Review, 31*, 100339. DOI: 10.1016/j.edurev.2020.100339

Zhang, S., Shan, C., Lee, J. S. Y., Che, S. P., & Kim, J. H. (2023). Effect of chatbot-assisted language learning: A meta-analysis. *Education and Information Technologies, 28*(11), 15223–15243. Advance online publication. DOI: 10.1007/s10639-023-11805-6

Zhang, Y., Wei, J., Chen, J., Wang, Y., & Zhang, Y. (2020). The application of artificial intelligence in the education of children with autism spectrum disorder: A review. *Frontiers in Psychology, 11*, 1338. DOI: 10.3389/fpsyg.2020.01338

Zhao, J., Wang, T., Yatskar, M., Cotterell, R., Ordonez, V., & Chang, K. W. (2019). Gender bias in contextualized word embeddings. *NAACL HLT 2019 - 2019 Conference of the North American Chapter of the Association for Computational Linguistics: Human Language Technologies - Proceedings of the Conference, 1.* DOI: 10.18653/v1/N19-1064

Zhao, M., Kumari, P., Madhavan Perumal, E., & Hou, Z. (2024). Developing generative AI functionalities in a social LMS. *Discover Artificial Intelligence, 4*(1), 99. DOI: 10.1007/s44163-024-00168-7

Zhu, C., Sun, M., Luo, J., Li, T., & Wang, M. (2023). How to Harness the Potential of ChatGPT in Education? *Knowledge Management & E-Learning, 15*(2), 133–152. DOI: 10.34105/j.kmel.2023.15.008

Zhu, Q., Yuan, N., & Guan, D. (2019). Cognitive Driven Multilayer Self-Paced Learning with Misclassified Samples. *Complexity, 2019*(1), 8127869. DOI: 10.1155/2019/8127869

Zimmerman, B. J. (2002). Becoming a self-regulated learner: An overview. *Theory into Practice, 41*(2), 64–70. DOI: 10.1207/s15430421tip4102_2

Zohuri, B., & Mossavar-Rahmani, F. (2024). Revolutionizing education: The dynamic synergy of personalized learning and artificial intelligence. *International Journal of Advanced Engineering and Management Research*, *9*(1), 143–153. DOI: 10.51505/ijaemr.2024.9111

About the Contributors

Aras Bozkurt is a researcher and faculty member at Anadolu University, Türkiye. With MA and PhD degrees in distance education, Dr. Bozkurt's work focuses on empirical studies in areas such as distance education, online learning, networked learning, and educational technology. He applies critical theories like connectivism, rhizomatic learning, and heutagogy to his research. Dr. Bozkurt is also interested in emerging research paradigms, including social network analysis, sentiment analysis, and data mining. Dr. Bozkurt's studies also cover the integration of artificial intelligence technologies into educational processes in the axis of human-machine interaction. His dedication to advancing the field is reflected in his editorial roles as the Editor-in-Chief of Open Praxis and Asian Journal of Distance Education, as well as his roles as an associate editor for prestigious journals like Higher Education Research and Development, Online Learning, eLearn Magazine, and Computer Applications in Engineering Education.

Munir Ahmad is a seasoned professional in the realm of Spatial Data Infrastructure (SDI), Geo-Information Productions, Information Systems, and Information Governance, boasting over 25 years of dedicated experience in the field. With a PhD in Computer Science, Dr. Ahmad's expertise spans Spatial Data Production, Management, Processing, Analysis, Visualization, and Quality Control. Throughout his career, Dr. Ahmad has been deeply involved in the development and deployment of SDI systems specially in the context of Pakistan, leveraging his proficiency in Spatial Database Design, Web, Mobile & Desktop GIS, and Geo Web Services Architecture. His contributions to Volunteered Geographic Information (VGI) and Open Source Geoportal & Metadata Portal have significantly enriched the geospatial community. As a trainer and researcher, Dr. Ahmad has authored over 50 publications, advancing the industry's knowledge base and fostering innovation in Geo-Tech, Data Governance, and Information Infrastructure, and Emerging

Technologies. His commitment to Research and Development (R&D) is evident in his role as a dedicated educator and mentor in the field.

Samet Aksoy graduated from the Department of Special Education at the Faculty of Education, Anadolu University in 2024. In the same year, he began his master's studies in the Department of Autism Spectrum Disorder Education at the Institute of Educational Sciences, Anadolu University, and is currently continuing his education. His academic interests include children with autism spectrum disorder, technology-assisted instruction, and social skills training.

Alper Altunçekiç completed his primary, secondary and high school education in Sivas. In 1997, he started his university education at Gazi University Faculty of Education. He successfully completed his master's degree in 2003 and his doctorate in 2010 and received the title of doctor. He started working as a lecturer in 2002. He gave lectures in the field of computer technologies. The author, who has studies on mobile learning, distance education, self-efficacy and science education, has recently developed mobile applications for mobile technologies and mobile learning environments. He continues his studies on this subject in order to increase mobile learning environments and to use them more effectively. She has also worked on personalized learning methods and developed applications to carry out distance education and online lifelong learning activities. In addition to his educational activities, he has also participated in joint projects with many public institutions and organizations that have developed themselves in software.

Manal Aqil is a lecturer at University of Management and Technology, Sialkot-Pakistan.

Emine Hande Aydos completed her undergraduate education in 2010 at METU Early Childhood Education; her master's degree (2013) and PhD in 2019 at Hacettepe University in the field of early childhood education. Her main areas of work are children's rights, child neglect and abuse, children's literature, and teacher education. In this context, she has participated as a fellow/researcher in numerous national and international projects supported by TÜBİTAK and other institutions related to her areas of expertise. Additionally, she has been involved in planning teacher education programs focused on pedagogical documentation, utilizing and monitoring web-based teacher education modules, and conducting intervention studies Since 2021, she has been working as an Assistant Prof. Dr. at Istanbul Kültür University, Faculty of Education, Early Childhood Education programme.

Halil Ibrahim Bulbul is currently working as a Prof. Dr. at Department of Computer and Instructional Technologies of Gazi Education Faculty of Gazi

University. He has been teaching various graduate and undergraduate level computer courses within the department. He received his Ph.D. degree from Ankara University, Ankara, Turkey, M.S.c. degree from California University of PA, U.S.A, in 1997 and 1990, respectively, and his B.S. degree from Gazi University, Ankara, Turkey, in 1985. His research interests include computer network, computer hardware, educational technologies, e-learning, we based education, distance education, educational software design, database management systems, machine learning, data maining, information security, information security policies and standards, smart grids security, renewable energy systems, occupational standards and vocational qualifications system. Books, articles, etc. related to the above-mentioned subjects. Various publications and ICMLA, ICRERA, icSMART GRIDS etc. He is a member of the organizing committee at the National and International Conferences he organizes. He has carried out various national and international projects supported by the state and private sector. Tübitak, Ministry of Industry, Kösgep, National agency etc. arbitrator, panelist and Commissioner etc. in organizations. carries out its duties. He has published some books and various indexed articles and conference papers, He has joined and completed various projects in national and international levels supported by government and private sectors. Currently he is a staff of Gazi Education Faculty, He is board members of Distance Education Committee at Higher Education Council and He is working Distance education Coordinator of Ahmet Yesevi University.

Mert Çetinok holds a Bachelor's degree in English Language Teaching from Gazi University, Ankara, Türkiye, which was competed in 2021. Mert Çetinok earned a Master's degree from the Foreign Languages Teaching Department at Yıldız Technical University, İstanbul, Türkiye. Since 2023, Mert Çetinok has been serving as an English language instructor at the Turkish Air Force Academy. His academic interests focus on language education, aviation English, and the educational technology in language instruction.

Şule Çinar Yağci is a French instructor at Zonguldak Bülent Ecevit University within the School of Foreign Languages. She holds a master's degree in teaching French as a Foreign Language (FLE) from Istanbul University and is currently pursuing her doctorate in foreign language education at Gazi University. Her research interests include the integration of artificial intelligence and digital tools in language teaching, intercultural communication, and didactic methodologies for teaching FLE. She has published several articles in national and international academic journals and has contributed to scientific works on innovative approaches in language education.

Bimol Chandra Das is a Business Analyst and MS Business Analytics student at Trine University, Detroit, specializing in AI and ML applications in business and healthcare. He holds a B.Sc. in Statistics from the University of Dhaka. His research focuses on predictive analytics, big data, financial and marketing analytics, consumer behavior, supply chain optimization, and sustainability in healthcare and transportation. Bimol has co-authored peer-reviewed studies on Electronic Health Records (EHR) optimization and AI-driven business growth. Passionate about bridging data and decision-making, he leverages AI to enhance data management, security, and business efficiency. Contact: bdas23@my.trine.edu.

Nazmi Dinçer, holds a Ph.D. in Educational Technology at Bahcesehir University, works as an English instructor at Turkish National Defence University, Air Force Academy. He has been teaching at the department of foreign languages for several years and currently runs courses that equip prospective pilots with the skills to communicate with air traffic controllers and based on ICAO standards. His research focuses on educational technology with a focus on foreign language education, aviation communication, and pilots' training.

İrem Doğaç completed her B.A. in Teaching English as a Foreign Language (ELT) at İzmir Democracy University in Turkey. Her research interests lie in second language acquisition, material development for teaching, and integrating AI in education. She has been working as an English Teacher in İzmir Private Turk College.

Betul Ersoz graduated from Marmara University's Computer and Instructional Technologies Education Department with a bachelor's degree in 2012. She completed her Master's degree in Management Information Systems at Gazi University in 2017. She completed her doctorate at Gazi University Computer and Instructional Technologies Education Department in 2025. Her research interests include artificial intelligence, explainable and generative AI, web technologies, and information systems.

Vasfiye Geçkin completed her B.A. and M.A. in Teaching English as a Foreign Language at Boğaziçi University (Turkey) and her Ph.D. degree in Linguistics from Universität Potsdam (Germany) and Macquarie University (Australia). She worked as a post-doctoral research fellow on the project 'Second Language Tutoring using Social Robots' at Koç University (Turkey). Her research interests include first and second language acquisition, reading and writing in a second language. Currently, she works as an Assistant professor at the Department of Foreign Language Education in Izmir Democracy University, Turkey.

Hamdi Gönüldaş, graduated from Ondokuz Mayıs University's Faculty of Education, Department of Teaching Individuals with Intellectual Disabilities, in 2012. He worked as a special education teacher for two years. At the beginning of 2014, after leaving the teaching profession, he successfully completed his foreign language education and started his Master's degree at Anadolu University Institute of Educational Sciences, Department of Special Education, Education of the Mentally Handicapped Programme. In 2017, she received her master's degree and in 2018 she started her PhD in the same programme. He is currently working as a research assistant. His scientific interests include children with special needs and teacher training programmes.

İlyas Gürses graduated from Marmara University's Bachelor's Program in Special Education for Individuals with Intellectual Disabilities in 2016. Following his undergraduate education, he continued his academic career with a focus on working with individuals with special needs. In 2023, he completed the Master's Program in Autism Spectrum Disorder at Hacettepe University, deepening his theoretical knowledge and practical skills in the field of autism. He is currently pursuing his doctoral studies in the Education of Individuals with Intellectual Disabilities Program at Anadolu University. In his academic and professional work, he focuses particularly on early intervention methods and assessment processes for children with autism spectrum disorder. He aims to contribute to the field through both academic research and applied projects.

Maida Maqsood did MS in English from Government College Women University, Sialkot. Throughout her academic journey, she has achieved notable successes that have strengthened her foundation in literature, education and linguistics. Her Master's research reflects her dedication to exploring critical themes in literature with the use of linguistics style. Additionally, her active participation in different conferences and seminars, such as The International Conference on Modern Trends in Applied Linguistics, and 7th ASNeT International Multidisciplinary Academic Conference 2024 (AIMAC 2024) highlight her commitment to staying updated with current trends in her field.

Marcos Merino is a pianist and composer with extensive teaching experience. Holds a Ph.D. in Education (UAM), a Master's in Jazz Studies (UNT), and a Bachelor's degree in Jazz Piano Performance (Conservatori del Liceu). As an educator, he has been part of the faculty at Universidad de las Américas (Quito, Ecuador), the Conservatorio Superior de Málaga, Centro Universitario de Artes TAI, and Universidad Alfonso X. He is currently a faculty member at Universidad Rey Juan Carlos (Madrid). Internationally, he has taught at various institutions in

Colombia, Ecuador, Hong Kong, and China. As part of the Erasmus+ university teaching program, he has collaborated with the following institutions: Taller de Músics (Barcelona, Spain), Conservatori Superior de València (Valencia, Spain), Conservatorio Giovanni Battista Martini (Bologna, Italy), The Royal Academy of Music (Aalborg, Denmark), and the Estonian Academy of Music and Theatre (Tallinn, Estonia).

Ali Orhan received his PhD in the Department of Curriculum and Instruction and is working at Zonguldak Bülent Ecevit University in Türkiye. His research interests focus on higher-order thinking skills such as critical thinking and problem solving, foreign language teaching, curriculum development and evaluation, meta-analysis, flipped learning, and online learning.

Selin Özer, graduated from Anadolu University Faculty of Education, Department of Special Education Teaching in 2021. In the same year, she was accepted to Eskisehir Osmangazi University Special Education Master's Programme with Thesis. She completed her master' degree in 2024. She is currently continuing her doctoral education in the same field. Since 2022, she has been working as a research assistant at Anadolu University Faculty of Education, Autism Spectrum Disorder Education Department. Her scientific interests include children with autism spectrum disorder, their education and technology-assisted education.

Halil Öztürk graduated from Ankara University's Faculty of Educational Sciences, Department of Teaching Individuals with Intellectual Disabilities, in 2011. He worked at a special education and rehabilitation center for one and a half years, gaining experience with various disability groups. In 2013, he transitioned to academia as a Research Assistant at Muğla Sıtkı Koçman University. He completed his Master's degree in Special Education at Dokuz Eylül University in 2016 and earned his Ph.D. in Special Education at Anadolu University in 2024. His research focuses on learning disabilities, autism, stakeholder collaboration, counseling, and the integration of technology in special education. He currently continues his academic work in the Department of Special Education at Muğla Sıtkı Koçman University.

Sara Redondo Duarte is currently an assistant professor at the Faculty of Education (Department of Educational Studies) at Universidad Complutense de Madrid (Spain). She holds a PhD in Education, a Master's degree in Educational Technology, and a Master's degree in Business Administration and Management. She enjoyed a research fellowship at the Educational Research and Documentation Center of the Ministry of Education in Spain from 2005 to 2008. Most of her professional career has been devoted to faculty development and management of educational innovation projects. She is a member of the consolidated research group Technological Development, Socio-cultural Exclusion and Education (DETECESE) at Universidad Complutense de Madrid. Her lines of research focus on faculty development, educational project management and the didactic use of technologies. Previously, she has held university management positions as Director of Educational Innovation and Faculty Development, and Director of Student Experience (among other positions) at Universidad Europea. She is co-author of several publications of the Eurydice Network (European Commission), the Spanish Ministry of Education and papers in educational research journals. She has received recognition for good practices in university leadership and management from Universitat Politècnica de Catalunya (2021) and the Management Excellence Club (2019) in Spain. She has been honored at the International e-learning Awards in the 2018, 2019 and 2022 editions.

Sunagül Sani-Bozkurt is a faculty member and researcher at Anadolu University, Education Faculty, Department of Special Education. Dr Sani-Bozkurt's research interests are autism spectrum disorder, assistive technologies, evidence-based practices, technology supported environment design and applications in the field of special education

Ömer Toprak has a bachelor's degree in special education and a bachelor's degree in psychological counseling and guidance. He completed his master's degree in the field of education of the mentally disabled and continues his doctoral education. He is working on individualized education programs.

Sevcan Yagan, graduated from Cukurova University Preschool Teaching undergraduate programme between 2002-2006, Anadolu University Institute of Educational Sciences Preschool Education master's programme between 2007-2010 and Hacettepe University Institute of Educational Sciences Early Childhood Education doctoral programme between 2011-2014. Between 2006-2014, she worked as a research assistant at Anadolu University Faculty of Education, Preschool Education undergraduate programme; between 2014-2016, she worked as an assistant professor at Istanbul Okan University School of Health Sciences, Child Development programme; between 2016-2021, she worked as a doctoral faculty member at Istanbul Kültür University Faculty of Education, Preschool Education undergraduate programme. Since 2021, she has been working as an associate professor at Istanbul Kültür University, Faculty of Education, Preschool Education undergraduate programme. She has been working on gender in early childhood education; qualified parent-child relationship; fatherhood, rights-based education and children's rights, democracy and value education in early childhood.

Atakan Yaşar is currently pursuing his Master's degree in the Department of Computer Education and Instructional Technology at Uludağ University. He received his Bachelor's degree from the same department in 2020, graduating as the third-ranked student in his cohort. His academic interests focus on instructional design and personalized learning, with an emphasis on integrating artificial intelligence, virtual reality, and interactive technologies into educational contexts. He provides private instruction in educational technologies and conducts research on the design of learner-centered digital environments. At present, he is actively engaged in five academic initiatives, including two conference papers, a graduate research project, a book chapter, and a faculty-level project supported under the GAP program.

Nuray Parlak Yilmaz is an associate professor at Bursa Uludag University Faculty of Education Department of Computer Education and Instructional Technology. She completed her undergraduate education at Ankara University, Faculty of Educational Sciences, Department of Curriculum and Instruction. Master's and PhD degrees are in the field of educational technology. Topics she has worked on include instructional design, ICT teaching, and technology integration in education.

Index

Symbols

A

F

G

H

I

T

www.ingramcontent.com/pod-product-compliance
Lightning Source LLC
LaVergne TN
LVHW062328300926
849161LV00007B/1616